MDF
24
P-51 MUSTANG

# THE NORTH AMERICAN AVIATION
# P-51 MUSTANG
## A COMPREHENSIVE GUIDE
## Part 2 Merlin Powerd

by Malcolm V. Lowe

SAM PUBLICATIONS

**SAM** PUBLICATIONS

# MDF 24
# The North American Aviation P-51 Mustang (Part 2: Merlin Powered)
by Malcolm V Lowe

First produced in 2014 by Media House, under licence from SAM Publications Limited
Media House, 21 Kingsway, Bedford, MK42 9BJ, United Kingdom

© 2014 SAM Publications Limited
© Malcolm V. Lowe – Text & Photographs
© Andy Evans – Colour Artwork
© John Fox – Cover Artwork
© Chris Sandham-Bailey – Understanding the Subject Drawings
© Michael Benolkin Cybermodeller Online – P-51C Walkaround

ISBN 978-1-906959-04-3

Typeset by SAM Publications, Media House, 21 Kingsway, Bedford, MK42 9BJ, United Kingdom
Series Editor – Andy Evans
Studio Manager – Jonathan Phillips
Printed and bound in the United Kingdom by Stephens & George

## The MDF Series

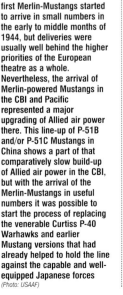

Allison-engined Mustangs had already performed important service in the CBI when the first Merlin-Mustangs started to arrive in small numbers in the early to middle months of 1944, but deliveries were usually well behind the higher priorities of the European theatre as a whole. Nevertheless, the arrival of Merlin-powered Mustangs in the CBI and Pacific represented a major upgrading of Allied air power there. This line-up of P-51B and/or P-51C Mustangs in China shows a part of that comparatively slow build-up of Allied air power in the CBI, but with the arrival of the Merlin-Mustangs in useful numbers it was possible to start the process of replacing the venerable Curtiss P-40 Warhawks and earlier Mustang versions that had already helped to hold the line against the capable and well-equipped Japanese forces
*(Photo: USAAF)*

# Contents

# Preface

Beautiful, purposeful, and iconic. There are so many superlatives that can be used to describe the fantastic P-51 Mustang. Hugely successful during World War Two, it is an aircraft that receives admiration and respect even seventy or more years after its creation. During the considerable time that I have had the pleasure to research the story of this magnificent warplane it has been my privilege to become involved with several veterans' associations that are linked to the Mustang. One of these is the 339th Fighter Group Association, an organisation dedicated to one of the Eighth Army Air Force's premier fighter units. Based at Fowlmere in Cambridgeshire, a location that I know well, the 339th successfully operated the Mustang in the final stages of the air war over Europe on bomber escort missions and accounted for a very respectable score of Luftwaffe aircraft in the air and during strafing attacks against ground targets. One of the unit's accomplished pilots was Lt Col Joseph L. Thury, whose well-known P-51D Mustang named 'Pauline' is pictured here. Officially a P-51D-10-NA, serial number 44-14656, coded 6N-C, this aircraft is fully representative of the well-equipped, potent USAAF Merlin-powered Mustang force in the latter part of World War Two

*(Photo: Steve Ananian, 339th Fighter Group Association).*

North American Aviation's fantastic P-51 Mustang is rightly regarded as one of the finest warplanes ever made. Originally designed to meet Britain's desperate need for modern fighter aircraft in the face of the overwhelming threat posed by Nazi Germany, the Mustang grew into a superlative warplane that can rightly be said to have contributed massively and centrally to the winning of the air war in the Second World War. Indeed, the Mustang is as popular today as it has ever been, and the type has moved seamlessly from excellence in the front-line during World War Two into legendary status in the decades following the end of that conflict.

The Mustang began life powered by the Allison V-1710 inline engine, and entered service in that guise during 1942 with the RAF. The creation, development and service use of the early, Allison-engined Mustangs was covered in the first part of this two-part 'Modellers Datafile' on the iconic North American Mustang. Without doubt the Mustang, in its various production forms, was one of history's great warplanes, and it was initially thanks to British needs that the aircraft was created in the first place. Its designer and manufacturer, North American Aviation, Inc., of Inglewood, California, became – thanks in large part to the Mustang – one of the world's leading producers of high-performance front-line combat aircraft.

This volume covers the Mustang after the versions that were Allison-powered, and therefore its subject matter is that of one of the finest warplanes ever made. The work that was carried out – both in the US and in Britain – to integrate the excellent Rolls-Royce Merlin engine with the superbly-designed Mustang airframe led to a thoroughbred that has few peers. Indeed the creation of the Merlin-powered Mustang can rightly be said to have been a 'Marriage made in Heaven'. Manufactured under licence agreements in the US by Packard as the V-1650, the Merlin proved to be simply the right power plant in the right airframe. Flown by skilled and highly-motivated pilots, and looked after by equally capable ground crews, Merlin-Mustangs subsequently made a terrific contribution to the war effort against Nazi Germany and Japan. Indeed, in its P-51D/K series form the Mustang was a superlative fighter at all altitudes, arguably one of the best if not the best fighter that the Allies produced during World War Two. It combined the beautifully-designed Mustang airframe with high-quality manufacture, and an excellent engine.

Continuing – or perhaps one should say 'sideways' – development, led to the curious but effective twin-engined Twin Mustang. This unusual 'twin' is also covered in detail in this volume. The deletion of camouflage paint during Merlin-Mustang construction meant that the majority of Merlin-powered Mustangs went to war looking shiny and colourfully-marked, in contrast to the often drab-painted Allison-Mustangs that preceded them on the production line. The modelling section in this book certainly proves this point, and I am indebted to my fellow modellers for their contributions to those pages.

Although this Book is not intended to be a 'be-all and end-all' on the Merlin-powered Mustangs, or indeed their twin-engined derivatives, there is a wealth of information contained in these pages that will hopefully prove invaluable to historians, enthusiasts and modellers.

*Malcolm V. Lowe*
Poole, Dorset, May 2014.

# Glossary of Terms

2nd TAF ......Second Tactical Air Force
A .................Attack (US)
A&AEE........Aeroplane and Armament Experimental Establishment
AB...............Air Base
ACC.............Army Co-operation Command
ACG ...........Air Commando Group
ACS.............Air Commando Squadron
ADC ...........Air Defence Command
ADGB..........Air Defence of Great Britain
AFB ............Air Force Base
AFDU ..........Air Fighting Development Unit
AI ...............Airborne Interception (radar)
AMI ...........Aeronautica Militiare Italiana
ANG ...........Air National Guard
AST.............Air Service Training
ATS .............Air Technical Section
ATSC...........Air Technical Service Command
AURI...........Angkatan Udara Republik Indonesia
BAC.............British Air Commission
BCOF ..........British Commonwealth Occupation Force
BPC.............British Purchasing Commission
BG...............Bombardment (or Bomb) Group
BS ...............Bombardment (or Bomb) Squadron
BuNo ..........Navy Bureau of Aeronautics Serial Number
BW .............Bombardment (or Bomb) Wing
CAC ...........Commonwealth Aircraft Corporation Pty., Ltd.
CBI .............China-Burma-India (Theatre)
COIN ..........Counter-Insurgency
Col. .............Colonel
D/F .............Direction-Finding
DoD ...........Department of Defense (US)
ETO ...........European Theatre of Operations
F .................Photographic (US); after 1947, Fighter
FAB.............Fuerza Aérea Boliviana
FAC .............Forward Air Control
FAD ...........Fuerza Aérea Dominicana
FAG.............Fuerza Aérea Guatemalteca
FAREP ........Fighter Airplane Range Extension Program
FAS .............Fuerza Aérea Salvadoreña
F-AWS ........Fighter-All Weather Squadron
F-AWW ......Fighter-All Weather Wing
FBG.............Fighter-Bomber Group
FBS .............Fighter-Bomber Squadron
FBW ...........Fighter-Bomber Wing
FC ...............Fighter Command
FEAF ..........Far East Air Force(s)
FG ...............Fighter Group
FG(P) ..........Fighter Group (Provisional)
FIS .............Fighter-Interceptor Squadron
FIW ...........Fighter-Interceptor Wing
FMS ...........Foreign Military Sales (plan)
FS ...............Fighter Squadron
FS(AW) ......Fighter Squadron (All Weather)
FS(C) ..........Fighter Squadron (Commando)
FS(P) ..........Fighter Squadron (Provisional)
FW .............Fighter Wing
FW(AW) ....Fighter Wing (All Weather)
FY ...............Fiscal Year
GIAP...........Guards Fighter Aviation Regiment (Soviet Union)

GR...............Groupe de Reconnaissance (France)
hp ...............horsepower
HVAR ..........High-Velocity Aerial (or Aircraft) Rocket
IAF .............Israeli Air Force
IDF/AF ........Israeli Defence Force/Air Force
IJAAF ..........Imperial Japanese Army Air Force
ILS .............Instrument Landing System
JG ...............Jagdgeshwader (fighter wing) (Germany)
Lt. Col. ........Lieutenant Colonel
MAP............Military Assistance Program (US)
MAP............Ministry of Aircraft Production (UK)
MDAP.........Mutual Defence Assistance Program
MoS ...........Ministry of Supply (UK)
MTO ...........Mediterranean Theatre of Operations
NAA ...........North American Aviation, Inc.
NACA .........National Advisory Committee for Aeronautics
NEI .............Netherlands East Indies
NG .............National Guard
NII VVS ......Soviet Air Force research and evaluation institute
OD .............(Dark) Olive Drab
OG .............Observation Group
OS ...............Observation Squadron
OTU ...........Operational Training Unit
P .................Pursuit (Fighter) (US)
PG...............Photo(graphic) Group
PoW ...........Prisoner of War
PR...............Photographic Reconnaissance
PRG ...........Photographic Reconnaissance Group
PRS.............Photographic Reconnaissance Squadron
RAAF ..........Royal Australian Air Force
RAF ...........Royal Air Force
RAP ...........Reimbursable Aid Program
RCAF ..........Royal Canadian Air Force
RG...............Reconnaissance Group
RS ...............Reconnaissance Squadron
RNEIAF ......Royal Netherlands East Indies Air Force
RNZAF ........Royal New Zealand Air Force
RoKAF ........Republic of Korea Air Force
RP...............Rocket Projectile
RSwAF ........Royal Swedish Air Force
SAAF ..........South African Air Force
SAC.............Strategic Air Command
SAR ...........Search and Rescue
shp .............Shaft Horsepower
SWPA .........South-West Pacific Area
TAC.............Tactical Air Command
Tac/R .........Tactical Reconnaissance (sometimes written TacR)
TBO ...........Time Between Overhauls
TNI/AU ......Tentara Nasional Indonesia - Angkatan Udara
                (Indonesian Air Force)
TRG ...........Tactical Reconnaissance Group
TRS.............Tactical Reconnaissance Squadron
UN .............United Nations
US...............United States
USAAC ........United States Army Air Corps - to 1941
USAAF ........United States Army Air Force(s) - from 1941
USAF ..........United States Air Force - from 1947
USMC.........United States Marine Corps
USN ...........United States Navy

# Introduction and Acknowledgements

The story of the superb North American Mustang can be quite neatly broken down into two main parts. Firstly came the early-World War Two Mustangs with their Allison V-1710 engines. These excellent low-level performers were the subject of Part 1 of this two-part 'Modellers' Datafile' on the Mustang, which specifically covered these Allison-powered Mustangs. They were followed (although there was naturally an overlap between the two) by the superlative, all-round excellent performer that was the Packard Merlin-engined Mustang of the later World War Two period. The Merlin-Mustang has come to be regarded, rightly, as one of the finest warplanes of all time – but this accolade has all too often been at the expense of the Allison-engined Mustangs, which were fine if understated combat aircraft in their own right.

Both Allison-engined Mustangs and Merlin-powered Mustangs served with great distinction in the Second World War, the first Allison-powered examples entering service in 1942, while Merlin-Mustangs served from late 1943/early 1944 onwards. Both types flew in the front line up to the end of the conflict. Merlin-engined Mustangs returned to combat on a large scale with participation in the Korean War of 1950 to 1953. Indeed, Merlin-engined Mustangs went on to serve with many, diverse air arms around the world in the post-war period, a chapter in the life of the Mustang that is as big a subject as the British and US operational use of the Mustang during World War Two. In civilian ownership, ex-military Mustangs became a central feature of air racing in the US in the years after World War Two, and the 'Warbird' movement has ensured that even today, a handsome number of Mustangs remain in airworthy condition.

The Mustang was originally created as a private-venture project by North American Aviation, Inc. (NAA), a company that was not officially recognized in its own country as worthy of designing fighter aircraft. The Mustang grew out of Britain's overwhelming need for large quantities of modern high-performance fighters in the early stages of World War Two. It was

*The Allison-engined Mustang has always been overshadowed by the exploits of the Merlin-powered Mustangs that came after it. Nevertheless, the Allison-Mustang was the aircraft that Britain ordered from North American Aviation in 1940, and the type went on to serve very usefully with the RAF especially in the specialized Tac/R and armed reconnaissance roles. Indeed, some examples were still in RAF service at the time of the ending of the Second World War in Europe in May 1945. The Allison-Mustang seen here belonged to the RAF's well-known No.2 Squadron (often written as II Squadron) and was photographed during 1942 – the year in which the Allison-Mustang first entered front-line operational service with the RAF. That was a full year before the Americans put the Mustang into service themselves*
(Photo: R.L. Ward Collection)

"Following the Elm Canal on strafing mission, the P-51 streaked low over Holland, Germany, France, and back to England. Speed took it past flak batteries before they could go into action...evaded enemy pursuits...the Mustang's heavy firepower blasted 3 seaplanes, 4 barges, 2 trains. The only thing that hit it was a Channel seagull, into which it ran!"
*Army Air Forces report*

U.S. ARMY OFFICIAL POSTER

Give us MORE P-51's

not, as incorrectly claimed by many published sources, the product of a British requirement or specification. Rather, it was one of the very few successful warplanes in history that was conceived without an official specification ever being raised before its creation. Indeed, it was born as the result of amicable and unofficial negotiations between North American's company officials and British government representatives in the US. Britain wanted NAA to licence-produce examples of the Curtiss

P-40 series, an aircraft type that Britain had selected as a major front-line type for future RAF usage. The personnel of NAA had other ideas, and instead of licence-building the rather archaic and out-dated P-40, instead came up with their own advanced, forward-looking design, which grew into the Mustang. The end result was one of history's great aircraft, which became a vital element of the growing and eventually overwhelming Allied aerial domination as World War Two drew to its ultimately successful conclusion.

The first Mustang was completed in a very short period of time – less than 120 days - and its performance proved to be better than that of most if not all European counterparts of the time (and certainly far better than the P-40), flying faster and carrying more fuel. It has passed into the popular mythology of World War Two that Reichsmarschall Hermann Göring, the chief of Nazi Germany's Luftwaffe, claimed that when he saw USAAF-operated Merlin-Mustangs flying freely over Berlin, he knew that the war was lost for Germany. Perhaps one of the great injustices that has been done to the Mustang over the years is the extraordinary myth that suggests that the Mustang's design was based on that of the antiquated Curtiss P-40, or even – quite

unbelievably – that the Mustang was a derivative of Germany's Messerschmitt Bf 109. Both these 'myths' about the Mustang are complete nonsense, but it is interesting to see how such untruths often gain their own momentum by the number of times that they are copied (often nowadays on the Internet) by so-called 'experts' from one dubious source to another.

One statement that cannot be disputed concerning the Mustang is the skill, determination and courage of those who took this superb aircraft into battle, and the quiet behind-the-scenes professionalism of those who worked on the aircraft and prepared them for combat, often in the most appalling conditions 'in the field'. This applied to both the Allison-engined and Merlin-powered Mustangs, but without doubt the mating of the excellent Rolls-Royce Merlin engine with the basic Mustang airframe created a warplane of extraordinary capability and performance that literally became a significant – some would say vital - tool in the Allied arsenal as World War Two wore on. Nevertheless, it is interesting to note that originally the Mustang's own 'local' armed forces in the US had little or no interest in the type. This delayed the service introduction by at least a year, if not longer, of the Mustang into US Army Air

The Curtiss P-40 was the aircraft that British purchasing representatives asked North American Aviation to build under licence for the RAF. NAA's thankful unwillingness to do so led to the company instead designing the excellent fighter that became the Mustang. The P-40 was a widely-used if unspectacular performer, which was easily bettered on all counts by the Mustang, particularly in its Merlin-Mustang form. Later production models of the extensive P-40 family from the P-40D onwards were known as the Curtiss Model 87 series, and were called Warhawk by the USAAF and Kittyhawk by the RAF and Commonwealth. This P-40K Warhawk, serial number 42-49756, was assigned to the 15th Fighter Group and with the name 'Stinger' was flown by the Seventh Army Air Force's top ace, Robert W. Moore, who later in the war also flew Mustangs – and achieved the majority of his aerial victories in the P-51D *(Photo: USAAF)*

The Merlin-engined Mustang continued to serve with the USAAF (and its successor, the USAF) after the end of World War Two, albeit less and less in a front-line capacity. Showing their later 1940's vintage (note the red stripe across the bars of the fuselage national insignia, and the post-war 'Buzz Number' prefix 'FF' on the fuselage sides), these smart late-model P-51D Mustangs (by then known as F-51D Mustangs – the nearest aircraft was built as a P-51D-30-NA) were performing in a second-line capacity in the Continental US when photographed *(Photo: USAF)*

Force(s) front-line units. Once the aircraft was finally in combat with the USAAF during 1943 it did not take American pilots long to realize the excellent capabilities of the Mustang - which must have led many of them to wonder why Britain's Royal Air Force had already operated the Allison-engined Mustang for a whole year before the US forces took the type into combat.

Apart from the obvious alterations in armament from one version to the next within the production run of Merlin-engined Mustangs, and the various changes that turned the type into a twin-engined fighter as the P/F-82 Twin Mustang, there were few if any major alterations to the basic layout of the Mustang in its Merlin-powered versions. Without doubt, one of the yardsticks by which a successful aircraft design can be judged, is the amount that its airframe is altered by necessity during production – and therefore in the case of the Merlin-engined Mustang, there were few significant alterations that actually needed to be made to the size and general layout of the Merlin-Mustang throughout its production run – except for the very obvious change in configuration with the introduction of the 'bubble canopy' layout of the P-51D. The radical alterations that were made to the basic layout of the Mustang to create the 'lightweight' P-51H, as related elsewhere in this book, were made by choice rather than necessity – and actually turned out to be less than successful, and in the event proved to be largely unnecessary. A literally 'sideways' development of the Mustang line led to the unusual but generally successful Twin Mustang of the post-war years.

The USAAF entered combat over Europe in 1942 without a long-range bomber escort fighter worth the name, and commenced operations under the misguided assumption that fleets of heavily-armed, high-flying heavy bombers, would always successfully fight their way to their targets. This policy quite rapidly proved to be flawed, and as Germany's air defence network of radar, anti-aircraft guns and home defence fighters improved from late 1942 and into 1943, so the losses of US heavy bombers mounted. The need for a long-range bomber escort fighter suddenly became a real necessity for the Americans. They were fortunate that salvation was to hand in the form of the Mustang, but it took quite a change in thinking and a major revision of tactics before the Merlin-engined Mustang was able to gain widespread service in the USAAF as a bomber escort over Europe – and later over the Pacific as well. In that role the Mustang excelled. It had the range to escort the US heavy bombers to their targets and back, especially once the

need for external, jettisonable long-range fuel tanks had also been met (which was a separate but no less important battle within the US military) – and it could easily look after itself when confronted by German (and later Japanese) fighters. Indeed, the extensive and very successful use of the Mustang by the USAAF ensured that the air war over Europe ended before the Germans could bring into widespread service some of the interesting and advanced projects that they were working on.

The Merlin-engined Mustang was a truly remarkable aircraft. Its story is the focus of this second part of the two-part 'Modellers' Datafile' on the Mustang, which specifically covers the Merlin-powered Mustangs and the unusual Twin Mustang.

## Acknowledgements for Parts 1 and 2 of the Mustang 'Modellers' Datafile'

It has been my pleasure – and privilege – to research the story of the Mustang for over two decades. During that time a great many friends, acquaintances and colleagues have assisted with information, documents, and photographs. As for the writing of these two Parts in the 'Modellers' Datafile' series on the Mustang, I have received help from many friends. A number of specialists in their particular fields have been especially forthcoming, including specifically Richard L. Ward, and Chris Ellis. Dick Ward was particularly supportive in pointing my ever-growing number of enquiries in the right directions, and by giving great assistance with the provision of photographs and illustrations. Considerable help was similarly rendered by John Batchelor, with information, photographs and sources.

A very special word of thanks must be expressed to Jerry Day of Oklahoma City in the US. Jerry and his team look after the famous racing Mustang 'Miss America' on behalf of Dr Brent Hisey, and I particularly express thanks to Jerry, Dr Hisey, and the whole 'Miss America' team for their invaluable help – not just with background material on racing Mustangs, but also on many of the technical aspects of the Mustang and its operation. Jerry Day was additionally of great help with checking Mustang facts and figures in my text.

From amongst my 'local' circle of aeronautical colleagues, special mention must go to Tony Blake, Tony Brown, Ian Claxton, Pete Clifford, the late Derek Foley, the late John Neale, Jim Smith, Andy Sweet, and Clifford Williams. Particularly helpful was an expert local to me on many aspects of the USAAC and USAAF, Gordon Stevens, who opened his vast archive of US-related information and photographs especially

Nice in-flight formation view of three Merlin-engined P-51Ds from the 20th Fighter Group's 77th Fighter Squadron. They are carrying 108 US gallon compressed paper long-range fuel tanks beneath their wings, these external jettisonable fuel tanks allowing the Eighth Army Air Force's Mustangs the ability to escort heavy bombers to such distant targets as Berlin from bases in England – an incredible achievement for their time. They are P-51Ds 44-14975/LC-K, 44-15605/LC-M, and 44-15321/LC-S. All are from the P-51D-15-NA NAA Inglewood production block. Eighth Air Force fighter units such as the 20th Fighter Group played a significant role in the winning of the air war over Germany and Occupied Europe in the latter stages of World War Two
*(Photo: Arthur E Sevigny, 20th Fighter Wing Association)*

for my Mustang research. Several friends from elsewhere in the UK were also involved with assistance, including Mick Gladwin of www.airrecce.co.uk. Les Wells of the IPMS (UK) Eighth Army Air Force Special Interest Group similarly supplied excellent information and references. Special thanks must additionally go to Richard Haigh, latterly of the Rolls-Royce Heritage Trust. The famed British test pilot Capt Eric Brown has also been a great help over the years.

Assistance has additionally come from all corners of the globe with information, photographs and background material on the Mustang in its many guises and areas of service. Particular individuals include Graham Lovejoy in New Zealand; Srecko Bradic in Serbia; Miroslav Khol and Pavel Jicha in the Czech Republic; a large number of American friends including Bob Avery, Scott Hegland and Jack McKillop, together with Ron Kaplan of the US National Aviation Hall of Fame, and Nancy Parrish of the Wings Across America organization in remembrance of women pilots in the US during World War Two; Jean-Jacques Petit in France; Peter Walter, 'Misty', and colleagues in Germany; Nikolai Baranov and Alexei Goss in Russia; Martin Kyburz in Switzerland; and my many friends in Canada, including William Ewing, Patrick Martin and particularly R.W. (Bill) Walker whose knowledge of Royal Canadian Air Force Mustangs is encyclopedic. Also especially helpful in the latter country was Ron Dupas, who assisted with many leads and photographic sources through his website www.1000aircraftphotos.com . I am similarly indebted to Christopher C Clarke, whose father, Flt Lt Fred 'Freddie' Clarke, was involved in the air battle on 19 August 1942 near to Dieppe during which Fg Off Hollis Hills of No.414 Squadron, Royal Canadian Air Force, shot down the first enemy aircraft ever credited to a Mustang (as related in Part 1 of this two-part 'Modellers' Datafile' on the Mustang, which covered the Allison-powered Mustangs).

Sincere thanks must also go to Peter Randall, whose excellent website www.littlefriends.co.uk contains a goldmine of detailed information on Eighth Army Air Force fighter units and their aircraft and pilots. Peter generously supplied photographs and much background information on this fascinating subject. Sadly three great friends and acknowledged specialists who it was my privilege to be acquainted with, Jerry Scutts, Paul Coggan, and the famed historian of all things USAAF, Roger A Freeman, all passed away some time ago during my initial writing of the text.

A great deal of the research relating to the creation of the Mustang was undertaken in the National Archives at Kew, London, and thanks go to this organization for its excellent facilities. This depository holds a considerable amount of documentation that concerns the British purchasing efforts in the US during the period from 1939 onwards. There are many letters and other documents that relate specifically to the birth of the Mustang in the archives at Kew, and these also confirm the name of the body that Britain established in the US in late 1939 to perform the buying of US war material – the British Purchasing Commission.

A number of veterans' associations also provided great help and advice. These include the 339th Fighter Group Association (particularly my great friend and former World War Two Mustang pilot Stephen C Ananian), the 20th Fighter Wing Association (Arthur E Sevigny), and that of the 55th Fighter Group (Russell Abbey). Unfortunately, some US veterans' groups are not so willing to be helpful or are happy to deal with British historians, but in contrast the aforementioned are excellent organizations with a sense of the significant history that they represent.

During the writing of the two Parts of this 'Modellers' Datafile' on the Mustang, considerable assistance was rendered with the checking of text and facts by Lucy Maynard, and by my father, Victor Lowe, himself an aviation historian of long-standing.

Sideways development of the Mustang led to the unusual, but generally successful, P/F-82 Twin Mustang. Developed during 1944 as a very long-range escort fighter, primarily for operations over the vastness of the Pacific, the type only saw front-line service after World War Two had ended. As an interim night-fighter, Twin Mustangs played their most important role for the Americans, and were very active during the early stages of the Korean War. Affording an excellent comparison between the 'normal' Mustang and the unusual 'twin' that was derived from it, an early Twin Mustang (actually one of the two original XP-82 Twin Mustang prototypes, serial number 44-83887, which first flew in August 1945) flies in formation with a P-51D Mustang *(Photo: NAA)*

# Merlin-Mustang Development

## Chapter 1

The Merlin-engined Mustang was a great warplane – and indeed, some would argue, the greatest warplane of its generation. Merlin-engined Mustangs gained their greatest fame when operated by fighter units of the US Army Air Force(s). Indeed, much of the type's totally justified fame has derived from the highly successful exploits of Mustang-equipped US fighter units in the skies over Europe, China and the Pacific during World War Two. Ironically, however, the USAAF was at first disinterested in the Mustang, and only late in the day recognized its true potential. Indeed, all the impetus to re-engine the Mustang with the superlative Rolls-Royce Merlin engine came from Britain – the country for which the Mustang had been designed and built in the first place, and which did not have a pressing need to re-engine the Mustang in the first instance. The original, Allison-engined Mustang configuration suited Britain's RAF very well, and it was only through personal and company initiative that the Merlin-Mustang was born.

On 30 April 1942, British test pilot Ronald Harker visited the RAF's Air Fighting Development Unit at Duxford airfield in Cambridgeshire. Harker was a service-liaison company test pilot for the famous British engine designer and manufacturer Rolls-Royce. It was his brief to fly examples of the aircraft then in RAF service or set to become operational (whether they were Rolls-Rolls powered or not), as well as any available captured enemy aircraft. His visit to Duxford on that day was specifically to fly the Allison-engined Mustang Mk I, which was on the verge of becoming fully operational with the RAF's No.26 Squadron. Harker flew Mustang Mk I AG422, and his impressions of that half-hour long flight, and the action that followed them, were to help change the course of World War Two. Harker found the Mustang to be a fine performer at low to medium levels, but he recognized, from a practical perspective, that the Mustang would benefit from the installation of an effective, powerful, high-altitude rated engine. Rolls-Royce, his employer, had such an engine then in continuing development. This was the 60-series derivative of the already famous and highly successful Rolls-Royce Merlin inline engine. Developed from the Merlin engines that had powered Supermarine Spitfires and Hawker Hurricanes during the early war years and most notably during the Battle of Britain, the

60-series Merlins were aimed specifically at giving the Spitfire an improved high-altitude and all-round performance, particularly to counter the Luftwaffe's excellent Focke-Wulf Fw 190 single-engined fighter. They included improved supercharging, using a two-stage, two-speed supercharger with automatic control.

Harker wrote a very important report about his experiences of flying AG422, which was dated 1 May 1942. It was addressed to his superiors and colleagues at Rolls-Royce, including senior managers at the company's main offices at Derby. In the days that followed there was considerable activity at Rolls-Royce, and much communication between the company and the Ministry of Supply and other government bodies, as the momentum began with a view to Rolls-Royce obtaining one or more examples of the Mustang to re-engine with a Merlin power plant. There was an additional and very important ingredient that made the possibility of the creation of a Merlin-engined Mustang a reality in the summer months of 1942. This was the potential of US production of the 60-series Merlin by the Packard Motor Car Company of Detroit. Packard had been producing the Merlin in its Mk XX form for some time, having signed agreements with Rolls-Royce for the manufacture of the Merlin in the US during 1940. Packard-built Merlins were already successfully powering Canadian-built Hurricane fighters, and would go on to power Canadian-built Lancaster four-engined bombers later in the war. The RAF was able to overcome initial worries over the possible disruption of supplies of 60-series Merlins for the Spitfire Mk IX if the Mustang was re-engined with the Merlin, particularly when Rolls-Royce appeared certain that Merlin production would keep up with demand if the engine was mass-produced in the US. In any case there was a growing disquiet amongst some in the RAF and Air Ministry in London as to the supply of fighter aircraft for the RAF in1943, particularly in the face of the Luftwaffe's excellent Fw 190. Although there was great hope for the Spitfire IX, which did indeed prove to be a very capable opponent for the Fw 190, it was expected that there would need to be other fighter types with increasingly good performance if the Allies were to stay ahead of the Germans. The possibility of a high-performance Merlin-powered Mustang more and more appeared to be a possible and increasingly attractive solution for the RAF.

**One of the five prototype/development Mustangs that were employed in Britain as flying test-beds for the Merlin installation into the Mustang airframe by Rolls-Royce. This aircraft, AM203, was the third Merlin-powered Mustang Mk.X to fly. It made its first flight under Merlin 65 power in December 1942. This useful side view of the aircraft on the ground clearly shows the highly modified nose contours of the Merlin installation, including the very prominent 'chin' air intake and the lack of an intake of any kind above the nose** *(Photo: M.V. Lowe Collection)*

## Conversion Work Commences

The task of actually fitting a Merlin engine to a Mustang airframe began at Rolls-Royce in the summer of 1942. Fortunately the Allison V-1710 and the Merlin were similar (but not identical) dimensionally, and the Rolls-Royce team attempted to install the Merlin and its associated equipment into the space normally taken up by the Allison V-1710. The work involved considerable replumbing for the engine's fuel, cooling and related functions, with the intention of keeping in place the Mustang's established layout of the mid-fuselage mounted radiator and oil cooler, with the famous under fuselage intake. It was also intended to fit a new propeller with an increased diameter of 11 ft 4 in (3.45 m) compared to that installed on Allison Mustangs. The original intention was to use the first Mustang that was loaned to Rolls-Royce, Mustang Mk I AG518, for the initial Merlin installation. However, by June 1942 that aircraft did not represent the most up-to-date production standard (it was from the initial Mk I production run of 320 Mustangs), and it was replaced by AM121 which was from the second batch of Mustang Mk I airframes. AM121 arrived at Hucknall on 7 June, and was followed on 26 June by AL963 and by AL975. All three of these Mustangs were initially put through their paces to ascertain their own characteristics and basic performance, no two aircraft even from the same production run being identical – a point that is true for any and every series produced aircraft type. AM121 was found to have a maximum speed of 371 mph (597 km/h) and a maximum take-off weight of 8,620 lb (3,910 kg). During August two further Mustang Mk I were allocated to Rolls-Royce, these being AM203 and AM208.

The first aircraft to be converted was AL975. It had flown for four hours and twenty-five minutes before being retired from Allison-engined flying of all types on 2 July to be converted to Merlin power. The work was carried out at Hucknall by Rolls-Royce engineers, with the company's Installation Design Department making the necessary drawings. The Merlin 61 was initially the chosen engine type to be installed. Some thought had been given to a 20-series engine for one of the conversions, and it had been hoped that the further developed Merlin 65 would be available. In the end a Merlin 65 was the type used in the initial conversion, as this mark began to become available in small numbers. It was potentially a more powerful engine than even the significant Merlin 61, and had improved gearing ratios for its two-stage supercharger and other developments. It fitted into the Mustang's cowling contours without any particular problems (the Merlin and Allison V-1710 were similar in general size, although the Merlin was heavier by some 300 lb or 136 kg), but modified engine mounts were needed and a huge amount of replumbing and rewiring was necessary. One very necessary change was to the carburettor intake housing. The Allison V-1710 used a simple downdraught carburetion system that called for the intake to be on the top of the cowling – which was one of the distinguishing features of all of the Allison-engined Mustangs. The Merlin, on the other hand, had an updraught SU-type carburettor that necessitated the associated air intake to be located below the engine. This resulted in the nose contours being considerably altered – the Rolls-Royce engineers were primarily concerned with the installation rather than the aesthetics of the whole process, and the result on AL975 was a rather ugly chin that blunted the aircraft's otherwise advanced streamlining and good looks. This large chin intake also provided air for the engine's intercooler radiator. In fact the removal of the original intake from the top of the nose improved forward vision slightly for the pilot. This was the case even though the thrust line of the Merlin was actually elevated slightly compared to the installation of the Allison engine. A larger cooling radiator for the engine had to be installed due to

the greater cooling requirements of the Merlin, and so a different radiator was fitted in the lower fuselage behind the cockpit. Its shape remained annular, however, as in the Allison-engined Mustangs, with the oil cooler in its centre as before. This oil cooler radiator was slightly smaller than previously. The main cooling radiator was made by Morris Motors, to the specific design required by the Rolls-Royce engineers. For the moment, the distinctive main cooling air intake below the fuselage for these radiators was to remain largely unaltered, but there were later to be big changes in this area. The exact size of propeller that would be needed to take up the Merlin's considerably increased power compared to the Allison engine was not decided on for sure before the conversion was completed, and so two different units were to be tried out. One was a Rotol purpose-made four-bladed unit of 11 ft 4 in (3.45 m) diameter, the other was the four-bladed Rotol arrangement of 10 ft 9 in (3.28 m) that was then being fitted to production Spitfire Mk IX aircraft. Work progressed comparatively quickly. By early October 1942 the installation was ready, and ground running at Hucknall commenced. AL975 by then had a new designation, being called a Mustang Mk X – as were the four subsequent Merlin conversions. This was in line with the Packard Merlin-powered Canadian-built Hurricanes, which were designated Hurricane Mk X. AL975 also had a 'G' prefix added to its serial number, signifying that it had to be guarded at all times when on the ground if away from its usual factory location or base – it was a very important aircraft.

## First Flight of a Merlin-Mustang

On 13 October 1942, AL975/G, piloted by Rolls-Royce's chief test pilot at Hucknall, Capt R.T. Shepherd, made a rather inauspicious first foray into the air under its new power. To begin with, the new Merlin-engined Mustang actually performed somewhat sluggishly. Its new fuel tank and pumping system were not ready, which restricted its maximum ceiling temporarily to 18,000 ft (5,486 m) and a top speed of only 376 mph (605 km/h). The aircraft also suffered problems with its new cowling panels during the first flight. With the Merlin 65 installed it was hoped that 427 mph (687 km/h) at 21,000 ft (6,400 m) in full supercharger mode could be attained. During subsequent test flights the shape of the lower nose intake was altered with a more flattened underside, and the exit outlet for the main intake beneath the fuselage was changed. On the seventh flight the purpose-built 11 ft 4 in (3.45 m) diameter propeller was installed instead of the Spitfire-sized propeller installation used up till then. Various tinkering with the cowling and other aspects subsequently took place, including

All the pioneering work to re-engine the Mustang from Allison to Merlin power began in Britain, well ahead of official interest in the US. The first aircraft to be modified by Rolls-Royce in Britain was AL975, which began life as a Mustang Mk.I, but first flew under Merlin power on 13 October 1942. It is seen here displaying the many alterations in the nose area that the change of engine type entailed. Particularly noticeable are the different engine mounts and the rather ugly 'chin' that the whole installation included, for the repositioned carburettor air intake and to provide air for the engine's intercooler radiator (Photo: via Chris Ellis)

alterations to a set of prominent louvers on the fuselage sides behind and below the exhausts, which were intended to be an outlet point for air that had passed through the intercooler radiator. However, with the intended fuel tanks and pumps at last installed, and the Spitfire-type propeller unit reinstalled, a speed in full supercharger of 422 mph (679 km/h) was achieved on 13 November with the full supercharging working. This was a cause for considerable celebration. Although the projected maximum speed had not quite been achieved, nevertheless the Merlin Mustang was proving itself to be a genuine 400 mph-plus fighter. Although several existing aircraft types were quite capable of gaining that sort of speed in a dive, few contemporary fighters could achieve it in level flight. Indeed, it had become something of a 'holy grail' amongst fighter designers to try to break the 400 mph (644 km/h) barrier in level flight. The Rolls-Royce conversion of the Mustang was certainly in that class.

The Merlin 65 fitted to AL975/G later had to be replaced, and although another Merlin 65 was fitted, this aircraft was eventually flown with a Merlin 70-series motor for development work on that particular engine type (it was finally damaged beyond repair when its Merlin 71 failed during a later test flight, the aircraft having flown a total of 195 hours and 30 minutes on Merlin development work). By then a second Merlin-Mustang Mk X had flown. This was AM208, which flew for the first time under Merlin 65 power on 13 November 1942. The conversion work carried out

on this aircraft was similar to that on AL975/G, but was significantly different in having the movable section of the radiator air inlet below the lower fuselage permanently closed. Being a Mk I (like all five Rolls-Royce conversion aircraft), it was built with the movable inlet characteristic of that production model, but Rolls-Royce discovered that the permanent closing of this movable section of the inlet did not adversely affect performance. In the end this modification was carried out to all the Rolls-Royce conversion aircraft except for AL975/G. Rolls-Royce in fact considered that the movable intake section was not necessary at all – except possibly for enhanced engine cooling when the aircraft was stationary on the ground - and could not find a good reason why it was able to open as wide as it did (13 in or 33 cm in the fully open position).

After initial flight testing AM208 was transferred to Boscombe Down on 28 November, where it was used for performance trials until the following April. It was here that the true potential of the Merlin installation came into its own. Flying at a maximum weight of 9,100 lb (4,128 kg), AM208 achieved a maximum speed of 433 mph (697 km/h) at 22,000 ft (6,706 m). This was with full supercharger - the second stage of the supercharging being set to engage at 15,500 ft (4,725 m) - and a combat boost rating of +18 lb. It was a considerable triumph. The projected maximum speed of 427 mph (687 km/h) was thus exceeded, and it was believed that this was due to the permanent closing of the movable section

Rolls-Royce pioneered the installation of the Merlin engine into the basic Mustang Mk.I airframe, as can be seen here in left-hand side view detail of one of the Mustang Mk.X aircraft. A large amount of design and engineering work was needed to get to this stage, not just in the integrating of the Merlin which was a very different engine to the Allison V-1710 for which the Mustang's front-end had originally been designed. The new engine mounts, re-routed plumbing and four-bladed propeller are particularly evident. This installation gave a very prominent 'chin' to the Mustang, with a bulky lower nose air intake for the large box beneath the engine which was the intercooler/fuel cooler radiator
*(Photo: R.L. Ward Collection)*

of the radiator intake. A maximum altitude of 39,000 ft (11,887 m) was also achieved, and a time of 11.3 minutes to 30,000 ft (9,144 m). These were all spectacular figures for their day, and signalled the excellent possibilities for any production configuration that might be developed of the Merlin-engined layout for the Mustang.

Unfortunately, flight testing also uncovered several important problems with the new Merlin-engined Mustang. Whereas the Allison-powered Mustang was a generally pleasant aircraft to fly, with few real vices, the Merlin Mustang was a completely different beast. It was found quite early on during Rolls-Royce's testing that it was quite a handful for its pilots. The increased power, and other changes such as trim and loading considerations brought about by the installation of the completely different engine type, together with the introduction of the four-bladed propeller (Allison Mustangs used three-bladed units) conspired to give the aircraft some uncomfortable habits. These mainly concerned directional stability. The testing of AM208 at Boscombe Down introduced these problems to service test pilots, some of whom were singularly unimpressed. The aircraft was found to sideslip during manoeuvres, something that was not present with the Allison-Mustang, and directional trim was very different to the previous Mustang versions, particularly with power applied. In an effort to solve the problem, it was proposed that the fin area of the aircraft should be augmented. This took the form of an overall increase in the chord of the fin, giving several additional square feet in area, but ultimately the addition of a small triangular dorsal fin-type extension extending forward from the base of the fin was eventually found to be of some help. This additional fitment is most closely associated with the much later, P-51D and Mustang Mk IV series Mustangs, but it was also fitted to some earlier Merlin Mustangs as well.

A further serious difficulty was encountered during the early testing of the Rolls-Royce converted Mustangs. It was found that in some flight regimes, especially in high-speed dives, the main undercarriage doors became unlocked and extended when a particular yawing motion was encountered. The problem was eventually traced to the door locking mechanism and was rectified, although some instances continued to occur. Indeed, the trouble appears to have persisted for some time, because later on some operational Merlin-Mustang production aircraft suffered airframe failure and break-up in flight that was eventually

attributed to the undercarriage doors extending in flight.

The third Rolls-Royce Mustang Mk X conversion to fly was AM203, which first flew on 13 December 1942. It too was fitted with a Merlin 65 engine, and had the 11 ft 4 in (3.45 m) propeller assembly. Unlike the initial two aircraft, it was intended for and carried out service evaluation with the AFDU at Duxford (and later at Wittering). Prior to delivery there it did, however, achieve 431 mph (694 km/h) in full supercharger at 21,000 ft (6,400 m), but with the Spitfire Mk IX-size propeller installed the top speed was increased by 3 mph (5 km/h). This aircraft was painted with a special 'high-speed' gloss finish, in comparison to the usual matt paint of service aircraft, to see if the gloss surface could improve the type's maximum speed. The special finish was created by Sanderson and Holmes of Derby. In subsequent trials it was found that this finish did not improve the aircraft's maximum speed at all. AM203 was later fitted with the increased area fin previously described, which did not improve the type's flight characteristics.

The fourth Rolls-Royce conversion was AL963. It too flew with a Merlin 65, and initially took to the air after conversion on 21 January 1943. It was primarily used for trials with an SU fuel injection pump, the purpose being to aid in the development of fuel injection systems that were compatible with the expanding science of the two-speed, two-stage type engine that was now making older forms of inline engine - such as the Allison V-1710 with its simpler single-stage supercharger – obsolete. This test work in fact helped along the development process on the even more advanced Merlin 100-series engine that Rolls-Royce was also working on. The appearance of this aircraft went through some important changes, due to the repositioning of the intercooler radiator from under the engine to the intake beneath the fuselage where the main engine cooling radiator and oil cooler were situated. This led to a redesign into a more streamlined shape of the prominent chin that was otherwise so characteristic of the Rolls-Royce Mustang conversions. AL963 was also fitted with a dorsal extension forward of the fin leading edge as an attempt to improve directional stability – this conversion might also have been applied to AL975. The aircraft's fin later had its chord increased. AL963 flew for the last time in January 1944.

Although the Merlin installation was obviously developing into a successful practical reality, Rolls-Royce had considerable misgivings as to what the next step might be. In an internal memo dated 1 July 1942, discussions involving the well-known US pilot

Thomas Hitchcock, the company, and Brig Gen A.J. Lyon (from the Air Technical Section of the Eighth Army Air Force in Britain) were outlined. It was stated that if acceptance for the new installation and configuration was allowed to take place in the US, there was the possibility that at best time was going to be wasted, and at worst it might turn out that the idea would "..not be favourably received by strong vested interests". By that stage even Rolls-Royce, thousands of miles away from the anti-Mustang feeling at Wright Field and in other sections of the US military, knew of the reality of the situation. In fact, the idea began to grow that Eighth Fighter Command in Britain should take a look at the Merlin-Mustang, with serving AAF officers seconded to Boscombe Down to observe the planned British military trials. It was at one time proposed (and later acted on) that two of the converted aircraft should be turned over to the AAF for trials to be conducted under American parameters – but in Britain, and definitely not in the US. At the same time, North American Aviation could be kept abreast of developments, while attempts were made to get the Merlin Mustang started on its long road to military acceptance in the US. It was even proposed that one or more of the Rolls-Royce converted Merlin-Mustangs should serve on operational trials with Eighth Army Air Force fighter units in Britain as a comparison with existing types.

There were certainly fewer misgivings amongst British procurement agencies compared to their US counterparts. Once the Merlin-Mustang configuration had started to take shape, the Ministry of Aircraft Production began to look favourably at the possibility of an initial production run of 500 Merlin-engined Mustangs. It was beginning to appear as if the Merlin-powered Mustang could help to alleviate the 'fighter problem' for 1943 that senior RAF and government personnel had been starting to become worried about as 1942 progressed. Amongst the many letters and telegrams that were sent between interested British officials during those hard-working summer months of 1942, there was even the allusion that thought should be given to licence-manufacture of the Mustang in Britain, using parts supplied by NAA. A potential source for British assembly was identified, this being Air Service Training at Hamble in Hampshire. The whole idea was to ensure deliveries to the RAF of Merlin-Mustangs, while at the same time trying to stay out of the procurement issues in the US, and side-step the increasingly perceived strong American opposition to the Mustang.

The final example of the five Rolls-Royce Mustang Mk X conversions was AM121. This aircraft had originally been intended to be the first to be converted, but because it was an NA-83 from the second batch of Mustang Mk I airframes it went through a longer period of performance testing prior to conversion. It was found to be 730 lb (331 kg) heavier than the earlier Mk I aircraft from the original production series (NA-73), and it first flew under Merlin 65 power in February 1943 after conversion. The test pilot was Capt Shepherd, as with all the first flights of all five Mustang Mk X aircraft. By then much of the basic testing of the Merlin

installation and compatibility with the Mustang had been carried out by Rolls-Royce, and AM121 was therefore briefly used for propeller development work. This included a spell with Rotol on the creation of special finishes for propeller blades. At some point the aircraft appears to have been fitted with a wider cord fin. AM121 was later turned over to the Eighth Army Air Force's VIII Fighter Command Air Technical Section at Bovingdon on 18 April 1943, where it served in US colours and markings, after apparently spending some time with the RAF's AFDU. It had a mishap and ended up on its nose while bearing the codes 'VQ-R' (the 'VQ' coding appearing on some aircraft assigned to the Air Technical Section) whilst seemingly engaged in further propeller trials. It underwent a considerable amount of evaluation with the ATS, where its long range and endurance were of particular interest. However, the aircraft's poor directional stability was a major stumbling block with the ATS pilots and other VIII FC personnel who flew it. According to historian Roger Freeman in 'The Mighty Eighth War Manual', the aircraft was eventually reduced to spares at Bovingdon in August 1944. Nevertheless, it provided much useful evaluation for those at Bovingdon who were at the sharp end of the shooting war in Europe, in contrast to the desk-flyers at Wright Field back in the US. One other Mustang Mk X also reportedly flew briefly with the AAF in England. This was AM203, the third Merlin-Mustang to fly in England, which was seconded to the Americans in Britain during the first part of 1943 again for evaluation purposes.

## Developments in the US

Like any good aircraft manufacturer, North American Aviation was keen to promote its products, and look at ways of improving them or modifying them to meet specific developing requirements. The considerable interest that was shown in Britain during the early summer of 1942 in the creation of a Merlin-engined development of the basic Mustang layout was keenly watched by the company – although it was clear that there was no specific USAAF need for such an aircraft. Nevertheless, thanks to the work of Thomas Hitchcock and Philip Legarra (an NAA technical representative in the UK), the concept of a Merlin-Mustang was one that grew increasingly important to the company. Information was made available to NAA by Rolls-Royce on the Merlin conversion programme at Hucknall, and with substantial lobbying taking place in the US inspired by Hitchcock and a small group of others, the USAAF slowly started to take an interest. NAA eventually received a contract for the conversion of two Allison-engined Mustangs into Merlin configuration on 25 July 1942, and work began in earnest in September 1942. This was sometime after Rolls-Royce had started its conversion work on the first Mustang Mk X AL975, and Legarra in particular was frustrated at the lost time and the apparently slow progress with the conversion work at Inglewood, which had little official prompting to spur it along. On returning from the US in early September 1942 Legarra was disappointed to note that the Mustang had the lowest priority that

A large amount of work needed to be carried out by NAA to create the production-standard Merlin-powered Mustang layout. NAA later stated that the whole job expended 223,000 man hours to get the configuration right. What is probably the first prototype XP-51B aircraft displays here one of the stages in the whole process, with an interim lower fuselage radiator intake, although the photograph appears to have been 're-touched' to hide and enhance some details. Interestingly the wing 20 mm cannons are apparently not present, but the aircraft bears an earlier style of fuselage national insignia than the picture of a US prototype aircraft elsewhere in this Chapter where a later form of US national insignia with side bars is present and yet the cannons are still fitted. This possibly points to the fact that the cannons originally fitted to these aircraft were at first removed but then re-installed at a later date in these prototype aircraft as a possible production armament configuration for the P-51B that was not taken up
*(Photo: NAA)*

could be granted to an aircraft. However, more positively, USAAF Gen 'Hap' Arnold was indoctrinated – apparently by the US Ambassador in London, John G. Winant – about the qualities of the Mustang when he visited London in June 1942.

Fortunately, NAA at Inglewood was by that time working on its own Merlin-Mustang conversions, having received the contract for this work in July 1942. Although the project went comparatively slowly, NAA was interested as much in the aerodynamics of the Merlin installation as in the actual installation itself. Edgar Schmued and his team had successfully designed a beautifully clean and advanced airframe while creating the Mustang, that now had to be transformed to take the Merlin engine while not losing any of the Mustang's aerodynamic qualities. This was somewhat different to the Rolls-Royce approach, where the emphasis was on making the concept of a Merlin-engined Mustang work rather than on the long-term aerodynamics of the installation. In fact the whole job was quite a difficult task for NAA, because the redesign of the Mustang layout necessary to re-engine the aircraft was not simply a case of installing the Merlin where the Allison had been so neatly and effectively mated into the airframe. The chosen engine for the NAA work was the Packard-built derivative of the Merlin 61. In American designation terminology that was the Packard V-1650-3, which is now almost universally referred to as the Packard Merlin but which at the time was known and referred to in many documents simply as the V-1650.

The Packard Company was only in the early stages of adapting to the building of the Merlin 61 when the requirement for the type came from North American. The Merlin was already successfully in production at Packard's Detroit facilities as the V-1650-1, which was equivalent to the low- and medium-altitude British Merlin XX (the Packard-built version of this engine was known to the British, when installed in British or Commonwealth-operated aircraft, as the Merlin 28). The Merlin 61 was a very different engine to the Merlin XX, and a great deal of effort was needed for Packard to get the Merlin 61 production off the ground. It was early Packard-made examples of this engine type that reached NAA for installation in the Merlin-Mustang conversions that the company was undertaking, and therefore the whole process involved evolving technology that was not at that time tried and tested in combat. In essence the V-1650-3 was similar in configuration to the Merlin 61, and featured a two-stage, two-speed supercharger that was to become so important in the Mustang's subsequent surge in performance at higher altitudes compared to the Allison-engined versions. There was considerable liaison between Rolls-Royce and Packard on all aspects of the Packard licence-production of the Merlin, and Rolls-Royce had a talented advisor, J.E. Ellor, working with Packard in Detroit - although, due to the distances involved, the very different work practices

between the two companies, the differing ways in which Rolls-Royce noted alterations compared to the Packard practices, and many other factors under wartime conditions, the liaison between the two was sometimes carried on under difficult circumstances. Packard found that early models of the V-1650-3 when bench-run were troublesome and did not at first give the required power output, although continuing development work in Detroit gradually overcame these difficulties.

## North American's Two Merlin-powered Prototypes

The two Mustangs that were chosen by NAA for the prototype conversion into Merlin power were the two aircraft that the company had retained from the batch of 150 Mustang Mk IA that were originally destined for the RAF, when that batch was broken up following the US entry into World War Two and 55 examples were transferred as P-51s to the USAAF. The aircraft in that production batch received US as well as RAF serial numbers, because they were ordered for Britain under the then-new 'Lend-Lease' arrangements. The two NAA aircraft were 41-37352 and 41-37421. Both were armed with two 20 mm cannons in each wing, as was the case with the other aircraft in that production batch. Under the USAAF's procurement policies, a new designation was sanctioned for the two aircraft, as they were effectively going to be of a 'new' pursuit type. Thus they were initially designated XP-78, and that nomenclature was employed in a considerable amount of documentation that related to them at the time. However, in the end the established type designation P-51 continued to be used for the planned new Mustang version with Merlin power, and so the two aircraft adopted the intended P-51B designation that was eventually given by the AAF to the initial production model of the Merlin Mustang. The two prototype aircraft were thus eventually simply designated as XP-51B, with the 'X' standing for 'experimental prototype'. They received the company designation NA-101.

It was a considerable task to convert the aircraft to Merlin power. Indeed, it was subsequently said by North American Aviation that the task expended 223,000 man hours to get the configuration right. The first aircraft to be converted was 41-37352, which pioneered the V-1650-3 installation. As was the case with Rolls-Royce, NAA's designers and engineers discovered that a redesign of the engine mounts and cowling was needed, and a considerable amount of relocating of ancillary equipment and pipework was necessary. The forward fuselage also had to be strengthened to hold the heavier Merlin (which weighed some 1,690 lbs or 766 kg dry compared to the 1,335 lb or 605 kg of the Allison V-1710). In order to keep the nose as 'clean' as possible, the intercooler required to cool the fuel-air mix from the engine's supercharger was located in the intake duct for the radiator and oil

A factory photograph of the cockpit interior of a P-51B. Like all combat versions of the Mustang, this version had a well thought out interior, with everything within comparatively easy reach. Much of the interior design could be attributed to Edgar Schmued, and it was certainly one of the neater World War Two fighter cockpits. The interior colour was generally dark green, the widely misinterpreted US 'Interior Green' shade not having been brought into widespread use at that time, although it was introduced in the later P-51D manufacture. The partially obscured gunsight appears to be an N-3B reflector sight, the standard issue for the P-51B/C series; although some later examples of these marks appear to have had the N-9 gunsight instead. A number of Mustangs also carried an additional simple 'ring and bead' sight in case the more sophisticated gunsight went wrong
*(Photo: NAA)*

converted Mustangs than the prominent 'chin' of the Rolls-Royce machines. North American's designers also tinkered with the thrust line of the engine, giving a slight downward appearance to the cowling panels compared to the panel line joints that run horizontally along the fuselage of Merlin-Mustangs up to the firewall. A four-bladed, cuffed Hamilton Standard propeller unit was fitted. Performance-wise, NAA appear to have hoped (as conveyed in a letter from Brig Gen Lyon to Ernest Hives of Rolls-Royce on 4 September 1942) that the Packard Merlin-powered Mustang would reach 445 mph (716 km/h) at 28,000 ft (8,534 m).

Rolls-Royce was far ahead of NAA in being the first to get a Merlin-powered Mustang into the air, achieving this on 13 October 1942. North American Aviation accomplished the same feat on 30 November 1942, when Robert Chilton took 41-37352 into the air for its maiden flight from Mines Field under V-1650-3 power. The flight was reasonably successful until the engine started to overheat, necessitating a rapid cessation after some 45 minutes of flight and an urgent investigation into what had happened. After some examination it was found that the radiator had become partially clogged, the result of dissimilar metals in the cooling pipework reacting with the engine's coolant to form and dislodge residues that caused the system to become contaminated and fouled. It was some weeks before the aircraft flew again, by which time the necessary alterations had been made to the cooling pipes and a different radiator assembly had been trialled.

It was in fact some time before a satisfactory intake shape below the belly could be found for the new installation. The intake needed to be larger due to the greater cooling needs of the V-1650-3 which called for a different radiator design and larger pipework. A number of designs were test-flown before the shape was perfected. A problem with the initial shape was intake 'rumble', which was caused by turbulent boundary layer air along the lower fuselage intermittently entering the intake, and to explore the problem a full-size Mustang was installed in the huge wind tunnel at NACA's Ames facility in California. NAA's Ed Horkey actually sat in the cockpit of the aircraft while it was tested in the wind tunnel up to a simulated 500 mph (805 km/h) so that he could experience the 'rumble' effect that Chilton had discovered during the initial test flying. Eventually NAA developed the well-known fixed intake shape with its distinctive slanted lip, incorporating an all-important gap between it and the lower fuselage, allowing only clean airstream air to enter. A substantial gutter around the upper extremity of the intake's structure helped the previously troublesome boundary layer air to escape along the fuselage sides. This was similar but by no means identical to the shape that had been pioneered on the A-36A and P-51A configurations, and was so characteristic of the series-production Merlin-Mustangs – although it now appears that some of the first production Merlin-engined aircraft (early P-51Bs) actually flew with an interim shape of intake.

An image that amply illustrates the result of all the hard work. A brand new Mustang Mk.III, recently delivered to Britain (although the photo actually carries the date April 1945), with its forward fuselage showing off the neat Packard V-1650 (Merlin) installation that was the result of the Rolls-Royce and NAA work to integrate the Merlin to the Mustang airframe. The close-cowled engine installation and small unobtrusive intake below the nose are particularly noticeable in this view. The four-bladed Hamilton Standard propeller unit, in this case with blade cuffs, was also a major feature of the new Merlin installation
*(Photo: R.L. Ward Collection)*

cooler beneath the fuselage. This intake then went through a laborious process of redesign and tinkering to get the shape right, while also giving enough cooling air for all the different elements located within it. The carburettor air intake on top of the nose of the Allison-engined Mustangs was moved – in much the same way that Rolls-Royce also did – to beneath the nose for similar reasons to those that Rolls-Royce discovered. The lower nose layout from that start was, however, much neater on the NAA's

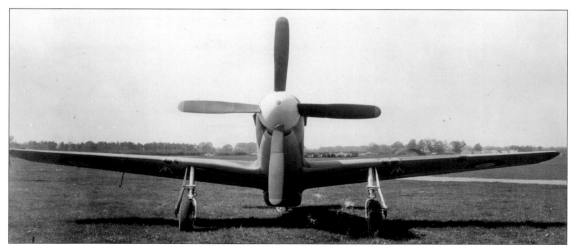

The first production versions of the Mustang that developed from the work of Rolls-Royce and NAA into the creation of a Merlin-engined Mustang airframe were the P-51B and P-51C. This smart Dallas-built P-51C-10-NT, 43-24943, illustrates the beautifully clean lines of the new nose arrangement with a production-series Packard V-1650-3 (Merlin) installed. The aircraft is overall 'natural metal' except for the aluminium-painted parts of the wings, with a Dark Olive Drab anti-glare panel ahead of the windscreen (Photo: NAA)

The positioning of the radiator itself within the intake area also caused problems for NAA. Originally the revised radiator arrangement was placed on its side so as to fit into the existing space, but this did not work satisfactorily and a new radiator design from the Harrison Division of General Motors with an upright fitting had to be pioneered. This also necessitated the repositioning of the oil cooler. In fact the whole of the Mustang's lower fuselage had to be altered to suit the aerodynamics of the new installation that had been developed. As previously related, North American's designers were very concerned with the aerodynamics of the whole re-engining process, and had to get the shape of the aircraft right once the Merlin and its related equipment had been successfully installed. Edgar Schmued actually visited Rolls-Royce in England in March 1943 while this process was going on. Eventually the fuselage beneath the cockpit was deepened, and for production aircraft the position of the wing was slightly lowered by 3 in (7.62 cm) and altered relative to the Allison-engined Mustangs. Therefore the fuselage of the Merlin Mustang P-51B series was substantially different to the Allison-engined P-51A and its predecessors in many respects, even though the two still looked similar.

The second XP-51B, 41-37421, first flew in February 1943. As a measure of how slow this development process was for NAA, in the three months following the first flight of the XP-51B, only 35 flights were accomplished, whereas during the initial three months of Rolls-Royce's flight-test programme 46 flights were made at Hucknall, plus other flying at Boscombe Down. Increasingly, however, the XP-51B started to fulfil NAA's hopes for the Merlin-Mustang combination. Eventually a speed of 453 mph (729 km/h) with full supercharger was achieved at 28,800 ft (8,778 m), and with the endurance of some four hours on internal fuel being carried over from the previous Mustang marks, the Merlin-Mustang combination was set to be a winner. While NAA worked hard on the development process for the Merlin-Mustang, Packard was also working overtime to get the V-1650-3 into production. This too proved to be a difficult process, but the value of the engine and its projected installation in the Mustang was at last starting to stir many in the AAF. In June 1943 Packard received a substantial contract for 13,325 V-1650-3 engines.

## Merlin-Mustang Production Commences

Unfortunately the procurement process of the Merlin-Mustang itself was entangled in the mire of politics and extraordinary blindness that seemed to equip many in the Army Air Force's development, testing and procurement offices. As noted in the Introduction, even the purchase of Allison-engined Mustangs for AAF service was a difficult process. The intended order for 1,200 Allison-engined Mustangs, which eventually materialised as only 310 P-51A aircraft, became mixed up with the initial procurement for the intended opening production model of the Merlin-Mustang. This was to be the P-51B, following the abandoning of the originally-planned P-78 designation. Although the testing of the two XP-51B aircraft by NAA became increasingly successful and fulfilled the performance intentions of the company, ironically the P-51B layout had already been ordered into production. In December 1942 the first significant order for Inglewood-built P-51B-NA Mustangs was made – an order for these aircraft had been provisionally sanctioned in August 1942, conditional on the success of the intended Merlin installation by NAA. However, in a strange quirk of financial gymnastics, although the initial aircraft (P-51B-1-NA and P-51B-5-NA) were ordered under FY 1943 funding, some of the subsequent P-51B-10-NA production was allocated from the FY 1942 procurement. In fact the possibility of orders for the P-51B came along at a good time. In November 1942 there was the start of a significant shake-up of the procurement procedures for combat aircraft as a part of a larger reform of the way that procurement was handled for the US armed forces. Henceforward, civil servants were given far more responsibility in the whole process, in order to try to ensure a better supply of the most needed war material. This had the long-term effect of significantly reducing the damaging individual influence of some officers such as those at the Materiel Command.

With the prospect at last of large-scale orders for the Mustang, North American Aviation was already in the process of altering its production resources to fit the new more healthy procurement

A P-51B or P-51C Mustang is run-up prior to being prepared for overseas shipment by sea. It was important to properly prepare the aircraft before being shipped, with preventative covering to avoid the worst of the salt water conditions, and the preparation of working parts to ensure that they functioned as intended on arrival. For the engine, a procedure was tried which involved running the engine with 65 octane fuel as an inhibitor prior to loading onto the transport ship, which theoretically protected the engine until it could be run on 100 octane (or the preferred 130 octane) after safe arrival. Noteworthy in this picture while the procedure is being tried are the ground personal with fire extinguishers, just in case (Photo: via Chris Ellis)

Illustrating the classic planform of the Merlin-powered Mustang, an early P-51B flies over snow-covered terrain probably somewhere in California during a test flight. Beneath the wings are two jettisonable 75 US gallon long-range fuel tanks. The worn nature of the uppersurface Olive Drab paint is noteworthy, this particular paint finish always giving trouble and wearing very easily into a worn and faded appearance. NAA intended for the upperwing surface in particular of every Mustang to be kept as clean and as smooth as possible due to the peculiarities of the laminar flow wing, but camouflage paint made this very difficult to achieve, let alone the demanding operating conditions that many Mustangs flew in *(Photo: NAA)*

at well over 20,000 ft (6,096 m), and a war emergency rating of +18 lb boost available for short periods. A maximum altitude was attainable of just short of 40,000 ft (12,192 m). These performance and range figures were a quantum leap in American fighter design, and placed North American Aviation literally miles ahead of all other pursuit manufacturers in the US.

Dimensionally, the wingspan of the P-51B/C was the same as the previous Allison-engined Mustangs, indeed the span of the Mustang was constant from the NA-73X to the later production models with Merlin power. The exact figure was 37 ft 0.3 in (11.29 m), the 0.3-in actually being 5/16-in. However, the length of the P-51B/C was slightly greater than the previous Allison-engined Mustangs – an important point that many historians completely overlook. The Allison-engined Mustangs were 32 ft 2.88 in (9.83 m) in length, the 2.88-in actually being 2 7/8-in. However, the Merlin Mustangs were slightly longer, at 32 ft 3.3 in (9.84 m), the 3.3-in actually being 3 5/16-in.

As previously related, some thought had been given to the Mustang being assembled in Britain from parts supplied by North American Aviation, in order to circumvent the opposition to the Mustang in the US. In the event NAA did not appear to have liked the idea, the company being at great pains to point out that its production schedules were based around the delivery schedules agreed with Packard, and that all Merlin-Mustang production would be Packard Merlin powered (including any examples required by Britain) – and that thought would only be given to the type being assembled elsewhere in the event of Packard being unable to supply sufficient engines on time. This in fact turned out to have some irony attached to it. Although the idea of assembly in Britain was never taken up, Packard did fall behind in delivering engines on time, resulting in some completed Mustangs being stored at Inglewood while they awaited their engines, and the original delivery timetable to the USAAF being a little behind schedule. In a further twist to the tale, the idea of Mustangs being assembled in Britain received a body blow from another quarter. The original thinking by the Ministry of Aircraft Production in Britain was for Air Service Training at Hamble to assemble the aircraft. However, it became obvious that the job would not just be assembly, but that a considerable amount of engineering work would need to be undertaken as well. This prompted Sir Frank Spriggs, the chief of the group of companies to which Air Service Training belonged, to state in a meeting with Sir Wilfred Freeman at the Ministry of Aircraft Production on 25 February 1943 that he had no further interest in the project and wished to be relieved of responsibility for it. Eventually no decision was reached as to who might build Merlin-Mustangs in Britain, but the problem was finally solved when North American Aviation got into the full-scale building of the type once the large-scale US orders were forthcoming.

Eventually, 1,988 P-51Bs were built at Inglewood under the NAA designations NA-102 and NA-104, and 1,750 P-51Cs came off the production lines at Dallas with the NAA designation NA-103 and NA-111. The NA-111 block numbered 400 aircraft, and was from 1944 procurement. The first production P-51B-1-NA to fly did so at Mines Field on 5 May 1943 – NAA having received the first production V-1650-3 engines for these aircraft in April 1943 - and the initial P-51C took to the air in Dallas three months later on 5 August 1943. The first deliveries to the USAAF were made in June 1943 - by then the mire of service testing had started to be straightened out. Elements of the 354th Fighter Group became, later that year, the first front-line USAAF group to fully equip with the type.

climate. During 1940 the company had expanded significantly by starting the building of a brand new production facility just outside Dallas, Texas. Initially this factory was delegated to take over NA-16 series Harvard/Texan production from Inglewood – and there were serious delays in the production of these types due to this, as noted in correspondence by the British Purchasing Commission at that time. However, with Dallas up and running successfully from 1941, there was eventually additional capacity available at the new factory complex for further manufacture, and some of the Merlin Mustang production was delegated to that facility. The P-51B equivalent that was made at Dallas was the P-51C, which was practically identical to the P-51B production model from Inglewood. Similarly, the manufacture of NAA's other major on-going project, the B-25 Mitchell twin-engined medium bomber, was increasingly delegated from Inglewood to a manufacturing facility at Kansas City, Missouri.

The P-51B in its production form was powered by the Packard V-1650-3 of 1,595 hp to 1,600 hp with maximum boost (1,380 hp for take-off), with a Bendix starter and a Bendix PD.18.A1 or PD.18.C1A carburettor, driving a Hamilton Standard cuffed four-bladed constant-speed propeller unit of 11 ft 2 in (3.4 m) diameter. It was armed, like the Allison-engined P-51A, with two 0.5-in machine guns in each wing. The internal fuel capacity was 184 US gallons in two wing fuel tanks, and (in all but the earliest production aircraft, although some were later retro-fitted) an 85 US gallon fuel tank (of which approximately 65 US gallons were usable) behind the cockpit. This additional internal fuel tank, although helping to considerably extend the Mustang's range, proved troublesome in giving centre of gravity problems and some handling difficulties when full. Like the P-51A, the P-51B could carry a 75 US gallon drop tank beneath each wing, but the wing was sufficiently stressed to be able to carry external fuel tanks of up to 150 US gallons. This gave a theoretical range, on internal fuel, of 850 miles (1,368 km); and with the 75 US gallon underwing tanks, of some 1,240 miles (1,995 km) – which was a breathtaking amount compared to all other Allied fighters. Its maximum speed was in the region of 440 mph (708 km/h) at 30,000 ft (9,144 m), with the V-1650-3 giving its maximum output

# Initial USAAF Operations

## Chapter 2

Widely regarded as the true pioneer in taking the Merlin-engined P-51 into combat, and thus starting the process by which the Mustang was to make such a significant contribution to the Allied cause in the air war, was the 354th Fighter Group. One of this unit's early P-51B Mustangs is seen here almost certainly at Boxted in the early weeks of 1944 (the photograph was passed for publication by the US censor on 20 January 1944). Underlining the fact that the 354th FG was actually a tactical, Ninth Air Force group that was effectively 'on loan' to the Eighth Air Force for bomber escort duties, this aircraft carries eight mission markers on its nose in the form of bomb symbols. A 355th Fighter Squadron P-51B-1-NA, 43-12451, it was coded GQ-I and at one stage in its career was named 'Live Bait' and 'Gwendolyn' when flown by 1st Lt Clayton Gross, a six aerial victories ace. Gross claimed four Bf 109s while flying this aircraft. Its former pilot, 1st Lt Gil Talbot, had originally named it 'Peggy' and claimed an Me 410 while flying it, although it is possible that Talbot might have been piloting an anonymous P-51B coded GQ-U for the latter claim
(Photo: USAAF)

**B**earing in mind the somewhat troubled procurement history of the Mustang for the US military, when the first Merlin-powered P-51B Mustangs started to leave the production lines at Inglewood in May and June 1943, it was by no means certain that they would ever be used as long-range bomber escorts. At that time the heavy losses of the Schweinfurt and Regensburg missions of 17 August 1943 were several weeks in the future, and the Eighth Army Air Force was continuing its policy of daylight strategic bombing of Germany from England without fighter escort all the way to and from its targets. The P-47 Thunderbolt had only recently started to provide any kind of cover at all from English bases for the Eighth Air Force's bombers, and the P-38 Lightning was still several months from its first genuine long-range bomber escort missions over north-west Europe. In the hierarchy of the Army Air Force, the Mustang still faced opposition or indifference in many quarters, even though it had been ordered into fairly wide-scale production as the P-51B with Merlin power. It must be remembered that the long-range escort fighter had never come into the thinking of the USAAF's strategists or their predecessors in the Army Air Corps, and the Army Air Force in any case was still considered, in mid-1943, to be a part of the Army (which indeed it was on paper) and intended in large part to support the Army's ground forces.

The USAAF's Directorate of Ground Support under Brig Gen D.M. Schlatter was responsible for allocating combat aircraft types

to specific roles, and the Merlin-engined P-51B was originally recognised principally as a tactical fighter and reconnaissance aircraft. It is therefore not surprising that when the first Merlin-Mustangs started to arrive in Britain in October and November 1943, they were not intended at all for escorting bombers – or indeed for any other purely fighter role. The first USAAF group that was intended for the type was the 354th Fighter Group. This unit, comprising the 353rd, 355th and 356th Fighter Squadrons, was to be assigned to the British-based tactical Ninth Army Air Force, and was intended for close air support of Allied ground forces particularly during the coming intended assault on the German-held French coast on the opening of the long-awaited 'second front'.

Originally activated on 15 November 1942 at Hamilton Field, California, the 354th followed a route somewhat similar to that of many of the fighter groups that were created at around that time to bolster the rapidly-growing Army Air Force. A period of training for its newly-assigned pilots was carried out in the Bell P-39 Airacobra, and the group filled in before being sent overseas by providing aerial defence of the western US, which was conducted partly as a training assignment. At last preparing during October 1943 to depart for England, many of the group's first cadre of pilots were assigned when the group was at Tonopah, Nevada, some having only just newly-graduated at flying training schools such as that at Luke Field, Arizona. Much time was spent on

An in-flight view of a Merlin-engined Mustang assigned to the unit that began the process of establishing the Mustang's fame as one of the truly excellent fighters of all time. Wearing the 'AJ' fuselage code of the 356th Fighter Squadron of the famed 354th Fighter Group, this P-51B-1-NA is fully representative of the early Merlin-powered Mustangs that the group took into combat during the pioneering days of the type's combat indoctrination over North-west Europe. From the first main production batch of Merlin-Mustangs, 'Miss Pea Ridge' wears the white nose, wing and tail bands of these early Merlin-engined Mustangs in the ETO, which were worn as additional recognition features to ensure that the Mustangs were not mistaken as German fighters
(Photo: USAAF)

training before the personnel of the group headed across the US by train – minus their Airacobras - to the famous Camp Kilmer in New Jersey. Camp Kilmer was the starting point for many overseas deployments of US combat groups heading for Europe by the northern route. On 21 October the group's personnel sailed for Britain aboard the Union-Castle Line troop-ship MV 'Athlone Castle' (and not HMS (!) 'Athlone Castle' as claimed by some writers). After a 12-day voyage as a part of a convoy, the ship reached Liverpool. The first stop for the group's personnel in England was the airfield at Greenham Common, Berkshire, and it was expected by members of the group that they would be assigned P-47 Thunderbolts for ground-attack missions over the Continent. It was something of a surprise to the group's officers when they were told that the unit would be equipped with Mustangs. This was an aircraft type with which few if any of the group's pilots were familiar.

## Merlin-Mustangs become Bomber Escorts

As a backdrop to these initial developments, however, some high-level manoeuvring was taking place. Those at the top in the Eighth Air Force had already come to realize that proper, comprehensive escort for their increasingly beleaguered daylight bomber force was essential. By the final months of 1943, some raids were undergoing losses of approaching ten per cent, a figure much above which losses were considered to be prohibitive. Tightly packed formations of B-17 Flying Fortresses and B-24 Liberators were proving to be unable to fight off Luftwaffe fighters, despite their heavy defensive armament and in spite of the claims by the bomber advocates that the bombers would always be able to defend themselves and successfully bomb their targets in broad daylight. The Eighth Air Force was having to go through what would be called today a major reality check, and the Merlin-engined Mustang appeared to be a potential answer to the growing difficulties – in being an aircraft with excellent range and good all-round performance, even at high altitudes. The arrival in Britain of initial deliveries of the Merlin-Mustang looked promising – but

these were intended, by the desk-flyers back in the US, as ground-attack aircraft for the Ninth Air Force. Something had to be done, and so in a series of deals that were struck, the precise background of which has never completely come into the open, the Eighth and Ninth Air Forces worked out some compromises. Temporarily, the Ninth Air Force's 354th Fighter Group and its prized Mustangs would be attached to the Eighth Air Force, but the 354th would return to the Ninth's full control in the future, when the Eighth had its own Mustang groups assigned – so long as the Mustang doubters back in the US could be persuaded to assign Mustang units as fighter and not as fighter-bomber groups.

Further deals also related to other incoming groups, but in the short-term the 354th became the first Mustang group to take the Merlin-Mustang into combat over north-west Europe. The 354th therefore found itself in a totally different kind of war to the fighting that it had expected, under a completely different command. The leader of the Eighth Air Force's VIII Fighter Command from August 1943 was the talented and pragmatic Maj Gen William Kepner, who was subsequently to oversee the great build-up of US fighter forces in Britain, and the decisive effect it was to have on the air war over north-west Europe. In the short-term, it was intended to get the 354th FG equipped with P-51Bs and combat-ready in the shortest period of time – no mean feat for a group that had not flown Mustangs before. The unit moved from its temporary base at Greenham Common to the Essex airfield of Boxted around the middle of November 1943. Its CO, Col Kenneth Martin, was asked by IX Fighter Command (which the unit still technically belonged to) how long it would take to get the Mustang into combat. He answered two weeks, and he was to be proven right, even though this sounded highly optimistic. The first Merlin-Mustangs arrived for the 354th just before the move was made to Boxted, and some pilots of the unit were also able to get in some time on Allison-engined Mustangs of the Middle Wallop-based 107th Tactical Reconnaissance Squadron, which was just taking the F-6B reconnaissance version of the Allison-powered P-51A into combat. (It has been suggested, in at least one

published source, that these Allison-Mustangs were loaned by the 10th Reconnaissance Group – which is completely incorrect, as the 10th did not even exist at that time!). Once at Boxted the 354th put in a rapid and extensive period of training, and remarkably was ready for the first planned operation, on 1 December. On that day, 24 P-51Bs of the unit flew the familiar 'shake-down' mission over nearby enemy-held territory in Belgium and the Pas-de-Calais in France. The group was accompanied by a highly-experienced and gifted air leader, Lt Col Donald Blakeslee of the veteran 4th Fighter Group, which had grown out of the original American-manned Eagle Squadrons of the RAF from earlier in the war. At that time the 4th FG was operating Thunderbolts, but it subsequently converted to Mustangs in 1944 and became one of the leading exponents of Merlin-powered P-51s in the coming months. This initial mission was comparatively successful, and, to put it in its historical context, it was flown only days after the first genuine Mustang bomber escort missions in the CBI theatre that were carried out in late November 1943 by the less-capable (in terms of bomber escort capability) Allison-engined Mustangs of the 311th Fighter-Bomber Group. The first genuine Mustang bomber escort over Europe was flown on the 354th Fighter Group's second mission, on 5 December. On that day the VIII Fighter Command put up a covering force of P-38 Lightnings, P-47 Thunderbolts and 36 Mustangs from the 354th to escort US heavy bombers on a raid over Amiens in France. This was comparatively uneventful. The third mission, on 11 December, was a milestone for the Eighth Air Force and for the Mustang, for it was the first Mustang bomber escort into Germany. The target was Emden, but the 354th lost its first Mustang without any significant contact with the Luftwaffe. The Mustangs flew with 75 US gallon external fuel tanks, which were now starting to reach England in useful quantities. Kiel was visited in the next escort on 13 December at just about the Mustang's extreme range with 75 US gallon drop tanks. Another Mustang was lost, and some inconclusive combats took place with twin-engined Messerschmitt Bf 110 heavy fighters. 16 December saw the Mustangs shepherding the heavy bombers to Bremen. During that escort the 354th achieved the first Mustang aerial victory over north-west Europe, when Lt Charles Francis Gumm, Jr., shot down a Bf 109. A graduate of the Luke Field flying training programme in Arizona and from one of the 354th Fighter Group's original cadres of pilots, Gumm was a 1st Lt from the 355th Fighter Squadron, and was subsequently to become one of the first aces of the Merlin-powered Mustang, when he achieved his fifth victory near Brunswick on 21 February 1944. He eventually achieved six confirmed aerial victories, but sadly was killed in a Mustang flying accident on 1 March 1944.

The Mustangs flew several more missions before the end of the

year, but by early 1944 the 354th was still the only Mustang-equipped VIII Fighter Command group. Although several German fighters had by then been downed, the 354th had also lost several Mustangs, including three on the 20 December Bremen mission. Worryingly, all losses up to that point appeared to have been through mechanical problems rather than enemy action. One of the losses was the CO of the 353rd FS, Maj Owen Seaman, who had attempted to ditch his Mustang in the North Sea with engine problems. Although the lower fuselage radiator intake was one of the innovations in the Mustang design and helped the type's performance and streamlining, it also made the Mustang almost impossible to ditch. Indeed, instructions were issued to US pilots later in the war to avoid ditching a Mustang at all costs unless it was absolutely necessary. Historian Roger Freeman could only find one example of a successful ditching of a Mustang, and normal practice came to be a bale-out once sufficient height had been gained. British experience was similar, the RAE at Farnborough conducting tests in late 1943 that led to the issue of a report at the end of the year that recommended a bale-out over water on all accounts from a stricken Mustang if there was enough height.

Other problems plagued the early Merlin-Mustangs during their initial operations as bomber escorts. Most of these were associated with the cold thin air that the aircraft operated in, and which proved so troublesome for the P-38 Lightning as well. High flying was not a problem for the B-17 Flying Fortress and B-24 Liberator bombers of the Eighth Air Force (although it was very

Famed recipient of the Medal of Honor for his outstanding and courageous airmanship on 11 January 1944 in defending B-17 Flying Fortresses of the 401st Bomb Group from multiple fighter attacks, James H. Howard of the 354th Fighter Group was the only Mustang pilot in Europe to be awarded the United States' highest military award for gallantry. The P-51B that he was flying on that famous occasion remains anonymous, but Howard is seen here, still the centre of media attention, several weeks later seated in the cockpit of his P-51B-5-NA 43-6315 AJ-A named 'Ding Hao!', with his then rank of Lt Col painted beside his name. Note the Malcolm Hood fitted to this aircraft *(Photo: USAAF)*

A probably staged but nonetheless busy ground crew scene at Boxted around 'Peggy', one of the best-known of the early Merlin-powered Mustangs that was allocated to the 354th Fighter Group and their pioneering bomber escort work from late 1943 onwards. The aircraft is being fitted with 75 US gallon long-range fuel tanks below the wings, and was a part of the 355th Fighter Squadron. A P-51B-1-NA, serial number 43-12451, it was coded GQ-I and at the time of this photograph it was allocated to 1st Lt Gil Talbot and named 'Peggy'. It later passed to 1st Lt Clayton Gross and re-named 'Live Bait' and 'Gwendolyn'. If the claims of these two pilots are put together, 'Peggy' was responsible for the destruction of five German fighters, four Bf 109s and an Me 410. It is adorned with the white nose, wing and tail bands of these early Merlin-engined Mustangs in the ETO, which were added as additional recognition features *(Photo: USAAF)*

One of the finest exponents of the Merlin-Mustang in combat over Europe was Capt Dominic Salvatore Gentile of the 336th Fighter Squadron of the famed 4th Fighter Group. Based at Debden in Essex, the 4th FG was one of the true high-flyers of the Eighth Air Force, and vied with the P-47 Thunderbolt-equipped 56th FG to be the top-scoring fighter group in VIII Fighter Command. Don Gentile's famous Mustang was named 'Shangri-La' and was a P-51B-5-NA, serial number 43-6913 and coded VF-T. It is seen here in the spring of 1944 at the time when the Mustang was starting to make an enormous impact on the air war over Germany. Gentile's final confirmed score was 21.833 aerial victories and six on the ground. He had formerly flown with one of the Eagle Squadrons of US volunteers in the RAF, the Spitfire-equipped No.133 Squadron, with which he had achieved the first two of his aerial victories *(Photo: USAAF)*

Although usually committed to bomber escort work, Eighth Air Force Mustang units were often called upon to perform tactical missions as well, a role that became increasingly important as the war progressed particularly in attacks on German airfields as a part of their escort missions deep into Germany. During the D-Day period in June 1944 many of the Eighth Air Force's air assets were specifically committed to the support of Allied ground units in the bitter fighting in Normandy, and in combating German fighters that attempted to intervene. This evocative scene at Bottisham in Cambridgeshire during June 1944 shows Mustangs of the 361st Fighter Group's 376th Fighter Squadron (coded 'E9') taxiing out ready for take-off on one such mission. All the Mustangs are marked with black and white so-called 'invasion stripes'. The P-51B-10-NA serial number 42-106707 in the foreground, coded E9-S and named 'Sleepytime Gal' was assigned to Lt Clarence E. Sullivan, Jr. *(Photo: USAAF)*

demanding for their crews), but the high altitudes and freezing temperatures were far more of a challenge for the Mustang. Congealed oil due to the cold, frosted windscreens, and coolant leaks were only some of the difficulties that faced maintenance crews and VIII FC technical staff, and a number of fixes were attempted to cure the problems. Serious too was the jamming of guns. The P-51B was comparatively lightly armed, with only four 0.5-in machine guns compared to the Thunderbolt's eight, and when some of these tended to jam during missions it further decreased the fighter's potential effectiveness. This problem was caused by two separate problems - one was the effect of lubricating oil congealing (and not icing-up, as claimed in several published sources) due to the cold at high altitudes if the Mustangs' electric gun heaters were not switched on in time before the aircraft gained height, or before the guns were fired at altitude. The other problem was the jamming of the guns due to the awkward canted-over seating of the guns, and the equally-awkward curved ammunition feed chutes. Much of the gun-jamming took place when the guns were fired while the aircraft was manoeuvring and pulling 'g'. The result was the holding back of the moving ammunition belt due to centrifugal force, causing the breech mechanism of the gun to jam. As described later in this Book, solutions were eventually found to these problems. Nevertheless the 354th FG had to ground some of its aircraft in early 1944 due to these serious difficulties. Problems were also encountered with the P-51B's Packard V-1650-3 power plants. Actually getting these engines into production had been a major task, and the production engines were different in a number of respects to the initial prototype examples that were virtually 'hand-made'. One problem was oil loss from the engine's breather system which proved to be difficult to rectify, and indeed Rolls-Royce in Britain became involved with attempts to solve this and other problems with the early Merlin-engined Mustangs. A number of Merlin-Mustangs were seconded to the company, the first of these being P-51B-1-NA 43-12425, which was delivered to Hucknall on 7 October 1943. At least 11 more Merlin-Mustangs eventually found their way to Rolls-Royce at different times

subsequent to this. A further problem encountered with Mustangs regarded spark plugs. American spark plugs proved to be inferior to British examples, and until US-manufactured plugs could be brought up to the same standard, British plugs of the RC5/2 variety were used.

Although these initial problems with the Merlin-Mustangs appeared serious, in reality solutions were found to most of the difficulties, and in the opening weeks of 1944 the Merlin-engined Mustangs started to come into their own. This was achieved with great dash and daring from the pilots of the escort fighters, and for the first time the fight was being taken to the Luftwaffe over its own territory. Indeed, it had already started to become noticeable (even at this early stage) that intercepting Luftwaffe fighters tended to keep their distance when escort fighters were present, preferring to find unprotected parts of bomber formations or lone stragglers to concentrate on. The presence of the escorts was thus starting to have a psychological effect on some German fighter pilots, who were increasingly not having things all their own way in their attempts to stop the heavy bombers from reaching their targets. In the vanguard of the Eighth Air Force's efforts was the 354th Fighter Group, and in January 1944 some epic air battles took place that set the scene for how the air war over Germany would subsequently take place. The first of these occurred on 5 January, the group's 12th mission. As a part of the 111-strong protection cover for a 245-aircraft force of heavy bombers attacking Kiel, many of the 41 354th FG Mustangs became embroiled in a major battle with Messerschmitt Bf 110 heavy fighters that were attempting to attack the bombers as they turned for home. The ensuing action was the first real victory for the Mustang escorts. Up to that time the lumbering Bf 110 fighters, which had enjoyed so much success earlier in the war, had often been able to cause considerable damage to the bomber formations. Now the tables were suddenly turned. The Mustangs got in amongst the German twin-engined fighters, which were absolutely no match whatsoever for the agile and aggressively-flown Mustangs. 14 Luftwaffe aircraft were claimed by the 354th without loss, but more importantly the Bf 110s were unable to

successfully press home their attacks on the US bombers. It was an action that effectively spelt the beginning of the end for the Bf 110 as a bomber interceptor. In many subsequent actions the Bf 110s were brought down in significant numbers by the US escorts, resulting in this aircraft type being completely withdrawn from bomber interception duties except as a last resort as 1944 wore on.

The next major action for the 354th took place on 11 January, and this mission proved to be one of even greater significance for the Mustang. On that day the 354th escorted the heavy bombers to Halberstadt and Oschersleben, the latter being a major production centre for the potent Focke-Wulf Fw 190 fighter. The Luftwaffe responded in force to this raid, and several major air battles took place. Again the 354th caught several Bf 110s together with the similarly outclassed twin-engined Messerschmitt Me 410, and also brought down a number of single-seat fighters. The overall score for the group was 16 destroyed for no losses, with several pilots scoring well. However, the big story of the day did not break for a time, until members of the B-17-equipped 401st Bombardment Group made it known that one of the Mustang pilots had single-handedly fought off repeated attacks against their Flying Fortresses. The pilot concerned was the modest but highly-capable Maj James H Howard. Leading the 354th on that (and several other) days, ex-'Flying Tiger' Howard had found himself alone when other members of the group had become involved in dog-fights elsewhere along the bomber stream. Even though several of his Mustang's machine guns had jammed, finally leaving only one working, Howard successfully drove off attacks by a number of German fighters of different types, shooting down several. For his actions that day, Howard was subsequently awarded the Medal of Honor, the United States' highest military award for gallantry. Very few fighter pilots received this award, and Howard's was the only one that was made to a fighter pilot in the ETO. Nevertheless, although his gallantry and great airmanship from that famous encounter cannot be disputed, historians have subsequently argued over how many aircraft Howard actually shot down that day, and of what types. Howard's actions were witnessed by the crews of several bombers, and he himself made claims of two destroyed. Unfortunately some writers have subsequently claimed that he shot down no fewer than eight enemy fighters, which is nonsense. The Luftwaffe's own records most definitely do not support that claim, and subsequent investigations have officially credited Howard with three victories (two Bf 110s and an Fw 190). Some writers have also trumpeted that Howard fought off "a whole group of Bf 110s", which again misunderstands the fact that the 401st BG came under attack from several aircraft types while Howard was defending its bombers. If the three victories that Howard is officially credited with are correct from that mission, then this makes Howard the first Merlin-Mustang ace, for they would add to his first victory on 20 December 1943 (a Bf 109), and his next victory on 30 January 1944 (a Bf 110), giving him a total of five before anyone else in the 354th FG. (It has sometimes been claimed that Lt Charles Gumm was the first Merlin-Mustang ace, but his fifth confirmed victory did not come until 21 February). In any case, Howard's actions on 11 January significantly helped to develop the Mustang as the great fighter that it came to be regarded as, and gained it a great deal of publicity, but in the wider context of the air war over north-west Europe it was obvious that the Luftwaffe now had a deadly adversary, that would only grow in strength and numbers in the coming months.

The 354th Fighter Group subsequently continued its increasing prowess with the P-51, and was duly joined by other groups that either arrived in the ETO fresh with new Mustangs, or subsequently converted onto the type as Mustangs became available in growing numbers. The next group to join the Eighth Air Force with Mustangs was the 357th Fighter Group. This unit, like the 354th, was originally assigned to the tactical Ninth Air

Force as a ground-attack unit, the desk-flyers back in the US still regarding the P-51 purely as a tactical aircraft. Just before this time, the Eighth had received yet another P-47 unit, the 358th Fighter Group (which had become operational on 20 December 1943), but not surprisingly by early 1944 VIII Fighter Command preferred to have all the Mustangs that it could lay its hands on, and a further deal was struck in which the 357th with its precious Mustangs joined the Eighth, while the 358th with its Thunderbolts was reassigned on 1 February a fighter-bomber group within the Ninth Air Force. The 357th thus became, in early February 1944, the first all-Mustang unit to actually belong to the Eighth Air Force, and it certainly was not the last. It had been activated on 1 December 1942, and had originally trained on Bell P-39 Airacobras at a number of bases in California and elsewhere in the western US before moving to England in November 1943. In late January and early February 1944 it exchanged bases with the 358th FG, and moved into its wartime home of Leiston in Suffolk which was to become one of the centres of excellence of Mustang operations in the ETO. The group comprised the 362nd, 363rd, and 364th Fighter Squadrons, and flew its first mission on 11 February 1944, the familiar 'shake-down' over northern France, on this occasion the mission acting as a diversion for a B-24 Liberator bombing raid. The group was led by Maj Jim Howard of Medal of Honor fame, continuing the practice of experienced officers accompanying 'rookie' groups during their initial combat indoctrination. The 357th FG became one of the Eighth Air Force's crack fighter units in the coming months, and was continually in combat until 25 April 1945, mounting 313 missions with the Mustang.

In the coming months an increasing number of Mustang-equipped groups started to join the Eighth Air Force, or existing units began to convert onto the Merlin-Mustang from their P-47 Thunderbolts or P-38 Lightnings. Thus by late 1944, the Eighth Air Force's fighter groups were almost exclusively equipped with Mustangs, the last groups to convert onto the P-51 (except for the 56th FG, which flew P-47s to the end) being the 78th and 356th Fighter Groups, which transitioned onto Mustangs from P-47 Thunderbolts in the final weeks of 1944. A more complete break-down of the magnificent 14 Mustang-equipped fighter groups of the Eighth Air Force may be found in the Appendices at the end of this Book. With the consequent build-up of Mustangs in the ETO, so the fortunes of the Luftwaffe began to seriously take many turns for the worse. A growing number of US pilots started to gain impressive scores against the enemy, and many of the German losses were irreplaceable as experienced pilots started to be shot down in increasing numbers.

1944 was the significant year in which the Merlin-Mustang rose to ascendancy as a supreme escort fighter. A growing number of US fighter pilots began to exact a heavy toll on the Luftwaffe's fighter arm, which was to be a key ingredient of the eventual Allied aerial victory over the Germans in the later stages of World War Two. Amongst the many Eighth Air Force pilots who became 'aces' with five or more aerial victories, 1st Lt Gilbert O'Brien can be seen in the cockpit of his P-51B 'Shanty Irish'. O'Brien flew with the high-scoring 357th Fighter Group from Leiston in Suffolk, and achieved seven confirmed aerial victories between March and July 1944. This particular Mustang was a P-51B-5-NA, serial number 43-6787, coded G4-Q (Photo: USAAF)

## External Fuel Tanks

It was not just the appearance over Germany of the Merlin Mustangs with their excellent endurance and high-altitude combat capabilities that started to win the war for the Allies in the skies over north-west Europe and particularly over Germany itself. In the US, interested parties had at last started to take the initiative over the heads of the increasingly sidelined Material Command to get the USAAF fit for the kind of real air war that was being fought. In the autumn of 1943 a programme had been introduced by Brig Gen Muir S. Fairchild, to have external fuel tanks developed and made operational for US fighters. Material Command had, not surprisingly, lagged behind with this issue as well as so many others, even when combat reports from the Pacific of the effectiveness of locally-produced drop tanks for P-47 Thunderbolts had started to reach the US. Fairchild was a man with huge influence, and he was also pragmatic enough to see how the air war was developing. Fairchild had been Director of Military Requirements at the HQ of the USAAF in Washington, D.C. in August 1942 as a Maj Gen when he had written to Oliver Echols at Material Command showing his surprise at the apparent slowness in the procurement of the Mustang. Now, in 1943, Fairchild once more needed to take the initiative to get things done. He and his staff officers instituted a programme called FAREP (the Fighter Airplane Range Extension Programme), which centred around the design and manufacture of jettisonable external long-range fuel tanks for USAAF fighters. Fairchild had in mind Europe as well as the Pacific, and it was the growing success of this programme that helped to give all USAAF escort fighters (P-38, P-47 and P-51) more range. In the case of the P-47, the programme included not just drop tanks, but the installation of underwing pylons as well, as these had not been included in early P-47 production (although it soon was!). The P-47's range was virtually doubled, allowing Thunderbolts to escort heavy bombers deeper into Germany. In these early days of the range extension programme, the external

fuel tanks that were most readily available were teardrop-shaped 75 US gallon aluminium tanks, that had been created initially as ferry tanks for the P-40 Warhawk and P-39 Airacobra. They were, however suitable for range extension on combat missions, and Fairchild's programme resulted in the adaptation of these tanks and their production being substantially increased. Efforts were made to develop purpose-built tanks as well, resulting in several new shapes eventually coming to the fore. One was a metal 110 US gallon tank, while in Britain, thanks to the efforts of the paper specialist company Bowater, a compressed paper fuel tank of 108 gallons was developed. Production of the latter was rarely to exceed demand in the coming months, but eventually the 'battle of the long-range fuel tanks' was won, with many thousands of all the new types being manufactured. It was not, however, simply a question of hanging these tanks beneath the most convenient location under an aircraft. Much thought had to go into plumbing in fuel lines to connect up to the tanks, flight testing had to be carried out both in the US and Britain to check the feasibility of the new installations and to ensure that they were safe for combat use, and testing was needed to find out just how far each fighter type could fly at different boost settings with the additional fuel loads. It was also necessary to develop a pressurised fuel system so that fuel could be drawn from the tanks.

On 27 September 1943 a milestone had been reached with the first really long-range escort over north-west Europe, when British-based Thunderbolts with long-range fuel tanks got as far as Emden on the north-western fringe of Germany. Four Eighth Air Force Thunderbolt groups, the 4th, 56th, 78th, and 353rd, had covered the bombers on the Emden raid, and thus for the first time were able to provide escort all the way to the target and back. Three of the groups used 75 US gallon tanks, while the 4th employed the new 108 US gallon tanks. The raid was psychologically a great success for the bombers, and for the US fighters it resulted in several successful air battles with Luftwaffe fighters, 21 being claimed for the loss of one Thunderbolt. But the real importance of this raid was that it had showed how effective proper fighter escort for the bombers could be – indeed, it demonstrated that escort fighters all the way to the target and back were forever-after essential. Following the mauling that the Eighth Air Force bombers had received in the summer of 1943, the advent of real fighter escort suddenly held the promise of getting the US strategic bombing campaign in the ETO back on track. It also demonstrated to the Luftwaffe that the American fighters were becoming, day by day, a thoroughly formidable opponent, with the range to take the fight to the Luftwaffe over its own home ground. Now the US fighters were

able to range freely over the skies of Germany, which must have been a chilling thought for those in Germany's military who were sensible enough to recognise the huge significance of that simple fact. One wonders, however, if the success of this mission was ever noticed by the many doubters of effective escort fighters back in the US, particularly the desk-flyers at the Material Command at Wright Field, who had done so much to stall the advent of the escort fighter in the USAAF. When it entered service several weeks after the Emden raid, the Merlin-

Mustang could reach targets such as Emden virtually without the help of drop tanks, but with the addition of external fuel tanks it would certainly go much further. Indeed, the Merlin-Mustang was starting to move into its most successful profession as a long-range escort in early 1944 as the long-range fuel tanks programme started to really get into gear, and thence the long distance and long endurance given by the humble but all-important drop tanks proved to be a vital part of the overall Mustang winning picture.

**Although P-51B production was commenced at the time when Dark Olive Drab uppersurfaces and Neutral Grey undersides were standard for US fighters, the general official deletion of camouflage led to 'natural metal' finish Mustangs proliferating as the war progressed. Some units were less than enthusiastic about sending gleaming and very conspicuous un-camouflaged Mustangs into combat, and so several Eighth Air Force groups began 'in the field' re-adoption of camouflage. In the case of the 357th Fighter Group, a number of the group's aircraft received a locally-applied coat of dark green paint on their uppersurfaces, probably using RAF paints which were in plentiful supply. Looking somewhat the worse for wear, Lt John Howell's P-51B named 'Shoo Shoo Baby' shows to advantage the field-applied camouflage. The Mustang was officially a P-51B-10-NA, serial number 42-106447, coded C5-L of the 364th FS** (Photo: USAAF)

**Amongst the great exponents within the Eighth Air Force of the Merlin-engined Mustang in Europe was the 355th Fighter Group, based at Steeple Morden in Cambridgeshire. One of that group's Malcolm Hood-equipped Merlin-Mustangs, P-51B-15-NA serial number 42-106950, named 'The Iowa Beaut' from the 354th Fighter Squadron is shown here, formating very close to the camera aircraft. Although it has sometimes been claimed that the Mustang on the occasion of this and several other similar photographs was being test flown to slow time a new engine, the aircraft is carrying 108 US gallon compressed paper underwing drop tanks, suggesting that it was being used for other purposes at the time** (Photo: USAAF)

# Service Excellence in Europe

## Chapter 3

From February 1944 onwards, major daylight air raids took place leading to large air battles over Germany which were to have dramatic effects on the German ability to wage war in general, and on the Luftwaffe in particular. One of the objectives of the combined bombing offensive of the British and US forces was the destruction of the major part of the German aviation industry, and this took the form in February 1944 of the so-called 'Big Week' of major bombing raids by the Eighth Air Force on many aircraft factories across Germany.

It was during this period of early 1944 that the Merlin-Mustang began to win its spurs and to take the fight dramatically and increasingly successfully to the enemy. The first actual raid of the famed and significant 'Big Week' was mounted on 20 February, and with only bad weather hampering efforts, raids continued until 25 February with several major factories being badly damaged. These raids had an important effect on German war production at the affected plants, although from the late summer of 1943 the Germans had been gradually dispersing their aircraft production and completion facilities, making it harder for the Allies to make any decisive long-term blows. The escort fighters were very busy during those raids, however, and made claims for some 208 German fighters for the loss of 40 of their number. Such losses as these were starting to be a major headache for the Luftwaffe. Unlike the Allies, the Germans did not have a large and on-going capability to replace pilot losses, whilst the demise of experienced pilots was a considerable practical and psychological blow. The losses in aircraft were also important, for although at that stage in the war the numbers could be made up, increasingly the quality of manufacture of German fighters tended to suffer due to the dispersal programme and the almost continual bombing of factories and infrastructure. A further series of massive daylight air raids was staged in March 1944, as the US heavy bombers made a concerted series of attacks on the capital of Nazi Germany, Berlin. These commenced on 4 March, and again the bombers received a thorough escort from the fighters, which were already coming to be called the 'Little Friends' of the

lumbering B-17 Flying Fortresses and B-24 Liberators that they were now much more effectively protecting. Even so, the US forces certainly were not in the ascendancy by any means yet, and the Eighth Air Force endured its largest ever loss of bombers in aerial combat – 69 – on the infamous 6 March Berlin raid. This mission was directed against specific military or industrial targets – as were the vast majority of the Eighth Air Force's daylight bomber efforts in the ETO – with the Erkner ball bearing plant a specific objective. The 730 B-17s and B-24s were escorted by a force that totalled just over 800 fighters from the Eighth and Ninth Air Forces (illustrating that the Ninth could also perform escort work when required) and the RAF, with 100 of these being Mustangs from the 4th, 354th and 357th Fighter Groups. Unfortunately the bombing was not particularly accurate, and 11 escorting fighters were lost. However, the escorts claimed 81 German aircraft, many of these being the now-outclassed Bf 110s whose ranks were swelled by Bf 110 night fighters - the use of these aircraft as day fighters, hopelessly burdened by their radar equipment, being a particularly desperate measure. Providing target and target withdrawal support for the bombers were the Mustangs, no other Allied single-seat fighter being able to fly as far as Berlin and back at that time. The 357th and 4th Fighter Groups were in the thick of the action in and around Berlin, with the Mustangs seriously outnumbered but well able to look after themselves. The 357th destroyed at least 20 of the enemy for no losses, while the 354th made claims for seven German fighters. The 4th FG had only recently transitioned onto the Mustang from the P-47 Thunderbolt (its first missions with the P-51B were flown in late February 1944), but this group was to eventually top all the Eighth Air Force's Mustang units in terms of aerial kills, and a fierce but friendly rivalry grew between the 4th with its Mustangs, and the 56th FG with its beloved Thunderbolts, as to which could achieve the most aerial victories.

The epic air battles that took place over Germany in the early months of 1944 were the largest of the war up to that time, and they confirmed without any doubt whatsoever the absolute

A beautiful in-flight view of what many regard to be the classic Mustang, the P-51D. Certainly for the USAAF, this aircraft was a real war-winner in the skies over Europe and the Pacific. Although P-51D Mustangs were delivered to the USAAF in 'natural metal' finish, with the uppersurfaces of the wings filled and sprayed in silver paint, some units preferred to repaint the uppersurfaces of their aircraft as an aid to camouflage. One of these groups was the 361st Fighter Group of the Eighth Air Force. A well-known P-51D-5-NA, serial number 44-13926 coded E2-S of the 375th Fighter Squadron, shows off its recently-painted uppersurfaces. The actual colour used on this and other Mustangs of the 361st FG has been the subject of argument for many years. Several in-flight colour photographs were taken of these aircraft at the time which suggested that the colour was dark blue, but it is now generally accepted that the shade was dark green or even regulation Olive Drab. The extreme nose and spinner were yellow, the assigned identification colour for the 361st FG *(Photo: USAAF)*

Fitted with a British-made rearwards-sliding Malcolm Hood, 'Lady Patricia' taxies out for a sortie aided by a ground crew member directing the pilot from his position on the left wing. The forward view for the pilot in any aircraft equipped with a tail wheel can be at best marginal, particularly for ground handling, and so any help from ground crew members as shown here was always appreciated. The aircraft has had the upper portions of its black and white 'invasion stripes' painted out roughly with dark green or Olive Drab paint, showing that the photograph dates from a little later after the immediate D-Day period in June 1944. The aircraft is from the 363rd Tactical Reconnaissance Group, a Ninth Air Force reconnaissance unit which had formerly been a fighter group, but switched roles in late August and early September 1944. The 'B3' code was then assigned to the 161st Tactical Reconnaissance Squadron. Although starting life as a P-51B-15-NA, this Mustang has been converted into an F-6C reconnaissance aircraft – note the camera window and fairing next to the number '3' on the fuselage side
*(Photo: USAAF)*

necessity for long-range escort fighters for the US heavy bombers, and the fact that the Mustang was by far the best fighter for that particular role. Nevertheless, there were still many problems to be overcome, and malfunctions were still quite common – on the 6 March Berlin mission, for example, the 357th Fighter Group's contingent was depleted by 15 Mustangs that had to abort for various technical difficulties or other problems. Losses took place as well, with the CO of the 354th FG, Col Kenneth Martin, being brought down on 11 February in an aerial collision with a Bf 109 and spending the rest of the war as a PoW. Without doubt, however, the escort fighters were having a major effect in how the air war was starting to develop from that time onwards to the end of the war, with the Luftwaffe being faced down over its own territory by an increasingly numerous and deadly foe. Many American pilots started to amass major scores of aerial victories. One of these was the 4th Fighter Group's Capt Dominic Salvatore Gentile. Don Gentile was one of the American pilots who had joined the British and Commonwealth forces early in World War Two whilst his country stayed out of the conflict, joining the RAF in September 1940. Eventually transferring to one of the three Eagle Squadrons – No. 133 Squadron - of the RAF that were manned by US personnel, Gentile scored his first two aerial victories in a Spitfire Mk Vb of No.133 Squadron near Dieppe on 19 August 1942 – the day of the disastrous British and Commonwealth landings at Dieppe, and the very day when Fg Off Hollis Hills of No.414 Squadron achieved the first-ever aerial victory in a Mustang. Gentile subsequently transferred to the USAAF when the Eagle Squadrons were absorbed to become the nucleus of the 4th Fighter Group in September 1942, and he duly scored 4.333 victories in P-47 Thunderbolts with the 4th FG's 336th Fighter Squadron. When the 4th FG rapidly transitioned onto the Mustang in February 1944 Gentile became one of the Merlin-Mustang's greatest early exponents on escort missions. His first kills in a Mustang came on 3 March (two Fw 190s), beginning a remarkable scoring run of 15.5 victories in just over one month. His final kills were three Fw 190s on 8 April, bringing his combined score to 21.833 aerial victories. Needless to say his exploits gained him considerable fame and Press attention, and he was rotated back to the US on leave later in April 1944

although he did not subsequently see any further combat in the war. He was one of many Eighth Air Force Mustang pilots who amassed considerable air-to-air scores in 1944, as the Merlin-engined Mustang really proved its worth on escort missions and the other diverse tasks that it was called upon to do in the ETO.

## Dangerous but Important Ground Victories

It was not just in the air that the American fighters put the Luftwaffe to the sword as 1944 progressed. Maj Gen Kepner was a keen advocate of taking the fight to the Luftwaffe wherever possible, not just in defence of the heavy bombers but on its home ground as well. The gaining of air superiority and the ultimate defeat of the Luftwaffe was a major objective for the Allies if the much-vaunted 'second front' was to be opened in North-west Europe in 1944. Allied leaders meeting in Casablanca and Washington in 1943 had developed their intention to launch an invasion of the European mainland during 1944, and air superiority was seen as a key issue that the Allied air arms had to ensure, if there was to be any hope of such a major undertaking succeeding. Indeed, it became a stated objective not only of VIII FC, but of the Eighth Air Force itself, to take the war aggressively to the Germans whenever and wherever possible. In January 1944 the leadership of the Eighth Air Force underwent a significant shift. On 6 January 1944 Lt Gen James H. Doolittle became its new head. 'Jimmy' Doolittle was a towering figure in the USAAF, whose no-nonsense, pragmatic approach was a world away from that of the desk flyers and vested interests back in the US. At once the nature of the task of the escort fighters changed. Hitherto, the bomber escort work that had developed during the previous six months or so had involved the fighters staying with the bombers as much as possible, and only straying away from them to chase away and engage attacking German fighters. Now, with Doolittle in charge, the whole picture changed. Subsequently the escorts were able to fly ahead of the bombers and seek out the Luftwaffe, to chase the German fighters to their destruction, and if fuel permitted, to shoot up anything on the ground if the bombers were considered safe after leaving their designated targets. With the advent of the Merlin-powered Mustang, with its great range and firepower, the capability to do this grew more and more as 1944 progressed.

The first Allied aircraft to touch down in Southern France following the Allied landings of August 1944 was a Mustang. Actually beginning life on the Dallas P-51C production line, the Mustang belonged to the 111th Tactical Reconnaissance Squadron, and was being flown by US Navy pilot Robert Snowden on detachment to the 111th. Short of fuel, he landed on a partly-built airstrip that was still under construction. The Mustang was named 'Val Gal II' after Snowden's wife. Val Snowden worked in the Chance Vought factory at Stratford, Connecticut, and posed as a 'Rosie the Riveter' for a wartime publicity poster
*(Photo: USAAF)*

An obviously posed but nonetheless interesting detail view of a Mediterranean-based P-51B/C of the 332nd Fighter Group with several of the unit's pilots. The only Black American (to use a modern-day term)-equipped fighter group that saw combat in World War Two, the 332nd FG spent much of its time as a part of the Fifteenth Air Force on bomber escort and related duties. This view clearly shows the gun ports of the two wing-mounted 0.5-in machine guns, and the smart flying gear of the pilots. The pilot on the left wears RAF-style flying boots with flying gloves and has the sleeves rolled-up of his flying suit, which appears to be the regulation-issue AN-S-31 Summer Flying Suit, together with RAF Type B flying helmet. The Mustang is named 'Skipper's Darlin' III' and was the personal mount of Capt Andrew Turner
*(Photo: USAAF)*

On the way back to England from the infamous 6 March Berlin mission, elements of the 357th FG went down to lower altitudes to take on some Luftwaffe fighters. Led by Maj Thomas Hayes of the 364th FS, the Mustangs subsequently shot up a Luftwaffe airfield at Ulzen, inflicting unspectacular but nonetheless important damage. This was possibly the first time that a Luftwaffe airfield in Germany had been attacked by Mustangs. In the weeks that followed, as the escort fighters started to fly more and more over Germany, and the opportunities to follow Doolittle's freer approach to escort work became more frequent if fuel levels permitted, Luftwaffe airfields increasingly became the targets for attack by the escorts. In fact attacks by Mustangs on Luftwaffe airfields were pre-dated by similar operations by P-47 Thunderbolts. Although at first most attacks were on an opportunistic basis, in time the whole operation became more organised – particularly as it started to become obvious to VIII Fighter Command that shooting up the Luftwaffe on its own bases could become a part of the wider plan to defeat the Luftwaffe altogether. Indeed, on days when the bombers could not fly because of predicted bad weather over their briefed targets, the escorts were freed up to go off on their own and carry out their own fighter sweeps.

In an effort to encourage the ground strafing of airfields, VIII FC took the unusual step of awarding ground 'kills' the same standing as aerial victories, allowing pilots to reach the mythical and generally sought after ace status solely through ground victories. In the event some groups aggressively went after ground targets on their way back from bomber escort work, although ground strafing was in reality a very hazardous business. Luftwaffe airfields were generally well defended with light anti-aircraft guns of various calibres and installations, and when the threat from marauding Mustangs and Thunderbolts became more serious as 1944 continued, so airfield defences tended to be increased even

more. This started to take a toll on the attacking US fighters, and although some spectacular results often came from airfield attacks, so the number of losses grew. At one stage it was four times more likely for a US pilot to be brought down by light anti-aircraft fire around airfields or other high-value installations than by the actions of Luftwaffe fighters, and some group commanders were reluctant to sanction the type of ferocious ground attacks that other groups came to revel in.

Although the Mustang was as suitable as any other Allied fighter for the type of aggressive, offence-driven work that airfield attacks and other ground strafing involved, it had one drawback that all liquid-cooled inline-engined fighters suffered. This was simply that a hit from enemy fire in the coolant piping or radiator could effectively bring the aircraft down, because a serious loss of coolant would soon result in an overheating and seized engine. This drawback did not affect the enormous P-47 Thunderbolt with its large, air-cooled radial engine, and in many ways the Thunderbolt was more suited to the type of ground-attack that Mustangs were tending to indulge in virtually every day by the autumn of 1944. Nevertheless, the Mustangs and Thunderbolts of the Eighth Air Force were able, with their almost incessant pursuit of the Luftwaffe both in the air and on the ground, to help significantly to turn the tide for the Allies in the air war over continental Europe. Although the Luftwaffe remained a force to be reckoned with, its many previous all-conquering successes from earlier in the war were long in the past as 1944 wore on, and it started to be very dangerous for aircraft wearing German insignia to take to the skies at all in many parts of the rapidly shrinking Third Reich. This, coupled with the whittling away of the Luftwaffe's prowess by the RAF from 1941/1942 onwards, and the increasing capability of the Soviet armed forces in the east, meant that air superiority started to become very patchy for the Germans as 1944 continued.

In addition to the American fighters being more numerous, often more aggressively flown by better-trained pilots, and overall with a better firepower for fighter vs. fighter dog-fighting, the USAAF also gained a further advantage for its pilots as the air war over Europe persisted. This was the introduction of the so-called 'g-suit'. Developed to allow pilots to pull more 'g' in aerial manoeuvres by preventing the pilot from blacking-out in tight turns, the g-suit was an important innovation that further tipped the balance in air combat away from the Luftwaffe. In Britain as well as the US, attempts were made to develop a flight suit that would prevent blood from draining away from the pilot's brain during tight turns, by putting pressure on the lower parts of the pilot's body at the appropriate times to prevent him from losing consciousness. A British system called the Frank suit used water to achieve the desired results, and was tested by the 4th FG in March and April 1944. However, the weight and comparative cumbersomeness of this suit caused it to be rejected in favour of the US Berger suit, which used a system of compressed air. The 339th FG was the first to try out this suit in the Eighth Air Force,

Former P-51B-1-NA serial number 43-12102 is shown in this image during the development work for the definitive P-51D layout. Interestingly this aircraft still retained some of the features of the P-51B, such as the inboard placing of the wing-tip navigation lights, which on the final P-51D configuration were relocated at the extreme wing-tip. Nevertheless it looked to all intents and purposes in general form to resemble the layout of the P-51D that it pioneered. Note the Douglas SBD Dauntless in the background. *(Photo: NAA)*

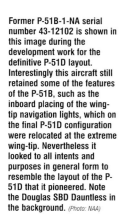

Constant improvement of the basically sound Mustang design to meet combat experience and evolving needs led to what many believe to be the best of the Mustang breed, the P-51D and P-51K series. The transition from the P-51B/C to the 'D' model Mustang involved a number of modifications, including an increase in the wing gun armament and major changes to the fuselage in the cockpit area and in the rear fuselage compared to the P-51B. This aircraft, 43-12102, was one of the trials Mustangs that was used in the P-51D development programme and was effectively the flying prototype for the new layout. It was a former P-51B-1-NA, but was given a full makeover including the cut-down rear fuselage and new rearwards-sliding clear unframed 'bubble' or 'all-round' vision canopy. It is seen here flying over rugged southern California countryside on a photo sortie for the cameras during the development work for the definitive P-51D layout. *(Photo: NAA)*

although it had already been used by some Ninth Air Force units. Eventually the Berger suit was standardised, and duly proved to be another useful tool in the Allied fighter pilots' armoury.

## The Definitive P-51D

Without doubt the P-51B/C Mustangs were highly successful in the bomber escort role, as well as proving to be good tactical aircraft as well, and the type continued in combat well into the last few months of the war. However, by the time that the early Merlin-powered Mustangs were proving themselves over North-west Europe in the big air battles of early 1944, North American Aviation was already working on a much improved Mustang. One problem with many of the fighter aircraft of the late 1930's and early 1940's era was the high rear fuselage line behind the cockpit, resulting in poor rearwards vision. In a fighter aircraft the pilot needs to be able to see as much of the 360 degrees around his aircraft as possible, but the rear was a problem for many of the fighters of that era. Even the Supermarine Spitfire, Messerschmitt Bf 109 and Republic P-47 Thunderbolt, good fighters though they were, nevertheless had the 'razorback' type spine that restricted rearwards vision. The solution was simple and obvious, but would require considerable re-engineering on all these types to create the desired effect. This involved cutting back the high rear fuselage line, lowering the spine of the rear fuselage, and the installation of a clear rearwards-sliding 'all-round' vision canopy. As an interim, as described later in this Chapter, a neat 'blown' rearwards-sliding canopy was made available for the P-51B/C series by a British company. Known as the 'Malcolm Hood' after its designer and manufacturer, the Malcolm hood did away with the heavily-framed, multi-panel sideways-opening cockpit canopy of the P-51B/C, and with the installation of a simple rail to allow it to slide backwards to open and forwards to shut, the new canopy was a major improvement. Nevertheless it was only an interim solution, and the Malcolm hood in reality was never available in the numbers necessary to 're-canopy' all the P-51B and P-51C-model Mustangs that were made. In any case, North American Aviation being the good manufacturer that it was, had rapidly began to try fix the problem altogether by designing a new Mustang fuselage arrangement. In the Spitfire and Thunderbolt, the razorback rear fuselage was replaced on later production models by their manufacturers with a cut-down rear fuselage and the installation of a new teardrop-shaped rearwards-sliding cockpit cover. In effect NAA went for the same approach, and in so doing created the definitive Mustang shape. Work on the new development as a company venture commenced in the autumn and early winter of 1943, and at least one P-51B was taken from the Inglewood production line and duly modified to take in the new refinements and modifications. It was a P-51B-1-NA, serial number 43-12102.

As well as this, two P-51B-10-NA airframes, 42-106539 and 42-106540, were used for engineering and mock-up installation work. The flying prototype, 43-12102, took to the air for the first time on 17 November 1943. Wind tunnel work and flight testing immediately showed that the modified rear fuselage and new cockpit canopy were a vast improvement over the P-51B/C arrangement, and provision was made for tooling up for production at once of the production version which was to be designated P-51D. By this stage North American Aviation had little trouble in getting new orders for the Mustang, a far cry from the situation earlier in the war. The new P-51D model was included in FY 1944 funding, apparently at the expense of some planned P-51B production (indeed, there is a story that the very first production P-51Ds were actually P-51B look-alikes, it taking several aircraft before the definitive P-51D layout could be fully instituted on the Inglewood production lines). The initial P-51D-5-NA was serial number 44-13353. In addition to manufacture at Inglewood, the P-51D was also made at the NAA factory at Grand Prairie (Dallas). Further, a version of the P-51D specific to the Dallas production line was also produced. This was known as the P-51K, and was similar to the P-51D except for its propeller type. The P-51D was fitted with a Hamilton Standard four-bladed unit similar to that of the P-51B/C, usually with blade cuffs. However, fears over the availability of this unit – Hamilton Standard propellers were almost universal on US combat aircraft in World War Two alongside Curtiss Electric units – led to the adoption of a four-bladed uncuffed slightly lighter Aeroproducts unit of 11 ft (3.35 m) diameter as an alternative for the P-51D. Some

The flying prototype for the P-51D development programme, former P-51B-1-NA serial number 43-12102, flies over southern California during the development of the P-51D-series layout. It was painted in basic Olive Drab and Neutral Grey finish, and displayed the cut-down rear fuselage line and new rearwards-sliding clear unframed 'bubble' canopy that were incorporated in the P-51D production layout. These changes gave the pilot a much better all-round view than had existed in the P-51B/C series (and indeed in the Allison-engined Mustangs), where the rear fuselage line was of the high 'razorback' design *(Photo: NAA)*

Supreme elegance. With a Southern California landscape as its backdrop, a P-51D-10-NA serial number 44-14214, makes a test flight before delivery and flies a neat formation for the camera aircraft. The painted silver upperwing surfaces of this aircraft are very apparent in this view. This production block was the first to fully introduce the 'fin fillet' ahead of the vertical tail to try to improve the P-51D's somewhat marginal directional stability, as illustrated by this aircraft. The directional stability problem was a feature for all Merlin-engined Mustangs, but was especially marked on the P-51D/K series with their cut-down rear fuselage line that exacerbated the difficulty. Interestingly, some pilots who were used to the somewhat more directionally stable P-51B preferred that earlier mark of Merlin-Mustang, while pilots who had experienced the much more docile and directionally far more stable Allison-engined Mustangs found the P-51D to be something of a wild beast and virtually like a different aircraft altogether – although most pilots nevertheless found the P-51D to be a superb fighting machine (Photo: NAA)

production Mustangs from the Dallas production were fitted with this propeller arrangement, and these were the Mustangs that were built under the designation P-51K. In addition, the blown teardrop-shaped cockpit cover that was introduced on the P-51D was in fact produced in two separate shapes. Again the anomaly was in the Dallas production, the cockpit cover fitted to many Dallas-built P-51D and P-51K being of a slightly altered shape with a slight step at its rear end. In spite of the fuselage modifications of the P-51D/K series, the fuselage 'length' remained the same as that of the P-51B/C series.

NAA also took the opportunity of the new P-51D version to incorporate several other changes, which had become necessary in the light of combat experience. One of them was the very necessary sorting-out of the armament problems, particularly gun jamming. The wing of the P-51D, although being the same span as that of all previous Mustangs, was actually altered in several respects, and some tinkering with the geometry of the main undercarriage also took place. Most importantly, the wing structure was strengthened to allow a bomb of up to 1,000 lb (454 kg) to be carried under each wing, and a stronger pylon just outboard of the main undercarriage was introduced. The whole gun installation area was also significantly changed. The four-gun, canted installation of the P-51B/C that had caused so many problems in service was completely replaced by a six-gun arrangement. This consisted of three 0.5-in M2 Brownings installed in each wing, in line with the leading edge, in an upright position. At a stroke the gun jamming during manoeuvring problem of the P-51B/C series was virtually eliminated. The ammunition bays and related hatches in the wings had to be changed due to this arrangement. The 85 US gallon fuselage fuel tank that was introduced on the later P-51B was installed as standard in the P-51D.

Just as significantly, the P-51D had a 'new' engine. For some time Packard had been working on introducing a slightly different version of the V-1650, and this was produced as the V-1650-7 specifically for the P-51D. It was generally similar to the V-1650-3 of the P-51B/C series, but had improved and altered supercharger drive gear ratios, slightly different connecting rods, and detail differences. Most importantly it was able to deliver 1,720 hp with maximum boost (war emergency rating of +18 lb boost available for short periods), and 1,490 hp for take-off, giving the P-51D a maximum speed of 437 mph (703 km/h) at 25,000 ft (7,620 m). This was just slightly less than the P-51B/C, and indeed the V-1650-7 was a lower altitude rated engine, but the overall gain in power improved all-round running including the all-important take-off performance. With two 1,000 lb (454 kg) or two 108 US gallon drop tanks the P-51D took off with more power compared to the P-51B. Nevertheless the P-51D's climb rate was not as good as that of the P-51B, mainly because of the increased weight of the new version, which was some 450 lb (204 kg) heavier under some operational loadings than its predecessor. The maximum range, however, was at least 1,650 miles (2,655 km).

The P-51D began replacing the P-51B on the Inglewood production line in February 1944, and the type was introduced at Dallas to supersede the P-51C from circa September 1944. The P-51D was built under several NAA designations, NA-106, 109, 111, 122, and 124. The P-51K was NA-111. Production totalled 7,956 P-51D (including 1,454 at Dallas) and 1,337 P-51K. Further, ten Dallas-built P-51Ds were completed as two-seat TP-51D aircraft and – as related later in this Chapter – there were also dedicated reconnaissance conversions under the F-6 label. The TP-51D had full dual-controls fitted, the rear occupant being seated in the space where the 85 US gallon fuselage fuel tank and radio equipment would normally have fitted, the latter being relocated. Several more two-seat trainer Mustangs were also made, it is believed as field modifications, and long after the war a number of two-seat conversions were accomplished by Temco and Cavalier (as described later in this book) – none of these are to be confused

The company photographers of North American Aviation took every advantage of the usually beautiful Southern California weather to take excellent, clean and clear in-flight photographs of the Mustang line in a large number of company publicity photographs. Even with the characteristic Mustang peculiarity of the famous lower fuselage radiator air intake, there is no doubting that the P-51D was an elegant, many would say beautiful, aircraft. The cleanest of them all were the initial production P-51D-5-NA aircraft, which did not have the dorsal fin extension ahead of the tailplane or 'fin fillet' that was introduced a little later in production to aid in directional stability. This example is one of these early P-51D Mustangs, serial number 44-13366, displaying in particular the cut-down fuselage line behind the cockpit and sliding clear unframed 'bubble' or 'all-round' vision canopy that together were major developments in the P-51D series compared to all previous production Mustangs (Photo: NAA)

with the unit-modified two-seat P-51B/C models that were used as operational trainers, 'hacks', joy-riders and beer-carriers by Eighth Air Force Mustang groups late in World War Two.

The new teardrop-canopy, six-gun P-51D started to arrive in England for the Eighth Air Force in May and June 1944. By then Europe had the priority for new Mustang deliveries, as the Mustang more and more proved its worth in air-to-air combat in the skies over North-west Europe. Initially the new aircraft found their way to group and squadron commanders, who were able to use the new big view from their cockpits to keep an eye on their own fighters, the bombers they were defending and the overall picture of air battles as they took place. In practice the P-51D was found to be just slightly slower than the P-51B/C at altitude, but its strengthened wing allowed greater loads to be carried – indeed, much later in the P-51D production, 'zero-length' mountings for up to five unguided air-to-ground rockets were included on the production line (in theory, three of these could be carried in addition to the usual pylon just outboard of the main undercarriage legs, or all five if the pylon was not attached). The P-51K started to reach England in the autumn or early winter of 1944. In practice, at operational level, the earlier P-51B/C continued to serve well into the P-51D/K era, and very often squadrons would fly mixed formations of the two distinct types. Some pilots actually preferred the P-51B/C layout, while many new pilots arriving later in 1944 or early 1945 flew nothing but the P-51D series. In the field some P-51B/C airframes were re-engined as maintenance demanded with the newer V-1650-7 engine, and it seems likely that some P-51Ds ended up with the earlier V-1650-3 engine for the same reason. Later P-51D and P-51K aircraft were also fitted with an excellent new gunsight, the K-14, which for its day was a major advance on previous equipment. A computing

'gyroscopic' gunsight which was a significant aid in deflection shooting, it gradually replaced the previous N-9 reflector sight which was used in some P-51B/C and early P-51D aircraft (the earlier N-3B was standard for the P-51B and P-51C). It was another input from the British into the Mustang story, having been based upon a British design and originally used in bomber gun turrets. The K-14 was a bulky piece of equipment that was difficult to locate on the coaming above the Mustang's instrument panel; eventually an installation pioneered by the 357th FG gained widespread acceptance.

Interestingly, however, the loss of the high fuselage line behind the cockpit resulted in the P-51D series being something of a handful as far as directional stability was concerned. This problem had already been apparent in the P-51B and P-51C series, the Merlin-engined Mustangs in general being somewhat wilder to fly than the beautifully-handling Allison-engined Mustangs. North American tried a number of solutions to this problem, but the eventual fix that appeared to offer the best way to meet the problem was the addition of a dorsal extension from the fin leading edge. This 'dorsal fin' was introduced on the production line later in 1944, but some of the aircraft in the initial 44-13… series were retrofitted in the field with this dorsal extension – and, as described elsewhere, a similar extension was also tried out on the P-51B and P-51C series aircraft as well, tailored to the different rear fuselage line of those fighters. In fact later production P-51D/K series aircraft incorporated a number of further minor equipment or instrumentation improvements compared to the earlier production examples, some in the light of combat experience.

Most significantly, however, virtually all those who flew the P-51D in combat found the aircraft to be superb. It combined range,

External, jettisonable long-range fuel tanks became a vital part of the overall picture of outstanding success for the USAAF's bomber escort fighters in the latter stages of the Second World War. The compressed paper 108 US gallon drop tank illustrated here was one of several types of external fuel tanks that could be carried by the Merlin-Mustangs of the Eighth and Fifteenth Army Air Forces, one under each wing *(Photo: Malcolm V. Lowe Collection)*

Mass production, 1940's style. There were certainly no robots or computer-automated processes at the time of Mustang manufacture, and although Mustangs were built on a production line, the methods of construction resulted in each aircraft being virtually a hand-made product. In this staged but no less interesting NAA company image, a basically finished P-51D fuselage assembly, complete with tailplane, is hoisted over the wing structure onto which it will be lowered and attached. The Mustang's wing was a strong, one-piece all-metal construction, its design being based around the special laminar-flow airfoil shape developed by NAA and NACA engineers. The wing was actually manufactured in two sections, the left-hand and the right-hand mainplanes, which were then bolted together at the centre line to create the one-piece structure, to which the main undercarriage, self-sealing fuel tanks, flaps and ailerons, and other major fittings were then added. The fuselage-to-wing connection was made at four principal attachment points *(Photo: NAA)*

speed and manoeuvrability in an excellent airframe that was easily the match of any piston-engined fighter that it came across - and if speed could be built up in a dive or the adversary could be lured into a turning dogfight, the Mustang could also battle it out with a new menace in the skies over Europe, the early German jets. Truly the Mustang had grown into a magnificent fighting machine.

## Merlin-Mustangs and Jets

The prowess of the aggressively-flown US-operated Mustang escorts was therefore not simply restricted to often successful dealings with the Luftwaffe's piston-engined fighters. In the background to the air war that was raging over continental Europe as 1944 wore on, a threat was materialising from the advanced aircraft types that German engineers and designers were developing. In the summer of 1944 the Messerschmitt Me 262, powered by two Junkers Jumo 004 turbojet engines, made its combat debut, as did the rocket-powered Me 163. The jet age was dawning, and it was – in the long term – bad news for the piston-engined fighter. Although combat aircraft such as the Mustang were certainly the ultimate expression of the piston-engined fighter, the jet engine threatened to eclipse the type very soon. The jet aircraft of the summer of 1944 onwards were not particularly reliable, fuel-efficient or combat-ready, but they were a sudden shock to the Allies and they definitely represented the shape of things to come. In the skies over Europe during the summer and autumn of 1944 the opening encounters took place between the American escort fighters and the first German jets. These advanced aircraft could have posed a considerable threat to the growing Allied air supremacy over mainland Europe, had they been available in significant numbers or developed further from

their initial rather crude layout. The operational fighter version of the Me 262, the Me 262A-1a, had a top speed of 540 mph (870 km/h) at 19,685 ft (6,000 m), while the Me 163B could reach the then incredible 593 mph (954 km/h) at 29,528 ft (9,000 m) – although the latter could only manage this for short periods due to its critically short endurance on full power. The Me 163 was also dangerous to operate, its volatile liquid fuels posing a considerable risk to its ground crews and pilots.

Nevertheless, this new breed of fighters became a potentially large threat to the Allies, and in their use against the US bombers and fighters they started to score successes as 1944 wore on. Amongst the first casualties were three 352nd FG Mustangs that are believed to have been shot down by Me 163s in early August 1944. It was the Mustang, however, that alone amongst the Allied fighters probably had the most realistic chance of taking on these new fighter types, and the very first to be brought down fell to the guns of a P-51 on 16 August 1944. On that day Eighth Air Force heavy bombers raided targets in south-eastern Germany, and were covered by a number of fighter groups including the Mustang-operating 359th FG from East Wretham, Norfolk. Amongst the Luftwaffe aircraft that responded to the raid were several Me 163Bs of JG 400. A number of these rocket fighters intercepted the B-17s that the 359th was covering. No piston-engined fighter, not even a Mustang, could conceivably catch an Me 163 with its rocket motor running, but the German pilots of these machines had a restricted endurance due to the limited fuel capacity of the type and the high burn rate of the fighter's rocket fuel. The 359th FG's Lt Col John Murphy and his wingman Lt Cyril Jones caught two of the rocket fighters as they manoeuvred, presumably with their power off, to engage the bombers. Jones scored hits on one Me 163 apparently without result, but Murphy was able to engage in a turning fight with a second rocket fighter. The tailless German fighter could not hope to out-turn a Mustang, and Murphy shot down his quarry to record the first success of the Eighth Air Force over the new breed of German fighters. Murphy was flying P-51D-5-NA 44-13966 coded CS-K on that significant mission.

On 29 August the first Me 262 jet fighter was destroyed by Eighth Air Force fighters, when P-47D Thunderbolts of the 78th FG from Duxford caused one of the German jets to crash-land near Brussels after a chase in which no shots were fired but in which the heavy Thunderbolts had dived on the Me 262 and had succeeded in catching up with their quarry. The kill was shared by Maj Joe Myers (CO of the 82nd FS) and another 78th FG pilot. Diving in the direction of an Me 262 and thus gaining a speed build-up was one of the best ways of engaging these fast fighters, but other means were discovered, including attacking the jets at their potentially most vulnerable moments. The first major

An interesting contemporary view inside the NAA Dallas (Grand Prairie) factory, with production of the P-51D or P-51K well under way (Dallas made both P-51D and P-51K Mustangs). The Mustangs are essentially complete but minus their propeller units, and with a protective coating over their cockpit transparencies. Particularly noteworthy is the primed wing uppersurface of each Mustang, probably using yellow-tinted zinc chromate primer, in preparation for aluminium (silver) paint to be sprayed on, with the forward panel lines having already been filled with putty. In the background are AT-6F-NTs intended for the Soviet Union, 'AT' (for 'Advanced Trainer') being the designation under which these Texans were being built at the time. Mustangs underwent few major changes throughout the entire production run of the Merlin-Mustang line, apart of course from the cutting down of the fuselage line behind the cockpit and the installation of three machine-guns in each wing in the P-51D. There were, however, several detail enhancements which aided the overall performance. A small but important change, for example, that was incorporated during the P-51D production was an alteration to the ailerons. Aileron effectiveness was somewhat poor in some flight regimes on earlier Mustangs. In the P-51D, better seals were attached to the leading edge of each aileron's balance strip. Three hinge bearing attachments were also added instead of the two previous attachments, the effect of these slight but important alterations being the requirement for less stick force to be used to allow the Mustang to manoeuvre, giving a gain in combat effectiveness especially in dog-fighting – an activity that the Mustang was already very competent in. *(Photo: NAA)*

It was not long before the P-51D started to make its presence felt as deliveries began to be made to the Eighth Air Force. Eventually all but one of the Eighth's fighter groups flew Merlin-Mustangs, and the type proved to be a great success over North-west Europe. Interestingly, however, some pilots who 'cut their teeth' on the earlier Merlin-Mustangs, the P-51B and P-51C, preferred those earlier marks compared to the later P-51D - despite the latter having heavier firepower that was also less prone to jamming than in the earlier versions. Eighth Air Force Mustangs became a very familiar sight above the English countryside, especially over East Anglia. In this image, Capt Reps P Jones of the 77th Fighter Squadron flies P-51D-10-NA, serial number 44-14823, LC-F 'Miss Miami'. As a carry-over from the days when the 20th FG flew P-38 Lightnings, many of the unit's Mustangs carried geometric symbols on their vertical tails to signify which squadron they belonged to in addition to the assigned squadron code letters *(Photo: Arthur E. Sevigny, 20th Fighter Wing Association)*

An early exponent of the Merlin-Mustang when the type first became available to the Eighth Army Air Force in England, the 357th Fighter Group initially flew the P-51B - but like other Mustang fighter groups of the Eighth it eventually operated the P-51D as well (the two types often overlapped, although by the latter stages of the war in Europe the P-51D easily predominated in terms of numbers). Taxiing past the photographer in this image was one of the group's P-51D Mustangs from the 362nd Fighter Squadron, actually a P-51D-20-NA serial number 44-63195. Coded G4-K, the aircraft was named 'Marymae' and was usually flown by Lt Richard Potter from Toledo, Ohio *(Photo: Malcolm V. Lowe Collection)*

Without doubt the outstanding success of the Eighth Army Air Force's fighter effort against Germany's Luftwaffe was due to the fantastic qualities of the Merlin-Mustang in the various marks that flew with the Eighth's fighter groups, but excellent leadership also played a key role. One of the Eighth's finest fighter leaders, and an unerring champion of the role of the escort fighter, was the famed Col Don Blakeslee. A part of the equally famous 4th Fighter Group but often seconded elsewhere to aid other groups, Blakeslee was one of America's top fighter pilots from any era. Formerly with the RCAF and then the RAF, Blakeslee was the CO of the 4th FG for most of 1944. In this view he is leading a formation of Mustangs from each of the three squadrons of the 4th FG, presumably for a photo-call. His immaculate P-51D-5-NA, 44-13779, did not have the fin fillet but wore all the regulation recognition markings of the mid-1944 era, including the well-known red nose of the 4th FG *(Photo: USAAF)*

Sitting peacefully in the summer sunshine prior to 14 August 1944 when it had a taxiing accident, an early P-51D of the 361st Fighter Group shows off the lines of the early production P-51D Mustangs, without the dorsal 'fin fillet'. A P-51D-5-NA, 44-13708 named 'Duchess of Manhattan', it was assigned to the 374th Fighter Squadron of the 361st Fighter Group at Bottisham in Cambridgeshire, and has the regulation yellow extreme nose and spinner as assigned to this group – all of the Eighth Air Force's fighter groups used coloured noses of one form or another for identification. Its pilot was Capt Henry B Lederer, and the 'Duchess' was his wife, who came from Manhattan *(Photo: USAAF)*

combat success by Mustangs over the Me 262 came on 7 October, when Lt Urban Drew of the 361st FG from Little Walden, Essex, shot down two of the German jets. On this occasion Drew used a tactic that was to become an important means of combating the German jets, of catching them when they were most vulnerable at or near their own bases when they were landing or taking-off. Flying his colourful P-51D-15-NA 44-14164 coded E2-D and named 'Detroit Miss', Drew caught the Me 262As at their home airfield of Achmer and brought down both as they were taking-off. Although this proved to be one of the best ways to combat the German jets, it sometimes came at a considerable price due to the impressive array of light anti-aircraft weaponry that was deployed at many German air bases as they came under increasing attack by the American fighters. Indeed, so tempting and at the same time vulnerable were the Me 262s when landing and taking off

that a number of long-nose Focke-Wulf Fw 190D fighters were assigned specifically to airfield defence at some Me 262 bases in order to take on any Allied fighters that were waiting for the opportunity to strike at the jets. Much of the initial fighter operations by the fighter-configured Me 262s (many were diverted for use as fast fighter-bombers) were carried out by Kommando Novotny, a semi-autonomous operational evaluation unit which was led by the high-scoring Luftwaffe fighter ace Walter Novotny. On 8 November 1944 Novotny was shot down and killed in an Me 262A by Mustangs, the kill being shared by two Eighth Air Force pilots who included the 20th Fighter Group's Lt Ernest Fiebelkorn. The top-scoring ace of the 20th FG with nine aerial victories, Fiebelkorn sadly lost his life in Korea in 1950 while flying a night-fighter F-82G Twin Mustang with the 4th Fighter-All Weather Squadron. His shoot-down of Novotny was illustrative of the ever-

The very smart and well-kept Mustang of the 4th Fighter Group's CO, Don Blakeslee, formates for the camera. Donald Blakeslee (to give him a more complete rendering of his name) finished the war with 14.5 aerial victories, some of these achieved while flying Spitfires earlier in the conflict, but it is his outstanding leadership qualities that have earned him a rightful place amongst the great fighter pilots of all time *(Photo: USAAF)*

growing problem that the Luftwaffe was having to face as 1944 wore on – the loss of valuable and irreplaceable experienced pilots in what had become for the Luftwaffe an increasingly deadly air war even in their own airspace.

## Mediterranean Merlin-Mustangs

In the Mediterranean and Southern Europe, four fighter groups flew the Merlin-Mustang for bomber escort and related tasks. The four groups concerned were the 31st, 52nd, 325th, and 332nd Fighter Groups. All of these had some combat experience prior to their time on the Mustang, but they became Mustang operators specifically under the organisation that was the Southern Europe equivalent of the ETO's strategic Eighth Army Air Force, the Fifteenth Army Air Force. Activated on 1 November 1943 out of a major reorganisation of US air assets in the MTO, the Fifteenth Air Force was planned to be a B-24 Liberator and B-17 Flying Fortress-equipped strategic force, that would primarily bomb Axis targets in northern Italy, the Balkans, and southern and central Europe – the areas that were out of reach of the Eighth Air Force's bombers, except during the 'Frantic' shuttle missions via bases in the Ukraine. Both the 31st and 52nd Fighter Groups had started

With its 'bubble' cockpit canopy partly covered as a protection against the notorious British weather, P-51D-10-NA 44-14519 had been sitting idle for some time – as evidenced by the down position of the wing flaps and the large wheel covers just visible in this view behind the flaps, showing that hydraulic pressure had bled off. The aircraft belonged to the 363rd Fighter Squadron of the 357th Fighter Group at Leiston in Suffolk, and had the red and yellow nose and spinner colours of that unit. It was named 'Daisy Mae' and was usually flown by Lt Alan Abner
*(Photo: R.L. Ward Collection)*

their combat careers with the Eighth Air Force in England during 1942 flying Spitfires, but had subsequently shipped out to North Africa later in 1942 and had fought through the campaign there, and later in Sicily and Italy still with Spitfires under the tactical MTO-based Twelfth Army Air Force. However, both were eventually chosen for long-range bomber escort operations in support of the Fifteenth Air Force's heavy bombers, it having become obvious to the leadership of the Fifteenth that fighter escort was just as necessary in the MTO as it was in Northern Europe. Many Merlin-Mustangs destined for Southern Europe staged through a major air depot, the 36th Air Depot, at Maison Blanche in modern-day Algeria. These aircraft were shipped by sea, and had to be put together in the somewhat spartan conditions in North Africa before being ferried to their units – sometimes by the very pilots who were to fly them in combat. The 31st FG (comprising the 307th, 308th, and 309th Fighter Squadrons) was assigned to the Fifteenth Air Force in April 1944, and the 52nd (comprising the 2nd, 4th, and 5th Fighter Squadrons) followed during May. At that time the 31st FG was newly based at San Savero in Italy, its home for much of the rest of the war, while the 52nd was newly-installed at Madna, south of Termoli, again its 'home from home' for the following months. Both units were in action straight away, the need for bomber escort being paramount. The 31st flew its first big operation on 21 April, a bomber escort to the infamous Rumanian oil installations at Ploesti, while the 52nd flew its first major mission – also to Ploesti – on 18 May. Helping the two groups with their operational transition onto the Mustang was Maj James Goodson, a veteran of the RAF Eagle Squadrons and an accomplished pilot with the 4th Fighter Group in England. While flying with the 31st FG on 23 April he shot down two Bf 109Gs between the famous landmark of Lake Balaton in Hungary and Wiener Neustadt in Austria, the

latter being the objective of the bombers. Goodson stayed with the Fifteenth from 12 April to 10 May, his two victories on 23 April contributing to his overall total of 14 aerial victories (nine in Mustangs), plus 15 ground victories. Both the 31st FG and the 52nd FG were awarded two Distinguished Unit Citations apiece for their sterling escort work on behalf of the Fifteenth Air Force's bombers, which increasingly had a positive effect on the effectiveness of the Fifteenth's strategic bombing effort.

Two further groups became Merlin Mustang operators under the Fifteenth Air Force in the early summer of 1944. They were the 325th and the 332nd, and with the existing two groups they formed a part of the Fifteenth Air Force's 306th Fighter Wing. Unlike the 31st and 52nd they had no connections with the Eighth Air Force. The 325th was already a part of the Fifteenth Air Force, having operated P-47 Thunderbolts in Italy from late in 1943 primarily for bomber escort work. In fact the unit was a veteran of the North African and Italian campaigns, having firstly operated P-40 Warhawks within the Twelfth Army Air Force from April 1943. In late May 1944 the 325th began to convert onto the Mustang, and its P-51s subsequently sported the famous 'checkertail' yellow and black markings that were the trademark of this group. Based at Lesina in Italy, the 325th (comprising the 317th, 318th, and 319th Fighter Squadrons) duly participated in many of the long-range bombing raids of the Fifteenth Air Force, the heavies sometimes striking at targets in Germany itself including the very long distance to Berlin. Some of these missions could easily be of seven hours duration, putting strain on aircraft and pilots just as in North-west Europe, with the added 'pleasures' at the Italian air bases of sometimes awful weather conditions and less than ideal facilities. The tour of duty for MTO fighter pilots was also longer than for their Northern Europe counterparts, and many flew 300 hours plus before being rotated home.

Several Mustangs brought together for a gathering of representatives from three of the Fifteenth Air Force's fighter groups in Italy. Nearest to the camera is a 308th Fighter Squadron, 31st Fighter Group P-51D coded HL-Z adorned with that group's distinctive red diagonal tail stripes, with next to it a 4th FS, 52nd FG P-51D coded 'WD'. Next in the line is a red-tailed 332nd FG P-51D with a '7' on the fuselage. Although not receiving the media attention of the more glamorous exploits of the Eighth Air Force's fighter groups in England, the Fifteenth Air Force's Mustang groups in southern Europe made a significant contribution to the air war over Europe *(Photo: USAAF)*

Nice formation view of Italian-based 308th Fighter Squadron, 31st Fighter Group Mustangs, two of which are immediately recognisable. HL-C, 44-13311, a P-51D-5-NA named 'OKaye', was flown by Capt (later Maj) Leland P. Molland, who finished the war with 10.5 aerial victories. HL-B, P-51D-15-NA serial number 44-15459, named 'American Beauty', was the personal aircraft of Capt John J. Voll, the top-scoring ace of the Fifteenth Air Force, with 21 aerial victories - all of these were achieved in Mustangs. Each aircraft wears the distinctive red diagonal tail stripes that identified the 31st Fighter Group *(Photo: USAAF)*

A useful detail view of the cockpit area of the P-51D of 1st Lt Bob Goebel. An 11 aerial victories ace, Robert John Goebel flew with the 308th Fighter Squadron of the 31st Fighter Group from Italian bases during the period April to September 1944. He was among the many talented exponents of the Mustang in the MTO, with the 31st FG being one of the crack fighter units of the Fifteenth Air Force primarily on bomber escort work. Some of the group's Mustangs can be seen in the background with the red diagonal tail stripes of this unit prominently displayed. The Mustang that Goebel is sitting in is a P-51D-5-NA, serial number 44-13500 (and not 44-13300 as sometimes claimed), coded HL-D and named 'Flying Dutchman' *(Photo: USAAF)*

The fourth and last Fifteenth Air Force Merlin Mustang unit to enter combat was the 332nd Fighter Group, which was unique amongst USAAF front-line groups in being predominantly black-American manned. Originally operating P-39 Airacobras with the tactical Twelfth Air Force in early 1944, the 332nd converted onto P-47 Thunderbolts for a very brief period before transitioning onto the Mustang in June 1944. Again assigned to the Fifteenth Air Force in May 1944, the 332nd unfortunately had to face a considerable amount of unnecessary prejudice during the time of its operations, and often its claims for aerial victories were turned down. The 332nd flew its first major operation on 7 June with the P-47, the customary 'shake-down' fighter sweep, in this case in the Bologna area. The final mission with the P-47 was flown on 30 June, by which time several bomber escorts had been flown, and the first major operation with the Mustang was undertaken on 6 July. The 332nd comprised the 99th, 100th, 301st, and 302nd Fighter Squadrons, it being unusual for a fighter group to have four assigned squadrons – the 99th FS in fact had already flown P-40 Warhawks as a part of the 79th FG in North Africa and Italy. Based at Ramitelli, the 332nd performed fighter escorts and ground strafing like the other three Fifteenth Air Force Mustang groups, and gained a Distinguished Unit Citation for its escort of the heavy bombers to Berlin on 24 March 1945, one of the longest raids that the Fifteenth Air Force ever carried out.

Like their counterparts in the ETO, the Fifteenth Air Force's pilots found the Mustang ideal for bomber escort and ground strafing, and it was easily the equal of any fighters that it came across in aerial combat. Over Southern Europe this included Italian and Rumanian fighter aircraft in addition to German, but encounters with German jets were not uncommon in the final months of the war. The first Me 262 to be shot down by Fifteenth Air Force Mustangs was brought down by two pilots of the 31st FG on 22 December 1944, while they were on a reconnaissance over southern Germany. The Fifteenth, like the Eighth Air Force, flew 'Frantic' shuttle bombing missions, staging through air bases in the Ukraine. The first was on 2 June 1944, when the 325th escorted heavy bombers to Poltava and Mirgorod (the fighters landed at Piryatin), attacking Debrecen in Hungary on the way. This initial MTO 'Frantic' ended on 11 June; two further shuttle missions were flown by the Fifteenth Air Force, one in July and the final one in August 1944. A considerable number of pilots became aces while flying the Merlin-Mustang with the Fifteenth Air Force, but highest-scoring of all was Capt John J. Voll of the 308th FS, 31st FG. As a 2nd Lt Voll achieved his first aerial victory on 23 June 1944, an Fw 190 north of Bucharest, Rumania, and his scoring run continued until 16 November when he brought down four German aircraft north of Aviano in Italy. These gave him a total of 21 aerial victories in the Merlin-Mustang, making him one of the highest-scoring Mustang pilots in terms of aerial victories of all time (in fact jointly second, alongside Lt Col John C. Meyer of the Eighth Air Force's 352nd Fighter Group). Appropriately, one of his assigned Mustangs was a P-51D-15-NA 44-15459 coded HL-B and named 'American Beauty'.

## Ninth Air Force Merlin-Mustangs

In addition to the significant work that Mustangs performed as bomber escorts in the ETO and MTO, and in successfully shooting up many ground targets such as airfields, the P-51 also played an important role specifically as a ground-attack aircraft. Three groups within the tactical Ninth Army Air Force, the 363rd, 354th, and 370th Fighter Groups, operated the Mustang primarily in a dedicated tactical fashion – although even they on occasion were called upon to provide escort duties, and as we have already seen, the 354th actually operated with the Eighth Air Force from December 1943 onwards specifically on bomber escort work until the Eighth had enough of its own Mustang groups. In reality, such was the pressing need for tactical fighters before, during and after

Wearing its smart black and white so-called 'invasion stripes', an early P-51D-5-NA, 44-13550, coded A9-M of the 380th Fighter Squadron of the 363rd Fighter Group is seen here in the period after D-Day. A Ninth Air Force fighter group, the 363rd flew its Mustangs mainly on tactical missions in support of ground forces, but later became a reconnaissance-dedicated unit. This early P-51D does not have the dorsal fin extension or 'fin fillet' that was fitted to later P-51D models to try to improve directional stability. Its upper surface 'invasion stripes' have also been somewhat crudely painted out with dark green paint, the fate of these identification stripes in the period after D-Day on the uppersurfaces of those aircraft bearing them
(Photo: USAAF)

the D-Day period, that on occasion fighter groups of the Eighth Air Force were detached to operate on purely tactical missions additional to their bomber escort work.

The 354th Fighter Group, after playing such an important role in introducing the Merlin Mustang to bomber escort work, more and more reverted to its originally intended role of tactical operations as April 1944 wore on. On 15 April the group flew its last mission from Boxted, a fighter sweep to Luftwaffe airfields in northern Germany around Rostock. Gradually the group then made the move to an advanced landing ground at Lashenden in Kent, from where it was nearer to the Continent as the pace of tactical operations picked up while preparations for the invasion of Europe increasingly took place. Nevertheless, the 354th FG continued to escort the heavy bombers whenever required, and on 4 May the group was a part of a major bomber escort effort to Berlin. D-Day itself, 6 June 1944, saw the 354th in action right at the start. On the late evening of 5 June, the group's Mustangs took off to give cover to Douglas C-47 transports carrying airborne troops and towing gliders from a rendezvous over Portland across to the area of 'Utah' Beach in the early hours of 6 June. The Mustangs staged back via Stoney Cross in the New Forest, but flew their second mission of the day, again covering paratroop-carrying C-47s, in the early morning of 6 June. In the days that followed the 354th was involved in various dive-bombing attacks, and on 14 June escorted Ninth Air Force medium bombers in a raid near Caen. Five intercepting Bf 109s were shot down on that occasion. In keeping with other tactical air assets, the 354th eventually moved over to the Continent, making its final missions from Lashenden on 22 June before starting to move over to A-2 Criqueville in Normandy. It was from here, on 4 July 1944, that the 354th mounted a very special mission. Several weeks earlier the group had converted one of its veteran 'war weary' P-51Bs, 43-

6877, into two-seat configuration, for instructional purposes and joy-riding. However, on 4 July the Mustang was used to fly none other than the supreme Allied commander, Gen Dwight D Eisenhower, in a flight from Criqueville over the then-front lines and particularly around the Saint-Lo area. The pilot for this epic and rather risky flight was Maj Gen Elwood Quesada, the head of IX Fighter Command. The Mustang was subsequently appropriately named 'The Stars Look Down'.

From A-2 Criqueville the 354th duly followed the fighting, and made several more base moves before ending the war in Ansbach and Herzogenaurach in Germany. For a short period, the group was forced to give up its prized Mustangs when it converted onto the P-47 Thunderbolt (the first P-47 mission was flown by the group on 26 November 1944), but normal operations were restored when Mustangs were again flown by the group in combat from 16 February onwards. In a repeat of its operations on D-Day, the 354th, alongside the huge aerial assets that the Allies could muster by that point in the war, flew cover for Operation 'Varsity', the Rhine Crossing on 24 March 1945. Perhaps unsurprisingly, the top Mustang aces of the Ninth Air Force flew with the 354th FG. At the head of them was Maj Glenn T Eagleston of the 353rd FS, who achieved 18.5 aerial victories in Mustangs between 5 January 1944 (an Fw 190 near Meldorf during the famous Kiel raid that helped establish the Mustang as a successful escort fighter) and 25 March 1945 (a Bf 109 near Aschaffenburg) - and a further two victories in Korea flying F-86A Sabres.

The second of the Ninth Air Force's Mustang groups was the 363rd Fighter Group (380th, 381st, and 382nd Fighter Squadrons). Originally activated in March 1943, this group moved to England in late 1943 and entered combat with the Merlin-Mustang in February 1944. Based initially at Keevil in Wiltshire but from late January/early February at Rivenhall in Essex, the first Mustangs

Among the many unsung heroes in the story of the Mustang are the test pilots who flight-tested the aircraft when they had originally been built, and the ferry pilots who flew them to their first intended destination after construction and testing. In this image, ferry pilot Florene Watson warms up a P-51D prior to a delivery flight. The contribution by female pilots to America's war effort has, sadly, largely been forgotten. The WASP organisation provided ferry pilots in a similar fashion to the ATA in Britain, and female pilots were more than capable of handling even a potentially wild beast like a Merlin-engined Mustang (Photo: wingsacrossamerica.org via Nancy Parrish)

Photographed at BAD 1 at Burtonwood in early 1945, this brand new Mustang shares the flight line with several other US types prior to onwards assignment. The Base Air Depots at Warton and Burtonwood in northern England reassembled and prepared Mustangs that had been shipped to Britain via Liverpool, for onward assignment to combat units. Those who worked at these Base Air Depots, some of whom were civilian employees, normally receive little mention in histories that have the World War Two period as their subject matter *(Photo: Gordon Stevens Collection)*

Weather Scout. Normally assigned to Capt John W. Simpson (ex-356th FG), this P-51D-20-NA serial number 44-72239 was a part of the 1st Scouting Force/857th Bomb Squadron, and is seen on a captured former Luftwaffe airfield. It is representative of the exceptional but rarely mentioned work of the Scouting Force Mustangs in the Eighth Air Force, which were primarily tasked with weather scouting in advance of heavy bomber missions. Named 'Zoom Zoozie', this aircraft carries the red bordering to the vertical tail that was a feature of 1st Scouting Force markings, and a red spinner and white nose band *(Photo: USAAF)*

did not arrive for the group until 24 January. The initial mission was flown on 24 February, and several pilots from the 354th FG gave the group a helping hand for the first operations. A number of bomber escorts were flown, but in mid-April the group departed Rivenhall for the advanced landing ground at Staplehurst in Kent, ready for more tactically-orientated missions connected to the coming Invasion. Thereafter the 363rd began to move over to the Continent from late June, although the group was also temporarily involved in combating V1 flying bombs, its base in Kent being in the firing line for these unmanned devices. Eventually the 363rd moved in to A-15 Maupertus, now the site of Cherbourg airport, in late June and early July 1944, and subsequently used A-7 Azeville from the following month. The group employed its Mustangs primarily for tactical missions in support of US ground forces, but in late August and early September the group's role was completely changed when it became the 363rd Tactical Reconnaissance Group, primarily flying F-6C and F-6D Mustangs until the end of the war.

The third of the trio of Ninth Air Force tactical Mustang groups was the 370th Fighter Group. This unit was a long-standing P-38 Lightning group, that started to fly the Mustang in the latter stages of the war. Activated comparatively late, in July 1943, the 370th (comprising the 401st, 402nd, and 485th Fighter Squadrons), moved to England in early 1944, and was equipped with Lockheed P-38 Lightnings before, during and after the D-Day period, subsequently following the Allied advance across Europe. In early 1945, as more and more Mustangs became available, the group gradually converted to the P-51D principally during February and March 1945. At that time the unit was based at Zwartberg in Belgium, and its Mustangs subsequently saw considerable action

during the Rhine Crossing on 24 March 1945, and supported the 2nd Armoured Division in its drive into the Ruhr. It finished the war at Y-99 Gütersloh in Germany.

In addition to these dedicated tactical assets, it is often forgotten that Mustangs of the Eighth Air Force played a highly important role before, during and after D-Day by performing many tactical missions against German forces in northern France quite in addition to their normal bomber escort duties. These involved a wide range of targets but importantly included rail and communications, as the Allies attempted to stop German reinforcements reaching the main area of battle in Normandy. During that time the Eighth Air Force's heavy bombers were often also brought in to provide extra support against tactical targets in the immediate area of the ground fighting. Indeed, so important was the Eighth Air Force in this sphere that later in the year, two of the Eighth's fighter units, the 361st and 352nd Fighter Groups, were actually stationed on the Continent to be near to the front lines so that they could specifically provide tactical support. A significant part of the 361st moved from Little Walden to A-64 Saint-Dizier late in 1944 and came under the control of XIX Tactical Air Command, and in mid-February 1945 relocated into Belgium to be based at A-84 Chièvres. The 352nd FG was normally based at Bodney in Norfolk, but a major part of its air echelon moved to Y-29 Asch in late 1944 to come under temporary control of IX Tactical Air Command, and thence to Chièvres in late January/early February 1945. The move of both these units to the Continent was specifically occasioned by the German offensive in the Ardennes, and both groups were able to provide much-needed additional air support to the hard-pressed US ground forces when the weather permitted. Unfortunately, the deployment had a particularly tragic consequence. Amongst those deployed with the 352nd FG contingent was Maj George Preddy, Jr. At that time Preddy was the leading Mustang ace in terms of aerial victories, with 21.833 victories. On Christmas Day 1944 Preddy and other pilots of the 352nd deployment were airborne over the battlefield, and Preddy shot down two Bf 109s south-west of Koblenz. Unfortunately, while crossing the front-line near Liège he was shot down by ground fire and killed. Tragically, the ground fire that brought down his Mustang came from a US Army anti-aircraft battery. No one subsequently bettered Preddy's 23.833 aerial victories in the Mustang, and he remains to this day the top-scoring Mustang pilot in terms of aerial victories. He also had five ground victories to his credit, and one wonders how many more aerial victories he would have achieved if he had not been brought down in this disastrous 'friendly fire' incident.

## Little-known Merlin-Mustang Operations

There were a number of units that flew the Mustang in a combat environment, but which to this day are rarely publicised and their exploits little known. A typical example is the P-51-operating weather scouting force of the Eighth Air Force. The need for this small but important organisation arose primarily from the vagaries of the weather over North-west Europe. All too often, early Eighth Air Force daylight bombing raids were thwarted by cloud cover over the intended target areas, even when it had been expected that weather would be fine enough to allow bombing to take place. In those far distant days, meteorology was nowhere near as precise or based on the large amount of data that is available nowadays, and there were certainly no satellites to allow an overall picture of the weather in areas distant to one's own location. The RAF already had a functioning weather data-gathering programme when the Eighth Air Force began operations in 1942, but thanks to the efforts of several individuals, notably Col Bud Peaslee, the USAAF in England eventually also developed its own organisation. This included specially-converted B-17 Flying Fortresses for long-range weather reconnaissance, especially out over the Atlantic, de Havilland Mosquitoes borrowed from the British for target-related flights over Occupied Europe, and P-51 Mustangs. The P-51s were ideal for target weather assessment ahead of the bomber stream, and were often (but not always) flown by former bomber pilots who had converted onto the P-51 at the training base at Goxhill or, later, at operational unit level. Goxhill was home to the 496th Fighter Training Group, which provided theatre operational indoctrination training for newly-arrived pilots as well as more general training duties – its assigned Mustang training squadron was the 555th.

The weather scout Mustangs would normally arrive in the target area some 15 minutes ahead of the leaders of the bomber stream, giving vital weather data to the raid's lead crews by coded radio message, and loitering in the target area to advise on bombing results to oncoming formations, give information on variations in the weather, and other relevant facts such as the extent of smoke-screens and fighter opposition. Being armed and also escorted by standard Mustang fighters, the weather scouts could shoot their way out of dangerous situations if intercepted. Their presence in the target area ahead of the bombers did not necessarily give the game away as to what the target was to be to the German defences because they looked like a part of the normal fighter escort – and thus making them more suitable in the latter respect than Mosquitoes, which were sometimes used for these tasks, often escorted by Mustangs. The first solely P-51 weather scouting mission was flown on 16 July 1944, using a provisional flight of Mustangs that had been formed at Steeple Morden within the 355th Fighter Group, and in August/September 1944 this flight became the 1st Scouting Force. It subsequently moved to Honington to operate within the 364th FG, which was one of the Eighth's fighter units delegated to the B-17-operating 1st Bombardment Division (later Air Division). Eventually the other two Bomb Divisions of the Eighth Air Force also had their own Scouting Forces – the B-24-operating 2nd Bomb Division was assigned the 2nd Scouting Force based at Steeple Morden with the 355th FG, led by Lt Col John Brooks who had formerly flown

Liberators with the 389th Bomb Group; and the 3rd Bomb Division (originally some B-24 units but eventually all B-17-equipped) received support from the 3rd Scouting Force, which flew as a part of the 55th FG at Wormingford. Operations were mounted in close liaison with the bombardment units, and often consisted of two flights of four Mustangs, which included the weather scouts themselves and their escorts. Most if not all of the Mustangs used were of the teardrop-canopy P-51 type. The Mustangs were generally very successful in this role, and they apparently did not require any specific modifications to allow them to perform the weather scouting mission – although nothing could be done on many occasions about the poor weather over North-west Europe! The weather scouts were not intended as fighter pilots and were briefed to avoid combat unless it became necessary – nevertheless, scouting pilots sometimes had little choice but to engage in combat, with some 17 aerial victories being attributed to them by the end of the war. By then the 1st Scouting Force had become a part of the 492nd BG's 857th Bomb Squadron (which was attached directly to the 1st Air Division from March 1945) and had moved to Bassingbourn (home of the 1st Air Division's 91st Bomb Group) during that month, while the 3rd Scouting Force had – on paper at least – become a part of the 862nd BS of the 493rd BG. These were rare cases of front-line Merlin Mustangs being on the 'books' of operational bombardment units.

In addition to the Eighth Air Force weather scouts, the Ninth Air Force also operated a similar unit that was associated with Mustangs. This was the 9th Weather Reconnaissance Squadron (Provisional), and like its equivalents in the Eighth Air Force it flew Mustangs ahead of planned bomber missions (but in this instance

Different marks of Merlin-Mustang often flew together in combat, and this neat formation from the Eighth Army Air Force's 339th Fighter Group includes three P-51D Mustangs in company with a Malcolm Hood-equipped P-51B. The aircraft are from the 505th Fighter Squadron of the 339th Fighter Group, up from Fowlmere and sporting that group's distinctive red and white nose and spinner markings. Nearest the camera is 'Pauline', a P-51D-20-NA, serial number 44-72437 coded 6N-C, which was the assigned aircraft of Maj (later Lt Col) Joseph Thury, the squadron CO. Thury began using this particular Mustang in the spring of 1944 following a previous 'Pauline', which dates the picture to that period – illustrating the fact that P-51B Mustangs were still current as front-line types even at that late stage in the proceedings. Joe Thury was a famed strafing ace, with an eventual total of 25.5 ground victories plus 2.5 aerial victories *(Photo: Steve Ananian, 339th FG Association)*

The Eighth Air Force produced many high-scoring air aces during the major air battles that took place over Germany in 1944 and early 1945. Amongst these was Lt Col John C Meyer of the Eighth Air Force's 352nd Fighter Group. One of Meyer's several Mustangs is seen here, a P-51D-10-NA, serial number 44-14151, named 'Petie 2nd' and coded HO-M. It wears the distinctive dark blue nose and spinner of the 352nd Fighter Group, together with the unusual style of representing the aircraft's code letters that was prevalent in this group, with the aircraft's individual letter placed on the fin. Meyer was one of the top exponents of the Mustang, scoring 21 aerial victories (plus others while flying the P-47 Thunderbolt) as well as 13 ground victories. His eventual score was 26 aerial victories – in keeping with a number of World War Two fighter pilots he also served in the Korean War, where he flew F-86A Sabres *(Photo: USAAF)*

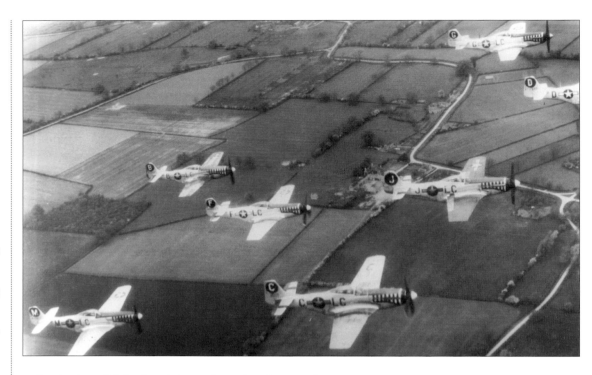

medium bomber or light bomber missions, and ground-attack sorties) to report on local weather conditions and other relevant information. Its aircraft usually acted in pairs, one for the reconnaissance task and one to provide cover. Originally operating a mix of early-mark Merlin-Mustangs, some of which were decidedly war weary, the squadron had a large influx of P-51D Mustangs when the 354th Fighter Group temporarily operated P-47 Thunderbolts late in 1944 and had to give up its beloved Mustangs.

Operationally, Mustangs were also used for various other tasks in the ETO, most notably as radio relay aircraft. These were Mustangs that were detailed to orbit well away from the aerial activity during raids, and relay radio messages as required between the bomber stream and other Allied aircraft, or other locations when required. The actual training of pilots to fly Merlin-Mustangs initially took the form of a number of fighter training groups in the continental United States, with in-theatre indoctrination taking place at dedicated local training units. In the US, several training groups had Mustangs on their books, particularly as the type became more numerous when deliveries of Merlin Mustangs increased. Units such as the 372nd Fighter Group at Esler Field, Louisiana, and the 53rd Fighter Group at Fort Myers, Florida, had Merlin-Mustangs on their roster. Within the Eighth Air Force in England, the 496th Fighter Training Group at Goxhill provided theatre operational indoctrination training for newly-arrived pilots – however, in late 1944/early 1945, the individual fighter groups of the Eighth Air Force were given responsibility for operational training and theatre indoctrination

for new incoming pilots. This initially appeared to be an extra burden that the groups themselves could little do with, but eventually it became a valuable part of each group's activities, and new pilots were able to assimilate the particular procedures and spirit of their new posting much more easily. Most if not all of the 14 Mustang fighter groups in the Eighth Air Force converted a small number of war weary P-51B/C Mustangs into two-seaters to help with this process.

## Merlin-Mustangs Triumphant

There can be little if any doubt that the advent of the Mustang as an escort fighter in the Eighth Air Force saved the US strategic bombing campaign over North-west Europe. That campaign went from strength to strength as 1944 continued, with the bombers consistently getting through to their targets despite the best efforts of the Luftwaffe, which the Mustangs were always able to cope with. In general, the greatest danger to the bombers became anti-aircraft fire (it had always been a danger from the first), which could not be combated in any particularly successful way. But against the Luftwaffe the Mustang was always on a par with any piston-engined fighters that the Germans could operate, even the excellent inline-engined Fw 190D which began operations in September 1944. A considerable number of US pilots became aces while flying the Mustang in air-to-air combat, and the actions of the Mustangs in attacking anything that moved on the ground as a part of their escort duties ensured that the Germans were always under pressure. Co-operation with the Soviet Union following complicated negotiations had resulted in the Eighth Air Force

flying several 'Frantic' shuttle missions in the summer of 1944, in which the great range of the Mustang had allowed Soviet air bases in the Ukraine to be reached by the fighters in concert with the heavy bombers. Of the seven 'Frantic' shuttle missions that were flown, four were performed by the Eighth Air Force. The first was in June/July 1944 (21 June to 5 July) and involved the heavy bombers of the 3rd Bomb Division carrying on to Italy after stopping over in the Ukraine. The fighter force for this first 'Frantic' comprised the three squadrons of the 4th Fighter Group (334th, 335th, and 336th Fighter Squadrons), together with a squadron of the 352nd FG. The total flight time for the fighters between the 4th FG's base at Debden in Essex, and the Ukrainian air base at Piryatin, was almost seven and a half hours. Although other fighter groups covered the bombers and then returned to England, the bombers flew on with their escort from the 4th FG, after bombing a synthetic oil facility south of Berlin. The escorting Mustangs had to fight off some German fighters over Poland, and the whole force then landed in the Ukraine – the bombers heading for Poltava and Mirgorod. Some Mustang ground crews had flown in the bombers to give maintenance cover for the fighters after landing, prior to

Allied airpower was eventually so successful in establishing air superiority over German-occupied territory as the war continued that even German airspace itself became a dangerous place for Luftwaffe aircraft of any kind, operational or training. As the Germans became more desperate, some bizarre experiments were tried out to try to make a difference to the course of the war. Here, a roving 55th Fighter Group P-51D piloted by 1st Lt Bernard H. Howes of the 343rd Fighter Squadron has chanced upon a Mistel guided bomb combination of KG 200 near Hagenow featuring a piloted Messerschmitt Bf 109F attached to a Junkers Ju 88A bomber, on a ferry flight from Kolberg to Tirstrup in Denmark on 3 February 1945. In this still from Howes' gun camera, a crew member is very wisely exiting the contraption while Howes presses home his attack and shoots down the Heath-Robinson device *(Photo: USAAF)*

the next leg of the mission on 26 June. Before then the Germans successfully bombed the airfields at Poltava and Mirgorod, inflicting substantial losses on the parked B-17s, some 70 being destroyed or badly damaged – actually the costliest endeavour of the Eighth Air Force's whole bombing campaign, although thankfully casualties amongst personnel on the ground were light. The remaining bombers and fighters then made their way to Italy on 26 June, the Mustangs landing at Lucera – two Mustangs were left behind in the Ukraine. The Mustangs then escorted Fifteenth Army Air Force heavy bombers on 2 July, before the whole force returned to England on 5 July. This had been a something of a logistical nightmare, but three more 'Frantic' shuttles were flown by the Eighth Air Force (in August and September 1944), again with fighter cover from Mustangs.

By the latter stages of 1944 Allied ground forces were closing in on Germany itself from the west and the east, and Allied air superiority over the battlefield and in general in the wider air war was starting to be almost universal. Despite the dispersed German aircraft industry continuing to produce large numbers of fighter aircraft, the inferior quality of many of these aircraft due to poor manufacturing practices and quality control, the effects of Allied bombing on factories and parts suppliers, and the difficulty of delivering the finished machines to operational units due to marauding Allied fighters seemingly being everywhere, were all having a serious effect on the Luftwaffe's ability to successfully wage war. Combined with this was an increasingly successful Allied bombing campaign against the German oil and aviation fuel industry, and the crippling losses of experienced and capable pilots, and it is not hard to see that the Luftwaffe was in an increasingly difficult position as the war reached its critical stages. But it was certainly not a beaten force even as 1945 dawned, and the Allies did not let up on the incessant hammering away at its capability and production bases. On 1 January 1945 the Luftwaffe showed that it could strike back by mounting a major attack on Allied airfields on the Continent (Operation 'Bodenplatte'),

A number of Eighth Air Force units flew other fighter types before transitioning onto the Mustang. One of those was the 364th Fighter Group at Honington in Suffolk, which entered combat with the P-38 Lightning before transitioning onto the Mustang in combat from July 1944. Some of the unit's pilots achieved aerial victories in both types, including Capt Ernest Bankey, Jr. Originally flying P-38s, and then Mustangs with the 385th Fighter Squadron, Bankey later flew with the group's headquarters section and achieved 9.5 aerial victories (8.5 in Mustangs) plus 8 ground victories. He is seen here with 'Lucky Lady VII', a P-51D-25-NA, serial number 44-73045 coded 5E-B, which he flew late in the war and which he piloted to shoot down two Bf 109s on 16 April 1945. The Mustang wears the blue and white nose markings of this group. Rear view mirrors were often a matter of taste, Bankey preferred the style seen here *(Photo: USAAF)*

Carrying a pair of the famed 108 US gallon compressed paper drop tanks, one beneath each wing, 'Dallas Doll' of the Eighth Air Force's 353rd Fighter Group awaits its next mission. The aircraft is a P-51D-10-NA, serial number 44-14495, of the 352nd Fighter Squadron, based at Raydon in Suffolk, and wears the black and yellow nose and spinner markings of that fighter group. It was flown by Lt Frank Bouldin, Jr. *(Photo: USAAF)*

Prominently displaying the 'WZ' fuselage code letters of the 78th Fighter Group's 84th Fighter Squadron, this 'War Weary' P-51B has had a mishap probably during the early part of 1945. The use of 'retired' front-line Mustangs for training purposes was of great importance not just for new pilots joining a fighter group. Some groups, like the 78th, only started to fly the Mustang operationally quite late in the war, necessitating considerable familiarisation flying being required even for some established pilots before combat could be undertaken - the 78th was a successful user of the P-47 Thunderbolt to the final weeks of 1944 before transitioning completely onto the Mustang *(Photo: USAAF)*

although the long-term value of this undertaking was highly questionable because the Allies were easily able to make up losses, a situation that the Germans were hard pressed to achieve.

Nevertheless, on several occasions later in 1944 the Luftwaffe had risen in strength to attempt to combat Allied daylight bombing, and several major air battles had ensued that were reminiscent of the big air battles over Germany of the opening months of 1944. On 2 November, the Luftwaffe attempted a large scale interception of 683 B-17s attacking the oil facility at Merseburg, near Leipzig in eastern Germany, including the employment of fairly large numbers of Me 163 rocket fighters. For some time the Germans had not attempted a large-scale interception of the heavy bombers, but on that day several epic air battles ensued. These ended in disaster for the Germans, with Eighth Air Force fighters claiming 134 German aircraft in the air, a total possibly approaching half the attacking force of some 300 Luftwaffe fighters. This was an important defeat, and the Luftwaffe only attempted three further large scale interceptions of the heavy bombers until the New Year, although to be fair the weather hampered many subsequent operations. At that time the average number of fighters available to each of the Eighth Air Force's fighter groups was 86, and Gen Doolittle remained concerned that a major effort by the Luftwaffe to saturate a bomber mission and bring down 100+ bombers remained a possibility. In fact Luftwaffe commanders had plans such as that in mind, and it is perhaps just as well that these never actually happened. One of the reasons for this was the pounding that Luftwaffe airfields were often taking at the hands of the marauding American fighters, and the effect that the Allied bombing was having on oil supplies.

In an effort to make the escort cover for the bombers more effective, on 10 October 1944 the fighter groups of VIII Fighter Command had been sub-divided into three Fighter Wings (the 65th, 66th, and 67th) which were operationally linked to the 2nd, 3rd and 1st Bombardment Divisions (later Air Divisions) respectively. This allowed for a simplified chain of command and easier planning of the direct fighter support for operations, with the groups within each fighter wing theoretically escorting the bomb groups within its associated bomb division. In practice fighters often supported the bombers from divisions other than that they were linked to, and of course in the heat of battle the fighters would come to the aid of any bombers that were under attack. In fact quite elaborate systems for the escorts had been devised to allow for penetration, over-target, and withdrawal support, so that by the early weeks of 1945 the whole question of bomber escort had developed into a detailed and well-tailored process that was poles apart from the situation that had existed when the Eighth Air Force first went to war without any escort at all for its bombers.

It was not just in the air that the American fighters were gaining impressive victories. Ground strafing had become more and more successful as the war continued, and not just airfields were attacked by the wide-ranging Mustangs. Just about any target that seemed to be of military value was fair game to the Mustangs, and in February 1945 as a part of Operation 'Clarion' the Eighth Air Force's fighter groups attacked transportation and communications targets wherever anything worth shooting at was seen. The only low point for the Mustangs came with the growing appearance of the twin-engined Messerschmitt Me 262A jet fighter during February 1945, as more of these jet fighters started to join front-line fighter units rather than production of this advanced aircraft being solely committed to bomber derivatives. When aggressively flown the Me 262A was easily the match for Mustangs in terms of speed and overall performance, but its turning circle was much more than that of the Mustang and several Mustang pilots were able to bring down these impressive aircraft in turning dog-fights. Overall, however, Allied air superiority was almost complete by this stage in the war. It was extremely dangerous for anything wearing German national insignia to venture into the skies, and even training aircraft apparently well out of the way in southern Germany were highly likely to find a Mustang on their tails if they dared to venture aloft during daylight hours. Indeed most ferrying of German aircraft had to take place at night, but even on their own airfields the Luftwaffe front-line aircraft were highly vulnerable. Allied strafing of German airfields reached a crescendo as the war moved into March and April 1945. Any attempt that the Luftwaffe might have been planning to mount any last-minute defence was shattered by several incredible attacks by Mustangs on Luftwaffe airfields at that time. One of the most notable was on 10 April, when the German jet fighters had a particularly successful day against the Eighth Air Force's heavy bombers. However, the Mustangs were waiting for the jets as they returned to their airfields, and claims were subsequently made for 20 of the advanced aircraft. But the real destruction that day was wrought at several Luftwaffe air bases. The 339th Fighter Group in particular made claims for 94 destroyed, with Lt Col Joseph Thury adding four to his growing score – he eventually finished the war in second place within the ranks of Eighth Air Force ground strafers with 25.5 destroyed. On 16 April, however, despite orders that ground strafing should cease, the Eighth Air Force achieved a stunning victory. Four Mustang groups, the 4th, 78th, 339th, and 353rd Fighter Groups, each claimed over one hundred aircraft destroyed on the ground, and the day's total claims ran to 752! This type of destruction was utterly disastrous for the Luftwaffe, and during the month of April claims were made for some 1,400 German aircraft on the ground. It was truly the end for the Luftwaffe. The cost, however, had been high. Many more Mustang pilots were lost in strafing attacks than were shot down in aerial combat, and the leading Eighth Air Force Mustang 'strafer' did not survive. He was Lt Col Elwyn Righetti, the CO of the 55th Fighter Group, who only entered combat in late 1944 but quickly became legendary for his strafing attacks on Luftwaffe airfields. He eventually achieved 7.5 aerial victories but scored 27 strafing victories, including nine on the day that he was shot down, 17 April 1945.

The exact number of German aircraft that Eighth Air Force Mustangs destroyed is impossible to calculate, particularly as claims tended to be greater than actual German losses, but a figure of 4,163 ground victories by all 15 VIII Fighter Command groups in all aircraft types flown has been widely suggested. Aerial victories have similarly been proposed to have exceeded five thousand. The top-scoring group that flew Mustangs was the 4th Fighter Group, but the 4th also flew P-47 Thunderbolts in its early combat career. In terms of aerial victories in the Mustang alone, the 357th FG must rank as number one, and its 364th Fighter

Squadron was one of the highest-scoring Mustang squadrons of the war with some 211 aerial victories alone, and at least 17 aces in its ranks.

## Reconnaissance Mustangs

The Allison-engined Mustang had found a particular niche for itself in the low-level armed tactical reconnaissance role, and it distinguished itself greatly in this task for both the RAF and the USAAF. It was a hard act to follow, but as more Merlin-engined Mustangs became available, so reconnaissance versions of the Merlin-Mustang fighters were developed and built by North American. The reconnaissance versions of the Mustang were designated F-6 (with 'F' meaning 'Photographic'). The original Allison-engined reconnaissance-configured P-51 was the F-6A, and the reconnaissance conversions of the P-51A were the F-6B (and NOT F-6A, as incorrectly claimed in scores of published sources). Following on from these were three specific reconnaissance models based on the Merlin-Mustangs. These were the F-6C, for reconnaissance configurations based on the P-51C AND the P-51B; the F-6D for reconnaissance examples based on the P-51D; and the F-6K for reconnaissance examples of the P-51K. In reality these three Merlin-powered reconnaissance models were not made as separate reconnaissance versions on their own assembly lines in the North American Aviation factories, but were 'converted' on the production line and/or after completion into reconnaissance configuration on an 'as needed' basis. A breakdown of identified serial numbers is included in the Appendices at the end of this book, but the precise number of 'conversions' is impossible to 'exactly' track-down (although many historians claim to have done so). Widely accepted figures are for 71 P-51B-10-NAs and 20 P-51C-10-NTs configured as F-6C aircraft from existing P-51B/C manufacture, with 136 or possibly 146 P-51Ds finished as F-6Ds and 163 P-51Ks configured as F-6Ks. In any case, aside from the camera installations in these aircraft and the associated wiring, and their camera controls in the cockpit, these aircraft were similar to standard fighter Mustangs and were fully armed, and in many cases they operated alongside normal Mustang fighters in the reconnaissance units that they were assigned to (this even extended to French post-war use, when reconnaissance-equipped and standard fighter Mustangs served in the same units). The reconnaissance configuration for the F-6C (ex-P-51B and P-51C) was for two rear fuselage-mounted cameras, usually two K-24s or a K-22 and a K-24, although the configurations varied. One of the camera ports was visible low in the rear left-hand fuselage side for the oblique camera, the other was behind the outlet flap of the lower fuselage radiator intake fairing looking vertically downwards. Some also had a camera mounted behind the pilot in similar fashion to the Tac/R Allison-engined Mustangs. In fact a number of camera combinations were used, and some field and depot modifications were made to standard fighter Mustangs to convert them into camera-equipped aircraft which sometimes had non-standard

features. The F-6D and F-6K could also carry, in addition to the two K-24 cameras of the F-6C, a much larger K-17. This also took photographs obliquely to the left, and its port was highly visible on the left-hand fuselage side on the aircraft that were fitted with this camera, because it was situated across the rear bar of the blue and white US 'star and bar' fuselage national insignia. The K-17 used much larger roll film size than the K-24, having a negative dimension of nine-inches (23 cm) square from which very high-quality and detailed black and white photographs could be made. However, not all F-6D/K Mustangs carried this camera. The window for the vertical K-24 camera in the rear fuselage of these Mustangs was often fitted with a special cover, which could be opened when the camera was being used, but which was usually closed to prevent dirt from obscuring or damaging the camera window when the aircraft was taxiing. In addition to these formal reconnaissance camera configurations, some later standard P-51D/K fighter Mustangs were fitted with a strike camera (often a K-25) mounted behind the pilot's seat looking to the left and slightly downwards, which could be used during missions for taking photographs of anything of interest. These strike cameras were often also used for rather less official purposes, frequently for taking air-to-air shots of fellow Mustangs for the family photo album or for squadron colleagues.

In North-west Europe, a comparatively large number of squadrons actually flew the reconnaissance-configured Merlin Mustangs. However, in Southern Europe, only one squadron took these marks of Mustang into combat. That was the 111th Tactical Reconnaissance Squadron, which had flown Allison-engined reconnaissance-configured Mustangs from its time in North Africa and Sicily in the summer of 1943. The 111th began receiving Merlin Mustangs in the summer of 1944, when many of its remaining Allison-engined Mustangs were getting very worn. The 111th (appropriately nicknamed the 'Snoopers') continued in combat in the Mediterranean and Southern European combat areas right to the end of the war – eventually flying reconnaissance-configured Merlin-engined Mustangs in Italy, through France from southern France northwards, and eventually into Germany itself. Originally a member of the 68th Observation (later Reconnaissance, then Tactical Reconnaissance) Group, the 111th TRS fought on into 1945 as a separate squadron assigned directly to the XII Tactical Air Command following the disbanding of the 68th in 1944. In fact the 111th went through a number of direct assignments as required, including an organisation called the Provisional Reconnaissance Group, but on 20 April 1945 it was assigned while in France to the new 69th Tactical Reconnaissance Group, and in July 1945 to the 10th Reconnaissance Group. At one time the squadron had a number of US Navy pilots assigned. Many bases were used by the squadron and its detachments, including Pomigliano, Santa Maria, Galera, and other locations in Italy, Borgo on the island of Corsica, and in France at Saint-Raphael, Valence, Dijon, and Azelot. A Distinguished Unit Citation was awarded to the 111th for operations over Germany in

During late 1944/early 1945, the individual fighter groups of the Eighth Army Air Force were given responsibility for operational training and theatre indoctrination for new incoming pilots, allowing the inexperienced pilots to assimilate the particular procedures and spirit of their new posting much more easily. Most if not all of the 14 Mustang fighter groups in the Eighth Air Force converted a small number of 'war weary' P-51B/C Mustangs into two-seaters to help with this process within their so-called 'Clobber Colleges'. Some of the trainers were however kept as single-seaters, including this 55th Fighter Group P-51B-1-NA, serial number 43-12438, which has an added 'fin fillet' and wears that group's 338th Fighter Squadron 'CL' code. The training Mustangs were generally individually coded in a different manner to the operational Mustangs, as shown by the '5' numbering of this crashed example. Many wore the letters 'WW' on their vertical tails to signify their retired or 'war weary' status
(Photo: USAAF)

One of the most colourful and eye-catching Mustangs of all time was the P-51D named 'Big Beautiful Doll' that was the personal Mustang of John D Landers, who flew with several fighter groups in Europe and the Pacific and who was eventually the CO of the Eighth Air Force's 78th Fighter Group at Duxford. This iconic aircraft was the epitome of the flamboyant and aggressive flyers who took the Mustang to war and achieved such great success not just in Europe but in all areas where the Mustang went to war. 'Big Beautiful Doll' was a P-51D-20-NA, serial number 44-72218, which bore Landers' then-rank of Lt Col on the canopy frame and carried the full late-war markings of the 78th Fighter Group. He was group CO of the 78th FG from February 1945, and achieved the rank of full Col in May 1945. The nose markings were black and white, edged in red, with a black rudder *(Photo: R.L. Ward Collection)*

February 1945, and the squadron served briefly in Germany at Fürth near Nuremberg as a part of the Allied occupation forces from July to October 1945. The 111th was finally inactivated in mid-December 1945 at Creil in France and eventually returned in May 1946 to the control of the Texas National Guard. During the later months of its existence it flew a complete mixed-bag of reconnaissance Mustangs, including some F-6Cs with Malcolm hoods. A number of its Mustangs appear to have eventually passed to the 34th PRS. Despite the primary mission of the squadron, like all the observation units, being tactical reconnaissance with the secondary role of ground-attack, one pilot of the 111th managed to join the ranks of the small number of Mustang reconnaissance aces in aerial combat. He was Lt Valentine Rader, who achieved 6.5 victories between 22 February and 10 April 1945 in F-6Cs while the squadron was operating over German soil.

The 69th Tactical Reconnaissance Group that the 111th TRS was eventually assigned to in 1945 was a latecomer to the action in Europe. Originally activated in September 1941 as the 69th Observation Group, the group stayed in the US and acted primarily in a training capacity, while also providing anti-submarine cover along the US Pacific coast after the Pearl Harbour attack. In January 1945, having been redesignated as the 69th Tactical Reconnaissance Group as early as August 1943, the group began training with reconnaissance Merlin-Mustangs, and moved from its final base in the US, Key Field, Mississippi, to Europe in February and March 1945. Temporary residence was taken up at Nancy, but the group was only in action for a short time, and ended the war at Haguenau to the north of Strasbourg in France. The group was assigned to the Ninth Air Force, and flew the usual round of photo and visual reconnaissance missions until the end if the war. The group's squadrons included the 111th (as previously related), 10th, and 22nd, Tactical Reconnaissance Squadrons, and the 34th Photographic Reconnaissance Squadron. The first three of these flew the F-6, although the latter was primarily a Lockheed F-5 unit but appears to have later taken on some of the Mustangs of the 111th.

Previous to this, the reconnaissance versions of the Merlin-Mustang had been in service with a number of initially British-based units for many months. Allison-engined reconnaissance Mustangs had equipped the 107th Tactical Reconnaissance Squadron of the 67th Tactical Reconnaissance Group, which was initially based at Membury and then from December 1943 at Middle Wallop in southern England. This squadron was highly active with its Allison-engined F-6B Mustangs up to and during the D-Day period, but increasingly obtained Merlin-powered reconnaissance Mustangs as well. The squadron continued to operate these to the end of the war, initially moving from Middle

Wallop to northern France after D-Day, at first being based briefly at A-4 (Deux Jumeaux) from late June onwards. The squadron ended the war, after numerous base moves, at R-11 Eschwege in Germany. The group that it was assigned to during all that period, the 67th TRG, received a Distinguished Unit Citation for its reconnaissance work from mid-February to mid-March 1944 along the coast of northern France in the run-up to D-Day, and had several other reconnaissance Mustang units attached. These included the 109th TRS, a National Guard squadron from Minnesota which joined the group in November 1943 having been called to active duty in February 1941. The squadron followed a similar path to the 107th TRS, and also ended the war at Eschwege in Germany. Additionally assigned to the 67th Tactical Reconnaissance Group, although actually a part of the 10th Photo Group for the latter stages of the war, were the 12th and 15th Tactical Reconnaissance Squadrons, which flew F-6 Mustangs in 1944 and 1945. Another squadron of the 67th TRG, the 33rd Photographic Reconnaissance Squadron, is also believed to have flown F-6 Mustangs although it was principally equipped with F-5 Lightnings. This squadron in fact went through a host of assignments and reassignments during its time in the ETO as operational requirements demanded. Eventually the 67th TRG was redesignated as the 67th Reconnaissance Group in June 1945, its job well and truly accomplished.

As previously related, the Mustang-equipped 363rd Fighter Group had its role completely changed in August 1944, and was reassigned from being a fighter-bomber group to become a reconnaissance unit under the designation 363rd Tactical Reconnaissance Group. The group's assigned squadrons also underwent a change of designation on 25 August 1944, becoming the 160th Tactical Reconnaissance Squadron (ex-380th FS), 161st TRS (ex-381st FS), and 162nd TRS (ex-382nd FS). In keeping with other Ninth Air Force tactical reconnaissance units the 363rd TRG subsequently flew in support of Allied ground forces, specifically aiding with its aerial reconnaissance activities the US Ninth Army. To that end the group continued to be based on the Continent, firstly at A-35 Le Mans in France but then including a number of base changes to keep up with the ground fighting and Allied advances. Its constituent squadrons started at A-38 Montreuil in France, but again moved forward as the ground war progressed – although the 162nd TRS only remained a part of the group for several weeks before going through a number of direct attachments to higher echelons and finishing the war as a part of the 10th Photo Group at R-28 Fürth in Germany. The group's Mustangs flew tactical reconnaissance sorties but also performed artillery spotting and related activities, in addition to carrying out ground strafing where appropriate. To this end a mixed-bag of Mustangs was

The Eighth Air Force eventually had a number of colourful and highly-capable rank pilots in the forefront of leading its Mustang force in the increasingly triumphant combat over Germany's Luftwaffe during the final months of World War Two. One of these was Lt Col John D Landers, seen here in the cockpit of his P-51D-20-NA serial number 44-72218, coded WZ-I and named 'Big Beautiful Doll', of the 78th Fighter Group. Landers was one of the highest-scoring Eighth Air Force pilots, with 14.5 aerial victories and 20 ground strafing victories, although six of the aerial victories were achieved in the Pacific while flying Curtiss P-40E Warhawks with the 49th FG *(Photo: R.L. Ward Collection)*

operated, both fighter versions and various marks of F-6 as well. One of the 162nd TRS's pilots, Lt Joe Waits, who also flew with the 15th TRS, became an ace with 5.5 aerial victories, a rare achievement amongst the Ninth Air Force's reconnaissance pilots.

Perhaps the best-known of the US Mustang reconnaissance units in the ETO was the 10th Photo Group. This unit was activated as the 73rd Observation Group in September 1941, but through various reorganisations was re-created as the 10th Photographic Group (Reconnaissance) in December 1943 while on paper based at Key Field, Mississippi, a centre of reconnaissance training and administration in the US. The unit moved to England in January and February 1944, and eventually took up residence at Chalgrove in Oxfordshire. Its large number of constituent units included several F-6 equipped squadrons, including most significantly the 12th and 15th Tactical Reconnaissance Squadrons. Both had previously been assigned to the 67th Tactical Reconnaissance Group, but joined the 10th on 13 June 1944, although they remained on paper assigned to the 67th for several further weeks. The 15th TRS moved in to Chalgrove in late June 1944 from its previous base of Middle Wallop. The squadron had already flown missions over northern France from late March and several of its pilots had achieved aerial victories. It

flew its first Tac/R missions with the 10th on 29 June. The 12th TRS similarly joined the 10th Photo Group in mid-June but was rapidly sent over to France from Middle Wallop to A-9 Le Molay to provide reconnaissance coverage for Gen Omar Bradley's US First Army forces in their fighting in the Normandy 'Bocage', and to cover Operation 'Cobra' and the break-out around the French town of Saint-Lo in July 1944. The 15th TRS in particular was a highly-aggressive squadron and very often became involved in aerial combat, even though the brief of the Tac/R units always remained that of getting the intelligence first and foremost. In total four of its pilots became aces, including Capt John Hoefker with 8.5 aerial victories in F-6C and F-6D aircraft, and Capt Clyde East who achieved the incredible score of 13 victories. This was an exceptional score for a Mustang reconnaissance pilot, and was only one short of the 14 gained by Edward McComas with the 118th TRS in China. East began his scoring on D-Day, 6 June 1944 by shooting down an Fw 190 near Laval while the 15th was still a part of the 67th TRG, and continued with his aerial victories right up to the last day of the war on 8 May 1945. He was the quintessential reconnaissance pilot, having originally flown with the RCAF and had actually at one time been a member of No.414 Squadron – which flew Tac/R Mustang Mk I aircraft and one of whose pilots,

The famous 'Big Beautiful Doll' of John D Landers later in the war, compared to the previous two images. A P-51D-20-NA serial number 44-72218, coded WZ-I, it eventually sported this revised colour scheme with the wing-tips also wearing the 78th Fighter Group's black and white identification markings, the rudder completely in black with the serial number repainted solely on the fin, etc. Landers became the CO of the 78th FG in February 1945, his 'Big Beautiful Doll' having already become something of a flagship for the unit *(Photo: Malcolm V. Lowe Collection)*

Reconnaissance-configured Mustangs played an important part for the Allies not just in the air war but in providing aerial intelligence for all branches of the armed forces. This was especially true in the run-up to D-Day in June 1944 and onwards to the end of the war. Allison-engined Mustangs pioneered the use of the Mustang as a tactical reconnaissance aircraft, making the Tac/R armed reconnaissance role their own. Later, Merlin-engined Mustangs joined this effort, and also played an important part in providing strategic reconnaissance cover for heavy bomber raids as well. This image shows a shiny new Inglewood-built reconnaissance-configured F-6D, serial number 44-15453, formerly a P-51D-15-NA which will have been converted on the production line into reconnaissance layout. Two camera windows can be seen in the rear fuselage, on and below the rear of the national insignia. North American Aviation's standard of workmanship was generally excellent, and the Mustang was certainly one of the best-made combat aircraft of World War Two *(Photo: NAA)*

Hollis Hills, had achieved the first-ever Mustang aerial victory back in 1942. After the war East remained a reconnaissance pilot, and flew reconnaissance Mustangs in Korea with the USAF before also flying intelligence-gathering sorties during the Cuban Missile Crisis in October 1962.

In keeping with other tactical reconnaissance assets, the 15th TRS also eventually moved over to France, taking up residence at A-27 Rennes/Saint-Jacques in August 1944 where the HQ of the 10th Photo Group and the 12th TRS were also located. From there onwards the squadron lived a nomadic life, like the 12th TRS following the advancing Allied armies. During the German Ardennes offensive of late 1944 (the so-called 'Battle of the Bulge'), the reconnaissance Mustangs of the 10th Photo Group flew whenever possible, maintaining contact with scattered US ground forces and observing where practicable German troop movements in the appalling weather conditions prevalent at that time. By early May 1945 the 15th had taken up residence at Fürth, where the 12th TRS also came to see out the final days of the war. Both squadrons flew a mix of F-6C and F-6D reconnaissance Mustangs, these two types being equally capable in the tactical recon role.

One further reconnaissance group flew the Mustang. This was the Eighth Army Air Force's 7th Photo Group - officially the 7th Photographic Group (Reconnaissance) - based at Mount Farm in England. The 7th PG in fact had a long history that stretched back to 1943, the group having originally been activated as the 7th Photographic Group on 1 May 1943 and moved to England in July of that year. The various operational squadrons of the 7th predominantly flew Lockheed F-5 Lightnings and reconnaissance Supermarine Spitfires during their wartime service, on long-range strategic reconnaissance missions and damage assessment sorties following heavy bomber raids as opposed to the shorter-range tactical reconnaissance of the Ninth Air Force's recon units. However, in early 1945 the group started to receive a number of P-51D and P-51K Mustangs. This was not primarily for reconnaissance purposes, for the group continued to successfully operate the F-5 Lightning until the end of the war. However, the unit's Lightnings had started to take particularly high losses in the latter stages of the war, especially due to Me 262A jet fighters which were able to catch the high-flying Lightnings with some ease. Mustangs were therefore taken on charge by the group specifically to provide its own escort for its reconnaissance Lightnings, which they did until the end of the war. Squadrons within the group that are known to have flown the Mustang escorts include the 22nd Photographic Reconnaissance Squadron (not to be confused with the 22nd TRS, which flew with the 69th Tactical Reconnaissance Group previously mentioned). The 7th Photo Group moved to Chalgrove late in March 1945 but flew the escort Mustangs up to and including its final operations.

## The Final Victory over Europe

It was to be reconnaissance Mustangs of the USAAF that had the last say in the air war over North-west Europe. In early May 1945 elements of the 10th Photo Group were based in south-eastern Germany, with many of the unit's photo Mustangs stationed at Fürth airfield. On the final day of the war in Europe, 8 May 1945, with German personnel surrendering to British or US forces wherever possible to avoid being captured by the Russians, a huge amount of aerial activity took place around Fürth. German aircraft began appearing from many locations, including the so-called Protectorate of Bohemia and Moravia (the former Czechoslovakia), in an effort to surrender to any available US forces before the Russians could get their hands on them. From nowhere, Fw 190s, Ju 87s and a wide miscellany of other aircraft started to fill the skies. Many of the locally-based US units, including the 12th and 15th Tactical Reconnaissance Squadrons, became involved in the curious occupation of rounding up these surrendering stragglers and escorting them to local US-held airfields. However, although Mustangs of these two squadrons successfully guided in a number of Luftwaffe aircraft and flew many patrols even though the war was officially ending, some of the German pilots were not so keen to surrender. A number of dog-fights took place during the day even into the evening, with several German aircraft being shot down by the reconnaissance pilots. At roughly 2000 hours on the evening of 8 May, two Mustangs of the 12th TRS were patrolling along the River Danube when they were 'bounced' by five Fw 190s. In the ensuing moments Lt Robert C. Little manoeuvred in behind one of the Focke-Wulfs and shot it down. He was probably flying his assigned Mustang, Dallas-built F-6C-1-NT 42-103206, and coded ZM-G. It is now widely regarded as the very last aerial victory of World War Two in Europe.

Photographed with the historic terminal building and control tower of Speke airport, Liverpool, in the background, several Mustangs from different sources were gathered. At the end of the war in Europe, a considerable number of Mustangs became redundant overnight. Many were scrapped while others were assigned to the Allied occupation forces in Germany. Some – only a comparatively small number - were returned to the US. A number of explanations have been offered over the years to explain this particular gathering, particularly as the aircraft are a real mixed bag. In the foreground is a reconnaissance F-6K, serial number 44-12527, wearing the tail markings and 'QL' code of the 22nd Tactical Reconnaissance Squadron, 69th Tactical Reconnaissance Group, Ninth Air Force (note the two-camera installation in the rear fuselage). Two other reconnaissance Mustangs of that group are also in the line-up, and behind them is an Eighth Air Force 'CY' coded P-51D of the 343rd FS of the 55th FG. It is assumed that the aircraft are being prepared for return to the US *(Photo: USAAF)*

# Service Excellence World-wide

## Chapter 4

The overwhelming success of the Merlin-powered Mustangs over North-west and Southern Europe has tended to overshadow the achievements of the Merlin-Mustangs in other parts of the world. This is not only true of the China-Burma-India (CBI) theatre, where Merlin-Mustangs supplanted their earlier Allison-powered predecessors from mid-1944 onwards especially in China. It was also the case in the Pacific, where Allison-Mustangs had not previously operated, but where Merlin-powered Mustangs performed long-range bomber escort as well as tactical missions with great capability much later in the war.

## Aerial Warfare in the CBI

Allison-engined P-51s of the 23rd and 311th Fighter Groups had represented a major extension of the USAAF's firepower in the CBI after they had become operational there in the latter part of 1943, as described in Part 1 of this two-part 'Modellers' Datafile' on the Mustang, which covered the Allison-Mustangs. Following on from this, Merlin-powered Mustangs subsequently served with three US fighter groups in the CBI, as well as two air commando units and two little-publicised joint Chinese-American fighter groups. It is true, however, that the CBI theatre was often overlooked in terms of procurement, leading to the much-quoted remark that this was a 'forgotten' area of conflict. Certainly the allocation of Mustangs, once the worth of the type had at last been recognised by the USAAF, tended to be biased towards Europe. It was not until the summer of 1944, several months after the Merlin-powered P-51 had started to make its mark for US units over North-west Europe, that Merlin-Mustangs were able to make an impact in India and particularly China.

In spite of this, Merlin-engined Mustangs did start to arrive in the CBI – albeit at first in small numbers – during the first half of 1944. Amongst the early recipients was the veteran 23rd Fighter Group, which was already successfully flying Allison-engined Mustangs. The first four Merlin-Mustangs were received by the 23rd during February 1944. These were flown in from India late in that month, Col Clinton Vincent (one of the foremost pilots of the 23rd FG, but at that time head of the 68th Composite Wing of which the 23rd was a part) leading the aircraft into Kunming after a delivery flight from India. The first squadron of the group to receive these aircraft the following month was probably the 76th Fighter Squadron, which at that time was still flying Allison-engined Mustangs. During the remainder of 1944 a trickle of

Aggressive and ultimately successful American air power in the Far East during World War Two was never better represented than by the 'shark-mouthed' Merlin-Mustang of one of the top US fighter pilots in this large theatre of war. Photographed in this publicity image was Maj (later Col) David L Hill, who ultimately became the Commanding Officer of the 23rd Fighter Group. A distinguished pilot and fighter leader, 'Tex' Hill originally served with the US Navy, but resigned his commission during 1941 to fly with the American Volunteer Group (the famed 'Flying Tigers') against the Japanese, piloting early Curtiss P-40s. Later joining the USAAF, Hill rose to command the 23rd FG in November 1943, a unit that was to become a highly successful exponent of the Merlin-Mustang. He ended the war with 15.25 aerial victories to his credit, although only one of these is known to have been achieved while flying Merlin-Mustangs
*(Photo: USAAF)*

Mustangs was delivered, allowing the group to considerably enhance its combat effectiveness, although Allison-Mustangs and particularly P-40s continued to be operated alongside the new arrivals until later in the year. The fighting in China was intense during several specific campaigns and offensives, with Chinese forces backed by American units taking on the Japanese in a number of particular areas. In mid-1944 the 23rd was involved in the defence against a major Japanese drive down the Hsiang Valley in the Hunan Province of China which began on 17 June 1944. In spite of bad weather conditions and heavy ground fire, the 23rd provided air support for Chinese ground forces and repeatedly struck at enemy troops and transportation. The group was rewarded for its considerable efforts with a Distinguished Unit Citation.

Operating conditions in China were very different compared to those that had been encountered in India. Although some of the Indian bases were somewhat spartan, at least many were established airfields with some measure of facilities and many had reasonable runways (although this did tend to depend on the weather). In China, however, the air bases were often dramatically different. Some were built by local Chinese labour which, although usually very enthusiastic, was often unable to make anything more than flying strips with primitive conditions. Even the more established bases lacked anything but the most basic facilities, and the whole adventure became a real test for the Mustangs. That the

P-51 came through often with flying colours was a testament to the hard-pressed ground crews and maintenance personnel who worked on them, as well as the Merlin-powered Mustangs proving to be able to operate in less than ideal conditions. Added to these factors was the reality that virtually all supplies had be flown in from India over a part of the Himalayas (the famous 'Hump' route), or by equally perilous overland routes. Poor quality airfield surfaces, sometimes inferior or even contaminated fuel, and the long distances involved in some missions – coupled with the threat of Japanese attack against the more forward airfields – made for a very different war to that being waged in Europe.

The overall aviation organisation that was tasked with taking the war to the Japanese in China was the Fourteenth Army Air Force, which had been activated in China in March 1943. It was headed by the unique Maj Gen Claire Chennault, who had built a formidable reputation earlier in the war with his leadership of the 'Flying Tigers'. The 23rd Fighter Group, together with the 311th FG which had moved in from India in the summer of 1944, plus the little-known 51st FG and the even lesser-publicised 3rd and 5th Fighter Groups (Provisional) – the latter two being jointly Chinese and American-manned – all operated in the later stages of the war with the Fourteenth Air Force, together with the 2nd Air Commando Group. Each of these units eventually flew Merlin-Mustangs, and their considerable presence for ground-attack and fighter missions was a major problem for the Japanese, who

gradually lost aerial supremacy even over their own rear areas as the Mustangs with their great range covered more and more of the vast Chinese interior.

The 76th and 74th Fighter Squadrons of the 23rd transitioned onto the Merlin-Mustang as 1944 progressed, but it was not until the autumn of that year that the group's P-40-operating 75th FS began to convert to the P-51, showing how difficult it was to obtain significant numbers of Merlin-Mustangs in the Chinese theatre, despite the desire of Chennault to obtain as many as possible of the potent North American fighter. The complete transition of the unit onto the Mustang did not take place until October or November 1944. The 23rd continued to be headquartered at Kweilin as it was during its Allison-Mustang days, and the unit flew many significant missions with the Merlin-engined P-51, including several successful attacks on Japanese airfields and installations. In these strikes the range and excellent performance of the Mustang proved vital, no other fighters in-theatre being able to perform such attacks while at the same time being capable of looking after themselves if intercepted. Notable but by no means unusual was the attack on Nanking and its surrounding areas on 8 December 1944, when a number of Japanese airfields were shot up and attacks made on river traffic, several of the Mustangs carrying bombs while others flew as top cover. In effect the 23rd's Mustangs were able to mount such raids as a combined attack and fighter force, and it was just this type of action that sapped the Japanese resources and made even their rear areas a dangerous place to be. Nevertheless the Japanese remained a formidable force in some parts of China, and several major counter-offensives were made by Japanese forces during 1944. Indeed, a successful Japanese attack was made in the direction of the 23rd's headquarters at Kweilin, which eventually fell in September 1944 to the Japanese after stubborn defence by American and Chinese forces. In fact several Fourteenth Air Force airfields were captured during that period. The 23rd moved its headquarters to Liuchow and then to Luliang, never to return to Kweilin.

A number of 23rd FG pilots achieved considerable successes while flying the Merlin Mustang, and just as in Europe the quantity of aces piloting the type started to grow. Perhaps the greatest exponent was Capt John 'Pappy' Herbst of the 74th FS, 23rd FG. Although somewhat older at 34 than the majority of the 23rd's pilots when he joined the group in May 1944, Herbst was an exceptional and experienced pilot who flew Merlin-Mustangs with the 23rd to great success. In addition to a possible aerial victory in the Mediterranean under conditions that are still shrouded in mystery, and several kills achieved whilst flying P-40Ns with the 23rd's 74th FS, Herbst scored the majority of his victories in the P-51B/P-51C. These started on 17 June 1944 when he was temporarily with the 76th FS of the 23rd, and continued into early

1945 when he scored the last of his 18 aerial victories in the CBI on 17 January by shooting down a Nakajima Ki-44 Shoki 'Tojo' near Kiangwan airfield, making a total of 14 in the Mustang. This allowed Herbst to become the leading ace in terms of aerial victories in the CBI.

However, ground-attack was virtually as important a mission for the China-based Merlin-Mustangs as aerial combat, and the role played by these aircraft was significant in blunting several Japanese offensives and aiding Chinese and American ground forces, in addition to shooting up many enemy-held airfields. The Mustangs often carried bombs, or rockets on 'zero-length' rocket rails, although the use of the long three-tube bazooka-type rocket installation much publicised in recent years as being extensively used by Mustangs was in fact not as widespread – the P-51B/P-51C in particular suffered from instability problems when carrying these particular weapons, aggravated by the centre of gravity difficulties caused by the fuselage fuel tank installation in those marks of Mustang. The cumbersome three-tube installation also proved to be drag-producing, and inaccurate. In similar fashion to the situation that was encountered in Europe, the P-51B/C suffered from gun-jamming problems with the four angle-mounted 0.5-in wing-mounted machine guns, a problem that was only really solved for good with the arrival of P-51D/K Mustangs with their six-gun wing armament in which all six machine guns were mounted upright with no ammunition feed problems.

Additionally a member of the 23rd Fighter Group from mid-

The Merlin-Mustang was the mount of several well-known aces in the CBI and Pacific areas. One of these pilots was Maj (later Lt Col) John Coleman Herbst, who ran up an impressive score of victories over the Japanese while flying Merlin-Mustangs. Originally serving with the Royal Canadian Air Force, a route into the war that several well-known American pilots took while their country was still neutral, 'Pappy' Herbst eventually joined the USAAF and flew with the 23rd Fighter Group, eventually leading its 74th Fighter Squadron. He became a ranking exponent of the P-51B/C, achieving the majority of his 18 aerial victories while flying the type. He is seen in this image seated in his well-known P-51B 43-7060 named 'Tommy's Dad'. Built as a P-51B-5-NA, with the fuselage fuel tank fitted it would have been known as a B-7-NA *(Photo: USAAF)*

The famous 'shark-mouth' adorned many Merlin-Mustangs in the CBI. The tail markings on this P-51B or P-51C, with a yellow band accompanying the tail number '261', suggests that the aircraft operated with the 51st Fighter Group's 26th FS - although even to this day, there is some confusion as to the allocation of markings to fighter squadrons in the CBI at specific times *(Photo: USAAF)*

1944 was the 118th Tactical Reconnaissance Squadron. Yet another National Guard squadron that had been federalised and duly saw overseas combat, the 118th was attached to the 23rd FG on or around 16 June 1944. Formerly a part of the Connecticut National Guard, the squadron was ordered to active service in February 1941. After several designation and base changes in the continental US during which anti-submarine coastal patrols were flown and much training carried out, the squadron moved to the CBI in early 1944 and was at first stationed in India, where it initially operated with P-40s under the Tenth Army Air Force. However, having become a part of the Fourteenth Army Air Force in June 1944, the unit was duly stationed alongside the fighter squadrons of the 23rd FG in China, and was eventually fully equipped with Merlin-Mustangs. Despite it being designated as a reconnaissance unit, the 118th performed a great deal more than simply that role. For most of its time in China it flew as a fighter and ground-attack squadron, in addition to performing reconnaissance tasks, and achieved a great deal of success. The squadron particularly made a name for itself in anti-shipping attacks, using its Mustangs for skip-bombing to considerable effect along the long Chinese coastline. Much of the success of the 118th was due to its exceptional commander, Maj (later Lt Col) Edward McComas. Not only was McComas an able leader, he also proved to be a gifted fighter pilot, who eventually rivalled and equalled 'Pappy' Herbst as the leading exponent of the Mustang in the CBI. On 16 October he was part of an armed reconnaissance flight to Japanese-held Hong Kong which was intercepted by a number of Japanese fighters. McComas shot down one of the hapless Nakajima Ki-44 Shoki 'Tojos' for his first aerial victory. This was the start of a remarkable scoring run that resulted in 14 victories in just over two months. This notable record included five Nakajima Ki-43 Hayabusa 'Oscars' on 23 December, making him one of the few pilots in China to claim five victories in a single sortie. His final victim was an 'Oscar', also over Hong Kong, on 24 December. All his victories are believed to have been achieved in the P-51C, although the 118th later converted onto the P-51D – as indeed did all the squadrons of the 23rd Fighter Group, apparently starting with the 75th FS early in 1945. In total, the four squadrons of the 23rd finished the war with 467 confirmed aerial victories (this is the 'official' figure quoted by Frank Olynyk in his book 'Stars and Bars', although adding up the scores of the 23rd FG's four squadrons comes to 491.75, and veterans of the unit claim considerably more), plus at least 320 ground victories, and more than 131,000 tons of Japanese shipping sunk, in addition to countless vehicles and enemy troops. This was at the cost of some 110 aircraft lost in aerial combat, and achieved in more than 24,000 combat sorties. The 23rd had certainly continued with great success the traditions of the American Volunteer Group in China.

Additional to the 23rd FG, Merlin-Mustangs were also flown by the 311th FG and the 51st FG in China. The 311th had already established itself as a successful Mustang unit with its many achievements in Allison-engined Mustangs which it started to fly in 1943. The first Merlin-engined Mustangs started to reach the 311th during the spring of 1944, with the squadrons of the 311th transitioning onto the P-51B/P-51C between May and August/September of 1944. This gave the group the opportunity to fly the Merlin-Mustang operationally prior to the unit's move to China to become a part of the Fourteenth Army Air Force in August 1944. The group continued to fly attack and fighter missions, with the Merlin-engined Mustangs considerably enhancing the unit's capabilities compared to the Allison-Mustangs, especially for escort work and operating at higher altitudes. Merlin-engined Mustangs of the group also carried out many successful tactical missions against Japanese ground targets when eventually based in China. The 530th FS, which had flown the P-51A from India as described in Part 1 of this two-part 'Modellers' Datafile' on the Mustang, which covered the Allison-Mustangs, became particularly successful with the P-51B/P-51C. It became necessary for squadrons of the 311th to operate from a remote Chinese-held airbase at Hsian in northern China, from where many operations were flown against the Japanese rear in the Yellow River area using the comparatively primitive conditions at the base. The first squadron of the 311th to operate from there was the 530th, which was detached to Hsian between October 1944 and February 1945, and carried out a highly successful series of three raids during the Christmas 1944 and New Year 1945 period against the Japanese air base at Tsinan. The raids were mounted at extreme range, with the Mustangs having to fly with 110 US gallon external fuel tanks and using their guns alone to create havoc amongst the local Japanese air assets.

The success of these attacks underlined the growing US aerial dominance over the Japanese during that period in many areas of China. Just as in Europe, Mustangs were successfully helping to wrest control of the air from the enemy, which became a significant factor in loosening the Japanese hold over the occupied areas of China. The 530th was relieved at Hsian in February 1945 by the 528th FS of the 311th FG, but by that time an old hand with the Mustang had successfully added to his score of aerial victories. The pilot concerned was James England, who had become the top-scoring ace amongst Allison-engined Mustang pilots with his eight aerial victories in the P-51A while operating from India. By then promoted to Major, England achieved two further aerial victories in the P-51C, the final being on 18 December 1944 near Hankow airfield, to give him a final total of ten and making him one of the most accomplished all-round fighter pilots in the CBI theatre.

As well as the 23rd and 311th Fighter Groups, the 51st FG also flew Merlin-Mustangs in China. Like other US units in the CBI, the 51st similarly flew a long and little-publicised war there, having arrived as early as March 1942. Originally activated as the

Several 'natural metal' P-51B and/or P-51C in the CBI. The forward fuselage 'shark-mouths' and tail vertical tail markings suggest allocation to the 51st Fighter Group's 26th FS *(Photo: USAAF)*

51st Pursuit Group in January 1941 under the command of Col Homer Sanders, the group became the 51st Pursuit Group (Fighter) in March 1941 and spent several months training for combat whilst also acting as a part of the west coast defence force while stationed at March Field, California (according to the unit's diaries, several of its Curtiss fighters were somewhat ironically deployed for a time at Mines Field, Inglewood, the home of North American Aviation). The three squadrons of the group were initially equipped with early-model P-40s, and the 51st came to be called "Homer's Volunteer Group" due to its willingness to move overseas for combat following the Pearl Harbour attack. The group moved by ship to Australia in January 1942 with a consignment of P-40s, and eventually reached India via Ceylon in March of that year. It was redesignated as the 51st Fighter Group in May 1942, and subsequently defended the Indian side of the 'Hump' aerial supply routes. The group was headquartered at Dinjan in India from October 1942, but in October 1943 the 51st was transferred to China and became a part of the Fourteenth Army Air Force. Henceforth the group's headquarters were sited at Kunming, and the 51st subsequently guarded the eastern end of the 'Hump' route, in addition to flying a range of fighter and ground support missions for US and Chinese forces. Like the 23rd and 311th Fighter Groups, the 51st started to receive Merlin Mustangs during 1944, and by the latter stages of the year had received sufficient to virtually retire its venerable P-40 Warhawks. By the early weeks of 1945 the Merlin-Mustang was numerically becoming the most important US fighter in the CBI theatre. The component squadrons of the 51st were the 16th, 25th and 26th Fighter Squadrons, which flew the P-40 and then the P-51, and the 449th Fighter Squadron which was exclusively a P-38-equipped squadron.

## Merlin-Mustangs and Chinese Pilots

Similarly little publicised participants in the CBI theatre were the two joint Chinese and American-manned fighter groups, the 3rd and 5th Fighter Groups (Provisional). These were a part of the Chinese-American Composite Wing, and like other US fighter groups in the CBI theatre, they originally flew P-40 Warhawks, but later received Merlin-Mustangs. The squadrons within these two groups were jointly commanded by an American and a Chinese officer, and their personnel were usually mixed between the two nationalities (although the Chinese personnel were a very diverse group, from many different parts of the vast Chinese hinterland). Formed in August 1943, the most successful in terms of its use of the Mustang was the 3rd FG (P). This group consisted of the 7th, 8th, 28th, and 32nd Fighter Squadrons (Provisional). The latter two squadrons were activated in August 1943 but the former two were activated in October of that year in India, before moving to China in January 1944. Initially based at Kweilin, both subsequently made many base changes to suit the ground war situation in China, with the 8th FS (P) operating in the area of the Yangtze River. At that time all the squadrons of the group were equipped with P-40 Warhawks, but in late 1944/early 1945 Merlin-Mustangs started to become available, and these were subsequently operated alongside the Warhawks. The Mustangs allowed the Chinese and American pilots to perform much longer-range missions than had been possible with the P-40, and ground-attack missions were flown against many far-flung Japanese installations, including important enemy airfields in the Hankow area. Unfortunately a Japanese offensive to capture the Allied airfields in the Laohokow area forced the 8th FS (P) to fall back to Ankang in March 1945, and thereafter a shortage of fuel was a constant problem for some of the Chinese-American units. In May 1945 the 8th was still flying a handful of Warhawks, in addition to a mixed-bag of F-6 and other Merlin-Mustangs. Although Japanese air activity was generally on the wane in China by that

time, several pilots from the 3rd FG (P) scored aerial victories in the Mustang. These included the group's highest-scoring ace to achieve all his victories in the group and to achieve victories in Mustangs, Lt Heyward Paxton, Jr., who scored three victories in January 1945 in P-51C Mustangs. He was a pilot of the 7th FS (P), and finished the war with 6.5 victories – again underlining the comparative scarcity of Japanese aerial opposition. Paxton was shot down on 14 January 1945 in the vicinity of Hankow airfield, but successfully returned to friendly lines after some two weeks despite being injured. Pilots in this theatre were just as likely to achieve ground victories, due to the considerable number of Japanese airfields that were targets for the far-ranging Mustangs, and one of the 7th FS (P)'s pilots holds a particular distinction. With 31.5 ground victories, Capt Thomas Reynolds was the highest-scoring ground victories ace in the whole of the USAAF. Some 25 of these were achieved in Mustangs, in addition to possibly three of his four aerial victories. The top-scoring Chinese pilot in the Chinese-American Composite Wing was Capt Kuang-Fu Wang, who was the Chinese CO of the 7th FS (P) from March 1945 to the end of the war. He achieved 6.5 aerial victories, one of these (a Nakajima Ki-44 Shoki 'Tojo') in a P-51K on 7 March 1945 although the others were scored in P-40N Warhawks.

The joint Chinese-American 5th Fighter Group (Provisional) comprised the 17th, 26th, 27th, and 29th Fighter Squadrons (Provisional). Like the 3rd FG (P), the 5th was activated in India, before moving to China which it carried out in the middle of 1944. The 17th FS (P), for example, was activated on 11 March 1944, but moved from India to Ling-Ling in China at the end of May 1944. At the time of its creation the group was equipped with P-40 Warhawks, but re-equipment with Mustangs followed on much later. However, the group was in the thick of the fighting well into 1945, and received a Distinguished Unit Citation for its ground-attack work during the fierce fighting sometimes called the battle of Chihkiang in April and May 1945. The group did not produce any P-51 aces, again showing the predominantly ground-support nature of the unit's work.

## Reconnaissance Assets

The use of reconnaissance Merlin-Mustangs in the CBI is rarely mentioned in histories of the Mustang, but was nonetheless important. The little-documented 8th Photo Reconnaissance Group provided reconnaissance cover for the extensive region of the CBI theatre, with its headquarters at Bally in India, but its squadrons were located all over the vast CBI area. The 8th was activated as the 8th Photographic Reconnaissance Group on 1

The impact of the Merlin-Mustangs in the CBI was immediate. They were able to fly all the variety of missions that Merlin-engined Mustangs flew in Europe, and take on any Japanese aerial opposition with great capability. The 311th Fighter Group was one of the recipients of Merlin-Mustangs in the CBI. This unit had already established itself as a successful Mustang unit with its various achievements in Allison-engined Mustangs which it started to fly in 1943. The first Merlin-powered Mustangs started to reach the 311th during the spring of 1944, and the unit used the Mustang's range and combat capabilities to great effect while based in China. Here a yellow and black-tailed P-51C-10-NT, 42-103896 named 'Princess' of the 530th FS, 311th FG, flies escort for a C-47 transport over China. The date of the image is generally accepted to be 24 July 1945, although this could be the date of release of the image for publication. In common with many CBI Mustangs, it carries an MN-26C d/f loop on its fuselage spine, indicative of extra navigation equipment being carried due to the miles of rugged and inhospitable terrain that these aircraft operated over in the CBI
*(Photo: USAAF)*

Probably photographed at Pungchacheng in China during 1945, this line-up of Merlin-Mustangs was from the 311th Fighter Group. The nearest aircraft is a P-51K-1-NA, 44-11444, named 'The Worldly Wench' and wearing the black and yellow tail markings plus white spinner of the 529th Fighter Squadron. 'My Ned' in the background is from the 530th FS. The 311th FG fought a long war with the Mustang, having originally started with Allison-engined Mustangs in 1943 (Photo: R.L. Ward Collection)

October 1943, and moved to India in February-March 1944. It covered the whole area of the CBI, including Burma, India, China, French Indochina, and Thailand, and carried out photo-reconnaissance, visual reconnaissance and mapping, in addition to performing ground-attack work and carrying out some escort missions for Allied bombers. The group was redesignated as the 8th Reconnaissance Group in June 1945. In effect this unit 'mopped up' several reconnaissance squadrons that were already operating in the CBI before its arrival, and eventually it contained the 9th, 20th, 24th, and 40th reconnaissance squadrons – these squadrons used a variety of different designations due to the diverse nature of the tasks that they performed. The 24th, for example, was a combat mapping squadron and primarily flew the Consolidated F-7, the photo/mapping version of the Consolidated B-24 Liberator four-engined heavy bomber. Of the 8th's four squadrons, the 20th Tactical Reconnaissance Squadron was most closely linked to the Mustang, by flying the F-6D during 1945. Prior to being assigned to the 8th PRG in April 1944, the squadron had been assigned directly to the Tenth Army Air Force, but had also been a part of the 5306th Photographic and Reconnaissance Group (Provisional) for a few weeks in early 1944. It had arrived in the theatre in late 1943, and used a variety of bases during its time in the CBI, including Dinjan in India, but flew detachments from various locations as operational circumstances demanded, including Myitkyina and Akyab in Burma. The squadron flew the P-40 during much of its time in the CBI, in addition to the F-6, and did not have any aces amongst its ranks and so has gone little-noticed by historians.

Two Air Commando Groups also flew the Merlin-Mustang in the CBI. One of these was the 1st Air Commando Group, which had successfully operated Allison-engined Mustangs during 1944 as described in Part 1 of this two-part 'Modellers' Datafile' on the Mustang, which covered the Allison-Mustangs. The group received Merlin-engined Mustangs predominantly in 1945, having transitioned onto the P-47 Thunderbolt, although for some of that period it acted mainly in a training capacity. Similarly Merlin-powered Mustang-equipped was the 2nd Air Commando Group, which was new to Mustang operations when it was activated on 22 April 1944. This group included in its ranks the 1st and 2nd Fighter Squadrons (Commando), which were both originally activated in April 1944 under a different title. In keeping with the 1st Air Commando Group, the 2nd ACG included within its inventory not only fighter squadrons, but also liaison and troop carrier elements, and like the 1st ACG it was also an early exponent of the kind of combined forces operations and close air support that are familiar today. The 2nd moved to India in September to November 1944, and was headquartered at

Kalaikunda in India from that period to the end of the war – although in practice its assigned units flew from a variety of airfields and airstrips near to the front lines when required. The unit's Merlin-Mustangs were in action from early 1945 onwards, and from February 1945 were officially stationed at Cox's Bazaar in India. Operations were flown over a wide variety of targets, and once more due to the comparative scarcity of Japanese aerial opposition by that time there was ample scope for the P-51D Mustangs of the two squadrons to concentrate on many diverse ground targets. Support was provided for the Allied forces crossing the Irrawaddy River in February 1945, and attacks were made as far away as Thailand, again the excellent range of the Mustang proving to be of great value.

## Pacific Merlin-Mustangs

In the vast Pacific battleground, Allison-engined Mustangs did not participate and so it was solely Merlin-engined Mustangs of the USAAF that made the P-51's presence felt in that part of the World War Two air war. Even then, it was not until later in 1944 that Merlin-Mustangs started to arrive in any meaningful numbers. Somewhat ironically, given the type's great successes as escort fighters during that period over North-west Europe and Southern Europe, many of the first Merlin-engined P-51s to fly combat in the pacific did so as reconnaissance aircraft and as fighter-bombers. By the time of the Merlin-Mustang's appearance in the Pacific, the air war in that vast area had already raged for almost three years. The principal USAAF fighters that were involved in the air war against the Japanese in the Pacific were - to begin with - the P-40 Warhawk and P-39 Airacobra, while later the P-47 Thunderbolt and P-38 Lightning became the main US fighters. The P-40 and P-39 helped to hold the line until the P-47 and P-38 could be developed and deployed in large numbers, although the P-40 continued to play a part in limited numbers until well into the final phases of the Pacific war. In stark contrast to the situation in Europe, the P-38 Lightning found a particular niche in the Pacific and was highly successful. However, advances in Japanese fighter technology also took place during that period, and by the later stages of the war the Japanese were developing a number of excellent piston-engined fighter designs although unlike the Germans, the Japanese were never able to successfully develop and deploy jet or rocket-powered fighters.

The employment of the Merlin-Mustang in the Pacific was effectively in two very different combat areas, resulting in very different sets of parameters for the Mustangs depending on where they were operating. In the south-west Pacific (often called the South-West Pacific Area, or SWPA), Merlin-Mustangs eventually flew with units of the Fifth Army Air Force. This air force had been

The 75th Fighter Squadron was the last of the 23rd Fighter Group's squadrons to transition onto the Mustang, doing so in late 1944. This 75th FS Mustang appears to be a P-51K with its uncuffed propeller blades, and illustrated the rather colourless mid-1945 markings of the squadron with a black tail and plane-in-squadron number ('56') on the nose without the famous 23rd FG 'shark-mouth', but bearing the tiger shark squadron badge on the fuselage side *(Photo: R.L. Ward Collection)*

in the thick of the fighting in the New Guinea area and in the defence of Australia since 1942 (the Fifth was actually created in February 1942). Under the very individual and successful leadership of Lt Gen George C. Kenney, the Fifth had been a part of the Allied effort alongside British Commonwealth and Dutch efforts to halt the Japanese advances in New Guinea and to successfully defend northern Australia, and then gradually to take the fight to the Japanese in their many conquests in the SWPA. Into this large area of operations the Merlin-Mustang was eventually introduced, although by then the P-47 Thunderbolt and P-38 Lightning were already well established there and highly successful. On the other hand, in the other main area of operations for the Mustang in the Pacific, namely the central Pacific and eventually over Japan itself, the Mustang with its great range capabilities was to prove highly valuable as a very long-range bomber escort – although the type was in combat for only a matter of months in that area. The USAAF organisation that operated in the central Pacific was the Seventh Army Air Force. Originally activated as the Hawaiian Air Force in November 1940, elements of this organisation were the very first US personnel to fight when Japanese forces struck by air against Pearl Harbour and other installations in Hawaii on 7 December 1941, with several locally-based US fighter pilots scoring aerial victories during the Japanese attacks. The Seventh Army Air Force was formally created from this organisation in February 1942, and initially provided air defence for the Hawaiian islands. However, from mid-1943 the Seventh took on a more offence-based role, and eventually provided bomber escort for B-29 Superfortress bombers of the Twentieth Army Air Force, with which it became closely associated.

Within the SWPA, the Merlin-Mustang first came to prominence within the Fifth Army Air Force as a reconnaissance aircraft. The first Mustangs to join a unit of the Fifth Air Force were the reconnaissance-configured F-6D Mustangs that began to equip the 82nd Tactical Reconnaissance Squadron of the 71st Tactical Reconnaissance Group in November 1944. The lateness of

this arrival underlines the fact that Merlin-Mustangs destined for operations in Europe had considerable precedence over any planned deliveries for the Pacific. Gen Kenney had long argued for Mustangs to join the Fifth Air Force, but it was only after he had been replaced in June 1944 by Lt Gen Ennis C. Whitehead that the prospect for Mustangs operating in the SWPA started to become a possibility. The 82nd TRS had latterly flown reconnaissance-configured Bell P-39N and P-39Q Airacobras, which although not sparkling performers had nonetheless acquitted themselves well in the tactical reconnaissance role - so long as there were not too many Japanese fighters around. The arrival of sufficient numbers of F-6D Mustangs in October and November 1944 allowed the squadron to re-equip with Mustangs, and these represented a quantum leap forward in capability over the venerable but generally well-liked Airacobras. Certainly several members of the squadron needed some refresher training on operating a 'taildragger' after being familiar for so long with the tricycle undercarriage Airacobra. While the 82nd was transitioning onto the Mustang the 71st TRG moved from Biak, an island off the New Guinea coast, to Leyte in the Philippines, in early November 1944, with the 82nd also making the move to the Philippines during that time, and eventually being based at San Jose, Mindoro, and later at Lingayen on Luzon in the Philippines. This placed the 82nd near to where the action was increasingly taking place, as Allied forces worked on the difficult task of removing the Japanese occupiers from the extensive Philippine islands. Like their fighter-reconnaissance counterparts in Europe, in addition to reconnaissance missions the unit's Mustangs participated in fighter missions as well as ground-attack sorties when required. Just before Christmas 1944 Capt William A. Shomo became the squadron's commander. Before joining the newly-formed Army Air Force in the summer of 1941, Shomo had studied at the Cincinnati College of Mortuary Research and had trained as a licensed embalmer. He had been with the 82nd since November 1943, and had flown the P-39Q Airacobra throughout many of the subsequent weeks, but the type was duly largely superseded by the

Merlin-Mustangs assigned to the 2nd Air Commando Group in India wore distinctive markings. This P-51D-15-NA, serial number 44-15338, photographed in India in early 1945, featured black lightning bolts on its fuselage and wings in addition to an exclamation mark on its vertical tail and individual identification number '84'. The Air Commandos made good use of their Merlin-Mustangs especially in the ground-attack role *(Photo: R.L. Ward Collection)*

The Air Commandoes used the Merlin-Mustang in the Pacific principally for providing support for ground forces, with fighter missions against enemy aircraft being only a part of their assigned task. The 3rd Air Commando Group, which included in its list of assigned squadrons the 3rd and 4th Fighter Squadrons (Commando), operated in the Philippines against the Japanese after moving there in late 1944/early 1945. One of the unit's Merlin-Mustangs was the famous 'Jumpin' Jacques' from the 3rd FS (C), which carried that squadron's blue and yellow tail markings and blue nose trim, in addition to the black theatre fuselage bands. It was a P-51D-20-NA, 44-64076 *(Photo: USAAF)*

F-6D. On 10 January 1945 he led a fighter-reconnaissance mission to the Japanese-held Tuguegarao airfield on Luzon. Discovering an obsolete Aichi D3A 'Val' dive-bomber in the vicinity of the airstrip he shot it down over the Cagayan River south of the air base. This was the first Mustang victory in the Fifth Air Force, and indeed in the Pacific as a whole. The next day was rather more historic, however.

Returning to the Tuguegarao area the following morning, Shomo led wingman Lt Paul Lipscomb in a two-ship armed-reconnaissance to take a look at the airstrips at Laoag and Atarri. While flying along the northern Luzon coastline, Shomo and Lipscomb chanced upon a formation of 12 Japanese fighters escorting a single Mitsubishi G4M 'Betty' bomber. Just what the purpose of this formation was, and whether or not the 'Betty' was actually on a bombing mission or was carrying an important person has never been determined. However, displaying the kind of aggressiveness characteristic of Mustang pilots in Europe and the Mediterranean in their dealings with the Luftwaffe, Shomo and Lipscomb did not hesitate to attack the Japanese formation despite being considerably outnumbered. In the subsequent completely one-sided encounter, Shomo shot down the 'Betty' plus six of the escorting Kawasaki Ki-61 Hien 'Tony' fighters. Lipscomb added to the rout by downing three more of the escorts. The remaining Japanese aircraft fled, while the Mustang pilots photographed the scattered wreckage of their prey. This remarkable feat was all the more notable because the 'Tony' was one of the best of the Japanese fighters of the later war period, but the aircraft that Shomo and Lipscomb brought down were apparently not flown as aggressively as the two reconnaissance Mustangs. For his shoot-down of the seven Japanese aircraft Shomo was subsequently awarded the Medal of Honor, the highest US military award. As with Maj Jim Howard in England exactly a year earlier, Shomo was subsequently the subject of considerable media activity following the award of this decoration. He was promoted to Major several days after the famous combat, and received a shiny new P-51D-20-NA (serial number 44-72505) to replace the rather more humble F-6D (44-14841, named 'Snooks – 5th') that he was flying when he scored his seven victories. The new aircraft was adorned with full unit markings and the name 'The Flying Undertaker', which was not carried by the F-6D that he had flown during his M of H-winning encounter.

Shomo's well-known combat was, however, not typical of aerial activity in the SWPA as 1945 wore on. Japanese air assets had been considerably depleted in the preceding year, there was less opportunity for reinforcements to arrive from Japan, and the chances for air-to-air combat were increasingly few and far between. Shomo did not subsequently add to his overall total of eight aerial victories, but his unit continued in combat virtually to the end of the war. Indeed, a second reconnaissance squadron within the 71st TRG also flew the Mustang in this latter stage of the war. This was the 110th Tactical Reconnaissance Squadron, which was a National Guard unit that had been federalised in

December 1940 having previously been a part of the Missouri National Guard. Eventually assigned to the 71st, the 110th TRS received F-6D and P-51D Mustangs in 1945, having previously operated the P-39 Airacobra and P-40 Warhawk. Later stationed at Lingayen in the Philippines from 20 January 1945 like the 82nd TRS, both reconnaissance squadrons eventually moved north to the island of Ie Shima in July 1945. This was in line with the movement of many of the air assets of the Fifth Air Force to the central Pacific at that time to assist directly in the war against Japanese forces nearer to the Japanese home islands, after the air war in the Philippines had been all but completed. By that period the 71st TRG that both the 82nd and 110th still belonged to, had been redesignated as the 71st Reconnaissance Group in May 1945.

Alongside the reconnaissance squadrons of the 71st TRG, one further unit took the Merlin-Mustang into combat in late 1944 and early 1945 in the Philippines. This was the 3rd Air Commando Group, which had amongst its assigned squadrons the 3rd and 4th Fighter Squadrons (Commando). At first equipped with P-40 Warhawks when initially activated in May 1944 under a different title, both squadrons later transitioned onto the P-51D, and moved with the 3rd ACG to the Philippines in late 1944/early 1945. Initially stationed at Leyte (from December 1944 for the 3rd FS (C), and at the same location from January 1945 for the 4th FS (C)), the two squadrons played very much the same role as the two Air Commando Groups in the CBI, providing support for ground forces with fighter missions against enemy aircraft being only a part of the task performed by the Mustangs of both squadrons. In any case, Japanese aerial opposition proved to be as scarce for the Air Commando pilots as it was by that time for the other US pilots in the Philippines, and the two squadrons of the 3rd ACG as a whole only achieved eight aerial victories up to the end of the war – this compares, for example, to the 39th Fighter Squadron's haul of 186, this squadron being a part of the 35th Fighter Group which saw combat throughout the New Guinea campaigns earlier in the Pacific war with other fighter types prior to the reconquest of the Philippines. The Mustangs of the 3rd ACG eventually ranged over long distances in search of the Japanese, and even flew some long-range missions to the island of Formosa (now Taiwan), involving flights of some seven hours. Amongst the personalities of this unit was Maj Walker Mahurin, who was the CO of the 3rd FS (C) in the early months of 1945, having taken over the squadron earlier in 1944. Mahurin was a high-scoring fighter pilot who had achieved 19.75 victories while flying P-47 Thunderbolts with the 56th Fighter Group of the Eighth Army Air Force from England. Shot down in March 1944 over France, he had successfully avoided capture with the aid of French civilians and had eventually returned to the US. Subsequently posted to the Far East, he became the squadron commander of the 3rd FS (C) in July 1944, and shot down a Mitsubishi Ki-46 'Dinah' twin-engined reconnaissance aircraft over northern Luzon on 14 January 1945. This was his only aerial victory in the SWPA, although several years later he shot down 3.5 MiG-15 jet fighters over Korea during

the Korean War while flying F-86 Sabres. Another pilot who had scored aerial victories over Europe but later flew with the 3rd ACG was Lt Louis Curdes. Having achieved eight aerial victories in the Mediterranean with the 82nd Fighter Group flying P-38 Lightnings, Curdes similarly found his way to the 3rd ACG after being shot down, in his case over Italy although he succeeded in escaping having been taken prisoner. Curdes scored his only aerial victory over the Japanese, a Mitsubishi Ki-46 'Dinah', on 7 February 1945 off Formosa while with the 4th FS (C). He did however also gain considerable fame by bringing down on 10 February 1945 a US-operated C-47 transport that was trying by mistake to land on a Japanese-held airstrip on Batan Island in the Philippines; the C-47 landed in the sea following some accurate gunfire from Curdes, and its crew and passengers were rescued.

Following several changes of location in the Philippines, the 3rd Air Commando Group, like a number of the other aerial assets of the Fifth Army Air Force, eventually moved to the island of Ie Shima to be nearer to the Japanese home islands. This took place in August 1945, very near to the end of the war. By that time the Mustang had become much more widespread as a fighter in the Fifth Air Force, due to the conversion of two of the crack fighter units of the Fifth onto the Mustang as many more new P-51D/K Mustangs at last started to become available in the early months of 1945 to fighter units in the Pacific. The two groups concerned were the 35th and the 348th Fighter Groups. Both these units were seasoned veterans of the fighting in the SWPA, and had fought through all the large air battles of 1943 and 1944 that had brought about the growing demise of Japanese aerial opposition in the New Guinea and Philippines areas. Both were equipped with the massive P-47 Thunderbolt, but as the P-51D/K started to become available, the transition began onto the smaller and potentially more potent North American fighter. The 35th FG had originally flown P-39 Airacobras but by the start of 1944, the P-47 Thunderbolt had become the standard equipment of the group. In the spring of 1945 the group began to transition onto the Mustang while newly-based on Luzon in the Philippines. The 348th FG was

a veteran of P-47 Thunderbolt operations, having flown the type throughout its combat period in New Guinea, operating there from mid-1943 onwards. By the spring of 1945 the group was, like the 35th FG, also based on Luzon in the Philippines (which had only recently been recaptured) when it transitioned onto the Mustang. The lack of Japanese aerial opposition in any numbers by that time resulted in both groups finding little chance to fully exploit the capabilities of the P-51, but like other Fifth Air Force units it eventually moved north where the action was mainly taking place as 1945 wore on. Nevertheless, fighting continued in parts of the Philippines right up to the end of the war, although Japanese opposition consisted mainly of fanatical but increasingly isolated ground forces. The 35th FG (comprising the 39th, 40th, and 41st Fighter Squadrons) moved from its final base in the Philippines at Clark Field in late June 1945 and took up residence on the island of Okinawa, which had only recently fallen to US forces (the final Japanese resistance on the island only ended on 22 June). The 348th FG (unusually comprising four squadrons, the 340th, 341st, 342nd, and 460th Fighter Squadrons) left its final headquarters in the Philippines, Floridablanca on Luzon, in early July 1945 and made the equally long move to Ie Shima island. Ie Shima itself had been taken by US forces at the start of the Okinawa campaign in April 1945.

From their new bases, which were well within range of the Japanese home islands for the long-legged Merlin-Mustangs, the 35th and 348th returned to the fighting. In addition to missions over Japan proper, both groups also ranged over Formosa and French Indochina to the west, and considerably added to the growing US air superiority over all these areas. Several of the successful pilots of these two groups who had come to prominence during their time on the P-47 Thunderbolt had the chance to add to their score of aerial victories while flying the Mustang, although for some giving up the beloved Thunderbolt was a regrettable turn of events. One of the characters of the 348th FG was Lt Col William Dunham, who had risen to being the group's deputy commander near to the end of the war, having been one of its highest-scoring

Partnering the 15th Fighter Group on Iwo Jima was the 21st FG, one of whose Merlin-Mustangs is shown here having suffered a mishap that could have been much more serious than it appears to have been. Named 'Little Angel' the 104', it belonged to the 21st FG's 46th FS, and was a P-51D-20-NA, serial number 44-63532. Both the 15th FG and the 21st FG were a part of the Seventh Air Force's VII Fighter Command, but came under the administration of the Twentieth Air Force for B-29 support operations *(Photo: USAAF)*

pilots in the P-47 with 15 confirmed victories. After briefly returning to the US, he went back to the Pacific in May 1945 to fly the Mustang, and added to his score on 1 August 1945 by shooting down a Nakajima Ki-84 Hayate 'Frank' of the IJAAF over Take Island off the coast of Kyushu. The 'Frank' was one of the best Japanese fighters of the late war period, and combined excellent climb rate with manoeuvrability. It was a match for a Mustang in a close dog-fight, but the tried and tested means of fighting the Japanese, of engaging and disengaging at will without getting involved in a climbing turn or close manoeuvring suited the Mustang even in its encounters with this fine Japanese fighter, which had first entered service in the summer of 1944.

## Merlin-Mustangs in the Seventh Air Force

In their operations over the Japanese home islands with the P-51, the 35th and 348th Fighter Groups were by no means the first to fly the Merlin-Mustang over Japan proper. For several months before their arrival, the Seventh Army Air Force's 15th and 21st Fighter Groups had been in action with the Merlin-powered Mustang. Beginning life in the central Pacific in Hawaii, the Seventh Air Force had eventually moved north to take the fight to the Japanese. The 15th Fighter Group in fact can lay claim to being the one fighter group in the USAAF that was in action from the start of the American involvement in World War Two right to the end of the war in the Pacific. When the Japanese struck at Pearl Harbour on 7 December 1941, the then-15th Pursuit Group was equipped with early-model Curtiss P-40s, and many of its aircraft were destroyed on the ground during the Japanese attack. Several of its pilots did, however, manage to leave the ground and fight back against the attacking Japanese aircraft. One of the successful pilots that fateful day was Lt George S. Welch, of the 15th PG's 47th Pursuit Squadron. Welch managed to achieve four confirmed victories in a P-40 on 7 December, and he eventually scored 16 aerial victories in a combat career that continued into September 1943 – although none of these were achieved in Mustangs. The following year he joined North American Aviation as a test-pilot, and was at the controls of the first XP-86 Sabre jet fighter when it made its maiden flight in October 1947. The 15th Pursuit Group duly provided the air defence for the Hawaiian Islands subsequent to the Pearl Harbour attack, and was eventually re-equipped and later flew P-39 Airacobras and later marks of P-40 Warhawks. Although elements of the group saw some action in the central Pacific, it was not until the group started to receive P-51 Mustangs in late 1944 that it was able to foresee a considerable amount of combat. Becoming a part of the Seventh Army Air Force in 1942, the group was redesignated as the 15th Fighter Group in May 1942, and consisted of the 45th, 47th, and 78th Fighter Squadrons during its time with the P-51. The 21st Fighter Group, on the other hand, was activated in Hawaii quite late in the war on 21 April 1944, and after initially providing air defence for the Hawaiian islands it started to receive P-51 Mustangs in numbers early in 1945 in preparation for a move north. Its assigned squadrons

during its Mustang period were the 46th, 72nd, and 531st Fighter Squadrons.

On 19 February 1945, the US invasion of the island of Iwo Jima in the Bonin Islands group began. Although only a small island, approximately five miles (8 km) at its longest aspect, it was a strategically vital point of land in the vast Pacific Ocean. It was the site of Japanese airfields and the home of Japanese fighters that could disrupt US B-29 Superfortress bombers on their way to bomb Japan at extreme range from their bases further away in the Pacific (the B-29 force eventually used the islands of Saipan, Guam and Tinian as their principal bases), but in US hands it could become a major air base for bombers and also for escort fighters too. The fighting to take the island was fierce, but as soon as it was possible, USAAF air assets started to move in – even before the remaining Japanese on the island had surrendered. These included elements of the 15th and 21st Fighter Groups, which started to fly into Iwo Jima with their new P-51D/KMustangs at the first opportunity. The 15th was officially headquartered at South Field, Iwo Jima, from 6 March, while the 21st was initially based at Central Field, Iwo Jima before moving to South Field in July 1945. Unfortunately the group's arrival was a little premature. During the night of 26/27 March, just after the headquarters had been established, some 300 Japanese soldiers broke into the area of the central airfield on the island, where the 21st FG had been settling in. During the ensuing fighting 11 of the group's pilots were killed together with several ground personnel from the group and other US servicemen. Fortunately the attack was repulsed, and during that period the Mustangs of the two groups successfully joined in with the final fighting on the island and over other nearby targets (including Japanese positions on the neighbouring island of Chichi Jima) by mounting ground-attack sorties in support of the US ground forces.

The main purpose for the Mustangs on Iwo Jima was to provide very long-range escort to the Boeing B-29 Superfortresses of the Twentieth Army Air Force's XXI Bomber Command, that were mounting long-range raids on the Japanese home islands from Saipan, Tinian and Guam in the Mariana Islands to the south of Iwo Jima. These raids were meeting increasing opposition from defending Japanese fighters, and a number of changes of tactics had been forced upon the B-29 force in order to increase the accuracy and effectiveness of these raids, and to keep losses to a minimum. As far as meeting the defending Japanese fighters was concerned, the Mustang with its excellent long-range capabilities was the ideal fighter to escort the B-29 bombers, and also coming into prominence as 1945 wore on was the very long-range version of the P-47 Thunderbolt, the P-47N. Able to stay aloft for some eight hours, the P-47N was a formidable weapon, the culmination of all the combat experience and development work on the P-47 up to that time. Although the Mustang had truly proven its worth as a bomber escort in Europe by this stage of the war, the escort missions that were being contemplated for the Iwo Jima-based Mustangs were like nothing seen in Europe. These were to be approximately eight-hour-long missions, with the best part of each flown over water. In effect this was the pinnacle of bomber escort. Nothing like it had been tried before, and has certainly never been tried since. Logistically there were many problems to overcome. One was navigation. Flying and navigating a single-seat, single-engine fighter over the distances involved, particularly over featureless ocean, was a new phenomenon, and in the event navigation was undertaken on some of the forthcoming missions by the B-29 bombers themselves, one or more of which would specifically 'escort' the fighters. The US Navy also supported when possible the very long raids of the B-29 force, by stationing submarines or surface ships along the planned flight paths of the raids in order to be able to pick up air crews unlucky enough to come down in the sea – although even then the distances involved were huge, and the Navy could not be everywhere.

The big day came on 7 April 1945. On that date the first true very long-range bomber escort was flown by the Iwo Jima Mustangs. Both the 15th and 21st Fighter Groups were involved, and they escorted the B-29 Superfortresses of the XXI Bomber Command's 73rd Bomb Wing (comprising the 497th, 498th, 499th, and 500th Bomb Groups, which were based at Isley Field, Saipan). In fact the 7 April raid was not only important because it had fighter escort – it was flown to the two most important industrial targets in XXI Bomber Command's targets folder. While B-29s of the 313th and 314th Bomb Wings went after the Mitsubishi engine factory at Nagoya, the 73rd Wing headed for the massive Musashi factory complex in a suburb of north-western Tokyo. This complex was a major engine plant of the Nakajima Company, producing more than a quarter of all engines for Japanese warplanes. It was a target that had almost legendary status in XXI Bomber Command, where it was known as Target No.357. It was certainly on a par with locations such as Marienburg, Rostock, Ploesti, Dessau and the scores of other industrial and aviation-related targets that the heavy bombers of the Eighth and Fifteenth Army Air Forces had been pounding away at in Europe for well over a year by that time.

The 7 April mission proved to be a success. The round trip was some 1,500 miles (2,415 km), and 108 Mustangs were involved of which 97 were effective. The 73rd Bomb Wing B-29s bombed from some 18,000 ft (5,487 m) and inflicted considerable damage to the Nakajima plant, with heavy damage caused to the machine shops which seriously slowed assembly. The escorts were kept busy too. In the comparatively clear conditions over Japan the Mustangs were able to spot Japanese fighters as they massed to attack the lumbering Superfortresses, and a number of significant air battles ensued. It was the first time that US escort fighters had flown over the Japanese home islands in this fashion, and like the Eighth Air Force fighters on their first major forays above Berlin over a year earlier and the significance that had on Germany's war effort, it was truly the beginning of the end for the Japanese now that the Americans could place effective fighter cover for the B-29s over Japan itself. In the dog-fights that ensued both the 15th and 21st scored victories. Maj James Tapp of the 15th FG's 78th FS achieved four victories, while squadron-mate Capt Robert W. Moore of the 78th FS shot down two Mitsubishi A6M3 'Hamps' in the Choisi area during some furious aerial fighting in the vicinity of Tokyo. The 21st FG made claims for five Japanese fighters. In contrast to these successes, two Mustangs were lost but one of the pilots was picked up safely when he was forced to ditch on the way home. It had been a major effort to put up this type of fighter cover, but the success of the two fighter groups was rewarded when they were each awarded a Distinguished Unit Citation for their participation in the 7 April raid.

This successful attack was followed up five days later by a second B-29 strike on the same location which created even more damage, and effectively ceased production at the Nakajima plant. The 12 April mission was also a success for Maj James Tapp, who shot down a Kawasaki Ki-61 Hien 'Tony' in the Tokyo area to become an ace. He was in fact the first ace of the 15th FG, and the first for the Seventh Air Force. Tapp eventually ended the war with eight aerial victories, all scored while flying Mustangs with the 15th FG. On 25 May the 15th FG became embroiled in some major

A well-known posed - but nonetheless interesting - view of a Mustang being waved off for a long-range mission. The aircraft belongs to the 506th FG, the last group to become operational on the Mustang, and shows the very late war colours of this fighter group of solid colour tailplanes rather than the striped tailplanes of several weeks earlier. The 506th flew very long-range missions against Japanese targets in the latter stages of the war, having flown its first operations in May 1945. Clearly visible beneath the right-hand wing is a metal 110 US gallon drop tank, the largest such jettisonable fuel tank that was normally carried by Mustangs during World War Two on very long-range operations *(Photo: USAAF)*

With the stark Iwo Jima landscape as a backdrop, two Mustangs from the 21st Fighter Group's 46th FS are readied for another long-range mission. Both are from the 44-63… batch of 1,000 P-51D-20-NA, a fair proportion of which found their way to the Pacific, while others were assigned to the Eighth Air Force in Europe *(Photo: USAAF)*

dog-fighting over and around Kashiwa airfield, and two Mitsubishi A6M 'Zekes' were shot down over the airfield itself by Capt Robert Moore of the 78th FS to become an ace and bring his overall score at that point to six. He eventually finished the war with a total of 12 aerial victories, 11 of which were achieved in Mustangs. This also made him the top-scoring ace in the Seventh Army Air Force. Some of these scores of aerial victories appear small in comparison to those achieved in Europe by Eighth Air Force pilots, but they were no less significant, and in similar fashion to those over Europe they added to the growing demise of enemy aerial opposition which was a vitally important part of the eventual Allied victory. Indeed, the very long-range escort missions flown by Mustangs in the central Pacific in support of the B-29 Superfortresses were some of the most epic fighter operations of the whole war, and were certainly not for the faint-hearted. Even flying in an undamaged aircraft over the vast expanses of the Pacific was a taxing occupation, but in aircraft that had received battle damage or had developed a technical fault the experience was highly demanding. Sometimes known as Empire Missions, the very long-range B-29 strikes hit back at the heart of the Japanese Empire and inflicted considerable damage on the infrastructure of the Japanese industry on the home islands that was supplying Japan's military.

Nevertheless, a further modification of tactics resulted in the B-29s concentrating largely on incendiary attacks against major Japanese cities, rather than solely on pin-point strikes against factories or similar targets. Although these incendiary attacks were not new (the first had been flown, against Tokyo, on 9 March 1945), following the destruction of significant point targets like the Nakajima plant at Musashi the bombers were unleashed on the Japanese cities in area bombing with incendiary bombs. This rendered escort impossible when the raids were carried out at night, thus allowing the Iwo Jima fighter force to be freed up for fighter sweeps across the Japanese home islands and other areas without the need on every mission to protect the bombers. However, in addition to the obvious dangers and hardships of the long-range missions from Iwo Jima, there were other factors that made the Mustang operations difficult. One was the interminable volcanic dust that blew around the island or was whipped up by propellers, which could fill air intakes and made maintenance a difficult task. Another potential hazard was the weather. Violent storms were sometimes encountered, and on 1 June a Superfortress escort mission turned into a disaster when the Mustang escort flew into a huge mass of cloud. A number of elements attempted to abort the mission, but in the ensuing series of collisions in the clouds no fewer than 27 Mustangs were lost

World War Two was brought to a close with the dropping of the two atomic bombs on Hiroshima and Nagasaki in August 1945 and the subsequent Japanese surrender, but the Mustang had contributed greatly to the overall defeat of the Axis powers in all parts of the world where there had been significant fighting. The end of the conflict, however, left the many Mustangs around the world with their main reason for existence suddenly concluded. These apparently brand new Merlin-engined Mustangs, all from Inglewood P-51D-20-NA production, were photographed just after the atomic bombs were dropped, seemingly prior to unit assignment although it is thought that at least one of them had been delegated to the 348th FG *(Photo: USAAF)*

with only five of their pilots surviving, the largest single loss of Mustangs in the theatre.

The 15th and 21st Fighter Groups were joined by a further Mustang-equipped group in April 1945, this being the highest-numbered group to fly the Mustang, and the last to be formed on the P-51 specifically for combat. The 506th Fighter Group was activated on 21 October 1944, and after training in Florida the group moved to the Pacific in February to April 1945. Based initially on Tinian, the group was officially headquartered at the recently-completed North Field, Iwo Jima, from 24 April, and comprised the 457th, 458th, and 462nd Fighter Squadrons. During that time there were several administrative alterations to the command structure within the Seventh Air Force, and on paper at least the 506th came under the administration of the Twentieth Air Force, although controlled by VII Fighter Command as also were the 15th and 21st Fighter Groups. The group flew its first mission on 18 May, which was a fighter sweep against Japanese targets in the Bonin Islands. However, despite the B-29 bomber force being concentrated for the most part on incendiary raids during mid-1945, there were also a number of specific missions flown to high-value targets when weather conditions allowed and where pin-point bombing was required. The 506th gained a Distinguished Unit Citation for its escort cover of B-29s during 7-10 June 1945, when targets for the Superfortresses - including groups of the 58th Bomb Wing - included the army arsenal and other industrial areas at Osaka. The 506th could also boast the final P-51 Mustang ace of World War Two. He was Capt Abner Maurice Aust, Jr., of the 457th Fighter Squadron. Aust achieved his first victories on 16 July, when he shot down three Nakajima Ki-84 Hayate 'Franks' between Akenogahara and the city port of Tsu south of Nagoya. He followed this up on 10 August during a fighter sweep over the home islands (a planned B-29 raid that day had been put on hold due to the Japanese apparently showing signs of making peace), when he shot down two Mitsubishi A6M 'Zekes' in the Tokyo area.

The dropping of the atomic bombs by specially-configured B-29s of the 509th Composite Group on Hiroshima (6 August) and Nagasaki (9 August) at last brought some of those at the head of Japan's military to their senses, and the possibility of an end at last to World War Two grew more likely. On 14 August 1945, while Japanese officials examined the American surrender terms communicated several days before, aerial activity was still taking place over areas controlled by the Japanese and over the Japanese home islands themselves. In one of the last actions to take place of the whole war that involved Mustangs, a flight from the 110th Tactical Reconnaissance Squadron including the unit's CO, Maj George Noland, became involved in an air battle with several Japanese fighters over Japan. Noland, flying Dallas-built F-6K 44-12833, shot down two of the Japanese aircraft, with six of the Japanese being claimed by the reconnaissance pilots. These were quite probably the last enemy aircraft credited to Mustang pilots in the Second World War. It was almost three years to the day since Flying Officer Hollis Hills in his Allison-engined No.414 Squadron Mustang Mk I had shot down near Dieppe in France the first enemy aircraft to fall to the guns of a Mustang. It had been a long war for the Mustang, but the final victory that it had so helped to win was not far away. On 15 August 1945 Mustangs were again in action over the Japanese home islands, with the 15th FG making a fighter sweep in the Nagoya area. During that day the Japanese finally accepted the Allied surrender terms, and the Second World War came to its end with the signing of the formal Japanese surrender aboard the USS Missouri on 2 September 1945 in Tokyo Bay.

The top-scoring ace of the Seventh Army Air Force was Capt (later Maj) Robert 'Todd' Moore of the 15th Fighter Group, with 12 aerial victories, 11 of these being achieved in Mustangs. Moore originally flew P-40 Warhawks with the 45th Fighter Squadron, but later flew Mustangs with the 78th FS before returning to the then-Mustang equipped 45th FS. He named his assigned aircraft 'Stinger', and he is seen here with P-51D-20-NA 44-63483 'Stinger VII' of the 45th FS, with which he achieved six victories
*(Photo: USAAF)*

# The RAF's Merlin-Mustangs

## Chapter 5

It was in order to satisfy Britain's increasingly desperate needs for significant numbers of modern, high-performance fighters to counter Nazi Germany that the Mustang had been created in the first place. As described in Part 1 of this two-part 'Modellers' Datafile' on the Mustang, which covered Allison-engined Mustangs, the RAF first began to operate the Mustang in the summer of 1942. The type proved to be an excellent Tac/R (Tactical Reconnaissance) aircraft, able to fulfil this demanding mainly low-level, long-range role whilst at the same time being capable of looking after itself with ease if confronted by the Luftwaffe. Indeed, Allison-Mustangs continued with the RAF in this vital tasking right up to the end of the war in Europe, and the RAF in fact could have done with many more of these excellent low-level aircraft – the ending of Allison-Mustang production in the US being quite unwelcome for the British in that respect.

However, although Allison-engined Mustangs persisted in RAF service in North-west Europe, albeit in dwindling numbers, right to the end of World War Two, the British also operated a significant number of Merlin-powered Mustangs as well. This included both 'razorback' and bubble-canopy aircraft, and of course the famous Malcolm Hood of British design and manufacture was comparatively widely used on P-51B/C Mustangs of the USAAF in Europe as well as on their British counterparts. British procurement of the Merlin-Mustang started somewhat later than that for the USAAF. The initial, Inglewood-built P-51B Mustangs that were intended for the RAF were known as the Mustang Mk III. Later, Britain also received Dallas-built P-51C models, but these were similarly known as Mk III Mustangs. At least 18 RAF squadrons eventually flew the Mk III. Serial numbers allocated for the Mk III production began with FB100, and 1,011 Mk IIIs were actually intended under Lend-Lease for delivery to Britain (at least, that is the number of serial numbers that were allocated in

several major blocks of serials, but a number of P-51Bs were later given British serial numbers in the batch SR406 to SR440, while some were not delivered through cancellation or due to crashes - for example to KH687 - before delivery; a more complete listing of the British serial numbers is included in the Appendices at the end of this Book), and there was some 'juggling' of the planned British contract aircraft to fulfil USAAF needs. It has also been suggested that some negotiation between British and US officials resulted in a number of 'deals' being struck, in which some Spitfires were allocated to US fighter units in return for British use of a number of the Mk III-type Mustangs. The number of Mk III Mustangs that actually reached Britain was probably something over 900 (910 has been suggested by a number of historians), but may well have been around the 850 mark.

In any case, initial deliveries of the Mustang Mk III were made in late 1943, and prior to operational entry, as was customary and necessary, trials on the new Mustang type were conducted at the A&AEE at Boscombe Down. The first Mk III to reach Boscombe Down was FX908 in October 1943, and was followed by approximately 11 other Mk IIIs in the following months. Testing confirmed a number of performance figures, including a maximum take-off weight of 9,190 lb (4,168 kg), which showed some growth compared to the figure of 8,622 lb (3,911 kg) for the Allison-engined Mustang Mk I. The Mk III's range on internal fuel of 150 gallons (682 litres) was found to be 1,045 miles (1,682 km), which was easily more than any contemporary British fighter. Maximum speed, tested with FX953, was 450mph (724 km/h) at 28,000 ft (8,534 m) – an excellent figure for its day. Attempts were made to try to overcome the gun jamming problems that were encountered principally by US-operated P-51B/C Mustangs. To this end a Mustang Mk III (FZ103) was used for gun-heating experimental work, and also had a device fitted for assisting the

The Mustang was originally designed and built for British front-line use, and Allison-engined Mustangs served the RAF well from the summer of 1942 onwards, the first operations of RAF Mustangs being flown in May 1942. Britain later became a major user of the Merlin-Mustang as well, with the type entering British service in late 1943/early 1944. This included employment in the Mediterranean as well as North-west Europe. In the MTO, No.260 Squadron, one of whose Mustang Mk.III fighter-bombers is seen here wearing the squadron's 'HS' code letters, was an important user while based in Italy. There is some debate amongst historians as to whether it was No.260 or No.213 Squadron which was the first to fly the Mustang Mk.III in actual combat in the MTO. No.213 Squadron, based in Egypt, received some Allison-engined Mustangs as a prelude to Merlin-Mustang operations, and has often claimed to have been first - having been considerable but friendly rivalry between these highly-professional and successful units *(Photo: Malcolm V. Lowe Collection)*

belt-feeding of the guns. Unfortunately while flying during these trials in July 1944 one of the Mustang's wings detached, and the pilot was lucky to survive the subsequent involuntary bale-out. Trials with a variety of weapons were also carried out, including underwing 500 lb (227 kg) bombs, but for some reason attempts were made to fly with a bomb under one wing, and an external fuel tank under the other – perhaps not surprisingly this created unenviable directional characteristics.

Aircraft intended for operational units were initially assigned to squadrons of No.122 Wing at RAF Gravesend in Kent (most of the British bases subsequently used by RAF Merlin-Mustangs were officially under RAF administration, unlike those British airfields where many US Merlin-Mustang units operated which were nominally US-controlled). No.122 Wing was assigned to the 2nd Tactical Air Force and comprised Nos.19, 65 and 122 Squadrons, all of which were previously equipped with Spitfires. The first aircraft to arrive did so just before Christmas 1943, and was allocated to No. 65 Squadron. The early British Mustang Mk IIIs were not fitted with the additional 85 US gallon fuselage tank that was to prove troublesome in US service, resulting in their endurance being less than that of the Mustangs serving with US squadrons. This did not pose a serious problem because the RAF did not at that time have a long-range fighter requirement on the scale of the USAAF's growing and increasingly perceived needs, and in the event US fighter units as previously described came to have specific priority on P-51B/C output. Indeed, the USAAF received some of the Mustangs originally intended for Britain when US production began to lag behind the suddenly-expanding US requirement for the Merlin-Mustang as a bomber escort in Europe. Illustrating how valuable the Mustang had suddenly become to the Eighth Air Force's bomber campaign, the USAAF actually requested that a number of the RAF's Mustang Mk III squadrons should fly as escorts in support of some of the early 1944 US bomber missions. This was all a far cry from the opposition that the Mustang had initially received from some in the Army Air Force.

## Important Differences

Unfortunately the Mustang Mk III suffered from several teething problems as it entered RAF service. The use for the pilot of British oxygen equipment coupled to the US system installed in the Mustang resulted in the need for a number of alterations. Oil and coolant leaks were also encountered, with the propeller shaft having a particular tendency to throw oil. This was eventually traced to poor seals, worsened by the RAF practice of diluting lubricant with fuel to allow easier starting in cold weather – a practice that North American Aviation back at Inglewood could never have foreseen. Although the Mustang's cockpit was comparatively roomy, particularly compared to types such as the Messerschmitt Bf 109, an early problem noticed by RAF pilots as well as their US counterparts was the lack of visibility and

restriction of head movement by the heavily framed sideways-hinging canopy of the P-51B/C. Help was already at hand, however. The British company of R. Malcolm Ltd. forever associated itself with the Mustang story by designing and producing a neat, unframed bulbous canopy which came to be known as the 'Malcolm Hood'. This excellent piece of engineering not only improved visibility in all possible directions manyfold, it also had the merit of allowing easier ingress and egress of the Mustang by replacing the cumbersome framed canopy of the standard production P-51B/P-51C, and it gave a little more headroom for taller pilots. Initial tests (it is widely believed that Mustang Mk IA FD473 was involved in an early installation) proved the effectiveness of the new canopy, and production was initiated – although these canopies were always in short supply, and were much sought-after. They started to reach RAF units in around February 1944.

British and Commonwealth pilots, particularly those who were used to the comparatively docile and pleasant-handling Allison-engined Mustang, found the new Merlin-powered Mustangs something of a handful until their handling and power-on vices had been encountered and mastered. Nevertheless the Mustang was popular with many pilots who had previously flown the Spitfire, for a number of specific reasons. The former's wide-track landing gear was far more suited to the rather austere airfields that the tactical Mustang pilots sometimes encountered. Similarly, the far greater endurance and range of the Mustang was a step up compared to the Spitfire, and it certainly had a roomier cockpit in comparison with the Spitfire. All things are relative, however, and many of the former Spitfire pilots were loath to give up their beloved Supermarine fighters until the Merlin-Mustang had thoroughly proven itself.

The RAF first took its Merlin-engined Mustangs into combat on 15 February 1944, when Nos.19 and 65 Squadrons flew a morning sweep over the northern French coast. This was a fairly typical shakedown exercise, but in the afternoon of the same day the two squadrons were in action again, when they escorted US heavy bombers attacking V1 launch sites in the Pas-de-Calais area. This was the start of comparatively regular escort duties with US bomber units during the next few weeks, which gradually became more ambitious and longer-legged. On the 8 March USAAF Berlin mission, RAF Mustangs flew to meet returning Eighth Air Force bombers 120 miles (193 km) west of the German capital. Although the British contribution was often no more than some three dozen Mustangs on these operations, and they were rarely situated to engage Luftwaffe fighters, they did occasionally deter them from the US formations. In the event this escort work did not last long, and by April the Eighth Air Force's Mustang force had grown to several operational squadrons which could cover the demands of bomber escort themselves, in concert with existing P-47 Thunderbolt and P-38 Lightning units. This allowed the RAF squadrons to be redirected to operations of a more tactical nature,

A neat echelon formation of No.19 Squadron Mk.III Mustangs with Malcolm Hoods. This famous RAF unit made good use of its Merlin Mustangs, serving as a part of 2nd TAF during and after the D-Day period, and later flying as a part of the Peterhead Wing in Scotland from February 1945. The Malcolm Hood conferred a number of benefits in increased vision for the pilot, but because of its shape it also gave a little more room in the cockpit for tall pilots *(Photo: R.L. Ward Collection)*

as the run-up to the planned invasion of the north of France continued. By that time the RAF had received sufficient Merlin-Mustangs to establish a second British-based three-squadron wing, No.133 Wing. Like No.122 Wing, it was assigned to the 2nd Tactical Air Force, and was based at Coolham in Sussex from early April 1944. It comprised one British (No.129) and two Polish-manned squadrons (Nos.306 and 315), and like those of No.122 Wing they had previously been equipped with Spitfires. Indeed, the Polish connection with the Mustang was a significant one. Many Polish nationals had joined the RAF to continue the fight against the Germans after their country had been overrun in September 1939, and eventually the Polish contingent within the RAF numbered several fighter squadrons. The Poles fought bravely and with considerable tenacity, and their operations while flying Mustangs are an often overlooked but nonetheless significant part of the Mustang's story.

## Fighter-bomber Operations

With the USAAF increasingly able to meet its requirement for Mustangs to escort its daylight heavy bomber raids from England, the spring of 1944 saw the RAF's Mustang Mk IIIs employed primarily in tactical missions across the Channel. These included a large number of targets, and the Mustangs would often carry two 500 lb (227 kg) bombs, although escort missions were also flown for Allied medium bombers performing tactical missions. On

occasion the RAF's Mustangs additionally escorted RAF Coastal Command strike aircraft and flew anti-shipping patrols, for which the Mustang's endurance made it ideal. In the spring of 1944 the Polish-manned No.316 Squadron converted to the Mustang Mk III from Spitfires and was initially tasked primarily to give cover for Coastal Command strike aircraft (particularly Bristol Beaufighters) operating off the Dutch and German coastlines.

The coming of D-Day on 6 June 1944 witnessed the RAF's Merlin-Mustangs – like the existing Allison-engined Mustangs of the RAF – fully involved in the intense aerial activity of the Allied invasion. By that time No.122 Wing had relocated from Gravesend to Ford in Hampshire (later the site of the infamous open prison). The Mustangs flew cover for the second wave of troop-carriers and glider-towing transports, and also escorted Coastal Command Beaufighters. Two pilots of No.129 Squadron succeeded in jointly shooting down a Focke-Wulf Fw 190. On 7 June, a number of No.133 Wing's Mustangs became involved in some of the most intense aerial fighting of the D-Day period. In a number of air battles inland from the Allied beach-heads, 17 Bf 109s and Fw 190s were claimed shot down, albeit for the loss of four Mustangs. During subsequent days both Wings had a number of successful engagements with the Luftwaffe – it is something of a myth that the Luftwaffe was not active during the D-Day period, for several air battles and smaller skirmishes took place during that time, even before Luftwaffe reinforcements

Probably photographed at a Maintenance Unit in Italy or the Middle East, this RAF Mustang MK.III, serial number FB33?, carries underwing long-range fuel tanks with prominent shackles attached. Although RAF Mustangs generally did not fly the type of long-range bomber escort missions more commonly pursued by US Mustangs, they were sometimes called upon to perform this type of work, and were often involved in protecting medium bombers *(Photo: R.L. Ward Collection)*

could arrive in the Northern France area. Nevertheless, the RAF Mustangs were primarily tasked with tactical missions, which they performed with great capability, and air-to-air combat was not officially encouraged unless really necessary. During that time the Mustangs remained based in Southern Britain, although on occasion Mustangs would stop off to refuel at the increasing number of airstrips that the Allies were creating in Normandy following the invasion. Eventually, in keeping with other Allied tactical air assets, a move was later made over to the Continent. Starting on 25/26 June, No.122 Wing gradually moved some 60 of its serviceable aircraft over to an area inland from the Normandy beachhead, to the airstrip at Martragny (B-7) between the historic towns of Bayeux and Caen.

No.133 Wing, however, remained in England, moving temporarily to Holmsley South in Hampshire later in June (c.22 to 25 June), before a move to Ford before the end of the month. The wing was later employed, as a supplement to the Air Defence of Great Britain organisation (the temporary and much disliked renaming of RAF's Fighter Command) to mount defensive action against the increasing threat of V1 flying bombs. Under Operation 'Diver', the Mustangs operated with other RAF fighters and in concert with anti-aircraft guns against these unmanned and unguided weapons, which were being dispatched against England and especially London in growing numbers from launch sites in North-eastern France. During July, No.316 Squadron was moved from its base at Coltishall in Norfolk to join in these defensive sorties, temporarily operating from West Malling in Kent and then Friston in Sussex. In two months the squadron's pilots set the highest score for V1 flying bombs shot down by any Mustang squadron by downing (or at least claiming) 74, before returning to Coltishall in the autumn. The highest-scoring V1 ace in the squadron was W/O Tadeusz Szymanski, who brought down eight (some sources list nine) of the weapons, in addition to 1.5 aerial victories against real aeroplanes. In fact bringing down flying bombs was hazardous work due to the risk of the V1 exploding when fired at. Mustangs had something of a speed advantage amongst Allied fighters and could catch flying bombs in a shallow dive, the V1s normally flying at speeds approaching 400 mph (644 km/h). If gunfire did not work, some pilots resorted to trying to send the bombs out of control by tipping them over with their wingtips – one of Szymanski's successful encounters ended this way. The Mustangs often flew standing patrols, and under the guidance of ground-based radar could be vectored onto the small fast-moving targets. In the continuing attempt to gain greater speeds for the Mustangs some experimental but not particularly successful use was made of the then new 130 octane

fuel (rather than the 100 octane normally used – unfortunately the higher-rated fuel sometimes caused engine damage including burnt-out valves). Nevertheless, Merlin-Mustangs proved to be useful against the flying bombs, bringing down at least 258. This total included five destroyed by the 363rd Fighter Group of the Ninth Air Force which also became involved in anti-V1 work for a short time. Only Spitfire Mk XIV and Hawker Tempest Mk V fighters achieved more successes against the flying bombs, and 21 Mustang pilots became V1 aces, of which 16 were Poles. This significant contribution to the defence of London and the Home Counties by the Mustang-flying Polish airman is sadly all too easily overlooked nowadays.

On the Continent, No.122 Wing's Mustangs were at the same time continuing their tactical work in support of the Allied armies. In mid-July the wing began to move from B-7 to a new landing ground, B-12 near the commune of Ellon just beside the road from Bayeux to Villers-Bocage. This was to keep up with the changing ground situation as Allied forces began to move outwards from the initial gains in that area following D-Day. No.19 Squadron was the first to move on the 15th, but the action was premature and the Germans successfully shelled the area during the night, killing several squadron personnel and damaging a number of Mustangs. Further shelling followed as Mustangs from the wing's other two squadrons arrived, and it was only on the 19th that the wing could properly take up residence. It was while flying from Ellon that Mustangs of the wing employed 1,000 lb (454 kg) bombs for the first time. This was a major development for the Mustang Mk III, which could just about manage two of these bombs, but because of the local tactical situation the Mustangs did not need to fly with full fuel tanks on all missions, allowing the carriage of these weapons. Nevertheless, longer missions were also frequently carried out. On 2 August Mustangs of the wing escorted de Havilland Mosquitoes of No.2 Group which were carrying out a precision raid on a barracks in Poitiers south of the River Loire. As

Photographed on or just after D-Day in June 1944, this Mustang Mk.III, serial number FZ196, was assigned to No.306 Squadron, a Polish-manned RAF squadron. Operating the Merlin-Mustang from the spring of 1944 until early 1947, this unit was one of several Polish-manned Mustang squadrons in the RAF. The aircraft carries full black and white 'invasion stripes' on its fuselage and wings, and the code UZ-D
*(Photo: R.L. Ward Collection)*

Squadrons of the 2nd TAF closely followed the fighting on the ground after D-Day in June 1944, and were often required to operate from very austere landing grounds that were hastily prepared by engineers, or from battered former Luftwaffe airfields. Here, Mustang Mk.III FZ190 coded QV-A of No.19 Squadron, RAF, is being worked on at the Advanced Landing Ground numbered B-12 at Ellon. A ubiquitous RAF-style starter trolley is in the foreground – it is plugged into the Mustang's fuselage just below the letters 'QV'. Situated to the south of Bayeux in Normandy (in the north of France), Ellon was used from mid-July 1944 onwards by No.19 Squadron and was one of the hastily constructed landing grounds that, once the fighting had moved on, quickly returned to its previous relative tranquillity. The battered church in the background was later repaired and is there to this day *(Photo: R.L. Ward Collection)*

the ground situation became more fluid, the Mustangs were able to extend their coverage as the Allies began to break out, and an important new mission became the bombing of barges on the River Seine to prevent them being used by the retreating Germans. This sometimes involved the use of 1,000 lb (454 kg) bombs, but during this time several of the wing's Mustangs came under attack from US-operated fighters, the old problem of aircraft recognition for US pilots once again apparently coming to the fore. A result was the abandoning of the standard upperwing red and blue circular national insignia on some aircraft in favour of red/white/blue roundels in an attempt to prevent these occurrences.

Many ground-attack sorties were flown by the wing's Merlin-Mustangs against German ground forces, and on some occasions large numbers of German fighters were encountered, the Mustangs being able to look after themselves in these encounters. On 20 August, for example, Nos.19 and 65 Squadrons fought a large air battle with Fw 190s during a fighter sweep in the Paris and Fontainebleau areas, the Mustangs claiming nine confirmed victories for the loss of one of their own. Three of the Focke-Wulfs were claimed by No.65 Squadron's Flt Lt L.M.A. Burra-Robinson which made him a Mustang ace, having previously shot down two Heinkel He 111s in April 1944. By that time the ground situation was improving steadily for the Allies, and the wing moved to keep up with the advances that were being made. This resulted in a brief move to Saint-André (B-24) in early September, before the wing moved to B-40 Beauvais to the north of Paris. Even this was too slow to keep up with the Allied armies, and from 9 September the wing moved into B-60 Grimbergen to the north of Brussels in Belgium, illustrating how fast the Allies were moving forward at that time. However, while at Grimbergen, although tactical operations continued - including attacks on the rail network - the Mustangs were additionally tasked with air cover for the massive Allied airborne operation to capture bridges in Holland over the River Rhine. This involved operations over Nijmegen and Arnhem, and a number of air battles ensued with German fighters. However, despite their presence being of importance to these operations, a major change for the three Mustang squadrons was about to take place.

By September 1944 RAF Bomber Command was increasingly carrying out daylight raids against targets in the western part of Germany. Fighter escort and support was necessary for these missions, and to meet this growing requirement No.122 Wing's Mustang squadrons were withdrawn from Belgium in late September and their involvement with 2nd Tactical Air Force ended. The final Mustang aerial victory for the No.122 Wing Mustangs on the Continent was achieved by No.122 Squadron on 27 September with the shoot-down of a Bf 109G in the Arnhem area. The three No.122 Wing squadrons then left Grimbergen,

Nos.19 and 122 on the 28th and No.65 Squadron the following day. They joined No.150 Wing to become a part of the Air Defence of Great Britain organisation, and were subsequently based at Matlask in Norfolk. The Mustangs were replaced within No.122 Wing at Grimbergen by Hawker Tempest squadrons (Nos.3, 56 and 486 Squadrons). The following month No.133 Wing, still with Mustangs, was also moved into East Anglia, taking up station at Andrews Field in Essex, where it was later joined by the former No.122 Wing squadrons and No.316 Squadron from Coltishall to form a 'super' wing of seven Merlin-Mustang squadrons. This allowed for simplified maintenance, supply and administration, and also provided the luxury of concrete runways for the winter months, a facility unavailable at the Norfolk airfields.

Nevertheless, with the increasing need for long-range fighters at that stage in the war, the RAF proceeded to convert six further fighter squadrons to Merlin-Mustangs during late 1944/early 1945. These included Nos.64, 118, 126, 165, 234, and 309 Squadrons. All were former Spitfire operators, except for the Polish-manned No.309 Squadron, which had temporarily converted onto Hawker Hurricanes from its venerable Allison-engined Mustangs before the changeover occurred. In late 1944 a second 'super wing' was formed, this time at Bentwaters in Suffolk, which was an airfield originally constructed for US heavy bombers but never used to house them. This expansion of the RAF Mustang Mk III fighter force to some 250 aircraft during the autumn of 1944 was made possible by substantial further deliveries of new Mustangs from the US. Many of these aircraft were from NAA's Dallas production, Dallas manufacture of the 'razorback' Mustang continuing for a several months (up to July 1944) after the Inglewood facility had changed over (in February/March 1944) to the 'bubble' canopy P-51D. In the event over a third of the total Dallas production was supplied to Britain. It is interesting to note that by that time the USAAF in Europe had largely re-equipped its combat squadrons with the newer P-51D model.

## Merlin-Mustangs compared to Axis fighters

In an interesting series of comparative trials, the Air Fighting Development Unit (AFDU) conducted a comprehensive test with a captured Bf 109G-6 and a late production Mustang Mk III. These trials also included comparisons with a captured Fw 190A, and several Allied fighters as well, including the Spitfire Mk IX, Spitfire Mk XIV, and Tempest Mk V. The AFDU report was dated 8 March 1944, and it sung the praises of the Mustang. Regarding the Bf 109, it was found that the altitude for maximum performance from the Bf 109G's Daimler Benz DB 605A engine was 16,000 feet (4,877m), but at that height the Mustang was 30 mph (48 km/h) faster in level flight. The Mustang was also faster, by 50 mph (80 km/h) at 30,000 feet (9,144 m). Like several other Axis fighters, the

Well-known for its 'shark-mouth' decorated Curtiss P-40 Kittyhawks in the Middle East, No.112 Squadron, RAF, began flying Merlin-powered Mustangs as replacements for the Kittyhawks in the summer of 1944. By that time the squadron was involved in operations in southern Europe, and successfully continued the 'shark-mouth' tradition by painting its Mustangs in the same way. The Mustang did not have the pronounced 'chin' air intake of the Kittyhawk, but nonetheless the effect was still very impressive, as displayed here by Mustang Mk.III, FB241/GA-Q. Mustangs bearing the individual letter 'Q' in No.112 Squadron were usually flown by Flt Lt Raymond Hearn, one of the unit's most celebrated pilots
*(Photo: R.L. Ward Collection)*

Bf 109 had a slightly better rate of climb up to some 20,000 feet (6,096 m), but from there upwards the Mustang gained a slight advantage. When 'zoom climbed' (employing speed obtained in a dive to increase the speed of climb) there was no noticeable difference in their respective rates. In a dive the Mustang Mk III could draw steadily away from the Bf 109G. In turning manoeuvres the Merlin-powered Mustang could out-turn the Bf 109, but there was little to choose between them in rate of roll. The firepower of the Messerschmitt was much heavier than the Mustang, with three 20mm cannon and two 13mm machine guns (although operationally the Bf 109G would need underwing 'gondolas' to mount the additional two 20mm cannon, in the Rüstsatz 6 add-on modification, thus slightly impairing overall performance), but the German fighter had nothing like the Mustang's endurance, showing only some 90 minutes under combat conditions – a paltry amount compared to the long-legged Mustang. The Bf 109's cockpit was also far more cramped, and its pilot also had a comparatively restricted view from the cockpit. In the trials made with the Fw 190A, which was perhaps the most formidable of German fighters in the mid- to late-war period, the Mustang was found to be nearly 50 mph (80 km/h) faster up to 28,000 feet (8,534 m), which increased to an excellent 70 mph (113 km/h) above that height. Little overall difference was found in rate of climb, but there was a slight advantage for the Mustang in turns. The German fighter had a vastly superior rate of roll, but the Fw 190 was very capably out-dived by the Mustang. Overall the Mustang came out very well from these comparative trials, and compared to the Tempest and Spitfire Mk XIV which were said to have in comparison 'no endurance' (!), the Mustang looked very good with its excellent range capabilities. Indeed, the report concluded: "The Mustang III is a delightful and easy aircraft to fly. Its advantages over the Spitfire IX lie in a considerably greater range and greater all-round speed. It can outstrip the Fw 190 in a dive, followed if desired by a shallow climb. Its only serious drawback is a slightly less rate of climb than the Spitfire IX, particularly at height." However, bearing in mind the speed of the Mustang, particularly in a dive, the report also concluded: "A pilot needs to understand the effect of compressibility speed. Practices should not be attempted."

## Fighter Command Merlin-Mustangs

The two Fighter Command Mustang airfields, Andrews Field and Bentwaters, were the main source of RAF long-range fighters for the remainder of hostilities in North-west Europe. Each had over 120 aircraft, illustrating how important it was to base these large numbers of Mustangs at sites once considered for heavy bombers, as there was enough room to house so many fighters and the infrastructure needed to operate them. The principal task of the Mustangs was to escort RAF heavy bombers to the Ruhr and further-flung targets involving deep penetration into hostile airspace. Compared to the experiences of the US escort Mustangs, the RAF's escort missions were more often than not comparatively uneventful in respect of contact with the enemy, although in the

final six months of the war the Luftwaffe began to take an active interest in the somewhat looser formations of the RAF Lancaster and Halifax bombers that were the subjects of the escort missions. However, by that time the German fighter force was considerably depleted, resulting in few large air battles compared to the situation for American Merlin-Mustang escort pilots earlier in 1944.

Nevertheless, some major dogfights did take place. On 12 December 1944, over 80 Mustangs from Andrews Field provided cover for 140 Lancasters of No.3 Group flying to bomb the Ruhrstahl steelworks at Witten. On that occasion the Luftwaffe responded in force with a mass attack from above by 40 to 50 Bf 109s. The Merlin-engined Mustangs engaged in combat, claiming five of the enemy plus two 'probables' for the loss of one Mustang, but the attack resulted in eight bombers being lost and the fighter attack helped to scatter the bombing, resulting in substantial damage to the town itself with no hits on the steelworks. On 23 March 1945 Luftwaffe jet fighters made their first concerted attack on an RAF daylight bomber formation. Mustangs from Bentwaters were on hand to observe 15 to 20 Me 262s come rapidly in on the flank of a Lancaster force bombing a bridge at Bremen. The Mustangs immediately dived after the jets but the superior speed of the Messerschmitts allowed most to escape. Nevertheless, Flying Officer A Yeardley of No.126 Squadron was able to open fire on one of the jets, which was observed to dive into the ground. This was the first known jet victory achieved by an RAF Mustang. The Andrews Field and Bentwaters squadrons were even more successful on 9 April when three of the twin-jets were claimed during an attack by around eight to ten Me 262s on RAF No.5 Group Lancasters bombing oil storage tanks and U-boat shelters at Hamburg. Several of the escorting Mustangs from Nos.64, 306 and 309 Squadrons engaged the jets, and three of the Messerschmitts were shot down by Polish pilots of No.309 Squadron. The following day, while on an escort to Leipzig, RAF

Displaying to advantage the 'shark-mouth' painted on the lower forward fuselages of many of its Mustang Mk.IIIs, this No.112 Squadron Mustang was photographed at Lavariano in Italy in the summer of 1945 after the end of the war. There were slight variations in the mouth design from one aircraft to another
*(Photo: R.L. Ward Collection)*

Proudly displaying a red and white Polish insignia on its nose, Mustang Mk.III FZ149/UZ-W was operated by the Polish-manned No.306 Squadron, RAF. The aircraft has a white spinner, nose and wing identification bands, and the then-standard scheme of Dark Green and Ocean Grey on its uppersurfaces, and Medium Sea Grey underneath, although it may have originally have been painted in the US equivalents to these paints. It also has a Malcolm Hood. The location of the photograph was originally thought to be Church Fenton but is now believed to be Andrews Field, in October 1944 *(Photo: R.L. Ward Collection)*

Several MK.III Mustangs from No.309 Squadron, RAF, lined up in December 1944 or January 1945. This was one of the Polish-manned squadrons of the RAF, and a number of the unit's Mustangs can be seen, including WC-J, WC-F, and SR418/WC-D. No.309 was unique amongst the Polish squadrons in flying Allison and Merlin-engined Mustangs during its long time on the type, having originally become a Mustang-operator in the summer of 1942
*(Photo: R.L. Ward Collection)*

Mustangs had their only known combat with Messerschmitt Me 163 rocket fighters. One was intercepted, and as it attempted to dive away from the bombers it was somehow caught and shot down by an Australian pilot, Flying Officer John Haslope of No.165 Squadron. On return to Bentwaters his Mustang Mk III was found to be in a very poor state of repair, with several inches more dihedral on the wings where Haslope had managed to pull out of the dive that had given him enough speed to catch the rocket fighter. It was the seventh and last Me 163 that was confirmed destroyed by Mustang pilots, the others falling to the guns of US-operated Mustangs. Haslope was awarded the DFC for his achievement, but sadly having become a civil airline pilot after the war he was tragically killed in Australia during 1951 while flying a Trans-Australia Airlines Douglas DC-3 airliner.

In addition to the Mustang III, the British also received significant numbers of the 'bubble' canopy P-51D/K, which became known as the Mustang Mk IV in British service (interestingly, the designation Mk IVA has sometimes been used for the P-51K examples, and some official documents of the period refer to this designation, although it is often ignored by historians). The USAAF had overriding priority on the P-51D/K models, but a very early Mustang Mk IV (TK589, the first Mk IV to arrive in Britain, ex-44-13332, without a fin dorsal extension) had reached Boscombe Down for evaluation as early as June 1944. It was discovered in the A&AEE's testing that the Mk IV was the heaviest of all the Mustang operational variants to serve with the RAF, weighing in at 9,982lb (4,528 kg) maximum with its internal fuel tanks full (at least 220 gallons effective – c. 1,000 litres). It was also found to be 25 mph (40 km/h) faster than earlier Mustangs. Nevertheless, Boscombe Down test pilots additionally discovered that the Mk IV had a number of vices compared to the Mk III, and limits were placed on the amount of 'g' that could be pulled in dive pull-outs due to elevator vibration – one wonders if the loss of Col Thomas Christian, Jr., the CO of the Eighth Air Force's 361st Fighter Group during a dive-bombing attack in August 1944 had any bearing on these conclusions. Four Mustang Mk IVs eventually served at Boscombe Down. Sadly one of these, KH648, was involved in a fatal accident in January 1945 when a gun bay panel departed the aircraft. This was one of four Mustangs of all types that were lost during their time at Boscombe Down, but the

only one that ended fatally.

In total, Britain received or was due to receive 876 Mk IV Mustangs, comprising 281 Mk IV and 595 Mk IVA (as with the Mk III, that is the number of serial numbers that were allocated). Serial numbers began with KH641. Although many of these reached Britain for the gradual re-equipment of the Mustang Mk III squadrons, in practice the two types operated alongside each other in some squadrons – and, as related later in this Book, some were sent to the Far East where they were simply scrapped due to the end of the war. At least another 56 Mk IV intended deliveries were cancelled. The British Mk IV Mustangs were generally similar to their US-operated counterparts, but one difference was in the installation of APS-13 tail warning equipment. Sometimes called a 'tail warning radar', this was not a 'radar' in the modern sense with a large dish antenna and radome, but was a simple sender/receiver that somewhat crudely warned of aircraft to the rear. It visibly consisted of several small antennae projecting from the side of the fin on each side, and was installed on later US-operated Mustangs. Although the installation appears to have been carried on machines supplied to Britain, it was not wired in, as confirmed by a number of former British Mustang pilots.

A little-known aspect of the operations of the British-based RAF Merlin-powered Mustangs concerned operations near and over German-occupied Norway. As previously related, RAF Merlin-Mustangs sometimes flew as escorts for Coastal Command strike aircraft. Included in these operations were long-range missions from Scotland to the Norwegian coast, where the Coastal Command aircraft – Beaufighters and Mosquitoes including those from the well-known Banff Strike Wing – were tasked to attack German shipping including freighters carrying vital iron ore to Germany. Usually employing RAF Peterhead as their base, the Mustangs were often detached from squadrons based further south or were from temporary squadron-strength deployments, but in early 1945 the Peterhead detachment grew into a wing with the arrival of firstly No.65 (in January) and then No.19 Squadron (in February), both Mustang-equipped. Indeed, as stated earlier, No.65 had been the first RAF squadron to equip with the Mustang Mk IV. These Norwegian operations were particularly arduous for the Mustangs and their pilots. Flights across the North Sea between Scotland and Norway involved some two to two and a

Photographed at Lüneburg in Germany during May 1945, this No.126 Squadron, RAF, Mustang Mk.III was coded 5J-A and is believed to have been KH430. The aircraft illustrates the drab colouring of end of war era British Mustang Mk.III aircraft. Although the Mk.III Mustangs were intended to be painted in the US with American paint equivalents of British shades, some appear to have been re-painted in Britain with Dark Green and Ocean Grey on their uppersurfaces, and Medium Sea Grey below, although the use of mixed grey shades seems to have persisted even at that late stage of the conflict
*(Photo: M. Robinson via R.L. Ward)*

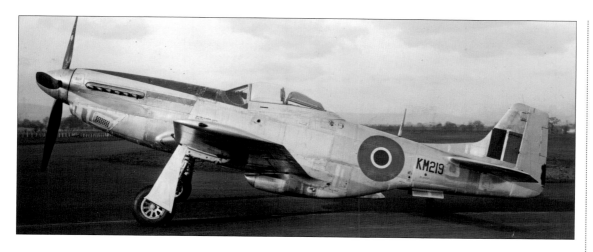

Unfortunately looking rather the worse for wear following its delivery voyage across the Atlantic by sea, Mustang Mk.IV KM219 shows off the lines of the RAF's equivalent to the P-51K with Aeroproducts propeller. These aircraft were sometimes known as Mk.IVA Mustangs, and the photograph was dated March 1945. A number of detail points can be seen in this picture, including the shroud around the six exhaust stacks (which was not fitted to all Merlin-engined Mustangs), the underwing pylon (only one of these was ever fitted under each wing, and the design went through a considerable evolution, with the final P-51D/K style being different to those fitted to previous marks), and the fuel filler port and ground line point just at the rear end of the sliding cockpit cover
*(Photo: R.L. Ward Collection)*

half hours over the open sea, and the flight out in company with the strike aircraft had to be made at as low a height as possible to avoid radar detection. Once over Norwegian waters, the RAF aircraft were at the mercy of anti-aircraft fire, as well as defending Luftwaffe fighters. These included Bf 109Gs and Fw 190As of the composite fighter wing JG 5, and some intense air battles ensued. The Bf 109G enjoyed a somewhat better turning circle at low speeds than the larger and heavier Mustang, and at the low levels that many of these combats took place the Germans were at an advantage of acceleration and climbing speed. The results were sometimes even in these low-level encounters, as discovered by the US Eighth Air Force's 4th Fighter Group which fulfilled some of these escort missions in August 1944 when the RAF Mustangs were otherwise engaged with anti-V1 operations. Indeed, almost right up to the end of the war intense operations were carried out along the Norwegian coastline, with Nos.19 and 65 Squadrons continuing to duel with JG 5 well into April 1945. Amongst the successful RAF pilots was the commanding officer of No.19 Squadron, Sqn Ldr Peter Hearne, whose final score in Mustangs was five aerial victories, making him a member of the select group of RAF Mustang aces.

Similarly little-known was the use of the Merlin-Mustang as a target-marker for heavy bombers. This was accomplished by the renowned RAF bomber pilot Wing Commander Leonard Cheshire, who had recognised the possibility of using a fast single-engined aircraft to accurately mark targets for oncoming heavy bombers. The Mustang appeared to be the ideal aircraft for the job, combining speed, range, and the ability to fight its way out of a difficult situation if the need arose. Cheshire first used a Mustang, borrowed from the USAAF and operated from RAF Woodhall Spa in Lincolnshire, to mark the Siracourt V-weapon storage site for No.617 Squadron and its Lancaster bombers on 25 June. Makeshift smoke-marking equipment was installed under the Mustang's wings and Cheshire successfully marked the target for the heavy bombers, despite having had no prior knowledge of flying the Mustang. The raid was a success, the Lancasters hitting

the site with 12,000 lb (5,445 kg) 'Tallboy' bombs. Following this accomplishment, Cheshire used a Mustang on two further occasions, in early July 1944, to mark targets for No.617 Squadron. Wing Commander J.B. Tait, who took on some of Cheshire's responsibilities when Cheshire's tour of duty ended, also used a Mustang as a target marker on at least one and possibly more occasions.

Before the end of the war in Europe, several further RAF squadrons were able to convert to the Mustang. Some began flying straight away the Mustang IV, while other flew a mix of the Mk III and Mk IV. They included No.154 (which only flew the type for a short time before disbanding at the end of March 1945), the Canadian-manned Nos.441 and 442 (although the former had received only a few examples before hostilities ceased, and did not fly them in combat), No.611 of the Royal Auxiliary Air Force, and the Polish-manned No.303. The latter flew one of the final RAF Mustang missions of the war, when it participated alongside other Mustang-equipped Polish squadrons including No.309 in an escort for RAF heavy bombers on 25 April in a raid on the famous mountain retreat of Adolf Hitler at Berchtesgaden. At the time of VE-Day in May 1945 there were 16 RAF Merlin Mustang squadrons in Britain with approximately 320 aircraft – although in comparison at that time the Eighth Air Force had around 1,600 Mustangs at its disposal.

## Merlin-Mustangs over the Mediterranean and Southern Europe

In addition to operations over North-west Europe, Merlin Mustangs also served with RAF and Commonwealth squadrons in the Mediterranean and Southern Europe theatre. The principal British tactical fighter in the MTO had for some time been versions of the Curtiss Kittyhawk (the RAF's equivalents of the Curtiss P-40 Warhawk family). A number of British squadrons had successfully operated the Kittyhawk in North Africa and in the early stages of the Italian campaign, but during 1944 as more Merlin-Mustangs became available the Mustang began to replace

Proudly showing the distinctive shark's teeth and eyes marking carried by many No.112 Squadron aircraft, Mustang Mk.IVA (P-51K) GA-S, serial number KH774 with Aeroproducts propeller, is illustrated wearing camouflage finish in this rare air-to-air image during 1945. The date of the photograph is believed to be May 1945
*(Photo: Malcolm V. Lowe Collection)*

Showing the uncuffed Aeroproducts propeller unit of the P-51K/Mustang Mk.IVA, this natural metal aircraft of No.112 Squadron wears the famed shark's teeth and eyes marking (otherwise known as a 'shark-mouth' or colloquially 'shark mouth') carried by many of the unit's Mustangs
*(Photo: Malcolm V. Lowe Collection)*

The Mustang Mk IVA of Wing Commander B. Eaton from No.239 Wing which included No.112 Squadron. It carried the name 'Marisa' on the 'bubble' canopy frame and Eaton's initials 'BAE' on the fuselage side, a privilege of RAF Wing Commanders
*(Photo: Malcolm V. Lowe Collection)*

Wing Commander James Storrar flew a personalised 'bubble' canopy Merlin-Mustang while in command of No.239 Wing in Italy during 1946, similar but not identical to this Mustang, KM232, which he flew earlier in Britain
*(Photo: Malcolm V. Lowe Collection)*

No.112 Squadron, a pioneer in the art of carrying 'shark mouth' insignia on the prominent lower fuselage air intake of its Kittyhawks. A real veteran of the fighting in North Africa and then Italy, No.112 received its Mustang Mk IIIs in the summer of 1944. Eventually several further squadrons converted to the Mustang Mk III in the MTO, including No.213 Squadron from the early summer of 1944, No.249 in the early autumn (this squadron received its first Mustangs in early September, to eventually replace its Spitfire Mk V complement), No.3 Squadron, Royal Australian Air Force (in November 1944), and No.5 Squadron, South African Air Force (in September 1944). All were operational on the type by the end of 1944, by which time some 277 Mustang Mk IIIs had been delivered in the MTO, and had become accustomed to flying tactical missions against a whole range of targets including communications, airfields, troop concentrations and armour and the many other tasks that fell to the capable and versatile Merlin-Mustangs. Some of these were flown with the aid of forward air controllers, who pin-pointed targets by radio from spotter light aircraft such as Piper L-4 Cubs or Austers. Level and dive-bombing missions were performed, and sometimes the Mustangs carried a 1,000 lb (454 kg) bomb beneath each wing, this being the maximum ordnance that could be safely carried although 500 lb (227 kg) bombs were far more common. Underwing unguided rocket projectiles were often available. These were usually mounted on individual launch rails, and were a somewhat cumbersome fitting that reduced the Mustang's performance and manoeuvrability – although this was not considered to be a

the venerable but much-loved Kittyhawk. The first MTO RAF squadron to re-equip with Merlin-Mustangs was No.260 Squadron, based at Cutella in southern Italy. This squadron received its first Mustang Mk IIIs in the spring of 1944, the transition from Kittyhawk to Mustang taking several weeks and involving some of the squadron's pilots picking up their new aircraft from Casablanca in North Africa where they had been shipped. No.260 Squadron was a part of No.239 Wing, which had slogged through the campaign in North Africa as a part of the RAF's Desert Air Force. Other constituent parts of this wing also converted to the Mustang during 1944. These included the famous

serious problem due to the relative lack of enemy fighter activity. Escort missions were also flown in support of Allied medium bombers and occasionally heavy bombers. Aerial combat against German and Republican Italian forces was particularly infrequent, and there was little chance for any of the British and Commonwealth pilots to run up impressive tallies of aerial victories.

In addition to operations over Italy, the MTO-based British and Commonwealth-manned Mustang squadrons also flew in combat over the Balkans from bases on the Adriatic coast of Italy. Some of these missions were in support of Yugoslav partisans, and in June 1944 a separate organisation within the Allied aerial command structure, the Balkan Air Force, was formed to specifically oversee these operations. Within the Balkan Air Force's No.283 Wing, Mustangs operated primarily with Nos.213 and 260 Squadrons. Indeed, in the spring of 1945 No.213 Squadron temporarily moved over to Yugoslavia in support of local operations against the increasingly isolated German occupying forces. During late 1944/early 1945 the 'bubble' canopy Mustang Mk IV started to become available, so that by the end of the year 46 had been delivered to the RAF and Commonwealth units in the MTO, with numbers increasing after the New Year to the extent that some of the squadrons had virtually fully re-equipped with this type by the time of the end of hostilities. As an illustration of how effective the Mustangs were as a part of the Allied tactical air effort in the Mediterranean theatre, on 5 May 1944 a combined force of Mustangs and Kittyhawks bombed – and successfully breached – the Pescara dam in Italy during an action that has subsequently received little publicity, but which was as audacious as the highly celebrated dams raid by No.617 Squadron Lancaster bombers in May 1943.

It is no reflection on the relative skills or tenacity of British fighter pilots compared to their American counterparts to point out that few RAF pilots actually became Mustang aces in aerial combat. RAF Mustangs were more often than not involved in tactical missions, where combats with enemy fighters were far fewer than in the large air battles at high altitude in which US Mustang pilots were often engaged. The top-scoring RAF Mustang ace was Flying Officer Maurice Pinches of No.122 Squadron. His 6.333 victories (some sources attribute him 6.5) were achieved mainly over Normandy in the D-Day period, including a Bf 109 on 17 June near Dreux. Just behind him was the Greek-born Flt Sgt Basilios Vassiliades of No.19 Squadron, who gained six (actually five and two shared) of his nine victories in Mustangs. There were seven recognised RAF Mustang aces (i.e. pilots who scored five or more aerial victories in Mustangs), although a number of other pilots who were aces in their combined scores while flying a number of operational types achieved some of their kills in

Mustangs. The highest-scoring Polish pilot who flew with the RAF, for example, was Wg Cdr Stanislaw Skalski, who rose to lead No.133 Wing. His total score was 22 victories (although some sources attribute him with 24), of which two of these were achieved in the Mustang Mk III (on 24 June 1944, when two Bf 109Gs that he was manoeuvring to attack collided in mid-air).

In contrast to the situation in Europe, British and Commonwealth air forces did not employ Mustangs in the CBI or Pacific during World War Two. However, some US-built Mustangs were nearing their combat debut with the Royal Australian Air Force as the war in the Pacific drew to a close in August and September 1945. In fact, Nos.84 and 86 Squadrons, RAAF, briefly flew the Mustang during that period - but did not play any part in the conflict with the Mustang. In the CBI, RAF-operated Hawker Hurricanes, Supermarine Spitfires and Republic Thunderbolts bore the brunt of the air war for the British alongside their American allies, with considerable use being made of these types over Burma - all three provided sterling service in that theatre. It is a little known fact, however, that there was a plan for the Mustang to operate over Burma with British forces as 1945 wore on. To that end a considerable number of Mustang Mk IV aircraft was sent to India by sea for assembly and making ready for combat. Some of these were put together at Dum Dum airfield, Calcutta, which was a convenient point for the assembly of the Mustangs. However, the end of World War Two immediately made these aircraft redundant. Many were new Mk IV aircraft, in the KM serial number range, but this did not save them from being scrapped. The Americans certainly did not want them back, even though they had been supplied under Lend-Lease, for the USAAF by then had more than enough Mustangs - many of which were, in any case, becoming redundant because of the end of the war and the anticipated coming into service of the first front-line jet fighters. Sadly up to 350 Mustangs (and possibly more than this) were simply broken up in India, having never had the chance to fire their guns in anger.

The right-hand side of Mustang Mk.IVA KM272 'Dooleybird' of No.19 Squadron, RAF. In recent years the colouring of the edge of the Olive Drab anti-glare panel ahead of the cockpit and around the cockpit canopy framing has created considerable debate, with one source claiming that it was yellow. However, the original images of this aircraft were supplied by the aircraft's pilot, who stated that the colouring of this edging was medium blue, as in the colouring of the nose markings. What is beyond doubt is that the name 'Dooleybird' was not carried on the right-hand fuselage side. This highly individually-painted aircraft was famously featured as one of the colour scheme options in the 'Matchbox' model kit of the Mustang back in 1973
(Photo: A.S. Doley via R.L. Ward)

One of the most colourful of the British and Commonwealth-operated Mustangs was 'Dooleybird', the aircraft often flown by Flt Lt A S Doley of No.19 Squadron in 1945. A former P-51K with Aeroproducts propeller (and therefore really a Mustang Mk.IVA although usually called a Mk.IV), the serial number was KM272 and the squadron codes were QV-V. The nose and spinner markings were medium blue and white. Note the ubiquitous RAF starter trolley behind the aircraft's right-hand undercarriage leg
(Photo: A.S. Doley via R.L. Ward)

# Post-War Merlin-Mustang Service

## Chapter 6

There is no doubt that the Allied victory in World War Two was achieved by a combination of many different factors, but one of the significant combatants in the conflict's air war was undoubtedly the Mustang. This amazingly successful warplane was certainly one of the most important participants in the winning of the air war over the Axis powers. It is impossible to say exactly how many enemy aircraft were shot down by Mustangs, particularly as some claims were far in excess of verified enemy losses, while some definite shoot-downs were never credited. Some theatres of war during World War Two also had their own unique scoring and counting methods. However, an often-quoted figure for Mustang air-to-air kills is at least 4,950, plus at least 4,131 ground victories, and some 230 V1 'flying bombs' shot down. The number of aerial victories was probably considerably higher than this, bearing in mind that some historians believe that the Eighth Army Air Force alone achieved over five thousand aerial victories. Whatever the exact figure might have been, the Mustang's contribution to aerial supremacy for the Allies in World War Two was hugely significant, and was definitely a prominent aspect, amongst many, of the final Allied victory.

Without doubt the Allied success in World War Two was only won at great cost, and the transition into the post-war world was no less difficult and demanding. In the euphoria of victory the first thoughts of many servicemen was to return home, and resume the lives and careers that they had been leading prior to being drafted or volunteering for military service. Nevertheless some career-minded personnel determined to stay on in the military, but the post-war reality was that most of the victorious countries began – some sooner than others – to cut back on their military organisations. Many of the famous units that had been so successful during the war were disbanded or amalgamated with others, and their equipment withdrawn from service.

In the case of the American fighters that had contributed in no small part to the final victory, the coming of peace brought significant changes almost as soon as the war ended. Production ceased quite rapidly of the piston-engined fighters. In the case of the P-51D series, manufacture at Dallas ceased almost as soon as the war against Japan ended, whilst at Inglewood the production lines finished a little more slowly, but the last Mustang examples were completed within weeks of the conflict ending. As far as front-line service was concerned, the Lockheed P-38 Lightning, for example, very rapidly disappeared as a front-line fighter in the inventory of the USAAF, although some examples of the F-5 reconnaissance versions of this type did soldier on for a time. The P-47 Thunderbolt also started to disappear comparatively rapidly, although that particular type found a new career with the National Guard (later Air National Guard) – and many examples were supplied to friendly countries under the various mutual defence aid schemes that the US pursued after the war. For the Mustang there were similarly many cutbacks, but at the same time a whole new career beckoned with the National Guard, and, for a time, the type successfully continued in front-line service.

## Allied Occupation Forces

In the immediate post-war period, there was a very considerable run-down of active units. In the ETO, the triumphant Eighth Army Air Force was earmarked for operations against Japan following the defeat of Germany. On 16 July 1945 this air force was transferred, on paper without its former active units, to Okinawa in order to become a new combat force against the Japanese, operating B-29 Superfortresses. In the event this combat deployment never materialised due to the surrender of Japan, but in Europe the units that had been a part of the Eighth

Post-war flying in the US must have been a very pleasurable experience. This beautiful in-flight view shows an F-51D-30-NA 44-74825, photographed over Yerba Buena Island and Treasure Island, in the vicinity of the city of San Francisco, on 24 June 1951. On this occasion the aircraft was being flown by Brig Gen John Felton Turner, who at that time was the commanding officer of the 144th Fighter Wing, Air National Guard. The tail tip and wing-tips were red
*(Photo: William T. Larkins)*

It is unfortunate to relate that far too many Mustangs ended up like this one at the end of the Second World War, discarded and looking for a new home. Sadly many were simply scrapped. This Mustang is a Dallas-built P-51C-10-NT, serial number 44-10911, and was one of the high-numbered Fiscal Year 1944 P-51C batches. It had undergone conversion into a reconnaissance Mustang, as evidenced by the camera window in the lower rear fuselage, making it an F-6C-10-NT *(Photo: R.L. Ward Collection)*

Air Force were transferred back to the US where many were disbanded or retitled. This happened firstly with the heavy bomber units, while many of the fighter groups followed later in 1945. VIII Fighter Command continued to exist until inactivated in England on 20 March 1946. By that time many of the famous fighter units of the Eighth and Ninth Air Forces were either inactivated, or were in the process of moving back to the US. Some of the fighter groups had continued to fly in the immediate post-VE-Day period, or had opened the doors of their airfields to allow the local public to take a look at their war-winning aircraft – there had often been a good relationship between the American GIs and the local population. However, this was by no means the end of the story for the Mustang in Europe. As a part of the Allied military administration that was put in place at the end of the war to govern Germany until such time that the Germans were adjudged capable and responsible enough to administer themselves, a substantial Allied occupation force was deemed necessary.

To that end a considerable military presence was needed to reside in-country, and that included aviation elements in addition to ground forces. In the west, Germany was split into three zones – British, French, and US-administered. Delegated as a part of the occupation forces, three Mustang-operating former Eighth Air Force fighter groups were earmarked to serve in Germany – these were the 55th, 355th, and 357th Fighter Groups. In the event all three served in Germany for some time after the war ended, although all three were considerably undermanned compared to their personnel levels at the height of their operations during the war itself. The 55th moved from its wartime base at Wormingford in Essex to R-70 Kaufbeuren in Germany during July 1945, and then relocated to Y-90 Giebelstadt in April 1946 before being inactivated there in August 1946. The 355th had been based at Steeple Morden in Cambridgeshire during World War Two from July 1943, but moved to R-77 Gablingen near Augsburg in southern Germany during July 1945 (although some elements of the group apparently moved over to the Continent just prior to this), before relocating to Schweinfurt in April 1946. The group

was eventually transferred to the US in August 1946 without its equipment, prior to being inactivated in November 1946. The 357th FG was another of the famous Mustang-equipped fighter groups of the Eighth Army Air Force, and flew from Leiston in Suffolk from February 1943 following its assignment to the Eighth Air Force after being traded for the P-47 equipped 358th FG. Elements of the group moved to R-85 Neubiberg in Germany during July 1945, and the unit remained there until inactivated on 20 August 1946. All three fighter groups came under the USAAF's occupation forces which formally grew, in the summer of 1947 after these Mustang units had left, into the well-known United States Air Forces in Europe (USAFE).

In addition to the three former Eighth Air Force fighter groups, several Mustang-equipped Ninth Air Force groups also participated in the Allied occupation forces in Germany (the Ninth Air Force itself was inactivated in Germany on 2 December 1945). These included the 10th Photo Group, which had a number of reconnaissance Mustang squadrons assigned and had fought a long war across Europe after D-Day. Redesignated as the 10th Reconnaissance Group in June 1945, the group was headquartered at R-28 Furth in the post-war period, before spending several weeks at Fürstenfeldbruck (later to become a major NATO air base) between April and June 1947. The group was then transferred to the US, minus its aircraft and manpower, but was remanned and equipped with F-6 reconnaissance Mustangs. It subsequently became the 10th Tactical Reconnaissance Wing in the summer of 1948, and was stationed at a number of air bases in the continental US including Pope AFB, North Carolina, where it was inactivated in April 1949. Other former Ninth Air Force Mustang units that formed a part of the Allied presence in Germany after the war included the 363rd Tactical Reconnaissance Group, which ended the war at Brunswick in Germany. The group became the 363rd Reconnaissance Group in June 1945, and before returning to the US in December 1945 where it was inactivated, it was stationed at several locations in Germany including Eschwege and Darmstadt. The same was true for the 370th Fighter Group, which ended the

Photographed post-war, this P-51D-30-NT, serial number 45-11664, had been converted into a reconnaissance-configured F-6D, as evidenced by the camera window fittings in the rear fuselage. This aircraft would, on paper at least, have been redesignated as an RF-51D as a result of the shake-up in designations that took place following the 1947 creation of the US Air Force as an independent organisation. It carries on the rear fuselage the words 'Enlist in the AAF Guard the Victory' *(Photo: R.L. Ward Collection)*

war at Y-99 Gütersloh in Germany. The group remained in Germany until it redeployed to the US in September to November 1945, and was inactivated on 7 November 1945. Whilst remaining in Germany it was successively stationed at Sandhofen and Fritzlar. In addition to these units, a Fifteenth Air Force fighter group that had flown Merlin-Mustangs in the MTO, the 31st Fighter Group, also operated the type in the post-war period as a part of the Allied forces in Germany. The 31st had ended the war at Mondolfo in Italy, and had subsequently moved to Triolo from where it returned to the US in August 1945 and was inactivated in November of that year. However, it was newly activated in Germany in August 1946 at Giebelstadt, and spent a brief period there before being based at Kitzingen from September 1946 until June 1947 when it was transferred back to the US. Even then, the unit's association with the Mustang did not cease there, for it was assigned at that time to another of the new USAAF commands, Tactical Air Command, and initially flew P-51D Mustangs at Turner Field (later, Turner AFB) in Georgia until these were replaced by Republic F-84 Thunderjets during 1948 – by which time the independent US Air Force had been born.

Elsewhere in the world, the Mustang similarly fulfilled the important role of occupier and peacekeeper. In the Far East, following the defeat of Japan a substantial Allied occupying force was established in Japan, again with a military administration to try to put the defeated country onto a peaceful and proper peacetime footing and bring it back into some form of civility. Many of the USAAF's Mustang-operating units that had fought the Japanese during the latter stages of the war subsequently joined the Allied occupying forces. These included the Fifth Air Force units that had flown the Mustang near to the end of the war, including the 71st Reconnaissance Group, the 35th and 348th Fighter Groups, and the 3rd Air Commando Group. The 71st RG had ended the war on Ie Shima, and had latterly flown reconnaissance sorties over the Japanese home islands in order to locate Prisoner of War camps in addition to flying combat reconnaissance and strafing missions as well. The group joined the Allied occupation forces by moving to Japan in October 1945, taking up residence at Chofu and soon after at Tachikawa – three of its squadrons, the 8th, 25th and 82nd flying Mustangs in the post-war period. The group was then inactivated in February 1946, but was activated again in Japan at Itami on 28 February 1947 when the need for reconnaissance assets both for the occupation forces and to carry out wider surveillance missions became greater. The group was successively based in Japan at Johnson Army Air Base and then at Yokota, and became the 71st Tactical Reconnaissance Wing in August 1948. It was equipped in its new life with a variety of reconnaissance types from late 1947 onwards, including reconnaissance Mustangs – its 25th Tactical Reconnaissance Squadron in particular operating Mustangs at Itami. The wing was later inactivated after being non-operational

from later in 1948.

Regarding other ex-Fifth Air Force assets that also provided occupation force support after the war ended, the 3rd Air Commando Group moved from Ie Shima to Chitose, Japan, in October 1945, and remained there until March 1946 when it was inactivated. Its Mustang-operating 3rd and 4th Fighter (Commando) Squadrons actually flew from Atsugi, Japan, for a short time in late September 1945. The 35th Fighter Group moved from Okinawa to Irumagawa in October 1945, and stayed there until moving to Yokota in March 1950. By then it had been redesignated as the 35th Fighter Wing in August 1948, and later as the 35th Fighter-Interceptor Wing in January 1950, and had been in the process for some time of converting onto the first real front-line jet fighter of the USAF, the Lockheed F-80 Shooting Star. However, events subsequently overtook the USAF units stationed in that part of the Far East, and with the start of the Korean War in June 1950 the 35th duly converted back onto the Mustang for combat operations over Korea – as described later in this Book. The group returned to Johnson Air Base in Japan in May 1951 and subsequently flew Mustangs alongside Shooting Stars as a part of the air defence of Japan until moving to Yokota in August 1954. It eventually transitioned onto the F-86 Sabre the following year. The 348th Fighter Group, on the other hand, only had a comparatively short tour of duty in Japan. The group moved to Itami in Japan from Ie Shima during October 1945 and stayed there until inactivated in May 1946, but continued to fly Mustangs during that period. All of the former Fifth Air Force Mustang units that thus formed a part of the Allied occupation forces in Japan came under the administrative control of the Far East Air Forces.

In Korea, formerly under Japanese 'overlordship', there was also a major Allied presence, and here a unit that had not flown the Mustang during the war nevertheless operated the type post-war. That was the 475th Fighter Group, which had been well-known during the hostilities as a P-38 Lightning unit, indeed one of the most famous of the Fifth Air Force's fighter groups. One of its pilots, Maj Thomas McGuire, Jr., had become the second-highest scoring ace in the USAAF with 38 aerial victories as well as being a recipient of the Medal of Honor. However, post-war the P-38 Lightning was quite soon withdrawn from USAAF front-line service, and even the 475th FG eventually gave up its beloved Lightnings for the Mustang. The group moved to Kimpo, Korea, in September 1945 after the end of the war from its base at Ie Shima (it had previously operated in the Philippines, but like other Fifth Air Force assets had moved further north near to the end of the war), and converted onto the Mustang in 1946. It stayed in Korea on peace-keeping duty with the Far East Air Forces until August 1948 when it deployed to Itazuke, Japan, and was finally inactivated at Ashiya in Japan at the start of April 1949.

Post-war Mustangs sometimes took on colourful markings, as evidenced by this example which has so far defied positive identification, although a number of theories have been put forward for its credentials. It carries the 'Buzz Number' prefix 'FF' on its fuselage side which was adopted for the Mustang following the creation of the US Air Force in 1947, and also exhibits the prominent lettering 'USAF' beneath its left-hand wing. It has uncuffed Hamilton Standard propeller blades *(Photo: R.L. Ward Collection)*

At the end of World War Two there were some 5,500 Mustangs in the USAAF's inventory. These mostly comprised Merlin-Mustangs, particularly but not exclusively P-51D and P-51K teardrop-canopy models. Around a fifth of these were new aircraft that had been completed near to the end of the war, and which had only flown at most for a few hours. A major depository for the latter was at Newark, New Jersey, where substantial numbers of new or almost-new Mustangs were kept, apparently redundant due to the end of the war and the increasing appearance of the initial generation jet fighters. Newark had been, in fact, the main staging point for Mustangs intended for shipment by sea to Britain during the war, and was the airfield that the aircraft were flown to prior to being prepared for shipment. There was to be, however, a major new career for these aircraft. With the coming of peace, the National Guard started to regain the units that had been called to active duty during the conflict, and a major re-equipment and upgrading programme was initialled as the National Guard was effectively reborn in the months following the cessation of hostilities. A major plan was put in place in October 1945 for the reorganisation of the air units of the National Guard to give a proper national coverage. This plan was subsequently amended several times, but it formed the basis of the way in which the National Guard's air assets grew over the coming years. Those years were to feature the Mustang and Thunderbolt in large numbers, and the first NG unit to fly the P-51D was the 120th Fighter Squadron of the Colorado National Guard. This squadron was granted federal recognition on 30 June 1946, and was based at Buckley Field, Aurora, Colorado. It was correctly named the 120th Fighter Squadron (SE), the 'SE' standing for 'Single-Engine', and was followed by the 109th FS (SE) of the Minnesota NG at Holman Field, St Paul, and the 110th FS (SE) of the Missouri NG at Lambert Field, St Louis, in September 1946. Observant readers will have noticed that this latter squadron already had a distinguished association with the Mustang. As the 110th Tactical Reconnaissance Squadron, it had flown F-6D Mustangs as a part of the 71st Tactical

Reconnaissance Group in the Philippines in 1945, as described earlier in this Book. Eventually a significant number of National Guard squadrons re-equipped with the Mustang, some 700 Mustangs being made available from the stockpiles at the end of the war to equip National Guard units, including some of the Mustangs held at Newark, New Jersey.

## The US Air Force is Born

Whilst all this was taking place, the USAAF itself went through some significant changes. For many serving officers, and politicians, the creation of an independent air force had seemed a desirable end for many years, and the experience of World War Two heightened this apparent need. The USAAF remained throughout the Second World War a part of the US Army, which it was subordinate to and theoretically was supposed first and foremost to support. The winds of change were blowing following the end of the war, however, and in 1947 the legislation was put in place to radically shake up the US armed services and to create an independent air force. This took place in the summer of 1947, the National Security Act that established the new US Air Force as an independent entity - equal to the US Army and the US Navy - being signed into law by President Harry S. Truman on 26 July 1947. Several weeks later, on 26 September 1947, Gen Carl Spaatz became the first Chief of Staff of the US Air Force. Spaatz in fact had previously been one of the advocates of the 'bomber will always get through' theory that wartime experience had thoroughly discredited, but by 1947 he had luckily realised that fighter aircraft can play a part in warfare too.

The establishment of the independent USAF created many changes to the force and its procurement goals and expectations. An obvious difference took place the following year, when in June 1948 the whole designation system for the USAF's aircraft changed. The old, out-dated title of 'pursuit' for fighter aircraft was dropped once and for all, and all existing aircraft with the 'P' prefix were redesignated as 'F' for 'Fighter'. For the Mustang this meant a change from P-51 to F-51. The

Several California Air National Guard F-51s run their engines at Van Nuys Airport, California, in or around 1950. The P-51 (from 1948, F-51) was a stalwart of the early post-war period in National Guard (after 1947, Air National Guard) service. The aircraft belong to the 195th Fighter Squadron – the nearest aircraft, with incomplete ANG markings, is a Dallas-built F-51D-30-NT, 45-11631 *(Photo: USAF)*

use of 'F' for 'Photographic' was dropped at the same time, with the reconnaissance Mustangs henceforth being known as RF-51 Mustangs rather than the previous F-6. In practice the old titles still continued to be used by some for a time after this, and many aircraft did not have the painted data information on their port fuselage sides changed at all. On the other hand, the 'Buzz Number' prefix 'PF' that was worn on the fuselage sides and underwing locations of Mustangs post-war together with the 'last three' numbers of the individual aircraft's serial number, was changed to the new prefix 'FF'. There was also a significant reorganisation of USAF combat organisations as well during 1947/1948, with the old group structures henceforward being called wings – therefore, for example, Fighter Groups were increasingly renamed as Fighter Wings. The change of name did not alter the actual flying make-up of each organisation, however, as the new fighter wings continued to have (usually) three squadrons attached to them, just like the previous groups. In line with these various name and institutional changes, the National Guard was officially renamed as the Air National Guard in 1947, but this title was already being used unofficially prior to that time.

In total, 75 NG/ANG squadrons eventually flew the Mustang of various different marks, with 44 starting with the P/F-51D as their initial or early equipment, and the type lasted for over ten years in NG/ANG service. In addition, six of these squadrons flew the reconnaissance RF-51D. This meant that the Mustang was assigned as the main mission aircraft to more NG/ANG squadrons than any other aircraft type. A brief listing of the 75 squadrons is included in the Appendices at the end of this book. The Mustang remained in ANG service well into the 1950's, although the whole procedure was very considerably shaken up for many squadrons with the onset of the Korean War in June 1950. It suffices to say that during and after the Korean War period, a major process of re-equipment took place in which the existing Mustangs were eventually replaced by jet fighters where their squadron remained as a fighter unit. The final ANG unit to fly the Mustang was the 167th Fighter-Interceptor Squadron of the West Virginia ANG. This was highly appropriate – this squadron could trace its ancestry back to the 369th Fighter Squadron of the 359th Fighter Group, which had flown Mustangs with the Eighth Army Air Force in England during the latter stages of World War Two. The 167th had in fact flown Mustangs on two separate occasions post-war, and on finally giving up the Mustang in 1957 it flew for a short time the North American T-28A Trojan prior to becoming an F-86H Sabre unit. The final airworthy Mustang on its inventory, F-51D-25-NA 44-72948, was flown into Museum retirement in January 1957.

### The USAF's Strategic Air Command
However, the ANG service of the Mustang was not the only post-war use that the type was put to by the US prior to the start of hostilities in Korea in mid-1950. As a part of the significant reorganisation and restructuring that the USAAF went through after the end of the war, a new command was created to

encompass the long-range, heavy bomber assets of the AAF. These basically included the long-range Boeing B-29 Superfortress because, even though the B-17 Flying Fortress and B-24 Liberator had been the core of the USAAF's strategic bomber arm during World War Two in the ETO, and for much of the time in the Pacific (particularly the B-24, prior to the arrival of the B-29), in the post-war period the B-29 Superfortress completely supplanted these types as the new primary heavy bomber of the USAAF – until the advent of the jet age in bomber operations. In its early days, Strategic Air Command (SAC) initially had fighter units specifically assigned to protect its heavy bombers, and to begin with this included the Mustang. Created in March 1946, SAC eventually had two fighter groups assigned that operated the Mustang. These were the 27th and 33rd Fighter Groups. The 27th FG (522nd, 523rd, and 524th Fighter Squadrons) already had a substantial connection with the Mustang. As the 27th Fighter-Bomber Group, it had operated the A-36A Invader in the MTO during World War Two, long before it became a fighter unit with SAC. Becoming operational within SAC in July/August 1947 as the 27th Fighter Wing, the unit was based at Kearney Army Air Field, Nebraska, but converted onto the F-82 Twin Mustang (described later in this book) during 1948, although it continued to have some Mustangs on strength in the later 1940's. The 33rd FG (comprising the 58th, 59th, and 60th Fighter Squadrons), had operated in the MTO and then the CBI during World War Two, but not with Mustangs. It was, however, activated in Germany with P-51D Mustangs in August 1946 at R-85 Neubiberg (later from July 1947 at Bad Kissingen) as a part of the newly-formed United States Air Forces in Europe, and flew with the Allied occupation forces there until transferred to the US in 1947 where it joined SAC. Initially equipped with Mustangs, the group became the 33rd Fighter Wing in October/November 1947, and was stationed at the infamous Roswell Army Air Field (later known as Walker Air Force Base) in New Mexico from September 1947 during the period immediately after the reputed UFO activity there of July 1947. It later converted during 1948 onto the Republic F-84 Thunderjet. The 82nd Fighter Wing (95th, 96th, and 97th Fighter Squadrons) also flew P-51D Mustangs for a time during its SAC assignment in 1948/1949, having previously operated P-51H Mustangs (as explained later in this Book). It was inactivated in October 1949.

A very wide variety of other USAAF/USAF units flew Mustangs after World War Two, although many of these only had the Mustang as their main mission equipment for a short time, or flew the Mustang while principally equipped with other types. The 18th Fighter Group (later 18th Fighter Wing/Fighter-Bomber Wing), for example, flew Mustangs from 1947/1948, having had no previous association with the type – it had operated P-38 Lightnings during World War II, and had then been a part of the Allied liberation forces in the post-war Philippines. This group, however, was later to have a very profound association with the Mustang, as described later in this book. Also illustrative of post-war Mustang operators was the 21st Fighter-Bomber Wing. As the 21st Fighter Group, this unit had successfully operated the

Two-seat Mustangs were made in comparatively small numbers, with a batch converted from NAA Dallas production, but other conversions were undertaken, some at unit level. This included work by the Temco Aircraft Corporation following World War Two, and the two-seat Mustang illustrated with its tail wheel locked down, 44-84662, is widely believed to be one of the Temco-converted machines. It is a TF-51D, and at the time of the photograph it was assigned to the North Dakota Air National Guard based at Fargo, North Dakota. It was sometimes flown by D.J. Hegland, and this particular photograph is one of a sequence that were taken of this specific aircraft in flight; the date of the photograph is believed to be some time just before the Korean War, although the original print of this picture is dated on its reverse side **August 1953** *(Photo: Collection of D.J. Hegland (Lt Col USAF, Ret.) via Scott Hegland)*

Mustang in the Pacific during the closing stages of World War Two as a part of the Seventh Army Air Force. Following the end of the war the group had undergone a number of changes, although it did not serve as a part of the Allied occupation forces in Japan. Instead it moved from Iwo Jima to Isley Field, Saipan, in December 1945, then to Guam in April 1946. It was finally inactivated on Guam in October 1946, having briefly re-equipped with P-47 Thunderbolts in the summer of 1946. The group had thus provided part of the aerial defence of the strategically important islands of Iwo Jima, Saipan and Guam in the post-war period. On 1 January 1953 the group was activated again, this time as the 21st Fighter-Bomber Wing, and was initially based at George AFB in California. Prior to fully equipping with F-86 Sabres the wing was issued with F-51 Mustangs, one of the last regular USAF units to equip with the by-then somewhat venerable Mustang. Having re-equipped with Sabres, the 21st was later assigned to US Air Forces in Europe and was subsequently stationed at Chambley Air Base in France from late 1954.

## British Merlin-Mustangs after VE-Day

The Mustang only persisted for a comparatively short time in British service following the end of World War Two. With the advent of the jet-powered Gloster Meteor and de Havilland Vampire, and later still the famous Hawker Hunter, the RAF increasingly converted its front-line squadrons to jet power, particularly its home-based units. Nevertheless the Mustang still had a part to play, and several squadrons continued to use the type in 1946, especially overseas. In Italy, Allied forces persisted on Italian soil for some time after the end of the war. This was not the same type of occupation force scenario as existed in Germany and Japan, however. For although the Italian state under Benito Mussolini had been a full member of the Axis powers, the Italians had capitulated in 1943 and some Italians had subsequently fought on the Allied side during the continued fighting in Italy up to VE-Day in May 1945. In practice British forces stayed on just as long as was necessary, and in the immediate post-war period the Italian reconstruction proceeded rapidly - a new Italian air force was set up comparatively soon after hostilities ceased, and Italy later became an export user of the Mustang – as described later in this book.

Several RAF squadrons continued to fly the Mustang from Italian soil in the months following the end of the war in Europe. These included the veteran Nos.112 and 260 Squadrons, which had operated Merlin-engined Mustangs in combat up to the end of the war. In August 1945 No.260 Squadron disbanded, its final equipment being Mustangs. No.112 Squadron lasted a little longer, disbanding in December 1946, with the ultimate dispersion of its remaining personnel and aircraft during the following month. An RAF squadron that had not flown the Mustang in combat, No.250, temporarily operated the Mustang in Italy post-war. This squadron had flown the Curtiss Kittyhawk in combat right up to the end of the war, and only converted to Merlin-Mustangs during August 1945. It flew these until disbanded at its final base, Treviso, in January 1947. Another veteran of the fighting in Italy and the Balkans, No.249 Squadron, had converted to Spitfires from its Mustangs in the period just before VE-Day, but reverted to Mustangs for a short time in the summer of 1945 prior to being disbanded in mid-August 1945. A further squadron that flew Merlin-powered Mustangs with the RAF in Italy was No.93 Squadron. This unit was formed in January 1946 at Lavariano by the renumbering of No.237 Squadron, a former Spitfire operator. It flew Mustangs until being disbanded in December 1946.

Elsewhere, two squadrons finished the war with Allison-engined Mustangs. As described in Part 1 of this 'Modellers' Datafile' on the Mustang, which covered Allison-engined

Showing a variety of marking styles, four National Guard Mustangs hold formation in the era just prior to, or during, the period when the Air National Guard was formed in 1947. They therefore carry the 'NG' abbreviation before 'ANG' became the recognised fuselage appellation. At least two of the P-51s belong to the Michigan National Guard
*(Photo: USAF)*

Mustangs, these were Nos.26 and 268 Squadrons – the latter giving up its final Mustangs in August 1945 in Germany, while the former, having spotted for naval guns in action against German enclaves in the Bordeaux area near to the end of the war, finally started re-equipping with a dedicated reconnaissance version of the Spitfire Mk XIV in June 1945. A third squadron, No.285, also had a number of Mustangs on strength at the end of the war, including some Allison-engined examples. This squadron was a training unit that provided target-towing aircraft for gunnery practice, and aircraft for simulated attacks for training purposes. It was based at North Weald in the final months of the war although it had detachments at several other bases, and it disbanded in June 1945.

A number of front-line squadrons based in Britain continued to fly Merlin-Mustangs after the end of the war in Europe. These included Nos.19, 64, 65, 118, 122, 126, 165, 234, and 611, and the Polish-manned Nos.303, 306, 309, 315, and 316. The latter five units continued to fly Merlin-engined Mustangs until each was disbanded in late 1946 or the first days of 1947 and its personnel either returned to their homeland or stayed on in Britain. However, the longest-lived of all the post-war RAF Mustang squadrons was No.213 Squadron in the Middle East, and this squadron actually fired its guns in anger in troubles totally unrelated to World War Two. Like many of the other post-war RAF Mustang squadrons, No.213 had gained a distinguished war record, having operated Merlin-Mustangs from May 1944 onwards. The squadron flew in Italy and the Balkans under the Balkan Air Force, including a spell stationed in Yugoslavia itself near the end of the war at Prkos, before returning to Italy in the immediate post-war period for stationing at Biferno. However, from September 1945 it was based in Palestine where a completely new and ultimately deadly conflict was going through its initial phases. The unit's Mustangs were involved in peace-keeping operations of a sort, including occasionally shooting up dissident locals, and were based at RAF Ramat David south-east of Haifa (now a major Israeli air force base). By that point much of the squadron's equipment comprised Mustang Mk IVs, including a number of P-51K equivalents. Eventually No.213 was earmarked for re-equipment with the Hawker Tempest and ultimately moved to Nicosia on the island of Cyprus in September 1946. It finally ceased Mustang flying in February 1947, the last RAF squadron to operate the fighter that Britain had had such a role in creating.

Some Mustangs remained in RAF service on paper until later in 1947, but the Mustang era in the RAF was finally at an end. Operationally the Mustang had therefore lasted in RAF front-line operations from May 1942 until late 1946/early 1947, a momentous period in the history of the RAF and a proud one for all the RAF units that had flown the Mustang in anger.

# Lightweight Mustangs

## Chapter 7

One of the criticisms that had been levelled at the Mustang almost right from the start was that it was a comparatively heavy aircraft. Certainly some of the type's detractors at Wright Field in its early days cited the comparatively heavy production versions of the Mustang as a reason for the USAAF to avoid operating the type, but in reality the Mustang turned out to have more than enough power from its installed engine types to allow it to fly and fight on a par with any piston-engined fighters that it met. Many things are relative, of course, and in comparative terms the Mustang was smaller and considerably lighter than both of its contemporaries in the USAAF fighter inventory, the P-47 Thunderbolt and the twin-engined P-38 Lightning. Nevertheless, North American Aviation was equal to the challenge of developing the Mustang layout further, and in response to British interest in a remodelled layout specifically to give a lower maximum take-off weight and increased manoeuvrability, the line of lightweight Mustangs was born. The new production layout, and the prototypes that preceded it, took the Mustang design down a completely new path, that of a lightweight fighter.

In any case, NAA was a good manufacturer in that it was not afraid to explore new avenues, and the concept of a lightweight fighter development of the Mustang appeared to potentially open up new possibilities for the Mustang series. Certainly combat experience in the early years of World War Two pointed to several specific criteria, including increased rate of aileron roll and fast climb rate, and the various ingredients that appeared desirable were duly incorporated by NAA's designers into a lightweight family of fighters that were based on – but in reality were considerably different to - the established production models of the Mustang series. The excellent design work that Edgar Schmued and his colleagues had carried out on the Mustang during the hectic days of 1940 had given birth to an exemplary fighter, but any good designer knows that even the best designs can be improved upon, or can take into account developing technology for better derivatives down the line. Schmued had some ideas in mind about lightweight fighter design even as the Mustang was taking shape on the drawing boards at NAA in the spring and summer of 1940, and his visit to Britain in the spring of 1943 included important discussions about the intended lightweight fighter development of the Mustang. He also used his visit to Britain to see various British production facilities, including those of Supermarine, the producer of the Spitfire, and to discuss performance and operational reports of the latest Allied and enemy fighters. The Royal Air Force was desirous for a flight stress maximum loading for a new fighter layout of 6g (this was lower than that of 7.333g required by the USAAF), but the idea of lightening the Mustang's structure to the reduced load limits and providing more power to give a better climb rate coupled with enhanced manoeuvrability effectively gave birth to the subsequent series of Mustang lightweight designs. Early Mustangs with the Allison V-1710 engine had a comparatively poor climb rate especially as height increased, and the exemplary German Focke-Wulf Fw 190 had a rate of aileron roll twice that of the early Mustangs. Both of those factors needed to be addressed in any further Mustang development work, although the climb rate improved somewhat with the installation of the Packard V-1650 in the P-51B onwards, particularly at higher altitudes. Schmued and his design team duly worked hard on the light fighter concept, and in effect they went on to create one of the few lightweight piston-engined fighter designs ever to achieve production status.

## Development

The lightweight Mustang family began with the XP-51F. In the event this and all the subsequent lightweight versions were basically a new design, even though they bore the name Mustang and had a general resemblance to the established P-51 production

The lightweight P/F-51H was an important development of the Mustang line that "seemed like a good idea at the time", but in reality struggled to find a role in the changing world of air warfare in the latter stages of World War Two and its aftermath. It was in fact virtually a new aircraft that drew on the basic Mustang layout but with many changes. Allowing a direct comparison to be made between the two related types, an F-51H lightweight Mustang (in the foreground) flies in company with a standard F-51D. The different fuselage and tail contours are readily apparent. The lightweight Mustang is an F-51H-5-NA, while the standard Mustang is a very late production F-51D-30-NA
*(Photo: USAF)*

layout. In reality they had no commonality in their major components with any of the existing Mustang production versions. Work progressed rapidly on the whole lightweight fighter project at Inglewood during 1943, the programme having commenced in earnest during January of that year. NAA's designers looked for weight-saving in all areas of the Mustang's airframe, and substantially changed the wings, fuselage, tail, undercarriage, and cockpit. Even the famous lower fuselage air intake for the engine's cooling radiator was redesigned. The existing structure was simplified where possible and smaller or lighter components were introduced in some areas. The wing's famous laminar flow section was made proportionately thinner, and with smaller main wheels and new brake assemblies for the main undercarriage and altered main undercarriage legs it was possible to do away with the prominent leading edge kink that was so characteristic of the inboard plan view of the standard Mustang's wing shape. The four-gun wing armament of the P-51B/C series was retained, but the XP-51F pioneered the teardrop canopy configuration that was also introduced on standard production Mustangs of the P-51D/K series. Power for the XP-51F was provided by the Packard V-1650-3 as used in the P-51B/P-51C production series. This engine type turned a three-blade propeller unit of 11 feet (3.35 m) diameter on the XP-51F of the Aeroproducts Unimatic series with large hollow blades, which saved a little weight and marked a return to the three-blade configuration of the early production Mustangs. The troublesome fuselage fuel tank of the Merlin-Mustang line was deleted, and the radiator configuration was re-modelled, with the oil cooler removed from the lower fuselage location altogether and replaced by a different process of heat exchange employing a heat-exchanger system. A simplified hydraulic system compared to that of the P-51B/C series and its predecessors was also introduced.

Under contract no. AC-37857, three XP-51Fs were ordered in July 1943, with the serial numbers 43-43332 to 43-43334. These received the NAA charge number NA-105 (NAA charge numbers and designations became somewhat more standardised as the war progressed, although the sequential numbering system continued to be spread across several production types). The initial XP-51F, 43-43332, first flew on 14 February 1944. NAA test pilot Robert C. Chilton was at the controls and all went well to begin with. Flight testing eventually led to a maximum speed of 493 mph (793 km/h) being attained, making the XP-51F by far the fastest so far of the various Mustang versions. Perhaps more importantly, 20,000 feet (6,096 m) was reached in climb tests just over two minutes quicker than the latest production Mustang, the P-51D. The weight-saving programme had certainly been successful, for the XP-51F's maximum take-off weight was 7,610 lb (3,452 kg), as compared to the figure of 9,190 lb (4,168 kg) for the Mustang Mk.III (P-51B/C). The third XP-51F was the next to fly, on 20 May 1944, with the second machine following two days later. Of the three, the first prototype was later transferred to NACA at the end of April 1945, after extensive company testing (it appears to have made 147 flights with the company during that period). The second was transferred to Wright Field in July 1944, while the third XP-51F was shipped to Britain where it became FR409.

The XP-51F was just the start of the lightweight Mustang programme, and was followed by the XP-51G. This version was similar to the XP-51F in many respects (although it included a small extension to the fin that was not present on the XP-51F), but it had a completely different engine. The power plant chosen was the Rolls-Royce-manufactured Merlin RM.14.SM (Merlin 100) engine of 1,690 hp at 18,000 ft (5,486 m) and configured for 150 octane fuel. Examples of this engine were specially supplied to the US for the XP-51G programme. This was the highest

specification engine yet fitted to a Mustang at that time. A four-blade Aeroproducts Unimatic A-542-B1 propeller unit was chosen to pull the power of this engine configuration. Also ordered under contract no. AC-37857, the two XP-51G had the serial numbers 43-43335 and 43-43336. The former first flew on 9 August 1944 in the hands of NAA test pilot Ed Virgin. Early in its test programme it was fitted with a five-blade Rotol propeller unit of wooden lamination construction. On 12 August Bob Chilton took the aircraft aloft with this propeller installation, and discovered that a very wild beast had been created. At cruising speed the aircraft was completely directionally unstable. Fortunately he was able to get the aircraft back on the ground without mishap, and the initial four-blade Aeroproducts propeller unit was reinstalled. The second XP-51G was initially flown by NAA test pilot Joe Barton on 14 November 1944. This aircraft is often credited as having been shipped to Britain in November 1944 for testing at Boscombe Down with the British serial number FR410 and known as a Mustang Mk.IV. However, no test reports from Boscombe Down have ever surfaced for this aircraft, and it appears that it was flown by NAA test pilots in the US including Bob Chilton as late as April 1945.

The final experimental lightweight Mustang version was the XP-51J. Procured under the same contract as the XP-51F and XP-51G, the 'J' model was unusual in marking a return to the Allison V-1710 power plant as used on the early production Mustangs. However, the V-1710 that was installed in this experimental version was a very different animal to that in the early Mustangs, being the V-1710-119. This highly-developed version of the V-1710 marked the appearance of a two-stage, two-speed supercharger to

the V-1710 line. Allison had been well behind Rolls-Royce in the development of a two-stage supercharger for the V-1710, and it was not until very late in the war that the V-1710-119 appeared. However, this supercharger was nowhere near as successful an installation as that in the Merlin and Packard V-1650, and relied on a hydraulically-activated supercharger that appeared to suffer unintentionally from variable speeds. The 'dash 119' also featured water injection to increase boost. In theory it was rated at 1,720 hp war emergency power with water injection at 20,000 ft (6,096 m), but the engine proved troublesome - resulting in the trials of the XP-51J being not terribly thorough. The engine installation in the aircraft was, nevertheless, very neatly accomplished, with the chin-mounted carburettor air intake so characteristic on Merlin-engined Mustangs being done away with due to the repositioning of the relevant ducting to the lower fuselage radiator air intake. A four-bladed Aeroproducts propeller unit was fitted as also used on the XP-51G.

Two XP-51J were built, serial numbers 44-76027 and 44-76028. The first of these was flown by NAA test pilot George Welch on 23 April 1945, while the latter first flew with NAA test pilot George Krebs in charge on 29 January 1946. By that time there was little purpose to the XP-51J programme with the war over and Mustang production having ceased, and both aircraft were transferred to Allison for development work, the first aircraft being delivered to Indianapolis in January 1946 (although there is conflicting information that both aircraft were delivered to the USAAF in February 1946 before being turned over to Allison). The XP-51F, XP-51G, and XP-51J experimental lightweight Mustangs were not terribly successful, although the XP-51G was the fastest of all Mustangs, on one occasion being recorded as attaining 498 mph (801 km/h) at approximately 20,000 ft (6,096 m). Bob Chilton later pointed out that the XP-51F was the version of Mustang that he enjoyed flying the most, with its performance that was quite different to that of the previous Mustang models. Nevertheless, the endurance of the three different experimental types was restricted due to the deletion of the fuselage fuel tank, each could only be fitted with rather flimsy underwing pylons, and only two machine guns could be installed in each wing. The old problems of directional stability were also still present. None of the three lightweight versions appeared to be the basis of a viable production model, but valuable lessons were learned by North American Aviation about just what could feasibly be done with the Mustang structure to lighten it, and the result was the only lightweight Mustang derivative to enter production, the P-51H.

## P-51H Production

This lightweight Mustang combined some of the weight-saving features of the experimental lightweight models, but included major compromises to make it into a viable combat aircraft. Contract no. AC-1752 covered the manufacture of 2,400 P-51H

(NA-126), the agreement being dated 26 April 1944. There was no prototype for the P-51H, as the development work carried out on the other lightweight Mustangs prepared the way for P-51H production to commence without further prototypes being necessary. The initial aircraft of the contract was serial number 44-64160, a P-51H-1-NA, and it first flew, with Robert Chilton at the controls, on 3 February 1945. The initial P-51H production aircraft were somewhat austere examples of the type, and an ongoing engineering puzzle that had not been resolved by the time that production started was the size and shape of the vertical tail for the P-51H. This resulted in some of the first series aircraft having an interim tail shape, both fin and rudder, and eventually a design was settled on that included a 'tall tail' that appeared to solve some of the directional stability problems that had existed for all the Merlin-engined Mustangs. Some of the development work on that tail layout was carried out using a converted P-51D-5-NA, serial number 44-13253, and it was not until early in the P-51H-5-NA block that the final tail shape was standardized. Some of the earlier P-51H aircraft were later retrofitted with the production-style design.

All P-51H production aircraft were built by North American Aviation at Inglewood. However, the planned 2,400 production series never to come to fruition. The end of the war effectively curtailed production, and although the final examples were built up to November 1945, this was mainly to use up existing major components and to wind-down the whole Mustang production programme. The manufacturing of the P-51H continued until 9 November 1945, when the final Mustang was completed ready for flight-testing and hand-over to the USAAF. In total, 555 P-51H were completed, the highest numbered P-51H that was finished being 44-64714, a P-51H-10-NA. All other intended production aircraft were cancelled. At that point manufacture of Mustangs by NAA thus ended for all time. Production of the Mustang as a whole had therefore lasted a little less than five years, the first series production Mustang from Inglewood having initially flown in April 1941. However, it must be remembered that the total of 555 P-51H aircraft represents what was actually completed – NAA had many more aircraft in preparation, and the necessary components were being prepared for the manufacture of a proportion of the remaining P-51H aircraft in the original contract total. As with other aircraft manufacturers the world over on the Allied side, the successful conclusion of World War Two for the

Allies was a significant headache for North American Aviation, as the massive wartime orders suddenly started to come to an end. Many, like NAA with the P-51H, found themselves in the midst of production and it was not easy to simply finish half-way through a job - particularly when it resulted in many lay-offs of the skilled and dedicated workers who had toiled so magnificently during the war to produce the required aircraft and war material. It also meant in many cases paying component manufacturers for parts that were suddenly no longer needed as production ground to a halt on many major aircraft programmes. In the case of North American Aviation, it was fortunate that the company had the beautiful and ultimately highly-successful P-86 (later F-86) Sabre

The interior of the lightweight P-51H was somewhat different to the wartime combat versions of the P-51 up to and including the P-51D, and appears less well thought out although it apparently reflected the latest thinking on instrumentation and control layout based on combat experience. When the third XP-51F prototype, 43-43334, was evaluated at Boscombe Down as FR409 from August 1944 following shipment to Britain, a criticism of the type was the cockpit interior layout. In this image the pilot's 'office' of an early P-51H, actually P-51H-1-NA 44-64170, can be seen *(Photo: NAA)*

150 POUNDS SAVED IN WINGS

80 POUNDS SAVED IN FIXED EQUIPMENT

130 POUNDS SAVED IN ENGINE SECTION

30 POUNDS SAVED IN FUSELAGE

300 POUNDS SAVED IN LANDING GEAR

This specially-annotated NAA company illustration shows the significant improvements in weight saving of the lightweight P-51H compared to the P-51D. The aircraft used for the illustration itself was the much-photographed fifth production P-51H-1-NA, 44-64164 *(Photo: NAA)*

The design, layout, outline and overall appearance of the lightweight Mustangs went through a number of phases, while NAA's designers worked with the concept of developing the basic Mustang layout into a truly lightweight design, with lower maximum take-off weight and increased manoeuvrability being some of the aims. This drawing shows one of the many stages that the concept went through while it evolved, with a different cockpit canopy layout and what appears to be a slightly redesigned air intake beneath the fuselage
(Drawing: NAA)

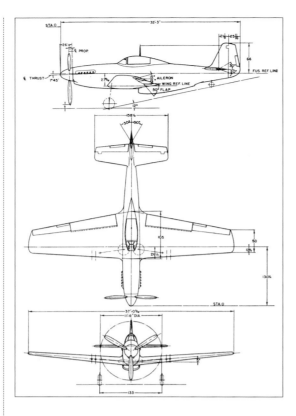

jet fighter project to be getting on with, which was in its early stages as World War Two suddenly ended. Nevertheless, a significant proportion of NAA's workforce faced redundancy due to the ending of World War Two. The company had grown into one of the US aviation industry's giants during the war, and near to the end of the war employed some 91,000 workers – many of these faced an uncertain future as the first weeks of peace commenced.

The P-51H was powered by a Packard V-1650-9 engine (equivalent to the Rolls-Royce Merlin 100-series) with a two-speed, two-stage supercharger. Its normal rating was up to 1,830 hp at sea level, but it could reach 2,270 hp for short periods with water injection 'war emergency' boost. It had a Bendix PD.18.C3A automatic updraft fuel-injection carburettor, but also featured a piece of equipment that caused no end of problems. This was a Simmonds engine pressure regulator/boost control, which

normally maintained engine manifold pressure, and if shut down before the engine was stopped after flight would work fine. However, if it was not shut down prior to the engine being stopped, when the engine was started again next time around the regulator would engage at the setting that it had been stopped with, resulting in a number of P-51H standing on their noses on start-up with the engine suddenly and unexpectedly reaching high rpm straight after being started. It became normal, and safe, practice, for ground crews to stand to the right of the aircraft on start-up, for if it suddenly stood on its nose, the duly shattering propeller blades would fly in pieces off to the left-hand side of the aircraft. The propeller unit fitted to the P-51H was the four-blade Aeroproducts Unimatic A-542-B1 of 11 ft 1 in (3.38 m) diameter as also installed on the XP-51G and XP-51J. With this combination the P-51H could reach 487 mph (784 km/h) at 25,000 ft (7,620 m) – this made it the fastest of all the 'series production' Mustangs.

Unlike the experimental lightweight Mustangs, the P-51H carried a fuselage fuel tank, of 50 US gallons. It was of a completely different design to that in the P-51B, P-51C, and P-51D series, and did not cause the centre of gravity and manoeuvrability problems that were encountered with those versions. It was additional to the P-51H's wing fuel tanks, of 104 US gallons in the right-hand wing, and 102 US gallons in the left-hand wing. With these installed the P-51H had a range of 850 miles (1,368 km), but this could be extended with external fuel tanks. The poor underwing pylons of the experimental lightweight Mustangs were replaced on the P-51H with more substantial units that could carry drop tanks of up to 110 US gallons – or a 1,000 lb (454 kg) bomb under each wing. In terms of armament, the P-51H carried three 0.5-in M2 Browning machine guns in each wing, mounted in similar upright fashion to those of the P-51D series. Again reflecting combat experience with other Mustang versions, these were set to converge at 800 yards (c. 800 m). A K-14A or K-14B gunsight was installed for sighting the guns. Three 'zero-length' fittings each for an unguided rocket for air-to-ground work could be installed beneath each wing (or up to five if the pylon was not fitted). Some (but certainly not all) P-51H were fitted with cameras. The installation and location in the rear fuselage was similar to the vertical and oblique cameras as carried in the F-6D/K reconnaissance Mustangs. The P-51H featured a teardrop-shaped cockpit canopy that resembled that of the P-51D and was slightly different to that of the XP-51F, and the cockpit interior

The P/F-51H was a very elegant aircraft in flight, especially in its 'natural metal' finish with black anti-glare panel ahead of the cockpit. This view shows the well-known and much-photographed fifth production P-51H-1-NA, 44-64164
(Photo: NAA)

was somewhat modified from that of the P-51D to try to make it more comfortable and pilot-friendly for long-range bomber escort missions.

In terms of construction, the P-51H was a totally all-metal aircraft (except for some small parts made from plastics), with no fabric-covered control surfaces (indeed, many existing P-51D series Mustangs after the war had their fabric-covered tail control surfaces replaced with all-metal units). The P-51H in effect was based on the XP-51F, but had a slightly longer fuselage of 33 ft 3.25 in (10.14 m) – the wing span remained exactly the same as the foregoing production Mustangs. As far as weight was concerned, the P-51H was certainly lighter than the standard production Mustangs, and weighed in at only just over 7,000 lb (3,175 kg) empty, and 9,250 lb (4,196 kg) maximum with its internal fuel tanks full. This was 732 lb (332 kg) lighter than equivalent figures for the Mustang Mk.IV. It has sometimes been claimed that the P-51H entered front-line USAAF service in 1945, and that some examples saw action near to the end of the war. This is completely untrue. No P-51H ever flew in combat, even though 370 examples had been delivered to the USAAF by the end of the war against Japan. In truth the type was only just entering service with second-line units when the war ended, and AAF testing of the P-51H in any case was still taking place at that time. Unfortunately, that service testing showed up several significant problems that resulted in the type never fulfilling a major role in the USAAF or its successor USAF.

The first service test examples of the P-51H to reach Wright Field did so in the spring of 1945, and to the proving grounds at Eglin in Florida during June 1945. At Eglin one of the intended evaluation programmes was to fly the P-51H against examples of the P-51D, P-47N Thunderbolt and P-38J/L Lightning, and gain comparative data of the merits of the new lightweight Mustang. The end of the war against Japan, however, led to these trials never being completed, and in reality only comparative tests were flown against the P-51D. Nevertheless they included much interesting data in comparison between the two distinct types of Mustang. The P-51H scored well in terms of its better stability with its internal fuel tanks full, due in the main because of the better layout of the fuselage fuel tank. For bomber escort missions the P-51H was found to have the excellent range of 1,890 miles (3,042 km) with two 110 US gallon underwing fuel tanks, although it was never, of course, put to the test under actual combat conditions. In comparative trials with an example of each type flown straight and level, the P-51H was able to outdistance the P-51D at all heights, its more powerful engine, improved supercharger performance and lighter weight giving it a distinct edge. In fact four P-51H were used for these trials, three H-1 and one H-5, with at least one of them apparently being assigned to the 611th Base Unit at Eglin. The P-51H-5 proved to be the most satisfactory amongst the four of these lightweights.

However, problems were encountered with the P-51H as a type that rendered it rather unsuitable for combat. One of the difficulties encountered was with buckling of the wings. Pulling 9g was found to considerably crease the wing skin and over-stress the wing structure. This was, admittedly, a problem with all production Mustang models, but the lightened wing of the P-51H appeared to be more prone than most to wing damage during stress. At least two P-51Hs were employed for stress testing, one of them (44-64162, the third production P-51H-1-NA) specifically for wing stress testing, but the difficulty was never satisfactorily resolved. In addition, the rear fuselage assembly of the P-51H was also found to slightly buckle when high-g manoeuvres were attempted. The latter was addressed with some local strengthening on aircraft where it had not already happened, although again it was a potentially serious problem. There were also difficulties with the undercarriage, both the main and tail wheel arrangements.

A rarely-seen view of the lightweight P/F-51H is the type's underside. This image clearly shows the straight wing leading edge of this Mustang variant, which was one of the main distinguishing points between the lightweight Mustangs and their better-known, 'normal' Mustang stable mates. Noteworthy also are the various underwing attachment points for external stores. The specific aircraft in the image is the fifth production P-51H, 44-64164
*(Photo: NAA)*

The tail wheel down-lock was a constant source of difficulty, as it often failed on the ground especially during taxiing, resulting in tail wheel undercarriage collapse and resultant heavy damage to the rear fuselage. No attempt ever seems to have been made to remedy this situation. The main undercarriage suffered from a retraction peculiarity. If the action of raising or lowering the main undercarriage was interrupted for any reason, the retraction system failed at once, resulting in one leg going up while the other went down. Nothing could be done to remedy the situation in flight, resulting in several aircraft landing on one main gear leg only. Even more seriously, the cockpit canopy had a tendency to fly off in flight. P-51H pilots were the first Mustang flyers to regularly wear a 'bone-dome' helmet due to this potentially very hazardous problem. The P-51H also introduced some rather advanced wheel brakes. These were Goodyear 'Three-Spot' brakes, that were very different to the multiple disc brakes of the P-51D. They worked quite well, but were more easily burned out by extensive use compared to those on the P-51D. There were other difficulties, including the locking latches on various panels, and a problem with engine surge near full throttle in the low cruising power range of the engine. Some modifications also needed to be made to the horizontal tail, especially the trim tabs which appeared inadequate. The P-51H-5 series introduced a number of improvements which rectified some of these shortcomings, but overall the P-51H in general seems to have been a rather problematic aircraft. Nevertheless, the final report on the P-51H, issued by the Air Proving Ground Command at Eglin Field in October 1946, was comparatively praiseworthy of the P-51H's attributes, especially its speed and range, and its comparative stability as a gun platform. Nevertheless it was considered to have insufficient advantage over the existing P-51D to warrant standardisation.

## US Service of the P-51H

The first USAAF unit to receive examples of the P-51H was the 412th Fighter Group. This unit is famous as having been the first to introduce jet fighters to the Army Air Force, when it took on

The well-known and much-photographed fifth production P-51H, 44-64164, was delivered to the USAF at Moffett Field, California, in June 1945, although it later spent a short period of time with NACA (Photo: NAA)

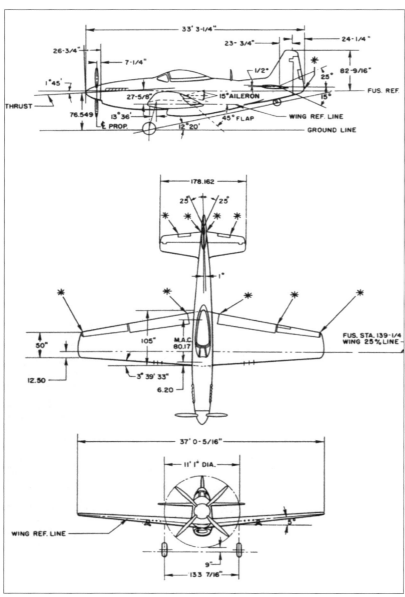

This general arrangement drawing shows the P/F-51H layout from an NAA P/F-51H Manual. Note the dimensions, which are sometimes incorrectly quoted in some published sources. Also noticeable are the small main undercarriage wheels, the revised (straight) wing leading edge shape, the tall tail, and the revised lower fuselage air intake (Drawing: NAA)

charge a small number of very early Lockheed P-80 Shooting Stars near to the end of World War Two and prepared to fly in combat with this type in Italy. Activated in November 1943, the group was based at a number of airfields in California during its comparatively short life (it was inactivated in July 1946), and was originally intended to be the first jet unit to fly the Bell P-59 Airacomet. However, this very early jet fighter proved to be something of a disappointment and was long in its gestation. At the end of World War Two, a squadron that had flown reconnaissance F-5 Lightning's in Europe as a part of the 10th Photo Group and then the 363rd Tactical Reconnaissance Group deployed back to the US. This was the 39th Photographic Reconnaissance Squadron, and from November 1945 until July 1946 it was attached to the 412th FG. During that time it took on charge a number of P-51H Mustangs as well as F-6D Mustangs, and appears to have had some P-80 Shooting Stars on strength or temporarily assigned as well. It was stationed at Santa Maria Army Air Field from October 1945, and at March Field, California, from December 1945 until July 1946. During that time it put the P-51H through an operational work-up, checking tactics for escorting USAAF long-range bombers, and using P-80s for simulated attacks to develop tactics for escort fighters such as the P-51H to combat jet fighter attacks on heavy bombers. As can be seen, this trials work prior to front-line operational service was after the end of World War Two, again underlining that no P-51Hs ever saw combat in that war. Just why a photographic reconnaissance squadron was tasked with this work has never been satisfactorily explained, as the P-51H never played a significant role as a photo-ship during its operational service. The squadron was redesignated as the 39th Tactical Reconnaissance Squadron in December 1945.

The P-51H never played a particularly significant part in the post-war USAAF, although it did serve with a number of front-line units. The first of these was the 57th Fighter Group. This unit was activated on 15 August 1946 at Shemya in the Aleutian Islands by a re-numbering of the 343rd Fighter Group. It comprised the 64th, 65th, and 66th Fighter Squadrons. The 57th FG in fact had existed before that time as a P-40 Warhawk and later P-47 equipped fighter-bomber group in North Africa and later Italy during World War Two. Almost at once the 'new' 57th FG began receiving P-51H Mustangs, these aircraft having been adapted for cold weather operations in Alaska at Spokane in Washington. Four examples were received in the initial days of the 57th FG's existence, but it was not until October that year that the group began building up any great number of these aircraft. One of the initial four Mustangs was lost in an accident occasioned by engine problems within days of its arrival, and the lightweight Mustang in general did not have a very happy time in the bleak coldness of Alaska and particularly the Aleutians. The group was tasked with the air defence of the Aleutian chain of islands, and support of ground units in the area, which appeared to be something of a backwater to which the lightweight Mustangs had been quietly consigned. Indeed, Shemya proved to be an impossible base for Mustang operations with its at best difficult weather conditions, and the 57th FG deployed to mainland Alaska in March/April 1947, remaining headquartered at Elmendorf AFB until it was inactivated there in April 1953 – by which time the Mustangs were long since replaced by jets. The squadrons of the 57th in fact deployed where necessary with their Mustangs, at one stage the 64th Fighter Squadron during 1947 found itself based at Nome which was as close as the P-51H ever got to the mainland Soviet Union, only some 150 miles (241 km) away. The 57th FG sometimes put up some impressive formations of Mustangs, on 8 August 1947 making a mass interception of B-29 Superfortresses of the 7th Bombardment Group which were making their way to Fairbanks, Alaska, from their home in Texas. A period of alert followed during 1948 due to the commencement of the blockade of Berlin by the Soviet Union, but the group started to convert to the F-80 Shooting Star during that year having been redesignated as the 57th Fighter Wing in March 1948. By that time the P-51H had been renamed as the F-51H in line with the changes that took place following the formation of the independent USAF in 1947. The group's remaining F-51Hs (28 had been lost in accidents or lesser mishaps) were later passed to Air National Guard squadrons.

As described earlier in this book, the organisation that was created after World War Two to manage and operate the USAAF's long-range bomber assets, Strategic Air Command, had assigned early in its existence several fighter groups specifically to escort its bombers. Three of these groups were operators of the P-51D Mustang, but two were also equipped for a time with the P-51H. The first of these was a very famous fighter group from World War Two, the 56th Fighter Group. This unit had flown the Republic P-47 Thunderbolt throughout all of its time in Europe with the Eighth Air Force from 1943 to 1945, and had been one of the most successful fighter groups of the Eighth during that time. However, post-war reality resulted in the group transitioning onto the P-51H in September 1946, having been reactivated on 1 May 1946 after

returning home from England during October 1945 and being inactivated that month. Many of the first P-51H Mustangs for the group were assigned from storage at Kelly Field in Texas, the well-known post-war holding area for redundant Mustangs. The 56th FG comprised the 61st, 62nd, and 63rd Fighter Squadrons, and these were fully equipped with the P-51H by the end of October 1946. The 62nd FS duly deployed to Alaska in December 1946, and ran into the same problems of appalling weather and marginal operating capability that the 57th Fighter Group found in the same area. In fact the 56th FG did not operate the P-51H for long, as the P-80 Shooting Star started to re-equip the group in the spring of 1947. However, the 62nd FS deployed to Grenier Field, New Hampshire, where it aided in the transition of a newly reactivated group, the 82nd Fighter Group, onto the P-51H. The 82nd Fighter Group (95th, 96th, and 97th Fighter Squadrons) had flown P-38 Lightning's in the MTO during World War Two, but was reactivated in April 1947 with P-51H Mustangs as a part of SAC and based at Grenier Field. It became the 82nd Fighter Wing in July 1947, and deployed some of its lightweight Mustangs to Alaska in March/April 1948 as a result of the tension in Germany over Berlin, amid fears that the Soviet Union might also try to provoke problems in Alaska too. This did not materialise, and the 82nd eventually deployed back to New Hampshire during the summer of 1948. However, the group began to re-equip with the P-51D Mustang as its lightweight Mustangs were gradually taken away to arm Air National Guard squadrons. The 82nd FW was finally inactivated in October 1949.

## Air National Guard Lightweights

By that time the P-51H had been redesignated the F-51H and had gained a new lease of life, within the Air National Guard. As previously related, the P-51D had served in the National Guard and then the ANG from 1946 onwards, but in 1948 the lightweight F-51H also started to equip Guard squadrons. The first of these was the 166th Fighter Squadron of the Ohio Air National Guard at Lockbourne AFB, which transitioned onto the F-51H in October 1948 having previously flown the F-51D. This was one of the many ANG squadrons that was later called to active duty during the Korean War, and transitioned onto jets although remaining in the continental US. It was returned to state control in November 1952 and reverted back onto the F-51H at Youngstown in Ohio, although redesignated as the 166th Fighter-Bomber Squadron. The squadron returned to the Lockheed F-80C Shooting Star in March 1954. The Korean War was to have a profound effect on the

Wearing full unit markings, a California Air National Guard F-51H formates on the camera ship with a part of the San Francisco Bay area in the background. The Mustang wears the insignia of the 194th Fighter-Interceptor Squadron/Fighter-Bomber Squadron, and is an F-51H-5-NA, serial number 44-64255. The 194th flew F-51H from the summer of 1952 to supplement its existing F-51D Mustangs *(Photo: William T. Larkins)*

operations of the F-51H in ANG service. Although initially some of the early ANG squadrons that transitioned onto the type in the later 1940's did so with aircraft taken out of storage or assigned to the ANG when F-51H-equipped regular Air Force fighter units like the 57th and 82nd Fighter Wings relinquished their lightweight Mustangs for other types, there was a separate and major allocation of the F-51H to ANG squadrons as a result of the start of the Korean War in mid-1950. From the first, the F-51H was not seen by the USAF as combat-worthy for the Korean conflict, but the F-51D certainly was. At that time a considerable number of ANG squadrons were equipped with F-51D Mustangs or early jets, and these were suddenly required for combat service in Korea. The solution was to remove the F-51Ds and jets from ANG Squadrons, send them to Korea - and replace them in the ANG with F-51H lightweight Mustangs. This resulted in the second influx of P-51Hs into ANG service. Many of the aircraft that subsequently served with the ANG came from storage, most being at the large depository at Kelly AFB in Texas. All of these lightweight Mustangs needed to be refurbished and brought up to the latest equipment levels, or at least to be checked over, and to this end each aircraft was given a permit after inspection for the long move by air to California to be worked on. There they went through the workshops of Grand Central Aircraft at Glendale or the Pacific Aeromotive Corporation at Burbank, before being released for duty in the ANG.

In total, seventy-five ANG squadrons eventually flew the Mustang, both original (F-51D/RF-51D) and lightweight (F-51H), and included amongst those were 61 that operated at least one example of the F-51H, either as the main part of their equipment or for some of them in very small numbers or just as a single example. Some of these F-51H squadrons also flew the F-51D – indeed, several squadrons flew F-51D and F-51H Mustangs at the same time, which must have posed interesting logistical and servicing problems, there being little commonality between the two. A brief listing of the overall total of 75 squadrons that flew the Mustang in its F-51D, RF-51D, and F-51H forms is included in the Appendices at the end of this Book. At least one of these squadrons, the 131st Fighter-Interceptor Squadron of the Massachusetts ANG, had an aerobatic team (named the 'Rainbows') comprising F-51Hs. Some of the squadrons did not receive F-51Hs until quite late in the service career of the type, with several transitioning onto them in 1952. Some used their F-51Hs as target-tugs, sometimes with improvised target-towing equipment.

A further unit that flew the F-51H was the 85th Fighter-Interceptor Squadron. This USAF unit was a part of the Air Defense Command (ADC), the major organisation that was tasked from 1946 with air defence of the continental US. The 85th FS was a seasoned combat veteran from World War Two, having flown P-

40 Warhawks and then P-47 Thunderbolts in North Africa and Southern Europe as a part of the 79th Fighter Group. It had been inactivated in July 1947, but was activated again on 1 November 1952 and came directly under the control of the 33rd Air Division. It was equipped with F-51H Mustangs at that time, and was stationed at Scott AFB, Illinois. Some of its Mustangs came from the ANG's 113th FIS of the Indiana ANG, which had previously been based at Scott AFB having been called to active duty due to the Korean War in February 1951. The 85th FIS only flew the P-51H for a comparatively short time, and moved on to the F-86 Sabre during 1953. Amongst the final units to operate the F-51H was the 112th Fighter-Bomber Squadron of the Ohio ANG, which ceased F-51H operations in April 1956. In even this matter, however, the lightweight F-51H was eclipsed by the earlier F-51D, which continued in ANG service until 1957. Several H-model Mustangs were used for a number of trials and development work, including one example which was bailed to the famous US naval fighter manufacturer, Grumman, for development work associated with the Grumman XF10F Jaguar variable-geometry naval jet fighter project. Five P-51H flew with NACA at various times for assorted trials work, although one of these sadly crashed in a fatal accident in May 1948. Two of the five received NACA numbers, NACA 110 and NACA 130. The latter, serial number 44-64415, an F-51H-5-NA, was flown at Moffett Field, California, with a Grumman F8F Bearcat naval fighter in a comparative research programme with examples of the Sabre jet fighter.

One point that does need clearing up relating to the lightweight Mustangs in terms of manufacture concerns the planned production model of the Mustang designated P-51M. Countless published sources have claimed that this version of the Mustang was going to be a Dallas-built P-51H, and that only one example was completed before production contracts were curtailed by the end of World War Two. Although it is true that only one P-51M was finished and found its way onto the books of the USAAF, it is untrue that this mark had any close connection with the lightweight P-51H. In reality the P-51M was to be a re-engined version of the P-51D, built at Dallas with the Packard V-1650-9A engine installed. This was a similar engine to the V-1650-9 of the P-51H/F-51H series, but did not feature water injection. The P-51M was therefore a P-51D/K in all but the choice of engine, and was not a lightweight version. It is true that only one example, serial number 45-11743, was completed and accepted by the USAAF, as a P-51M-1-NT. However, at least 63 further examples of this version appear to have been completed or at least neared completion right at the end of the war, but were not accepted by the Army Air Force as they were no longer required, and were presumably scrapped. The actual story of these aircraft - and their fate - remains a point of controversy amongst historians. These were in any case the last Mustangs to

Seen here not long after the end of World War Two and presumably before the creation of the independent USAF, P-51H 44-64180 was being used as a recruiting poster by proclaiming "Enlist in the AAF now, be a guardian of victory". It belonged to a base unit at Bolling Field, Maryland, and carried the 'Buzz Number' PF-180, wartime and immediate post-war US national insignia without the later red horizontal bars, and was the first P-51H-5-NA
(Photo: R.L. Ward Collection)

be built at the NAA Dallas facility, in around September 1945. On the other hand, the Dallas-built P-51H look-alike that was genuinely envisaged was to have been the P-51L, powered by a Packard V-1650-11 engine, but although 1,700 production examples appear to have been planned this version was never built. Neither was the P-51E, because that designation was never given to a production version of the Mustang. There has been speculation that the P-51E was to have been the Dallas-built equivalent of the P-51D, but in the event that Mustang version was simply manufactured as the P-51D-NT series.

## The British Connection

Considering that the British interest in the creation of a lightweight Mustang had been one of the important factors that had motivated NAA into developing the lightweight Mustang series, only a very small number of lightweight Mustangs were ever allocated British serial numbers or were painted in British markings – and none ever saw active service with the RAF. Only the third XP-51F prototype, 43-43334, appears to have been shipped to Britain, although some mystery surrounds the XP-51G 43-43336. Some sources claim that the latter was actually supplied to Britain. It was allocated the British serial number FR410 and appears to have been called a Mustang Mk.IV, but records show that it was flying in the US as late as April 1945 and was apparently never delivered. The XP-51F 43-43334 definitely did reach Britain, where it was allocated the British serial number FR409. Some sources claim that it was called a Mustang Mk.V by the British, but this term does not appear to have been widely used. FR409 arrived in Britain in the summer of 1944, and served briefly at the A&AEE Boscombe Down for a short time from 21 August 1944. There it was found to have a loaded weight with 150 gallons (682 litres) of fuel of only 7,669 lb (3,479 kg), making it the lightest Mustang in Britain and comparing with the equivalent weight for the Mustang Mk.IV (P-51D/K) of 9,982 lb (4,528 kg) maximum. Boscombe Down's test pilots were suitably impressed with the aircraft, which they found easy to fly with good handling characteristics. The excellent all-round view was also noteworthy. However, one criticism concerned the layout of cockpit controls. NAA had re-worked the cockpit interior of the lightweight Mustangs, giving a somewhat different layout to controls and instrumentation in the lightweight models compared to the previous production

Mustangs. This was done mainly to make the cockpit a better working environment for long-range missions, and was to an extent based on combat experience with the P-51D and earlier models. Nevertheless, the cockpit layout in the P-51B/C series, and in the P-51D/K, was excellent, and the re-working for the lightweight Mustangs generated criticism from some pilots. There has also been some mystery surrounding a P-51H that was allocated the British serial number KN987. It is believed that this aircraft was for evaluation purposes, but, like the XP-51G FR410, there is no evidence that it ever spent any time in Britain.

## Final Merlin-Mustang US Service

During the latter stages of their USAF service, some Mustangs were becoming somewhat weary. On 19 January 1953 the USAF ordered that all existing Mustangs in service should have their tail wheel retraction mechanism disengaged and the tail wheel undercarriage locked in the down position. During the period after the Second World War many Mustangs had traded in their fabric-covered tail control surfaces for metal-covered units, and some Mustangs had been converted as fast target-towing aircraft for use at gunnery meets. As more and more examples were retired, a considerable number of airworthy airframes were stored in the open at Kelly AFB in Texas, from where a gradual process of selling off at least some of the lower-time airframes began in the later 1950's. Officially, the end for the Mustang in USAF service came on 27 January 1957. On that day, F-51D-25-NA, 44-72948, a veteran of the West Virginia ANG, was flown to the premises of the Air Force Museum by Maj James L Miller. In fact the flying career of '948' was not quite over, because the aircraft subsequently flew again the following month in honour of the debut of the film 'Battle Hymn', which detailed the experiences of an American aviator who had much influence on the Republic of Korea Air Force, Dean Hess. For the Mustang there had therefore been just over thirteen years and nine months of service with the USAAF and then the USAF, following the combat debut of the first Mustangs in US service from 9 April 1943 onwards. This was not quite, however, the end of the story for the USAF's involvement with the Mustang, because as described later in this book, limited further developments took place during the 1960's.

The Mustang story in US military service came to a significant moment on 27 January 1957. On that day, F-51D-25-NA, 44-72948, a veteran of the West Virginia ANG, was flown to the premises of the US Air Force Museum by Maj James L Miller, officially marking the end of active Mustang service in the USAF. The Museum is located at Wright-Patterson AFB, the old Wright Field where the original testing and evaluation of the Mustang for the US services was carried out. It has since been re-named as the 'National Museum of the United States Air Force'. As for Mustang '948', it subsequently flew again the following month, in honour of the debut of the film 'Battle Hymn', which detailed the experiences of an American aviator who had much influence on the Republic of Korea Air Force, Dean Hess (Photo: USAF)

# Twin Mustangs and Further Developments

## Chapter 8

Quite probably the most high-profile Twin Mustang was P-82B serial number 44-65168 named 'Betty Jo', which was specially prepared to accomplish a very long-distance publicity flight. It was fitted with extra fuel tanks in the fuselage space behind the pilots' seats, some of its military equipment was removed, and four oversize 310 US gallon drop tanks were suspended from the outer wing pylons (two of these pylons were installed beneath each wing). On 27/28 February 1947 the aircraft flew non-stop from Hawaii to New York's La Guardia airport in a time of just over 14 hours, 30 minutes, after a flight of at least 4,968 miles (7,995 km) at an average speed of some 342 mph (550 km/h). The Twin Mustang was flown by Lt Col Robert E. Thacker, with Lt John Ard as co-pilot, and was named 'Betty Jo' after Thacker's wife – although, as seen here, originally the name was incorrectly painted as 'Betty Joe'! Militarily the flight was of little value as it did not represent a combat configuration for the Twin Mustang, but it achieved loads of column space in the 'popular press' of the time
*(Photo: USAAF)*

A primary motivator behind the development of what became the Twin Mustang, was the rise to great significance during World War Two of the bomber escort fighter. Although NAA had successfully built into the P-51 Mustang from the start an excellent endurance, even with the addition of external fuel tanks the Mustangs operating in Europe were likely to be flying at the extremes of their range and endurance capabilities if bombers attacking very far-flung targets were to be escorted all the way. In 1943, any concepts for further extending the range of the Mustang must have seemed like a good idea to North American Aviation's engineers, and preliminary thought was given to the creation of a separate but related escort fighter derivative that was additional to the lightweight Mustang development process described in the previous Chapter. The creation of a very long-range escort fighter eventually became even more a good idea when the likelihood of extreme long-range missions across the vast emptiness of the Pacific became more of a possibility as the war progressed. One of the main problems in the Pacific war was the question of distance. The huge mileage between US-held bases and the Japanese homeland was a major consideration for the USAAF, and although from 1944 the B-29 Superfortress bomber with its long-range capability could fly those distances, there needed to be fighters with similar range that could stay with the bombers. American bomber assets gradually came into the range of attacks on Japan itself due to the 'island hopping' campaign that the US undertook across the Pacific, which involved gradually wresting control from the Japanese of islands ever closer to the Japanese home islands that could then be used as air bases. Even so the distances involved were still large, and the need gradually developed for a fighter able to cover those vast distances. In 1943 these long-range Pacific operations were still some time in the future, but North American Aviation began looking at possible ways to further extend the Mustang's excellent range capabilities. At that time the Mustang was yet to prove itself as a pre-eminent long-range escort, but NAA always had the capacity of forward-thinking, and the idea of creating a very long-range fighter drawing on aspects of the Mustang design began to take shape.

## The Creation of the Twin Mustang

During the New Year period of 1944 the company put forward a number of long-range fighter proposals to the USAAF. These aroused sufficient interest for the go-ahead of the construction of a number of prototypes, under Contract no. AC-2029 of 7 January 1944. Two prototypes were envisaged under NAA number NA-120 of a long-range fighter of very novel layout. Someone at North American – it has never become conclusively obvious exactly who - had reasoned that the excellent long-range abilities of the Mustang could be considerably enhanced by mating two Mustang fuselages to a common centre section and horizontal tail, with a new undercarriage arrangement. Although the ensuing twin-engined, twin-fuselage layout has been much praised by many writers, one cannot help thinking that the resulting airframe had more than just a little of the Heath-Robinson about it, and it definitely looked as if it was two existing aircraft bolted together rather than being a brand-new design resulting from a blank sheet of paper. Certainly the aircraft's two crew members had a lot of daylight between them, with the pilot situated in the left-hand fuselage, and the right-hand fuselage cockpit being inhabited by a co-pilot with a basic set of controls and gauges. The latter crew member would be able to aid in navigation and act as a second pilot which would considerably ease the strain and fatigue of single-pilot operations over the long stretches of Pacific Ocean – although he was very much only along for the ride during any aerial combat. The twin-engined layout would also potentially add a large margin of safety particularly for over-water operations. At some stage early in the design of the type, the name Twin Mustang was coined and quickly became established for the new development.

A large amount of the development and engineering work on the planned Twin Mustang took place in the first half of 1944, at the time when the P-51B was starting to establish the Mustang's reputation as a superlative combat aircraft in the skies over Europe. By the time of this picture on 19 June 1944 (the month of D-Day), this full-scale mock-up was ready for USAAF inspection. Noteworthy are the ports in the centre section wing leading edge for six 0.5-in machine guns, and a pod shape beneath the centre section *(Photo: NAA)*

The two initial Twin Mustang prototypes were designated XP-82 and allocated the serial numbers 44-83886 and 44-83887. They were intended to be powered by two Packard-built Merlins, of the V-1650-23/25 series. These were 'handed' with opposite rotation, with a -23 fitted in one fuselage and a -25 fitted in the other, allowing for the virtual elimination of the problems of engine torque on take-off and in other flight regimes. The V-1650-23/25 was a similar engine type to the V-1650-11, had the same sea level power rating of the V-1650-9 as fitted to the P-51H lightweight Mustang of 1,830 hp, and it also featured the PD.18.C3A injection carburettor of the V-1650-9. The two fuselages themselves resembled those of the lightweight experimental Mustang prototypes but, in reality, the fuselage design was virtually new and had little to do with the previous aircraft. Countless writers have claimed that the Twin Mustang was simply two P-51H fuselages joined together but this is completely untrue, if anything the fuselage of the experimental lightweight XP-51F was the closest relative of the Twin Mustang fuselages, which anyway were longer. The undercarriage arrangement for the new fighter was also new, with each fuselage having its own tail wheel while the main landing gear legs were attached at the root of each outer wing panel and retracted inwards into the lower fuselage and wing centre section. The Twin Mustang thus had a four-point undercarriage configuration, which made for some interesting taxiing experiences for those unused to this type of arrangement. The outer wing sections retained the laminar flow configuration of the single-seat Mustangs, but the wing as a whole was a stronger entity able to carry greater loads. Internal armament for the Twin Mustang was to be carried in the new wing centre section which joined the two fuselages, doing away with guns mounted in the outer wing panels as in the conventional single-engined P-51 Mustang fighters. Underwing pylons were provided beneath the outer wing sections for the carriage of fuel tanks, bombs and/or rockets. Indeed, bearing in mind the considerable use, particularly of earlier Mustang models, as light ground-attack aircraft, NAA ensured that its new twin would be a well-armed machine for any particular role that it might be called upon to perform.

## Production Commences

While detail design work took place on the new twin-engined fighter, NAA received an initial contract on 8 March 1944 from the USAAF for 500 Twin Mustangs that would be designated P-82B (NA-123). These would be powered by V-1650-23/25 engines as in the two XP-82 prototypes (although interestingly 'handed' -19 or -9/-21 engines appear to have been specified, and it seems likely that some if not all the production P-82Bs used this combination), and incorporate a number of detail differences from the initial prototype aircraft. As a separate issue, two further prototypes, designated XP-82A (similarly designated NA-120), were additionally envisaged, powered by Allison engines. As with

the XP-51J experimental lightweight Mustangs, North American Aviation returned to the Allison power plant in the Twin Mustang as well. It has been argued by a number of writers that this was because of fears that Britain might revoke the manufacturing licence for the Merlin engine if and when the Second World War ended, and the Allison would be the obvious engine type to install instead. The engine chosen was the Allison V-1710-119, which was the two-stage, two-speed supercharged version of the Allison V-1710 that was also tried out in the XP-51J lightweight Mustang. This engine was a troublesome power plant, but fortunately many of the problems were ironed out before the Twin Mustang reached widespread service. In the XP-82A, two V-1710-119 were installed without being 'handed', which must have led to some hair-raising take-offs and landings with the torque from both engines pulling the Twin Mustang off in the same direction. Interestingly, some official Air Force documents of the time refer to at least one production version of the P-82 as the P-82Z, although this designation does not appear to have been used beyond official paperwork.

The first XP-82, 44-83886, flew for the first time on 15 April 1945. It was followed by the second XP-82 on 30 August 1945 and by the XP-82A 44-83888 later in the year. In fact only one of the

The second prototype for the P-82 series was the XP-82, serial number 44-83887, seen here during an early test flight. Both XP-82 prototypes were powered by V-1650-23/25 engines. Following development work with the manufacturer, this aircraft later served with NACA on research programmes *(Photo: NAA)*

The Twin Mustang assembly line at NAA's Inglewood facility. All Twin Mustangs were produced at Inglewood, and in comparison to the standard P-51 Mustang, the P-82 was a much more complicated aircraft to build. Nevertheless, manufacture was only cut-back due to the cancellation of orders at the end of World War Two, causing production to be made at a comparatively slow and leisurely pace (Photo: NAA)

The instrument panel of the P-82B, in the pilot's (left-hand) fuselage side. The cockpit layout was similar if a little more basic in the right-hand fuselage side in this model for the co-pilot/navigator. Noteworthy is the small panel to the left just below the main instrument panel, with switches for the bombs, rockets and guns, and warning lights for the undercarriage (Photo: NAA)

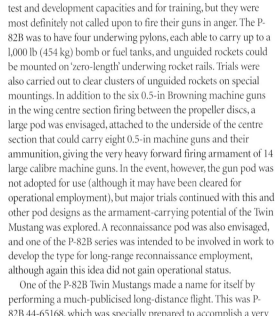

two Allison-powered XP-82As was ever finished, but the end of World War Two did indeed lead to problems over the continued licence-manufacture of Merlin engines in the US, and so this aircraft in effect proved to be the prototype for most of the production Twin Mustangs that followed. In fact the ending of Second World War led to a number of problems for the Twin Mustang programme. Significantly, the order for 500 of the V-1650-powered P-82B was cut, with just 20 examples being completed and readied for handing over to the USAAF. They were from the initial P-82B-1-NA (NA-123) block, starting with serial number 44-65160. Several of these aircraft subsequently served in

test and development capacities and for training, but they were most definitely not called upon to fire their guns in anger. The P-82B was to have four underwing pylons, each able to carry up to a l,000 lb (454 kg) bomb or fuel tanks, and unguided rockets could be mounted on 'zero-length' underwing rocket rails. Trials were also carried out to clear clusters of unguided rockets on special mountings. In addition to the six 0.5-in Browning machine guns in the wing centre section firing between the propeller discs, a large pod was envisaged, attached to the underside of the centre section that could carry eight 0.5-in machine guns and their ammunition, giving the very heavy forward firing armament of 14 large calibre machine guns. In the event, however, the gun pod was not adopted for use (although it may have been cleared for operational employment), but major trials continued with this and other pod designs as the armament-carrying potential of the Twin Mustang was explored. A reconnaissance pod was also envisaged, and one of the P-82B series was intended to be involved in work to develop the type for long-range reconnaissance employment, although again this idea did not gain operational status.

One of the P-82B Twin Mustangs made a name for itself by performing a much-publicised long-distance flight. This was P-82B 44-65168, which was specially prepared to accomplish a very long-distance publicity effort. It was fitted with extra fuel tanks in the fuselage space behind the pilots' seats, some of its military equipment was removed, and four oversize 310 US gallon drop tanks were suspended from the outer wing pylons (two of these pylons were installed beneath each wing). On 27/28 February 1947 the aircraft flew non-stop from Hawaii to New York in a time of just over 14 hours, 30 minutes, after a flight of at least 4,968 miles (7,995 km) at an average speed of some 342 mph (550 km/h). This was achieved even though three of the giant external fuel tanks would not jettison and had to be carried the entire distance, increasing drag and making the aircraft unstable. The Twin Mustang was flown by Lt Col Robert E. Thacker, with Lt John Ard as co-pilot, and was named 'Betty Jo' after Thacker's wife. The flight represented a new record between the two points, and it was arguably the longest flight at that time by a piston-engined fighter, although it was nowhere near the longest flight by a piston-engined combat aircraft – in November 1938 two Vickers Wellesley bombers of the RAF flew non-stop from Ismailia, Egypt, to Darwin, Australia, a distance of 7,157.7 miles (11,519 km). Indeed, militarily the flight of 'Betty Jo' was of little actual value, as the Twin Mustang in service would not have been able to fly combat with the four massive fuel tanks installed.

An interesting in-flight image of the high-profile P-82B Twin Mustang serial number 44-65168 named 'Betty Jo', which made the well-known (at the time) long-distance flight in February 1947 from Hawaii to New York's La La Guardia airport. As can be seen in this photograph, the Twin Mustang was heavily overloaded with underwing fuel tanks in order to achieve the non-stop flight. Although this publicity stunt proved that Twin Mustangs could fly a long way, the actual combat value was limited, as the aircraft certainly could not carry any useful load apart from fuel in this configuration, and in any case the increasing service introduction of jet fighters was rapidly bringing to a close the days of the piston-engined front-line day fighter *(Photo: USAAF)*

Even though the order for 500 P-82Bs had been drastically cut, a version of the Twin Mustang for purely long-range escort work was manufactured. This was the P-82E (NA-144), which was Allison V-1710-143/145 powered, and was built to a total of 100 aircraft starting with serial number 46-255. The P-82E was in effect an Allison-engined P-82B, and the order for 100 aircraft was made in November 1945 (the contract appears to have been effective from 12 December 1945). It can be argued that this order was part of a plan by the USAAF to help keep aircraft manufacturers alive in the immediate post-war period, due to the massive cancellations and cut-backs occasioned by the end of the war which had caused real problems for some companies. The Allison engines in the P-82E were 'handed' to reduce torque effects, and the whole combination drove the now well-established Aeroproducts propeller units – which of course were also handed to go with the alternative rotation of the engine versions, and were also fully-feathering. The P-82E (after mid-1948, F-82E) was built from early 1946 and eventually served successfully with one long-range bomber escort wing of Strategic Air Command.

### Night-Fighter Development

In addition to the long-range bomber escort role, the Twin Mustang was given a totally new role when the USAAF started to develop a completely different requirement. This was for a night-fighter to replace the Northrop P-61 Black Widow night-fighter of World War Two, which had continued in service post-war. The large, twin-engined Black Widow had been America's only purpose-built production night-fighter of the war, but had been successful in combat in both Europe and the Pacific. The first operational Black Widows had flown from the south of England in the summer of 1944, and the type had underlined the growing need for efficient night-fighters. The role of night fighting had in effect come of age during the Second World War, and had become an integral part of aerial warfare. At the end of World War Two there were two distinct types of fighter. On the one hand there was the day fighter such as the Mustang and Spitfire; and on the other hand, radar-equipped night-fighters such as the Black Widow and successfully adapted aircraft such as the de Havilland Mosquito. In the post-war years, the concept of night-fighting was much further developed, so that these distinct roles eventually came together. Increasingly, fighters needed to be able to fight by night and in bad weather as well as by day. Nowadays combat aircraft have all these qualities rolled into one, but in the later 1940's there was the need for a fighter that could fly and fight at night in the best tradition of the Black Widow. This role became known to the USAAF and its successor USAF as the 'all-weather fighter', and the Twin Mustang appeared to be a possible if interim solution to the need to eventually replace the Black Widow.

To that end two of the 20 P-82B Twin Mustangs were used for a development programme that involved the installation of airborne interception radar to the basic Twin Mustang layout. The two aircraft concerned were the tenth and eleventh P-82Bs, and they were converted by NAA with technical assistance from the USAF to P-82C and P-82D standard. The aircraft were identical in airframe and engines, but had different radar systems installed. The P-82C (44-65169) was fitted with SCR-720 radar (a type that dated back to usage in World War Two) in a large central pod, while the P-82D (44-65170) was equipped with the more modern APS-4 radar. The SCR-720 was similar to the equipment carried in the P-61 Black Widow. The pod housing it on the P-82C was a very elongated unit that extended out of front of the arc of the propellers, to reduce interference. Both aircraft were painted glossy black overall to fit in with their new role. The radar screen plus the controls for the radar equipment were installed in the right-hand fuselage cockpit of each of the two development aircraft, the crew member in that side of the Twin Mustang now being the radar operator rather than just a co-pilot or navigator.

The resulting night-fighter layout created considerable interest for the USAAF, again showing how far North American Aviation

The P-82B Twin Mustang 44-65168 named 'Betty Jo' - and its crew members - received much Press attention at the time of the aircraft's highly-publicized long-distance flight from Hawaii to New York's La Guardia airport in February 1947. The mis-spelling of the Twin Mustang's name is noteworthy - it was later corrected! *(Photo: USAAF)*

had come as a creator and manufacturer of fighter aircraft, compared to the company's pre-war status. Two specific marks of Twin Mustang night-fighter were ordered under the FY 1946 procurement. These were the P-82F (NA-149) which equated to the P-82D with a straightforward APG-28 tracking radar installation, 100 being ordered; and the P-82G (NA-150) equipped with SCR-720C radar equipment, of which fifty were built. It might seem that these were ridiculously small totals compared to the thousands of Mustangs that were ordered during the Second World War, and indeed they were, the USAAF having to operate with critically reduced budgets following the end of the war. The first P-82F was serial number 46-405, while conversely the initial P-82G was 46-355. Production of these aircraft progressed comparatively slowly, with engine deliveries from Allison being so delayed that some completed aircraft awaited their engines for some time, and production actually crept into the spring of 1949. All Twin Mustangs were built by NAA at Inglewood.

Although decidedly odd in appearance, especially the P-82G with its huge radar pod protruding forwards from the wing centre section beyond the engine nacelles, the Twin Mustang was a very capable performer. The P-82G was powered by the Allison V-1710-143/145 'handed' engines, like the P-82E and P-82F, which developed 1,600 hp each at take-off but with water/alcohol injection achieved 1,930 hp each at sea level for short periods. Maximum speed was in the region of 459 mph (739 km/h) at 21,000 ft (6,400 m). These engines, like the V-1710-119, had an up-draught carburettor that necessitated the associated air intake to be located below the engine. This intake was smaller and further back than that characteristic of Merlin-engined Mustangs, but it represented an important redesign for the V-1710 engine

layout. Hitherto V-1710 variants used in the early production Mustangs had a simple downdraught carburetion system that called for the intake to be on the top of the cowling – which was one of the distinguishing features of all of the Allison-engined Mustangs. The propeller type fitted was an Aeroproducts unit of 11 ft (3.35 m) diameter. The maximum take-off weight of the P-82G was a staggering 25,891 lb (11,744 kg).

Although built in comparatively small numbers the night-fighter Twin Mustangs were a useful - if rare - beast in the USAF's inventory. In addition to air-to-air missions with the established six 0.5-in machine guns in the centre wing, the Twin Mustangs were fully fitted out for air-to-ground work, and a variety of weapons could be carried beneath the outer wing sections including unguided air-to-ground rockets, bombs of up to 1,000 lb (454 kg) each on four underwing pylons, or of course fuel tanks, normally of up to 165 US gallons. The total internal fuel, in four self-sealing wing fuel tanks, was 576 US gallons (although one reputable published source claims 574 US gallons, but in any case not all of this potential load would have been usable), which gave the Twin Mustangs a range of some 2,240 miles (3,605 km). In line with other USAF aircraft types, the Twin Mustang was redesignated in mid-1948, all versions henceforth being called F-82 instead of the previous P-82. The initial 'Buzz Number' prefix for the Twin Mustang of 'PQ' was accordingly changed to 'FQ'. Although production was intended to be ended at Inglewood with the final F-82F and F-82G examples in 1948 (but, as previously related, some of these aircraft were not ready to fly until 1949), there was, nevertheless, one further Twin Mustang variant. This was the F-82H, which was a conversion of several existing F-82F and F-82G night-fighter Twin Mustangs specifically for operations in Alaska. The modification process included 'winterisation', which although rarely detailed, in fact included improved heating in the two cockpits, improved sealing of the cockpits and several other measures including the use of higher strength oil. In total, five F-82G and nine F-82F Twin Mustangs were modified to this standard.

## Twin Mustangs in Service

The day-fighter bomber escort version of the Twin Mustang, the P/F-82E, served principally with one USAF unit. This was the 27th Fighter Wing, which already had a long association with the Mustang. As the 27th Fighter-Bomber Group, it had flown the A-36A Invader dive-bomber in combat in the MTO during World War Two from 1943 to 1944. In the post-Second World War era it had renewed its association with the Mustang, becoming operational within Strategic Air Command in July/August 1947 as the 27th Fighter Wing. The unit had been based at Kearney Army Air Field, Nebraska, but converted onto the F-82E Twin Mustang during 1948, although it continued to have some Mustangs on strength as well in the later 1940's. The 27th was still based at Kearney (later renamed as an AFB) during March

Although smartly dressed in full USAF markings, this P-82B is representative of that early mark of Twin Mustang in being used solely for development work or other such tasks, as the P-82B did not fly with front-line units. Nevertheless, this version was useful in proving the viability of the Twin Mustang as a type, and its day fighter successor in the Twin Mustang line, the P/F-82E, certainly did see operational service (Photo: USAF)

1948 when it started to receive initial deliveries of F-82E Twin Mustangs. Comprising the 522nd, 523rd, and 524th Fighter Squadrons, the 27th FW fully converted onto the type during that year, and did a great deal to prove the Twin Mustang in service. The wing was combat-ready on the type by the end of 1948. In effect the 27th flew the Twin Mustang in the role that it had originally been intended for, namely the long-range escort of US strategic bombers. The wing was assigned to the Eighth Air Force of SAC, and became well-known for long-distance proving flights which explored the Twin Mustang's range and operational flexibility. In February 1949, 54 Twin Mustangs of the 27th set off on a long-range flight in stages that took them south from Kearney AFB to Panama and back, the whole exercise taking some ten days. A number of the stages in the journey were flown at night, and the whole exercise was flown without a bomber to escort the fighters and provide navigation. Such long-range flights were aided by the Twin Mustang having two crew members, for the co-pilot in the right-hand fuselage was able to take over and fly the aircraft from time to time to allow the pilot to rest. Indeed, the crew member in the right-hand fuselage had to fly the aircraft for the sake of safety during formation flying if his aircraft was the one on the extreme left of the formation. The F-82E could certainly be flown from the right-hand seat because all the relevant controls and instruments were provided (although some of these could be stowed away when not needed), together with the ability to lower the undercarriage in an emergency and perform other tasks as necessary. The occupant in the right-hand seat, however, had a rough time if his aircraft was rolled. Twin Mustangs tended to roll around the left-hand fuselage, and so the pilot had no particular problems, but the manoeuvre could be very uncomfortable for the occupant in the right-hand fuselage. In March 1949 the 27th FW moved from Kearney AFB to Bergstrom AFB in Texas, and in keeping with its mission, on 1 February 1950 the 27th was renamed as the 27th Fighter-Escort Wing, and its squadrons became Fighter-Escort Squadrons on the same date. However the time was by then

virtually up for the Twin Mustang as an escort fighter, as jets increasingly had the range and superior performance to provide cover for SAC's bombers, which in any case were to go through their own jet revolution. By the end of 1950 the 27th had fully transitioned onto the Republic F-84E Thunderjet, its Twin Mustangs being stood down on paper in August 1950. The wing at once showed its enhanced capability by deploying its Thunderjets from Bergstrom AFB to Europe in September 1950 in a mass flight that won for the unit the Mackay Trophy.

Although built in comparatively small numbers, the Twin Mustang night-fighters served in a wide variety of squadrons from 1948 onwards. It was the middle of that year before night-fighter Twin Mustangs started to become available in numbers, allowing several of the night-fighter squadrons to begin to transition onto the type and start to give up the Northrop F-61 Black Widow. The latter type had given sterling service in the immediate post-war era and was still in fairly widespread use in 1948, there being no single type that could replace it until the F-82 started to become available. In the event nine night-fighter/all-weather squadrons subsequently operated the Twin Mustang, in the continental US and in the Pacific and Korea – none served in Europe. The squadrons were the 2nd and 5th of the 52nd Fighter Wing (All Weather) to cover the eastern US; the 317th, 318th, and 319th Squadrons of the 325th FW (AW) in the western US; the 4th, 68th, and 339th Squadrons of the 347th FW (AW) in the Pacific; and the 449th Squadron of the 5001st Composite Wing in Alaska. It will be noted that several of these units already had a significant connection with the Mustang, the former two wings having flown the type, as the 52nd and 325th Fighter Groups, in the MTO during World War Two.

The actual designations of the squadrons that flew the Twin Mustang as a night-fighter needs a little explaining. All of the above squadrons operated the P-61 Black Widow prior to transitioning onto the Twin Mustang, and in effect the Twin Mustang subsequently bridged the gap in service between the Black Widow, which was a Second World War type, and the advent

This factory ramp view of 'PQ-255', the first of the P-82E long-range Twin Mustang day fighters, displays all the relevant features of the P/F-82E Twin Mustang. Particularly noteworthy are the gun ports in the centre wing section for the six 0.5-in machine guns, which fired between the propeller discs, the guns being staggered in their installation to allow for the ammunition feeds to reach each gun without interruption. Also visible is the neat installation of the 'handed' Allison V-1710-143/145 engines which rotated in opposite directions, the 'handed' Aeroproducts propellers, and the characteristic undercarriage arrangement (Photo: NAA)

The Twin Mustang was the most distinctive shape in the sky during the time of its operational service. The type's twin-fuselage layout is well illustrated in this image, seen from a rarely-photographed rear three-quarter angle. This particular aircraft is 'PQ-255', the first of the P-82E long-range day fighters *(Photo: NAA)*

of the all-weather-capable Lockheed F-94 Starfire. The Starfire was the first widely-operated USAF all-weather jet fighter, and was a two-seat, single-engined fighter that was developed from the P-80 Shooting Star series which had been the first jet fighter to operate in the USAAF. Some writers have therefore seen the Twin Mustang as an interim type until jets took over the night-fighter role forever, but in service the Twin Mustang nevertheless represented an improvement in capability from the earlier Black Widow. The advent of the so-called all-weather fighter resulted in a major change of designation in 1948 as the night-fighter Twin Mustang started to enter service. The units destined to operate the type were redesignated as Fighter Squadrons (All Weather). One of the first to take on this title was the 5th FS (AW), which was officially designated as such on 10 May 1948. On the same day the 2nd FS (AW) was also born. A further change took place in January 1950, when the name changed to Fighter-All Weather Squadron. Thus the 5th FS (AW) became the 5th F-AWS on 20 January 1950. In April/May 1951 the nameplate changed once more, those squadrons still flying the Twin Mustang at that time becoming Fighter-Interceptor Squadrons. In keeping with this, the wings that the squadrons were assigned to also changed their names, the 52nd for example becoming the 52nd Fighter Wing (All Weather) on 10 May 1948, and changing its name to the 52nd Fighter-All Weather Wing on 20 January 1950. In May 1951 it became the 52nd Fighter-Interceptor Wing, and was inactivated in February 1952 at the end of its association with the Twin Mustang. For the

record, the 52nd and its two Twin Mustang squadrons was successively based at Mitchell Field (later, AFB), New York, from June 1948, and at McGuire AFB, New Jersey, from October 1949 until it was inactivated.

As for the other Twin Mustang night-fighter/all-weather units, the squadrons of the 325th FW (AW) – later 325th F-AWW – took in a number of base changes during their time with the Twin Mustang. The 317th Squadron principally served at Moses Lake AFB, Washington from late 1948 until April 1950, subsequently moving to McChord AFB, Washington. The 318th Squadron was at McChord AFB from late 1948, and remained there while transitioning onto the F-94 Starfire in the early 1950's. The 319th, however, was much-travelled, starting at France Field in the Panama Canal Zone from early 1948 until April/May 1949. It was then stationed in the US at McChord AFB from May to September 1949, and subsequently at Moses Lake AFB where it eventually relinquished its Twin Mustangs. The 449th Squadron, on the other hand, was based throughout its time with the Twin Mustang in Alaska. One of the first all-weather fighter squadrons to receive the Twin Mustang, the squadron was aided in its transition onto the type by members of the 27th Fighter Wing, who had by then successfully taken on the day-fighter F-82E Twin Mustang. Indeed, most of the all-weather/night-fighter squadrons were assisted by members of the 27th as they converted onto the type from the F-61 Black Widow. Three crews of the 27th Fighter Wing flew in their F-82Es from their base at Kearney AFB in Nebraska during

The P-82E serial number 46-256 in flight, bearing a data measuring boom on its left-hand wing. Although representative of the P/F-82E series, this particular aircraft also served with the Lewis Research Centre of NACA between January 1950 and March 1954 on icing research, becoming NACA 133 and redesignated as an EF-82E. It is seen here comparatively early in its life and still bearing the early 'Buzz number' prefix 'PQ' that was used prior to the change in designations following the creation of the USAF *(Photo: NAA)*

September 1948 to Adak where the 449th FS (AW) was based. An intensive period of operations ensued in which each new crew destined for F-82 operations was put through its paces. Fortunately the Twin Mustangs operated without serious problems and some 49 days later the three crews from the 27th FW returned home. The 449th Squadron subsequently proved to be the longest-surviving Twin Mustang unit, continuing to fly the type until well into 1953 – the F-82 officially being retired in October 1953. By then the squadron had transitioned onto the F-94 Starfire. Based at Adak until March 1949, the squadron subsequently operated from Ladd AFB in Alaska throughout all its remaining time on the Twin Mustang. The squadron was assigned directly to Alaskan Air Command in September 1947, but joined the 5001st Composite Wing on 1 July 1949, which it stayed with into 1953 until joining the 11th Air Division in April 1953. Latterly the squadron was assigned examples of the rare 'winterised' F-82H.

The Twin Mustangs of the night-fighter/all-weather squadrons were involved during their operational time on the F-82 with developing tactics not only to get the best out of their Twin Mustangs, but also to work out tactics to deploy effectively with ground-based radars and other air defence systems. Although this co-operation was not new, having started to evolve during World War Two, much of the technology was moving forwards and the Twin Mustangs showed their potential effectiveness in a number of specific exercises. These included Operation 'Swarmer' in April 1949, which involved many USAF assets including Twin Mustangs from the 2nd and 5th Fighter Squadrons (All Weather). This exercise tested the effectiveness of the air defence network for the eastern US, and involved the Twin Mustangs forward-operating from Shaw AFB in South Carolina.

In addition to the front-line units, four Twin Mustangs served at different times with the NACA. The first of these was the XF-82 serial number 44-83886, which operated at NACA's Langley facility from June 1948 until October 1955 on a variety of projects. It became NACA 114 during that time. The second XF-82, 44-83887, served at NACA's Lewis Research Centre from October 1947 until July 1950, principally on ram-jet power plant research. The famous F-82B 44-65168, otherwise known as 'Betty Jo' which made the non-stop flight from Hawaii to New York in February 1947, served at the same NACA facility from September 1950 until June 1957. It replaced the XP-82 44-83887 on ram-jet trials and research when the latter was damaged during testing. 'Betty Jo' eventually became NACA 132. Finally, the F-82E 46-256 also served at the Lewis Research Centre between January 1950 and March 1954 on icing research, becoming NACA 133 and redesignated as an EF-82E. Although the Twin Mustangs that were based in the US never had to fire their guns in anger, the F-82s that operated in the Pacific had the accolade of taking the Twin Mustang into combat. The three Pacific-based Twin Mustang units, the 4th, 68th, and 339th Squadrons, were assigned at least on paper to the 347th Fighter Wing (All Weather). The 4th was based at Naha, Okinawa, throughout its time with the Twin Mustang, but a detachment was made to Itazuke in Japan in the initial stages of the Korean War.

This squadron in practice came under the umbrella of the 51st Fighter-Interceptor Wing, which was responsible for the air defence of the Okinawa area. The 68th was stationed at Ashiya, Japan, from May 1949 after a stay at Bofu, Japan, but moved to Itazuke in April 1950, and had close associations with the 8th Fighter-Bomber Wing. The 339th, which in practice was attached to the 35th Fighter-Interceptor Wing, was at Johnson AB, Japan, until March/April 1950 when the squadron moved to Yokota in Japan; it remained there briefly until August 1950 when a return was made to Johnson AB. This meant that the three squadrons were on hand when the Korean War began in June 1950, and all three subsequently played a part in the early stages of the conflict. Indeed, the Twin Mustang hit the headlines when the first air-to-air kills of the war were achieved by F-82s operating over Korea, as described in the following Chapter. The onset of the war resulted in the 347th Wing, which had become a Fighter-All Weather Wing in January 1950, being inactivated on 24 June 1950 (at least, that is what the official records say). The three Twin Mustang squadrons were duly assigned directly to the local Air Forces within the umbrella of Far East Air Forces. The 68th and 339th were assigned to the Fifth Air Force, and the 4th was assigned to the Twentieth Air Force. The Twin Mustangs subsequently distinguished themselves in combat, but a shortage of spares eventually compromised the operations of these aircraft.

## Birth of the Cavalier Mustang

Although the F-82 Twin Mustang left the USAF's inventory in 1953, and the final active Mustang was retired in 1957, this was by no means the end of the story for the Mustang line, and even its

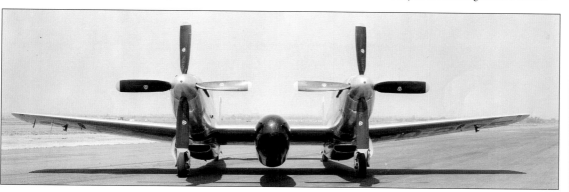

Wearing an overall black night-fighter finish, the one and only P-82C displays its distinctive side profile with the pod attached to the underside of its centre wing section for the SCR-720 airborne radar as one of the development aircraft for the planned night-fighter developments of the Twin Mustang layout. Serial number 44-65169, it was originally a P-82B before conversion, and its central pod containing the SCR-720 radar was smaller than the much longer pod of the P-82D which had the APS-4 radar fitted
*(Photo: NAA)*

connections with the US military continued several years after these retirements. In the late 1950's, many surplus Mustangs became available for sale to private individuals. In the US the available aircraft were from former-USAF stocks, but another excellent source of surplus Mustangs was Canada, where former Royal Canadian Air Force-operated Mustangs started to become available in increasing numbers in the late 1950's. At this stage in the Mustang's story a private individual became involved who had no connections to North American Aviation, but who was to have a profound influence on prolonging the life of the Mustang. He was David Breed Lindsay, Jr., and his companies, including Trans-Florida Aviation and the Cavalier Aircraft Corporation, became household names to many in the aviation business in the 1960's. Through the activities of these companies a number of Mustang airframes were 'reprocessed' to 'new' condition, mainly for civil use but a significant number were subsequently operated by military air arms.

This completely new branch of the Mustang story commenced in the late 1950's when USAF storage depots contained an increasing number of once front-line but by then out-of-date fighter aircraft. Sadly, many of these aircraft were eventually scrapped, but a significant number survived and were sold on to private individuals. Indeed, low-time Mustang airframes could be bought for as little as $800, although many sold for upwards of double that figure. Florida-based newspaper businessman David B. Lindsay, Jr., saw the market potential of some of the surplus aircraft, and quickly developed ambitious plans for ex-military Mustangs. His initial idea was to modify the Mustang airframe into a high-performance executive aircraft, which would be 'civilianised' and fitted out with the latest avionics and other

relevant equipment. Lindsay shrewdly realised that the Mustang could be a useful business asset, and the 'Cavalier' concept was born. In the following years his programme would significantly prolong, both in civil and later in military terms, the service life of the Mustang. Lindsay began by forming a company to undertake the task, Trans-Florida Aviation, Inc., based at Sarasota-Bradenton Airport, Sarasota, Florida, which acquired eight ex-RCAF P-51D Mustangs to commence the programme. These airframes were all ex-No. 443 Squadron aircraft with low airframe hours. On arrival at Sarasota the first of these P-51D Mustangs, serial number 44-73411, was completely stripped down. By that time Lindsay had formulated his own plans and concepts for the conversion of the new executive Mustang.

Following dismantling, 44-73411 was stripped of all military equipment, including the military radio set, and weapons-related fitments and installations. Lindsay somewhat ambitiously envisaged the aircraft as a two-seater, and so the large fuselage fuel tank, located behind the pilot's seat, was removed. This fuel tank, as related earlier in this book, had been somewhat notorious during the service life of the Merlin-engined versions of the P-51, its installation in the fuselage having caused centre of gravity problems and complicated the operational use of the type. The floor within the fuselage where the fuel tank had been installed was reinforced and a second, custom-built seat was fitted in its place. A well-appointed interior was installed, with upholstery and carpeting. As the noise level in the normal P-51D was too high for acceptable civilian operation, the entire cockpit was soundproofed with polyurethane foam and lots of sound-reducing tape. Lindsay himself designed the new instrument panel and cockpit side consoles. With a light grey basic colour the main instrument panel

In its overall appearance the Twin Mustang was hardly an elegant aircraft, and had something of the Heath-Robinson about it. The overall black colour scheme worn by many of the production aircraft and some of the development aircraft did, however, give more of a purposeful air to the type. This is the P-82C-NA development aircraft, serial number 44-65169, which was equipped with the SCR-720 airborne radar as one of the development aircraft for the planned night-fighter developments of the Twin Mustang layout *(Photo: NAA)*

was designed to include both engine and flight instrumentation. The principal flight instruments were mounted vertically at the top and centre of the panel ostensibly to avoid potential vertigo problems, with the engine instruments at the left and the radio controls to the right. The left-hand side console featured the throttle, undercarriage and flap controls, three trim wheels and the carburettor heat control. Lindsay's design was basically user-friendly and well thought-out, so that even inexperienced pilots after a short period of familiarization were able to become safely conversant with the cockpit layout. A variety of avionics options was available to potential customers. These included Collins Flight Directors, an autopilot, ILS (Instrument Landing System) equipment and an electric compass. Radio controls could be fitted in the front or rear crew stations, according to customer requirements. Individual 'demand'-type oxygen regulators were a standard fit, supplied from oxygen bottles installed in the rear fuselage, or a more complicated high-pressure oxygen system could be incorporated as required. Heat for cabin heating could be drawn from the radiator (as opposed to the manifold on the military P-51 models) and a new cabin ventilation system provided cool air flow when required.

## Two Crew Members

In effect Lindsay was creating in civil form what had already been made in military guise, because the concept of a two-seater Mustang was not new. As previously mentioned in this book, North American Aviation had manufactured a small batch of ten two-seat dual-control Mustangs under the designation TP-51D whilst standard P-51D production was underway. In addition, a number of 'field' modified Mustangs had flown as two-seaters during the latter stages of the Second World War, mainly with fighter groups of the Eighth Air Force. These were not alone. After the war, the Temco Aircraft Corporation also created a batch of two-seat Mustangs, primarily for military employment, by remanufacturing and converting a number of existing Mustang airframes. These were mainly for Air National Guard use, and approximately 15 were converted from F-51D airframes with dual controls. They were a full two-seat conversion, with comparatively comprehensive instrumentation for the rear crew member and a revised cockpit canopy.

Each Mustang airframes in Lindsay's programme received a total overhaul, with considerable work carried out on each airframe and even reskinning where necessary. The wing gun

ports were faired over, and the gun bays were lined and modified to take up to 400 lb (181 kg) of stowed luggage. The powerplant for the 'new' aircraft was based on the Packard V-1650-7 with the characteristic two-speed, two-stage supercharger, but with some equipment from the Merlin 620 series engine. This produced a powerplant rated at 1,595 hp at sea level take-off power. It allowed a power loading of only 7 lb (3 kg) per hp at the 'new' Mustang's 10,500 lb (4,763 kg) maximum take-off weight. A four-blade constant-speed Hamilton Standard 2D50-65 propeller unit was the standard fit.

The instrument panel of the P/F-82G, in the pilot's (left-hand) fuselage side. A small note below the lower line of instrument faces says 'radio call 63-55', which presumably identifies this aircraft as the first P-82G, serial number 46-355. Particularly noteworthy is the shape of the lower part of the pilot's seat and the control column. The pilot's cockpit of the P/F-82F was similar but not quite identical to this layout (Photo: NAA)

The distinctive planform of the Twin Mustang is well illustrated in this view of the one and only P-82D development aircraft with APS-4 radar housed in the long pod between the two fuselages. With its shiny all-black paint scheme, 44-65170 can be seen in flight over the Pacific coastline of the US on what was apparently a publicity flight, as this is one of a large number of photographs that were made of this aircraft at that time (Photo: NAA)

A revealing image of a fully operational P/F-82E, showing a number of transitional markings due to the creation of the independent USAF and the transition from Group to Wing reorganization within the new Air Force. The Twin Mustang is serial number 46-268, with the pre-USAF 'Buzz number' PQ-268 beneath its left-hand wing, and the new USAF 'Buzz number' prefix FQ-268 on its lower fin, in addition to the title 'U.S. Air Force' painted above this on the fin. The aircraft is from the 27th Fighter Group/Wing, whose 'Intelligent Strength' emblem it wears on the fuselage side beneath the cockpit. It also has the red horizontal bar across the otherwise dark blue and white national insignia, again signifying the period when the US Air Force had come into being *(Photo: USAF)*

The prototype airframe, 44-73411, was US civil registered as N550D. Unfortunately, in July 1960 and apparently re-registered as N551D, it was destroyed in a crash at Sarasota. Nevertheless, Trans-Florida duly modified and sold the other seven ex-RCAF airframes from Lindsay's initial purchase. With the sale of these aircraft, Lindsay began to recognize the potential for a production-line style 'processing' of further ex-military Mustangs. As a result, an additional Mustang was rapidly modified to act as an additional prototype and company demonstrator. This was an ex-Minnesota ANG F-51D, 45-11489, which was also registered N551D. During its modification process it was also fitted with a further new innovation – wing-tip fuel tanks. Trans-Florida duly expanded its business by buying up substantial supplies of Mustang spare parts, and acquiring further Mustang airframes – this time from ex-USAF stocks, and some already partly civilianized airframes from existing private civil owners. Indeed, the company was somehow able to obtain the ownership of the F-51 Mustang Type Certificate, and the name 'Mustang' was its registered trade mark.

During 1961, with five variants of the Cavalier design, Lindsay began to seriously market the Cavalier brand. The five Cavalier Mustang versions differed mainly in fuel-carrying capacity, and their designations reflected the Mustang's maximum range in miles according to the fuel capacity of that particular version. The basic model was the 750, which was equipped with two fuel cells totalling 184 US gallons capacity, while the 1200 version had two additional L-shaped 48 US gallon tanks in the former wing gun bays at the expense of luggage space. Similar to the 750 model, the

Cavalier 1500 was fitted with two additional 63 US gallon tanks, bringing the total capacity to 310 US gallons. The standard model was the 2000, which featured a 92 US gallon wing-tip tank on each wing, each with an electric dump valve allowing the pilot to dump all fuel in the tank during just three minutes' flight time if required. Additional further tankage gave the Cavalier 2000 a no-reserve range of some 2,000 miles (3,220 km). The Cavalier 2500, looked upon as the classic and most up-market model in the range, had a grand capacity of 484 US gallons. It was similarly equipped to the 2000, with the addition of two further internal 60 US gallon fuel cells.

In September 1967 David Lindsay changed the name of his company to the Cavalier Aircraft Corporation. The Cavalier Mustang, of whichever version, was sold as a package which included a full 'after sales' service. The Trans-Florida factory and warehouse at Sarasota eventually contained thousands of spare parts for the aircraft, some still in their original NAA packaging and with the relevant supporting documentation. It became the company's proud boast that it could airfreight any P-51 spare to anywhere in the world within one day of receiving the order. A new 490-page maintenance manual and a pilot's handbook, plus special covers for the main air intake and the cockpit canopy, all accompanied the machine on purchase from Cavalier. For potential operators, ground school and categorization flights were included in the price of $48,000 with full navigation and full radio fit (or $32,000 without radios). In addition, a 'new' fully-overhauled Packard V-1650-7 engine could also be purchased for $3,000. At first the Cavalier concept included the vertical tail of the P-51D layout, but by 1967 Trans-Florida was fitting the taller vertical tail similar to that of the lightweight P-51H series as standard - although customers could request the standard tail instead if required. Eventually the tall tail came to be a major distinguishing feature of the Cavalier Mustangs, and the increased vertical tail area certainly aided the directional stability of the Cavalier Mustang models.

Around the time of the creation of the Cavalier Aircraft Corporation, Lindsay began to market a new idea, that would allow a private owner to modify his existing standard Mustang into a Cavalier conversion without needing to have his aircraft pass through Cavalier's Florida factory. The idea was straightforward - the owner would purchase a kit of parts and instructions which enabled him to install wing-tip fuel tanks, a high-pressure oxygen system, the necessary items to make the aircraft into a two-seater with a custom-designed and built rear folding seat, the new Aeroquip fuel system, and the 14 in (35.6 cm) taller vertical tail that had become such a characteristic feature of the Cavalier series Mustangs. In the period up to 1968 Cavalier successfully sold several versions of its high-powered executive Mustang to civil

Even though it was never intended as a primary mission requirement of the Twin Mustang, in fact the type excelled at ground-attack work, and was much used in this demanding role during the early phases of the Korean War. Here, an anonymous Twin Mustang wheels away after a firing pass at a practice target in the US. The aircraft is definitely a night-fighter Twin Mustang, as evidenced by its black colour scheme and radar pod between the two fuselages *(Photo: USAF)*

owners in a number of the versions outlined above. In addition to buyers in the US, at least two Cavalier aircraft were sold to foreign customers. The first was 44-73206, a former P-51D-25-NA Mustang that was eventually purchased by the Director of Air Tahiti, Jean-Francois Lejeune, and registered F-AZAG. During December 1968 the Vice-President and General Manager of Cavalier, Lt Col Gerald Tyler, ferried Cavalier 2000, 44-74694 (US civil registered as N16S), across the North Atlantic from Newfoundland to Shannon, Ireland, direct en route to an Italian customer. Destined for a Florence-based ice-cream manufacturer, it was registered I-BILL on arrival. Tragically, the renowned 'Warbird' collector Ormond Haydon-Baillie was killed in this aircraft in West Germany in July 1977, shortly after he had purchased it.

## 'Official' Interest in the Cavalier Mustang

The successful conversion of standard Mustangs by Trans-Florida into comparatively high-performance civil aircraft not surprisingly soon started to attract military interest. The US Department of Defense (DoD), which had been created in the years following the end of World War Two, turned its attention towards the Cavalier Mustang in a practical way in 1966. Following a feasibility study it was decided that the Cavalier Mustang with suitable modifications was ideally suited for the then-developing COIN (Counter-Insurgency) role. At this time Trans-Florida was producing about four civil conversions per year, and had a workforce of some 70 employees. In the early weeks of 1967 the DoD contracted Trans-Florida, under a programme called Project Peace Condor, to remanufacture, militarize and modernize an undisclosed number of Mustangs for military use. The cost of a civilian conversion by that time had risen to between $60,000 and $100,000 depending on the requirements of the buyer. Although costs were not published for the military variant, it was estimated at the time that the price would be $180,000 per airframe. Though potential recipient nations at that time were only disclosed as 'South American', the bulk of the subsequently-created military Cavalier Mustangs went to Bolivia and El Salvador. Later some appeared in other locations, including Indonesia. The first DoD contract covered 12 airframes. These Mustangs were actually allocated new US military FY serial numbers, in the 1967 and 1968 fiscal year procurements, reflecting the fact that they were in effect 'new' aircraft.

The remanufacturing process for these Project Peace Condor airframes included complete dismantling of the airframe, a strengthening of the fuselage structure, plus the modification of wing spars, stringers and webs to strengthen the whole wing structure and allow for the installation of additional underwing weapons pylons. The standard Cavalier tall tail was also added for greater directional stability and thus to enhance the 'gun platform' performance of the aircraft. Merlin 620 series engines were installed in the Peace Condor aircraft - several of these were acquired from ex-RCAF Douglas C-54GM transport aircraft. The armament for the Peace Condor aircraft comprised six Browning

0.50-in. machine guns in the existing gun bays, but each had 2,000 rounds. The inboard underwing pylons were stressed to carry a 1,000 lb (454 kg) bomb, or a 110 US gallon fuel tank. Up to six further weapons stations could carry either LAU rocket pods each with 19 70-mm folding-fin unguided rockets, or individual 12.7-cm HVARs (high-velocity aerial [or aircraft] rockets). Interestingly, the gunsights fitted to these aircraft are reputed to have been the same as those installed in British Hawker Hunter jet fighters - 'Jane's' All The World's Aircraft' of 1969-1970 referred to this piece of equipment as being a British Mk IIIN type. An N-4 or N-6 gun camera was located in the left-hand wing. A comprehensive avionics package including Bendix equipment was also included. With the 110 US gallon drop tanks on the two inboard underwing pylons, the loiter time for these aircraft over a potential target area was an exceptional five hours. Each of the 'Peace Condor' Mustangs was configured as a two-seater, with the pilot in the front seat and an observer/forward air controller in the rear. One example, however, was completed with full dual controls and complete instrumentation in the rear crew position, and is sometimes

The instrument panel of the P/F-82G, in the radar operator's (right-hand) fuselage side. This was a very different layout to the pilot's cockpit of the P/F-82G, and comprised equipment (including the two screens in the centre right of the instrument panel) related to the radar equipment installed in the aircraft, which the crew member in the right-hand fuselage was responsible for *(Photo: NAA)*

A P/F-82E Twin Mustang, 46-275, of the 27th Fighter Group/Wing following the creation of the independent US Air Force. The 'Intelligent Strength' emblem of the 27th is proudly painted below the cockpit. This unit was the only major front-line operator of the P/F-82E and already had a proud tradition, having taken the A-36A Invader into combat for the USAAF in 1943 in North Africa while designated the 27th BG (Light) and later the 27th Fighter-Bomber Group *(Photo: R.L. Ward Collection)*

referred to as a 'Cavalier TF-51'. Initially the aircraft were finished in a colour scheme that included the wording 'US Air Force' on the fuselage sides, although they were not in fact destined for US military usage at all.

While the 'Peace Condor' work was going ahead, Lindsay pursued a private-venture single-seat counter-insurgency aircraft programme. The Mustang used as the prototype of this idea was an early P/F-51D, 44-13257. It was civil registered as N4222A, and amongst other modifications it was fitted with wing-tip fuel tanks each carrying 110 US gallons. The lower fuselage longerons were reworked and strengthened to a higher specification than the 'Peace Condor' aircraft, through the installation of external aluminium 'doublers' along each side. The aircraft was fitted with six underwing hardpoints (three beneath each wing) for a maximum load of some 5,000 lb (2,268 kg), being able to carry a 1,000lb ( 454 kg) bomb on the inner pylon under each wing, with the other two pylons beneath each wing capable of carrying up to 750 lb (340 kg), including rocket pods or bombs. Similar avionics to the 'Peace Condor' Mustangs, and a Stanley extraction seat, were also planned. During the latter part of 1967 Trans-Florida set about marketing the type, which went under the name Mustang II (although this term is also sometimes used for the 'Peace Condor' standard Mustangs as well). At that time the company still owned over 100 Packard V-1650 and Merlin engines and an enormous stock of Mustang spare parts and ancillaries, and had the ability to modify if required a large number of Mustangs to its planned new specifications. The prototype Cavalier Mustang II flew for the first time in December 1967, and some later military Cavalier Mustangs were fitted out to roughly that standard, but the type itself did not enter production as a separate Mustang mark.

Although at the time the 'Peace Condor' contract was fairly well publicized, other sales involving reworked Mustangs (presumably in the later years to Cavalier II standard) to undisclosed customers received rather less publicity and have been the source of considerable speculation and confusion in subsequent years. It is possible that Trans-Florida's first military customer was the Fuerza Aérea Dominicana (FAD). The Dominican Republic was an operator of ex-Swedish air force Mustangs (as explained later in this Book) and apparently began to have its Mustangs reworked by Trans-Florida in 1964. The FAD aircraft were remodelled to a standard possibly unique to that operator, and did not have the wing-tip fuel tank fittings. These Cavalier Mustangs were intended as additional aircraft to reinforce the existing fleet in the Dominican Republic or to act as attrition replacements. There is also evidence to suggest that Cavalier personnel might have done work on the FAD machines in the field in the Dominican Republic and, during the later stages of the company's operation, spares were supplied for FAD personnel to do their own maintenance work. Cavalier-modified Mustangs were also operated by Guatemala, although this appears to have been a reworking of existing in-service airframes rather than

'new' production. At least seven reworked Mustangs, including one TF-51D and a TP-51D which incorporated the fuselage longeron doubler modification, were delivered to the TNI/AU (Indonesian air force) as late as 1971.

As stated earlier, the retirement in 1957 of the last of the USAF's Mustangs was not quite the end of the story of US military use of the Mustang. This was because the Cavalier Mustang also served in small numbers in US service, albeit not in any front-line role. During 1967 the US Army ordered two unique Cavalier Mustangs for use as high-speed chase aircraft in support of the Lockheed YAH-56A Cheyenne fire-support/gunship helicopter trials. The two Mustangs were completed by Trans-Florida/Cavalier roughly to Cavalier Mustang II standard, but without armament. They were two-seat, but single-pilot operation aircraft, with the rear seat utilised by an observer/photographer to record events during the YAH-56A helicopter evaluation and trials programme. In fact the Cavalier Mustang triumphed in the US Army's requirements for this role after the North American T-28 Trojan and Beech U-21 King Air had been ruled out as potential chase aircraft. Utilized primarily for air-to-air photographic missions in company with a YAH-56A helicopter and containing additional flight-test equipment, the two Cavalier Mustangs were ideal for this role, as their flight characteristics were similar to those of the Cheyenne. The two aircraft, which appear simply to have been referred to as F-51D Mustangs in service, had the 'new' serial numbers 68-15795 and 68-15796 allocated. They featured reinforced wing main spars and were fitted with 120 US gallon wing-tip fuel tanks. Interestingly, these two aircraft worked alongside another Mustang, which carried the 'obsolete' serial number O-72990. In the event the Cheyenne helicopter never entered production, and following the termination of the AH-56A programme the two Cavalier Mustangs were used for a variety of communications duties and other tasks. These included trials with a 106 mm 'recoilless rifle' at the China Lake weapons proving grounds. These trials were to determine the accuracy of a flat trajectory, large-calibre recoilless airborne weapon, and one was fitted to 68-15795. Though the trials proved that the weapon was accurate and could be fired while airborne, the project was eventually terminated.

## The Unusual Turboprop Cavalier

The Cavalier Mustang programme was still very much in existence, however, and the next stage in Lindsay's Mustang conversion work was the most radical yet. Concurrent with the piston-engined Mustang II programme, Cavalier began to experiment with the complete re-engining of the Mustang. One of the problems that Cavalier was experiencing with its overall Mustang conversion programme was the difficulty of pushing the Merlin engine beyond its Second World War performance levels. Another consideration was the Time Between Overhauls (TBO) performance of the engine and airframe. A logical, but at the same time radical, step appeared to be the fitting of a new engine altogether in the Mustang. At that time, in the later 1960's, the turboprop engine was well established, and offered power output levels and reliability in excess of the piston engines of World War Two vintage. Lindsay therefore took the step of looking at the feasibility of installing a turboprop power plant into the Mustang airframe, and from this the Cavalier Mustang III concept was born. After studying various potential alternatives, the Rolls-Royce Dart R.Da.6 Mk.510 turboprop was selected for installation. A development aircraft, eventually registered N6167U, was earmarked for the considerable conversion work that was involved in this very radical plan. The new Cavalier variant was created out of this concept was called the Turbo Mustang III by Cavalier. The particular Dart turboprop engine that was chosen for installation in the development airframe was originally fitted to a Vickers Viscount 745 four-engined airliner of United Air Lines, Inc. The safety and reliability records of the Dart engine particularly impressed Lindsay, as the type had by then achieved over 45 million hours running time and an in-flight shutdown record of only one per 300,000 hours. Hitherto the Merlin or Packard V-1650 installed in the Cavalier series would operate for a maximum of 1,000 hours between overhauls. The turboprop Dart on the other hand would run for 6,000 hours. This could be achieved with minimal maintenance requirements, which was a good factor in itself, but was an important consideration for forward area military operations where maintenance equipment and back-up would be minimal. In addition, the mating of the turboprop engine to the Mustang meant the doing away with the radiator in its established and vulnerable position in the lower fuselage behind the cockpit and its associated and infamous belly air intake.

The Mustang III was certainly a very different beast to the Mustangs that had gone before it. A constant diameter, tube-like Viscount airliner engine cowling housed the Dart power plant in the demonstrator N6167U. The actual installation of this engine required much redesign and beefing-up of the Mustang forward fuselage, although maintenance for the engine was enhanced by the way the cowling opened out like flower petals in four main sections. It was intended that the production Turbo Mustang III would have a more powerful R.Da.7 Mk.529 turboprop, which would deliver 2,185 shp (shaft horse power) maximum cruise power against the 1,550 shp take-off rating of the Mk.510 engine. A British company, the Bristol Aeroplane Plastics Co., was lined up to supply plastic armour for the fuselage undersides, cowling and cockpit areas of the planned production aircraft. An 11 ft 6 in (3.5 m) diameter, four-bladed Dowty Rotol propeller unit with an advanced automatic synchronized power/pitch facility was fitted. The Dowty Rotol unit could be placed in flat pitch/maximum drag to facilitate deceleration and a shorter ground roll on landing. Production aircraft were intended to be fitted with the North American Rockwell LW-3B ejector seat.

Other features of the Turbo Mustang III included self-sealing full cells in the wing roots, two 120 US gallon wing-tip fuel tanks, and the provision for two 110 US gallon fuel tanks on the inboard underwing pylons. All the internal fuel tanks were lined with reticulated foam for fire suppression. As with the piston-engined Mustang II the fuselage longerons were reinforced, extra spars were installed in the wing to allow for the six weapons pylons, and a taller vertical tail was fitted. The avionics fitted were similar to the 'Peace Condor' aircraft.

A number of roles were envisaged for the Turbo Mustang, including short-range reconnaissance and Forward Air Control (FAC). The aircraft was intended to be versatile and could be configured in many different ways depending on its intended mission. Six 0.5-in machine guns as usual formed the type's main armament, while various types of bombs could be carried under the wings including the ubiquitous Mk 81 or Mk 82 low-drag 250 lb (113 kg) bombs. A variety of other ordnance was to be made available, including seven-tube LAU-59 or AERO-6A unguided rocket pods, or 19-tube folding fin LAU-3A rocket launchers, XM-75 grenade launchers, or SUU-11A 7.62 mm mini-gun pods each with 1,500 rounds. The maximum ordnance load was 4,500 lb (2,041 kg), but this limited the aircraft's range to some 200 miles (322 km), with a loiter time over the target of 90 minutes. When configured for a maximum 500 miles (805 km) range mission the ordnance was limited to 1,000 lb (454 kg) in low-drag bombs and six 0.5 in. guns with 1,200 rounds of ammunition. In its clean condition, the Turbo Mustang was the fastest of all the production Mustangs, with a maximum speed of 540 mph (869 km/h) at sea

A posed but nonetheless interesting detail view of the pilot and ground crew of an F-82F Twin Mustang night-fighter. The aircraft had the serial number 46-477 and wore the name 'Wimpy' just below the cockpit. There is no doubt that the Twin Mustang's finest hour was as a night-fighter, and it was at the end of the piston-engined night-fighter era - being replaced in USAF service mainly by the all-weather-capable Lockheed F-94 Starfire jet fighter. In the background of this excellent period image are several examples of another of North American Aviation's wonderful products - the superlative F-86 Sabre (Photo: USAF)

During the 1960's the Mustang gained a completely new lease of life with the activities of Trans-Florida Aviation and later the Cavalier Aircraft Corporation. This included the full reconditioning of some existing Mustangs into effectively new, upgraded aircraft, which received new US military serial numbers although they were not intended for US military service. One of these aircraft, serial number 67-14863, is seen outside the Cavalier Aircraft Corporation's Sarasota, Florida facility – by the time of this picture, the company had almost certainly changed its name from Trans-Florida Aviation
(Photo: via Chris Ellis)

Two Cavalier Mustangs fly in formation. Nearest to the camera is 67-22580, a single-seat Cavalier F-51D, while in the background is two-seat Cavalier TF-51D 67-14866. Note the long cockpit canopy of the latter, and the very prominent tall tails of both aircraft, which considerably improved the Mustang's well-known problems with directional stability. Of these two, neither served with the USAF but TF-51D 67-14866 was later delivered to Bolivia
*(Photo: via Chris Ellis)*

level. The empty weight was 6,800 lb (3,085 kg), whilst the maximum take-off weight was 14,000 lb (6,350 kg).

A production run of 2,000 Turbo Mustang IIIs was ambitiously envisaged by Cavalier over a four and a half year period, with major production back-up similarly ambitiously forecast from North American Rockwell (which was a successor to the original NAA company). These would have been essentially brand new aircraft, but using some Mustang components, and would therefore have been different to the cavalier Mustangs thus far produced which were all reconditioned former Mustangs. In the event, however, the whole plan never got off the ground. At Cavalier's request, the 'prototype' Turbo Mustang III conversion was demonstrated to Tactical Air Command officials at Langley AFB in Virginia during September 1968. At that time the USAF was looking for a potential interim AX tactical fighter for the USAF, able to perform the then increasingly in-vogue COIN mission. Although, unofficially, some interest was expressed, the headquarters of TAC officially showed no interest, and production orders were never placed. This was, basically, the end of the line for potential large-scale 'new Mustang' production.

## Piper Enforcer

Following its failure to impress the USAF with the Turbo Mustang, Cavalier was nevertheless undaunted. Indeed, the company subsequently even projected and built a new COIN aircraft based on the Mustang layout. Again drawing as closely as possible on the Mustang airframe, the new aircraft was powered by a different turboprop engine, the AVCO Lycoming T55-L-9. This powerful engine developed 2,535 shp, and was a step up again in the development of the Mustang into something that it was never envisaged to be in the first place. The name Enforcer appears to have been given to this project (although that is in some dispute amongst historians - this name is usually associated with what came after). Two prototypes were built by Cavalier, a single-seat

aircraft civil registered as N201PE and a two-seater registered N202PE. The type's armament, fuel provision, wig-tip fuel tanks and tall tail were all similar to the Turbo Mustang III layout. The second aircraft, two-seater N202PE, was evaluated by the USAF in 1971 as a potential off-the-shelf tactical aircraft for FAC and light strike missions, but was not ordered. This in effect was virtually the end of the Cavalier Mustang story, but there was a final twist in the tale. Unfortunately, the single-seat prototype N201PE was lost in an accident on 12 July 1971. Tailplane flutter caused an elevator to depart the aircraft, and the pilot safely ejected. By that time Cavalier had realised that it had insufficient capital to pursue the Mustang III programme, and the famous Piper Aircraft Corporation took over development of the Lycoming-powered Mustang later in 1971 after the project was sold by Cavalier. Piper subsequently designated the aircraft the Piper PA-48 Enforcer, and David Lindsay is believed to have acted as an unpaid consultant on the project. Even so, development was apparently suspended for a time, but the Enforcer was by no means dead.

To that end, work resumed on the Enforcer programme in the early 1980's with the construction of two further, second-generation Enforcers. Although Piper duly marketed these as 'new' aircraft, they did in reality still have considerable Mustang ancestry. The Enforcer programme was resurrected due to an $11.8 million contract, with Piper announcing the receipt of the USAF's contract on 4 September 1981. The go-ahead for the resurrection of the Enforcer seemingly arose due to pressure from some members of the US Congress for the Enforcer programme to be continued. It appears that during September 1981 a variety of P-51 components, including fuselage and wing parts, undercarriages and other pieces were delivered to the Piper Aircraft Corporation's Lakeland facility in Florida. This miscellany of parts came from Gordon Plaskett of King City, California, who owned a cache of Mustang components. It seems likely that some of these parts eventually found their way into the two new Enforcer prototypes, which were constructed during that period. Around twenty per cent of the PA-48 components are believed to have been compatible with those of the Mustang, but Piper was subsequently quick to point out that Enforcer was a new design.

The two new Enforcers were powered by a 2,445ehp Avco Lycoming T55-L-9 series turboprop engine with armour protection, which drove a four-bladed Aeroproducts propeller. The overall length of the new Enforcer was 34 ft 2 in (10.41 m), making it almost two feet longer than the standard P-51D Mustang. The wing span over the two wing-tip fuel tanks was 41 ft 4 in (12.6 m). The two new Enforcers were both single-seaters, and were fitted with completely revised avionics, a new cockpit canopy, new wing spars which were supposed to be good for some 14,000 hours, a larger fin and rudder, and a new aileron system and hydraulically boosted controls. The maximum take-off weight of

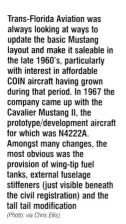

Trans-Florida Aviation was always looking at ways to update the basic Mustang layout and make it saleable in the late 1960's, particularly with interest in affordable COIN aircraft having grown during that period. In 1967 the company came up with the Cavalier Mustang II, the prototype/development aircraft for which was N4222A. Amongst many changes, the most obvious was the provision of wing-tip fuel tanks, external fuselage stiffeners (just visible beneath the civil registration) and the tall tail modification
*(Photo: via Chris Ellis)*

the new Enforcer was 14,000 lb (6,350 kg), with a maximum of 5,680 lb (2,576 kg) of ordnance on six underwing pylons (three for each wing). Gun pods, cluster bomb units, standard unguided bombs and unguided rocket pods of various different types could be carried. The inner pylon under each wing could carry a bomb of up to 2,000 lb (907 kg). Wing guns were not fitted. The prototype new Enforcer, c/n EN1 and civil registered as N481PE, flew for the first time on 9 April 1983. EN2, the second prototype which was civil registered as N482PE, followed on 8 July 1983. After company trials that were satisfactory and appeared to point to a potentially very successful design, both aircraft were evaluated

by the US DoD, including trials at Eglin AFB in Florida during May 1984. This evaluation was claimed at the time to have been thorough, but it is understood that the USAF did not apparently bother to fly the portion of sorties allocated to them at Edwards AFB in California. Perhaps not surprisingly, the design was rejected. The two new PA-48s were placed into storage at Davis-Monthan AFB in Arizona during August 1984, one of them subsequently passing to the USAF Museum at Wright-Patterson AFB – ironically the location of the early testing of the XP-51 and the place where official opposition had seemingly existed against the Mustang in the early 1940's.

# Conflict in Korea

## Chapter 9

When the Japanese surrendered in 1945 at the end of World War Two, the newly-formed United Nations developed plans for a trusteeship administration for the troubled Korean peninsula, with the Soviet Union administering the area north of the 38th Parallel and the United States the Korean territory south of that line. In 1948 two separate governments were established, creating two disparate Korean territories known generally as South Korea (officially the Republic of Korea, created in August 1948) and North Korea (officially the People's Democratic Republic of Korea, created in September 1948). The northern part came under the leadership of previous anti-Japanese communist elements, and the south under pro-American anti-communist Koreans. It was an uneasy settlement that did not appear to have much chance of success, especially as both of the Korean sides proclaimed their intentions to re-unify the Korean lands under their own political outlook.

Attempts were made by the United States to create a military organisation in South Korea, and some training overseen by US personnel was undertaken. As for the new country's air force, this was established with the donation of several former US aircraft that were mainly trainers and light liaison types. However, during the summer of 1950 a consignment of 10 Mustangs was given to the South Koreans. Sometimes called the 'Truman Gift', these ten Mustangs at once equipped the only real combat elements of the Republic of Korea Air Force (RoKAF). The aircraft themselves were hardly in pristine condition, most if not all having come out of storage in Japan where some are believed to have been used for target-towing. They were hastily prepared for transfer to the South Koreans. There were, however, few South Korean pilots who could fly the type successfully. A number of USAF volunteers therefore aided the South Koreans to get the aircraft airworthy and to begin training South Korean pilots. Several of the Americans were from

the 8th Fighter-Bomber Wing which helped to organise the programme, and a number of them would end up flying the Mustangs in combat in a short while. The whole endeavour came under the quaint Americanism of 'Bout One', and was the start of a long association with the Mustang for the South Koreans. Some of the training for the South Korean pilots took place at Chinhae; the majority of the Korean airmen were inexperienced, although a number of them had performed some flying under the Japanese. Principal amongst the Americans involved in this project was Maj Dean Hess, who was in effect to become the father of the RoKAF.

## The Shooting Starts

It was a miserable, rainy day, 25 June 1950, when a massive invasion of South Korea was launched by the North Koreans. The scale and initial success of this operation caught everyone unawares, particularly the Americans, and in a short time the South Korean forces were in full retreat. Allied units in the region were at once put on the highest state of alert. This mainly included US, British and Commonwealth occupation forces in Japan, which was the closest area where the US had a major military presence stationed in the region (the majority of US forces had been, somewhat unwisely, withdrawn from South Korea in 1949). An immediate consideration that grew hourly in importance as the North Korean invasion gained momentum, was the evacuation of US civilians from South Korea to the relative safety of Japan.

The US response to the North Korean invasion was immediate, but was complicated by reality. The majority of USAF units stationed in Japan were equipped with jets, which did not have the range to fly effective combat missions over to Korea and back. In South Korea itself there was a variety of airfields, many of which were generally in a poor state of repair, and certainly could not sustain jet operations until major work had been carried out on

The Korean War of 1950-1953 was the second major war for the Mustang. Conditions in Korea were often miserable for pilots, ground crews and aircraft alike, but the Mustang rose majestically to the challenge once again. It is often forgotten that a major user of the Mustang during the Korean War was the Republic of Korea Air Force (RoKAF), which was putting the type into service with US help during the period when the conflict began. Mustangs were in service with the RoKAF right to the end of the war, and continued in South Korean service for some time afterwards. This image shows an F-51D or K Mustang early in the RoKAF service of the type, with hand-painted South Korean insignia and individual aircraft number *(Photo: USAF)*

Nicely-adorned with unique 'shark-mouth' markings, amongst the most colourful and certainly the most striking of the USAF Mustang units that fought in the Korean War was the 12th FBS. This unit wore distinctive 'shark-mouth' markings on the lower nose of many of its Mustangs (except for those newly received by the unit) and was one of the first regular USAF squadrons that was committed to action in Korea following the North Korean invasion of June 1950 *(Photo: USAF)*

them. It was not clear at all just what the USAF's response to the invasion could be, except that something needed to be done quickly. In particular the evacuation of US citizens needed to be covered effectively by air and ground forces. For the South Koreans there was no choice but to commit any and all available forces. This included the combat initiation of any aerial assets, and to that end the small group of RoKAF Mustangs with their American helpers almost at once went into action, mainly in the ground-attack role. For some of the South Korean pilots this gave a whole new meaning to the concept of learning on the job.

The only fighter aircraft that the USAF possessed in the theatre that could operate from Japan and yet had the range and loiter capability to do any meaningful work over Korea was none other than the F-82 Twin Mustang. Thus the accolade of being the first US aircraft in action in the skies over South Korea fell to the black-painted Twin Mustang night-fighters of Far East Air Forces, which were abruptly called upon to enter combat in a completely unfamiliar operational scenario. The three squadrons of Far East Air Forces that were operational on the type at the start of the Korean War were the 4th Fighter-All Weather Squadron at Naha, on Okinawa Island; the 68th Fighter-All Weather Squadron at Itazuke in Japan; and the 339th Fighter-All Weather Squadron at Yokota, Japan. The latter squadron was generally responsible for the air defence of the Tokyo area, while the 68th Squadron included western Japan as a part of its responsibilities, and was therefore closest to the Korean peninsula. These units were equipped with the F-82G Twin Mustang, which had started to equip the Pacific all-weather fighter squadrons during 1949. In February 1950 the 339th Squadron finally retired its last Northrop F-61 Black Widow night-fighter, and all three of the all-weather fighter squadrons were officially equipped with the F-82G from March 1950 onwards – although crew training was still continuing when the Korean War broke out. At the end of May 1950 there were 32 F-82G actually assigned to the three operational Twin Mustang squadrons within Far East Air Forces.

During 25 June, the day that the North Korean invasion began, the bases where these three Twin Mustang squadrons were located were placed on a high state of alert.

At that time the 68th Squadron was still not up to full operational strength, necessitating the deployment of eight Twin Mustangs and crews from Okinawa to Itazuke. On 26 June the 339th also deployed eight aircraft and crews to Itazuke, but retained some of its aircraft for the air defence of Tokyo in case the North Koreans attempted an attack against a high value target on the Japanese mainland. The first fighter mission of the conflict was flown by a Twin Mustang of the 68th Squadron piloted by Lt George Deans with Lt Marv Olsen as radio/radar operator, who flew an armed reconnaissance to the 38th Parallel in the early hours of 25 June to check on initial reports that the North Koreans had moved south into the Republic of Korea. From the 26th, several Twin Mustangs began operating armed protection flights over South Korea (by day as well as by night), principally to cover the evacuation of US citizens. This evacuation took the form of seaborne assets using Inchon harbour, and aerial evacuation from Seoul, the capital of South Korea. Seoul lies in the west of South Korea comparatively close to the 38th Parallel, and it soon appeared likely following the North Korean invasion that it would fall to the communist invaders within a short space of time. A principal airport in the Seoul area, Kimpo, was rapidly handling a number of transport aircraft as the evacuation quickly gathered pace. The North Koreans at once attempted to interfere with the US evacuation, causing the USAF to begin overflying the area as soon as possible. The Twin Mustangs were able to loiter over the evacuation area using their long endurance, with top-cover flown by Japan-based Lockheed F-80C Shooting Star jet fighters – though the endurance of the latter was severely limited.

Although the North Koreans lacked any kind of substantial air power, they did have a number of Soviet-made combat aircraft on hand at the time of the invasion of South Korea. Yakolev fighters such as the Yak-9, and Illyushin Il-10 close-support aircraft, were

Two Mustangs from the 39th FIS (sometimes referred to as the 39th FBS) are readied in the open air for further action against the North Koreans. The aircraft on the left is a former Air National Guard aircraft (note the insignia of a Mustang-operating Indiana ANG unit on the aircraft's fuselage). The necessity of combat in the Korean War led to many ANG Mustangs being 'rounded up' for shipment to Korea to take part in the conflict *(Photo: USAF)*

The attrition rate for Mustangs during the Korean War was high. Employed principally for ground-attack, often close to the front lines, the Mustang was susceptible to ground fire due to its liquid-cooled engine installation. Even a hit from small arms fire could mean potential disaster if a coolant line was damaged. In this image a Mustang has made it home for its lucky pilot, although the aircraft appears to be in a rather poor state of repair. The twin aerial installation on the fuselage spine was somewhat unusual and was possibly associated with AN/ARA-8 homing equipment *(Photo: USAF)*

amongst the North Korean air assets. Some Lavochkin La-7 fighters might also have been included and were widely reported by US pilots, although this seems rather unlikely. There appears to have been a recognition problem amongst the American flyers, as the Yaks were inline-engined while Lavochkins were radial-engined. On the 26th the first North Korean aircraft were seen by the Twin Mustangs. The North Koreans had evidently received information about the US evacuation, as a number of North Korean fighters attempted to interfere with the ground operations. Several began to tangle with the Twin Mustangs, but fired inconclusively from long range. The Americans were under orders only to fire if fired upon.

## Twin Mustangs in Combat

On 27 June, however, things were very different. Again the North Koreans attempted to interfere with the US evacuation, but this time they made concerted attacks on Kimpo airfield. The USAF's covering aircraft intervened and a number of air combats ensued, during which the Twin Mustangs and Shooting Stars emerged with a tally of seven North Korean aircraft shot down without loss to themselves. Although there has been some confusion in the following years as to who shot down what and in which particular aircraft, it now appears that three of the kills were achieved by the Twin Mustangs. Airborne over South Korea that day were Twin Mustangs of the 68th and 339th Squadrons. At just before midday several North Korean aircraft attempted to raid Kimpo airfield. Waiting for them was a mixed force of F-82G Twin Mustangs from the 68th and 339th, and a number of combats ensued. A 68th Squadron Twin Mustang flown by Lt William Hudson with Lt Carl Fraser as radio/radar operator manoeuvred onto the tail of one of the North Korean aircraft and Hudson's accurate shooting brought it down. Somewhat bizarrely, Fraser later stated that he saw the North Korean pilot talking to his observer as the aircraft went down. That would mean that the fighter was actually a two-seat Yak-11 trainer, or (perhaps more likely) an Ilyushin Il-10 that was mis-identified by the American flyers. During the same engagement the 68th Squadron's Lt Charles Moran, whose Twin Mustang had been damaged at the start of the skirmish, also shot down a North Korean aircraft that was thought to be a Lavochkin La-7. The CO of the 339th Squadron, Maj James Little, was also credited with an La-7. In subsequent years it was widely believed that Hudson's victory was the first of what became the Korean War, and that he was flying F-82G Twin Mustang serial number 46-383, subsequently named

'Bucket of Bolts'. However, it now seems more likely that it was actually F-82G s/n 46-401 that Hudson and Fraser were crewing during the shoot-down incident. It is also possible that Little's kill was made moments earlier than Hudson's. Little in fact was already a seasoned fighter pilot, having achieved seven aerial victories against the Japanese while flying P-40 Warhawks with the 75th Fighter Squadron of the 23rd Fighter Group during 1943.

Whatever the actual course of events, the actions of the Twin Mustangs, plus the four victories achieved that day by F-80C Shooting Stars, were the start of the significant aerial activity over Korea by the USAF. Despite the efforts of the US fighters, however, major damage was caused at Kimpo by North Korean aircraft during the evacuation period. The 27th additionally marked the start, and the end, of the Twin Mustang's achievements as a fighter in the conflict, as no further aerial victories were subsequently achieved by the F-82 contingent. Nevertheless, the Twin Mustang went on to make an important contribution to the overall effort against the North Koreans in the following months, albeit mainly as a ground-attack aircraft. With Far East Air Forces suffering a major shortage of suitable combat aircraft at the start of the conflict, the Twin Mustangs were pressed into service as impromptu ground-attack aircraft, which became a role in which they excelled. They were able to employ their formidable forward-firing battery of six 0.5-in machine guns to good effect, and their ability to carry a substantial load under their wings allowed them to use a variety of air-to-ground ordnance. This included unguided rockets and bombs, but also involved the use of napalm. Indeed, the Twin Mustang became the first aircraft to widely use napalm during the Korean conflict, commencing in late June. Napalm proved to be of great effect against North Korean ground units, who feared its effectiveness. The napalm mixture was usually carried in converted long-range fuel tanks which would simply be dropped from comparatively low level over the battlefield.

The Twin Mustang force was in fact the pioneer of what became a massive air effort which grew rapidly as the conflict developed. A specially-convened meeting of the United Nations Security Council, at which the Soviet Union was not present, supported US efforts on behalf of the Republic of Korea, and asked for support for the South Koreans from member nations. Eventually a major effort was staged by a disparate selection of countries to militarily aid South Korea (some 16 countries eventually contributed), of which the US and British Commonwealth contributions were the largest. In its initial stages the war went from bad to worse for the South Koreans. The capital, Seoul, was taken (its location comparatively close to the 38th Parallel, on the western side of the Korean peninsula, remains to this day a vulnerable setting) and the increasingly successful North Korean forces pushed south, with seemingly little to stop them from capturing the whole of the Korean peninsula.

## A Second Major War for the Mustang

Help was eventually to hand, however, and the Mustang was to play a pivotal role in the UN operations in aid of the South Koreans. Indeed, what became the known as the Korean War was to be the Mustang's second major conflict, following its great success during the Second World War. In Korea, however, whereas the Mustang had been one of the superlative fighters of the world war, in Korea the F-51D version of the Mustang became a work-horse of low-level, ground-attack missions. This was because there was no other aircraft in the USAF's inventory that was numerous enough or suitable enough to fulfil this demanding role. Unfortunately, as experience during World War Two had shown, although the Mustang had excellent all-round performance and firepower, it was vulnerable to ground fire due to all the pipe-work in its structure that was a part of the liquid-

An F-51D Mustang of the 18th FBW is loaded with unguided rockets ready for another sortie against North Korean targets. The installation of up to five 'zero-length' rocket attachments under each wing by NAA late in the original P-51D production series proved to be very useful for operations in the Korean War, with much use being made of unguided air-to-ground rockets by the UN forces. This aircraft wears the F-51D/K's 'Buzz Number' prefix 'FF' *(Photo: USAF)*

cooling system for its Merlin engine. The radiator installation in the lower fuselage below and behind the cockpit was also in a vulnerable position for ground-attack missions where fire from the ground was likely to be accurate and intense. A hit in any of the coolant pipes or the radiator would usually result in a loss of sufficient coolant to cause the engine to seize, resulting in the often rapid demise of the aircraft.

In other words, the Mustang was not the ideal choice for ground-attack and close-support missions over Korea. The aircraft type that would have been more suitable was the P-47 Thunderbolt (after 1948, F-47), with its rugged construction and its big air-cooled radial engine that was not as susceptible to ground fire. Unfortunately, the F-47 was not available in particularly large numbers by mid-1950, having been in dwindling service in the Air National Guard after the end of World War Two – in addition, some Thunderbolts had been supplied to friendly nations elsewhere in the world, resulting in the type being

unavailable to US forces for widespread action over Korea. Of other fighters and fighter-bombers that were in existence at the time, the F-80C Shooting Star jet fighter was unsuitable for widespread use as a fighter-bomber due to its comparatively short endurance and relatively light weapons load – although the type did put in some service over Korea in this role. The F-51H lightweight version of the Mustang was still in service at that time, however, and the question has often been raised as to why that version of the Mustang was not used in Korea, instead of the F-51D. There were in fact several reasons for the lack of use of the F-51H in the Korean War. To begin with, the F-51H was only made in comparatively small numbers, and spare parts were not available in sufficient quantities to allow the relatively small force of F-51H Mustangs to operate effectively in a major combat environment. In addition, the F-51H was far too flimsy to operate in the harsh operating environment of Korea, where operations were often flown from austere air bases at which maintenance facilities were

A considerable contribution to the United Nations forces that fought in the Korean War was made by Britain and other Commonwealth countries. Included amongst these was South Africa, which had a close association with the Mustang during the war in Korea. In this image the first four F-51D Mustangs destined for the SAAF's contingent in South Korea receives a considerable send-off. The photograph was probably taken at Johnson AB in Japan during November 1950 where the South Africans initially trained - the Mustang was not a part of the SAAF's inventory otherwise. The Mustangs were supplied from US stocks *(Photo: USAF)*

at a premium – the problems with the collapsing tail undercarriage on these aircraft, for example, are referred to elsewhere in this book. They were simply not intended for the type of rough operations that the Korean War demanded. In comparison, even though the F-51D was far from ideal itself, it was available in sufficient quantities to allow for effective numbers to operate in Korea. In addition, there was no particular shortage of spares for the F-51D, unlike the dwindling situation with the F-51H, and it would certainly cope with the austere conditions in Korea far better than the lightweight F-51H. For these reasons it therefore made sense to standardise on the F-51D as the one main ground-attack and close-support type for the USAF and Allied countries in the Korean theatre. Lt Gen Earle Partridge, who headed the Fifth Air Force (which was primarily concerned with operations in the theatre during the war), requested soon after the North Korean invasion the immediate transfer of as many Mustangs as possible from the continental US to Japan, for deployment to Korea as soon as possible. According to USAF figures, in mid-1950 at the time of the start of hostilities in Korea, there were 764 Mustangs in the US with Air National Guard squadrons, plus some 794 more in storage at various locations in the US. This meant that a useful force of Mustangs could be made available for service in Korea, but a considerable amount of redeployment would be necessary to make these aircraft accessible for combat service. As noted in Chapter 7 of this book, a great many changes were duly made to the inventories of ANG squadrons. At that time a significant number of ANG squadrons were equipped with F-51D Mustangs or early jets, and these aircraft were now unexpectedly and abruptly required for combat service in Korea. The obvious solution was to remove the F-51Ds and jets from ANG squadrons and send them to Korea, while replacing them in the ANG with F-51H lightweight Mustangs. This resulted in the second influx of F-51Hs into ANG service as ANG F-51D Mustangs were taken out of service and prepared for movement overseas to Korea, while their place was taken in the ANG units by F-51H lightweight Mustangs.

## Merlin-Mustangs Enter Combat

Although the Mustang was not intended for air-to-air combat over Korea, during the early days of the US involvement the type did achieve a notable success. This was on 29 June, when Gen Douglas MacArthur was arriving at Suwon on a fact-finding mission having taken over as the supreme commander of allied forces in Korea. A variety of fighters were detailed to cover Macarthur's trip. Once more the North Koreans tried to interfere with proceedings, and several new air battles ensued. Again, as with the combats

involving the Twin Mustangs on 27 June, there remains to this day much confusion as to who was involved and in what, and who and what was shot down. What does appear to be agreed is that four North Korean aircraft were destroyed by several Mustangs. These F-51Ds were presumably 'Bout One'/South Korean Mustangs, because most US historians claim that the USAF did not have any operational Mustangs in Korea at that time. Aerial victories were subsequently credited to three USAF pilots, Lts Harry Sandlin and Orrin Fox of the 80th Fighter-Bomber Squadron, and Lt Richard Burns of the 35th FBS. These pilots were apparently seconded to the RoKAF as a part of the 'Bout One' programme. Burns was credited with an Il-10 while Fox shot down two Yak-9s, or possibly Il-10s – again, air-to-air identification appears to have been a challenge for the American pilots. Sandlin received credit for another member of the mysterious and probably mis-identified 'Lavochkin La-7' community. Other combats also took place during that day, and it is possible that two further North Korean aircraft were shot down by Mustangs. However, unfortunately due to the confused nature of the whole affair and the apparent lack of records to verify much of the action, there are some historians who now doubt altogether the role of the Mustang in the combats of 29 June, further clouding the issue of what actually took place on that day. What is subsequently confirmed is that on 30 June the South Korean Mustangs were moved to Taegu, which was an air base that was to become a well-known name in the following years. From there, combat operations were duly flown by the 'Bout One' aircraft in support of South Korean and US ground operations, especially elements of the US 24th Infantry Division (particularly the 21st Infantry Regiment) who were amongst the first US ground troops under Task Force Smith actually involved in the fighting on Korean soil in the early days of the war.

In addition to the initial combat operations of the RoKAF/'Bout One' Mustangs, a Commonwealth country was also joining in the effort during the early days of the war to try to stop the North Korean advance. This was Australia, which had a significant presence in Japan at the time as a part of the Allied occupation forces under the British Commonwealth Occupation Force (BCOF). Amongst the Australian air elements of this organisation was No.77 Squadron, Royal Australian Air Force, which was equipped with Mustangs. Based at Iwakuni in Japan, the squadron had been a part of the BCOF's air occupation contingent (sometimes referred to as BCAIR, or colloquially as the 'Commonwealth Forces of Occupation') for some time, and ironically actually flew what was supposed to be its last occupation force sorties from Iwakuni on 23 June, just two days before the North Koreans attacked. Instead of returning home,

No.2 Squadron, South African Air Force, operated Mustangs principally from K-10 Chinhae from late 1950 until December 1952. This South African Mustang is fully armed with underwing unguided rockets and a fuel tank probably filled with napalm. Note the unit insignia ahead of the cockpit on the fuselage side
*(Photo: via Chris Ellis)*

the Australians found themselves at once in a real shooting war. With the squadron committed by the Australian government in late June to the efforts to help South Korea, the unit's Mustangs were readied for action. Initially operating from Iwakuni and using the Mustang's legendary long-range capabilities to good effect, the Australian Mustangs were committed from 30 June. They flew their first real sorties on 2 July, providing fighter cover to UN-contingent aircraft. The initial combat mission for the Australian Mustangs was the next day, but although at first successful, the Mustangs soon proved to be vulnerable to North Korean anti-aircraft fire. Their first combat loss was on 7 July. No.77 Squadron was later attached to the USAF's 8th Fighter-Bomber Wing, and thence to the 35th Fighter-Interceptor Wing, during its service in Korea.

Feverish activity ensued at bases and depots all around the US in late June and early July 1950 to start the process of moving a substantial number of Mustangs from the US to Japan, for operation by the USAF over Korea. A procession of Mustangs was moved to the west coast of the US where they were eventually collected together at the naval air facility at Alameda, California. After preparation work, 145 Mustangs were craned aboard the US aircraft carrier USS Boxer (CVA 21). Some of the Mustangs were placed in the carrier's hangars below the flight deck, while others – suitably wrapped with a protective coating to prevent the worst excesses of salt water corrosion – were parked on the ship's flight deck. Also aboard the carrier were 70 pilots who were regarded as being familiar with the F-51. The ship sailed from Alameda on 15 July, and made the Pacific crossing to Tokyo in Japan in the rapid time of just eight days and 16 hours, arriving on 23 July. At first many of the pilots aboard the ship assumed that they would form the nucleus of a new, Mustang-equipped fighter group, but in the event most were dispersed on arrival to a number of existing squadrons, which began rapidly to convert onto the Mustang from their jet fighters. In addition to the Mustangs that were transported to the theatre by USS Boxer, a contingent of retired Mustangs was rounded up from various locations in the Pacific. These aircraft were additional to the 'Bout One' F-51Ds already referred to, and some were in a rather poor condition. Nevertheless, the situation on the ground in South Korea was rapidly worsening, and the USAF needed anything and everything that it could operate in order to put up some kind of aerial cover for the increasingly hard-pressed UN ground forces.

## USAF Mustangs in Korea

In July and August 1950, as a result of the activities across the Pacific and in the US to amass a viable strike force of Mustangs, the first USAF units began to transition onto the F-51D. Initially, on 3 July the 18th FBW gathered together a number of its experienced former Mustang pilots, principally from the 12th FBS,

and deployed them from Clark AB in the Philippines where the wing was based to Johnson AB in Japan. There they formed the 'Dallas' Provisional Squadron. This unit flew its first Mustang sorties over Korea on 15 July. On 10 July a further provisional unit, the 51st FS (Provisional) was formed under Fifth Air Force command, and this squadron located itself at Taegu in South Korea to commence operations. Sufficient Mustangs were by then starting to be put back into the air to allow the first regular USAF squadron to begin to convert onto the type. This was the 40th Fighter-Interceptor Squadron of the 35th FIW, based at Ashiya AB in Japan with F-80C Shooting Stars. Conversion from the F-80 onto the F-51 took place as rapidly as possible, allowing the squadron to move to Pohang, South Korea, on and around 16 July. Operations against North Korean ground forces began as rapidly as was feasible. Pohang was an austere air base in the extreme southern end of South Korea, and it needed much work by US engineers to get it into shape for Mustang operations. It later received the airfield coding K-3, in line with the assignment of identification code numbers to Korean air bases used by the USAF.

The early provisional units that flew initial combat operations in the Mustang did not last long. Indeed, the 'Bout One' and 'Dallas' organisations merged and were eventually combined with the 51st FS (Provisional) until the arrival from the Philippines of substantial elements of the 18th FBW which moved north to join in the fighting over Korea. These included the 18th Wing's 12th and 67th Fighter-Bomber Squadrons, which were able to take on charge some of the Mustangs that had been transported by USS Boxer from the US. Eventually the 51st FS (Provisional) was absorbed into the 18th Wing's establishment. Unlike the original 'Bout One' Mustangs, the USS Boxer Mustangs were generally in good shape, and a few of them only had a small number of hours flying time on their clocks. It is therefore something of a myth,

With the distinctive scenery of K-10 Chinhae's water and hills as a backdrop, a South African-operated Mustang prepares for a dawn take-off at the start of another hard day of ground-attack work against North Korean tactical targets. The South African Air Force's No.2 Squadron was attached to the USAF's 18th FBW during its operational period in Korea, principally based at Chinhae in South Korea, and equipped with Mustangs supplied from US stocks *(Photo: via Chris Ellis)*

Mud and often appalling weather characterized operations during much of the Korean War. In this image a SAAF F-51D or K of No.2 Squadron is worked on in the open air, with low cloud hugging the high ridges in the background *(Photo: USAF)*

Making ready for an early morning take-off in Korea, a No.2 Squadron, SAAF Mustang is run-up, its upper cowling panel temporarily removed. The underwing load carried by this aircraft of external fuel tanks (which were probably filled with napalm) and unguided rockets were fairly typical for the close-support work that Mustangs were principally used for in Korea
*(Photo: via Chris Ellis)*

A SAAF Mustang numbered '322' receives maintenance inside a hangar. This was a luxury, as most maintenance had to be performed outside due to the poor condition of the facilities at many Korean air bases, especially if there had been fighting nearby or if the air base in question had been attacked prior to falling into UN hands. Only the deepest maintenance could be carried out inside. This Mustang was a part of South Africa's contribution to the Allied effort during the Korean War and was operated by No.2 Squadron *(Photo: USAF)*

perpetrated by some writers, that the Mustangs that served in Korea were all barely-flyable relics that had seen better days. Without doubt some of the Mustangs were in the twilight of their careers, but others were in good shape to take on the North Korean invaders. This was just as well, for the North Korean advance was virtually unstoppable in the early weeks of the war, and it was only the intervention of a great deal of air power that went a long way towards preventing the North Koreans from being entirely successful in their drive through South Korea.

The 12th and 67th Squadrons entered combat as soon as possible after transitioning onto the Mustang (the 18th Wing's other squadron, the 44th FBS, stayed in the Philippines for local air defence there and retained its Shooting Stars). Based initially at Johnson AB in Japan after deploying from Clark AB in the Philippines, the 67th moved in early August 1950 to Taegu (which received the air base coding K-2). The 12th Squadron in effect absorbed the provisional 51st Squadron at Taegu on 4 August. With both squadrons thus located at Taegu, much work was needed to extend and improve the infrastructure at that base (as had also been the case at Pohang), particularly to house the two squadrons with their full complement of Mustangs. Together with the 40th Squadron, these two units joined the battle as soon as possible. The 40th, in fact, ended up having to defend the area of

its own base from a major North Korean advance along the eastern coast of South Korea. The enemy's push was met with intense activity from the Mustangs, which succeeded in breaking the North Korean advance while flying around 35 sorties each day in appalling weather with the cloud-base often at around 200 ft (60 m) or less.

The 12th and 67th Squadrons also flew a large number of missions as soon as they entered the fray. The dangers of operating the Mustang as a fighter-bomber in the face of extensive and often accurate anti-aircraft fire were illustrated very soon after the 67th Squadron began its combat deployment. On 5 August, while attacking a North Korean position near Hamchang, South Korea, the squadron suffered a significant loss. Maj Louis J. Sebille, the unit's CO, was shot down while making a repeat pass against the enemy forces that elements of his squadron were attacking, in an attempt to blunt a North Korean advance towards Taegu. Some writers have claimed that he was trying to deliver one of his two 500 lb (227 kg) bombs which had failed to detach on his first run. However, the 'Time' magazine report on the incident on 4 September 1950 quoted his wingman as saying that Maj Sebille radioed after his first pass that he had been hit, and was going round again to attack the enemy that had inflicted damage on his aircraft. Sebille's Mustang duly crashed directly into the North Korean position. For his actions, Maj Sebille was posthumously awarded the Medal of Honor. He thus became the third and final US Mustang pilot to receive this highest of all US military gallantry medals, after the awards to Maj James H. Howard and Capt William A. Shomo of the USAAF during World War Two. He was also the first USAF airman to be awarded the Medal of Honor following the creation of the independent US Air Force in 1947.

In the days that followed, several further squadrons converted onto the Mustang and joined the action over South Korea. These were the 39th FIS of the 35th Fighter-Interceptor Wing (as previously related, that wing's 40th FIS had already entered combat over Korea with the F-51D – the wing's other squadron, the 41st FIS, retained its F-80C Shooting Stars); and the 35th and 36th Fighter-Bomber Squadrons of the 8th Fighter-Bomber Wing. The 39th FIS was also an F-80 Shooting Star unit that made the transition rapidly onto the Mustang. The squadron received its 'new' Mustangs during the first days of August 1950 and moved into the increasingly busy Pohang airfield. The 35th and 36th FBSs

were similarly F-80-equipped prior to moving onto the Mustang. Based at Itazuke, the two squadrons received their Mustangs on and around 11 August; the wing's other squadron, the 80th FBS, retained its Shooting Stars and did not transition onto the Mustang. The 35th and 36th Squadrons initially operated from Tsuiki in Japan due to the congestion at the South Korean air bases, again utilising the Mustang's excellent range capabilities to fly over to Korea from Japan and loiter in target areas for considerably longer than the Shooting Stars would have been capable of doing. Eventually the 35th Squadron was able to move to Suwon in early October 1950, while the 36th moved later in October to Kimpo.

By that time in the war, a considerable amount of action had taken place. The initial North Korean advances had pushed a substantial way into South Korea, but a combination of air power and last-ditch defence by US and South Korean forces just succeeded in stopping the North Koreans. The US forces were able to establish a bridgehead at Pusan in July which aided considerably in this defence. On 15 September 1950 a major allied force was landed at Inchon in Operation 'Chromite'. This invasion force, principally made up of US Army and Marine Corps troops, aided by forces at Pusan, was able to push back the North Koreans. Air power was a vital ingredient in the success of the subsequent drive forward by combined UN forces, which successfully retook the South Korean capital Seoul, and then

drove north. The 38th Parallel was crossed, and the UN forces routed the North Koreans, successfully capturing the North Korean capital Pyongyang. For a time, Mustangs were actually based at Pyongyang while the advance continued. Unfortunately, the war then increasingly took on a much more sinister form. In early October, with the North Koreans falling back in increasing disarray, the Chinese warned the UN forces of Chinese intervention if the advance continued towards the North Korean border with communist China. In early November Chinese forces began to enter North Korea, and on 26 November the first major clashes began between Chinese and US troops.

By that stage the UN forces had total air superiority, the North Korean air force having been destroyed largely on the ground by UN air attacks. With Mustangs and other allied aircraft operating near the famed Yalu River border area with China, encounters with Chinese aircraft commenced. Worse, the Chinese aircraft were mainly Soviet air force MiG-15 jet fighters, flown by experienced Soviet pilots but seconded to the Chinese. This changed the whole nature of the air war. During the first days of November 1950 Mustangs of the 8th and 18th Wings started to encounter MiG-15s that were based across the Yalu River in Manchuria, and although at first the appearances of the MiGs were only periodic, soon the MiG-15 turned out to be a key adversary for the UN aerial forces. During late November the Chinese launched a major offensive into North Korea from Manchuria and immediately drove south,

Australian-built Mustangs were used operationally in Korea by No.77 Squadron, RAAF, which flew the type in combat from July 1950 until March/April 1951. Heading this line-up of Australian Mustangs being prepared for another mission is A68-765, a US-built F-51D which was one of 299 Mustangs that were supplied to Australia from the US, although some Australian manufactured Mustangs are also believed to have found their way to Korea
*(Photo: R.L. Ward Collection)*

retaking Seoul in January 1951. Fortunately the communist advance was eventually halted and the Chinese forces were pushed back to a line roughly equating to the 38th Parallel. Allied airpower, including the Mustang force, was a key to aiding the UN ground operations which eventually held the Chinese invasion. From the spring of 1951 the war continued as a partial stalemate, but there was no let-up for the Mustangs, some of which had been relocated several times to a number of air bases as the ground war moved forwards and then backwards.

In action, each Mustang typically carried a bomb of 500 lb (227 kg) or 1,000 lb (454 kg) beneath each wing on its main underwing pylon beside the undercarriage, accompanied by three unguided rockets outboard of this on 'zero-length' launchers (the cumbersome rocket rails tried out during World War Two, and the equally drag-producing and not well-favoured three-tube bazooka-type mountings of Second World War vintage were most definitely not used in Korea). Often just two rockets were carried beneath each wing in addition to the bomb. Probably the most effective weapon that was used in Korea by the Mustangs was, however, napalm. This highly flammable mixture was extremely effective against troops, burning everything where it landed and being almost impossible to extinguish until it had burned itself out. It was typically carried in converted underwing fuel tanks, and simply dropped from low level onto the target. The precise mixing up of chemicals that constituted the napalm mixture was made prior to the mission, and captured North Korean troops often talked of the fear and disarray that this weapon created in their ranks. Typical fighter-bomber missions for the Mustangs saw two or four aircraft working together (lone sorties were rarely flown by the fighter-bombers), and targets were often identified for the Mustangs by specially-configured North American T-6 Texans. The latter, referred to as 'Mosquitoes', were an invaluable addition to the USAF's operations, although ground spotters were often also used. Sometimes the Mustangs flew as escorts for USAF Boeing B-29 Superfortress bombers, but this was not by any means their main task. An interesting role that some of the Mustangs were involved in was the developing art of combat search and rescue, which first came into its own in the Korean War. Using early operational helicopters, sometimes covered by Mustangs which could shoot up any enemy troops in the vicinity, a number of armed rescues of downed aircrew were attempted behind the North Korean and Chinese lines. Air bases on the Korean peninsula that were used by the USAF Mustang force included Taegu (K-2), Pohang (K-3), Pusan (K-9), Chinhae (K-10), Suwon (K-13), Kimpo (K-14), Seoul (K-16), Hoengsong (K-46), and

Osan (K-55), in addition to the major North Korean location at Pyongyang (K-24) and the air base at Yonpo (K-27). The Mustang in fact was not alone as a propeller-driven aircraft in the overall UN tactical fighter-bomber effort against the North Koreans and Chinese over the battlefields. US Navy and Marine Corps F4U Corsairs and Douglas AD Skyraiders, plus British Royal Navy Fairey Fireflies, also contributed massively to the aerial offensive against the enemy.

## Twin Mustang Finale

The F-82 Twin Mustang similarly continued on operations in Korea, following the initial operations in June 1950 previously referred to. The type proved to be a very valuable asset for ground-attack work, but the Twin Mustang force was never very large and eventually a developing scarcity of spares and a growing shortage of Twin Mustangs themselves reduced their effectiveness and helped to put an end to their operations. Several Twin Mustangs were lost during the conflict, some disappearing without trace. On the night of 7 August 1950 a Twin Mustang piloted by Lt Charles Moran went missing during a night ground-attack mission. The Twin Mustangs sometimes flew alone on this type of work, and Moran's aircraft simply disappeared. Its wreckage was found some 18 months later. Moran was a serious loss to the 68th Squadron, in not only being an accomplished and experienced pilot, but in also having scored one of the three aerial victories credited to Twin Mustangs on 27 June, just after the start of the conflict. Another sad loss during this period was a renowned former Mustang pilot from the days of the Eighth Air Force in World War Two. One of the colourful characters of the 20th Fighter Group at King's Cliffe in England had been Lt Ernest Fiebelkorn. The top-scoring ace of the 20th FG with nine aerial victories, Fiebelkorn remained in the USAAF and then the US Air Force after World War Two, and eventually became a Twin Mustang pilot with the 4th Fighter-All Weather Squadron at Naha AB on Okinawa island. On the afternoon of 6 July four Twin Mustangs from the 4th Squadron left Itazuke in Japan to try to locate a major column of North Korean tanks that was heading south and which Fifth AF intelligence had so far failed to locate. The Twin Mustangs duly searched in vain for the tanks in poor weather conditions. Fiebelkorn volunteered to let down into the low cloud to try to find the tanks, but he and his radio/radar operator were never heard from again. The wreckage of their F-82G was not found until some time later when the UN forces eventually secured the area. Evidently the Twin Mustang had flown into a high peak in the poor visibility.

The 339th Squadron was the first of the three Twin Mustang units in the Korean theatre to give up its aircraft, in the spring of

Several Mustangs from the 39th FIS, based at Chinhae in the summer of 1951. The underwing external fuel tanks in the foreground were probably being stacked up ready to be made into napalm bombs. The nearest Mustang is an F-51D-25-NT, 44-84910/FF-910 *(Photo: USAF)*

1951. However, the 68th successfully retained its Twin Mustangs until the first half of 1952, and the 4th Squadron also kept some of the twin-engined fighters on its roster during that period. All three of the Twin Mustang squadrons eventually transitioned completely onto the Lockheed F-94 Starfire jet-powered night-fighter. One other Twin Mustang squadron can lay claim to having been active during the Korean War. This was the 449th Squadron at Ladd AFB near Anchorage in Alaska. The commencement of the Korean War saw the unit's Twin Mustangs policing the airspace along the border with the Soviet Union in that often forgotten outpost of the US. To better accomplish this task four of the squadron's Twin Mustangs were forward deployed to Nome, from where patrols and visual reconnaissance flights were made over the Bering Straits area. Some Soviet air activity was witnessed, but no trouble was encountered and the unit eventually began to transition onto the Lockheed F-94 Starfire.

## South African Mustangs in Combat

In November 1950 the USAF and Australian Mustang contingent in Korea was joined by a further Commonwealth country. This was South Africa, which delegated a fighter squadron to the conflict in Korea as a part of its commitment to the UN cause. The unit concerned was No.2 'Cheetah' Squadron, South African Air Force, which was made up of volunteers from the South African armed forces and equipped with Mustangs. The F-51Ds were supplied from US stocks, there being sufficient Mustangs available to do this by that time. The South African contingent sailed to Japan from Durban, South Africa, on 27 September 1950. Once in Japan the squadron moved to Johnson AB to receive its Mustangs and

perform training on the type, the Mustang not being a part of the SAAF's inventory at that time and therefore unfamiliar to many of the South African pilots. Initially 25 F-51Ds were made available to the South Africans, and after a period of training and working-up the squadron moved to Korea. The first base for the Cheetahs was Pusan (K-9), which was occupied at that time by the 12th FBS of the 18th FBW. The South Africans subsequently operated under the umbrella of the 18th Wing, and commenced operations on 19 November. A move was made soon after into North Korea as the UN forces advanced forward, the squadron moving in to Pyongyang (K-24). However, with the Chinese invasion and the subsequent pushing back of the UN forces, the South Africans pulled out of North Korea and returned south, taking part in the major aerial effort to try to halt the Chinese advance.

## Reconnaissance Mustangs

In addition to the role of fighter-bomber that the F-51D fulfilled in Korea with capability and great courage, the Mustang also flew for the Americans as one of the principal reconnaissance aircraft in the conflict. Several aircraft types operated in Korea in the reconnaissance role, but the Mustang became the principal land-based tactical reconnaissance aircraft, and as such added to the laurels of the F-51 in general during the Korean War. For daytime visual reconnaissance and photography of a tactical nature the USAF came to principally employ the Mustang, while for night-time reconnaissance a version of the Douglas B/A-26 Invader was employed. In fact the two types aided the whole reconnaissance effort by working hand-in-hand, the Mustangs by day and the Invaders by night.

Official photographers often have a tendency towards taking somewhat contrived images, but in this case the result is an interesting view of US-operated F-51Ds and their weaponry. Being worked on beside a large number of bombs are two late-production F-51D Mustangs from the 39th FIS (also sometimes referred to as the 39th FBS), the nearest being an F-51D-25-NA, 44-73888/FF-888. The stripes around the rear fuselage of this aircraft suggest that it is a command plane *(Photo: USAF)*

One of the main tactical reconnaissance assets for UN forces in the Korean War was the Mustang. Camera-carrying, reconnaissance Mustangs fought a long, lonely but nonetheless successful war in Korea, and were amongst the unsung heroes of the conflict. This RF-51D, serial number 44-14547, was built as a P-51D-10-NA and was converted to reconnaissance configuration. It is seen here bearing the name 'Symons Lemon' while operated by the 45th TRS, and bearing the RF-51D's 'Buzz Number' prefix 'RF'. The 45th TRS was established in September 1950 specifically for operations in Korea, and it was the final US-operated Mustang squadron that was active in the Korean War
(Photo: USAF)

When the Korean War began, however, the USAF only had one daylight tactical reconnaissance squadron available in Japan. This was the 8th Tactical Reconnaissance Squadron (later redesignated as the 15th TRS), which operated the Lockheed RF-80A, a camera-equipped version of the F-80 Shooting Star jet fighter. It was clear as soon as the conflict in Korea started that a considerable amount of tactical reconnaissance coverage was going to be needed, and one of the results of this was the establishment of the 45th TRS on 3 September 1950 at Itazuke. This unit was intended to be equipped with Mustangs, for tactical coverage of the battlefield and front line plus supply lines running north from the battlefield, while the RF-80A-equipped 15th TRS was tasked with coverage of potential targets deeper within North Korea itself such as airfields and communications, for which the superior speed of the jet would be of most value. However, there was a complete shortage of RF-51D camera-equipped Mustangs in Far East Air Forces, and the 45th TRS did not start to receive suitable Mustangs until November 1950. The squadron subsequently flew a mixed-bag of camera-equipped RF-51D and straight (non camera-equipped) F-51D Mustangs, the latter usually being the most prevalent. Some if not all of the RF-51Ds were actually Mustangs that were converted into the reconnaissance role in Japan, which therefore theoretically added to the overall total of actual reconnaissance Mustangs that were converted by NAA in World War Two from straight fighter Mustangs. Nevertheless, contrary to some published sources, the camera-equipped Mustangs in Korea were usually and probably always armed, as were their Second World War counterparts.

Initial operations for the reconnaissance Mustangs of the 45th TRS were often flown from Taegu (K-2), and at first involved single- or two-plane flights. Sometimes specific areas where enemy activity was suspected would be flown over in a search pattern that took in a 10 mile (16 km) radius around the suspected site of the enemy to catch up with any local movements that had taken place under the cover of darkness by the North Korean or Chinese forces. The communists would often only move any distance at night, and take cover during the day to avoid being spotted, but the reconnaissance Mustangs became very efficient at seeking out concealed enemy forces, and their pilots came to know their areas of operations very well. However, the vulnerability of the Mustang to ground fire resulted in several modifications in their tactics. From the spring of 1951, for example, missions would usually be flown with two aircraft, one going down low while the other stayed at a higher altitude to look out for signs of ground fire. Sometimes missions involved four aircraft for additional safety and enhanced capability to sight concealed targets on the ground. On occasion the Mustangs would act as target spotters (this was the 'Mosquito' mission otherwise usually flown by specially-configured T-6 Texans) for USAF fighter-bombers

(which were often Mustangs of the fighter-bomber squadrons), or for naval gunfire. Sometimes the reconnaissance Mustangs were able to shoot up targets of opportunity, but this was not their primary objective.

The unit that the 45th and 15th Tactical Reconnaissance Squadrons were eventually assigned to, in addition to the 12th TRS with its night reconnaissance Invaders was the 67th Tactical Reconnaissance Wing. This wing was formally activated on 25 February 1951 at Komaki AB, Japan, specifically for operations over Korea. It took over the activities of the 543rd Tactical Support Group, which had a headquarters at Itazuke that had overseen some of the reconnaissance effort up to that time. Operations by the new 67th Wing began at once in support of UN forces in Korea. The wing's headquarters moved to Taegu (K-2) in South Korea during March 1951, before moving on to Kimpo in August 1951, from where it saw out the war. The squadrons that were assigned to this wing flew from a variety of air bases in South Korea during that time, with detachments moving around as necessary. The 67th already had a considerable historical attachment to the Mustang – as recounted earlier in this book, as the 67th Tactical Reconnaissance Group it had included reconnaissance Merlin-Mustangs in its inventory during the war in Europe, right up to the end of the Second World War. The CO of the 67th TRW from the time of its activation in February 1951 was Col Karl L. Polifka, who was a celebrated reconnaissance pilot from the Second World War, and who sowed the seeds for the 67th to become a highly efficient organisation. Underlining how dangerous the reconnaissance task was in Korea, Polifka was killed on 1 July 1951 in a Mustang during a dangerous reconnaissance mission to the Kaesong area. Reconnaissance pilots flew a tour of 100 sorties in Korea, which was a high number to fly in the increasingly vulnerable Mustang.

## Aerial Combat

Although the main task of the Mustangs in Korea was of a tactical nature and did not primarily include air-to-air combat, it was inevitable that aerial combat would take place from time to time, and the USAF's Mustangs scored a number of aerial victories over North Korean propeller-driven aircraft during the conflict. There were also less conclusive encounters with MiG-15s, which the Mustang could certainly not out-run, but could engage in a turning fight if required that would considerably favour the propeller-driven aircraft. There are no definite records of Mustangs shooting down MiG-15s, but on at least two occasions USAF Mustang pilots managed a good burst of fire at a MiG-15 which was subsequently assessed as a 'probable' victory. One of these was on 7 November 1950 when several pilots of the 12th FBS scored numerous hits on a MiG-15 that had intercepted them from its base at Antung in Manchuria, just over the Yalu River border area (the MiG base at Antung was clearly visible to the USAF pilots when they were flying over north-western North Korea close to the Chinese border). An explosion was seen on the ground following this encounter, but the MiG was not definitely seen to crash and so the 'victory' was not allowed by the USAF.

Mustangs had some successes against propeller-driven North Korean aircraft, even after the confused aerial dog-fighting of the initial few days of the conflict over Korea. A successful day was 1 November 1950, when elements of the 67th FBS were attacking ground targets in the Yalu River area. The Mustangs were armed with two napalm tanks each and six 5-in (12.7 mm) unguided rockets, in addition to their six internal 0.5-in machine guns. The American fighter-bombers were attacked by North Korean fighters which were described by one of the American pilots, Capt Ross Flake, rather more accurately than in previous times as 'Yak-type North Korean fighters'. In the dog-fight that followed, the Mustang pilots proved far superior to their North Korean adversaries in terms of flying skills, and two of the Yaks (which were probably Yak-9s) were shot down, Capt Flake and Capt Robert Thresher being credited with the victories. The Mustang could certainly hold its own against this type of aerial opposition, even though the nimble Yak fighters were able to turn with the F-51Ds and had a creditable all-round performance. In total, 19 North Korean aircraft were credited to USAF Mustang pilots during the Korean conflict, although subsequent revisions have removed some of these victories. Much of the fighter activity over Korea for the USAF in the early days of the war was performed by the F-80C Shooting Star, but the intervention of the Chinese and Russians during November 1950 with the excellent MiG-15s necessitated a more advanced fighter being deployed by the Americans. This took the form of the superlative North American F-86 Sabre, and for the rest of the conflict it was the Sabre that equipped an increasing number of the USAF's fighter units in the Korean

theatre. The Sabre was the match for the MiG-15, and at the end of the war the Americans claimed a 10:1 kill ratio against the MiG-15 by the various marks of F-86 that were deployed in Korea. In fact subsequent revisions, and access to Soviet records following the end of the Cold War have led to this figure being revised to more like 5:1, which was still a very creditable ratio and one of the major explanations of the eventual failure of the communists to win the war in Korea. For the Mustang, there followed the somewhat unfortunate role of being used as bait while on their fighter-bomber missions over North Korea and particularly what came to be known as 'MiG Alley' in the Yalu River area, in the hope that MiG-15s would be lured into intercepting the F-51Ds while Sabres waited in the wings ready to pounce on the communist fighters.

## Mustang Operations Wind-Down

In reality the number of Mustangs actually used on operations over Korea started to diminish during 1951. The high point of the Mustang's deployment in the Korean War was probably reached in early December 1950, with six USAF fighter-bomber squadrons operating the type, plus one from Australia and one from South Africa, as well as the newly-arrived reconnaissance Mustangs of the 45th TRS. The first unit to transition from the Mustang to other types was the 8th FBW, which began to withdraw back to Itazuke in Japan on or around 8 December 1950 (the official records say 10 December 1950), to return to flying the F-80 Shooting Star. The Mustangs that its 35th and 36th TRSs had been flying were mainly retained in Korea, and distributed to other Mustang squadrons including those of the 18th FBW. In May 1951 the 40th FIS of the 35th FIW was also withdrawn, and rotated to Japan to begin conversion onto jets. The 35th Wing's 39th FIS was then attached to the 18th Wing, joining that wing's 12th and 67th FBSs on operations from a series of bases including Chinhae and Hoengsong (K-46) – the latter often acting as a forward staging base for the wing's Mustangs. During April 1951 the RAAF's No.77

This unusual photograph was snapped a split second after two napalm fire bombs were released over North Korea. One can be seen nearly vertical behind and below, and the second one released has just separated from the aircraft *(Photo: USAF)*

Squadron also ceased combat activities with the Mustang, and stood down so as to transition onto the Gloster Meteor F Mk 8 jet fighter. The squadron had been based for a short time on North Korean territory at Yonpo during the UN push into North Korea in the early winter of 1950, but had latterly used Pusan as one of its chief bases, while also employing Iwakuni in Japan for its principal maintenance centre. The squadron flew its last Mustang mission on 6 April, attacking a convoy of Chinese transport vehicles. Overall, the Australians had flown some 3,800 Mustang sorties, and used 56 Mustangs in Korea, of which 18 had been lost to all causes, with eight pilots killed and at least one taken prisoner.

During 1951 the need for Mustangs in Korea increased, but the number available began to seriously dwindle. Many of these Mustangs were by then becoming very war weary, although they were performing a very worthwhile service to the overall UN war effort. The Mustang fighter-bombers flew some of the missions in two major aerial campaigns, Operations 'Strangle' and 'Saturate', which aimed to bring pressure on the North Koreans to negotiate by interdicting supply lines and preventing supplies reaching the communist front lines in the increasingly static ground war. Eventually, in June 1952, the Mustang force began to wind down. The 39th FIS ceased Mustang operations during that month, and was re-assigned to the 51st FIW at Suwon (K-13) to re-equip with F-86 Sabres. Increasingly the fighter-bomber role over Korea for the USAF was taken over by the Republic F-84E Thunderjet, particularly longer-range penetrations over North Korea, allowing the remaining Mustang units to gradually draw down their operations. The 12th FBS ceased its Mustang operations in December 1952 and duly converted onto Sabres. It later flew from a new air base, with better facilities compared to many of the existing South Korean airfields, at Osan (K-55). In the same month, No.2 Squadron, SAAF, also ceased Mustang operations. The South Africans had operated with distinction during their time on the Mustang, and had continued to be attached to the 18th FBW during all their time in Korea, principally based at Chinhae (K-10) in South Korea. During its time with the Mustang, No.2 Squadron had been allocated further batches of Mustangs from US stocks but had lost 73 or 74 aircraft to all causes, with some 12 pilots killed and others missing or captured, in at least 10,373

sorties flown. The squadron transitioned onto the F-86F Sabre after finishing with the Mustang. A number of the South African Mustangs were returned to the USAF in December 1952 while No.2 Squadron converted onto the jets. At least two of these F-51Ds and probably more were then handed over to the RoKAF. The South Koreans continued to fly the Mustang up to the end of the war, principally using the air base at Kangnung (K-18), and by the end of the conflict they were the only UN forces still operating the type.

The final USAF fighter-bomber squadron to continue flying the Mustang in Korea was the 67th FBS of the 18th FBW. This squadron had previously flown the 10,000th sortie of the wing's Korean operations, and then the 45,000th, but eventually ceased Mustang operations in early 1953 to convert onto the F-86 Sabre. The final mission was flown on 23 January 1953, ending two and a half years of Mustang fighter-bomber combat over Korea. This left the 45th TRS as the only USAF unit still flying the Mustang over Korea at that time, albeit mainly on reconnaissance duties, but even that squadron was in the process of winding-down its Mustang operations. The unit had started converting onto the Lockheed RF-80C, the most up-to-date photo-reconnaissance version of the F-80 Shooting Star, in the late summer and autumn of 1952, and flew its final Mustang operations in February 1953. On 27 July 1953, an armistice was at last signed that ended the Korean War, although it was a conflict without a resolution, and ever since the Korean peninsula has been split between North and South Korea, with tension at times threatening to spill over into more conflict. For the Mustang the Korean War had been its second and last major war. The F-51D and RF-51D Mustangs that had been in action over Korea had performed a very significant job for the UN forces, although the type had taken a beating from anti-aircraft defences that underlined the Mustang's vulnerability to ground fire due to its liquid-cooled engine and radiator installation. Nevertheless the UN had achieved its immediate goals in Korea by the armistice of July 1953, and the Mustang had certainly been an important factor in the defeat of the North Korean and Chinese ground forces.

**Taken during September 1951, a U.S. Air Force North American F-51D Mustang taxis through a puddle. Not the most ideal situation but not enough to stop operations!** (Photo: USAF)

# Other Operators and Civil Service

## Chapter 10

Out of the total Mustang production run of over fifteen thousand examples, the vast majority of Mustangs were operated by or found their way onto the inventories of the US Army Air Force(s) or the Royal Air Force. However, in addition to these two principal air arms, as we have seen elsewhere in this book a number of other air forces flew Mustangs in smaller but no less significant numbers during World War Two or in Korea. British Commonwealth countries including Canada, South Africa and Australia used Mustangs that were in effect 'borrowed' from the RAF (the latter two also used Mustangs in Korea under different arrangements). On the other hand, France and China flew Mustangs during the later stages of World War Two, these countries using Mustangs that had been delivered by the US and painted in the markings of these operators. Some pilots whose countries had been occupied but who flew with the Allies also had time on the Mustang, notably the Poles.

Additional to these considerations, the Mustang was eventually flown by a diversity of countries around the world. This employment commenced after World War Two, when there were surplus Mustangs available for 'export' use, and a number of countries were in need of an aircraft of the Mustang's calibre. Indeed, it was in this context that the longevity of the Mustang was truly exhibited, with several countries flying the type well into the 1970's, and one - the Dominican Republic - using Mustangs as its main front-line combat aircraft until 1984.

The supply of some of these 'export' aircraft was undertaken by the US under the auspices of a number of mutual aid defence arrangements, with some of the aircraft involved changing hands for little or no money. Following World War Two several defence and mutual aid pacts were brought into existence by the US that drew in a number of countries, which subsequently benefited from the supply of US equipment. In the case of the Mustang this was most notably in Central and South America. Often cited as the reason for the supply of Mustangs to a number of Central American states is the so-called Rio Pact of 1947, but in reality there were several agreements under which Mustangs were supplied which were not necessarily related to the 1947 agreement. These included the umbrella American Republics Project which eventually grew into and was in part replaced by

Mutual Defence Assistance (usually simply known by its common abbreviation MDAP) and Military Assistance Programme (MAP) schemes. There were also related initiatives such as the Reimbursable Aid Programme (RAP) and the Foreign Military Sales (FMS) plan. Untangling which Mustang deliveries were covered by which programme is beyond the scope of this brief narrative, but it is worth noting that the US preferred to supply only Thunderbolts and not other types to the Central American and Caribbean states, a plan that was not achieved as the text of this chapter demonstrates.

Most 'export' Mustangs were of P-51D-lineage, because no lightweight Mustangs ever operated in a front-line context outside of the United States military, and it is believed that the same is true of the F-82 Twin Mustang. However, a number of Cavalier Mustangs certainly did see 'overseas' employment. Only one other country, namely Australia, actually built Mustangs additional to production in the US by North American Aviation, and apart from this Australian production for the Australian armed services, no Mustangs were built as such for export – except of course for the original country of delivery, Britain. Therefore all of the countries that flew Mustangs after World War Two except for Australia used 'second hand' Mustangs which had originally been built for US or British service.

## Australia (including local production)

Australia was the only country outside of the US where Mustangs were built in series production, making this country highly significant in the overall history of the Mustang. Australia already had important links with North American Aviation due to the Australian connection during the late 1930's with the North American NA-16 trainer. The developed NA-33 (NAA designation NA-16-2K) derivative of the NA-16 line was built in Australia as the Wirraway light combat and training aircraft. Constructed by Commonwealth Aircraft Corporation Pty., Ltd. (CAC) in Australia from 1939 onwards, the Wirraway gave important service during the Second World War in the Pacific area, and created a significant link between the Australians and the North American company. Australian pilots first became acquainted with the Mustang in combat in Europe, where some Australian pilots flew with RAF

Australia was not only an operator of Merlin-Mustangs, it was unique for an overseas country in being a Mustang manufacturer as well. In total 299 Mustangs were received by the Australians from US production, but an additional 200 were manufactured in Australia by the Commonwealth Aircraft Corporation. The Australian-built Mustangs were basically similar to their US-produced counterparts, except in detail and in the case of some examples, by engine mark. Illustrated is A68-565, a former P-51K from US production wearing the 'LB' codes of No.84 Squadron, Royal Australian Air Force
*(Photo: RAAF)*

squadrons. An Australian-manned Curtiss Kittyhawk squadron, No.450, received a small number of Mustangs (possibly only one) in either late 1944 or in May 1945 but did not become operational on the type before disbanding in August 1945. In contrast, No.3 Squadron, Royal Australian Air Force, flew Mustangs in combat in the Mediterranean theatre from late 1944 onwards. By then the Australian military was already well aware of the capabilities of the Merlin-engined Mustang, and the decision to build the type in Australia was made in April 1944, on the assumption of the necessary obtaining of the relevant production licences from NAA and the US government. The type's considerable range capabilities, which would be very useful in the Pacific theatre, were a major consideration in the Australian preference for the Mustang. It was initially intended to produce 690 Mustangs in Australia, to begin with by using knock-down parts from North American but later switching to full manufacture in Australia. CAC at Fishermans Bend, Melbourne, was lined up to make the Australian Mustangs, and a pattern aircraft was supplied from NAA production during 1944 to help with production start-up. This initial aircraft was allocated the Australian military serial number A68-1001, 'A68' having been selected as the Mustang serial number prefix within the Australian numbering system for military aircraft. It did not fly until April 1945 having firstly been used for much groundwork as production was set up. However delays in the whole programme meant that the first locally-built Mustang did not fly until late that same month.

As an interim, while manufacturing facilities were being established in Australia, Mustangs were ordered directly from the US. Eventually 298 Mustangs of P-51D and P-51K versions were delivered to Australia from standard US production, starting in April 1945. They comprised 84 P-51Ks (Australian serial numbers A68-500 to A68-583), and 214 P-51Ds (A68-600 to A68-813). However, although these were intended for the war against the Japanese, in the event the British and Commonwealth air forces did not use Mustangs in the CBI or Pacific during World War Two. Nevertheless, some of the US-built Mustangs that were supplied to Australia were nearing their combat debut with the RAAF as the war in the Pacific drew to a close in August and September 1945. Nos.84 (squadron code LB) and 86 Squadrons, RAAF, briefly flew some of the US-supplied Mustangs during that period - but did not play any part in the conflict with the Mustang. The end of the war significantly reduced the need for a large number of fighters to be operated by the Australians, and the intended local production of Mustangs was cut back accordingly. In the event only 200 Mustangs were completed in Australia, and of those, 80 were built up from 100 sets of components that were supplied by North American Aviation in order to start up the Australian production. Therefore, a total of 499 Mustangs, (299 from US production including the pattern aircraft, and 200 from Australian manufacture), actually received Australian military serial numbers.

The first Mustang to be completed in Australia was A68-1, which first flew in late April 1945. According to the logbook of pilot Flt Lt 'Jim' Schofield, the flight was made on 29 April 1945. Australian manufacture was broken down as follows. Initially, 80 Mustang Mk 20s were put together with the local designation CA-17 (serial numbers A68-1 to A68-80). These were made from 100 sets of components that were produced by North American Aviation and shipped to Australia. Next in the numerical sequence were 28 CA-18 Mustang Mk 22s (A68-81 to A68-94, and A68-187 to A68-200). Subsequently were 26 CA-18 Mustang Mk 21s (A68-95 to A68-120). Finally were 66 CA-18 Mustang Mk 23s (A68-121 to A68-186). All of these were Packard Merlin-powered, except for the Mk 23 which had Rolls-Royce produced Merlins. In fact all of the 200 were generally similar to the P-51D version of the Mustang, except for comparatively minor detail and equipment

changes. The most radically different was the Mustang Mk 22, which was a photo reconnaissance version and featured mountings and wiring for a variety of cameras including the ubiquitous F.24 in the fuselage aft of the radiator installation. Normally two cameras were carried, one vertical and one oblique, the latter looking out through a left-hand fuselage side window unique to this version – which was therefore different to the installations found on US-operated reconnaissance F-6 Mustangs. Due to the ending of the war the manufacture of the Australian Mustangs was made at a comparatively leisurely pace, and it is often said that this was partly to keep the CAC factory open for as long a period as possible.

The Australian manufactured Mustangs were dimensionally identical to their US-built equivalents, with similar performance capabilities. The Mks 20, 21 and 22 were powered by the 1,720 hp Packard Merlin V-1650-7 in similar fashion to the US-built P-51D (although there are repeated claims that some of the Mk 20s had the V-1650-3), but the Mk 23 was fitted with a 1,655 hp Rolls-Royce Merlin 70. Armament was identical to the P-51D. There was provision for underwing stores on the usual single underwing pylon beneath each wing, including the ubiquitous 75 or 110 US gallon external fuel tanks, or a 500 lb bomb. Some aircraft were also fitted with underwing zero-length rocket rails outboard of the pylon for up to six 5-in rockets (three beneath each wing).

The first Australian-manufactured Mustangs were accepted for RAAF service in June 1945, but as stated earlier no Mustang saw combat with Australian forces in the Pacific. The final deliveries from the first batch of Australian-manufactured Mustangs, the Mk 20, were made in the summer of 1946, but the very last Mustang that was manufactured in Australia was not handed over until August 1951. This was a Mustang Mk 22 A68-200, and it was the last Mustang to be built anywhere – until limited production began again in the early 2000's.

In Australian service the initial deployment in Nos.84 and 86 Squadrons, RAAF, was superseded by comparatively long-running operations with Nos.76, 77 and 82 Squadrons (No.81 Wing). These three squadrons were delegated to occupation duties, and were sent to Japan from 1946 as a part of the Allied occupation forces under the British Commonwealth Occupation Force (BCOF). Nos. 76 and 82 Squadrons left Japan in 1950 at the end of their deployment, but still in the area at the commencement of the Korean War was No.77 Squadron at Iwakuni in Japan. This squadron actually flew what was supposed to be its last occupation force sorties from Iwakuni on 23 June, just two days before the North Koreans attacked. With the squadron committed by the Australian government in late June to the military efforts to help South Korea, the unit's Mustangs initially operated from Iwakuni and employed the Mustang's legendary long-range capabilities to good effect. They flew their first real sorties in early July, and the squadron was later attached to the USAF's 8th Fighter-Bomber Wing, and thence to the 35th Fighter-Interceptor Wing, during its service in Korea. During April 1951 No.77 Squadron ceased combat activities with the Mustang, and stood down so as to transition onto the Gloster Meteor F Mk 8 jet fighter. The last Mustang mission was flown on 6 April. Overall, the Australians flew some 3,800 Mustang sorties, and used 56 Mustangs in Korea, of which 18 had been lost to all causes, with eight pilots killed and at least one taken prisoner. Most of the Mustangs used were US-built from amongst the 299 supplied from the US, but there is evidence that with them were several of the Australian-manufactured examples.

Other RAAF units that flew the Mustang, albeit not in combat, were Nos.75, 76 and 78 Squadrons, No.3 Squadron (a reconnaissance unit originally numbered No.4 Squadron, and not to be confused with the wartime No.3 Squadron in the Mediterranean), and several second-line auxiliary squadrons of

the Citizen Air Force manned by part-time territorial personnel. The latter were No.21 (City of Melbourne) Squadron, No.22 (City of Sydney) Squadron, No.23 (City of Brisbane) Squadron, No.24 (City of Adelaide) Squadron, and No.25 (City of Perth) Squadron. Three of these (Nos.21, 23, and 25) had transitioned onto the de Havilland Vampire by the mid 1950's, but No.24 Squadron did not finally gave up its much-treasured Mustangs until mid-1960 when the auxiliary squadrons of the Citizen Air Force lost their position as flying units.

Retired ex-RAAF Mustangs were held at a storage depot at Tocumwal, New South Wales. Six of these aircraft, A-68-1, -7, -30, -72, and -87 (all CAC-manufactured) had an unusual post-retirement career. In the early 1950's Britain selected several sites on the Australian mainland to conduct nuclear bomb tests. A feature of these tests was to determine the effects of a nuclear blast on military equipment. To that end, the six aforementioned Mustangs were selected to be parked near to the 'ground zero' at the test site at Emu in South Australia and subjected to the rigours of two nuclear explosions. The detonations took place in October 1953. Only one of the Mustangs was damaged to any large degree, and by 1967 the site was deemed safe so that the six aircraft were put up for sale by the Australian Department of Supply in May 1967. They were subsequently sold, five eventually being used by the Cavalier Aircraft Corporation in the US in its rebuild programme of Mustang airframes during the 1960's.

## Bolivia

The Mustang was an important aircraft to the Fuerza Aérea Boliviana (FAB) for well over two decades. In that time the Bolivian air force succeeded in operating a mixed bag of Mustangs from various sources, and the type saw combat on several occasions during its Bolivian service. This was particularly true following the establishment of military dictatorship in Bolivia from 1964 onwards, with a succession of régimes that were acceptable to the Americans in the following years.

Despite US attempts to standardise Central and South American countries on the Republic P/F-47 Thunderbolt, several instead eventually flew Mustangs, and this was particularly true of Bolivia. Despite persistent reports, Bolivia did not operate Thunderbolts, although one example did arrive in Bolivia but was not used operationally. Instead, the first deliveries to Bolivia of Mustangs apparently took place in the late 1940's, comprising a small number of examples, and was followed in the summer of 1954 by the acquisition of three further Mustangs. The latter comprised two single-seaters and a two-seat example, but their delivery was a slow process and two of them were only delivered in early 1955 (by which time the third aircraft had crashed, but was later replaced). It is believed that these were ex-RAAF aircraft,

obtained via a US organisation known as the American Aeronautics Corporation. Further deliveries took place in 1960, comprising a number of Mustangs that were just being retired by Uruguay, and reputably purchased for a token $1 each. The exact number of Mustangs involved in this transaction has been the subject of considerable debate and confusion amongst historians, the numbers stated being between four and eight. In reality at least four airworthy examples were definitively delivered, with possibly several more for spares. One of these aircraft is confirmed as FAB-506, a former P-51D-20-NA (44-63807) that had served in Uruguay as FAU-272 until 1960 before passing to Bolivia for $1.

Further F-51D Mustangs were delivered in the mid-1960's, these early Bolivian Mustangs being coded in the 'FAB-500' numbers range. Exactly how many additional Mustangs were received in the mid-1960's is a considerable mystery, and at least one historian doubts their existence altogether.

Bolivia became, later in the 1960's, one of the major customers for Cavalier Mustangs. These were supplied, as was the case with El Salvador, under the auspices of the Project Peace Condor programme. Up to nine Cavalier Mustangs, approximating to but certainly not identical to Cavalier Mk II configuration, were involved. This definitely included at least one two-seater (possibly as many as three), serial number 67-14866 (FAB-521). Confirmed serial numbers of the single-seat examples include 67-22579 (FAB-519) and 67-22581 (FAB-523).

In the later days of their Bolivian service the Mustangs and Cavaliers were concentrated into an Escadron de Caza within the FAB's Grupo 2, based principally at Colcapirua. They were eventually replaced beginning in 1977 with the sale of a number to Canadian private sources. Much earlier than this, a Bolivian Mustang was donated to Venezuela (which was not a front-line Mustang operator) as a part of a deal in the later 1960's that saw some F-86 Sabres and B-25 Mitchells (both of course, like the Mustang, North American Aviation products) passed to Bolivia from Venezuela.

## Canada

The Royal Canadian Air Force (RCAF) had a long and very fruitful association with the Mustang that lasted well into the 1950's. As related elsewhere in this book, the RCAF operated important numbers of Mustangs during World War Two in Europe, with five squadrons eventually flying the type including one that was amongst the first to operate the Mustang in front-line service. This wartime use was alongside the RAF as a part of the overall British and Commonwealth war effort employing aircraft that were effectively RAF machines 'loaned' for Canadian operations, but post-war the RCAF flew the Mustang in Canada itself.

The Canadian association with the Mustang as an operational

Canada was a major post-World War Two operator of Merlin-Mustangs. All 130 of the Mustangs that were supplied to Canada post-war came from US stocks. These Mustangs were supplied to Canada in the late 1940's and early 1950's and were generally in very good condition, coming as they did from stocks of low-time airframes in the US. This contrasted strongly with the Mustangs that were supplied from war-weary stocks in Europe to countries like Italy, many of which were in poor condition. This Canadian Mustang Mk IV, '9552' (believed to be ex 44-63872), exhibits what happens to a P-51D which has sat on the ground for some time allowing hydraulic pressure to drain from its systems, allowing the inner main undercarriage doors and the flaps to creep down *(Photo: R.L. Ward Collection)*

type began in 1942, when Nos.400 and 414 Squadrons were re-equipped with Mustang Mk Is, having previously flown the Curtiss Tomahawk. No.414 Squadron participated in the Dieppe operation in August 1942, one of its pilots, the American F/O Hollis Hills, scoring the first-ever Mustang air-to-air kill. Nos.400 and 414 Squadrons were army co-operation units, as also was No. 430 Squadron, RCAF, which similarly operated Mustangs – becoming operational in 1943. Later in the war in Europe, Nos.441 and 442 Squadrons, RCAF, were also equipped for a comparatively short time with Mustangs, the former not seeing combat with the type.

In the post-war period the RCAF underwent a certain amount of reorganisation, as the eventually large wartime complement of Canadian front-line squadrons was run down and priorities changed. Several Auxiliary Fighter Squadrons were created as a second-line active reserve but important home-defence force, and some flew Mustangs. The RCAF's post-war Mustangs were supplied from surplus US stocks after the war. Eventually 130 were earmarked for Canadian service, with initial deliveries taking place in 1947 with the balance following in 1950/51. Most if not all were P-51D-20, D-25 and D-30s from NAA Inglewood production. In Canadian service they received the designation Mustang TF (Tactical Fighter) Mk IV (the Roman numerals are sometimes replaced in Canadian sources by a numeral '4'), and the type was operated until the mid-1950's when jet equipment was gradually phased in and national defence priorities were reorganised. The Canadian serial numbers that were allocated for these aircraft were 9221 to 9300, and 9551 to 9600. Most of the survivors were disposed of later in the 1950's (although several were not struck off charge until late in 1960), with some being purchased by private buyers.

The Canadian Auxiliary Fighter Squadrons that flew the Mustang included Nos. 402 (City of Winnipeg), 403 (City of Calgary), 420 (City of London), 424 (City of Hamilton), 442 (City of Vancouver), and 443 (City of New Westminster) Squadrons. Interestingly, these units were allocated squadron code letters in similar fashion to those worn by wartime units – the identified codes being AC (402 Sq); AD (403 Sq); AW (420 Sq); BA (424 Sq); BU (442 Sq); PF (443 Sq) – the latter two squadrons were both based at Sea Island, British Colombia, and frequently exchanged aircraft. In addition, at least two - No.416 'Lynx' Squadron (coded AS), and No.417 Squadron (coded AT) – and possibly other front-line regular RCAF squadrons, also temporarily operated some of these post-war Mustangs. Canadian sources additionally refer to service by at least two Mustangs (9227 and 9553, at Arnprior) for weapons clearance and experimental work at the Central Experimental and Proving Establishment, which also used a Mustang (9555) at the Winter

Experimental Establishment at Edmonton, Alberta, for cold weather trials. Training work was performed by some Mustangs at the Canadian Joint Air Training Centre at Rivers, Manitoba, by No.1 (F) OTU at Chatham, New Brunswick, and by the Central Flying School at Trenton. No.102 (CR) Flight, at Trenton, employed at least two Mustangs as target–towers.

## China

Chinese pilots flew alongside their US counterparts with considerable if largely unheralded success in the Chinese part of the CBI theatre during the later stages of World War Two, as referred to in Chapter 4 of this book. It seems likely that a number of Mustangs (possibly as many as 50) were turned over to the Chinese during the latter stages of the war itself, rather than the Chinese pilots simply flying in 'borrowed' aircraft. At the end of the war, the USAAF had a large number of aircraft at various air bases on nominally Chinese territory. China at that time, it must be remembered, was not the large, unified entity that it is today. Effectively the Chinese who fought the Japanese were a disparate selection of Chinese groups, a coalition that did not last long after the end of the war. Not surprisingly the Americans came to recognise the US-leaning Chiang Kai-shek, who had been one of the principal leaders of anti-Japanese forces during the war, as the legitimate leader of all the Chinese when the war ended. A coalition of Chinese groups which supported the communist-inspired Mao Tse-tung, however, had other ideas, and fighting between these disparate groups led to full civil war in the period after the end of World War Two from 1946 onwards. The Americans supported Chiang Kai-shek's 'nationalist' Chinese with considerable amounts of military hardware. There were approximately one thousand USAAF aircraft of various types in or near Chinese territory at the end of the war, mainly those that had flown with 14th Army Air Force units (they included P-51B, P-51C, P-51D, F-6D, and some P-51K versions), and it appears that the Americans turned over most if not all of these to the Chiang Kai-shek air arm. They included not only Mustangs, but other combat and transport types as well. The details of this transaction have never fully come to light, nor has anything like an idea as to how many Mustangs exactly were involved. The Chiang Kai-shek forces subsequently flew some of these Mustangs against the Mao Tse-tung groups, but without much success, and it was not long before the US-supported forces were in full retreat. The nationalist fall-back did not cease until Mao Tse-tung's supporters has taken control of all of the mainland Chinese territory, the victory being completed during 1949, leaving only the island of Formosa (modern-day Taiwan) as the solitary remaining refuge for Chiang Kai-shek.

During the retreat of Chiang Kai-shek's forces a number of

The Dominican Republic's varied Mustang fleet became well-known for its longevity and the number of different and diverse sources that the aircraft came from. Dominican Mustangs arrived in all shapes and sizes over the years from the summer of 1948 onwards. In this image can be seen a pair of unidentified Dominican Republic-operated Mustangs, apparently photographed in late 1969. The Dominican Mustangs sported very distinctive camouflage schemes, and were subjected to a number of upgrades during their long service in the Dominican Republic
(Photo: R.L. Ward Collection)

Mustangs fell into communist hands, and it is possible that some were used against their previous owners. The retreat of Chiang Kai-shek to Formosa and the establishment of his Western-inspired Republic of China resulted in the creation of an air arm that lent very heavily on the Mustang as its principal fighter in the post 1949-era. This service appears to have lasted well into the mid-1950's when jet fighters from the US started to become available.

## Costa Rica

One of the least-known of Mustang operators, Costa Rica (the Fuerza Aérea Costarricense) operated four F-51Ds from early 1955 onwards. These are sometimes said to have been supplied under one of several mutual aid packages that the United States had formulated in the post-war period, particularly relating to Central and South American countries, but the actual picture is somewhat more complicated. A civil war had taken place in Costa Rica in 1948, and following the cessation of hostilities much of the Costa Rican armed forces had been disbanded. However, Costa Rica had had disputes with Nicaragua, its northern neighbour, for some time, and in early 1955 these spilled over into a Nicaraguan-backed invasion by 'rebel' forces. Costa Rica was unable to defend itself, and the United States stepped in to help with military aid. This included the supply of four Mustangs in January 1955, which were sold to the Costa Rican authorities for a nominal $1 each. It appears likely that the four aircraft were formerly operated by the 182nd Fighter Squadron of the Texas Air National Guard, and were flown to Costa Rica by USAF pilots from Kelly AFB in Texas. All four were F-51Ds, and they were locally numbered 1 to 4 in Costa Rican service. Following arrival they were operated against the Nicaraguan 'rebel' forces, although it is not clear how often they fired their guns in anger. It is speculated that they were flown by mercenary pilots, as the Costa Ricans did not have sufficient trained pilots to operate the Mustangs themselves – it is now believed that USAF pilots actually flew the aircraft in Costa Rica on patrol. This use must have been successful as the Nicaraguans subsequently withdrew. Nevertheless, one of the Mustangs was shot down. There are rumours that this Mustang might have been attacked by a Republic F-47N Thunderbolt that was supporting the rebel invasion, possibly one of the few if not the only occasion when a Mustang and a Thunderbolt met on opposing sides in combat.

## Cuba

One of the Central American countries whose use of the Mustang has been the subject of much speculation and rumour, Cuba was in a state of open revolution when a small number of Mustangs arrived on this Caribbean island. It has sometimes been reported that the prevailing pro-US régime that dominated Cuba in the 1940's received several Mustangs under the Rio Pact of 1947, but this appears to have been myth more than fact. In the early 1950's dissatisfaction with the autocratic pro-US régime of Fulgencio Batista led to full-scale revolt led by Fidel Castro. The rebel forces were able by various clandestine means to acquire a variety of weapons, and three Mustangs were obtained on the open market in the late 1950's, probably from civilian sources. The first of these is thought to have arrived in or just after May 1958 and was numbered '401'. The three Mustangs served with the Fuerza Aérea Rebelde (latterly also called the Fuerza Aérea Revolucionaria). After that time the Mustangs presumably continued in service until replaced by aircraft supplied from the Soviet Union, with whom Castro subsequently aligned himself.

## Dominican Republic

The story of the Mustang in the service of the Dominican Republic is worthy of a large book in its own right. This Caribbean island country holds the accolade of being the final front-line Mustang operator, keeping the type in continuous service from the late 1940's until as recently as 1984. A number of current airworthy Mustangs owe their existence to the long and somewhat treasured life that they had in Dominican service, the Dominicans operating a truly mixed bag of standard Mustangs and Cavalier Mustangs as well.

As explained in Part 1 of this two-part 'Modellers' Datafile' on the Mustang, which covered Allison-engined Mustangs, the story of the Mustang in Dominican Republic service dates back to the later 1940's. The Dominican Republic became unique in being one of only a very small number of countries to operate Allison-engined Mustangs, when this Latin American country received a small number from 1948.

However, that was only the start of the story. When Sweden began to run down its Merlin-Mustang force in the early 1950's, the Dominican authorities saw a chance to add further Mustangs to the inventory of the Aviacion Militar Dominicana (as it was by then called). In fact the Dominican Republic's dictator, Rafael Trujillo, at that time felt snubbed by the US, which had been slow in supplying a requested batch of Thunderbolts, partly due to fears that this would upset the relative balance of military forces in the Caribbean at the expense of Cuba (which during that period was a friend of the US). Negotiations took place during 1952 between the Dominican and Swedish authorities, and these were successfully concluded with the help of the Swedish export company Henry Wallenberg & Co. AB. This company actually purchased the Mustangs from the Swedish authorities in September 1952 on behalf of the Dominican Republic. The number involved was 32 (and not 44 as sometimes claimed), and they cost $15,500 each. As with other deals involving Swedish Mustangs, the Swedish company Svensk Flygtjänst AB was contracted to deliver the aircraft. They were dismantled and packed for delivery by sea, the cargo ship leaving Swedish waters in December 1952. Trujillo was not satisfied, however, and a further deal was concluded in late January 1953 for 10 further Mustangs, at what is believed to be the same price each as the original 32 aircraft. These were shipped in May 1953. The Dominican authorities still were not satisfied, however, and wanted several more Mustangs. The Wallenberg company agreed to this new demand in June 1953, but for some reason this deal fell through. The aircraft that were reserved under this final set of negotiations were instead kept in reserve, and may well have formed part of the order that was eventually sold to Nicaragua. Unfortunately the whole deal later became surrounded by controversy, with claims that Ramfis Trujillo, who was the son of the Dominican dictator Rafael Trujillo, might have made substantial monetary gain out of the whole situation by originally having the 42 Mustangs signed to him, and later selling them to the Dominican military at a much increased price.

There is no doubt that the Mustangs were the pride and joy of Ramfis Trujillo, much to the dismay of the Dominican pilots who considerably preferred the F-47D-30-RA and TF-47D-30-RA Thunderbolts that had been obtained by somewhat more legitimate means. Ramfis Trujillo had successfully made himself the head of the Aviacion Militar Dominicana, and the unit that the Mustangs were attached to was called the Escuadron de Caza Ramfis (the Thunderbolts were in the less grandly named Escuadron de Caza-Bombardero). The first batch of Mustangs arrived from Sweden in January 1953 and they were taken overland to the air base at San Isidro, near to the Dominican capital (named at the time Ciudad Trujillo but later renamed Santo Domingo de Guzman). Swedish technicians did an excellent job in getting the Mustangs airworthy and the pilots of the Aviacion Militar Dominicana checked out on the type. Finally the Thunderbolts were retired, in late 1957, due to the purchase prior to this from Sweden of de Havilland Vampire jet-powered fighter-bombers, but the Mustangs persisted in the fighter role as the main Dominican fighter type. Rafael Trujillo was assassinated in 1961, leading to a succession of juntas, coups and failed leaders, but the Mustangs persisted through it all in the service of the renamed Fuerza Aérea Dominicana. Two major upgrades were made of the Dominican Mustangs by Trans-Florida Aviation in the US when relations with the US warmed for a time following Trujillo's death. The first was in the early 1960's (several were being reworked in 1964) and the second was in the late 1960's (by which time Trans-Florida had become the Cavalier Aircraft Corporation, and carried out some of the work in the Dominican Republic as a part of Project Peace Hawk in 1968), during which it is believed several of the Mustangs (most reports state three) were retained by Cavalier as part-payment for the upgrade work. It appears that up to 18 Dominican Mustangs were involved in the latter programme, ostensibly to make them into Cavalier Mk II standard. Following the demise of the Trujillo dynasty the Mustangs were concentrated in a unit named unglamorously the Escuadron de Caza. It is possible that one or more of Haiti's Mustangs were obtained by the Dominicans for spares when they were retired in the mid-1970's.

During some of their operational life the Dominican Republic Mustangs were certainly kept busy, with a succession of coups, attempted coups and a major US intervention taking place in the country during their Dominican service. Nevertheless, a lack of money and a similar lack of support from the US for aid in the receipt of newer equipment meant that the Dominican Mustangs had to soldier on until 1984, although the standard of maintenance that the Dominican ground crews afforded the aircraft was of a very high order.

## El Salvador

Holding the distinction of being the final nation to fly the Mustang in combat in an out-and-out shooting war, El Salvador was an important Central American Mustang operator which used the type in a major conflict with neighbouring Honduras. El Salvador was also important in being one of two Central American recipients 'from the factory' of the Cavalier Mustang (the other was Bolivia). Although a comparatively small country, El Salvador was nevertheless comparatively densely populated, and made various attempts in the 1950's and early 1960's to modernise its out-dated armed forces. A result of this was the acquisition from the late 1950's onwards of Goodyear-built FG-1D Corsair fighters (plus, seemingly, some standard F4U-4 Corsairs), but rising tension with neighbouring Honduras, which was relatively well-armed, caused the Salvadorians to seek more airpower alternatives. As explained in Chapter 8 of this book, Trans-Florida Aviation in the US had embarked on a programme of updating the basic Mustang layout and turning it into a 1960's-standard combat aircraft. A number of countries around the world became interested in obtaining the Cavalier-refurbished and updated Mustangs, and in 1968 El Salvador successfully ordered a small batch of these Cavalier Mustangs. This was under the auspices of the Project Peace Condor programme, and amongst the aircraft ordered was one dedicated two-seater variant. The exact number eventually delivered to El Salvador is unfortunately open to debate, but the Salvadorian serial numbers that were allocated give a clue, these being FAS 401 to FAS 405 for single-seat Cavaliers plus FAS 400 which was reputedly a two-seat TF-51D, and a standard F-51D numbered FAS 406 (FAS = Fuerza Aérea Salvadorena). In addition, a further F-51D was donated by a private individual to replace FAS 402 which crashed in October 1968. The Mustangs and Corsairs were concentrated into the FAS Grupo de Combate's Escuadron de Caza. It appears likely that several further Mustangs were also obtained during that period (variously described at the time and since as numbering 11, 12, or 14 examples), and serial

numbers up to at least FAS 411 are known, these latter being standard F-51 Mustangs and not Cavalier Mustangs.

Tensions between El Salvador and Honduras centred on the number of Salvadorians who had gone to live in Honduras. Eventually relations boiled over due to a game of football. In the group qualifying stages leading up to the 1970 World Cup that was due to be staged in Mexico, El Salvador and Honduras unfortunately ended up playing each other to decide which one would occupy a place in the finals in Mexico from the Latin American qualifying competition. The first play-off match took place in Tegucigalpa, the capital of Honduras, in early June 1969 followed several days later by a second match in San Salvador. Crowd trouble and associated riots led to increased tension, and on 14 July 1969 the Salvadorian army invaded Honduras, ostensibly to protect its citizens. The resulting conflict has forever after been known as the 'Football War' (or 'Soccer War' to some Americans). Air action immediately followed, but the Fuerza Aérea Salvadorena did not fare too well, and one of its Mustangs (believed to be FAS 404, although there are conflicting reports about the dogfight) was shot down by a Honduran F4U-5N Corsair. The Salvadorians lost one or possibly two more Mustangs during the short war, although it is believed that at least one of these was to ground fire, while a two-seater was reported at the time as being interned in Guatemala.

This is now generally accepted to have been the last time that Mustangs flew in combat, and it was not a particularly auspicious end to the type's illustrious war record that spanned in time back to 1942. The aerial combats during the 'Football War' are also widely thought to have been the last time that front-line piston-engined aircraft met each other in anger (Mustang vs. Corsair). Mustangs remained in service with the Fuerza Aérea Salvadorena into the 1970's, until finally replaced by ex-Israeli-operated Dassault Ouragan jet fighters in 1974/1975, some of the Mustangs being sold to finance the new warplanes.

## France

French airmen fought in the RAF during World War Two from the time of the German occupation of France, and in units of the Free French forces under Allied control. Following the D-Day landings and the increasingly successful Allied liberation of German-occupied France, attempts were made by the French to reconstitute the French air force (Armée de l'Air) as a single unified entity and bring together into a new air force the diverse French aviation units and Free French elements that had thus far operated in a disparate fashion on the Allied side. In late 1944 and early 1945 the new Armée de l'Air began to receive equipment from the Allies solely for French usage and to operate an increasing number of front-line units and aircraft types. One of the latter was the Mustang, and France thus became one of the few foreign operators to fly the P-51 in combat during World War Two.

France was virtually unique in operating its Mustangs primarily as reconnaissance and target-spotting aircraft, although many of the Mustangs supplied to France were actually straight fighter models, some of which were later converted to reconnaissance configuration. French reconnaissance assets were collected into a unit called GR 33 (GR = Groupe de Reconnaissance), with this organisation's subordinate escadron (squadron) I/33 'Belfort' operating F-4 and F-5 Lightnings on long-range strategic reconnaissance. For tactical reconnaissance and battlefield support, the Groupe's second squadron, II/33 'Savoie', flew Supermarine Spitfires of various different marks including some Mk IXs. However, in the early weeks of 1945 the Spitfires started to be replaced by Mustangs. The initial batch of Mustangs was received from USAAF stocks in England in mid-January 1945, the first aircraft being transferred to Luxeuil airfield during that month (the date of arrival appears to have been 14 January, although USAAF records are not particularly clear on this matter). Most if not all of these Mustangs were straight fighter versions, although a promise on the supply of equipment to convert them into reconnaissance aircraft was also given by the Americans. The squadron had 12 aircraft by 11 February, these comprising a real mixed bag of Mustangs including P-51B/C and P-51D examples. The nominal operational strength of 18 aircraft was reached in early March, but sufficient cameras and related equipment to convert all the fighter examples into true reconnaissance Mustangs were not available, and so the French ended up flying camera-equipped Mustangs alongside straight fighter examples. Nevertheless operations commenced from Luxeuil in February, it is believed the first actual sorties being flown on the 19th of that month. The small French Mustang force was subsequently heavily involved in supporting French ground units, including the heavy fighting around Colmar in north-eastern France where the French 1st Army was in action alongside the US 7th Army against German forces. GR II/33 subsequently moved up to Colmar airfield in the second half of March 1945 and supported French units involved in the Rhine Crossing at the end of that month and the subsequent break-out into Germany proper. French Mustangs closely supported French 1st Army units, both in tactical reconnaissance and ground attack sorties, and worked with French-operated P-47D Thunderbolts by identifying targets and calling down precision strikes in virtually a forward air control role.

The small French Mustang force suffered a number of casualties before the end of hostilities, but an accepted total has never come to light. Although a number of the French aircraft had been converted into reconnaissance configuration as F-6 look-alikes, the type was almost universally known to the French as the P-51 or simply the Mustang. The fuselage code letters R7 were worn by the Mustangs of II/33. In common with US-operated P-51s, the small French Mustang force became a part of the Allied occupation organisation in western Germany after the end of the war. The first base used by the French Mustangs while carrying out this task was Lahr in the very western part of Germany south-east of Strasbourg, but a move was subsequently made to Breisgau (Freiburg) to the south of Lahr. Several of the squadron's Mustangs, however, were based in North Africa for a time after the end of the war in Europe on mapping duties, and to 'fly the flag' in the French north African colonies which had returned to French jurisdiction at the end of the war.

In December 1947 there were some fifteen Mustangs operational with four in reserve – included were P-51B/C and P-51D examples plus an odd F-6K (the latter, 44-12471, being a genuine US-converted F-6K). Several of the Mustangs also appear to have eventually been on the strength (on paper at

least) of I/33 (later 1/33) 'Belfort', although by the early 1950's many of the Mustangs were becoming decidedly 'war-weary' and moves began to be made to find a jet-powered replacement. The 'Savoie' squadron started to leave Breisgau in the spring and summer of 1950 as its occupation force role came to an end, with Cognac in western France becoming the unit's new base. The final French Mustangs were withdrawn in 1952, with the type being replaced, at least temporarily, by specially-configured jet-powered Republic F-84G Thunderjets from the summer of 1952. A real rarity amongst the French Mustangs was a two-seat liaison, 'hack' and training Mustang, which was converted from a P-51D. The conversion was definitely bizarre, with the rear part of the aircraft's 'bubble' canopy hinging upwards at the rear to allow the second occupant access into the rear seat – a true oddity amongst Mustangs.

## Germany and Japan

A number of Mustangs fell into enemy hands during World War Two, and both Germany and Japan were able to evaluate the type at close-hand. In particular the Germans eventually had a number of flyable Mustangs of various marks at their disposal. These aircraft came their way due to a number of shot-down examples being not too badly damaged, and subsequently being put back in the air.

Not surprisingly, the Mustang was of great interest to the Germans from the outset. It became a matter of some importance for the Luftwaffe not only to evaluate the Mustang, but also to teach its pilots how to tackle this highly-capable warplane. As Mustangs roamed more and more over enemy-held territory, so a small number of examples became available to the Germans due to operational losses or mechanical malfunction. The majority of Mustangs that came down over Occupied Europe were not in a fit state to be put back in the air, but there were at least two flyable P-51s available to the Luftwaffe by the summer of 1944. Many of the captured aircraft that the Germans were able to make airworthy were concentrated in a special unit which reported directly to the Luftwaffe high command. This was the 2nd Staffel of the Versuchsverband Oberkommando der Luftwaffe (2./Versuchsverband OKL), which used the fuselage identification code 'T9'. The captured Allied aircraft that it flew were painted in very distinctive colours with large German national insignia to avoid accidental shoot-downs by confused or trigger-happy German gunners. It eventually numbered amongst its ranks several Spitfires, Mustangs, and other frontline Allied types. It has become part of the folklore of the assumed mystery that surrounds this unit that it has come to be known unofficially as the 'Zirkus Rosarius', and there are persistent reports that its aircraft were used to fight against Allied

**French Mustang. A significant European operator of the Mustang was France, which used mainly reconnaissance-adapted Merlin-Mustangs in the latter stages of World War Two and in the post-war period – although some straight fighter versions were also flown. The principal operating unit was the Groupe de Reconnaissance GR 33, one of whose F-6D aircraft is seen here probably in 1945. Coded 'V', the Mustang belongs to ER 2/33 'Savoie', and proudly bears the coat of arms of the French Savoie department on its vertical tail**
*(Photo: Jean-Jacques Petit Collection)*

warplanes, flown by Germans and painted in spurious US or British markings. In reality the unit's aircraft were used to visit combat units to familiarise Luftwaffe aircrew with the type of aircraft that they were up against in aerial combat, and to allow some experienced Luftwaffe pilots to actually fly the aircraft for themselves – but not in combat. The Mustangs that the Germans made airworthy were a mixed bag, and included at least one former 4th FG P-51B. Indeed, most of the airworthy German Mustangs were of the 'razorback' layout, although in addition at least one P-51D is known to have existed in German colours. There is also some evidence that the major German military flight test and research establishment (Erprobungsstelle or E-Stelle) at Rechlin to the north of Berlin took a look at one or more of the captured Mustangs. At the end of the war advancing Allied forces 'liberated' a number of Mustangs that were found at German or occupied airfields. Interestingly, a number of these were on airfields in the so-called Protectorate of Bohemia and Moravia (the former Czechoslovakia, where the Germans had a number of aircraft companies which were forced to work for them within the overall German aircraft production organisation), and it is not clear why they were particularly concentrated in that part of the German occupied areas.

Japanese fighters began to encounter Allison-engined Mustangs for the first time in major combats during October and November 1943 over Burma. Like the Germans, the Japanese were very interested to find out more about the American fighter, but it was some time before an intact example came their way. This turned out to be a Merlin-engined Mustang, in fact a P-51C of the 51st FG. There is some confusion as to when the Mustang concerned, which was named 'Evalina', actually fell into Japanese hands. It landed virtually intact at Suchon airfield in China, and after repair it was ferried to Japan by Maj Yasuhiko Kuroe of the famous 64th Sentai, which had duelled with Mustangs over Burma from late 1943 onwards. The Mustang was delivered to a Japanese evaluation and test centre at Fussa (more recently

known as Yokota Air Base), where it was examined in detail. It was later moved to Akeno, and was flown in mock combat against a range of then-current Japanese fighters. Evaluation was made of the Mustang's systems and equipment, which were found to be considerably better than those in Japanese fighters. In particular the armour protection for the pilot was of great interest to the Japanese pilots who flew the aircraft, this item in particular being something that Japanese aircrew would have welcomed being much higher on the list of priorities for their own aircraft. Particularly worrying for the Japanese was the long-range capability of the Mustang, which it was noted would allow Mustangs to fly over Japan itself if any of the Pacific islands approaching Japan were captured by the Allies – something that indeed did happen as 1945 progressed. Ground crews were amazed by the Mustang's lack of major oil leaks in comparison to Japanese aircraft of that period. It appears that the Mustang was flown a great deal in Japanese hands, and was very well liked by those who flew the aircraft, until an obvious lack of spares finally grounded it. When Mustangs were eventually able to fly over Japan in combat during 1945 it seems likely that at least two further examples, this time of the P-51D series, were captured by the Japanese, although the story of these aircraft remains unclear.

## Guatemala

The Guatemalan association with the Mustang began in 1954, during a time of considerable political turmoil within Guatemala itself and with outside interference also taking place. For several years after 1944 rebels supported by the US had been trying to overthrow democratically-elected governments in Guatemala. Several attempts were made by the legitimate Guatemalan government after the mid-1940's to procure Mustangs, which was not surprising as the main fighter type in the Guatemalan inventory was the early 1930's-vintage Boeing P-26A. These requests, which included representations to Sweden, were turned down by the US which considered the legitimate government to be communist-inspired. Between 17 to 20 Mustangs were believed to have been involved in the thwarted deal with Sweden, at a price of around $700,000 for all the aircraft involved. Instead, in the early summer of 1954, two Mustangs were supplied by the US to rebel anti-government forces led by Colonel Carlos Castillo Armas. The two Mustangs were taken from Texas ANG stocks and were delivered to the rebels by USAF pilots. Castillo Armas, buoyed up by considerable arms supplies from the US via the CIA including the two Mustangs, mounted an ultimately successful invasion from neighbouring Honduran territory (known to the CIA as Operation 'Success') which began in June 1954. The rebel air force was bolstered by two or three more Mustangs which were supplied via Honduras although there was also considerable Nicaraguan involvement in Operation 'Success'. Indeed, it appears that Castillo Mustangs might have operated from Honduran and Nicaraguan air bases wearing fake Guatemalan insignia at the time of the coup attempt. This has led some writers to suspect that Honduras was itself a Mustang operator, but such does not appear to have been the case. Following the overthrow of the legitimate Guatemalan government by the US-supported anti-government rebels, the Guatemalan armed forces were reorganised and re-equipped with US-supplied hardware, which included 11 further Mustangs as well as the ex-Castillo aircraft. They mainly comprised F-51D Mustangs, but there was a two-seat example amongst them. At least 14 more Mustangs were supplied from 1957 into the early 1960's, in batches that included some examples that had been newly-retired by the Canadians. There are also rumours that some former Israeli Mustangs might additionally have been received.

In Fuerza Aérea Guatemalteca (FAG) service the Mustangs equipped one fighter-bomber squadron, identified by several writers as having the title of the Escuadron Costa Atlantico (this was during the late 1950's, later the unit appears to have been renamed the Escuadron de Ataque y Reconicimiento). They carried Guatemalan serial numbers beginning with 'FAG' and numbered in the three hundreds (for example, FAG-345 was a two-seat example; this aircraft was formerly 44-84660, a TF-51D which was originally a single-seat P-51D-25-NT before conversion into two-seat configuration). Guatemalan Mustangs became particularly high profile because they equipped an aerobatic demonstration team. Initially known as 'Los Machitos' from 1955, the name was changed to 'Los Cofres' in approximately 1957. During the early 1970's the unit, still Mustang-equipped, was known as 'Quetzales'. Unfortunately in early 1972 the team suffered a serious accident when three Mustangs collided during a display that they were putting on. It was during 1972 that most if not all of the remaining Mustangs were withdrawn from Guatemalan service, with August 1972 being the cut-off date for many.

## Haiti

One of several operators whose Mustang service is little-known, the Caribbean state of Haiti definitely flew at least four and probably six Mustangs. Initial deliveries were made in – apparently – the early 1950's, the first four aircraft seemingly arriving in 1951, and it is possible that up to six in total were obtained from the US. It is not clear if they were all obtained on the open market from private vendors. In Corps d'Aviation d'Haiti service the Mustangs were collected into a composite attack and training unit located at Bowen Field, Port au Prince. The surviving Mustangs remained in Haitian service into the mid-1970's, although their airworthiness for much of that period was certainly questionable.

## Indonesia

The establishment of Indonesia as an independent country from the former Netherlands East Indies in December 1949 (refer to the section on the Netherlands East Indies elsewhere in this chapter) resulted in a number of former NEI air assets being passed to Indonesia's fledgling air arm. Named the Angkatan Udara Republik Indonesia (AURI), this air arm received several former NEI ML-KNIL P-51D/K Mustangs, that had ironically previously flown in combat against the terrorists who had successfully fought for the establishment of the Indonesian state. The exact number of Mustangs remains open to speculation, although it is possible that at least 25 examples were involved, including both P-51D and P-51K models. In AURI service some of these aircraft quickly sported much more flamboyant markings than those painted on them by their former Netherlands East Indies owners.

The history of Indonesia subsequent to its creation has been one of long-running struggles with rebellious factions within the far-flung Indonesian republic, and various attempts by Indonesia's leaders - particularly Achmad Sukarno - to interfere with neighbouring foreign states. This kept the ex-NEI Mustangs very busy during their long Indonesian service. Seemingly at first assigned to No.1 Squadron of the AURI, the Mustangs also later equipped No.3 Squadron, and did not leave Indonesian service until – probably - the later 1970's. They were eventually supplanted in Indonesia in the ground-attack/COIN role by the Rockwell International OV-10F Bronco (which was a product of the group that North American Aviation had eventually been absorbed into), the Indonesians having eventually become more friendly with the US.

## Israel

A major Mustang operator, that used its Mustangs in combat in at least two wars, was Israel. Following the creation of the state of Israel in May 1948, the Israelis were attacked by several neighbouring countries, and needed to rapidly build an effective air force. Amongst several clandestine acquisitions of aircraft at that time from many different sources were at least two Mustangs, the first of approximately 45 to 50 Mustangs of various marks that the Israelis eventually operated – although some Israeli sources now claim that as many as 79 may have eventually reached Israel.

The initial two combat-worthy Mustangs were obtained in 1948. It is quite possible that two or three more Mustangs were also bought by the Israelis during that period, but two definitely reached Israel in time to participate in the initial fighting in what the Israelis call the War of Independence. They appear to have been shipped to Israel under the label of agricultural equipment in order to circumvent a US arms embargo on the Middle East. The first flight of a Mustang that was made in Israel was on 2 October 1948. Both of the Mustangs were assigned to the initial fighter unit of the Israeli air force (IDF/AF), No.101 Squadron. The first Mustang sortie that was flown by No.101 Squadron was on 18 October 1948, a reconnaissance mission over the Lebanese capital Beirut which then proceeded over Iraq, taking advantage of the excellent long-range capability of the Mustang. The two Mustangs subsequently flew further sorties in this initial conflict, and received the codings D-190 and D-191 (they also appear to have been coded 41 and 42 at some point in their Israeli careers). One of the bases used by the two Mustangs during this period was Hatzor. Unfortunately there were a number of incidents in which neutral aircraft were shot down by the Israelis. One of these involved a Mustang, when D-190 shot down an RAF reconnaissance de Havilland Mosquito PR Mk 34 of No.13 Squadron, RAF, on 20 November 1948. After several months of fighting the conflict eventually ended successfully for the Israelis during 1949. It was clear that the Mustang was of great value, and the Israelis subsequently made major efforts to procure further Mustangs.

It appears that several Mustangs were obtained from private owners in the US (possibly ex-racing machines) at that time. Some

Israeli historians have claimed that as many as 36 further Mustangs were obtained from private US sources in the early 1950's, in addition to the initial two that fought in 1948, and possibly two others that arrived during the War of Independence but were delayed from entering service due to a lack of spare parts. What is definitely known, however, following these initial acquisitions, is that a considerable windfall came in the early 1950's, with 25 F-51Ds supplied by Sweden. The first were delivered in December 1952. On acceptance by the IDF/AF they were allocated to No.101 Squadron, the original Israeli Mustang operator, which had a considerable number of Mustangs on strength in 1954, possibly approaching 60.

What is certain is that by the mid-1950's the Israeli Mustangs from several sources had already seen considerable action, even after the War of Independence. It was the Suez crisis of late 1956, however, that saw the Israeli Mustangs back in action in a significant shooting war. Although No.101 Squadron had been disbanded on the type in early 1956, its Mustangs had been distributed amongst two further fighter units, Nos.105 (which formed in June 1956) and 116 (which formed on the Mustang after the running down of No.101 Squadron's Mustang assets, and included a number of flying instructors in its ranks). Both of these were ready for action when the Suez operations began in late October 1956, some 29 Mustangs being available at that time. During the Suez operations they operated predominantly in the ground attack role against Egyptian targets, which were mainly military units on the ground as British and French air assets were used against Egyptian airfields. During the course of the Suez operations, which lasted into November 1956, the Israeli military admits to the loss of nine Mustangs (although persistent reports refer to seven) - illustrating the intensity of the short but hotly-contested operations that Israel's ground attack assets were involved in, particularly over the Sinai desert.

The Mustang remained in Israeli service following the Suez operations, albeit mainly in a second-line capacity. No.105 Squadron was disbanded soon after the Suez crisis finished, and the final main Israeli Mustang unit, No.116 Squadron, was relegated to second-line duties in 1958. However, although this is often stated as the end of Mustang operations in Israel, such was not the case. Several Mustangs remained in service, some as target-towers, but 15 January 1961 appears to be the cut-off time for the surviving aircraft.

## Italy

The Italian service of the Mustang is one of the least well-documented aspects amongst published sources of the foreign service of the P-51. It is often claimed, completely erroneously, that 48 Mustangs served with the Italian air force post-war. This is completely wrong, in reality approximately 173 Mustangs at one time or another served in Italy!

Like many countries, after World War Two the Italians found themselves short of modern front-line combat aircraft, despite having a number of indigenous types either in production or available at the end of the war. A significant part of the Italian armed forces fought with the Allies as the war in Europe came to a close, and the assorted aircraft types that were in service with the Allied-leaning Italian forces formed the basis of the post-war Italian air force. In keeping with several other countries, Italy subsequently became a beneficiary of one of the US military aid programmes that existed after World War Two. This led to the supply of military equipment that included a large number of Mustangs. Initially, however, the Italian acquisition of the Mustang was a somewhat difficult experience, similar to the problems encountered by the Swiss and the Swedes.

The initial batch of Mustangs for Italy comprised 50 aircraft, plus a mysterious converted two-seater for a total of 51 examples –

although some Italian sources claim that the two-seater was actually a part of the 50 aircraft first assignment. These Mustangs were delegated to the Italians in September 1947, but they were certainly not new aircraft - they were former USAAF Mustangs that were stockpiled in Allied-controlled western Germany. Many were war veterans (and some decidedly war-weary) following service with Eighth and Ninth Army Air Force units, and several had been neglected where they stood in various air depots or collection points. Nevertheless some were comparatively low-hours airframes, and most if not all were P-51Ds. The initial examples, assigned the Aeronautica Militare Italiana (AMI) serial numbers MM4234 and MM4235, were moved to Italy in September 1947. These first aircraft were prepared for service at Naples-Capodichino, and were comparatively slowly followed by the remaining aircraft, the final deliveries being made in the second half of 1948. The serial number range for these first 50 aircraft was MM4234 to MM4283. Some of the later aircraft were flown from Germany by the Italians themselves, the Americans being preoccupied with the blockade of Berlin and the Berlin Air Lift later in 1948. The first major Italian air force unit to transition onto the type was the 4° Stormo at Naples-Capodichino.

The first Mustangs for Italy was followed by a second batch, comprising 20 aircraft. They were allocated in February 1949, and received the Italian serials MM4286 to 4305 (it will be noted that there are two 'missing' serial numbers between this allocation and the first batch). These Mustangs again came from USAF storage facilities in Allied-controlled western Germany. It is believed that most if not all of these initial Mustangs from the first two batches were P/F-51D-20 and D-25-NA versions, most Italian historians now agreeing that at least 38 were of the latter mark.

This was only the start, however, and in later years a further 102 Mustangs were supplied to Italy. In contrast to the previous allocations, however, these later aircraft were delivered from the US, and were shipped across the Atlantic by sea. Deliveries began in September 1950, and continued into early 1951, with the aircraft being off-loaded in Brindisi harbour. The Italian serial numbers that were allocated to the main block of 100 aircraft were MM4306 to MM4405. The final two examples were MM4431 and MM4432 which arrived independently. However, just to cloud the picture, three further serials were allocated, MM4406 to MM4408, apparently to rebuilt aircraft. Whether or not the latter three were rebuilt from existing Italian airframes, or were pieced together from parts supplied by the Americans, is not clear. Of the main batch of 100 aircraft, all were of the P/F-51D-25 version, 56 being D-25-NA, and 44 being D-25-NT type Mustangs.

Italian Mustangs equipped Nos. 2°, 3°, 4°, 5°, 6° and 51° Stormi. A number of Mustangs were also used by training units. This included the Scuola Volo at Lecce-Galatina, and the SE (Scuola Elmas) at Cagliari-Elmas on the island of Sardinia. The 4° Stormo additionally flew several specially-equipped Mustangs for target-towing. At least one Mustang (MM4371, a former F-51D-25-NT) was converted for photo reconnaissance. Increasingly the Mustang was replaced by jets in Italian service, with types such as the de Havilland Vampire starting to equip Italian units from the early 1950's onwards. Nevertheless the Mustang continued in AMI service well into the 1950's, with most remaining examples being withdrawn in 1958 but some continuing on the books into 1959. Latterly some were used as fast transports and 'hacks' in the AMI's regional commands, with the type sometimes being used as personal transports by high-ranking officers. A small number were operated in Somalia while Italy looked after that country in a UN trusteeship agreement up to 1960. Although many of the Italian Mustangs were scrapped at the end of their service, a number were transferred to Somalia when that country gained its independence in 1960.

## Netherlands East Indies

In common with Britain and France, the Netherlands similarly established a purchasing organisation in response to its lack of significant numbers of modern combat aircraft. Although the Netherlands fell quickly following the German invasion of the country on 10 May 1940, the Dutch possessions in the Far East - the Dutch East Indies - remained free and determined to fight on. The Royal Netherlands East Indies Air Force (RNEIAF, or ML-KNIL in Dutch) was very poorly equipped, however - amongst its more modern types was the woefully inadequate Brewster Buffalo fighter. The Netherlands Purchasing Commission therefore attempted to acquire more modern combat aircraft in the United States, and sought firstly to procure Bell P-39 Airacobra fighters. This plan was however turned down by the Americans, but a curious arrangement was instead suggested whereby 100 Curtiss P-40Es destined for Britain would be redirected to the RNEIAF. The Dutch refused this option, however, and instead started to take an interest in the North American NA-73 project. The Dutch eventually decided on a requirement for 100 Mustangs, but nothing came of this idea, and the RNEIAF was totally ill-equipped when the Japanese struck the Netherlands East Indies in December 1941. Defeated and driven out of their colonial possessions, the Netherlands East Indies forces were obliged to fight on from Australia. The RNEIAF eventually flew a number of Curtiss P-40N Warhawks, which were outclassed and war-weary by 1945. A further request was therefore made to the Americans by the Dutch East Indies authorities for Mustangs, and this time they were lucky. 41 aircraft were earmarked for NEI service, and were redirected from existing contracts - many if not all were painted with Dutch flags on the North American production line. Deliveries appear to have commenced in March 1945, with the NEI Mustangs being gradually delivered to the Dutch maintenance facility at Bundaburg in Queensland, Australia. Royal Australian Air Force personnel apparently helped to put the aircraft together after they arrived by sea, and eventually the ML-KNIL received 40 Mustangs. They were serialled N3-600 to N3-640, which makes 41 - the 'missing' Mustang, N3-623, never made it to Dutch service. The final aircraft accepted into NEI service appear to have been delivered after assembly in March 1946. The 40 aircraft comprised ten P-51Ks (the initial ten aircraft of the batch), the rest being P-51D models. These aircraft exhibited a mixture of canopies, either the more widespread teardrop form or the 'Dallas' shape. Some of the 'Ds had uncuffed Hamilton Standard propeller blades while others had the more usual cuffed variety.

In RNEIAF service these Mustangs arrived too late to operate against the Japanese, but they instead formed part of the Dutch presence as the Netherlands East Indies were gradually returned to Dutch rule after World War Two ended. The Mustangs were flown from Australia by NEI pilots in April and May 1946 to Batavia (now Jakarta). The first NEI squadron to be fully equipped was No.121 Squadron, and later No.122 Squadron also operated some of the Mustangs. Unfortunately a major independence movement in the NEI had by then been established, many of whose members had collaborated with the Japanese occupying forces during the war. Trouble soon began, and the RNEIAF Mustangs were subsequently committed to action against terrorists in a variety of locations in what became a protracted conflict. The Mustangs almost exclusively flew ground attack missions, using a variety of weapons including free-fall bombs and unguided rockets in addition to the Mustangs' six 0.5 inch machine-guns. In addition, a handful of the Mustangs were specially configured to fly reconnaissance operations, with a camera-equipped reconnaissance pod fitted beneath the port wing of some aircraft, which operated with a unit named the PVA (Photo Verkennings Afdeling). Unfortunately outside pressure, somewhat ironically particularly from the US,

eventually led to the Dutch agreeing to the formal establishment of the republic of Indonesia, and a significant number of the remaining NEI Mustangs were passed to the newly-established Indonesian air arm.

## New Zealand

During World War Two the Royal New Zealand Air Force (RNZAF) operated the Vought F4U Corsair and Curtiss P-40 fighters of various marks with considerable success. However, during 1945 New Zealand successfully negotiated for the supply of P-51 Mustangs to enhance the RNZAF's capabilities in the Pacific. A total of 370 aircraft was envisaged, apparently to comprise 167 P-51Ds, with the balance being made up of the intended Dallas-built P-51M production model. In the event the P-51M was never mass-produced, and the war against the Japanese was finally concluded in September 1945 before the P-51D came into front-line RNZAF service. Nevertheless, an initial batch of 30 P-51Ds had been earmarked for delivery to the RNZAF, and these were duly received in August and September 1945 having been shipped from the US on two separate transport ships – but they were at once placed in storage. However, in the post-war years the New Zealand military activated the second-line reserve Territorial Air Force, and this subsequently operated a variety of aircraft types. In 1951 it was planned to equip several of the Territorial Air Force's squadrons with some of the stored Mustangs, and these aircraft started to be brought out of storage. They received the New Zealand serials NZ2401 to NZ2430, and were from NAA Dallas production within US procurement (all were in fact P-51D-25-NTs) – NZ2413, for example, was ex-45-11503. The first to fly was NZ2406 (ex-45-11495) in August 1951. The initial squadron to operate the Mustang was No.4 (Otago) Squadron of the Territorial Air Force, and subsequently Nos.1 (Auckland), 2 (Wellington) and 3 (Canterbury) Squadrons were also equipped. The type remained in service until October or November 1955 when the final examples in Territorial Air Force service were withdrawn, although four soldiered on until the early months of 1957 when the final example was withdrawn, as target-towers, fighter affiliation and communications aircraft with No.42 Squadron, RNZAF. Several of the New Zealand Mustangs were sadly involved in fatal crashes, and one (NZ2408, ex-45-11498) was almost accidentally shot down by a RNZAF de Havilland Vampire. While operating with No.2 (Wellington) Squadron, the Mustang was towing a target during a live firing exercise for Vampires when it was hit by cannon fire from one of the jets. Fortunately it was able to land safely but never flew again.

## Nicaragua

One of several countries that benefited from the comparatively large number of Mustangs that were disposed of by Sweden at the end of their Swedish air force service, Nicaragua became the largest operator of Mustangs in Central America and was eventually able to obtain examples from a number of sources. Ruled by a succession of dictators who were acceptable to the US, notably the notorious and tyrannical Somoza dynasty, Nicaragua was successful over a long period in obtaining US arms without any restrictions. This included a variety of Mustangs from at least two different sources. Although it is often thought that the supply of Mustangs to Nicaragua started with a major deal with Sweden in the latter half of 1954, in fact two Mustangs were apparently obtained by Nicaragua prior to this via the US through the CIA. In fact the story is slightly more complicated, the two Mustangs involved actually being supplied to US-backed Guatemalan rebel forces under Castillo Armas, in a deal that involved the Nicaraguan dictator Anastasio Somoza who was complicit in the Guatemalan coup of June/July 1954. The Nicaraguan military was obviously impressed with the Mustang, as negotiations began with the

Swedish authorities through the Henry Wallenberg & Co. AB company in Sweden for the purchase of Mustangs specifically for the Nicaraguan military. Wallenberg's representatives were successful in their negotiations and the deal was agreed in September 1954 for the supply of 25 Mustangs. These included both straight fighter, and camera-equipped reconnaissance Mustangs (known to the Swedish as J 26 and S 26 respectively). In the end there were 26 and not 25 Mustangs in this consignment, as Wallenberg apparently managed to obtain an additional Mustang from the Swedish military before the aircraft were shipped and it appears to have been added to the Nicaraguan order (this may well have been the final S 26 Mustang in Swedish service). In any case the 26 Mustangs arrived by sea in Nicaragua in January 1955, and were subsequently prepared for Nicaraguan service by US technicians. At least nine more Mustangs, from US sources, were also obtained by Nicaragua at various stages in the late 1950's. One former Swedish Mustang is rumoured to have been supplied by Nicaragua to Guatemala in late 1955, in return for a Republic F-47N that had been used covertly in Operation 'Success' in neighbouring Guatemala.

On several occasions a number of Nicaraguan Mustangs were used in combat, Nicaragua and its surroundings being particularly volatile during the Mustang period there. On at least two occasions in the late 1950's there were incursions into Nicaraguan territory from Costa Rica, in which the Mustangs played a small part in the Nicaraguan response. The most dramatic incident for the Nicaraguan Mustangs took place in 1957, when a significant clash occurred between Nicaragua and neighbouring Honduras over disputed territory. Nicaraguan pilots, however, appear to have much preferred the F-47N Thunderbolt to the Mustang. Nevertheless, several Mustangs were used for demonstration purposes at military events, and the Fuerza Aérea de la Guardia Nacional de Nicaragua operated a dwindling number of airworthy examples as more modern equipment was supplied by the US, including eventually North American T-28 Trojans. In the early 1960's (probably 1963, although again this fact is open to interpretation) possibly 20 or 21 of the surviving Nicaraguan Mustangs, including some non-airworthy examples, were sold to a US organisation known as the MACO Corporation.

## The Philippines

Some foreign-operated Mustangs led a very active life. This was especially true of those that were flown by the Philippines, and they were involved in a considerable amount of combat in the decade following World War Two. The sprawling island nation of the Philippines had been the scene of considerable Mustang activity during the later stages of World War Two, as described earlier in this book. USAAF-operated Mustangs had been an important part of the war against the Japanese in the Philippines, and had principally flown in fighter and armed reconnaissance roles in that part of the Southwest Pacific theatre. However, it was as a ground-attack type that the Mustang came to prominence over the Philippines in the decade after the war.

The nation of the Philippines as we know it today came into existence in July 1946. At that time there was still a comparatively large American presence in the area, following on from the significant US air, naval and ground activity in the Philippines during the war. The fledgling Philippine Air Force was brought into being in July 1947, and had as a part of its early equipment a number of P-51D Mustangs. These had been supplied from US stocks, and it is possible that some amongst them were combat veterans of the US operations in the area during the latter stages of the Second World War. In fact the Philippine military as a whole was heavily reliant on US assistance from the start, and it at once found itself in a major shooting war.

During the wartime Japanese occupation a major home-grown resistance movement had developed. Known under the name of Hukbalahap or Huks, this disparate resistance organisation had successfully harried the Japanese until the Philippine islands were gradually liberated by US forces later in the war. With the onset of peace in 1945, the Huks had expected to be a part of the Philippine leadership in the post-war period, and won several seats in elections following the Japanese defeat. However, the Huks were instead viewed as a threat by the new Philippine leadership, which governed with American support. Armed conflict between the Huks and the US-leaning Philippine forces soon erupted, and Philippine-operated Mustangs were in combat almost from the first. Huk forces were soon regularly the target of the Mustangs, which were operated exclusively in ground-attack missions due to the lack of airpower opposing them. There were eventually enough Mustangs to equip three squadrons, although the exact number of Mustangs that were operated has remained unclear. The Mustang-equipped units were the 6th, 7th, and 8th Fighter Squadrons. All were home-based in Manila, although many detachments were established around the extensive Philippines as required, as the Huks often operated in remote areas away from large towns. From 1950 American influence in the conflict became significant, as the Philippines assumed a new strategic importance to the US due to the commencement of the Korean War. The Philippine armed forces increasingly received American military and CIA assistance. A number of other aircraft types joined the Mustangs in the counter-insurgency war, including T-6 Texans which often identified targets for their North American stable mates. The Huks were renamed as the People's Liberation Army in 1950, but by 1954 their insurgency was defeated and the conflict closed in the autumn of that year. Philippine Mustang strength gradually ran down in the later 1950's and the type was eventually replaced by another North American product, the F-86F Sabre jet fighter, and therefore was out of service when internal revolt again flared up in the Philippines in the early to mid 1960's. Mustangs had proved to be very successful in the war against the Huks up to 1954, and some examples soldiered on to the late 1950's. In the ground-attack role the type had used various ordnance, including underwing unguided rockets mounted on 'zero-zero' rocket rails. A variety of individual aircraft numbering systems appear to have been used on the mustangs during their Philippine service. Reputedly at one stage the 6th FS had aircraft numbered in the 200 series, the 7th FS used numbers in the 300 series, and the 8th FS utilised 400-series numbers – although some aircraft were marked with a three-number code beginning with zero.

## Somalia

Italian Somaliland was occupied by British forces during World War Two, but was restored to Italian trusteeship under the UN in 1950. Between then and 1960, the country was under Italian administration. As a security force within the trustee territory the Italians established the Corpo di Sicurezza della Somalia. This organisation used several F-51D Mustangs from Italian stocks as a part of its air element, some of which were based at the capital, Mogadishu. The operating unit for at least some of the time appears to have been the Squadriglia Caccia Aviazione Somalia. The country eventually gained its independence in 1960, and received aid from the Italians before and immediately after independence. This included military assistance, and one of the aircraft types that was supplied by the Italians was the F-51D Mustang. It seems likely that eight examples were handed over to the Somalis (possibly numbered from 1 to 8), and formed the main part of the combat element of what became the Somali Aeronautical Corps. The surviving Mustangs were retired in or around 1968, this possibly coinciding with a left-wing coup in Somalia in the late 1960's, after which the country was increasingly aligned with the Soviet Union.

Sweden obtained, in several batches and as a result of wartime landings on neutral Swedish territory, 161 Mustangs plus others that were used for spares. In Swedish service the Mustang was known as the J 26 in its normal fighter configuration, but there was also a Swedish reconnaissance conversion known unofficially as the S 26. The reconnaissance-configured aircraft were flown by the Swedish reconnaissance wing F21, and as the Mustang shown here has the number '21' behind its fuselage national insignia it would appear to be a reconnaissance S 26 allocated to that unit
*(Photo: R.L. Ward Collection)*

## South Africa

In the latter stages of World War Two, the South African Air Force's No.5 Squadron transitioned onto Mustangs from the Curtiss Kittyhawk in the Mediterranean theatre during September and October 1944, and briefly continued to operate the type post-war. Two other South African squadrons, Nos.1 and 2 Squadrons, were delegated to receive the Mustang in Italy at that time, but did not fly the type in combat. South Africa was not an export operator of the Mustang post-war, until the Korean War resulted in the South Africans having one squadron of Mustangs in combat. As described in Chapter 9 of this book, South Africa delegated a fighter squadron to the conflict in Korea as a part of its commitment to the UN cause. The unit concerned was No.2 'Cheetah' Squadron, which was made up of volunteers from the South African armed forces and equipped with Mustangs. The F-51Ds were supplied from US stocks. Initially, 25 F-51Ds were made available to the South Africans, who subsequently operated under the umbrella of the 18th Fighter-Bomber Wing, and commenced operations on 19 November 1950. A long period of combat resulted, until December 1952 when No.2 Squadron ceased Mustang operations. The South Africans operated with distinction during their time on the Mustang, and continued to be attached to the 18th FBW during all their time in Korea, principally based at Chinhae (K-10) in South Korea in the latter stages of their Mustang operations. During its time with the Mustang, No.2 Squadron had been allocated further batches of Mustangs from US stocks but had lost 73 or 74 aircraft to all causes, with some 12 pilots killed in action and others missing or captured, in at least 10,373 sorties flown. The squadron transitioned onto the F-86F Sabre after finishing with the Mustang. A number of the South African Mustangs were returned to the USAF in December 1952 while No.2 Squadron converted onto the jets. At least two of these F-51Ds and probably more were then handed over to the Republic of Korea Air Force.

## South Korea

A country that flew the Mustang in combat was South Korea, whose Republic of Korea Air Force (RoKAF) was a major operator during the 1950's. As described in Chapter 9 of this book, the first Mustangs to reach the South Koreans did so in mid-1950, when 10 Mustangs (most probably all F-51Ds) were given to the RoKAF by the US from storage. These Mustangs formed the so-called 'Truman Gift', and were initially flown mainly by USAF pilots seconded to the RoKAF to aid that air force's pilots to transition onto the type, the RoKAF up to that time flying only trainers and liaison aircraft. The head of the US contingent, Maj Dean Hess, was instrumental in the establishment of the RoKAF as a viable fighting force, and the role of the US pilots and maintenance personnel was vital in helping the South Koreans to take on the numerically far superior North Korean forces.

During the Korean War from 1950 to 1953 the RoKAF operated the Mustang throughout the conflict, the US continuing to supply Mustangs to the South Koreans from existing stocks of former USAF aircraft. In addition, further Mustangs were passed to the RoKAF when the South African No. 2 Squadron gave up operating the type in Korea in late 1952. Historian M.J. Hardy in his book 'The North American Mustang' claims that the 10th and 11th Fighter Wings of the RoKAF flew the Mustang in combat, while other writers have named the 1st Fighter Squadron of the RoKAF as the principal South Korean squadron to operate the type. In reality the exact details of the South Korean Mustangs remain shrouded in some mystery, with few precise details of the RoKAF being available due to much secrecy surrounding this country's military organisations as a result of the continuing stand-off between North and South Korea. It does, however, appear that Mustangs remained in South Korean service after the end of the Korean War, possibly persisting in service until the late 1950's. An F-51D-25-NT, 44-84669, that flew with the RoKAF is exhibited at the Korean War Museum in Seoul, South Korea, as a reminder of the important role that the Mustang played in the early years of the RoKAF.

## Soviet Union

The Soviet Union was supplied with significant numbers of US warplanes during World War Two, following the attack on the Soviet Union by Germany in June 1941, in addition to considerable quantities of other war materials. As explained in Part 1 of this two-part 'Modellers' Datafile' on the Mustang, which covered Allison-engined Mustangs, a small batch of Allison-engined Mustangs was supplied to the Soviet Union by Britain in 1942. These aircraft were evaluated by the Russians but no further Allison-powered examples were subsequently supplied.

However, in addition to these deliveries of early British Mustangs, the Soviet Union also came by a further number of Mustangs much later in the war. These were all Merlin-engined Mustangs, and were aircraft that were left behind when the USAAF employed several air bases in the Ukraine for the 'Frantic' shuttle missions. The Americans had three air bases made available to them by the Soviet authorities in the Ukraine (which was of course a part of the Soviet Union at that time) – Poltava, Mirgorod, and Piryatin. A total of seven 'Frantic' shuttles were flown from early June 1944 onwards, and several unserviceable P-51 Mustangs were left behind by the Americans at the Ukrainian bases when they finally pulled out. Most of these would have been P-51D Mustangs, but some might well have been P-51B or 'C' versions. In addition, the Soviets are thought to have come across further Mustangs, presumably damaged or captured examples, as they advanced across Eastern Europe in the later stages of the war. Although evidence is scarce, it is possible that some of these variously-acquired Mustangs were subsequently made flyable, and evaluated by the Soviets. They did not as far as is known enter operational service and their later history in the Soviet Union remains unclear.

## Sweden

The major 'export' operator of the P-51 in Europe was the Kungliga Svenska Flygvapnet (Royal Swedish Air Force, or RSwAF). Eventually 161 Mustangs served with the RSwAF, although the

Mustangs truly served world-wide in the post-World War Two period. Amongst Latin and South American Mustang operators, Uruguay was originally intended by the US after the war to fly the P-47 Thunderbolt. Nevertheless the Fuerza Aérea Uruguaya received F-51D Mustangs from 1950, including '273' illustrated. The Uruguayan Mustangs were eventually replaced by the Lockheed F-80 Shooting Star jet fighter
*(Photo: M.V. Lowe Collection)*

actual total that was bought was a little higher than this, and the purchase arrangements were somewhat fraught with problems. None of these aircraft were new-build, they were all from former USAAF stocks and following Swedish service a number went on to operate elsewhere in the world.

Neutral during World War Two, but with links to all the major protagonists, Sweden increasingly became an arrival point and refuge for damaged combat aircraft that were unable to regain their own bases. As the conflict wore on, increasingly a significant proportion of these were American.

Amongst the ever-growing number of US warplanes that were arriving over Sweden as the conflict continued, a number of Mustangs were included. The first Mustang to descend on Swedish soil crashed in April 1944 and was written off. On 13 May 1944, however, a P-51B landed intact but critically short of fuel at Rinkaby airfield and its pilot was interned. The aircraft was from the 354th FG of the Ninth Air Force, which at that time was still performing some bomber escort work, and was named 'Z HUB' (serial number 43-6365). It was the first of several Mustangs that collected at Swedish airfields during the final twelve months of the war, allowing the Swedes to have five flyable Mustangs by October 1944 including several P-51Ds. These aircraft remained US property, and when flown they were piloted by interned American pilots in Sweden. One was destroyed in a fatal crash but in March 1945 Swedish pilots were cleared to fly the existing four flyable Mustangs in the country. By then the Swedish military was well aware of the capabilities of the Mustang, which appeared to be an excellent fighter with which to update Sweden's aerial combat capabilities. After some tortuous negotiations an agreement was reached in early April 1945 for Sweden to buy 46 Mustangs from US stocks for $70,000 each, together with the four surviving airworthy interned examples for $25,000 each. Some spares were also included in the deal.

On 10 April, a day after the contract was agreed, the first batch departed from Metfield in Suffolk and flew non-stop to Bromma near Stockholm in Sweden. Initially 10 Mustangs made the trip, followed by 18 on 13 April, 15 on 14 April, and three on 25 April. All the Mustangs were ferried by US pilots. It has always been rumoured that the 14 April consignment was intercepted by German fighters on the way to Sweden, resulting in an air battle during which two German fighters were shot down.

In Swedish service the Mustang was given the designation J 26, and the first unit to receive the newly-delivered aircraft was Flygflottilj F16 at Uppsala north of Stockholm. The three squadrons of this wing, 1/F16, 2/F16, and 3/F16, were fully

equipped with the type by the end of April 1945, replacing the wing's indigenous FFVS J 22 fighters.

In early 1946 representations were made by the Swedish government for more Mustangs. By that time hundreds of used, battle-worn Mustangs were stock-piled at air bases in Allied-controlled Germany, and the price had fallen to $3,500 per aircraft – although the quality of these war-weary Mustangs was in some cases very questionable. In the event 90 Mustangs were duly supplied by the US, these aircraft all being from war-weary surplus stocks at Nürnberg-Fürth airfield. The first of the 90 were flown to Sweden from Fürth in November 1946, arriving at Malmen on the 24th of that month. Some were found to need considerable overhaul work on arrival in Sweden, and the final examples were not ready for front-line squadrons until well into 1948. The final 30 airframes of this order were for spares. As a finale, Sweden later bought 30 further Mustangs, possibly to make up for the latter, and in March 1948 a contract was agreed between the Swedish government and US representatives for 30 Mustangs at $2,500 each. All of these aircraft were also eventually sourced in Germany from surplus US stocks.

Swedish procurement of the Mustang therefore consisted of four interned aircraft, the initial order for 46 Mustangs, followed by 90, and then the final 30. This makes 170 in total, but as nine were scrapped the final total was 161, of which 157 were actually purchased rather than from interned stocks. The figure of 157 is often quoted in published sources as the total that Sweden ordered, but as can be seen from the foregoing text, it was not quite as simple as that. In Swedish service the Mustangs were allocated the Swedish serial numbers 26001 to 26161. The initial four, 26001 to 26004, were the original four airworthy interned aircraft, of which the first flyable arrival in Sweden, 'Z HUB', was 26001. This aircraft, plus 26002, were the only P-51B-model Mustangs, all the rest being of P-51D-series (the other two interned aircraft were P-51D-5-NAs). In Swedish service, the original operational Swedish wing, F16, was eventually joined by another operational wing, F4, which was based near Ostersund. It received its first Mustangs for 1/F4 in May 1947, but was not fully operational on the type for many months after this. Mustangs were also allocated to F20, although this wing borrowed aircraft from F16 as necessary. Each wing was normally made up of three squadrons, and those that were Mustang-equipped on paper had 15 operational aircraft, plus several examples for the staff or headquarters flight of the wing. The peak was reached in July 1949, when 127 Mustangs were on strength as front-line aircraft. Some aircraft were converted by the Swedes to reconnaissance S 26 configuration.

A further RSwAF unit to fly the Mustang was F8, which employed the type in small numbers for liaison and communications flying, often in the hands of ranking officers.

The service of the Mustang as a front-line fighter in Sweden was comparatively short. From April 1952 F16 began converting onto the Saab J 29A indigenous jet fighter. The longest-lived of the Swedish Mustangs were the reconnaissance-configured S 26 Mustangs. The final examples in service of these were retired in October 1954, having been sold to Nicaragua, although the last flight of a Swedish reconnaissance Mustang was on 24 November 1954. It had been expected that this final Mustang would be kept for museum display in Sweden, but it too was sold via the Swedish export company Henry Wallenberg & Co. AB to Nicaragua. Swedish Mustangs were also supplied via Wallenberg to Israel (25), and the Dominican Republic (42), in addition to the 26 that were shipped to Nicaragua.

## Switzerland

In common with other European countries such as Italy and Sweden, Switzerland operated the Mustang post-World War Two as an interim fighter until the new generation of jet-powered combat aircraft became available in sufficient numbers, and to replace increasingly obsolete existing piston-engined types. In the event the Swiss obtained 130 Mustangs from 1948 onwards, all from existing ex-USAAF stocks, but in reality the Mustang was to soldier on in Swiss service for a decade. Nevertheless, in common with many other overseas operators of the P-51, the type came to be well-loved by its pilots and ground crews, and it represented the zenith of piston-engined fighter operations for the Swiss.

Prior to Switzerland becoming an official overseas operator of the Mustang, however, the type had become well known to the Swiss. Neutral in World War Two, Switzerland nevertheless lay geographically very close to many of the air battles that took place during that conflict, particularly later in the war when US heavy bombers raided targets deep in Germany from bases in England and the Mediterranean. On a number of occasions US aircraft, both bombers and fighters, landed in Switzerland due to battle damage, and in one of these instances the aircraft involved was a Mustang. Arriving on 19 July 1944, a 4th Fighter Group P-51B was in good enough condition to be subsequently tested by the Swiss armed forces and examined by representatives of the Swiss aircraft industry. The Mustang obviously impressed the Swiss, and with a large surplus of ex-USAAF Mustangs available after World War Two it was unsurprising that the Mustang was seen as a good prospect for Swiss service prior to new jet equipment becoming available. Post-war, Switzerland evaluated and later ordered from Britain the de Havilland Vampire first-generation jet fighter/fighter-bomber, but the Mustang appeared to be an excellent fighter type with which to modernise the Swiss fighter arm before the Vampires were delivered from Britain in significant numbers.

Switzerland was not in line for the type of US aid that was made available to many of the countries of Europe that had suffered wartime deprivations, and therefore actually purchased Mustangs from the Americans – although this was at a knock-down price. Like those Mustangs supplied to Italy and Sweden, however, the Mustangs concerned were not new. They were stockpiled in Allied-controlled western Germany (what became post-war West Germany), and to say that some of these aircraft were in poor condition is an understatement, many being war veterans (and some decidedly war-weary) following service with Eighth and Ninth Army Air Force units. Many had been neglected where they stood in various air depots or collection points, and it was some of these that the Swiss purchased. A Swiss delegation visited the US air depots at Oberpfaffenhofen and Nürnberg-Fürth airfields in southern Germany to survey the large numbers of former front-line fighters that were in storage. A deal was reached in December 1947 for the Swiss to buy 100 P-51D Mustangs, most if not all preferably of the D-20 and D-25 production series, plus tools, spare parts and replacement engines. In addition, a further 30 were also eventually procured, to act as spare parts sources for the better initial 100 airframes.

Purchased for $4,000 each (although it is not clear if that price also applied to the final 30 airframes), the 130 P-51 Mustangs appeared to represent a good-value, low cost solution to the impending fighter gap in Switzerland until the jet-powered de Havilland Vampire became available in numbers.

Although it was intended that the late-arrival 30 Mustangs would be used for spares, in fact the Swiss were very successful in procuring a good supply of separate spare parts and in the event some of the final 30 served in front-line units in similar fashion to the initial 100 better airframes. The Swiss air force (named the Schweizerische Flugwaffe after World War Two) numbered the 130 Mustangs J-2001 to J-2130 in the then-current Swiss numbering system. Mustangs duly served with the Swiss air force from 1948 to 1958. Altogether, five front-line fighter/fighter-bomber squadrons of the Schweizerische Flugwaffe flew the Mustang. These were Fliegerstaffeln (FlSt) 16, 18, 19, 20, and 21. Of these, FlSt 16 was a part of the Überwachungsgeschwader (UeG) at Dübendorf airfield. The UeG was the permanent, full-time part of the air force, with professional full-time military pilots assigned who were also responsible for pilot training. The other four Fliegerstaffeln had personnel attached who were 'part-time' military personnel under the Swiss system of citizen militia status. Several of the Mustangs were converted into reconnaissance platforms with a local modification to allow a camera to be carried in the rear fuselage. The Mustangs were well-liked in Swiss service, but the type was eventually replaced by the de Havilland Vampire and Venom.

## Uruguay

Another South American country that benefited from American military aid in the post-World War Two period was Uruguay. Suffering from a lack of modern fighter aircraft, Uruguay was offered Republic P-47 Thunderbolts by the United States in one of the post-war military aid programmes. Under a proposed delivery plan, 30 P-47Ds were to have been supplied in the immediate post-Second World War period. However, this offer was rejected, and in the event the Fuerza Aérea Uruguaya instead was eventually the beneficiary of F-51D Mustangs. Most historians agree that a total of 25 was supplied, starting in 1950. Numbers allocated in Uruguay were in the 260, 270 and 280 blocks. Most were subsequently operated by Grupo 2, some in the fighter-bomber role, with a number also flying with Grupo 1 late in the type's Uruguayan service. They persisted until the late 1950's when they were increasingly replaced by Lockheed F-80 Shooting Star jet fighters - although by then the F-80 itself was very outdated. Six or possibly eight of the surviving aircraft were sold to Bolivia in 1960 for a nominal $1 each.

## Venezuela

There have been persistent rumours and far more correct claims that at least one Mustang found its way into Venezuelan service. This little-known happening took place via Bolivia, when the Venezuelan air force was in the process of disposing of some F-86 Sabres and B-25 Mitchells to Bolivia and a Mustang appears to have gone the other way as a goodwill gesture, possibly in 1968. The aircraft concerned appears to have been a former Swedish-operated Mustang. It has also often been claimed that the three Mustangs that definitely did reach Fidel Castro's forces during the fighting in Cuba in the late 1950's were obtained with Venezuelan help.

It is often forgotten that air racing had been a major attraction in pre-World War Two America, and it was resurrected rapidly after the end of the war. Amongst the former military types that formed the basis of post-war air racing US-style was the Mustang, and a variety of different marks of P-51 duly competed in a wide variety of events. One of the successful early exponents was former P-51C, NX1202, in which Paul Mantz won the prestigious 1946 and 1947 Bendix Trophy long-distance races
*(Photo: R.L. Ward Collection)*

A considerable feat was achieved in January 1951, when a privately-owned Merlin-Mustang successfully flew the Atlantic Ocean non-stop between New York and London's new airport at Heathrow. The Mustang concerned was none other than N1202, the P-51C that had won the 1946 and 1947 Bendix Trophy races. Now owned by airline pilot Capt Charles F. Blair and renamed 'Excalibur III', the Mustang was flown by Blair across the Atlantic on 31 January 1951 at an unofficial solo record time of seven hours, 48 minutes. The crossing was made from Idlewild Airport in New York to Heathrow at an average speed of 442 mph (711 km/h). This remarkable non-stop flight was achieved with the 'wet' wing modification which had helped the aircraft to its Bendix Trophy successes, the total internal capacity available within the Mustang being 865 US gallons. Blair and 'Excalibur III' then flew into the history books by becoming the first to make a solo flight over the North Pole. This was achieved on 30 May 1951, from Bardufoss in Norway across the North Pole to Fairbanks, Alaska. This very long flight took 10 hours, 29 minutes to complete, over an incredible distance of 3,375 miles (5,432 km). Although not a world record, it was certainly the longest distance covered non-stop by a Mustang. The aircraft is seen here, wearing its smart red and white paint scheme, on arrival at Heathrow following the transatlantic flight. It survives to this day, and is owned by the National Air and Space Museum in the US
*(Photo: via Chris Ellis)*

## Privately-owned Mustangs

The long military service of the Mustang around the world has been matched, indeed extended, by the type's long-standing and continuing popularity in the hands of civilian owners. Without doubt this love affair between private owners and the Mustang has ensured the type's enduring survival well into the twenty-first century. Nevertheless, it probably breaks the heart of many enthusiasts and owners to be reminded that at the end of World War Two, significant numbers of Mustangs (and indeed almost all other types of US warplanes that had fought in the war) were simply destroyed. In Allied-occupied Germany, a considerable number of Mustangs were concentrated, partly because some Ninth Air Force combat units had ended the war there, and partly because the Mustang was one of the US front-line types delegated to occupation duties following the end of the war. When jet fighters started to arrive in numbers to update the US fighter capability in Allied-controlled Germany, many of the surviving Mustangs there were simply put out to pasture. Some were stored at air bases such as Nürnberg-Fürth, but others were destroyed using small explosive charges, often placed in the cockpit, after all usable parts had been removed - frequently those doing the demolition work were German hired-hands who had totally failed to do that type of work for the German armed forces during the war. In addition, large numbers of redundant military aircraft were stored in the US as 1945 wore on, often being transferred direct from the factory to storage facilities such as Kingman in Arizona. The fortunate Mustangs amongst these were bought by a small but

growing number of demobbed military pilots or entrepreneurs who saw a potential use for a high-performance warplane that was now increasingly unwanted by the military for which it had been built. At that time it was possible to buy a Mustang for only several hundred dollars (there is a popular legend, never officially verified, that at least one Mustang was bought from the war surplus officials at Kingman for only $25).

At first many privately purchased post-war Mustangs were intended for air racing, but others were bought as 'executive' transports and run-arounds – although the Mustang was not particularly suitable for the latter, particularly as it potentially had high running costs, something that was not a concern during military operations. With the coming of the Korean War in 1950 and the sudden need for Mustangs in the ground-attack role for close support of UN forces, many USAF personnel must have cursed that such a potentially valuable aircraft as the Mustang had been so depleted in numbers due to scrapping during those first few years of peace – leading, as related in Chapter 9, to the robbing of Air National Guard squadrons of any available P-51D-type Mustangs to fulfil the demands of combat in Korea. Since that time the value of Mustangs has steadily increased, and with the official release from US military service of the Mustang in 1957 more and more civilians have owned and cared for this increasingly iconic aircraft.

With the advent of the 'warbird' movement from the 1960's onwards, the value of most if not all surviving World War Two-era aircraft of any make and description has steadily increased.

With that increase in value has come the truly fortunate desire to ensure that no Mustangs, whatever their condition, are scrapped. Unfortunately space considerations do not allow for a detailed assessment of privately-owned Mustangs in this book, as the subject is truly vast and deserves a separate examination in its own right.

## Merlin-Mustangs for Air Racing

The Merlin-Mustang in its various versions has been a natural choice for air racing. Post-World War Two, in 1946 the US National Air Races were resurrected at Cleveland, Ohio, and at once the Mustang proved to be an excellent air racer, both in long-distance races and in the more dangerous closed-circuit pylon-type racing. Indeed, Mustangs came to dominate air racing in the US – with their owners sometimes considerably modifying their aircraft in order to gain more speed. During the 1949 National Air Races at Cleveland in early September 1949, the Bendix Trophy long-distance race witnessed one of the greatest Mustang speed performances of all time. Staged from Rosamond Dry Lake in California to Cleveland, over a distance of 2,008 miles (3,232 km), the first three places were taken by Mustangs, with top honours going to the well-known racing pilot Joe DeBona. He was flying an F-6C with a 'wet' wing modification civil registered as N5528N, and he covered the course in four hours, 16 minutes and 17 seconds at an incredible average speed of 470.136 mph (757 km/h) - surely one of the most impressive Mustang performances of all time. Air racing in the US continues in the present day, with Mustangs often proving to be successful at the annual air racing event at Reno, Nevada.

## The 'Warbird' Movement

Without doubt the fact that there are today so many airworthy Mustangs is thanks not only to the air racing population, but also to the growth of the warbird community. The use of the term 'warbird' appears to have arisen in the 1970's, and generally describes an ex-military aircraft preserved and operated by a civil owner. Of course there is a cross-over between the air racing and warbird communities in the US, and both have roughly similar goals, but certainly many warbird owners are very passionate about preserving the Mustang for prosperity in its original form, rather than as modified air racers. There are many expert restorers in the US and several other countries including Britain, which specialise in complete rebuilds from the ground up of historic aircraft, and paint shops that nowadays make authentic recreations of original colour schemes from the Second World War period.

Perhaps the most obvious and widespread of changes to non-racing Mustangs has been the provision of a second seat behind the pilot, and the fitting in some cases of rudimentary dual controls - although some two-seat conversions have gone all the way and resulted in the aircraft being made into a genuine two-seater with full dual controls. These conversions have been

Amongst the most famous of 'unlimited' racing Mustangs is the spectacular 'Dago Red'. Civil registered as N5410V, this aircraft has graced the air racing circuit in the US from the mid-1980's for a number of owners and pilots, after it had been rebuilt from a former racing aircraft using parts from other Mustangs. It is also one of the most successful racers in the Unlimited Class events down the years at the world-famous Reno air racing festival. In September 2008 it was in the forefront of the Mustang revival at Reno, taking second place in the Unlimited Gold final race behind Bill Destefani in the modified P-51D 'Strega' - and thus re-establishing Mustangs as the premier Reno racers after several years of domination by radial-engined Bearcat and Sea Fury racers. It is pictured here at Nellis AFB in October 2002 *(Photo: Malcolm V. Lowe)*

King's Cup winner. Merlin-Mustangs have featured prominently on the air racing circuit in the US since World War Two ended, but occasionally air races elsewhere in the world featured a Mustang. This smart red and white US civil registered Mustang, N6356T, spent some time in England during the late 1960's. It was actually a P-51D-30-NA, 44-74494, that saw little service with the USAAF but was operated in Canada by the RCAF as '9237' during the 1950's. Charles Masefield flew the aircraft to success in Britain in the King's Cup air race of 1967 *(Photo: via Chris Ellis)*

carried out by a variety of companies and individuals, resulting in few of these aircraft being similar and most being to varying specifications. The trend was institutionalised by Trans-Florida Aviation/Cavalier Aircraft Corporation in some of the Cavalier Mustang conversions and upgradings that were performed by that company in the 1960's. However, in recent years several organization, notably the Stallion 51 Corporation of Kissimmee in Florida, have offered conversion courses for pilots to transition onto the Mustang, and in that sense there has been a mini-boom in the provision of two-seat training on specially-converted Mustangs.

One of the most famous surviving Mustangs is 'Miss America', the well-known racing P-51D registered N991R. For over a decade it has been in the ownership of Dr Brent Hisey, and is raced regularly at Reno. The Mustang is pictured here in 2003 at Wiley Post Airport, Oklahoma City, where it is based. It was damaged in an accident during the 2002 Reno air races, but this image shows the Mustang following its rebuild and return to airworthy condition. It has been converted so that a second occupant can be seated in the cockpit, behind the pilot – many surviving airworthy Mustangs are configured in this way *(Photo: Jerry Day)*

# Mustang in Colour

## Chapter 11

A line-up of completed Merlin Mustangs at Inglewood, with FZ132, a Mustang Mk III intended for the RAF even though it wears US national insignia, the third in the line. Interestingly, that aircraft and the example nearest to the camera have a camouflage pattern that appears to be Dark Green and Dark Earth on their uppersurfaces, even though that colour combination had been dropped by the RAF in the mid-war period prior to the completion of FZ132. The middle aircraft in the line is destined for the USAAF and wears Dark Olive Drab and Neutral Grey camouflage
(Photo: NAA)

The first Merlin-powered Mustang variant for the US Army Air Force(s) was the P–51B. Seen on a test flight prior to delivery, this Mustang with the serial number 43-12408 was from the initial production batch made by North American Aviation at Inglewood, the P-51B-1-NA
(Photo: NAA)

A very colourful CO's kite. Sporting coloured bands to denote a command aircraft, Dallas-built P-51D-5-NT 44-11200 was flown by Lt Col (later Col) Claiborne H Kinnard, Jr., who was the 355th Fighter Group's commanding officer from February until 7 June 1945. The Mustang is pictured in Germany probably in June of that year. Kinnard was in fact a high-scoring ace, with eight aerial and 17 ground victories in Mustangs
(Photo: 355th Fighter Group Association via Peter Randall)

Beautiful detail close-up of the business end of 'Woody's Maytag', the P-51B, serial number 43-6520, coded WR-W of Capt Robert E. 'The Kid' Woody. An aircraft of the 354th Fighter Squadron, 355th Fighter Group, it is seen in this image at the unit's home base of Steeple Morden in Cambridgeshire. The aircraft's Crew Chief, S/Sgt Gertzen, can be seen pulling some maintenance on the Merlin engine. Very visible is the yellow-tinted zinc chromate primer colour on the engine bearer, and the similar colour on the inside face of the wheel cover
*(Photo: via Peter Randall)*

In the Eighth Air Force, one of the highest-scoring aces of the famous 4th Fighter Group was Duane Beeson, from Boise, Idaho. Finishing the war with 17.333 aerial victories over north-west Europe, Beeson achieved 5.333 of these in two different Mustangs. His personal P-51B-5-NA, 43-6819 named 'Bee', showed considerable wear and tear to its original paintwork *(Photo: USAAF)*

Showing off a very worn uppersurface coat of Olive Drab paint, P-51B 43-12201 was a P-51B-1-NA from the initial Merlin-powered Mustang production contract built by North American Aviation at Inglewood. It wears the red-bordered 'star and bar' US national insignia that was used for a short time during the summer of 1943 before the fully blue-bordered national insignia was introduced *(Photo: NAA)*

'Miss Rogers' was an early production P-51D that served with the 4th Fighter Squadron, 52nd Fighter Group, Fifteenth Army Air Force in the Mediterranean and southern Europe. Built by North American Aviation at Inglewood, the aircraft was a P-51D-5-NA. 'WD' was the code letter combination for the 4th Fighter Squadron *(Photo: USAAF)*

This well-known P-51D, serial number 44-13410, E2-C 'Lou IV', was flown by Lt Col Thomas J J Christian, the Group Commanding Officer of the 361st Fighter Group, Eighth Air Force. Sadly, Christian was killed in action on 12 August 1944, shortly after this photo was taken. This image is from a well-known series of colour photos that were taken of this aircraft and others from the 375th FS. It is one of the main sources of 'evidence' used for the argument of blue uppersurfaces on aircraft of the 361st FG. There has long been debate on this point, but historian Peter Randall (www.littlefriends.co.uk) is a supporter of the 361st FG's Crew Chiefs - who, when asked, always laugh and say "we NEVER had any blue painted a/c in the 361st". It is much more likely that the uppersurface colour, which was added at unit level to make the Mustangs' 'natural metal' appearance less conspicuous, was actually Olive Drab or a locally-sourced dark green shade *(Photo: USAAF)*

The personal P-51D-20-NA of Col William Clarke, the commanding officer of the 339th Fighter Group in the spring of 1945, seen at the 339th's base at Fowlmere in Cambridgeshire. Named 'Dotty' on its canopy frame for Clarke's wife Dorothy (and not 'Dolly' as often claimed), the aircraft was also called 'Happy IV'. It sports the red and white nose checks that identified the 339th FG
*(Photo: Steve Ananian, 339th FG Association)*

A bomb-carrying F-51D of the 18th Fighter-Bomber Wing's 67th FBS taxies out for a mission in Korea. The aircraft, 44-73000, bears the 'Buzz Number' 'FF-000', the 'FF' prefix denoting the F-51 in the post-war 'Buzz Number' sequence of codes. The 67th FBS was particularly successful in air-to-air combat over Korea, making a number of claims *(Photo: USAF)*

Much less well-known than the Mustangs operated by Eighth Air Force fighter units in the latter stages of World War Two, the P-51s of the Fifteenth Air Force nevertheless performed an important role in the air war over their particular area of responsibility, namely the Mediterranean and southern Europe. In this view the red-striped tail of 44-13464, the P-51D of Major Sam Brown, stands out to show that this aircraft belonged to the 31st FG, one of the Fifteenth's top combat groups. Assigned to the 307th FS, whose 'MX' code the aircraft wears, Brown finished his tour of duty in September 1944 with 15.5 aerial victories
*(Photo: USAAF)*

Nice air-to-air image of 'The Iowa Beaut', a North American Aviation Inglewood-built P-51B-15-NA, serial number 42-106950 – and definitely NOT a P-51C, as claimed in one recently published source. Photographed in the summer of 1944, it was operated by the 354th Fighter Squadron, 355th Fighter Group, based at Steeple Morden in Cambridgeshire. 'The Iowa Beaut' sports rough Olive Drab or locally-painted dark green uppersurfaces and ten 'kill' markings beneath its cockpit canopy, although the pilot or pilots who achieved those victories in the aircraft remains a point of some debate. At the time of the photograph, the Mustang was assigned to a virtually unknown pilot named Robert Hulderman (some historians call him Hulberman), but he was certainly not an ace. It is believed that some of the victories that were achieved in 'The Iowa Beaut' were scored by Capt Fred Haviland, Jr., a six aerial victories and six ground victories ace. This aircraft was also flown by an RCAF exchange pilot, Warren Peglar, during the summer of 1944 *(Photo: USAAF)*

The only P-82C Twin Mustang that was built shows off its glossy all-black exterior and the unusual lines of the Twin Mustang. With the serial number 44-65169 this aircraft started life as a P-82B, from a production block that was powered by the Merlin engine. It was converted to act as a night-fighter development aircraft, fitted with a large fairing attached to the wing centre section that housed an SCR-720 airborne radar, and was painted with the early-style post-war 'Buzz Number' 'PQ-169'. The Twin Mustang as a type eventually found its true role as a night-fighter *(Photo: NAA)*

With the war won, 'Wolverine' and 'Arlene' bask in the German sunshine in the summer of 1945. Assigned to the 354th Fighter Squadron of the 355th Fighter Group, both aircraft wear the red/yellow/red occupation forces' fuselage identification bands. 'Wolverine' was a P-51D-25-NA, 44-73156, assigned to Lt Ervin Nelson. 'Arlene' was a P-51D-20-NA, 44-72492
*(Photo: 355th Fighter Group Association via Peter Randall)*

Eighth Air Force Mustang units flew a variety of locally-modified two-seat Mustangs towards the end of World War Two. This was partly to provide operational conversion training to newly-arrived fighter pilots, following the decision to allow the fighter groups themselves adopt this role in late 1944/early 1945. In the foreground of this view is VF-4 of the 336th Fighter Squadron, 4th Fighter Group. The line-up appears to have been taken at Debden, home of the 4th FG, on 23 March 1945, possibly on the occasion of a group commanders' conference. The third Mustang in the line is P-51D-20-NA 44-72519 LC-D named 'Gumpy', which was assigned to Col Robert P Montgomery, the CO of the 20th Fighter Group at that time *(Photo: Arthur E. Sevigny, 20th Fighter Wing Association)*

Underlining the close connection between the heavy bombers and the Mustangs that became their protective 'little friends', several blue-nosed P-51s of the Eighth Air Force's 352nd Fighter Group fly in company with B-24 Liberators of the 458th Bomb Group in the late summer or autumn of 1944
*(Photo: USAAF)*

Mustangs of the 361st Fighter Group were much-photographed in flight. Very familiar because of this is the P-51D, 44-13357, B7-R 'Tika IV' of Lt Vernon R Richards from the 374th FS. Eighth Air Force Mustangs were eventually distinguished by coloured markings on their forward fuselages and spinners, which distinguished the unit (in this case, yellow for the 361st FG), with individual squadrons within each FG being marked out with code letters (here, 'B7' for the 374th FS). This aircraft was a P-51D-5-NA and therefore being an early production P-51D, it did not have the small dorsal extension to the fin which characterised later P-51D production aircraft *(Photo: USAAF)*

Royal Australian Air Force (RAAF) F-51D or K Mustangs from No.77 Squadron in maintenance at Iwakuni, Japan. No.77 Squadron was originally part of the British Commonwealth Occupation Force in Japan. By 1950 it was the only squadron representing the RAAF in Japan and was preparing to leave the country on 25 June 1950 – this plan was radically altered by the start of what became the Korean War. Between 2 July 1950 and 6 April 1951 the squadron flew 3,800 sorties (according to Australian records) before the unit converted to the Gloster Meteor F.8 jet. Note the yellow-tinted zinc chromate primer colour on the engine bearers and support frames of the two aircraft that have their engine cowling covers removed *(Photo: RAAF)*

Reconnaissance-configured, camera-carrying Mustangs were an important part of the tactical reconnaissance assets available to the United Nations forces during the Korean War. RF-51D 44-11913 'Tulie, Scotty & ?' (actually a former P-51K) displays the distinctive markings of the 45th Tactical Reconnaissance Squadron, which was stationed at Kimpo near Seoul following the United Nations' success in starting to push the North Korean forces out of what is now South Korea. This aircraft also displays the 'Buzz Number' prefix of that era for reconnaissance Mustangs of 'RF' *(Photo: R.L. Ward Collection)*

Featuring in a series of company publicity photographs, one of the early production lightweight Mustangs, P-51H-1-NA 44-64164, shows off the refined and rather austere lines of this version of the Mustang. The red, white and blue colouring on the spinner of this aircraft is thought to represent NAA's flight testing division *(Photo: NAA)*

There is only a small number of surviving F-82 Twin Mustangs, and most of them are non-airworthy museum exhibits or wrecks. One potentially airworthy example is F-82B 44-65162, the third production F-82B-1-NA, which for many years was in the hands of the famed Confederate Air Force at Harlingen, Texas, as N12102. It is seen here in happier days prior to an accident in October 1987 that rendered the aircraft unflyable and in need of extensive repair work *(Photo: John Batchelor)*

A post-war Mustang that graced British skies was the smart red-and-white US civil-registered Mustang, N6356T. Formerly P-51D-30-NA 44-74494, it flew with the RCAF as '9237' during the 1950s. In Britain it gained considerable fame when, flown by Charles Masefield, it won the King's Cup air race in 1967. The small emblem below the cockpit is that of the 'Tiger Club' *(Photo: Beagle Aircraft Ltd.)*

Twin Mustangs served with distinction, like the Mustang itself, in the Korean War. This 1950-era radar-equipped F-82G night-fighter, 46-376, operated with the Itazuke-based 68th F-AWS (Fighter – All Weather Squadron, sometimes written as 'Fighter (All-Weather) Squadron'), and wears the 'Buzz Number' prefix for Twin Mustangs of 'FQ' in red on its rear fuselages *(Photo: USAF)*

One of the last Mustangs of any type to receive a US military serial number, Cavalier Mustang 67-22581 operated in Bolivia before being sold to private ownership in late 1977 and civil-registered C-GMUS. It approximated roughly to Cavalier II standard and is seen here during 1984 still wearing its Fuerza Aérea Boliviana colours, but with Canadian civil registration and name 'What's Up Doc'
(Photo: John Batchelor)

Resplendent in this view wearing a somewhat fictitious 361st Fighter Group-like colour scheme, this Mustang is the well-known P-51D named 'Gunfighter' which was operated for many years by Brig Gen Regis Urschler, former commander of the 55th Strategic Reconnaissance Wing. Nowadays a part of the Commemorative Air Force Museum, it was later painted in 55th Fighter Group colours as a tribute to the predecessors of the 55th Strategic Reconnaissance Wing. It is a P-51D-25-NA, 44-73264, civil registration N5428V (Photo: John Batchelor)

Without doubt, one of the best-known of post-war civil-operated Mustangs was 'Ole Yeller', the Rockwell International-titled former P-51D-30-NA, serial number 44-74739 and civil registered as N51RH. Flown for many years by the legendary Robert A 'Bob' Hoover, the aircraft was often used as the lead-off aircraft for the Reno air races. It had in fact been converted into basic Cavalier Mustang configuration by Trans Florida Aviation in the early 1960's, and finally passed out of Hoover's ownership in 1999. It was later owned by John Bagley
(Photo: William T. Larkins)

# Colour Artwork

North American P-51D Mustang of the 308th Fighter Squadron, 31st Fighter Group, 15th US Army Air Force, Mondolfo, Italy 1944. The aircraft has an overall natural metal finish with red spinner, and red nose and tail flashes. Dark Olive Drab 41 anti-glare ahead of windscreen

North American F-51D Mustang of Grupo de Aviacion No.2 Caza/Grupo de Aviacion No.1 Rec/Tact, Fuerza Aérea Uruguaya, Glendale circa September 1950. The aircraft has an overall natural metal finish with a black anti-glare panel

North American F-6K Mustang J-2088 of the Swiss Air Force circa 1957. The aircraft has an overall natural metal finish with a blue anti-glare panel

North American P-51B Mustang 36500 of the 468th Fighter Squadron, 352nd Fighter Group, 8th US Army Air Force, Bodney, Norfolk, June 1944, as flown by Lt. Stanley 'Stan' Miles. The aircraft is finished in Dark Olive Drab 41 (close to FS34087) upper surfaces with Neutral Grey 43 (close to FS36173) lower surfaces with a blue forward fuselage and white codes with a yellow serial number, and carries black-white 'invasion stripes'

North American P-51B Mustang 106473 of the 362nd Fighter Squadron, 357th Fighter Group, 8th US Army Air Force, March 1944 as flown by 1st Lt John Forrest Pugh. The aircraft is finished in overall natural metal, with Dark Olive Drab 41 (or possibly RAF Dark Green) upper surfaces. The forward fuselage has a red and yellow diamond pattern

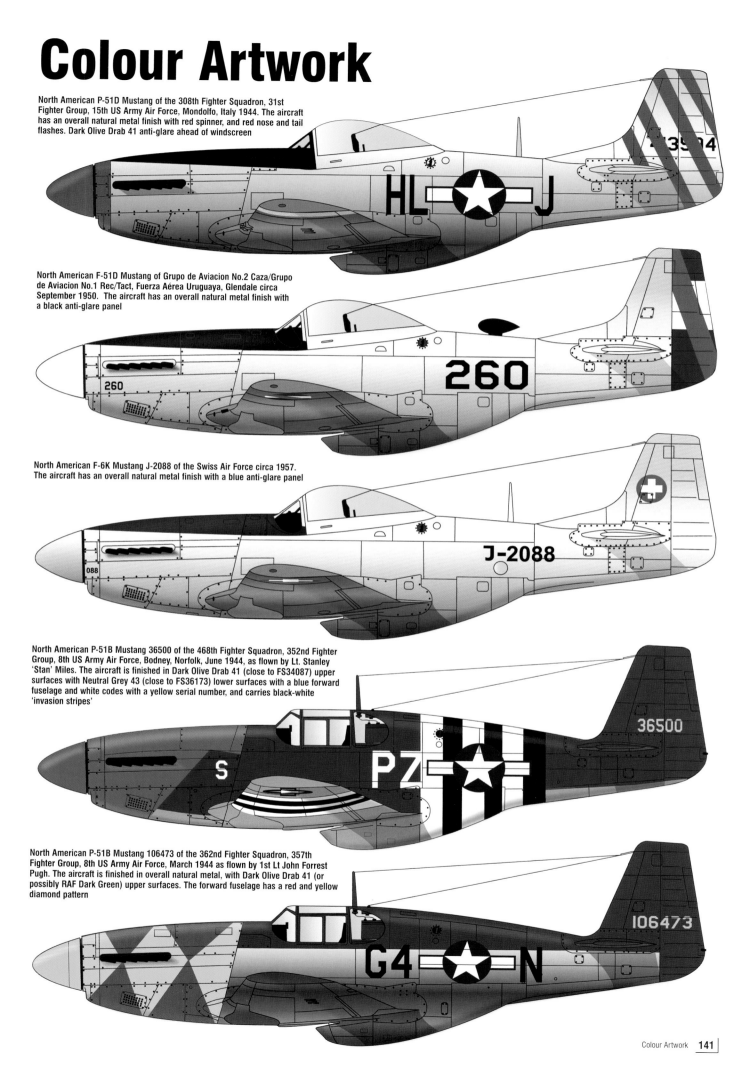

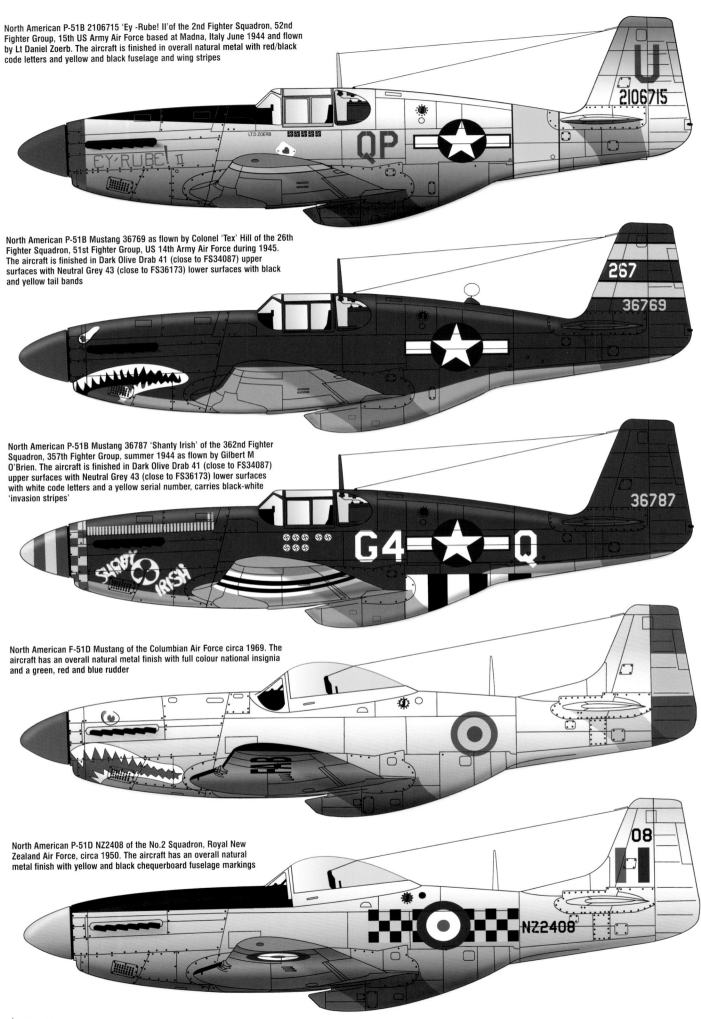

North American P-51B 2106715 'Ey -Rube! II'of the 2nd Fighter Squadron, 52nd Fighter Group, 15th US Army Air Force based at Madna, Italy June 1944 and flown by Lt Daniel Zoerb. The aircraft is finished in overall natural metal with red/black code letters and yellow and black fuselage and wing stripes

North American P-51B Mustang 36769 as flown by Colonel 'Tex' Hill of the 26th Fighter Squadron, 51st Fighter Group, US 14th Army Air Force during 1945. The aircraft is finished in Dark Olive Drab 41 (close to FS34087) upper surfaces with Neutral Grey 43 (close to FS36173) lower surfaces with black and yellow tail bands

North American P-51B Mustang 36787 'Shanty Irish' of the 362nd Fighter Squadron, 357th Fighter Group, summer 1944 as flown by Gilbert M O'Brien. The aircraft is finished in Dark Olive Drab 41 (close to FS34087) upper surfaces with Neutral Grey 43 (close to FS36173) lower surfaces with white code letters and a yellow serial number, carries black-white 'invasion stripes'

North American F-51D Mustang of the Columbian Air Force circa 1969. The aircraft has an overall natural metal finish with full colour national insignia and a green, red and blue rudder

North American P-51D NZ2408 of the No.2 Squadron, Royal New Zealand Air Force, circa 1950. The aircraft has an overall natural metal finish with yellow and black chequerboard fuselage markings

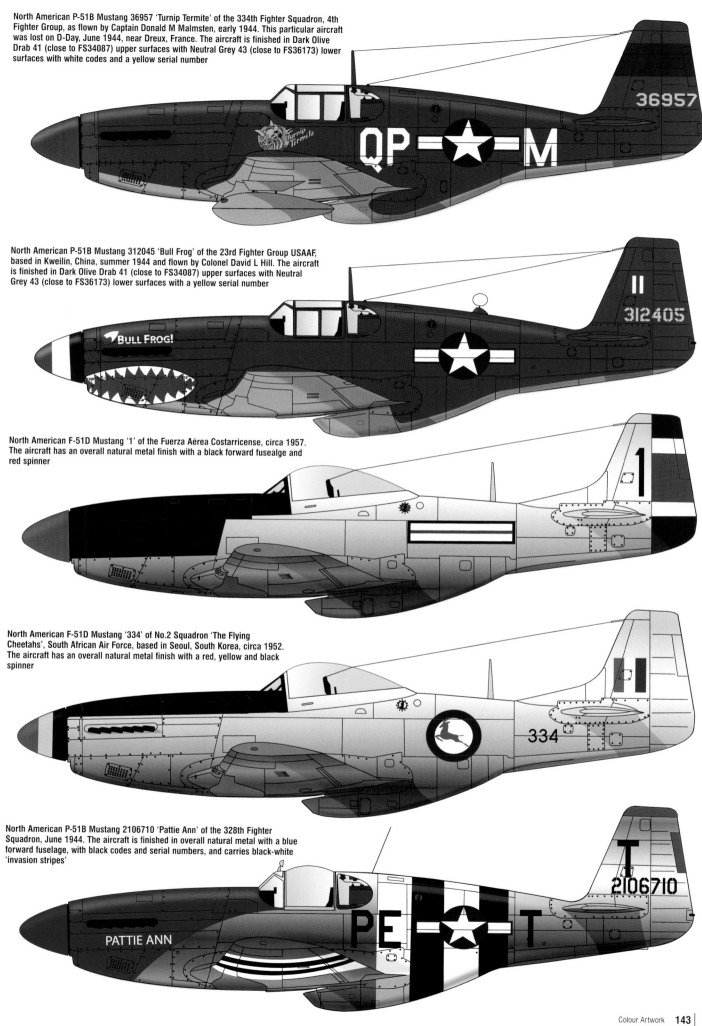

North American P-51B Mustang 36957 'Turnip Termite' of the 334th Fighter Squadron, 4th Fighter Group, as flown by Captain Donald M Malmsten, early 1944. This particular aircraft was lost on D-Day, June 1944, near Dreux, France. The aircraft is finished in Dark Olive Drab 41 (close to FS34087) upper surfaces with Neutral Grey 43 (close to FS36173) lower surfaces with white codes and a yellow serial number

North American P-51B Mustang 312045 'Bull Frog' of the 23rd Fighter Group USAAF, based in Kweilin, China, summer 1944 and flown by Colonel David L Hill. The aircraft is finished in Dark Olive Drab 41 (close to FS34087) upper surfaces with Neutral Grey 43 (close to FS36173) lower surfaces with a yellow serial number

North American F-51D Mustang '1' of the Fuerza Aérea Costarricense, circa 1957. The aircraft has an overall natural metal finish with a black forward fusealge and red spinner

North American F-51D Mustang '334' of No.2 Squadron 'The Flying Cheetahs', South African Air Force, based in Seoul, South Korea, circa 1952. The aircraft has an overall natural metal finish with a red, yellow and black spinner

North American P-51B Mustang 2106710 'Pattie Ann' of the 328th Fighter Squadron, June 1944. The aircraft is finished in overall natural metal with a blue forward fuselage, with black codes and serial numbers, and carries black-white 'invasion stripes'

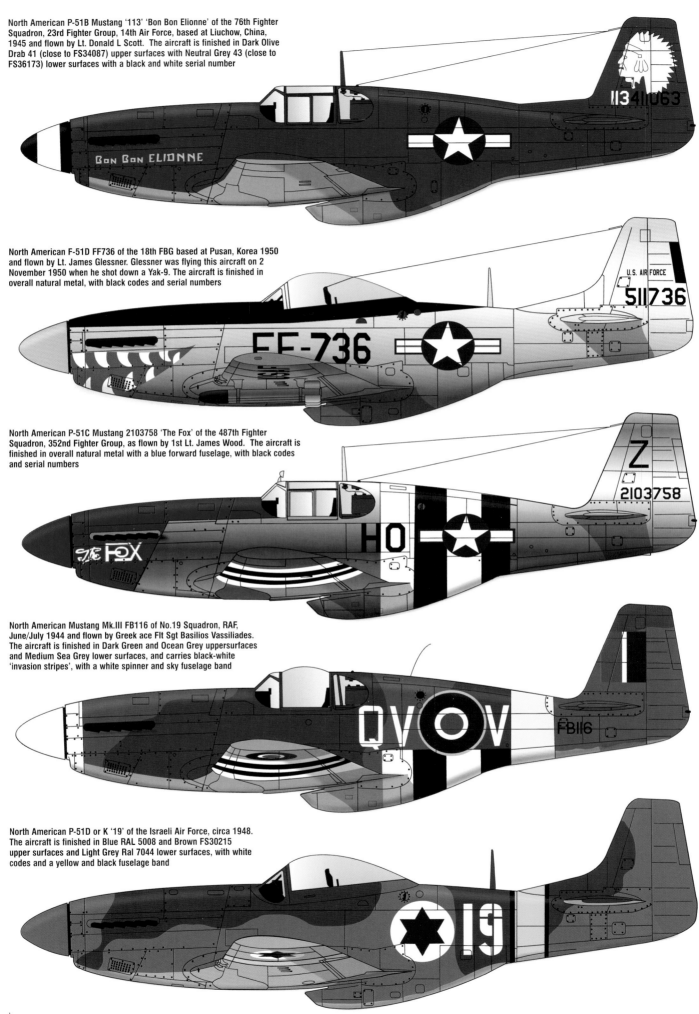

North American P-51B Mustang '113' 'Bon Bon Elionne' of the 76th Fighter Squadron, 23rd Fighter Group, 14th Air Force, based at Liuchow, China, 1945 and flown by Lt. Donald L Scott.  The aircraft is finished in Dark Olive Drab 41 (close to FS34087) upper surfaces with Neutral Grey 43 (close to FS36173) lower surfaces with a black and white serial number

North American F-51D FF736 of the 18th FBG based at Pusan, Korea 1950 and flown by Lt. James Glessner. Glessner was flying this aircraft on 2 November 1950 when he shot down a Yak-9. The aircraft is finished in overall natural metal, with black codes and serial numbers

North American P-51C Mustang 2103758 'The Fox' of the 487th Fighter Squadron, 352nd Fighter Group, as flown by 1st Lt. James Wood.  The aircraft is finished in overall natural metal with a blue forward fuselage, with black codes and serial numbers

North American Mustang Mk.III FB116 of No.19 Squadron, RAF, June/July 1944 and flown by Greek ace Flt Sgt Basilios Vassiliades. The aircraft is finished in Dark Green and Ocean Grey uppersurfaces and Medium Sea Grey lower surfaces, and carries black-white 'invasion stripes', with a white spinner and sky fuselage band

North American P-51D or K '19' of the Israeli Air Force, circa 1948. The aircraft is finished in Blue RAL 5008 and Brown FS30215 upper surfaces and Light Grey Ral 7044 lower surfaces, with white codes and a yellow and black fuselage band

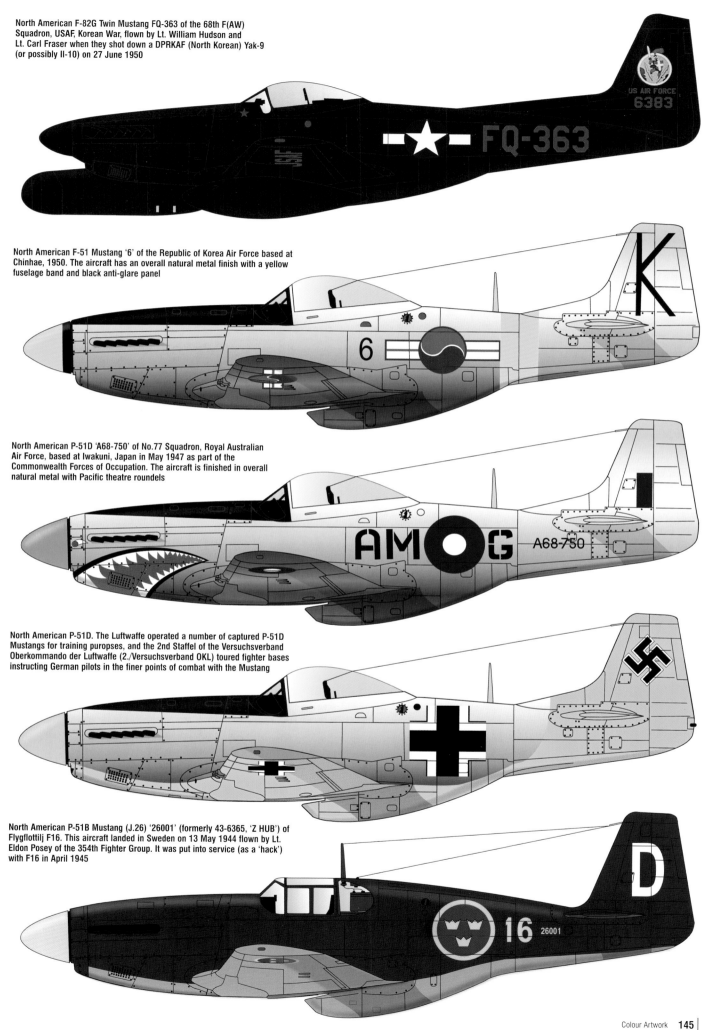

North American F-82G Twin Mustang FQ-363 of the 68th F(AW) Squadron, USAF, Korean War, flown by Lt. William Hudson and Lt. Carl Fraser when they shot down a DPRKAF (North Korean) Yak-9 (or possibly Il-10) on 27 June 1950

North American F-51 Mustang '6' of the Republic of Korea Air Force based at Chinhae, 1950. The aircraft has an overall natural metal finish with a yellow fuselage band and black anti-glare panel

North American P-51D 'A68-750' of No.77 Squadron, Royal Australian Air Force, based at Iwakuni, Japan in May 1947 as part of the Commonwealth Forces of Occupation. The aircraft is finished in overall natural metal with Pacific theatre roundels

North American P-51D. The Luftwaffe operated a number of captured P-51D Mustangs for training puropses, and the 2nd Staffel of the Versuchsverband Oberkommando der Luftwaffe (2./Versuchsverband OKL) toured fighter bases instructing German pilots in the finer points of combat with the Mustang

North American P-51B Mustang (J.26) '26001' (formerly 43-6365, 'Z HUB') of Flygflottilj F16. This aircraft landed in Sweden on 13 May 1944 flown by Lt. Eldon Posey of the 354th Fighter Group. It was put into service (as a 'hack') with F16 in April 1945

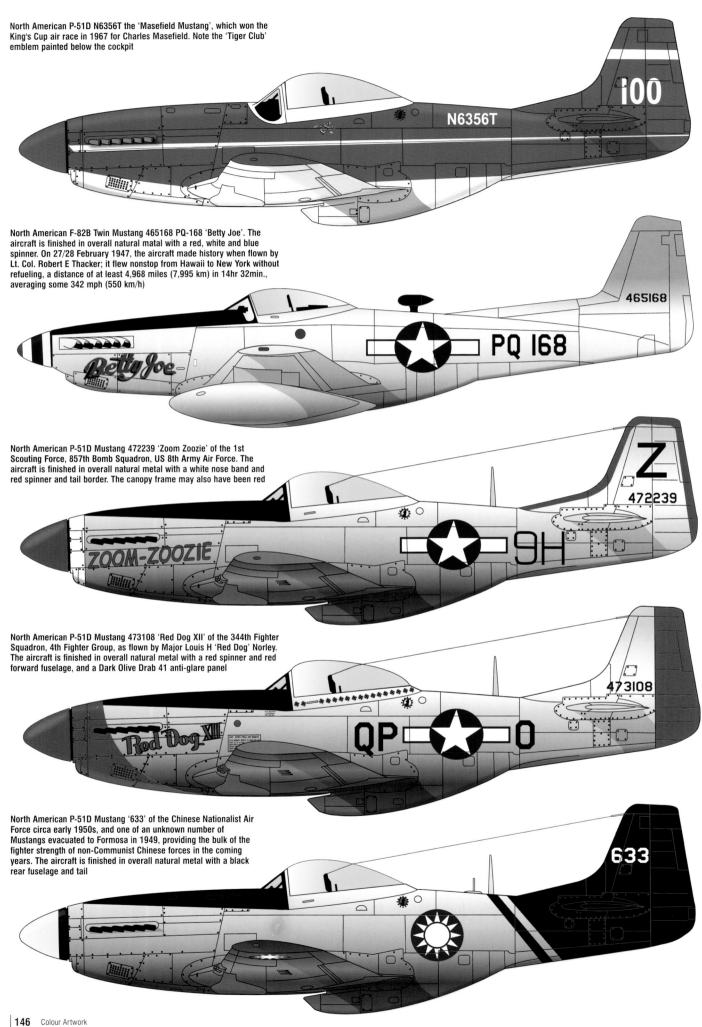

North American P-51D N6356T the 'Masefield Mustang', which won the King's Cup air race in 1967 for Charles Masefield. Note the 'Tiger Club' emblem painted below the cockpit

North American F-82B Twin Mustang 465168 PQ-168 'Betty Joe'. The aircraft is finished in overall natural matal with a red, white and blue spinner. On 27/28 February 1947, the aircraft made history when flown by Lt. Col. Robert E Thacker; it flew nonstop from Hawaii to New York without refueling, a distance of at least 4,968 miles (7,995 km) in 14hr 32min., averaging some 342 mph (550 km/h)

North American P-51D Mustang 472239 'Zoom Zoozie' of the 1st Scouting Force, 857th Bomb Squadron, US 8th Army Air Force. The aircraft is finished in overall natural metal with a white nose band and red spinner and tail border. The canopy frame may also have been red

North American P-51D Mustang 473108 'Red Dog XII' of the 344th Fighter Squadron, 4th Fighter Group, as flown by Major Louis H 'Red Dog' Norley. The aircraft is finished in overall natural metal with a red spinner and red forward fuselage, and a Dark Olive Drab 41 anti-glare panel

North American P-51D Mustang '633' of the Chinese Nationalist Air Force circa early 1950s, and one of an unknown number of Mustangs evacuated to Formosa in 1949, providing the bulk of the fighter strength of non-Communist Chinese forces in the coming years. The aircraft is finished in overall natural metal with a black rear fuselage and tail

# Modelling the Mustang in Popular Scales

## Chapter 12

## Cripes A' Mighty!

A 1:24 P-51D Mustang in the markings of 8th Air Force Ace Major George Preddy by Paul Carroll

### North American P-51D Mustang IV

Manufacturer: Trumpeter
Scale: 1:24
Kit Type: Plastic injection moulded with etch
Kit Number: TU02401

### Trumpeter

Trumpeter's big Mustang comes in a sturdy box containing fifteen sprues with one dedicated to rubber parts for various pieces of piping. There is a bag of springs and rods and an

8th Air Force Ace Major George Preddy

etched frame for the control surface hinges (**Photos 1, 2 and 3**). Trumpeter has produced a very nice set of cast rubber tyres with a diamond tread pattern, and although not to everybody's taste I feel that with careful sanding they really can look like the real thing. There is a film for the instrument panel, a decal sheet, a three-view colour scheme drawing and an instruction book together with three well cast resin figures. I do find Trumpeter's colour indications often spurious and somewhat vague and unhelpful, but good research material, including colour photographs, will usually overcome this sort of problem.

### Cockpit

Trumpeter provides a good basis for the cockpit, although I thought that the oxygen hose was too thin and lacked character so I replaced it with a piece of guitar string which replicates the texture of oxygen hose quite well. I also used MDC's excellent 1:24 Seat Harness set for USAAF fighters. I am slightly perplexed as to why Trumpeter provides etched hinges for the control surfaces but no harness or even buckles for the cockpit! There are a number of decals for the instrument panel, radio and cockpit walls that help to reproduce the Mustang's 'office' and the K14 gunsight is well represented. Using my trusty Waldron punch and die set I punched two small discs of clear plastic

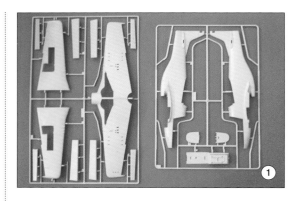

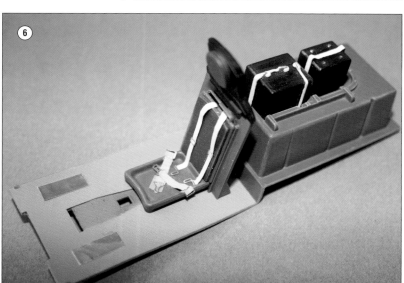

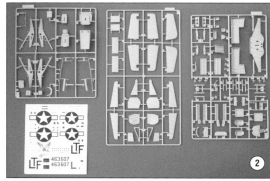

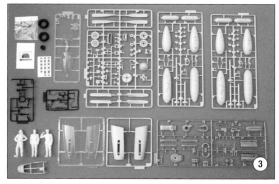

from the edge of the instrument film to reproduce the two lenses on top of the gunsight just below the reflector (**Photos 4 and 5**). As with all kits, the cockpit is what you make of it and Trumpeter provide enough material, minus that seat harness, to produce a very good representation of that part of the aeroplane. The floor in Mustangs was made of plywood and images show different shades depending on age and use. I painted mine Humbrol 63. I then used Xtracolor Interior Green for the cockpit and fuselage interiors. There are two metal heel plates just in front of the rudder pedals and I replicated these from pieces of aluminium food tray, which is a fantastic source of scale sheet metal! (**Photos 6, 7 and 8**)

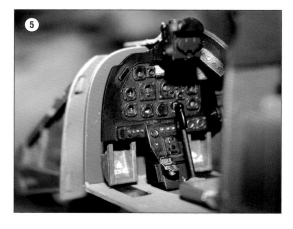

## Engine

The Rolls-Royce (Packard) Merlin replica in the kit goes together well and is a fair and reasonably accurate representation of the original. Obviously there are a lot of pipes and wires missing, but for the dedicated super detailer the kit engine provides a perfect starting point (**Photo 9**). The engine can be viewed through transparent plastic engine covers if so desired, but I chose to use the grey plastic parts, thus hiding it forever. I have always avoided working parts and feel that if you want to display the engine, leave the covers off (**Photo 10**). There is a slight gap between the engine cover and fuselage that is easily filled (**Photo 11**). The spinner and propeller assembly is positive, but I feel that the shape of the blades is slightly suspect, though not enough to detract from the overall appearance of the aeroplane.

## Airframe

On the whole the fit of the main airframe parts is very good. Aligning the two fuselage halves is critical to ensure that 'steps' do not develop. When the fuselage contains such a wealth of detail as this one in the form of engine, cockpit and bulkheads, even more care has to be exercised. In spite of such care, I had to resort to my 'big plane clamp' in the form of my trusty Black and Decker Workmate in order to line up the top and bottom of the model (**Photo 12**). Each subject needs a different approach and the Mustang's belly radiator proved to be a difficult shape to clamp. The tail wheel leg has to be glued between the fuselage halves and is vulnerable to breakage during the remaining construction. Yes, I broke it, so I drilled holes in the axle and the leg and used a piece of steel rod from the kit's hinge system, which I superglued into the two holes. This is a useful undercarriage leg repair system and pins or needles can also be used to reinforce the joint. The wing-to-fuselage joint was nearly perfect, as was that of the tailplanes-to-fuselage.

I used small pieces of aluminium tubing for the muzzles of the machine guns and also for the gun camera that was mounted in the port wing root. Note that the guns are staggered, with the longest protrusion being each of the outer barrels. There is a small airscoop on the port side of the kit that should be removed and filled for WWII era aircraft. The panels that cover the gun bays do not all fit as well as they should; again careful filling is necessary and I also blanked off the holes for the

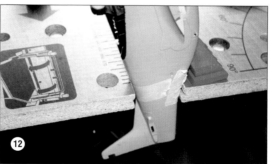

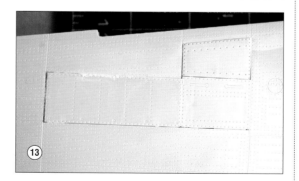

rocket pylons using scrap from the kit's sprues (**Photo 13**). Trumpeter supplies its customary hinge system and I chose to omit this feature, gluing control surfaces and flaps directly to the airframe. The main undercarriage is sprung and again I chose not to use this working feature in order to achieve a more realistic sit. A plethora of 'things under wings' is supplied and I selected the sixty-gallon metal tanks, as the subject that I had chosen appeared to be carrying these in a number of photographs.

## Markings

The Mustang carried some of the best nose art in WWII, but Trumpeter chose a fairly neutral subject in Glen Eaglestone's aircraft (**Photo 14**). Trumpeter's decals are reasonable offerings and have always worked well for me. However, the kit decal sheet fails miserably on the stars-and-bars, which are far too light in colour. This was enough to set me off on producing the aircraft of a personal hero, Major George E 'Ratsy' Preddy, third highest-scoring USAAF ace in the European Theatre of Operations. Eagle Strike produces an excellent sheet of three aircraft from the 352nd Fighter Group including George's Cripes A' Mighty (**Photo 15**). This aircraft - 44-14906/PE-P was the last he flew, and the fourth to bear the name.

## Painting and Decaling

I always fear natural metal finishes. I realise that to some this may seem irrational, but we all have these demons lurking and natural metal is one of mine. I thought long and hard about how I would attempt to clad my Mustang in faux aluminium. Eventually I sprayed the whole airframe with Tamiya acrylic aluminium from an aerosol can. This product is surprisingly good and beats airbrushing when you have too much real work to do, or do not have access to an airbrush. I hung the model from a beam in the garage using a coat hanger inserted in the tail. Tamiya's acrylic aerosol produced a deep, realistic metal appearance that to my eye looks like the finish that wartime Mustangs sported. The other main colour on the 352nd FG aircraft was medium blue which gave them their appropriate nickname, The Blue Nosed 'Birds' of Bodney.

I used Frisk-Film to mask off the main airframe in order to paint the blue nose. Once the film was in place I used a flexible curve with a piece of double-sided tape on the back to hold it firmly against the side of the nose as a guide for the brand new scalpel blade that I used to very carefully cut through the film. I cannot overstress the need for a new blade and gentle pressure or you will produce a new and unwanted 'panel line'. I masked the spinner at the same time, and for the blue I used another Tamiya aerosol. Eagle Strike make excellent decals but they are

rather affectionate! Once dipped in water and released from their backing sheet they have a tendency to adhere to fingers rather than models. To overcome this problem, simply ensure that you have a cotton wool bud at hand to cajole the decal onto the correct surface. Copious amounts of Micro Set will also help position the decals.

There are six red 'teardrop' decals which are supposed to be mounted around each gun; however, I chose to paint mine as I found it difficult to get the decals to conform to the compound curves in those areas. Once the decals had dried I set to work with a tube of Burnt Sienna watercolour paint that I ran into the recessed panel lines. Once dry I removed most of this with a dry cotton cloth, which I use for this task as it leaves a deposit where needed - a wet cloth will remove all of the paint. The guns and exhaust stacks were treated to a light spray of Tamiya smoke.

## Final Details

I decided that I would replicate the radio aerial wire using fishing line, and then had to face the challenge of drilling a hole in the canopy through which to pass it! I used a pin-vice with the finest drill bit in my possession and carefully drilled through the underside into the aerial fairing which is mounted on the outside of the canopy. I then drilled a small hole in the back of the pilot's seat, another in the front of the fin and then spent some minutes threading a length of fishing wire through the canopy. Once it was through the canopy I superglued one end into a pre-drilled hole in the back of the seat and let it set. Having placed the canopy on its rails I then superglued the other end through the hole that I had drilled in the leading-edge of the fin and pulled it taught.

There has been some debate as to whether Mustangs of this period had aerials that were mounted through the canopy. Having looked at hundreds of photos the one thing that is difficult to discern is the aerial wire between the cockpit and tail but I have found one clear photo showing such an arrangement. I am sure that the many fine aviation artists who have depicted this aerial arrangement have also done their research. I drilled it and fitted it anyway. And besides, you can hardly see it in some lighting conditions!

For the signal lights under the wing I used my Waldron punch-and-die set to remove three discs from the end of some developed film, each one a different shade. As digital photography takes over, I am beginning to hoard every last scrap of such material, including unsuccessful slides. The formation lights were painted with Tamiya clear red and green.

The cockpit canopy is separate from the frame and requires careful use of your chosen adhesive to join it. I would have preferred a one-piece canopy and frame. George Preddy's aircraft carried two rear-view mirrors on the cockpit frame, items that I fabricated from sprue and two fins from an AMRAAM missile. I used some chocolate-bar wrapper foil for the silver in the mirrors, and clear plastic punched from the excess left from around the kit's instrument film.

# Dominican Fighter - The Mustang's Last Ride

1:72 Fuerza Aérea de Republica Dominicana F-51D by Mark Taylor

### North American F-51D Mustang

Manufacturer: Airfix
Scale: 1:72
Kit Type: Plastic injection moulded
Kit Number: 02047

The Dominican Republic became one of the signatories of the Inter-American Treaty of Reciprocal Assistance, better known as the 'Rio Pact' after the location of the first meeting and signings. After this it was able to procure quantities of aircraft from the United States, which included twenty-five P-47Ds and thirty AT-6 trainers. In 1952 the Air Force managed to purchase twenty-five Vampires and thirty-two P-51D Mustangs from Sweden, when similar purchases from Japan and Canada were blocked by the United States. The last active use of the P-51D Mustang in a combat role was carried out by the Dominican Air Force when in 1983 a flight of Mustangs strafed a Cuban Intelligence-gathering ship that refused to leave Dominican Waters. By the end of their careers the Dominican Air Force had ten Mustangs that had survived an active service of thirty-six years. Of these nine were sold to Johnson Aviation for a sum of 3.6 million US Dollars, which was roughly the same amount that was paid originally for all the Mustangs bought in the 1950s. In all they were not a bad investment!

Since the re-emergence of Airfix onto the kit market I have built a few of their new-tooled aircraft such as the P-40B, Zero and MiG-15, and Airfix like a lot of manufacturers these days are taking note of reviews and criticisms and are constantly improving their new releases. Many people comment on the depth of the panel lines on Airfix aircraft, and on their earlier new releases these were quite pronounced, but on the new Mustang, I have to say that I feel that they are very acceptable, and allow for them still to be seen after either brush or airbrush painting. In the box you will find three grey plastic sprues, the extra sprue consisting of underwing stores of two 500lb bombs and six rockets along with an uncuffed, square-tipped Hamilton Standard propeller. A sprue of clear parts includes two types of canopy, windscreen, landing light and gunsight. The decal sheet has markings for two aircraft, one USAF Korean War Mustang of the 12th Fighter Bomber

The decal sheet, showing both sets of markings, stencils and instrument panel decal in the top left corner

Eduard's photo-etch set for the cockpit interior

The resin extras used

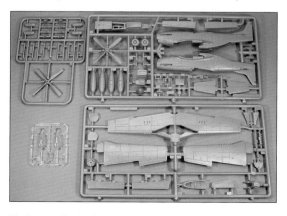

Plastic parts, showing the additional sprue top left

**Cockpit sidewalls, showing the level of moulded details**

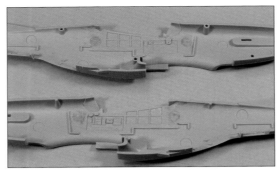

**The internal structure goes from the cockpit right back to include the rear wheel well**

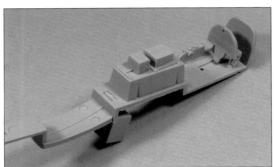

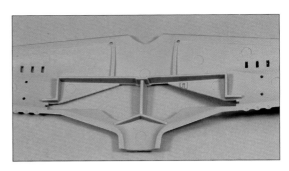

**The one-piece lower wing, note the opened spent case ejection ports**

**Detailing the cockpit with the addition of etched parts for the instrument panel, side console and battery boxes. Note the added wires for the battery box**

**The completed cockpit with the pilot's seat in place along with the joystick**

Squadron of the 18th Fighter Bomber Group, and one for the Dominican Republic Air Force. The sheet also includes a full set of stencils along with a decal for the instrument panel, this latter being a good inclusion for beginners or those who do not wish to invest in aftermarket accessories. The instructions are excellent with all colour call-outs for Humbrol Paints and three plan charts - two in colour for the individual aircraft markings and one in black and white showing stencil locations. To enhance this model further I decided to invest in the Quickboost replacement hollowed-out exhaust units and a replacement seat with back pad and harness. From Eduard came an etched set to improve the cockpit along with Kabuki masks for the canopy. Lastly from the Eduard 'Brassin' range came some replacement wheels, and although these were for the Tamiya kit, at the time of writing there were none specifically for the Airfix kit.

Construction began with the cockpit, and here Airfix have taken the decision to have the internal structure go from the engine firewall area all the way back including the fixture for the radiator assembly ending up at the rear wheel well. The Eduard coloured etched detail set gives you the full instrument panel and bomb arming panel beneath it, along with two replacement sidewalls for the cockpit. On looking at this set and the kit, I was torn between the two. The kit has some very nice, but limited, three-dimensional sidewall details, whereas the Eduard set has some lovely painted replacement panels that are really too flat (a limitation of the etching process). My decision was a compromise in using the best of both parts. The cockpit was part assembled by gluing in the

instrument panel (first sanding it down to accept the etched replacement later on) The mounting block for the seat was carefully carved away in preparation for the resin one, and the ejector pin holes were filled and sanded smooth. The left hand side console was kept, and the two boxes behind the pilot's seat had their dimensions reduced by carving away some of the plastic. This was done so that the replacement boxes in the Eduard set could be made to fit over them and have some form of structure to glue them to.

At this point the interior and pilot's seat were given a primer coat of Halford's Grey from a spray can, and when this was dry I then airbrushed the interior and seat with Vallejo Model Air Interior Green 010. The etched instrument panel and bomb arming panel were glued in place. I then constructed the battery boxes and fitted them over the plastic formers that I had left, and control wheels and levers from the Eduard set were fitted to the left hand side console. My attention then turned to the sidewalls, after picking out the box details with Citadel Paints' Chaos Black. I then painted the oxygen hose with their Catachan Green. Next I cherry-picked which items I was going to use off the etched set, these being the throttle quadrant, which was attached over the raised plastic detail, along with the oxygen regulator control and the radio switching panel, and again these were fitted over the existing detail to give a much more realistic three-dimensional effect to the cockpit.

It was now that I realised that I was losing out on some of the printed details on the etched set, these being the data panels that are fitted around the interior of the cockpit. Now, I had an etched set from Eduard in the past where the painted/printed detail came away from the metal. This got me thinking as to whether there was any way to shave off the printed panels that I wanted. So, taking a new small chisel blade for my craft knife I tried to shave off the panels and was quite successful. These were then affixed in the relevant places using superglue. The last item to paint and fit was the joystick and a word of warning here - this is a very fine moulding and even with delicate and careful cutting I still managed to snap it in half. The interior section had the pre-painted radiator fixed in place and then the whole structure was glued into the left side of the fuselage. When this was fully fixed I

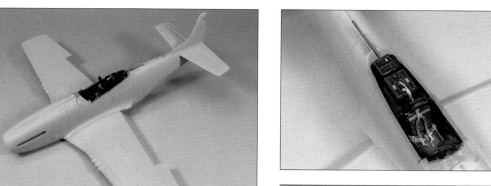

It finally looks like an aircraft! The cockpit is in place and the wings are fitted. Most joint seams have been smoothed by this stage

A top down shot of how the pilot's office looks in place

A shot of the underside showing the lowered flaps and the attachment of sway braces to the ordnance racks

went about joining the fuselage halves, starting with the nose section joint to the cockpit on the upper edge and to the opening for the wing join on the lower.

Liquid poly was brushed onto both sides of the joining edges and left for a few seconds, the sides were then pressed together and the joint straightened up so that there was as little a lip between them as possible. This was allowed to dry before tackling the rear joint in the same manner. When these had been allowed to dry sufficiently I went about the process of smoothing the joins with a combination of Squadron sanding sticks and small pieces of wet and dry abrasive paper, finally finishing off with a polishing stick. Prior to assembling the main wing a decision has to be made as to what underwing stores the aircraft is going to carry, either rockets or bombs. The supplied drop tanks I decided are not really an option for the Dominican fighter as the fuel capacity of the aircraft without them was sufficient for all their operations. This seems to be borne out by the few photographs to be found online that show either clean aircraft with no underwing stores or mounts for rockets or bombs. I decided to use the bomb mounts so opened up the relevant holes, and whilst doing this I decided to open up the spent case ejection ports for the wing guns. To do this I used a curved blade in my craft knife and gradually shaved the internal plastic down until just a thin film of plastic covered the ports. I then took a new long pointed blade and used it carefully to remove the remaining plastic covering the ports. When all of this was done the left and right wing upper pieces were glued onto the lower.

The visible joins were left to dry and then cleaned up in the same fashion as the fuselage joint as described above. I will point out that the joint around the projections for the wing guns is not very good and is very difficult to fill and clean up. To address this problem took some time, gradually closing up the gap as much as possible with liquid cement and waiting for it to dry. Then I used a combination of a sharp knife blade and fine strips of wet and dry paper folded to give a thin sanding edge to clean up the joint. The fit of the completed wing to the fuselage is very good and there is almost no gap in the upper wing joint to speak of. The horizontal stabilisers were cleaned up and fitted with no problems, as was the rudder. The radiator air intake scoop was fitted and also the chin scoop, again these exhibited a good standard of fit and gave no problems to align properly.

The entire model was given a final look-over to check for any imperfections or problems prior to being washed with detergent and then given a clean with a piece of kitchen roll dampened with a 50:50 mix of airbrush paint cleaner and water. All of the pieces to be attached later were also cleaned up in preparation for priming and painting. The cockpit had a piece of sponge inserted to protect it prior to the area being masked off for painting using Blu Tack. I wanted the option of leaving the canopy loose so as to be able to

display it in either the open or closed position. It was at this point that when I tried some dry-fitting that I realised that due to the thickness of the plastic on the lower canopy part 14B that it would not sit forward enough to close the gap with the front canopy and windscreen section. This was due to the inner face hitting the battery boxes. (Note: I imagine that this will not be the case with the unmodified interior). The thickness was also a problem when it came to having the canopy open as again it would not sit correctly in relation to the aircraft sides. This meant that if the canopy sat flush at its front when open, the rear would be up away from the aircraft body and vice versa. The solution was a lot of carving and sanding to thin the walls of the plastic down to a more scale thickness and a lot of test-fitting until the part would sit correctly in both positions.

The model and loose items were then given a coat of Halford's Grey primer from an aerosol can. When this had dried the airframe was once again checked for any imperfections, which showed that the front fuselage join still needed some attention to give a seamless finish. This was addressed by further sanding and polishing. A new coat of primer was then sprayed onto this area only and left to dry. When checked later I was happy with the resulting finish and the main painting could progress. I began by giving the whole model some pre-shading along the panel lines and wing roots with Vallejo Black Grey 056. This was followed by spraying White 001 with a couple of drops of US Light Grey 045 to take away the pure brightness of the white and give it a discoloured finish. The outer surfaces of the main undercarriage doors were also sprayed at this stage.

Looking at colour photos of Dominican Mustangs and allowing for differences in film stock colour and exposure it can be seen that the undersides can vary in shade from nearly pure white to a variation of light to mid greys. When the underside was completed and dried it was masked off in preparation for the upper camouflage. Some internet sources state that the colours used on these aircraft are the same as those on US aircraft operating in South East Asia during the Vietnam War. This I am unsure of as there seems to be a similarity, but again any differences could be down to variations in film and exposure.

The upper green was sprayed with Vallejo US Dark Green 016 as a match to Humbrol 116 on the paint chart. The lower section of the cockpit canopy, Part 14B, and the masked canopy parts were also painted at this stage. The patches of tan camouflage were masked off in stages and were sprayed with Vallejo Sandy Brown 034 for Humbrol 118. Both of these colours were lightened slightly with a

The aircraft with the decals applied and small detail painting completed

drop or two of white. All of the separate pieces to be added later were painted with their respective colours at this stage. When the model had been left long enough for the paint to dry the masking was removed and the full effect of the paintwork could be assessed. On inspection some of the green areas had a bit of inadvertent overspray of the tan paint. This was corrected by remixing a small amount of the green and turning down the pressure on the airbrush and touching in the required areas freehand.

The resin exhausts were hand panted with Citadel Boltgun Metal layered with thin washes of a mix of Terracotta and Dark Flesh to indicate a slight amount of rusting. The exhaust openings were picked out using Black applied with a very fine brush. The exposed area of the lowered flap hinges was hand painted with Mithril Silver, which gives a nice contrast to the camouflage on the wings. The whole aircraft and relevant loose pieces were given a couple of coats of Johnson's Klear and left to dry for twenty-four hours in preparation for applying the decals.

I had already decided to keep any weathering on the project to a minimum. I had initially thought that these aircraft would probably be in a very weary state given their age and usage, however, all the photographic evidence contradicts this idea. The aircraft look to have been very well cared for and do not show any real indication of daily wear and tear. Now here is a tale of why researching a subject is a must. Having decided to model the Dominican Air Force Mustang I went online to check out what few photographs there are of it in their service. I noted the colours, the lack of wear and tear on the airframes, the styles of the camouflage patterns and that no two schemes were the same. The one thing I overlooked was the markings themselves as I assumed that the marking chart in the instructions was correct.

It was only after I had started and positioned the upper left wing roundel that something nagged me at the back of my mind. I went back to my sources and noticed that the instruction chart is incorrect. A study of all the images I could find always showed that of the quadrants in the roundel, the upper left one as viewed is always blue. This means the only one shown correctly on the chart

is that on the left fuselage side. The one on the upper wing should show the blue quadrant in the upper left position pointing towards the front edge and left wing tip, and correspondingly the lower right wing as viewed from below shows the blue in the same position facing the wing edge and wing tip. Back to the aircraft and the fact that having only one set of decals and that the one applied was now incorrect and that I could do nothing to rectify it, I continued with the rest of the application. The decals performed well and settled down nicely with an application of Micro Sol setting solution. There is a method I use for decals that have a lot of clear backing film in order to prevent any chance of silvering due to trapped air, and this was used on the tail markings of this aircraft. Prior to dipping the decal and backing paper in warm water I take a sharp pointed craft knife blade and using the very tip make a series of pin-prick holes in the clear areas of the decal. This helps to serve two purposes, firstly after initial application of the decal it allows any trapped air to escape when it is pressed down onto the surface; secondly it also allows any setting solution to penetrate the decal easier.

The only weathering applied was some slight exhaust staining using a fine misting of a 50:50 mix of Vallejo Black Grey 056 and Rust 080, and a small amount of paint chipping on the left rear wing root where the pilot and ground crew would access the aircraft. The model was given another coat of Klear to seal and protect the decals. The area surrounding the wheel wells was masked off and the interior was sprayed with Vallejo Chromate Green 094. This was then given a wash of Citadel Badab Black and the area dry brushed with Codex Grey to bring out the raised details. The model and all the loose pieces were then given a final spray of Vallejo Matt Varnish 059 to return it to a more natural finish. When I was happy that all the parts were dry and finished I began to attach all the loose items to the main airframe. The oleo legs were glued in place and when dry the wheels were fixed into position, and the tail wheel was also attached at this stage. I feel that doing all of the undercarriage in one go allows me to check for the correct sit of the aircraft as it allows you time to adjust the leg and wheel angles or positions while the glue is still drying. The undercarriage doors were then fixed in place, and also the landing light.

The exhausts were glued into their openings and fit really well, and the propeller was attached. The front windscreen was glued into place and the rear clear canopy part was glued to the pre-painted and thinned-down lower section. The whole rear canopy section was then put in place and not glued. I was really pleased with the more natural sit of this part when comparing it to photographs of full-sized Mustangs. I was very pleased with how this model turned out and I found it a very enjoyable build. The breakdown of parts is near identical to the Tamiya Mustang in the same scale, and having built both now I feel that the Airfix kit compares very favourably, and at better than half the cost too. In fact the only real difference between the two is that the Tamiya model included the retraction arms for the inner main gear doors, but these could have been added using thin plastic rod. This kit for the money is, in my opinion, one of the best on the market.

# Stang!

'…an accurate model of an 'inaccurate' aeroplane…' by Mike Grant

**North American F-51D Mustang**

Manufacturer: Airfix
Scale: 1:72
Kit Type: Plastic injection moulded
Kit Number: 02047

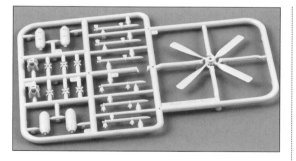

An additional sprue of rockets and an uncuffed prop is included in the F-51D boxing

W hen Airfix announced this kit, I must confess I was amongst the naysayers who questioned whether the modelling world really needed another 1:72 P-51D, after all there were several excellent Mustangs already out there! The article subject was built from the post-war F-51D boxing of the kit, which comes with Korean War and Dominican markings, and the box also contains a sprue specific to this version which carries the underwing rockets and an uncuffed prop.

There's a virtually unlimited number of colour schemes applicable to the P-51D and literally hundreds of aftermarket decal options, but a group build of 'Museum Displays' on the Unofficial Airfix Modellers' Forum inspired the choice for this model. On a recent trip to a museum in Mesa, Arizona, I'd taken some photos of an airworthy, restored P-51D carrying the name 'Stang'. While many Warbirds are finished in authentic colour schemes, in this case no attempt had been made to replicate a genuine WWII aircraft. The main camouflage colour was a vivid blue that contrasted nicely with the yellow nose and red-and-white nose art, itself rendered in a very 1980s looking script. This unconventional paint job appealed to my contrary nature, as did the prospect of trying to build an accurate model of an 'inaccurate' aeroplane. And, as a friend gleefully suggested, I could enter it in the civilian category at model contests and really upset the judges…

## Cockpit

'Stang' is a two-seater Mustang, so the first task was to convert the kit cockpit accordingly. I'm unsure as to whether the second seat is merely for a passenger, or whether there are some duplicate controls installed, and since an online search returned no photos of the actual interior some artistic liberties were taken. Airfix supply a very nice interior, with well defined sidewall details. Rudder pedals are moulded integrally with the instrument panel, for which a gauges decal is supplied. The pilot's seat is simplified but acceptable, although I opted to use a replacement from a scrap Academy kit, which included a seat harness. The radio equipment behind the seat was sawn off and the floor extended to accommodate the second seat. This was a resin item sourced from the spares box; it probably isn't correct but looks OK in-situ.

A replacement pilot's seat was sourced from the Academy P-51D kit, while the second seat was a resin item from the spares box

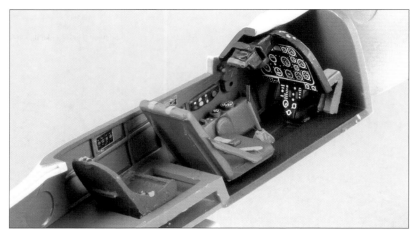

Strips of masking tape held the wings in place with correct dihedral while the glue dried

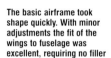

The completed cockpit looks suitably cluttered

The basic airframe took shape quickly. With minor adjustments the fit of the wings to fuselage was excellent, requiring no filler

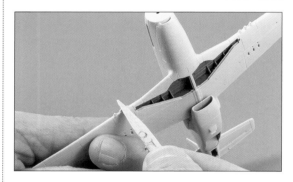

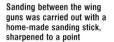

Sanding between the wing guns was carried out with a home-made sanding stick, sharpened to a point

The wing guns are little more than plastic nubs so they were sliced off, holes drilled and replacements from hypodermic tubing inserted

Micro-mesh cloths of successively finer grades were used to polish the plastic prior to painting

One of the complaints made of recent Airfix toolings is the thickness of the sprues where the parts connect, and that's certainly the case with the Mustang kit. For major parts such as wings and fuselage halves it's hardly an issue, but the smaller parts do require great care in separating them. In some cases a fine razor saw rather than a knife was used to prevent snapping, but even so the fragile joystick was an early casualty and had to be replaced with a scratchbuilt item. Most of the cockpit was airbrushed with Xtracrylix Interior Green (XA1117), followed by a pin wash of dark brown. The floor and some of the sidewall panels were painted black, and then various buttons and cables

picked out using Vallejo acrylics. Various placards from my own 1:72 cockpit decals sheet (CKP072) added a little extra clutter to the interior. Without thinking I went ahead and installed the clear gunsight (part 1D), and it wasn't until the model was finished that I realised this civilian restoration didn't carry one. Before joining the fuselage halves the radiator exhaust was glued to the underside of the cockpit floor, the part having previously been painted silver and given a dark grey wash to accentuate the detail. The inclusion of the grille is a nice touch from Airfix, as it is visible when viewing the model from the rear. It's also worth painting the tail-wheel bay at this stage as it's hard to access once the fuselage is complete.

## Main Assembly

The fit of the fuselage halves was exemplary, a fine bead of liquid cement quickly bonding them securely together. Airfix suggest the inclusion of the propeller assembly at this stage too, but I figured the fragile blades would be prone to snapping as the model was handled, so it was left off until later. The lower wing is moulded as one piece, to which the upper halves are attached, but not without first having drilled out the relevant holes for the underwing stores. There's some excellent detail in the wheel wells, which looks even better after a wash and some light dry brushing. The completed wing assembly can now be glued to the fuselage, although in my case it wasn't without its problems. Because the fit at the wing root was so tight, the wings were forced downwards resulting in a loss of dihedral. This was rectified by gradually shaving off styrene at the wing root mating surfaces until the wing unit slotted into place, although it still took a little wrangling to slide it into place below the belly intake. With care, though, the wing can be made to fit well enough to preclude the use of filler. Tailplanes and rudder virtually clipped into place, only minor adjustments being needed to ensure the elevators were exactly perpendicular to the fin. A really nice feature of the Airfix kit is the inclusion of a set of dropped flaps, which slot firmly into position so tightly that glue isn't required.

## Undercarriage

Besides the wing fit issue, the only other minor problem encountered during the build was with the undercarriage. There's nothing wrong with the accuracy or the detail; the parts are well moulded, and the wheels even have flat spots where they contact the ground. The problem derives from the softness of the plastic, as the main legs seem to lack rigidity, but with superglue, care in alignment and by leaving the model propped up off the ground while everything hardened, it does eventually come together. If you're modelling the kit with wheels up (and Airfix do supply a pilot figure) you'll have no problems, and kudos must be given to the manufacturer for the engineering of the undercarriage doors. They fit tightly in the closed position,

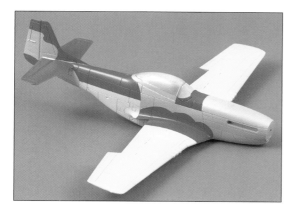

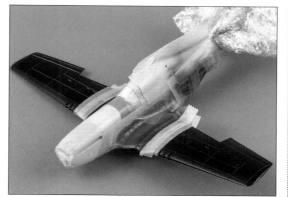

With the majority of masking removed, the model was beginning to look like its full-size counterpart.

Parafilm was used to mask the blue areas.

which came in useful at the painting stage for masking off the previously airbrushed wheel wells.

## Painting and Finishing

In common with many restored Warbirds, 'Stang's' paintwork is highly glossy. The plastic of Airfix's P-51D kit sports a slight frosted finish, which is very nice to work with and will look great under a coat of Olive Drab and Neutral Gray, but I felt the slight texture might detract from a shiny finish. Micro-mesh abrasive cloths were therefore used to polish the plastic prior to painting. The deceptively simple colour scheme is actually quite complex to reproduce. The fuselage is painted aluminium, while the outer wings are highly polished natural metal. There are irregular splotches of blue on the wings and fuselage, a yellow nose/spinner, and invasion stripes, so a lot of tedious masking was required. However it was minimised by some careful planning.

Firstly, a coat of Tamiya White Surface Primer was applied to the whole airframe, having been decanted from its aerosol can. The areas of invasion stripes on the wings and fuselage were then masked off with ParaFilm, as were the outer wings, and the fuselage sprayed silver. A mix of Tamiya AS-12 and a touch of light grey lacquer created the dullish silver shade I was looking for. The fuselage was then covered in ParaFilm and the irregular shapes of the 'camo' were cut out with a brand new #11 blade, before being airbrushed Tamiya X-14 Sky Blue. Once cured, this was covered and then the yellow nose and spinner sprayed. More masking followed before spraying the gloss black, which also formed the base coat for the wings. These were finished in Alclad Polished Aluminum, after which the model was given several coats of Johnson's 'Future'. As is often the case with a complex scheme, particularly on a small airframe like the Mustang's, the actual airbrushing time can be measured in minutes whereas several hours go into the masking procedure.

As far as I know there are no commercially available aftermarket decals for this particular aircraft, so artwork was drawn up using the many available online photos of 'Stang' as reference. Once sized to 1:72 the decals were output using an

ALPS printer. Although it has the ability to print white, the ink is not as opaque as that found on conventional screen-printed decals so I usually print duplicates of the white underlays and double them up on the model. With all markings in place a couple more coats of Future were applied, but after some deliberation I decided the model was too glossy. Although the real plane has a high gloss finish the model looked toy-like, so a few light coats of Tamiya semi-gloss varnish were airbrushed, though the polished wing areas were masked off first. I was much happier with the overall finish, and the final details and sub-assemblies were added to the model.

## Conclusion

OK, I was wrong: there was room for another 1:72 P-51D in the market after all. For me, the Airfix Mustang epitomizes enjoyable modelling. The kit is cheap, accurate, well-moulded with excellent detail but with just enough idiosyncrasies to challenge and maintain my interest. It would be nice if the panel lines were just a fraction finer, and if the sprue connections could be just a little thinner, but these are merely nit-picks of what is otherwise a very nice kit.

White underlay patches were applied first to build up the opacity of the markings

The ALPS-printed decal sheet with a few duplicate markings in case of mishaps.

# Mustang Mud Movers

A Quarter-Scale F-51 and a Photo-Recce RF-51

| North American F-51D Mustang Korean War |
| --- |
| Manufacturer: Tamiya |
| Scale: 1:48 |
| Kit Type: plastic injection moulded |
| Kit Number: 61044 |

## Tamiya

Although the USAF was well equipped with fast modern jets by the outbreak of the Korean War, the NA Mustang's 'long legs' and ordnance-carrying ability soon meant that it would prove its worth yet again. The USA was scoured for as many airworthy F-51 examples as possible, mainly from Air National Guard units, and some 145 were shipped to Korea from the USA, and ultimately equipped five USAF Fighter Bomber Wings, supplemented by South African and Australian-equipped Mustang units. Many more F-51s were later delivered to the RoKAF and the Mustang virtually became the exclusive equipment for the fledgling air force throughout the war.

## Modelling a RoKAF F-51
### by Ian Day

In order to vary the models built for this feature, Ian Day decided to finish his F-51 as one of the Mustangs flown by Major Hess, who was the advisor-in-chief to the 1st Fighter Squadron, RoKAF. Of course, in 1:48 scale, there is only one kit to choose – it has to be the Tamiya F-51 'Korean War Mustang' boxing. Complete with optional propeller blades and spinners, optional canopy hoods, HVARs, drop tanks and 500lb bombs, this superb kit has no equal in this scale and is literally a simple build-from-the-box project.

The cockpit interior was painted Interior Green, with a matt black instrument panel and gloss varnish instrument dial faces. ReHeat etched brass seat belts were added and the whole interior dry-brushed in light grey to pick out the detailing. The undercarriage door interiors were first painted a 'dirty green' colour and given a light dry-brushing of yellow and black. The whole area was then dry-brushed with Tamiya Aluminium XF-16, the finished effect being of a well used and well worn aircraft. These aircraft were used from temporary strips and were often parked on bare soil on open ground surrounding the field. Assembly was straightforward without any problems – and any filler.

First the fuselage halves were joined, followed by the tailplanes, which needed a small amount to be trimmed off the starboard unit's locating tab, front and rear, to ensure a perfectly seamless fit. The wings fitted to the fuselage perfectly, without any adjustments at all. The undernose intake and bomb racks were next, fitting into the pre-drilled holes. The canopy frame was first painted black on its mating surfaces and then the clear hood was attached. Similarly the windscreen was attached. When both were dry they were masked out using a combination of Tamiya masking tape and Maskol.

Painting started with the Olive Drab anti-glare panel on the cowling top, which when it was dry, was masked out. Then, Tamiya Silver X-11 was sprayed over the whole model. When this was completely dry, it was polished with 'SnJ' polishing powder, which has the effect of removing the slightly speckled finish you sometimes get with metallic paints. The wings (which on the real Mustangs were filled and painted silver on the production line to preserve the laminar flow) were then coated with Johnson's 'Future' and masked off. The various selected panels on the fuselage were also masked and the remainder of the fuselage was lightly misted over with Tamiya Smoke X-19. The panel lines and random other panels were given a slightly heavier 'misting' than others, which, when the masking was removed, gave a subtly contrasting natural metal effect. The exhaust manifolds, which had been left off until after painting, were now added.

When all the paint was dry, the RoKAF insignia and markings decals from the old AeroMaster decal sheet 48-099 were added. Weathering was confined to slight exhaust staining and cordite stains on the leading edges of the wings. The underwing stores were finally added, the 500lb bombs painted with olive green coloured bodies and dark green fins and the HVAR rockets with pale grey bodies, dull silver fins and Olive Drab warheads with natural metal tips. My only criticism with this Tamiya kit is the sprue tree attachment to the canopy hood. Regardless of how careful you are, cutting marks always seem to remain on the clear portion. A little redesigning of the mould would solve this, albeit minor, problem on an otherwise excellent kit.

## Modelling an RF-51
### by Neil Robinson

Not only was the F-51 the major USAF/UN ground attack fighter in the first year of the conflict, but it also proved to be an excellent photo-reconnaissance platform, which prompted Neil Robinson to modify the Tamiya kit into such an example. On September 1950, the 45th Tactical Reconnaissance Squadron was activated at Itazuke, Japan, initially equipped with 'straight' F-51Ds. The unit moved to K-2 Taegu in October, and in November received the first of the custom-built RF-51s, although because of shortage of the sub-type, in fact more operations were flown using standard F-51Ds rather than RF-51s! Despite being tasked with the deep penetration and tactical reconnaissance roles, the 45th's RF-51s retained full offensive armament capability, and although they were never committed to close support operations, they regularly attacked 'targets of opportunity'. It wasn't until mid-1952 that the 45th TRS exchanged their F/RF-51Ds for F-80Cs and RF-80As, by which time the old North American bird had flown many hundreds of hours in extensive coverage of North Korean supply routes and front-line situation evaluation.

## Modifying the Tamiya kit into an RF-51

As with all the best modifications, this is a relatively easy and straightforward exercise. Basically, the RF-51D (originally designated F-6D) carried three cameras built into the rear fuselage. A K-17 and a K-27 camera were fitted to aim out of the port fuselage half for high altitude work, with a K-24 camera mounted vertically downwards, for lower altitude work. I think it has been universally accepted that the Tamiya kit is probably the best 1:48 scale P/F-51D currently on the market, especially in the F-51D 'Korean War Mustang' boxing, which is what I used for the subject of this model. Building this kit is a real pleasure, and it goes together without any problems. Because the fit of the parts was so good, I was able to paint the 'natural metal finish' fuselage prior to fitting the wings, which received a duller 'painted silver' finish, using Dull Aluminium, to represent the laminar flow finish, with the exception of the flaps and ailerons of course, which were kept in the 'natural metal finish'.

The Olive Drab anti-glare panel in front of the windscreen appears to have come from two different aircraft, as the front section is darker than the rear section, so two 'shades' of Olive Drab were used. The propeller spinner, canopy hood sides, wing tips, tailplane tips and fin/rudder tip were painted medium blue prior to

the white decal polka dots being applied – each one separately! Both Hamilton Standard and Aeroproducts propellers were fitted to RF-51s, but the Aeroproducts blades supplied with the Tamiya kit feature 'squared-off' tips. The particular aircraft I had chosen to model had standard 'round-tipped' propeller blades, so a few minutes with the wet-and-dry was required to round the tips off. The larger of the two propeller spinners (part A1) was also used.

Drilling out the camera ports was done after the fuselage halves had been glued together, as I didn't intend (nor had I any information about) fitting representations of the cameras inside. Note that the upper fuselage-side port is much larger than the one below it, and it also has a surrounding fairing, presumably to help keep oil and dirt stains off the lens. For some reason the upper camera port surrounding fairing doesn't show up too well on the accompanying photographs of my model, but I assure you it is there, made out of a disc of thin plastic card, 'created' by a paper hole punch, with its centre drilled out. The underside camera port also appears to have a surrounding fairing too, which I 'created' in the same way. There is also a Direction Finding Loop and fairing just behind the aerial mast, which was made from a small section of shaped sprue and some fuse wire. The only other addition I made was to the cockpit interior, fitting some ReHeat brass etch seat belts. The Markings came from the AeroMaster decal sheet 48-009, 'Mustangs over Korea', suitably modified to represent 44-11911, 'Buzz Number' RF-911, based at K-14 Kimpo, South Korea, mid-1951.

# 'Alpine Air'

### An Unusual Take on a 1:48 P-51D by Mike Grant

| North American P-51D Mustang |
| --- |
| Manufacturer: Tamiya |
| Scale: 1:48 |
| Kit Type: Plastic injection moulded |
| Kit Number: 61040 |

## Tamiya

The impetus for this build of Tamiya's quarter-scale P-51D came from a discussion with a few friends at an informal model meeting in one of our homes. We settled on a plan to run a mini-contest amongst ourselves. We'd all build the same kit within a certain time-frame with the finished models judged independently by other modellers, and the winner would have dinner bought by the other entrants. Tamiya's Mustang was the subject we eventually decided on, and the only other requirement was that it should be finished in post-war markings.

I spent the next couple of weeks researching schemes and had almost settled on a USAF Air National Guard aircraft when I stumbled on a website about Swiss Mustangs. The particular aircraft I chose to model was one used by the Swiss to evaluate performance prior to placing a much larger order from the Americans, and was in a natural metal finish, rather than painted aluminium, including the wings. I was particularly

drawn to the wide red bands on the wings with the white Swiss crosses, and the similarly painted rudder – a black serial and a few stencils were the only other markings carried.

## Cockpit Construction

Tamiya's cockpit is certainly good enough to build and paint right out of the box, but I decided to replace the kit seat with a resin Ultracast item, which has finer detail and the advantage of a seat harness moulded on, sparing me having to add it from scratch or use photo-etch items. Sidewall detail is somewhat simplified and a little shallow but more than adequate. One thing that's apparent from studying photos of real P-51 cockpits is the amount of data placards that were used. I added several of these, using decals from my own cockpit-details sheet and custom making others (the ALPS printer is capable of printing a very nice silver). A couple of fuel gauges were added to the cockpit floor, although these were virtually obscured once the seat was in place. The radio equipment behind the seat is also well replicated, needing only some wiring adding.

The canopy spacer bar on part C1 should have lightening holes in it, so I drilled these out. Ultracast produce a lovely resin piece for this part but I didn't want to weaken or distort the kit

**Basic colours have been sprayed on the interior parts – US Interior Green and very dark grey**

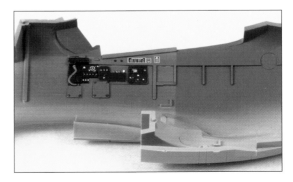

**Sidewall detail benefits from a wash to emphasise the recesses, and careful painting of the various panels and switches**

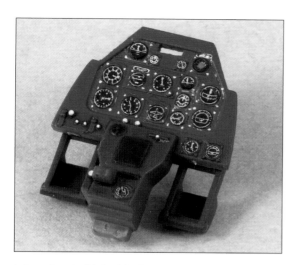

Instrument panel painted and decalled, and the big rudder pedals which attach to the back of it

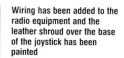

Wiring has been added to the radio equipment and the leather shroud over the base of the joystick has been painted

part by sawing off the spacer. My only gripe with this kit concerns the rear canopy which comes as two parts, the lower frame and the clear piece. Cutting the clear part from the sprue without damaging it or leaving a tiny burr of plastic is very difficult, and posing the canopy open places stress on the two-part assembly, pulling them apart. To avoid unsightly refractions along the rear canopy base I found it necessary to paint the lower edge of part D5 (or D3 if using the Dallas-built option) with black paint, before gluing it to the sliding frame.

## Fuselage and Wings

Tamiya's reputation for superb engineering is clearly justified when assembling the main airframe. Everything goes together with the finest of tolerances. The separate upper nose section with delicate rivet detail is a touch of brilliance – no sanding of the seam and subsequent elimination of surface detail. The big lower wing fits tightly to the fuselage, and the upper wing halves just drop into place without the need for any filler along the wing root seam; as far as I can recall, the only kit I've ever built where this has been the case. The tailplanes were less positive and needed holding in place while the glue dried to keep them at the correct 90° angle, but again there was little, if any, evidence of a gap. Separate flaps are a nice touch and again fit very well. In order to allow the flaps to be modelled closed the manufacturer has moulded a small indent at the flap roots to compensate for the wing-fillet trailing edge. On the full-sized aircraft there's no indentation, so if it disturbs you a corrected pair of resin flaps is available from Ultracast.

## Other Details

Alternative exhaust stacks are provided, although again I opted for an Ultracast resin set because of the superior quality. These are drop-in replacements for the kit parts and the stubs are already hollowed out. The undercarriage is also well represented with sharp wheel hub detail and tyre treads; unfortunately eliminating the mould seam around the circumference of the tyres eradicates some of that detail, so I reinstated it with a razor saw. Brake lines were added from fine solder, and the landing light (part D1) was enhanced with a Greif lens. Although drop tanks are included I wanted to leave them off my model, but I did want the pylons. Unfortunately the sway braces are moulded as part of the tanks, so the empty pylons need the braces adding, and I used fine solder for these. The barrels of the wing guns were drilled out, though they'd probably look better if replaced with hypo-tubing.

## Finishing

This is an ideal kit for a natural metal finish, since there's so little bodywork required, meaning less sanding and filling that can mar the surface. I use Alclad, which requires a primer, so a coat of Tamiya white Fine Surface Primer was applied directly from the spray-can. The outer wing panels and rudder were then airbrushed with Gunze Mr Color gloss white, a lacquer which dries instantly and is a bright white; this would be the underlying colour for the red areas of the national insignia. Once the white areas had been masked with Tamiya tape, airbrushing the Alclad began, using two shades: Aluminum, and Polished Aluminum. In reality there's very little difference between the two, so I masked off certain panels and lightly oversprayed the Alclad with thinned Tamiya Smoke. With the surrounding areas masked off it's very difficult to tell how much darker the panels are becoming, so I constantly peeled back the edges of the masks to check the contrast with the base Alclad. I was aiming for subtle shifts in colour rather than an obvious patchwork of metallic shades.

With all of the natural metal areas finished I sprayed a light

Ultracast's nice resin seat, painted and ready to install

Completed cockpit unit in place

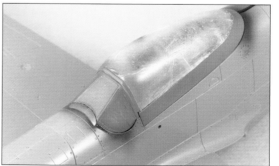

The canopy has been masked with Parafilm, and the interior frame colour of dark grey has been sprayed, prior to airbrushing the exterior with Alclad

Wing guns drilled out

A fine razor saw was used to rescribe the tread pattern lost after cleaning up the tyres

coat of Johnson's 'Future' to protect them, and then peeled off the tape to reveal the white insignia areas. Although I could have printed the white crosses as decals I chose to mask them, so the outlines were printed onto regular laser paper and covered with masking tape. These were carefully cut out with a new #11 blade, peeled off the backing paper and applied in their correct positions. The Alclad was masked off and the red airbrushed, again using a fast-drying hard gloss lacquer from Mr Color. Serials and stencilling were ALPS-printed and applied like

Tamiya White Primer reveals any flaws and is an ideal base for Alclad

The result of masking off selected panels and overspraying with Tamiya Smoke

regular decals, then I carefully ran a watercolour dark grey wash into the panel lines, which are deep but narrow, and hence perfect for highlighting. A light coat of satin varnish sealed everything in.

## General Notes

Switzerland acquired 130 P-51D Mustangs after WWII, and all were ex-US machines stationed in occupied Germany. All were former combat machines and some had been flown previously by US aces. These Mustangs continued to serve in a natural metal appearance with Olive Drab anti-glare panel. National insignia was initially a red square with white cross on four positions on the wings and an all-red rudder with a white cross. Later this was changed into roundel-type national insignia and the tail marking was moved from the rudder to the vertical stabiliser. The colour of the anti-glare panel was changed to blue RAL 5017. A number of machines received an experimental green camouflage to the upper surfaces. No specific information is available regarding this shade, although a guess might suggest it was an early NATO Green.

Areas to be later sprayed red are masked off

Creating the masks for the Swiss crosses, which were printed in outline form onto laser paper, covered in tape then carefully cut out

# The Ultimate 1:32 Mustang

by Dick Clark

**North American P-51D Mustang – Silver Edition**

Manufacturer: Tamiya
Scale: 1:32
Kit Type: Plastic injection
Kit Number: 25151

## Tamiya Silver Edition

Originally released in 2011, Tamiya's 1:32 P-51D is rightly regarded as being one of the best Mustang kits available. This 'special version' features plated parts to represent the bare aluminium panels of the late and post-war Mustangs. This presentation adds considerably to the cost of the kit, but does it add significantly to the quality and realism attainable?

## What You Get

The box itself is spectacular, but I approached opening it with some trepidation, my only experience of plated kits being the highly-polished chrome-effect on parts for custom car and dragster models built in my teens. This effect might need, I was sure, some toning down. I need not have worried. The plating Tamiya have applied is far more subtle. The finish even varies on some panels. All sprues are individually bagged, with clear parts and the various metal rods, nuts, bolts, etch and nylon poly-caps contained in a separate boxed section at one end. The parts are exquisitely moulded. There are several decal sheets, with added colour and placement sheets for the different aircraft offered in this boxing, as the original instruction booklet has not been altered. There is also a very useful colour booklet featuring a detailed history of the type, schematic drawings and two pages of thumbnail-sized photographs. The photos are especially welcome although, as the subject is a preserved example, they should not be taken as gospel, and further research is recommended.

My own in-depth research began, and I learned a great deal of

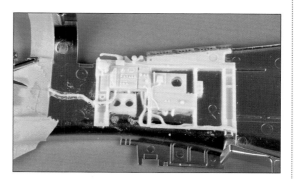

Starboard cockpit sidewall with resin and etch aftermarket parts

the incredible story of the 'Tuskegee Airmen'. It was my original intention to build the model as 1Lt Charles White's 'Creamer's Dream' with decals by Zotz, but as the serial number of this aircraft is unknown, it was impossible to determine which parts would be correct. Therefore the decision was made to build Capt Roscoe Brown's 'Bunnie', aircraft number 44-15569; with that number, everything is identifiable. I made a list of all the required alternative parts before starting the build, a decision which helped enormously.

## Into the Fray

It should be noted before any construction starts, that the plated finish is quite delicate and easily scratched, so handle with care at

The nearly completed cockpit and drive train assembly

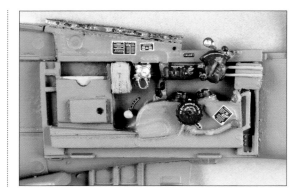

**Port cockpit sidewall after main painting and decaling**

**Further gaps at the front of the wing root, requiring the same treatment of carefully-applied filler and thin strips of Bare-Metal Foil**

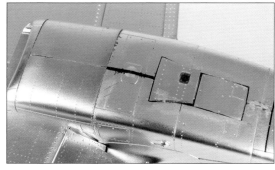

**The gap under the belly where I couldn't get the fuselage halves to close up completely. Note also scratches in the rather delicate plated surface; this will have to be disguised as weathering later on**

all times. Also note that CA glue will pit the finish, so this must be used sparingly and with extreme caution. Almost right from the start choices have to be made and alternative parts selected. This was brought home to me when I made an error at only stage 3, picking wrong parts for V7 and V8. I don't know how the error was made, but it was not discovered until Stage 6. Fortunately I was able to correct the error with some razor-saw surgery, but this may have been the source of other problems much later in the build, so be warned! The first four stages deal with the engine which, when assembled, was sprayed matt black then dry-brushed lightly with Citadel 'Boltgun Metal' to pop-out the detail and give it a slightly worn look.

There are more choices to be made at Stage 7 and at Stage 9 the correct seat has to be selected. In addition, the choice has to be made whether or not to add the pilot figure, as part Z12 should not be fitted if the pilot is required. In fact, this part appears to be only appropriate for an aircraft just about to depart on a mission, otherwise it may be left out anyway. If one is using the later, simpler seat (parts D19 and D21), there is an etched stay to add to either side. This is not mentioned in the instructions until Stage

11, but should really be fitted at Stage 9 as it will set the angle between parts D19 and 21, the seat and seat back.

At Stage 10, part D53 is not appropriate for all aircraft, especially earlier examples. Similarly, at Stage 11 there are choices to be made, not only with regard to parts used, but also where those parts are to be fitted. The beacon receiver, parts D7 and 10, is not required on all aircraft, and should be fitted to the sidewall on some and the floor as shown on others! I chose to use the kit control column rather than that included in the resin aftermarket set. At Stage 12 I really started to get into my aftermarket resin, with replacements for the radio and battery, with cables added from fuse-wire. Resin was also used for the gunsight (and this is another part where alternatives are offered). Part D5, which fits under the instrument panel shroud, is something of a mystery, being appropriate for some aircraft out of sequence to those suggested by following the developmental time-line - and, just to make itself even more confusing, may not always be fitted in the same place! The cockpit and drive-train assembles into a kit all of its own which can, when finished, be set aside while the fuselage sides are tackled. Before fixing anything to the sides, some painting is required. I used a black automotive primer on all the plated surfaces, having first experimented on an unwanted part.

The surface did not need any other special preparation. There are many alternative parts for the sidewalls. In this case resin replacements were used for most parts and fittings. Once the basics had been fixed, the sidewalls were primed in black, then Tamiya Zinc Chromate primer was airbrushed in a downward direction, allowing the underlying black to create shadows where the top colour was thinner. Gloss varnish was applied, and the stencils and placards added as further detail was built up. The 'BarracudaCals' stencils are superb, but note that many of them are in two parts. The first layer is the bare placard, over which the text is applied, so a drop of gloss needs to be touched on after the first part has set. The results are stunning! Only a couple of the very tiniest stencils were lost, too minute to keep track of!

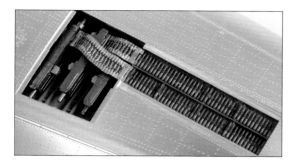

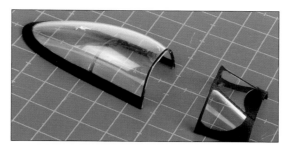

The starboard gun bay, every fifth bullet painted with a red tip to denote a tracer round

Before closing up the fuselage, make sure you've added all the bits of pipe and the engine cradle inside the engine bay. Stage 19 deals with the radiator/oil cooler ducting. Running a thin wash of black into the radiator faces makes the detail pop out; it all shows later so is worth making the effort. Stage 20 brings this all together, along with the panel designed to keep the changeable (open or closed) tail-wheel compartment in place. If one is adding the pilot, his arms need to be fixed in position before the cockpit/drive train assembly is fitted. I had intended fitting the pilot but changed my mind when I realised he'd hide most of all that lovely detail I'd added to the cockpit. Etched part b-8 is only required on later versions.

I had a problem when I joined the two fuselage halves, in that the belly would not close up properly around the radiator ducting. I suspect this may have been due to the etch panels fitted to either side of part R15 not being bent to the perfect curve, so be very careful when fixing these parts at Stage 19. This is where the plated finish becomes a problem, because of course one cannot simply fill and sand down in the normal fashion. In the end, filler was carefully worked into the bad join, smoothed before it had time to set, then covered with a thin strip of Bare-Metal Foil to blend it in.

I skipped Stage 23, fitting the exhaust stubs, until near the end of the build. Stage 24 gave me some problems. I would recommend fitting part V21, the coolant tank, to the pipe ends, leaving parts V22 and R21 until after Stage 26. At Stage 26, fit part V11 to the carburettor ducting (built up at Stage 25), then fit the ducting to the engine bearers and the engine compartment frame. This will give a much clearer location for part V22. I had great difficulty getting these parts aligned correctly. The alignment of V22 is also critical to the correct alignment of part V18 at Stage 27. Again, I had problems getting this all to align correctly; problems I didn't realise were there until I came to try to fit the cowling panels much later in the build. Much cursing and careful cutting away of misaligned parts was required to correct my errors here, so do take great care. I suspect that part V18 may have been deformed in the first place, adding to the problems, but I also think the error I made and had to correct right at the beginning with the engine assembly could have influenced these alignment problems.

Looking at the rudder and elevator assembly, one might think it all looks a bit strange, but follow the instructions and it all makes sense. I test fit everything (and, yes, I still make mistakes) and found that just push-fitting the assembled rudder and elevators was quite sufficient without applying any glue to the hinges. I'm not sure they would have retained their movement if I had tried to glue them. I also left Stage 32, the tail wheel assemblies, until later. Once the tailplanes are fitted, the whole fuselage can be set aside while the wings are assembled. I got rather confused assembling the armament; the instructions need to be followed very carefully to avoid getting the guns in the wrong order and the cartridge chutes on the wrong guns. Referring to the photos in the kit-supplied booklet, I picked out every fifth bullet head in the ammo trays to represent tracer rounds, though I'm not really sure if this would be appropriate for both runs of ammunition. It seems like overkill, but I guess they might have just had one type of belt. It looks cool, anyway.

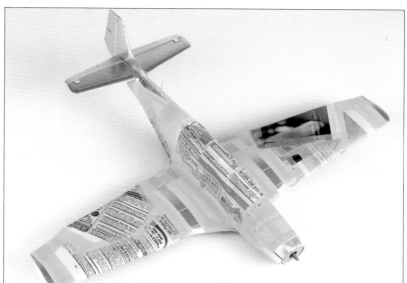

At Stage 40, fitting the upper wing halves to the one-piece lower wing leaves an inevitable join-line along the leading edge. This is an area where the plated finish really isn't helpful because, of course, one cannot sand away the joint seam without destroying the finish. I suspect Tamiya may not have thought of doing a version of this kit with this finish at the design stage, because it would have been much better to have made the leading edges (and wing tips) as separate mouldings with the join running along natural panel lines. This would also apply to the tailplanes, around the tail fin and underneath the tail, although it didn't matter in this case as these areas were to be painted.

I missed out the formation light lenses at Stage 44 until right near the end of the build. At Stage 46, I found fitting the wing assembly to the fuselage needed quite a bit of test fitting and fettling before the two would mate up. As it was, I needed to repeat my filler and Bare-Metal Foil trick at the front edge of the wing roots, though it was a lot fiddlier and consequently less successful here. On the other hand, the assembled air intake fitted a treat. In retrospect I feel I should have drilled out the gun muzzles before I fitted these panels to the wings; they would have looked better.

I had to jump forward to Stages 62/63 before painting (the sequence here seems quite illogical if the builder is to apply any paint to the model - and at the very least the anti-glare panel will need painting). I had decided to fit the lower cowling, part U4, permanently, though it still needs the locating pins SB4 and V30 to fit. Once this is fixed the other, removable cowling panels can be taped in place for painting. The last thing I did before painting was fit the windscreen. I masked the screen up using the kit-supplied masks to spray it matt black before fitting. Then, after fixing it in place, I removed this masking, re-covered the screen with Bare-Metal Foil to replicate the finish on the screen framing, masked the framing which was to remain bare metal and replaced the front screen mask for good measure. At this stage I reckoned I was about ready to paint. I assembled the closed main wheel doors and fitted them; they are a very close fit, masking off the wheel wells perfectly and allowing for masking the yellow stripe around the wing of the Red Tail version.

Back to the bare model after all painting has been completed, ready for the last leg.

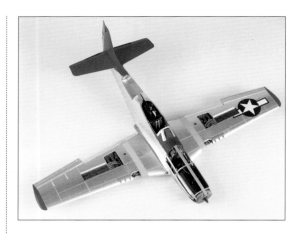

The number '7' decal I managed to break up. Thanks are due to Fundekals' excellent service in providing a replacement extremely promptly. Note also the fine stencil decal above the '7'

## Painting and Decaling

The wing stripes were primed with black auto-primer, to give a dark base for a stronger hue of yellow. Once the yellow had dried, these stripes were masked over and the other red areas primed with white (experimentation had shown that a black base resulted in much too dark a shade of red). When the red had set, the nose was remasked to apply the Olive Drab anti-glare panel. Before decaling, the entire airframe was given a coat of Tamiya gloss varnish, just to smooth out the surface.

There are a huge number of stencils to add to this model, whether one uses the kit decals or aftermarket items as I did. Fündekals claim they have researched and faithfully replicated the unique font North American used at this time; their version is certainly slightly different and was used throughout in the interests of authenticity and accuracy. I picked out some panel lines with a thin, light grey wash, but kept it light as these aircraft were maintained to a high degree of polish. Just removable or openable panels were given a darker wash to pick them out. On the prototypes the rivets were often puttied over, polished and painted with an aluminium dope; this is something else that can't be replicated without far too much risk to the metal finish, although thankfully the rivet detail, though very comprehensive, is also very restrained. So a couple more coats of gloss were applied for a final, polished look - and this did improve the appearance of the finish quite markedly.

## Final Details

Well, when I say final … there's quite a lot still to do, yet. Picking up the instruction sequence at Stage 49, the main gear doors need to be assembled then painted before moving on to Stage 50. While this was drying I built up the main and tail wheel assemblies, using the Scale Aircraft Conversion replacements for their extra strength (although the kit versions have a clever steel pin insert into the legs for added strength) and finer detail. You may note

that the main wheel tyres are mismatched; having read that this was often the case in the field, I decided that this would add another point of interest, so there's a block-tread tyre on one wheel and a diamond-tread on the other.

When it came to fitting the inner main gear door assembly, I found this needed quite a bit of fettling before it would slot in properly. Since I have no intention of swapping the up or down gear assemblies around, this was glued in place. The main gear legs tighten up beautifully when you do the little screw up, but I found that the cover panels were not a very secure fit, so they were glued in place as well. On the other hand, the tail wheel assembly fitted so tightly I didn't use any glue at all. To finish the undercarriage off, the wheels and tyres were given a light dry-brushing of brown muddy colour.

Pylons and drop tanks were next. I'd acquired BarracudaCast replacement ends for the large papier-mâché 108-gallon tanks before discovering that Bunnie was known usually to have carried the metal 75-gallon teardrop type. I skipped the propeller assembly until right at the end, as the blades would have been a serious hindrance. The canopy needed to have its frame covered in Bare-Metal Foil, so a rough template was made using the tracing-type paper that covers the decal sheets. The canopy was masked up for painting the frame the interior colour first, then this was removed and the foil applied.

The aircraft's aerial wire passed through the canopy. To achieve this, fishing line was superglued to a hole drilled in the top of the tail fin, then passed through the canopy and through another hole drilled in the seat headrest, where it was again glued and held taut while the glue set. The end was trimmed off and the canopy finally attached, slotting it into the upper fuselage panel; this panel was glued in place and the canopy given a tiny drop of glue at each front corner just to hold it in place. I applied some fairly heavy cordite staining under the wings. I'm not good enough with my airbrush yet to attempt this with it, and the pastel powders I usually use wouldn't adhere to this glossy finish. Areas of matt varnish were dry-bushed on using a cotton bud, and pastel powder worked into this. Contemporary photos show very little exhaust staining on the real thing, so just a mere hint of staining was applied by working in pastel powder as best I could.

Last, but not least, came the propeller assembly. The blades were sprayed matt black, glossed, decaled and matted before assembly; the spinner was sprayed red also prior to assembly. There are multiple choice options for prop blade decals; not all were applied, so references are needed here. The Fündekals options include gunsight calibration stencils for the rear face of the blades which, while they would have made an interesting extra detail, contained spelling errors which were the only criticism I could lay on these superb decals. So, having no evidence that they were featured on my prototype, I left these off. The prop is a firm push-fit onto the spine. Wingtip navigation lights, the underwing lights and the aerial mast were the final details to add. The gun cover panels have all been left separate.

## Conclusion

Phew! This was a bit of a marathon, especially with all those extra cockpit stencils and placards, but, oh boy, is it worth it! But is it truly the ultimate Mustang? Actually, in all honesty - probably not. It is a truly superb kit, which goes together almost faultlessly, and all those extra details lift it to a higher plane, if you'll pardon the pun. The plated finish is good, but possibly not the best way to achieve a bare-metal finish - and it's a lot more money for what you get. But for those who lack the skills to apply a really good bare-metal effect via painting, this is a very good alternative indeed. It could be better if the original kit had been designed with the finish in mind, with the leading edges moulded separately and other joins all made along natural join lines.

# 'Red Dog XII'

**A New Approach to 1:32 Modelling by Colin Pickett**

## North American P-51D Mustang

Manufacturer: Zoukei-Mura
Scale: 1:32
Kit Type: Plastic injection moulded with etch
Kit Number: 32004

### Zoukei-Mura

It's inevitable that comparisons will be made between this and the similarly scaled Tamiya kit, however, in my opinion, the scale is all that's comparable as the Zoukei-Mura kit concept is poles apart from Tamiya's. Tamiya's concept is to build a finished replica of the aircraft, whilst Zoukei-Mura's is actually to replicate the building. To make sense of this statement, the Zoukei-Mura kit is constructed along similar lines to the prototype and as such the build follows the actual production line sequence, with various

elements being built and then brought together near to the end, prior to final finishing and assembling. Whilst this does sound complex in the extreme it does have two functions. Firstly it builds a precise and detailed model and secondly provides a greater

The level of detail is amazing, as seen here by the tiny pistons in the engine

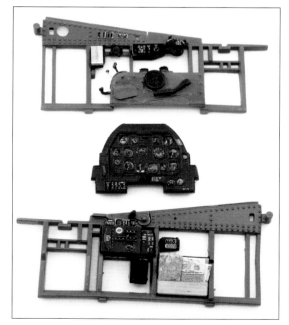

The kit seat with HGW harnesses, perfect for the scale

Cockpit sidewall and instrument panel with incumbent etch as well as scale maps in the map case from my spares box

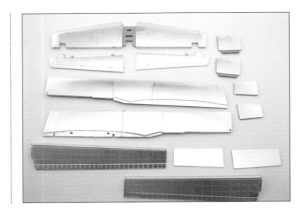

I pre-covered many of the panels with Bare-Metal Foil before installation

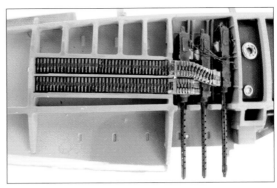

The gun bays in construction, with additional cabling

Internal wing structure with fuel tanks and gun bays, most of which won't be seen again

understanding of the type. As such I feel there is certainly a place for both kits in the marketplace as they cater for different tastes.

The Zoukei-Mura North American P-51D Mustang is packed in a reasonably large box simply jammed full of parts, with silver, black and grey sprues in abundance, along with the three types of canopy used on the D-Model. It's well worth sitting down for a couple of evenings to look at the sprues and instructions just to get to know your way around them. The kit's instruction book deserves mention as it's a reference in its own right, being made up of forty-six A4-sized colour pages featuring huge levels of detail, including pictures of the completed parts along with fine drawings and illustrations. This will become a document I'll revisit when making further Mustangs. It's also possible to buy the additional Zoukei-Mura Concept Notebook, produced to go alongside the kit. This gives a guide to the background of the kit and the company, and also features some stunning builds of the model as well as further reference photographs and drawings. Certainly if you want a good insight into the whole ethos of the Zoukei-Mura modelling ideology then this book will be an ideal work-along guide.

There are a limited number of add-on bits for the ZM kit, with Zoukei-Mura themselves cornering the market; however I found that the parts I chose to change were available for the Tamiya kit and so with a little adaptation I could get them to fit. In fairness to Zoukei-Mura the concept they have is similar to that of Eduard

and the Brassin range, where the kit itself will produce a very tidy model, but if you want that extra buzz, you simply buy in the extra bits from the range of upgrades they produce. The kit tyres looked a little artificial on the sprue, though at least they aren't vinyl. They do lack any weighted effect, although Zoukei-Mura do produce a set of weighted tyres if you want to keep things 'in-house'. I decided to swap these for a set of Brassin P-51D Wheels #632 015I that I found lurking in my stash. Although for the Tamiya kit, these have more sidewall detail, but are in need of adaptation to fit on the correctly tapered spindle of the Zoukei-Mura kit's oleo legs. A simple case of swapping the hubs did the trick. I decided that the gun barrels looked a bit under-detailed for the level of build I wanted so I purchased a set of Zoukei-Mura's own Metal Machine Gun Barrels. These are produced for them by Master and certainly look the part, and include new gas struts for the undercarriage doors too #SWS04-M03. In truth unless you are going to expose the barrels by removing a wing panel they are hidden in the wing, so the kit parts are fine.

## Construction

The kit instructions are set out in such a way that you can't help but treat each section as a separate model in its own right, and this way I found I researched and added detail to each element as I went along. As is my wont, or perhaps my downfall, I immediately deviated from the instructions and spent several hours assembling items such as the drop tanks, internal wing fuel tanks, oil tanks, oil cooler etc. I often do this with a kit from a manufacturer I've not used before, so I get a feel for the plastic and how it reacts to the various glues, so that when it gets to the major parts I have a good idea of how to get the best 'damage free' joints. It saves hours on filling and sanding later. I also spent time painting, applying washes of various tints and detail-painting various components, drilling out mounting holes and vent openings etc. Whilst it sometimes feels like I'm not making progress, when I get towards the end of a kit it all comes together quickly.

Returning to the instructions, things kick off with the engine, with a highly detailed replica Packard Merlin being the result. Whilst you can't see them on the completed model, the engine actually has tiny pistons moulded inside, adding to the interest level and you just know it's only a matter of time before someone decides to produce a cut-away style model from this kit revealing all (yes, I am sorely tempted). As it stands the kit has more than enough detail in this area from the box; however, there is always room for the dedicated super detailer to go to town. I added some bolt heads to the oil tank as well. The engine bearers are formed around the engine and fixed to the bulkhead, and section one is complete.

Next up came the cockpit, and I deviated from the kit in a couple of areas. Firstly I used a set of HGW harnesses on the kit seat. The kit allows for your personal taste in this respect as it comes with a seat with moulded-in harnesses, or one without.

The additional detail in the cockpit such as throttle cables and instrument cables helps to bring things to life

A view of the internal cockpit area and engine bulkhead

The Packard Merlin engine installed in the engine bearers on the bulkhead

The HGW harnesses are a little fiddly to put together, requiring you to thread the straps through the photo-etched metal buckles and then glue them in place. The effort is well worth an evening, and I'll be using them again in future projects of this size and scale. Another addition was the Zoukei-Mura etched set, which offers harnesses for the more traditional super detailer, as well as a huge number of additions for the cockpit area including a complete instrument panel with fuses, throttle levers and placards. Again not essential as the decal sheet provides an instrument panel but I though it worthwhile for the extra detail in this scale. I also added a set of maps to the map case just because I enjoy those little touches.

The cockpit floor is an item for debate, some aircraft having a black finish, others being left bare wood. I had the HGW decals from the seatbelt so I went with the bare wood as it gives some depth to the cockpit area. I also added a coiled cable for the radio microphone connection, which I posed on the seat ready for use. Whilst we are on the cockpit I feel the gunsight deserves a mention. The kit comes with two options, depending on the version you choose. For a change these actually look like a gunsight, complete with leather pad. I also added a pair of lenses to the top of the sight and painted the edges of the sight glass with transparent green paint to give it some depth.

With the cockpit together the action moves onto the radio and battery installation, and again this highly visible area received some detail from the etch set as well as some lead wire to replicate the connections and cables. Just to make things that little bit tougher I also wanted to use Bare-Metal Foil on the P-51D to give an appropriate finish to the model, and with this in mind I proceeded carefully to add foil before assembling the parts, using a sharp blade to cut out sections, and being careful to match and vary the 'grain' direction of the aluminium finish per panel – yes, this Mustang was foiled one panel at a time. The foil was polished into place using a cotton bud and a wooden cocktail stick employed to burnish it into fine detail such as rivets and panel lines. I also used a fibreglass polishing pen to add more wear in places. The edges were sealed with a coat of gloss enamel varnish.

Work then moves onto the radiators under the fuselage, before the engine assembly is mated to the cockpit section. This section is then clad in the exterior panels, which I'd pre-covered in Bare-Metal. And there lies my error. The tolerances in the parts are so fine that the thickness of the foil in the joins affected the fit … so it was a case of carefully trimming the foil away from the join where I could and then stripping and fitting the panels I couldn't manage. In addition to the aluminium foil, I also dressed the exhaust panels in chrome foil to give more variation. The tail assembly followed the same route, fitting onto the rear of the fuselage as per the real deal. I also fitted the windscreen transparency at this stage using Gator Glue, having previously painted the inside of the frames black and fitted the supplied masking set.

The kit had started to look like a Mustang. The wing is the next step, kicking off with painting the framework and spars, along with the fuel tanks before installing them, making up the wheel wells and the gun bays before adding the plastic skin panels to replicate that laminar flow wing. I added some more detail to the gun bays such as control cables and additional panels to the Browning guns themselves, as well as the Zoukei-Mura gun barrel set. The control column fits on top of the wing before the wing fits under the fuselage, to locate in the middle of the cockpit, and the joints between the wing and fuselage are covered with panels.

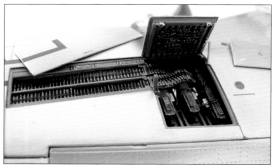

## Painting

The kit comes supplied with decals for three well known aircraft, however there's no reason to be restricted as there are a huge number of decals for 1:32 Mustangs available in the aftermarket, and I had to resist temptation to produce an RAF or RAAF version, given the small amount of conversion work required and the availability of the necessary parts on the aftermarket.

## The kit's options are:

- 'Miss Marilyn' P-51D-5-NA Sr.44-13837, 343rd Fighter Squadron, 55th Fighter Group, flown by Captain Robert Welch
- 'Old Crow' P-51D-10-NA Sr. 44-14450, 363rd Fighter Squadron, 357th Fighter Group, flown by Captain 'Bud' Anderson
- 'Red Dog XII' P-51D-25-NA Sr. 44-73108, 334th Fighter Squadron, 4th Fighter Group, flown by Major Louis Norley.

Choosing which option took a lot of deliberation, but in the end I settled for 'Red Dog XII', as I felt this gave the metallic finish the best setting.

With the bulk of the construction complete and the markings choice made I then finished off the foil covering and masked off for the Olive Drab anti-glare panel on the nose. The red sections were masked off and painted next; I used Tamiya X-7 to provide a deep gloss red. Finally the fuselage was masked off and the wings given a dusting of Xtracrylix Silver paint by airbrush to replicate the painted finish given to the wings to smooth the airflow over the wing, but without wiping out the metal effect of the foil. The decals came next, with no drama to report, these being in perfect register, gossamer thin and with a good depth of colour coupled with a minimal carrier film. Once a coat of Klear had sealed them in place I decided to proceed with weathering. With the odd exception I like my aircraft to have a slightly tired and distressed finish, because when you get up close to most aircraft they are simply grubby. To this end a wash was applied to the panel lines to bring them out, followed by a highlight with some thinned dark grey acrylic. The exhaust and gun port staining was created with a thinned coat of Tamiya Smoke and matt brown, and oil stains were added with a fine brush using Tamiya Smoke.

## Finishing

The undercarriage and wheels simply click into place with the brake lines attached followed by the undercarriage doors, which again fit positively in place. I added a small Little Cars lens inside the landing light to replicate a light bulb. I also added a similar lens to the rudder to replicate the light there. It was at this point I noticed that the make-up of the cowling parts, which whilst okay for use when the engine cover is fitted, don't resemble them whilst disassembled and placed around the aircraft for maintenance. After a bit of consideration I decided that I needed them in my planned diorama and set to with the razor saw to make things right. Not a major issue but one to note if you plan a similar setting. I decided to leave the front of the spinner off as I just couldn't bring myself to hide all that wonderful hub detail and I wanted to enhance the maintenance look. I added a small wire loop to the tail to aid attaching the aerial wire, and another to the rear of the headrest. A hole was drilled through the canopy with a pin drill to allow the wire to pass through, the actual wire being made up of a length of fine fishing line coloured with a black marker pen. With most finishing stages of a model I find that the completed article emerges over a number of hours of work, which I normally split over a couple of sessions to give my failing memory a chance to remember all the tweaks I wanted to add.

## Conclusion

Whilst the kit lacked the pure engineered precision of the newer Hasegawa or Tamiya kits, I actually felt this was a good thing, as I often find that the modern model kit is an assembling exercise rather than a building and learning curve. As far as value for money goes I think that the Zoukei-Mura Mustang scores really well, whilst the actual 'box cost' may put some off, you don't need to add anything else unless you are super-obsessive, the high parts count making for an extended modelling experience.

# Daisie Mae

**A Classic Mustang by Trevor Pask**

**North American P-51D Mustang**

Manufacturer: Hasegawa
Scale: 1:32
Type: Injection Moulded Plastic
Kit No: 04286

**Aftermarket:**

Kitsworld Decals #132002
Eduard #32506 seat belt seat belts USAF and USN WWII
Eduard #32010 P-51 Details for Hasegawa Kit

**A**lthough Revell pioneered the use of 1:32 from the 1960's onwards, it was the Japanese manufacturer Hasegawa that produced some of the first truly practical kits in this large scale.

The P-51 first appeared in 1976 and received rave reviews at the time for previously unheard of levels of detail. As with the 1:24 Airfix 'Super kits' of the same period, the smaller Hasegawa kit came with full engine detail, separate control surfaces, and removable access panels in the wings to reveal the guns and associated ammunition feeds. Additionally, unlike the bigger 1:24 Airfix kit of the same subject, the wheel wells were blanked off, and a reasonable amount of internal detail provided. Kits were beginning to get much better in the 1970s, but the P-51 presented the modeller with some serious detail.

Having set the standard, the Hasegawa kit has only recently been superseded by the efforts of Dragon and Tamiya. Both of these later kits are stunning pieces of engineering, and are superior in all respects to the Hasegawa version. The Hasegawa kit is, however, still in the catalogue, and despite the severe price rise in kits from this manufacturer, is still a relatively affordable option. The kit has also been issued in literally dozens of versions over the years, and older boxings can be picked up for very modest prices on the Internet, or tucked away in the back of traders' vans at summer air shows.

The kit used in this project was bought for a few pounds at Shoreham Air show in 2012. The show was delayed due to bad weather, but a 1:32 Hasegawa kit for £10 - if not quite worth the trip - was a compensation of sorts for surviving the vagaries of the late English summer weather. Dating from the early 1980s, the box of the bargain basement kit was battered, but the contents were still in their protective bags, and the decal sheet intact. None of the decal options supplied by Hasegawa in this version offered themselves as attractive subjects, but with a plethora of aftermarket sheets available for the Mustang, a post air show season modelling project immediately presented itself.

In common with many large scale kits from the 1970s and early 1980s, to a modern modeller, the Hasegawa P-51 has the feel of a smaller kit that has been scaled up. The detail is there, but it is vague in places, with the mouldings lacking the sharpness and solidity of a modern kit. Some aspects of the detail can be helped

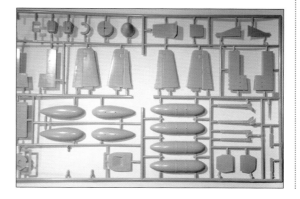

**Kitsworld's instruction sheets are well-presented in full colour**

**The Kitsworld decal sheet**

**Sprue layout is typical of the period**

Basic construction of the cockpit tub under way

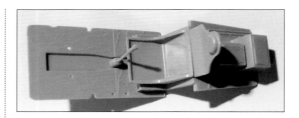

The fuselage halves ready to be joined. The engine provided by Hasegawa is a good idea, but is basic by modern standards. The engine needs to be fitted to the fuselage in order to provide a degree of structural stability, but in terms of detail, it is best simply painted black and fixed into position as a mounting block for the propeller

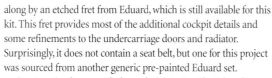

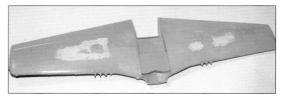

The removable panels in the upper wing were a good idea, but the fit is poor and they are best fixed shut, or left open and the detail inside enhanced

The lower wing component. For 1976, a one-piece moulding this size was impressive, as was the internal detail in the wheel wells

along by an etched fret from Eduard, which is still available for this kit. This fret provides most of the additional cockpit details and some refinements to the undercarriage doors and radiator. Surprisingly, it does not contain a seat belt, but one for this project was sourced from another generic pre-painted Eduard set.

Construction began with the cockpit interior. The Eduard elements integrated reasonably well with the plastic supplied by Hasegawa and with some carful painting, a good representation of the P-51's cockpit can be achieved. The engine is also supplied as a separate, if undersized component. This would have been a huge innovation when the kit was new, but to a modern eye appears to be gimmicky and simply complicates the engineering of the kit. The recommended approach is simply to paint the engine matt black and use it as a base for the propeller, and to add some structural integrity to the model.

The situation is similar with the removable wing panels, which perhaps are best described as a good idea a little ahead of their times. The panels do not fit well, and the detail they reveal is vague and in need of a lot of work. On this project, the panels were simply fixed down, and filler used to smooth the gaps over. This may seem like a strange approach, but the wings of most P-51s have a resin type filler applied to all panel joints, and were sanded down to achieve as smooth a surface as possible for the laminar flow wing to work to best effect. The gun bay panels were obviously left as removable items, but were engineered to fit very tightly.

World War Two fighters were relatively simple aircraft and even in a large scale a modelling project comes together very quickly once the interior details have been completed. A kit of the P-51's

size and vintage, however, does not simply clip together. Careful alignment of the components is required and some help in the way of heavy duty clamps is needed to hold everything together. A significant amount of filler is also required along every joint and it is a careful and messy evening's work to smooth this down. Some modellers used to more modern kits may find this work tiresome, but the only really challenging areas were around the radiator – a common area for problems on P-51 kits – and the gun bay access panels.

Halfords Grey Plastic Primer was used to prepare the model for the painting element of the project. While the painting instructions of many P-51 kits indicate that the aircraft had an overall natural metal finish, in practice just the fuselage tended to be unpainted. The wings as mentioned earlier had any gaps and imperfections carefully filled before being painted with an aluminium paint. The resultant contrast between the fuselage and wings was not standard, and varied depending on the paint used and the treatment of the fuselage. The P-51 in the RAF Museum, for example, has a highly polished body and quite dull wings. Other restored P-51s, however, have different appearances, and contemporary WW2 photographs are often difficult to interpret, but tend to indicate that many service aircraft were scruffier than the restored RAF example at Hendon.

Humbrol 11 Silver applied from an aerosol can was used to simulate the natural metal finish on the fuselage. This is a bright punchy shade, which appears to be correct for a model in this scale. It also has the added advantage of being available in a tinlet. Having an exact match in this form greatly assists any touching up which may be required by hand. The wings were painted with an airbrushed mixture of the same shade mixed 70/30 with matt white. This created a contrast between the two areas on the model, which while not being as vivid as that seen on some restored aircraft, approximated the finish seen on some aircraft during WW2.

The tail, canopy framing and nose areas were all masked up and painted when the main colours were fully dry. The tail was airbrushed, but the nose areas were carefully hand painted. Humbrol H66 Olive Drab lightened with a little matt yellow was used for the prominent anti-dazzle panel. Once dry this area was given a light touch with a sheet of very well worn fine wet and dry paper to 'distress' the paint and reveal a little of the aluminium colour underneath. It is important not to overdo this technique, but carefully done it can replicate the chipped and faded appearance of these areas on the real service aircraft. If the technique is used on any model, several coats of Johnson's Klear are necessary to protect any such distressed area as the affect of

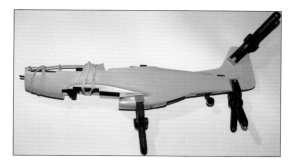

The two fuselage halves need a bit of gentle persuasion to come together

Masking the model up for painting – necessary even on an overall natural metal aircraft because the wings on many P-51s had their panel lines filled, were sanded smooth and then painted in a aluminium paint, which contrasted with the polished fuselage

the solvent in any varnish used later in a project, could lift or distort the base colour. A coat of Johnson's Klear is also, of course, an advisable preparation for the decals.

An aftermarket decal sheet from Kitsworld was sourced to provide an alternative finish to the options supplied with the kit. A huge variation of schemes were worn by the P-51, but the aircraft perhaps looked its best when it was primarily in a natural finish, with a reasonably sized piece of nose art with minimal other distractions cluttering the airframe. Kitsworld specialise in nose art decals, and the company was an obvious place to look for something interesting. The sheet for this project was chosen because it offered two 'pin up' nose art options on otherwise standard airframes, with the added interest of both images being both modern-looking and tasteful.

Looking through a number of manufacturers' catalogues, it is apparent that very few kits of the Mustang and similar WW2 fighters are released with 'pin up' nose art. It can only be suspected that the marketing of such kits would be problematic in some countries – especially as a large part of the model aircraft market is squarely aimed at younger people. A similar problem exists with models of historic F1 and other racing cars because of their association with tobacco and other dubious sponsors. It is sensible to ban tobacco advertising on public health grounds, but most thinking people would realise that Tamiya having to reissue the kits of James Hunt's 1976 McLaren M23 in a plain box with virtually no decals and no hint on the instruction sheet as to the red chevrons, which were typically painted on the car, is a step too far. Likewise, a WW2 P-51 in typical markings is probably not going to warp anyone's view of gender differences…

Most of the 'pin up' artwork on WW2 American aircraft was inspired by illustrations from Esquire magazine – the 'Loaded' or 'FHM' of the day. There are contemporary photographs of magazine pages taped to the side of an aircraft to guide the painter, who was often a ground crew member that had been trained as an artist – until the 1950s large street adverts in parts of the United States were commonly painted by hand. The illustrations in the magazines tended to be drawings themselves and were far less revealing than any images or photographs that were typically used in mainstream advertising from the 1960s onwards. The two aircraft featured on the Kitsworld sheet are good examples of the genre - 44-14519 B6-R of the 363rd Fighter Squadron 'Daisy Mae' flown by Lt Allen K Abner, and 44-14722 G4-N of the 363rd Fighter Squadron 'Temptation' flown by Lt Matthew S Martin. 'Daisy Mae' was selected for this project – partly because the image was the larger, but also because the figure was so modestly dressed as to push the boundaries of the genre in a direction it was not normally pushed!

The Kitsworld decals were of excellent quality – being perfectly printed and very thin. The aftermarket sheet does not provide any national insignia or stencils. These have to be sourced from elsewhere, and the decal sheet provided with the kit and the spares box provided everything else that was needed. The version of the kit used for this project dated from the early 1990s,

and typically for Hasegawa products of that period, contained decals which were very thick and needed soaking for at least five minutes before they could be persuaded to move on the backing sheet. Once on the model, however, use of Micro Set and Sol made the images behave and they settled down perfectly. Not every twenty-year old decal sheet leads to this outcome, but generic WW2 insignia and stencils for the P-51 are easily obtainable from aftermarket manufacturers.

Once all the decals were on, the model was dusted with Humbrol Satin Vanish varnish to seal the images in. With this task done, the lines were emphasized with a HB pencil, and ground-up pencil lead rubbed into the rivet and other recessed detail. As these typical artist mediums are not stable, they themselves were sealed in with another cost of the same varnish. The undercarriage bays, inside of the undercarriage doors, and legs received a wash of Games Workshop Grey Ink at this stage of the project. This medium is very useful to create a sense of depth and contrast, a necessary quality that needs to be created on a model of this type.

The model was completed with the addition of ancillary pieces such as the undercarriage doors and the canopy. The Eduard additions to the undercarriage were fiddly to attach, but added a veneer of detail that made the model just a little more eye-catching. The windscreen portion of the canopy was slightly too narrow for the recess on the fuselage. The fit was improved by a little late surgery to the cockpit decking, but the drama was a lesson in always ensuring that the canopy fits at an early stage of the build. The work required to make the canopy fit was minor, but it would have been much more straightforward at the start.

There are better 1:32 kits of the P-51 available, but the old Hasegawa kit builds up into an acceptable replica, and especially if one of the earlier versions of the kit can be sourced, it is the logical and affordable option for any modeller on a budget who wants to venture into large scale modeling. Some photo etch is recommended, but the large scale of the kit makes it an ideal introduction to that medium as well – a cockpit in 1:32 being a lot easier to work on than one in 1:72.

Had it not rained and the Vulcan been delayed, this particular kit may very well have remained unmade for a few more years!

# P-51C Walk Around

## Chapter 13

## North American P-51C-10NT Mustang, Warhawk Air Museum Nampa, Idaho

Photographs courtesy of Michael Benolkin of Cybermodeller Online   www.cybermodeller.com

The Warhawk Air Museum's P-51C is painted in the markings of Boise native and five-times WWII Fighter Ace Lt Col Duane W. Beeson. The 'Boise Bee' and Beeson flew with the 334th Fighter Squadron, 4th Fighter Group, 8th Air Force in England. 'Boise Bee' was restored to flying condition and made its first post-restoration flight in 2010 at the Reno Air Races.

- **1** As seen when displayed in the Warhawk Air Museum is P-51C Mustang 'Boise Bee'
- **2** Close-up of the 'Boise Bee' artwork and 'kill' markings
- **3** Low angle shot showing the port main wheel, undercarriage door and wheel well detail

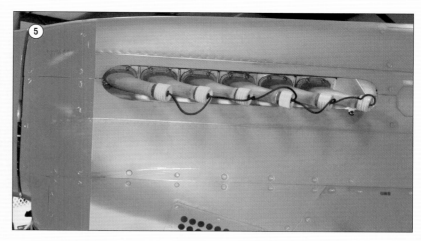

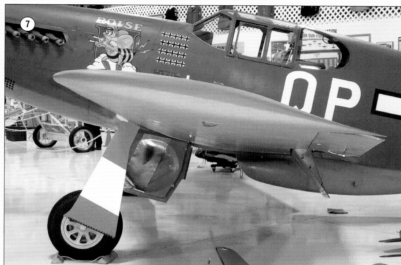

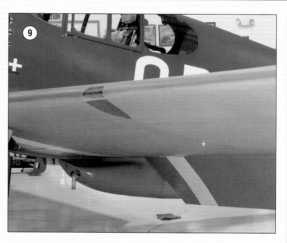

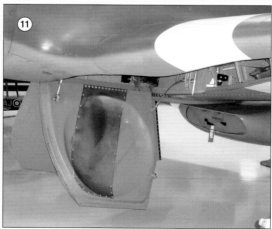

- **4** The deeper nose contour of the Merlin-engined Mustang is evident here, as is the spinner
- **5** The port side of the Merlin exhaust stack with 'plugs'
- **6** The cockpit glazing on the port side, and note the partly open side pane
- **7** A view of the port wingtip contour and undercarriage door shape
- **8** Port wing flap, fuel filler cap and body/wing join contour
- **9** Port wing light fairing and underfuselage radiator scoop
- **10** Port wing machine gun ports, and note the 'stepped' arrangement
- **11** Main wheel undercarriage doors

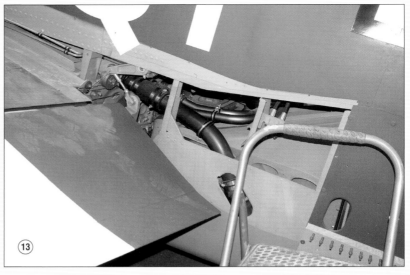

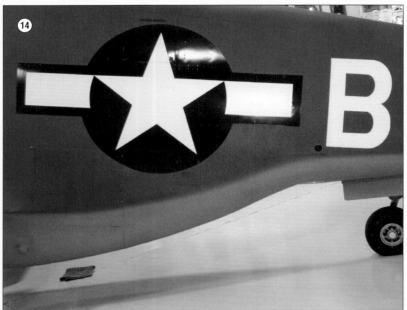

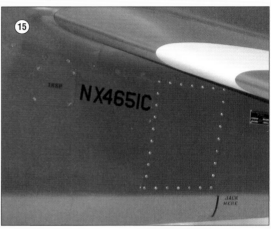

- **12** Main wheel and tyre
- **13** With the access panels removed you get a good view inside the fuselage. These are new items fitted during restoration to flying condition.
- **14** The port side national insignia and rear fuselage shape
- **15** Aircraft code in black just under the tail
- **16** Port side tailplane
- **17** Port side of the rudder
- **18** Starboard side of the rudder and note the trim tab

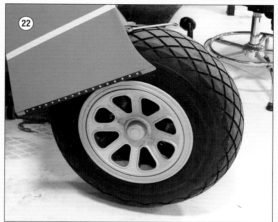

- **19** Starboard tailplane
- **20** Seen during restoration the starboard side 'Boise Bee' is exposed
- **21** Starboard side view of the tail wheel
- **22** Starboard side main wheel and tyre
- **23** Starboard side main landing gear leg
- **24** Pitot tube
- **25** Extended starboard side wing flap

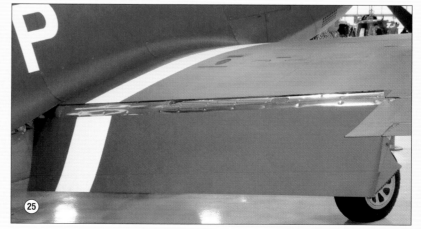

- 26 Starboard view of the canopy, wing and armament
- 27 The P-51's Rolls Royce Merlin engine exposed
- 28 Looking further aft on the starboard side toward the cockpit firewall
- 29 Panels removed, the 'Boise Bee' in maintenance

# Technical Diagrams

## Chapter 14

## Exploded View of P-51

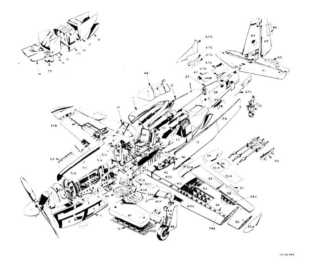

## Towing the P-51

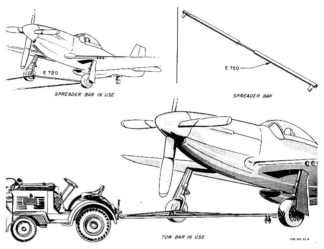

## The Engine Cowling

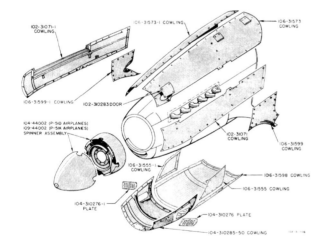

## Engine Mount Assembly

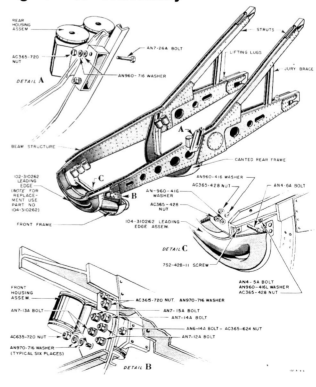

## Engine Exhaust System

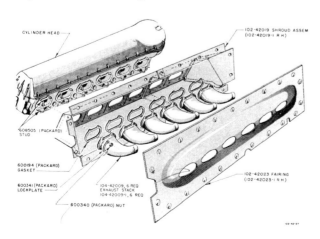

# Radiator Inlet Scoop

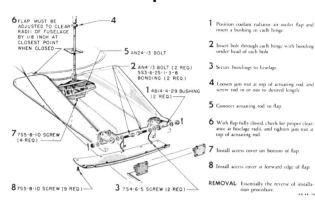

6 FLAP MUST BE ADJUSTED TO CLEAR RADII OF FUSELAGE BY 1/8 INCH AT CLOSEST POINT WHEN CLOSED

4
5 AN24-13 BOLT
2 AN4-13 BOLT (2 REQ.)
5S3-6-25-1-3-8 BONDING (2 REQ.)
1 4B14-4-29 BUSHING (2 REQ.)
7 7S5-8-10 SCREW (4 REQ.)
8 7S5-8-10 SCREW (9 REQ.)
3 7S4-6-5 SCREW (2 REQ.)

1 Position coolant radiator air outlet flap and insert a bushing in each hinge.

2 Insert bolt through each hinge with bonding under head of each bolt.

3 Secure bondings to fuselage.

4 Loosen jam nut at top of actuating rod, and screw rod in or out to desired length.

5 Connect actuating rod to flap.

6 With flap fully closed, check for proper clearance at fuselage radii, and tighten jam nut at top of actuating rod.

7 Install access cover on bottom of flap.

8 Install access cover at forward edge of flap.

REMOVAL: Essentially the reverse of installation procedure.

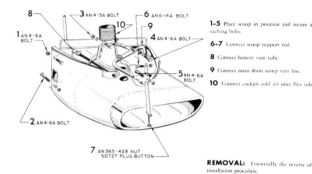

8
3 AN4-5A BOLT
6 AN6-14A BOLT
10
9
1 AN4-6A BOLT
4 AN4-6A BOLT
5 AN4-6A BOLT
2 AN4-6A BOLT
7 AN365-428 NUT 50727 PLUG BUTTON

1-5 Place scoop in position and secure attaching bolts.

6-7 Connect scoop support rod.

8 Connect battery vent tube.

9 Connect main drain sump vent line.

10 Connect cockpit cold air inlet flex tube.

REMOVAL: Essentially the reverse of installation procedure.

# Carburettor Air Induction System

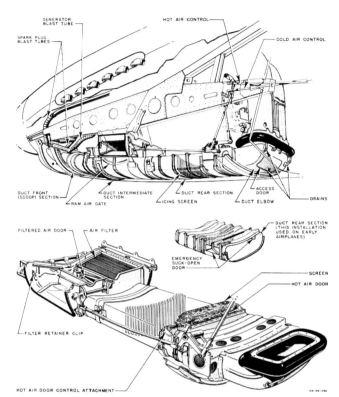

GENERATOR BLAST TUBE
HOT AIR CONTROL
SPARK PLUG BLAST TUBES
COLD AIR CONTROL
DUCT FRONT (SCOOP) SECTION
DUCT INTERMEDIATE SECTION
DUCT REAR SECTION
ACCESS DOOR
RAM AIR GATE
ICING SCREEN
DUCT ELBOW
DRAINS

FILTERED AIR DOOR
AIR FILTER
DUCT REAR SECTION (THIS INSTALLATION USED ON EARLY AIRPLANES)
EMERGENCY SUCK-OPEN DOOR
SCREEN
HOT AIR DOOR
FILTER RETAINER CLIP
HOT AIR DOOR CONTROL ATTACHMENT

# P-51 General Arrangement

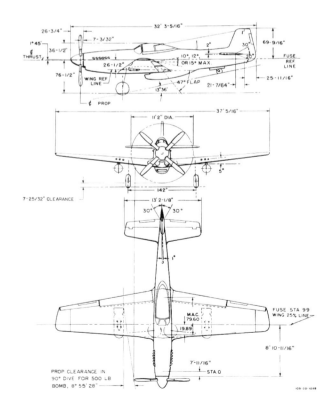

# Air Induction System – Early Aircraft

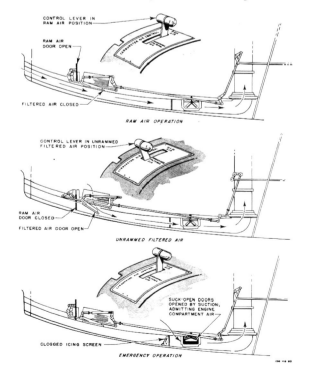

CONTROL LEVER IN RAM AIR POSITION
RAM AIR DOOR OPEN
FILTERED AIR CLOSED
RAM AIR OPERATION

CONTROL LEVER IN UNRAMMED FILTERED AIR POSITION
RAM AIR DOOR CLOSED
FILTERED AIR DOOR OPEN
UNRAMMED FILTERED AIR

SUCK-OPEN DOORS OPENED BY SUCTION, ADMITTING ENGINE COMPARTMENT AIR
CLOGGED ICING SCREEN
EMERGENCY OPERATION

# Engine to Firewall Connections

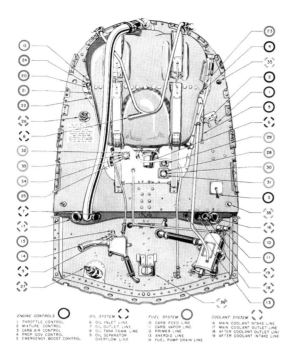

ENGINE CONTROLS
1 THROTTLE CONTROL
2 MIXTURE CONTROL
3 CARB AIR CONTROL
4 PROP GOV CONTROL
5 EMERGENCY BOOST CONTROL

OIL SYSTEM
6 OIL INLET LINE
7 OIL OUTLET LINE
8 OIL TANK FOAM LINE
9 OIL SEPARATOR
  OVERFLOW LINE

FUEL SYSTEM
10 CARB FEED LINE
11 CARB VAPOR LINE
12 PRIMER LINE
13 ANEROID LINE
14 FUEL PUMP DRAIN LINE

COOLANT SYSTEM
16 MAIN COOLANT INTAKE LINE
17 MAIN COOLANT OUTLET LINE
18 AFTER COOLANT OUTLET LINE
19 AFTER COOLANT INTAKE LINE

# Engine Instrument System

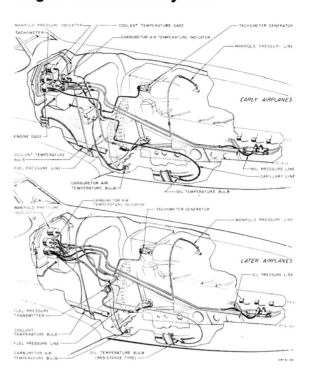

# Fuel, Oil and Coolant Drains

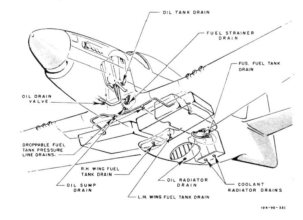

OIL TANK DRAIN
FUEL STRAINER DRAIN
FUS. FUEL TANK DRAIN
OIL DRAIN VALVE
DROPPABLE FUEL TANK PRESSURE LINE DRAINS.
R.H. WING FUEL TANK DRAIN
OIL SUMP DRAIN
OIL RADIATOR DRAIN
COOLANT RADIATOR DRAINS
L.H. WING FUEL TANK DRAIN

# Oil System

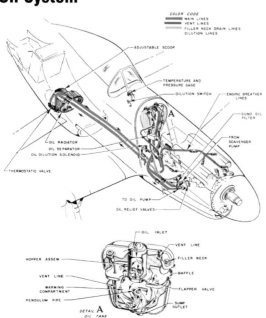

COLOR CODE
MAIN LINES
VENT LINES
FILLER NECK DRAIN LINES
DILUTION LINES

ADJUSTABLE SCOOP
TEMPERATURE AND PRESSURE GAGE
DILUTION SWITCH
ENGINE BREATHER LINES
CUNO OIL FILTER
FROM SCAVENGER PUMP
OIL RADIATOR
OIL SEPARATOR
OIL DILUTION SOLENOID
THERMOSTATIC VALVE
TO OIL PUMP
OIL RELIEF VALVES

OIL INLET
VENT LINE
HOPPER ASSEM
FILLER NECK
BAFFLE
VENT LINE
WARMING COMPARTMENT
FLAPPER VALVE
PENDULUM PIPE
SUMP OUTLET
DETAIL A
OIL TANK

# Cooling System

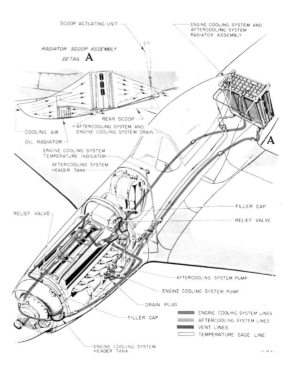

SCOOP ACTUATING UNIT
ENGINE COOLING SYSTEM AND AFTERCOOLING SYSTEM RADIATOR ASSEMBLY
RADIATOR SCOOP ASSEMBLY
DETAIL A
REAR SCOOP
COOLING AIR
OIL RADIATOR
AFTERCOOLING SYSTEM AND ENGINE COOLING SYSTEM DRAIN
ENGINE COOLING SYSTEM TEMPERATURE INDICATOR
AFTERCOOLING SYSTEM HEADER TANK
RELIEF VALVE
FILLER CAP
RELIEF VALVE
AFTERCOOLING SYSTEM PUMP
ENGINE COOLING SYSTEM PUMP
DRAIN PLUG
FILLER CAP
ENGINE COOLING SYSTEM HEADER TANK

ENGINE COOLING SYSTEM LINES
AFTERCOOLING SYSTEM LINES
VENT LINES
TEMPERATURE GAGE LINE

# Engine Bay – General Arrangement

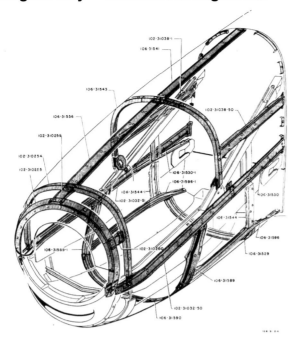

# Air Induction System – Late Models

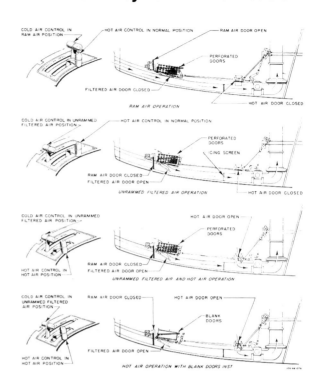

# Engine Bay – Fixings

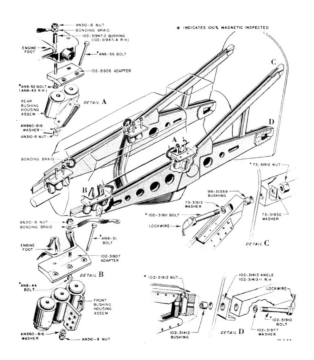

# Coolant Radiator

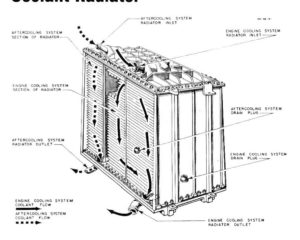

# Carburettor Air Control System

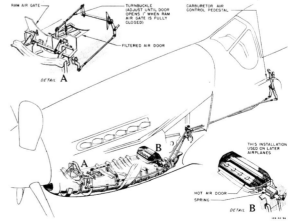

# Fuel System

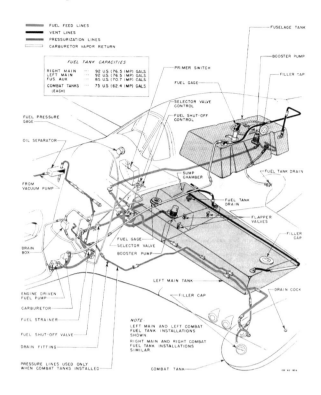

FUEL FEED LINES
VENT LINES
PRESSURIZATION LINES
CARBURETOR VAPOR RETURN

FUEL TANK CAPACITIES
RIGHT MAIN ··· 92 US (76.5 IMP) GALS
LEFT MAIN ··· 92 US (76.5 IMP) GALS
FUS. AUX ··· 85 US (70.7 IMP) GALS
COMBAT TANKS ··· 75 US (62.4 IMP) GALS
(EACH)

FUSELAGE TANK
BOOSTER PUMP
FILLER CAP
PRIMER SWITCH
FUEL GAGE
SELECTOR VALVE CONTROL
FUEL SHUT-OFF CONTROL
FUEL TANK DRAIN
SUMP CHAMBER
FUEL TANK DRAIN
FLAPPER VALVES
FILLER CAP
DRAIN COCK
LEFT MAIN TANK
FILLER CAP
FUEL GAGE
SELECTOR VALVE
BOOSTER PUMP
FUEL PRESSURE GAGE
OIL SEPARATOR
FROM VACUUM PUMP
DRAIN BOX
ENGINE DRIVEN FUEL PUMP
CARBURETOR
FUEL STRAINER
FUEL SHUT-OFF VALVE
DRAIN FITTING
COMBAT TANK

NOTE
LEFT MAIN AND LEFT COMBAT FUEL TANK INSTALLATIONS SHOWN
RIGHT MAIN AND RIGHT COMBAT FUEL TANK INSTALLATIONS SIMILAR

PRESSURE LINES USED ONLY WHEN COMBAT TANKS INSTALLED

# Propellor Installation – Hamilton Standard

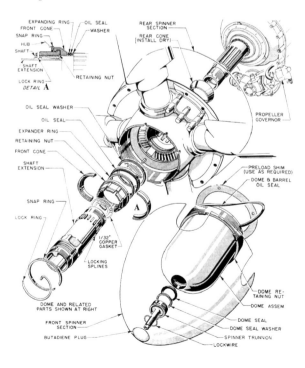

EXPANDING RING
FRONT CONE
SNAP RING
HUB
SHAFT
SHAFT EXTENSION
LOCK RING
DETAIL A
OIL SEAL
WASHER
RETAINING NUT
REAR SPINNER SECTION
REAR CONE (INSTALL DRY)
PROPELLER GOVERNOR
OIL SEAL WASHER
OIL SEAL
EXPANDER RING
RETAINING NUT
FRONT CONE
SHAFT EXTENSION
SNAP RING
LOCK RING
PRELOAD SHIM (USE AS REQUIRED)
DOME & BARREL OIL SEAL
1/32" COPPER GASKET
LOCKING SPLINES
DOME RETAINING NUT
DOME ASSEM
DOME AND RELATED PARTS SHOWN AT RIGHT
FRONT SPINNER SECTION
BUTADIENE PLUG
DOME SEAL
DOME SEAL WASHER
SPINNER TRUNNION
LOCKWIRE

# Propellor Govenor System

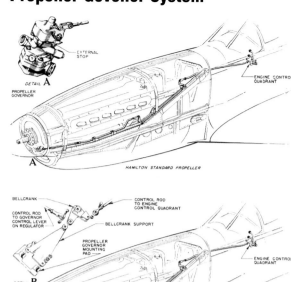

EXTERNAL STOP
DETAIL A
PROPELLER GOVERNOR
ENGINE CONTROL QUADRANT
HAMILTON STANDARD PROPELLER
A

BELLCRANK
CONTROL ROD TO GOVERNOR CONTROL LEVER ON REGULATOR
CONTROL ROD TO ENGINE CONTROL QUADRANT
BELLCRANK SUPPORT
PROPELLER GOVERNOR MOUNTING PAD
DETAIL B
ENGINE CONTROL QUADRANT
AEROPRODUCTS PROPELLER
B

# Spinner Installation – Hamilton Standard

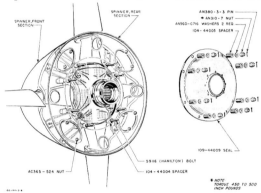

SPINNER, FRONT SECTION
SPINNER, REAR SECTION
AN380-3-3 PIN
AN310-7 NUT
AN960-C716 WASHERS 2 REQ
104-44005 SPACER
109-44009 SEAL
AC365-524 NUT
59116 (HAMILTON) BOLT
104-44004 SPACER
NOTE TORQUE 450 TO 500 INCH POUNDS

# Propellor Installation – Aeroproducts

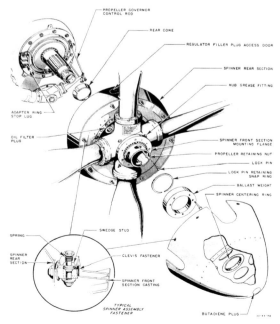

PROPELLER GOVERNOR CONTROL ROD
REAR CONE
REGULATOR FILLER PLUG ACCESS DOOR
SPINNER REAR SECTION
HUB GREASE FITTING
ADAPTER RING STOP LUG
OIL FILTER PLUG
SPINNER FRONT SECTION MOUNTING FLANGE
PROPELLER RETAINING NUT
LOCK PIN
LOCK PIN RETAINING SNAP RING
BALLAST WEIGHT
SPINNER CENTERING RING
SPRING
SWEDGE STUD
CLEVIS FASTENER
SPINNER REAR SECTION
SPINNER FRONT SECTION CASTING
TYPICAL SPINNER ASSEMBLY FASTENER
BUTADIENE PLUG

## Control Stick Mechanism

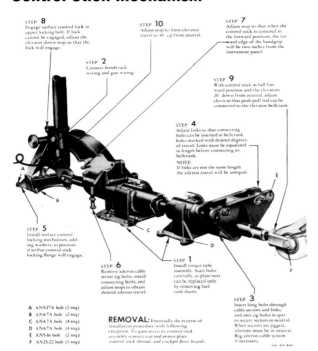

STEP **8**
Engage surface control lock in upper locking hole. If lock cannot be engaged, adjust the elevator down stop so that the lock will engage.

STEP **10**
Adjust stop to limit elevator travel to 10° up from neutral.

STEP **7**
Adjust stop so that when the control stick is centered in the forward position, the forward edge of the handgrip will be two inches from the instrument panel.

STEP **2**
Connect bomb rack wiring and gun wiring.

STEP **9**
With control stick in full forward position and the elevators 20° down from neutral, adjust clevis so that push-pull rod can be connected to the elevator bellcrank.

STEP **4**
Adjust links so that connecting bolts can be inserted in bellcrank holes marked with desired degrees of travel. Links must be equalized in length before connecting to bellcrank.
NOTE:
If links are not the same length the aileron travel will be unequal.

STEP **5**
Install surface control locking mechanism, adding washers, to position it so that control stick locking flange will engage.

STEP **6**
Remove aileron cable sector jig bolts, install connecting bolts, and adjust stops to obtain desired aileron travel.

STEP **1**
Install torque tube assembly. Start bolts carefully, as plate nuts can be replaced only by removing fuel tank doors.

STEP **3**
Insert long bolts through cable sectors and links, and into jig holes in spar to secure sectors in neutral. When sectors are jigged, ailerons must be in neutral. Rig aileron cable system if necessary.

A  AN5-17A bolt (2 req.)
B  AN4-7A bolt (2 req.)
C  AN4-7A bolt (4 req.)
D  AN4-7A bolt (4 req.)
E  AN5-16 bolt (2 req.)
F  AN25-22 bolt (1 req.)

**REMOVAL:** Essentially the reverse of installation procedure with following exception: To gain access to control stick assembly remove seat and armor plate, control stick shroud, and cockpit floor boards.

## Instrument Panel

**COCKPIT (Front)**

1. Selector Dimmer Controls
2. Remote Indicator Compass
3. Clock
4. Suction Gage
5. Manifold Pressure Gage
6. Airspeed Indicator
7. Directional Gyro
8. Artificial Horizon
9. Carburetor Air Temperature
10. Coolant Temperature
11. Tachometer
12. Altimeter
13. Bank-and-Turn Indicator
14. Rate-of-Climb Indicator
15. Oil Temperature, Fuel and Oil Pressure Gage
16. Engine Control Panel
17. Landing Gear Warning Lights
18. Parking Brake
19. Oxygen Flow Blinker
20. Oxygen Pressure Gage
21. Ignition Switch
22. Bomb and Rocket Switch
23. Chemical Release Switches
24. Cockpit Light Control
25. Gun, Camera and Sight Switch
26. Rocket Control Panel
27. Fuel Shut-off Valve
28. Fuel Selector Valve
29. Emergency Hydraulic Release

## Side Panel – Left

**COCKPIT (Left Side)**

1. Flare Pistol Opening
2. Cockpit Light
3. Coolant Radiator Air Control Switch
4. Oil Radiator Air Control Switch
5. Landing Light Switch
6. Left Fluorescent Light Switch
7. Mixture Control
8. Propeller Control
9. Throttle Quadrant Locks
10. Throttle
11. Microphone Button
12. Flap Control Handle
13. Carburetor Air Controls
14. Rudder Trim Tab Control
15. Aileron Trim Tab Control
16. Bomb Salvo Releases
17. Elevator Trim Tab Control
18. Landing Gear Control

## Side Panel – Right

**COCKPIT (Right Side)**

1. Oxygen Regulator
2. Emergency Canopy Release
3. Recognition Light Key
4. Canopy Crank and Lock
5. Circuit Breakers (under)
6. Right Fluorescent Light Switch
7. Electrical Control Panel
8. Rear Warning Radar Control Panel
9. VHF Volume Control Knob
10. VHF Control Box
11. IFF Control Panel
12. Detonator Buttons
13. Detrola Control Box
14. Cockpit Light

## Throttle Quadrant

**THROTTLE QUADRANT**

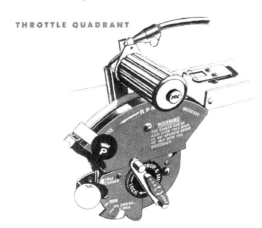

## Electrical Control Panel

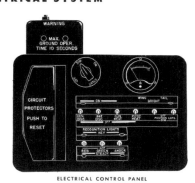

ELECTRICAL CONTROL PANEL

## K-14A Computing Sight

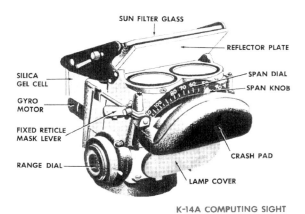

SUN FILTER GLASS
REFLECTOR PLATE
SILICA GEL CELL
SPAN DIAL
SPAN KNOB
GYRO MOTOR
FIXED RETICLE MASK LEVER
CRASH PAD
RANGE DIAL
LAMP COVER

K-14A COMPUTING SIGHT

## Canopy Release Cables

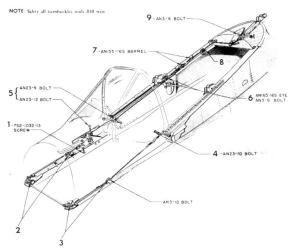

NOTE: Safety all turnbuckles with .040 wire.

9 - AN3-6 BOLT
7 - AN155-16S BARREL
8
5 { AN23-9 BOLT
   AN23-12 BOLT
6 AN165-16S EYE
  AN3-6 BOLT
1 - 752-1032-13 SCREW
4 - AN23-10 BOLT
AN3-10 BOLT
2
3

1  Attach clevis end of cable assembly to emergency release handle.

2  Pass cable over outboard side of pulley immediately forward of release handle, and string cable forward over pulley at right corner of firewall.

3  Continue cable across firewall and over pulley at left side; then run cable aft and under pulley adjacent to instrument panel.

4  Attach turnbuckle end of cable to left side emergency release slide.

5  Connect link to emergency release handle and attach aft end of link to right side emergency release slide.

6  Attach eye to fitting extending downward from right side emergency release slide.

7  Screw barrel onto eye; and screw terminal of aft release cable into barrel.

8  String cable aft and over outboard side of two pulleys aft of pilot's seat, and continue cable inboard to center pulley.

9  Run cable aft and connect to aft release slide.

REMOVAL: Disconnect cables at attaching points and draw out.

## Flare Gun

FLARE GUN

CAUTION: Insert the gun into the tube *before* loading it. Don't load the gun first, as there is danger of accidentally discharging the flare into the cockpit.

## Windshield Panels

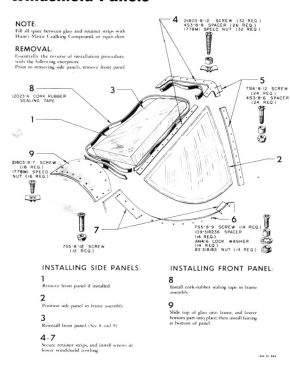

NOTE:
Fill all space between glass and retainer strips with Hunt's Mastic Caulking Compound, or equivalent.

REMOVAL:
Essentially the reverse of installation procedure, with the following exception.
Prior to removing side panels, remove front panel.

4  21803-8-12 SCREW (32 REQ.)
   4S3-8-8 SPACER (26 REQ.)
   1778MI SPEED NUT (32 REQ.)

8  12023-A CORK RUBBER SEALING TAPE
3
1
5  7S6-8-12 SCREW (24 REQ.)
   4S3-8-6 SPACER (24 REQ.)
9  21803-8-7 SCREW (16 REQ.)
   1778MI SPEED NUT (16 REQ.)
2
6  7S5-8-9 SCREW (14 REQ.)
   109-318236 SPACER (14 REQ.)
   AN416 LOCK WASHER (14 REQ.)
   83-318182 NUT (14 REQ.)
7  7S5-8-12 SCREW (12 REQ.)

INSTALLING SIDE PANELS:
1  Remove front panel if installed.
2  Position side panel in frame assembly.
3  Reinstall front panel. (See 8 and 9.)
4-7  Secure retainer strips, and install screws in lower windshield cowling.

INSTALLING FRONT PANEL:
8  Install cork-rubber sealing tape in frame assembly.
9  Slide top of glass into frame, and lower bottom part into place; then install fairing at bottom of panel.

## SCR-522-A and AN/APS13 Radio Installation – Late Aircraft

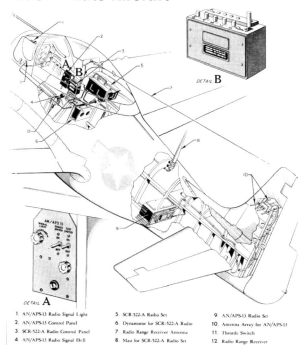

DETAIL B

AN/APS 13

DETAIL A

1. AN/APS-13 Radio Signal Light
2. AN/APS-13 Control Panel
3. SCR-522-A Radio Control Panel
4. AN/APS-13 Radio Signal Bell
5. SCR-522-A Radio Set
6. Dynamotor for SCR-522-A Radio
7. Radio Range Receiver Antenna
8. Mast for SCR-522-A Radio Set
9. AN/APS-13 Radio Set
10. Antenna Array for AN/APS-13
11. Throttle Switch
12. Radio Range Receiver

## SCR-695-A and AN/APS13 Radio Installation – Early Aircraft

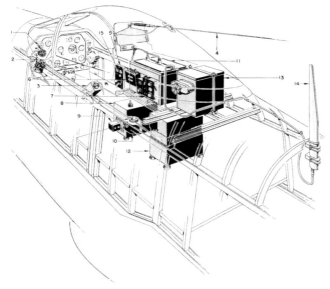

1. REMOTE CONTACTOR
2. THROTTLE SWITCH
3. DETROLA RECEIVER MODEL-438
4. DETROLA & SCR-274-N ANTENNA
5. 106-71154 PANEL ASSEMBLY
6. CONTROL BOX FOR SCR-522-A
7. CONTROL BOX FOR SCR-695-A
8. DYNAMOTOR FOR SCR-522-A
9. INDICATOR LAMPS SCR-695
10. INERTIA SWITCH SCR-695
11. TRANSMITTER RECEIVER SCR-522-A
12. RADIO SET SCR-695-A
13. BATTERY
14. ANTENNA FOR SCR-522-A
15. SCR-695-A DETONATOR BUTTONS

## Oil Coolant and Radiator Flap Actuators

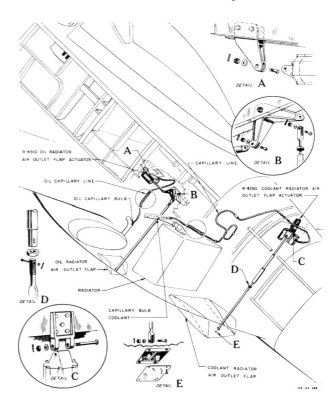

## Electrical Equipment

## Vacuum System

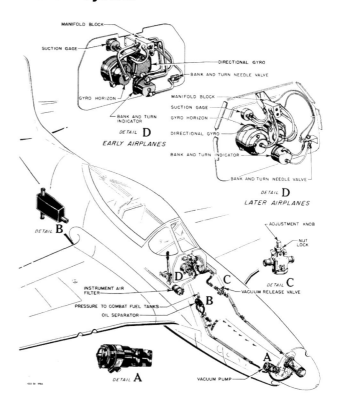

# Lubrication Chart

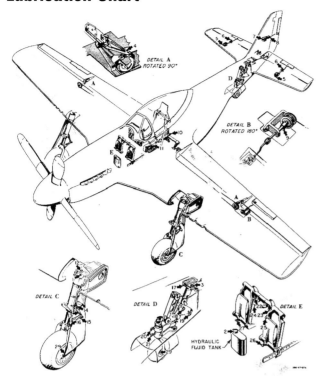

# Fuselage and Wing Connections

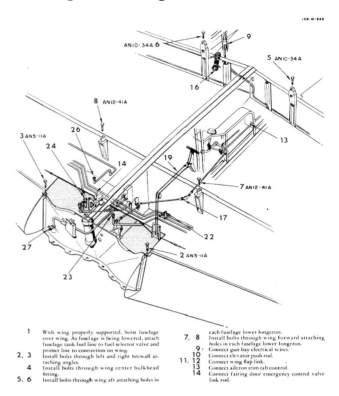

| | |
|---|---|
| 1 | With wing properly supported, hoist fuselage over wing. As fuselage is being lowered, attach fuselage tank fuel line to fuel selector valve and primer line to connection on wing. |
| 2, 3 | Install bolts through left and right firewall attaching angles. |
| 4 | Install bolts through wing center bulkhead fitting. |
| 5, 6 | Install bolts through wing aft attaching holes in |

each fuselage lower longeron.

7, 8    Install bolts through wing forward attaching holes in each fuselage lower longeron.

9    Connect gun bay electrical wires.

10    Connect elevator push rod.

11, 12    Connect wing flap link.

13    Connect aileron trim tab control.

14    Connect fairing door emergency control valve link rod.

# Hoisting Points

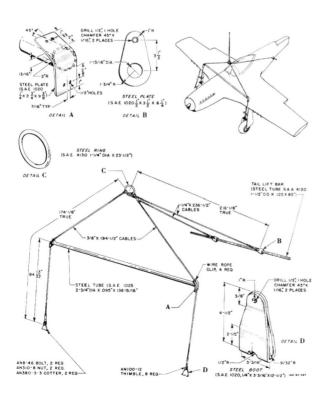

# Wing Panel Joins

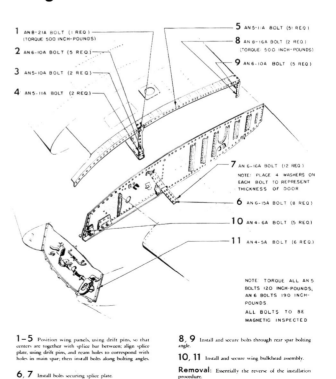

**1–5** Position wing panels, using drift pins, so that centers are together with splice bar between; align splice plate, using drift pins, and ream holes to correspond with holes in main spar; then install bolts along bolting angles.

**6, 7** Install bolts securing splice plate.

**8, 9** Install and secure bolts through rear spar bolting angle.

**10, 11** Install and secure wing bulkhead assembly.

**Removal:** Essentially the reverse of the installation procedure.

# Rear Fuselage Section

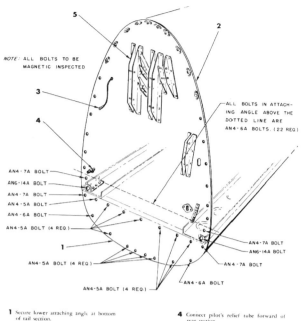

NOTE: ALL BOLTS TO BE MAGNETIC INSPECTED

ALL BOLTS IN ATTACH-ING ANGLE ABOVE THE DOTTED LINE ARE AN4-6A BOLTS. (22 REQ.)

AN4-7A BOLT
AN6-14A BOLT
AN4-7A BOLT
AN4-5A BOLT
AN4-6A BOLT
AN4-5A BOLT (4 REQ.)
AN4-5A BOLT (4 REQ.)
AN4-5A BOLT (4 REQ.)
AN4-6A BOLT
AN4-7A BOLT
AN6-14A BOLT
AN4-7A BOLT

**1** Secure lower attaching angle at bottom of tail section.

**2** Fit rear section to main fuselage attaching angle.

**3** Connect electric-disconnect plug on forward side of rear section bulkhead.

**4** Connect pilot's relief tube forward of rear section.

**5** Connect empennage control cables. (See applicable paragraph.)

REMOVAL: Essentially the reverse of installation procedure.

# Braking System

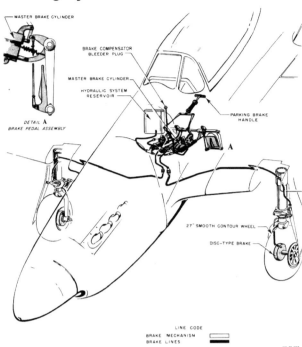

MASTER BRAKE CYLINDER

BRAKE COMPENSATOR BLEEDER PLUG

MASTER BRAKE CYLINDER

HYDRAULIC SYSTEM RESERVOIR

PARKING BRAKE HANDLE

DETAIL A
BRAKE PEDAL ASSEMBLY

27" SMOOTH CONTOUR WHEEL

DISC-TYPE BRAKE

LINE CODE
BRAKE MECHANISM
BRAKE LINES

# Wing Panel Assembly

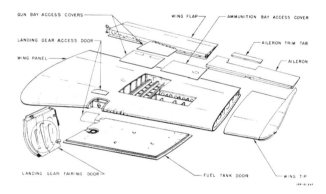

GUN BAY ACCESS COVERS
WING FLAP
AMMUNITION BAY ACCESS COVER
LANDING GEAR ACCESS DOOR
AILERON TRIM TAB
WING PANEL
AILERON
LANDING GEAR FAIRING DOOR
FUEL TANK DOOR
WING TIP

# Fuel tank Doors

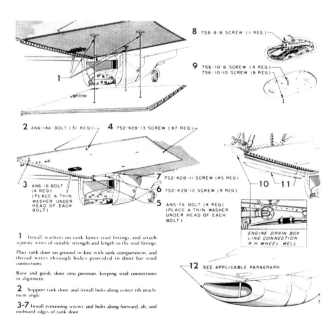

**8** 7S6-8-8 SCREW (1 REQ)

**9** 7S6-10-8 SCREW (4 REQ)
7S6-10-10 SCREW (8 REQ)

**2** AN6-14A BOLT (31 REQ)  **4** 7S2-428-13 SCREW (87 REQ)

**3** AN6-16 BOLT (4 REQ) (PLACE A THIN WASHER UNDER HEAD OF EACH BOLT)

**7** 7S2-428-11 SCREW (45 REQ)
**6** 7S2-428-12 SCREW (9 REQ)

**5** AN5-7A BOLT (4 REQ) (PLACE A THIN WASHER UNDER HEAD OF EACH BOLT)

**10 — 11**

ENGINE DRAIN BOX LINE CONNECTION R H WHEEL WELL

**12** SEE APPLICABLE PARAGRAPH

**1** Install washers on tank lower stud fittings, and attach separate wires of suitable strength and length to the stud fittings.

Place tank door on ground in line with tank compartment, and thread wires through holes provided in door for stud connections.

Raise and guide door into position, keeping stud connections in alignment.

**2** Support tank door, and install bolts along center rib attachment angle.

**3-7** Install remaining screws and bolts along forward, aft, and outboard edges of tank door.

**8** Connect bonding braid from booster pump to tank door.

**9** Install booster pump access door.

**10** Install engine drain box drain line.

**11** Install fairing over lower wing center bolting angle.

**12** Install radiator air inlet scoop.

REMOVAL: Essentially the reverse of installation procedure, with the following exceptions.

# Wing Tip Assembly

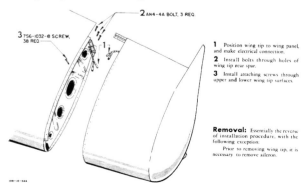

**2** AN4-4A BOLT, 3 REQ.

**3** 7S6-1032-8 SCREW, 38 REQ.

**1** Position wing tip to wing panel, and make electrical connection.

**2** Install bolts through holes of wing tip rear spar.

**3** Install attaching screws through upper and lower wing tip surfaces.

**Removal:** Essentially the reverse of installation procedure, with the following exception:

Prior to removing wing tip, it is necessary to remove aileron.

Prior to removing fuel tank doors, jack airplane, using wing jacking points at lower surface of each wing section immediately outboard of bomb racks, and jacking point on wing center rib.

Weight of airplane must be supported at center jacking point, with outer jacking points being used for balance only.

**CAUTION**

The foregoing jacking procedure should be closely followed, as the fuel tank doors form a structural part of the wing. Distortion and misalignment may result from improper support. To prevent sinking when jacking on soft surface, place suitable platform beneath jacking stand.

# Aileron Control System

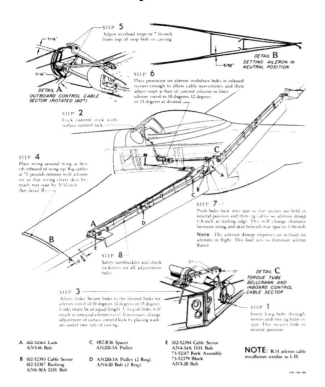

STEP 5
Adjust overload stops to 7/16-inch from top of stop bolt to casting.

7/16

7/16

5/32

DETAIL B
SETTING AILERON IN NEUTRAL POSITION

STEP 6
Place protractor on aileron, withdraw bolts in inboard sectors enough to allow cable movements, and then adjust stops at base of control column to limit aileron travel to 10 degrees, 12 degrees or 15 degrees as desired.

DETAIL A
OUTBOARD CONTROL CABLE SECTOR (ROTATED 180°)

STEP 2
Lock control stick with surface control lock.

STEP 4
Place string around wing at first rib inboard of wing tip. Rig cables at 70 pounds tension with aileron set so that string clears skin beneath rear spar by 5/32-inch. (See detail B).

STEP 7
Push bolts back into spar so that sectors are held in neutral position, and then rig cables so aileron droop 1/8-inch at trailing edge. This will change clearance between string and skin beneath rear spar to 3/16-inch.

Note: The aileron droop imposes an airload on ailerons in flight. This load acts to eliminate aileron flutter.

STEP 8
Safety turnbuckles and check locknuts on all adjustment bolts.

DETAIL C
TORQUE TUBE BELLCRANK AND INBOARD CONTROL CABLE SECTOR

STEP 3
Adjust links. Secure links to the desired holes for aileron travel of 10 degrees, 12 degrees or 15 degrees. Links must be of equal length. Unequal links will result in unequal aileron travel. If necessary, change adjustment of surface control lock by placing washers under one side of casting.

STEP 1
Insert long bolts through sectors and into jig holes in spar. This secures link in neutral position.

A 102-52364 Link
  AN5-16 Bolt

B 102-52393 Cable Sector
  102-52387 Bushing
  AN6-30A D.H. Bolt

C 4B2-R36 Spacer
  AN210-3A Pulley

D AN210-3A Pulley (2 Req.)
  AN4-20 Bolt (2 Req.)

E 102-52394 Cable Sector
  AN4-34A D.H. Bolt
  73-52317 Fork Assembly
  73-52379 Block
  AN5-20 Bolt

NOTE: R.H. aileron cable installation similar to L.H.

# Aileron Trim Tab Control System

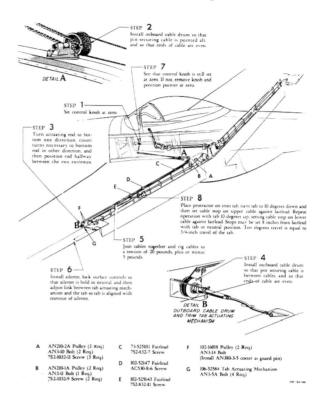

STEP 2
Install inboard cable drum so that pin securing cable is pointed aft, and so that ends of cable are even.

DETAIL A

STEP 7
See that control knob is still set at zero. If not, remove knob and position pointer at zero.

STEP 1
Set control knob at zero.

STEP 3
Turn actuating rod to bottom one direction, count turns necessary to bottom rod in other direction, and then position rod halfway between the two extremes.

STEP 8
Place protractor on trim tab, turn tab to 10 degrees down and then set cable stop on upper cable against fairlead. Repeat operation with tab 10 degrees up, setting cable stop on lower cable against fairlead. Stops may be set 8 inches from fairlead with tab in neutral position. Ten degrees travel is equal to 3/4-inch travel of the tab.

STEP 5
Join cables together and rig cables to a tension of 20 pounds, plus or minus 5 pounds.

STEP 6
Install aileron, lock surface controls so that aileron is held in neutral, and then adjust tab actuating mechanism and the tab so that tab is aligned with contour of aileron.

STEP 4
Install outboard cable drum so that pin securing cable is between cables, and so that ends of cable are even.

DETAIL B
OUTBOARD CABLE DRUM AND TRIM TAB ACTUATING MECHANISM

A AN210-2A Pulley (2 Req.)
  AN3-10 Bolt (2 Req.)
  7S2-1032-11 Screw (3 Req.)

B AN210-1A Pulley (2 Req.)
  AN3-11 Bolt (1 Req.)
  7S2-1032-9 Screw (2 Req.)

C 73-525101 Fairlead
  7S2-832-7 Screw

D 102-52147 Fairlead
  AC530-8-6 Screw

E 102-525143 Fairlead
  7S2-832-11 Screw

F 102-16018 Pulley (2 Req.)
  AN3-14 Bolt
  (Install AN380-3-5 cotter as guard pin)

G 106-52584 Tab Actuating Mechanism
  AN3-5A Bolt (4 Req.)

# Elevator Control System

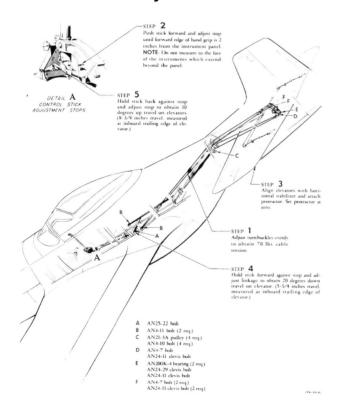

STEP 2
Push stick forward and adjust stop until forward edge of hand grip is 2 inches from the instrument panel.
NOTE: Do not measure to the face of the instruments which extend beyond the panel.

DETAIL A
CONTROL STICK ADJUSTMENT STOPS

STEP 5
Hold stick back against stop and adjust stop to obtain 30 degrees up travel on elevators. (8-3/4 inches travel, measured at inboard trailing edge of elevator.)

STEP 3
Align elevators with horizontal stabilizer and attach protractor. Set protractor at zero.

STEP 1
Adjust turnbuckles evenly to obtain 70 lbs. cable tension.

STEP 4
Hold stick forward against stop and adjust linkage to obtain 20 degrees down travel on elevator. (5-3/4 inches travel, measured at inboard trailing edge of elevator.)

A AN25-22 bolt
B AN4-11 bolt (2 req.)
C AN21-3A pulley (4 req.)
  AN4-10 bolt (4 req.)
D AN4-7 bolt
  AN24-11 clevis bolt
E AN200K-4 bearing (2 req.)
  AN24-29 clevis bolt
  AN24-11 clevis bolt
F AN4-7 bolt (2 req.)
  AN24-11 clevis bolt (2 req.)

# Flap Control System

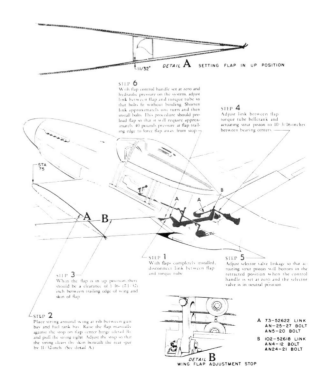

11/32

DETAIL A   SETTING FLAP IN UP POSITION

STEP 6
With flap control handle set at zero and hydraulic pressure on the system, adjust link between flap and torque tube so that bolts fit without binding. Shorten link approximately one turn and then install bolts. This procedure should preload flap so that it will require approximately 40 pounds pressure at flap trailing edge to force flap away from stop.

STEP 4
Adjust link between flap torque tube bellcrank and actuating strut piston to 10-3/16-inches between bearing centers.

STA 75

STEP 1
With flaps completely installed, disconnect link between flap and torque tube.

STEP 5
Adjust selector valve linkage so that actuating strut piston will bottom in the retracted position when the control handle is set at zero and the selector valve is in neutral position.

STEP 3
When the flap is in up position there should be a clearance of 1 16-(23/32)-inch between trailing edge of wing and skin of flap.

STEP 2
Place string around wing at rib between gun bay and fuel tank bay. Raise the flap manually against the stop on flap center hinge (detail B) and pull the string tight. Adjust the stop so that the string clears the skin beneath the rear spar by 11/32-inch. (See detail A).

DETAIL B
WING FLAP ADJUSTMENT STOP

A 73-52622 LINK
  AN-25-27 BOLT
  AN5-20 BOLT

B 102-52618 LINK
  AN4-12 BOLT
  AN24-21 BOLT

# Landing Gear Control System

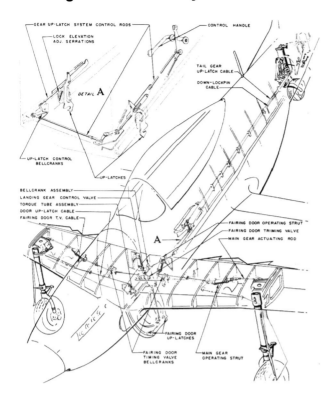

# Tail Gear Assembly

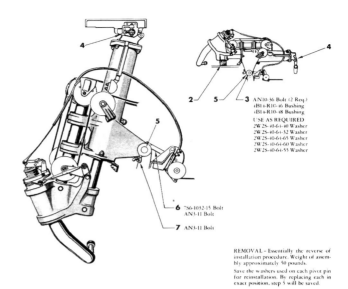

**3** AN10-16 Bolt (2 Req.)
tB14-R10-16 Bushing
tB14-R10-18 Bushing
USE AS REQUIRED
2W2S-40-64-40 Washer
2W2S-40-64-32 Washer
2W2S-40-64-65 Washer
2W2S-40-64-60 Washer
2W2S-40-64-55 Washer

**6** 7S6-1032-15 Bolt
AN3-11 Bolt

**7** AN3-11 Bolt

REMOVAL – Essentially the reverse of installation procedure. Weight of assembly approximately 50 pounds.

Save the washers used on each pivot pin for reinstallation. By replacing each in exact position, step 5 will be saved.

**1** Hoist or jack airplane tail to a convenient height (weight lift tube with 200 pounds). Remove fuselage access doors directly below horizontal stabilizers.

**2** Lift the assembly through the tail wheel opening, and place in gear up position. Place a temporary support over wheel opening to support assembly.

**3** Place bushings into the pivot bolt holes, and bolt to the support bracket.

**4** Remove support, release up-latch, and swing assembly 2 or 3 times from the up to the down position to

test alignment with locks.

**5** If necessary to correct alignment, replace temporary support, remove pivot bolts, and substitute thicker washers on one side and thinner washers on other until alignment is made. .010 max. side play.

**6** Attach hydraulic strut actuating arm.

**7** Connect fairing door actuating link.

**8** Refer to applicable paragraphs for cable installations.

# Main Wheels Maintenance

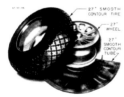

Figure 158—Main Wheel, Tire, and Tube

and fluid can flow freely to or from the brake. The fluid flows by gravity from the hydraulic system tank into the cylinder through port B, so that the master cylinder con-

stantly maintains the correct volume of fluid under all conditions. When the piston rod is pulled back, the valve seats on piston, and the brake pressure is directly proportional to the force applied to the brake pedals. The brake pressure flows through the outlets in the piston wall around past the parking brake stem assembly and out port A to the brakes.

    *(b)* INSTALLING AND REMOVING BRAKE MASTER CYLINDER. (See figure 156.)

    *(c)* ASSEMBLING AND DISASSEMBLING BRAKE MASTER CYLINDER (See figure 157.)

    *(d)* PARKING BRAKE VALVE—A parking brake valve is incorporated in each brake master cylinder. (See figure 157.) After braking pressure has been generated by the pedals, the parking brake is applied to lock pressure in the brake lines between the master cylinder and the brakes. The pressure in the brake lines holds the stem assembly seated until enough pressure is generated in brake cylinders to overcome pressure in the lines and

**1** Slide wheel parts over axle line up by rotating brake discs with the rollers inside the wheel hub and then push the wheel carefully over the discs.

**2** Insert outer bearing, install axle washer and nut and secure wheel as follows:
  a. Rotate wheel while tightening the adjusting nut. This will result in a definite drag or bind in the wheel bearing.
  b. Back off nut until nut is free.
  c. Again take up on nut until point is reached where there is a sudden definite increase in drag of nut.
  d. Continue to take up on nut until next cotter key hole is reached, then lock.

NOTE:
If next cotter key hole on axle is less than ¼ inch away from cotter pin hole in nut when making this final take up the nut should be taken up to the second locking position.

# Main Wheel Structure

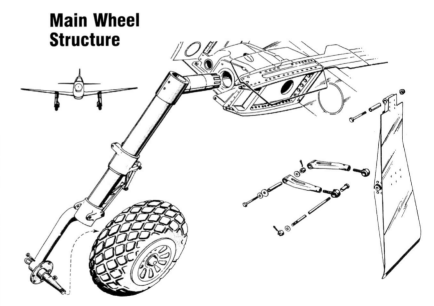

# Wing Structure

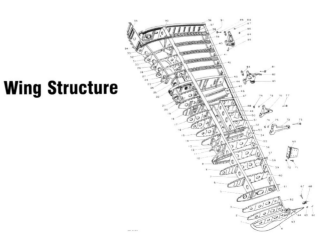

# Main Fuel Tank

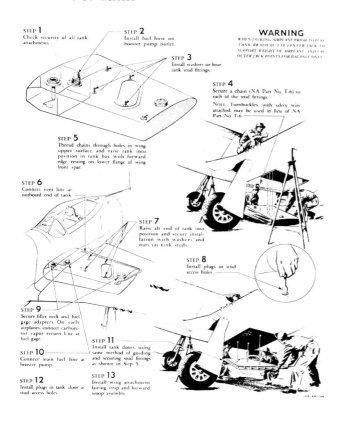

**STEP 1**
Check security of all tank attachments.

**STEP 2**
Install fuel hose on booster pump outlet.

**STEP 3**
Install washers on four tank stud fittings.

**STEP 4**
Secure a chain (NA Part No. T-6) to each of the stud fittings.
NOTE: Turnbuckles, with safety wire attached, may be used in lieu of NA Part No. T-6.

**STEP 5**
Thread chains through holes in wing upper surface, and raise tank into position in tank bay with forward edge resting on lower flange of wing front spar.

**STEP 6**
Connect vent line at outboard end of tank.

**STEP 7**
Raise aft end of tank into position and secure installation with washers and nuts on tank studs.

**STEP 8**
Install plugs in stud access holes.

**STEP 9**
Secure filler neck and fuel gage adapters. On early airplanes, connect carburetor vapor return line at fuel gage.

**STEP 10**
Connect main fuel line at booster pump.

**STEP 11**
Install tank doors, using same method of guiding and securing stud fittings as shown in Step 5.

**STEP 12**
Install plugs in tank door at stud access holes.

**STEP 13**
Install wing attachment fairing strip and forward scoop assembly.

**WARNING**
WHEN JACKING AIRPLANE PRIOR TO FUEL TANK REMOVAL, USE CENTER JACK TO SUPPORT WEIGHT OF AIRPLANE AND USE OUTER JACK POINTS FOR BALANCE ONLY.

# Auxiliary Fuel Tanks

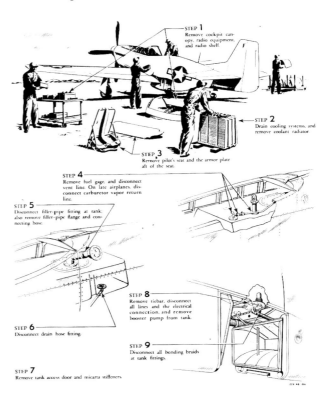

**STEP 1**
Remove cockpit canopy, radio equipment, and radio shelf.

**STEP 2**
Drain cooling systems, and remove coolant radiator.

**STEP 3**
Remove pilot's seat and the armor plate aft of the seat.

**STEP 4**
Remove fuel gage, and disconnect vent line. On late airplanes, disconnect carburetor vapor return line.

**STEP 5**
Disconnect filler-pipe fitting at tank; also remove filler-pipe flange and connecting hose.

**STEP 6**
Disconnect drain hose fitting.

**STEP 7**
Remove tank access door and micarta stiffeners.

**STEP 8**
Remove tiebar, disconnect all lines and the electrical connection, and remove booster pump from tank.

**STEP 9**
Disconnect all bonding braids at tank fittings.

# Gunnery Equipment

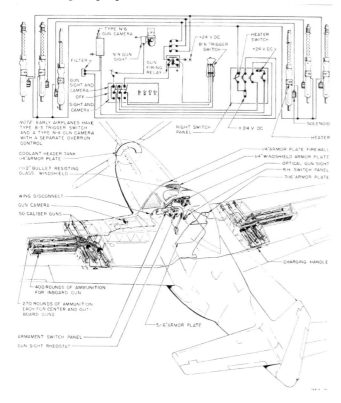

# Mechanical Bomb Release Mechanism

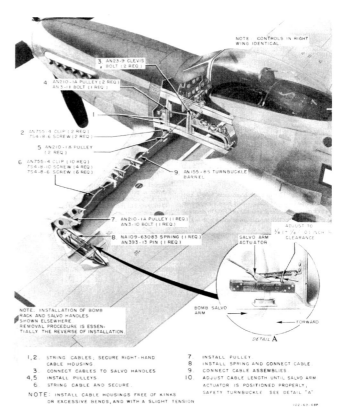

NOTE: CONTROLS IN RIGHT WING IDENTICAL.

3. AN23-9 CLEVIS
BOLT (2 REQ.)

4. AN210-1A PULLEY (2 REQ)
AN3-11 BOLT (1 REQ.)

2. AN755-4 CLIP (2 REQ)
754-8-6 SCREW (2 REQ)

5. AN210-1A PULLEY (2 REQ)

6. AN755-4 CLIP (10 REQ)
754-8-10 SCREW (4 REQ)
754-8-6 SCREW (6 REQ.)

9. AN155-8S TURNBUCKLE BARREL

7. AN210-1A PULLEY (1 REQ)
AN3-10 BOLT (1 REQ)

8. NA109-63083 SPRING (1 REQ.)
AN393-13 PIN (1 REQ.)

ADJUST TO .01 INCH CLEARANCE

SALVO ARM ACTUATOR

BOMB SALVO ARM

FORWARD

DETAIL A

NOTE: INSTALLATION OF BOMB RACK AND SALVO HANDLES SHOWN ELSEWHERE. REMOVAL PROCEDURE IS ESSENTIALLY THE REVERSE OF INSTALLATION.

1,2. STRING CABLES, SECURE RIGHT-HAND CABLE HOUSING
3. CONNECT CABLES TO SALVO HANDLES
4,5. INSTALL PULLEYS
6. STRING CABLE AND SECURE.
NOTE: INSTALL CABLE HOUSINGS FREE OF KINKS OR EXCESSIVE BENDS, AND WITH A SLIGHT TENSION

7. INSTALL PULLEY
8. INSTALL SPRING AND CONNECT CABLE
9. CONNECT CABLE ASSEMBLIES
10. ADJUST CABLE LENGTH UNTIL SALVO ARM ACTUATOR IS POSITIONED PROPERLY, SAFETY TURNBUCKLE. SEE DETAIL "A"

# Rocket Launcher Installation

AN 01-60JE-4
ARMAMENT GROUP

Section
Group Assembly Parts Li

# Bore Sighting System

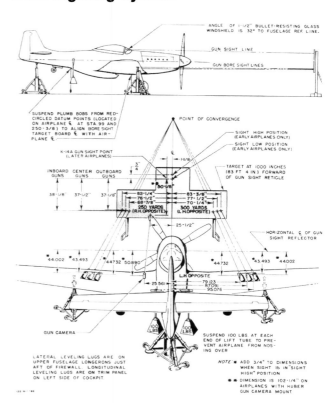

ANGLE OF 1-1/2" BULLET-RESISTING GLASS
WINDSHIELD IS 32° TO FUSELAGE REF LINE.

GUN SIGHT LINE

GUN BORE SIGHT LINES

SUSPEND PLUMB BOBS FROM RED-
CIRCLED DATUM POINTS (LOCATED
ON AIRPLANE ₵ AT STA. 99 AND
250-3/8) TO ALIGN BORE SIGHT
TARGET BOARD ₵ WITH AIR-
PLANE ₵

POINT OF CONVERGENCE

K-14A GUN SIGHT POINT
(LATER AIRPLANES)

INBOARD   CENTER   OUTBOARD
GUNS      GUNS     GUNS

SIGHT HIGH POSITION
(EARLY AIRPLANES ONLY)

SIGHT LOW POSITION
(EARLY AIRPLANES ONLY)

TARGET AT 1000 INCHES
(83 FT 4 IN.) FORWARD
OF GUN SIGHT RETICLE

38-1/8"  37-1/2"  37-1/8"

82-1/4"   83-3/8"
76-1/2"   77-1/2"
68-7/8"   70-1/4"
250 YARDS  300 YARDS
(R.H. OPPOSITE) (L.H.OPPOSITE)

25-1/2"

HORIZONTAL ₵ OF GUN
SIGHT REFLECTOR

44.002  43.493   44.732 50.890     44.732   43.493  44.002

L.H. OPPOSITE

25.561      79.123
87.091
95.076

GUN CAMERA

SUSPEND 100 LBS AT EACH
END OF LIFT TUBE TO PRE-
VENT AIRPLANE FROM NOS-
ING OVER

LATERAL LEVELING LUGS ARE ON
UPPER FUSELAGE LONGERONS JUST
AFT OF FIREWALL. LONGITUDINAL
LEVELING LUGS ARE ON TRIM PANEL
ON LEFT SIDE OF COCKPIT.

NOTE * ADD 3/4" TO DIMENSIONS
WHEN SIGHT IS IN "SIGHT
HIGH" POSITION
** DIMENSION IS 102-1/4" ON
AIRPLANES WITH HUBER
GUN CAMERA MOUNT.

# 75 Gallon Combat Tank

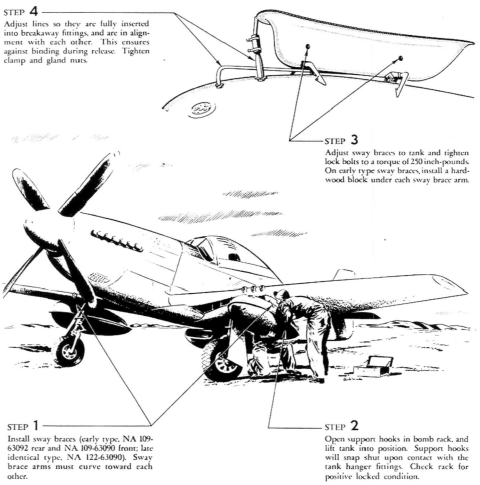

STEP 4
Adjust lines so they are fully inserted
into breakaway fittings, and are in alignment with each other. This ensures
against binding during release. Tighten
clamp and gland nuts.

STEP 3
Adjust sway braces to tank and tighten
lock bolts to a torque of 250 inch-pounds.
On early type sway braces, install a hard-
wood block under each sway brace arm.

STEP 1
Install sway braces (early type, NA 109-
63092 rear and NA 109-63090 front; late
identical type, NA 122-63090). Sway
brace arms must curve toward each
other.

STEP 2
Open support hooks in bomb rack, and
lift tank into position. Support hooks
will snap shut upon contact with the
tank hanger fittings. Check rack for
positive locked condition.

NOTE: If only one combat tank is
to be used on mission, plug pressure fitting in opposite wing to prevent loss of
system pressure.

109-48-192A

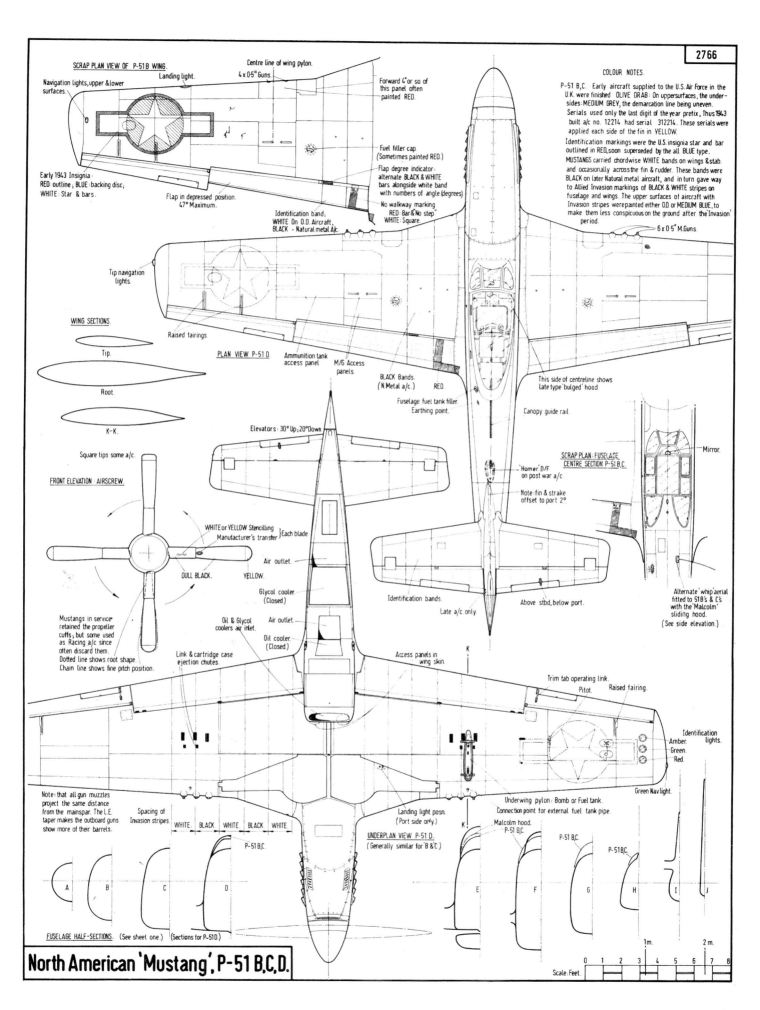

SCRAP PLAN VIEW OF P-51 B WING.

Navigation lights, upper & lower surfaces.

Landing light.

Centre line of wing pylon.
4 x 0.5" Guns.

Forward 4" or so of this panel often painted RED.

Early 1943 Insignia:
RED: outline; BLUE: backing disc; WHITE: Star & bars.

Flap in depressed position. 47° Maximum.

Fuel filler cap. (Sometimes painted RED.)

Flap degree indicator. alternate BLACK & WHITE bars alongside white band with numbers of angle (degrees)

No walkway marking
RED: Bar & No step
WHITE: Square.

Identification band;
WHITE On O.D. Aircraft,
BLACK - Natural metal A/c.

COLOUR NOTES.

P-51 B,C. Early aircraft supplied to the U.S. Air Force in the U.K. were finished OLIVE DRAB: On uppersurfaces, the undersides: MEDIUM GREY, the demarcation line being uneven. Serials used only the last digit of the year prefix. Thus 1943 built a/c no. 12214 had serial 312214. These serials were applied each side of the fin in YELLOW.

Identification markings were the U.S. insignia star and bar outlined in RED, soon superseded by the all BLUE type. MUSTANGS carried chordwise WHITE bands on wings & stab. and occasionally across the fin & rudder. These bands were BLACK on later Natural metal aircraft, and in turn gave way to Allied Invasion markings of BLACK & WHITE stripes on fuselage and wings. The upper surfaces of aircraft with Invasion stripes were painted either O.D. or MEDIUM BLUE, to make them less conspicuous on the ground after the 'Invasion' period.

6 x 0.5" M.Guns.

Tip navigation lights.

WING SECTIONS.

Tip.

Root.

K-K.

Raised fairings.

PLAN VIEW P-51 D.

Ammunition tank access panel.

M/G Access panels.

BLACK Bands. (N.Metal a/c.)    RED.

Fuselage fuel tank filler. Earthing point.

This side of centreline shows late type 'bulged' hood.

Canopy guide rail.

SCRAP PLAN: FUSELAGE CENTRE SECTION P-51 B,C.

Mirror.

'Homer' D/F on post war a/c.

Note: fin & strake offset to port 2°

Square tips some a/c.

FRONT ELEVATION: AIRSCREW.

Elevators: 30° Up; 20° Down.

WHITE or YELLOW Stencilling
Manufacturer's transfer } Each blade

DULL BLACK.    YELLOW.

Air outlet.

Glycol cooler. (Closed.)

Oil & Glycol coolers air inlet.

Air outlet.

Oil cooler. (Closed.)

Identification bands.

Above stbd, below port.

Late a/c only.

Alternate 'whip' aerial fitted to 51B's & C's with the 'Malcolm' sliding hood. (See side elevation.)

Mustangs in service retained the propeller cuffs; but some used as Racing a/c since often discard them. Dotted line shows root shape. Chain line shows fine pitch position.

Link & cartridge case ejection chutes.

Access panels in wing skin.

K

Trim tab operating link.

Pitot.    Raised fairing.

Identification lights.
Amber.
Green.
Red.

Green Nav light.

Note: that all gun muzzles project the same distance from the mainspar. The L.E. taper makes the outboard guns show more of their barrels.

Spacing of Invasion stripes.

WHITE  BLACK  WHITE  BLACK  WHITE

P-51 B,C.

Landing light posn. (Port side only.)

UNDERPLAN VIEW P-51 D. (Generally similar for 'B & C.')

Underwing pylon: Bomb or Fuel tank.
Connection point for external fuel tank pipe.

K

Malcolm hood. P-51 B,C.

P-51 B,C.

P-51 B,C.

FUSELAGE HALF-SECTIONS. (See sheet one.) (Sections for P-51 D.)

A   B   C   D   E   F   G   H   I   J

1m.    2 m.

0  1  2  3  4  5  6  7  8

Scale: Feet.

# North American 'Mustang', P-51 B,C,D.

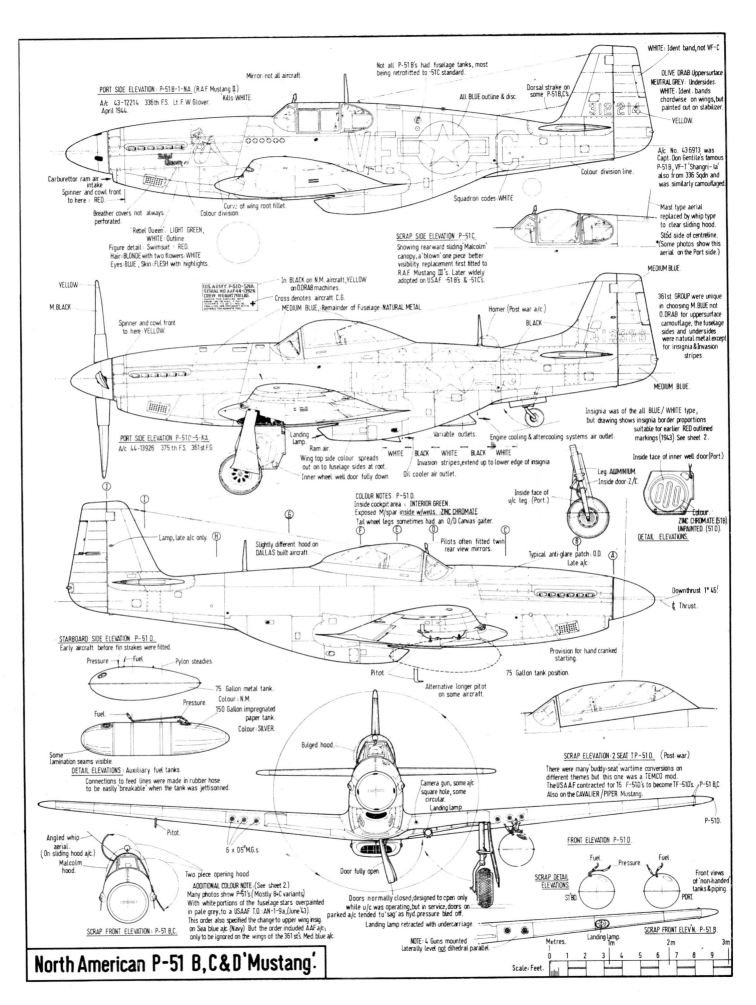

**PORT SIDE ELEVATION: P-51 B-1-NA. (R.A.F. Mustang II)**
A/c 43-12214. 336th F.S. Lt. F. W. Glover. April 1944.

Kills: WHITE.

Mirror: not all aircraft.

Not all P-51 B's had fuselage tanks, most being retrofitted to -51C standard.

WHITE: Ident band, not VF-C

Dorsal strake on some P-51 B,C's.

OLIVE DRAB Uppersurface
NEUTRAL GREY: Undersides.
WHITE: Ident bands chordwise on wings, but painted out on stabilizer.

All BLUE outline & disc.

YELLOW.

A/c No. 43-6913 was Capt. Don Gentile's famous P-51 B, VF-'T' 'Shangri- la' also from 336 Sqdn and was similarly camouflaged.

Colour division line.

Squadron codes: WHITE.

Carburettor ram air intake.
Spinner and cowl front to here: RED.

Breather covers not always perforated.

Colour division.

Curve of wing root fillet.

'Rebel Queen': LIGHT GREEN, WHITE: Outline.
Figure detail: Swimsuit: RED.
Hair: BLONDE with two flowers: WHITE
Eyes: BLUE, Skin: FLESH with highlights.

Mast type aerial replaced by whip type to clear sliding hood. Stbd. side of centreline.
*(Some photos show this aerial on the Port side.)

**SCRAP SIDE ELEVATION: P-51C.**
Showing rearward sliding 'Malcolm' canopy, a 'blown' one piece better visibility replacement first fitted to R.A.F. Mustang III's. Later widely adopted to USAF -51B's & -51C's.

YELLOW.
M. BLACK.

Spinner and cowl front to here: YELLOW.

U.S. ARMY. P-51D-5-NA.
SERIAL NO. AAF44-13926
CREW WEIGHT 200 LBS.

In BLACK on N.M. aircraft, YELLOW on O.DRAB machines.
Cross denotes aircraft C.G.

MEDIUM BLUE: Remainder of Fuselage: NATURAL METAL.

Homer (Post war a/c.)
BLACK.

MEDIUM BLUE.

361st GROUP were unique in choosing M. BLUE not O.DRAB for uppersurface camouflage, the fuselage sides and undersides were natural metal except for insignia & Invasion stripes.

MEDIUM BLUE.

**PORT SIDE ELEVATION P-51D-5-NA.**
A/c 44-13926. 375th F.S. 361st F.G.

Landing Lamp.
Ram air.
Wing top side colour spreads out on to fuselage sides at root.
Inner wheel well door fully down.

WHITE BLACK WHITE BLACK WHITE
Invasion stripes, extend up to lower edge of insignia.
Oil cooler air outlet.

Variable outlets.
Engine cooling & aftercooling systems air outlet.

Insignia was of the all BLUE/WHITE type, but drawing shows insignia border proportions suitable for earlier RED outlined markings (1943). See sheet 2.

Inside face of inner well door (Port).

Leg: ALUMINIUM.
Inside door: Z/c.

Inside face of u/c. leg. (Port.)

Colour:
ZINC CHROMATE. (51B)
UNPAINTED. (51 D.)
DETAIL ELEVATIONS.

**COLOUR NOTES: P-51D.**
Inside cockpit area: INTERIOR GREEN.
Exposed M/spar inside w/wells: ZINC CHROMATE.
Tail wheel legs sometimes had an O/D Canvas gaiter.

Lamp, late a/c only.

Slightly different hood on DALLAS built aircraft.

Pilots often fitted twin rear view mirrors.

Typical anti-glare patch: O.D. Late a/c.

Downthrust 1° 45'
¢ Thrust.

**STARBOARD SIDE ELEVATION P-51 D.**
Early aircraft, before fin strakes were fitted.

Pressure. Fuel.
Pylon steadies.

75 Gallon metal tank.
Colour: N.M.
Pressure.
150 Gallon impregnated paper tank.
Colour: SILVER.
Fuel.

Some lamination seams visible.

**DETAIL ELEVATIONS: Auxiliary fuel tanks.**
Connections to feed lines were made in rubber hose to be easily 'breakable' when the tank was jettisonned.

Pitot.
Alternative longer pitot on some aircraft.

Provision for hand cranked starting.

75 Gallon tank position.

Bulged hood.

Camera gun, some a/c square hole, some circular.
Landing lamp.

**SCRAP ELEVATION: 2 SEAT TP-51 D.** (Post-war).
There were many 'buddy-seat' wartime conversions on different themes but this one was a TEMCO mod. The USAAF contracted for 15 F-51D's to become TF-51D's. P-51 B,C. Also on the CAVALIER / PIPER Mustang.

P-51D.

Angled whip aerial.
(On sliding hood a/c.)
Malcolm hood.

Pitot.

6 x 0.5" M.G.s.

Two piece opening hood.

**ADDITIONAL COLOUR NOTE:** (See sheet 2.)
Many photos show P-51's (Mostly B&C variants) With white portions of the fuselage stars overpainted in pale grey, to a USAAF T.O. AN-1-9a, (June '43). This order also specified the change to upper wing insig. on Sea blue a/c. (Navy) But the order included AAF a/c; only to be ignored on the wings of the 361st's Med. blue a/c.

Door fully open.

Doors normally closed; designed to open only while u/c was operating, but in service, doors on parked a/c tended to 'sag' as hyd. pressure bled off.

**FRONT ELEVATION P-51 D.**
Fuel. Pressure. Fuel.

**SCRAP DETAIL ELEVATIONS.**
STBD.

Front views of 'non-handed' tanks and piping.
PORT.

**SCRAP FRONT ELEVATION: P-51 B,C.**

NOTE: 4 Guns mounted laterally level not dihedral parallel.

Landing lamp.
Landing lamp retracted with undercarriage.

**SCRAP FRONT ELEV'N. P-51 B.**

Metres.
0 1 2 3m
Scale: Feet.
0 1 2 3 4 5 6 7 8 9 1m 2m 3m

# North American P-51 B, C & D 'Mustang'.

# Merlin-Mustang and Twin-Mustang Specifications

Apart from the obvious alterations in armament from one version to the next within the production run of Merlin-engined Mustangs, and the various changes that turned the type into a twin-engined fighter as the P/F-82 Twin Mustang, there were few if any major alterations to the basic layout of the Mustang in its Merlin-powered versions. Without doubt, one of the yardsticks by which a successful aircraft design can be judged, is the amount that its airframe is altered by necessity during production – and therefore in the case of the Merlin-engined Mustang, there were few significant alterations that actually needed to be made to the size and general layout of the Merlin Mustang throughout its production run – except for the very obvious change in configuration with the introduction of the 'bubble canopy' layout of the P-51D. The radical changes that were made to the basic layout of the Mustang to create the 'lightweight' P-51H, as related elsewhere in the text, were made by choice rather than necessity – and actually turned out to be less than successful, and in the event proved to be largely unnecessary.

Nevertheless, despite the Mustang being one of the best-known warplanes of all time, there have still been a number of anomalies within published sources over the years as to what the size of the Merlin-engined Mustang really was. This has partly arisen due to the understandable tendency in many publications to round off the wingspan and lose the 5/16-inch over 37 feet.

However, as related elsewhere in this book, that 5/16-inch (closely equivalent to 0.3 inch) nevertheless existed in the official Manuals for the P-51 - with which the aircraft was maintained and looked after in the field. It is therefore included without hesitation in the following specification summaries.

A 311th Fighter Group, 14th Air Force Mustang escorting C-47's over China on July 24, 1945. *(Credit USAF Museum)*

## Specifications - P-51D Mustang

| | |
|---|---|
| **Dimensions** | Span 37 ft 0.3 in (11.29 m); length 32 ft 3.3 in (9.84 m); height 13 ft 8 in (4.17 m) |
| **Power plant** | One Packard V-1650-7 (Merlin) inline piston engine, producing 1,720 hp with maximum boost, and 1,490 hp for take-off |
| **Armament** | Six 0.5-inch machine guns, plus underwing stores of drop tanks, or two 500 lb (227 kg) bombs |
| | (or, later, two 1,000 lb (454 kg) bombs or up to ten 5-inch unguided air-to-ground rockets) |
| **Weights** | Empty 7,125 lb (3,232 kg); loaded 12,100 lb (5,489 kg) |
| **Performance** | Maximum speed 437 mph (703 km/h) at 25,000 ft (7,620 m); range c. 2,080 miles (3,347 km) with drop tanks; service ceiling 41,900 ft (12,771 m) |

## Specifications - P-51H Mustang

| | |
|---|---|
| **Dimensions** | Span 37 ft 0.3 in (11.29 m); length 33 ft 3.25 in (10.14 m); height 13 ft 8 in (4.17 m) |
| **Power plant** | One Packard V-1650-9 (Merlin) inline piston engine, producing 2,270 hp with maximum boost, and 1,830 hp for take-off |
| **Armament** | Six 0.5-inch machine guns, plus underwing stores of drop tanks, two 1,000 lb (454 kg) bombs, or up to ten 5-inch unguided air-to-ground rockets |
| **Weights** | Empty 7,040 lb (3,193 kg); loaded 9,250 lb (4,196 kg) |
| **Performance** | Maximum speed 487 mph (784 km/h) at 25,000 ft (7,620 m); range c. 1,160 miles (1,867 km) with drop tanks; service ceiling 41,600 ft (12,680 m) |

## Specifications - F-82G Twin Mustang

| | |
|---|---|
| **Dimensions** | Span 51 ft 7 in (15.72 m); length 42 ft 2.5 in (12.87 m); height 13 ft 10 in (4.22 m) |
| **Power plant** | Two Allison V-1710-143/145 inline piston engines, producing 1,600 hp each |
| **Armament** | Six 0.5-inch machine guns, plus underwing stores of drop tanks, or up to 4,000 lb (1,814 kg) of bombs or other stores |
| **Weights** | Empty 15,997 lb (7,256 kg); loaded 25,891 lb (11,744 kg) |
| **Performance** | Maximum speed 459 mph (739 km/h) at 21,000 ft (6,400 m); range c. 2,240 miles (3,605 km); service ceiling 38,900 ft (11,857 m) |

# Power for the Merlin-Mustang

The re-engineering of the Mustang's airframe to take the Rolls-Royce Merlin inline engine led to the transformation of the Mustang from a capable low-level fighter, reconnaissance and light attack combat aircraft with Allison V-1710 power, into a world-class all-level multi-role fighter. The story of how this was achieved is worthy of a volume by itself, and was mixed up in the strange and murky world of politics and favoritism that existed in the USAAF's procurement and testing offices, as well as parts of the US government. On an engineering level, for North American Aviation it was not simply a question of replacing the Mustang's original Allison V-1710 engine with a Merlin, for the whole process involved a major re-design exercise that resulted in the Mustang's airframe being tailored to the Merlin and its associated equipment. The Merlin-Mustang story was additionally a triumph of engineering and mass-production. The Packard Motor Car Company of Detroit, Michigan, was vital to this process, and it emerged from the Mustang era as a significant producer of aero engines – a process that sadly did not persist for the company into post-war success in that sphere. Packard was – and still is – best known as a producer of luxury cars. Having been formed as the Packard Motor Car Company in October 1902, the company was responsible amongst other work for the design of a famous car engine, the 'Twin Six', and development work on a ubiquitous

aircraft engine – the famed Liberty engine, which was developed during World War One and became one of the most widespread and well-known aero engines of its time. Packard also worked successfully on engines for maritime use, including V12 engines that powered US PT Boats during World War Two.

The company was therefore in a good position when the need for overseas production of the Rolls-Royce Merlin engine in the US became a matter of utmost importance at the end of the 1930's. British and Commonwealth needs for the Merlin, which was seeing increasingly widespread application in British warplanes was highly likely to outstrip potential production in Britain, and the US seemed a good possible source of license manufacture. A number of American companies appeared to be possible candidates but one of the main contenders, the Ford motor company, was unimpressed and did not want to build engines for Britain (indeed, Henry Ford believed that Britain would soon be overrun by Nazi Germany). Packard on the other hand was highly enthusiastic, and agreed to build the Merlin in the summer of 1940. Indeed, a specific division specializing in modern aero engine production was formed within the Packard organization. Britain's Ministry of Aircraft Production awarded its initial contract for production of the Merlin in late June 1940. During the same month, the Merlin was accepted as a stop-gap engine to power a proportion (actually some 1,258 fighters) of a

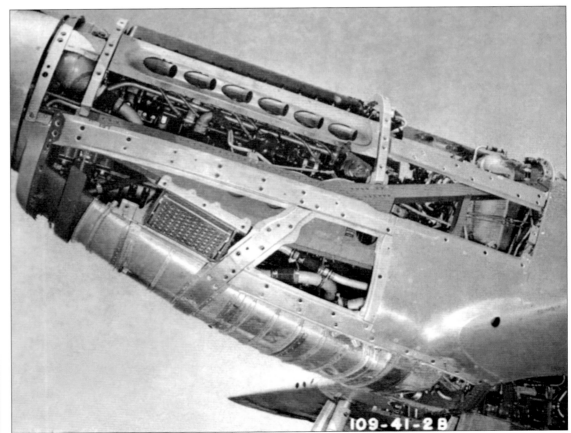

The 'business end' of a P-51D, showing the very neat and streamlined installation of the Packard V-1650-7 Merlin engine. The prominent framework around the engine featured attachment points for the removable cowling panels. Very obvious in this view is the air intake beneath the forward fuselage for the Bendix carburettor. This was and remains a major distinguishing point between Merlin-Mustangs and the earlier Allison-powered Mustangs, the Allison-engined aircraft having this intake above the nose rather than below it *(Photo: NAA)*

The starboard side of a Packard V-1650-3 Merlin as fitted in the P-51B/C series. This is probably a demonstration example as featured in the manufacturer's publicity. Although of course based on the successful and for its time advanced Rolls-Royce Merlin engine, Packard's V-1650 was a rather different beast. Built to American working practices and measurements, parts were rarely if ever interchangeable between the Rolls-Royce and Packard-built examples of the Merlin *(Photo: Packard)*

planned procurement of 3,000 warplanes intended for FY 1941 purchase for US military use. Even at that time it was realized that Allison was not going to meet all the US military inline-engine requirements with its V-1710 power plant. The Merlins for US employment turned out to be for the Curtiss P-40F version (and later the P-40L) of the otherwise Allison-engined P-40 Warhawk/Kittyhawk line.

The first Packard-built Merlin was ready for its initial tests in May 1941. The reasons for the apparent delay in getting the first engine ready lay in a number of factors, not least of these being the difficulties that Packard came across in adapting the Merlin to US production methods and requirements. The manufacturing practices of Rolls-Royce in Britain were considerably different to those of Packard, resulting in Packard needing some time to tool-up for production to begin. Many drawings were not clear enough for complete outsiders to comprehend, and some of the necessary calculations and dimensions were not present on Rolls-Royce drawings and literature. Packard had to make many of its own drawings, and found that even in apparently simple matters such as screw thread dimensions there were differences between US and British practices and usages. Although theoretically the British-built and US-built Merlins were interchangeable, in practice

there were significant detail differences between the two. Eventually Rolls-Royce had a permanent engineer based with Packard to try to help the whole process along.

In US designation parlance the Packard-built Merlin was called the V-1650. The initial production model was the V-1650-1, which equated to the Rolls-Royce-built Merlin XX and was later known as the Merlin 28 in British and Commonwealth use. It had a single-stage supercharger, was suitable for low and medium-altitude fighters, and was rated at some 1,250 hp at 11,500 ft (3,505 m). It was used in the Curtiss P-40F Warhawk (and also the P-40L derivative of the P-40F), where it did not appreciably improve the type's performance over the Allison V-1710-powered P-40E Warhawk. It was also installed in the Canadian-built Hawker Hurricane Mk.X and subsequent Canadian-built Hurricane marks (sometimes referred to as the Merlin 29 for later Hurricanes), and the Canadian-built Lancaster Mk.X four-engined bomber.

Such was the growing demand for aero engines that Packard actually ceased its luxury car production in early 1942 – a decision that the company no doubt later regretted. In the context of the Mustang, the next production model from the Detroit production lines, the V-1650-3, was the start of the company's association with the Mustang. Based around the

A rear view of a Packard V-1650-3 Merlin as installed in the P-51B/C series. According to Packard's own data, the weight of a V-1650-7 as fitted to the P-51D/K series with its associated mount and accessories was 2,200 lb **(998 kg)** *(Photo: Packard)*

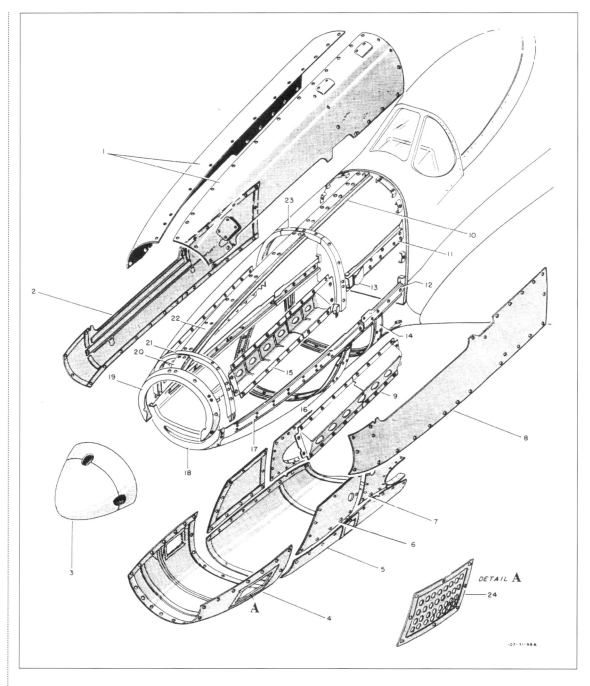

Merlin 60-series of Rolls-Royce that successfully transformed the Supermarine Spitfire into an excellent all-round fighter, the V-1650-3 was to give the first Merlin-powered Mustangs – the P-51B and P-51C - an excellent all-round performance to add to the Mustang's already exemplary range and endurance. A true two-stage two-speed supercharged V12 inline engine, the V-1650-3 was one of the finest fighter engines of its generation, although Packard's engineers did not just merely build what Rolls-Royce showed them, and indeed important development work on the supercharging for the Merlin series was performed by both companies. This helped to keep both the Spitfire and the Mustang ahead of German engine developments for Luftwaffe fighters, and was a key to the outstanding success of the Merlin-engined Mustang. At least one pattern Merlin was supplied to Packard at the commencement of the process that led to US production. The V-1650-3 was a true 1,600 hp-class inline piston engine with emergency boost, but further development led to the V-1650-7 of 1,720 hp which powered the P-51D and P-51K (and Australian-built Mustangs), and some later examples of the P-51B/C line.

The P-51D/K series Mustang was a superlative fighter at all altitudes, arguably one of the best if not the best fighter that the Allies produced during World War Two. It combined the beautifully-designed Mustang airframe with high-quality manufacture, and an excellent engine. Continuing development led to the V-1650-9 that powered the lightweight P-51H production model, which could produce an exceptional 1,930 hp with war emergency boost water injection. Packard received contracts for 75,986 Merlins during the war, of which somewhere over 50,000 (some sources suggest nearer to 60,000) were actually produced before the cessation of hostilities.

A number of propeller types were used during the Mustang production run, with Curtiss Electric units usually being fitted to Allison-engined Mustangs, and a variety of specific types for the Merlin-Mustangs. The unit of choice was made by the well-known propeller manufacturer Hamilton Standard, with the P-51B, P-51C, and P-51D mainly being fitted with various marks of the Hamilton Standard unit, with some variations in propeller blade being possible. In the P-51D, for example, the 11 ft 2 in (3.4 m) diameter Hamilton Standard Hydromatic propeller unit consisted of the hub type 24D50-87 or 24D50-105, with blades of type J-6523A-24, K-6523A-24, or 6547A-6. The former two types were of the distinctive paddle-type with shank cuffs, the 'J'-model blades having anti-icing provision. The 6547A-6 type blades were square-tipped and did not have cuffs or anti-icing provision. The blades in sets of similar type numbers were interchangeable. There was no provision for propeller feathering, and a governor within the hub unit regulated the angle of the propeller blades to maintain constant engine speed. The propeller blade angle variations that were required during these constant-speed operations were controlled by three forces – centrifugal twisting moment, which was used to move the blade angle towards low pitch; engine oil under pressure, circulated into the pitch mechanisms in the propeller hub, to supplement the centrifugal twisting moment; and engine oil under boosted pressure from the governor within the hub which balanced the centrifugal twisting moment of each blade and the oil under pressure. This was a slightly complicated system which nevertheless worked well, although it took a little getting used to for some pilots who were accustomed to simpler propeller control. The P-51K, on the other hand, was selected to have the alternative Aeroproducts propeller unit, but this was discovered to be somewhat troublesome compared to the increasingly tried-and-trusted Hamilton Standard Hydromatic unit.

British spark plugs were found to be better for the Packard Merlin engines than those manufactured in the US, and the USAAF ordered 100,000 British RC5/2 plugs during the period of the flight testing of the XP-51B Mustangs in the US - which would be the standard until better-quality or more suitable American examples could be made. In fact British plugs were subsequently extensively used on the Merlin-engined Mustangs, even those in US service. Excessive spark plug oiling was a relatively common occurrence on the early Merlin-powered Mustangs, particularly on the front cylinder of the left-hand row in the engine. This plug in particular was often changed much more frequently than those for the other cylinders. Long periods of cruising, necessary in particular on the outward-leg of bomber escort missions, would often complicate this situation. Pilots were advised to run the engine at high revs for short periods during long cruising periods in order to clear any possible excess build-up of oil in the engine cylinders. The problem of plug fouling was also exacerbated by choice of fuel.

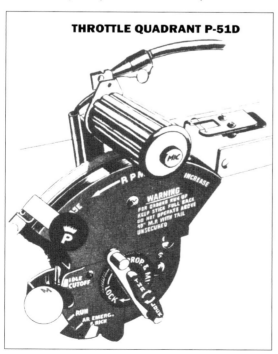

THROTTLE QUADRANT P-51D

The quality of aviation fuel available to the Allies during World War Two was of superior quality to that employed by the Germans, particularly later in the war when the Allied bombing campaign against Germany's oil industry proved to be increasingly successful. German aircraft generally ran on B4 (roughly 87 octane) or C3 (roughly 100 octane) fuel, and later in the war contaminated fuel became a problem for front-line units. The Merlin-Mustang by choice was fuelled by 130 octane fuel when available. This was generally the best rating available for the long-distance flights demanded of US escort fighters, mixing periods of cruise to and from the target with relatively short periods of excessive engine performance demanded during combat. Certainly the Eighth Air Force preferred this rating of fuel, but by mid-1944 an even higher-rated, 150 octane fuel was becoming increasingly available. This was subsequently widely adopted by the Eighth Air Force's fighter groups, but it was soon found that this high-rated fuel readily fouled with lead the engine spark plugs, resulting in a number of accidents. An additive was subsequently applied to the fuel, resulting in a 150 octane mixture known as PEP, and this was tentatively tried out by the 355th Fighter Group. Although more successful, it was found to cause harm to the valve seats within the engine, resulting in damage that would often require a complete engine change. With no obvious solution most fighter groups opted to return to the tried and tested 130 octane fuel, although this was in short supply in early 1945. From March 1945 it started to become more widely-available again, but some fighter groups

By the time that Mustang production had speeded up, much larger assembly lines at North American's factories with rather more professional equipment and moving trestles than used previously had been developed. In this picture, the engine installation (sometimes called a 'power egg') is being moved into place for mating onto the firewall of a P-51D or P-51K fuselage. The heavy engine installation is held by a moving frame-type crane suspended above the fuselage for ease of movement and installation
(Photo: NAA)

The Mustang's engine was finished as a complete unit for attaching to the fuselage firewall, with all the necessary bearers, attachment points, pipework and plumbing in place. In the first place this speeded up and simplified manufacture, and allowed for ease of engine changing when it became necessary. The transformation from Allison to Merlin power, however, caused various changes to be made to the attachment, pipework and thrust line of the engine installation, as well as the position of the carburettor air intake which was above the engine for the Allison V-1710, and below for the Packard V-1650. Here, a V-1650-7 is shown in its complete state having just been attached to the fuselage firewall, with the engine bearers and cowling attachment structure all a part of the overall engine package *(Photo: NAA)*

were able to obtain stocks more readily than others, resulting in some aircraft being fuelled up with the fuselage tank only containing the treasured 130 octane, the other fuel tanks being filled with the much less trusted PEP solution.

The P-51B had an internal fuel capacity of 184 US gallons in two wing fuel tanks, and (in all but the earliest production aircraft, although some were later retro-fitted) an 85 US gallon fuel tank (of which approximately 65 US gallons were usable) behind the cockpit. This additional internal fuel tank, although helping to considerably extend the Mustang's range, proved troublesome in giving centre of gravity problems and some handling difficulties when full. Like the P-51A, the P-51B could carry a 75 US gallon drop tank beneath each wing, but the wing was sufficiently stressed to be able to carry external fuel tanks of up to 150 US gallons. The 85 US gallon fuselage fuel tank that was introduced on the later P-51B was installed as standard in the P-51D.

As explained elsewhere in this Book, the addition of long-range fuel tanks that could be carried beneath the wings of the Merlin-Mustang was a major step towards the winning of the air war over Germany. In fact the use of long-range fuel tanks in this way had started with Allison-engined Mustangs, the P-51A being able to carry a 75 US gallon drop tank beneath each wing (the P-51A having been the first real Mustang fighter version). However it was with the Merlin-Mustang and the type's long-range bomber escort missions that the use of these tanks came into their own. Eventually the 75 US gallon drop tank was supplemented by larger underwing fuel tanks to give even more range - resulting in several new shapes eventually coming to the fore. One was a metal 110 US gallon tank, while in Britain, thanks to the efforts of the paper specialist company Bowater, a compressed paper fuel tank of 108 gallons was developed.

Production of the latter was rarely to exceed demand in the coming months, but eventually the 'battle of the long-range fuel tanks' was won, with many thousands of all the types developed being manufactured. It was not, however, simply a question of hanging these tanks beneath the most convenient location under an aircraft. Much thought had to go into plumbing in fuel lines to connect up to the tanks, flight testing had to be carried out both in the US and Britain to check the feasibility of the new installations and to ensure that they were safe for combat use, and testing was needed to find out just how far each fighter type could fly at different boost settings with the additional fuel loads. It was also necessary to develop a pressurised fuel system so that fuel could be drawn from the tanks.

As a footnote, Packard returned to making cars after World War Two, introducing its first all-new post-war model in 1948. Unfortunately the company was unable to capture a significant share of new car sales in contrast to its pre-war pre-eminence in the luxury car market, and a merger with Studebaker followed in October 1954. This did nothing to revive the flagging fortunes of the company, which had ceased to exist as a corporate entity by the end of the 1950's – a sad end to a company that had contributed so much to the Allied victory in the air war during the Second World War.

# Merlin-Mustang Armament

Allison-engined Mustangs featured several different internal armament 'fits', depending on which mark they were. These were explained in Part 1 of this two-part 'Modellers' Datafile' on the Mustang, which covered Allison-engined Mustangs. Of relevance to the story of the Merlin-powered Mustangs as far as armament is concerned was the Allison-engined P-51A, which featured two 0.5-in Browning M2 machine guns in each wing, and was the first true Mustang fighter. The guns were not installed upright, but instead were canted at an angle, in the direction of the outer wing. This two-gun installation was continued into Merlin-Mustang production, with both the P-51B and the P-51C also having this armament arrangement with two 0.5-in machine guns in each wing, canted over and not upright.

Therefore in the P-51B/C series and the equivalent Mustang III of the RAF, only four wing guns were fitted (two in each wing). These were the ubiquitous 0.5-in Browning M2 machine guns as used in many US warplanes of the World War Two era, but in

those marks of Mustangs the guns were sometimes prone to jamming. This was very unfortunate during combat. It was not specifically an icing-up problem, as claimed by some writers, but was the result of two separate problems. One was to do with icing, particularly the effect of lubricating oil congealing with the cold at high altitudes if the Mustangs' electric gun heaters were not switched on in time before the aircraft gained height, or before the guns were fired at altitude. The other problem was the jamming of the guns due to the awkward canted-over seating of the guns, and the equally-awkward curved ammunition feed chutes. Much of the gun-jamming took place when the guns were fired while the aircraft was manoeuvring and pulling 'g'. The result was the holding back of the moving ammunition belt due to centrifugal force, causing the breech mechanism of the gun to jam. It must be noted that this gun-jamming problem had not affected the Allison-engined P-51A in the same way that it did in the Merlin-powered P-51B/C, because the Allison-Mustangs tended to operate at lower altitudes and were much less used in

The ubiquitous 0.5-in Browning M2 machine gun was the internal gun armament of the Merlin-Mustangs, with two installed within each wing in the P-51B and P-51C, and three in each wing in the P-51D and P-51K. The guns were mounted upright in the P-51D and P-51K unlike the earlier aircraft, thus doing away with one of the causes of gun jamming in the earlier Mustangs. In each wing there was a main bay in which the gins were installed, plus a long span-wise bay adjacent to this where the ammunition was housed, as shown on the left-hand wing of this P-51D of the 20th Fighter Group in England
*(Photo: Arthur E. Sevigny, 20th Fighter Wing Association)*

Two 0.5-in M2 Browning machine guns were installed in each wing of the Merlin-engined P-51B/C series, in a curious canted-over fitting that also included rather tortuously curved ammunition feeds. This installation was prone to jamming. It had initially been pioneered in the Allison-engined P-51A, which had been the first true fighter model of the Mustang line. This illustration shows the gun installation and ammunition feed layout of the P-51A, as also used in the Merlin-engined P-51B/C series *(Drawing: NAA)*

the same type of close-in aerial combat that the later Mustangs tended to be involved in, and so gun-jamming had not been a particular issue for the P-51 – hence NAA had been happy to use the same armament arrangement in the P-51B/C series, unaware that the very different operating environment that these types flew in would lead to problems with this installation.

Eventually a number of fixes were tried in order to cure the problem. Some were very much 'home-made', but the most successful involved the use of an ammunition belt booster motor, as used in gun turrets or on belt feeds in awkward positions in the heavy bombers. The problem was solved altogether with the altered gun installation in the P-51D/K models of the Mustang for the USAAF and the equivalent

Mustang Mk.IV/IVA of the RAF. In these aircraft there were three 0.5-in machine guns in each wing, in a much altered and refined weapons bay, and they were mounted vertically with less curved ammunition belt feeds which appeared to solve much of the jamming difficulty. Pilots were also advised to turn on their gun heaters when the guns were charged during flight, to avoid any danger of oil congealing due to extreme cold at high altitudes prior to combat taking place.

In the P-51B series with its two machine guns in each wing, the maximum number of rounds was 1,260 – the inboard guns having 350 rounds each, the outer 280. In the P-51D series, there was a minimum of 1,840 rounds in total – the inboard guns having 400 rounds each, and the two outer guns 260 rounds

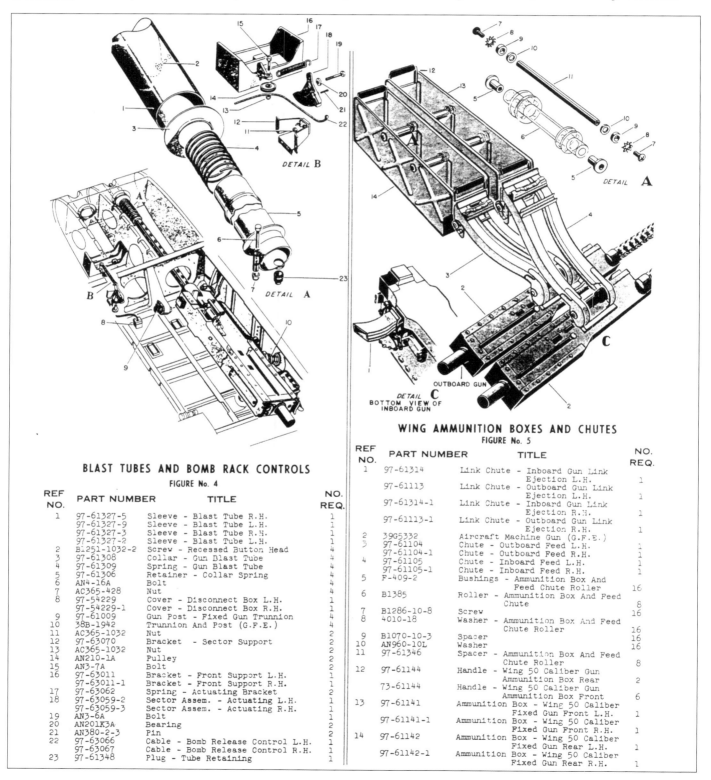

## BLAST TUBES AND BOMB RACK CONTROLS
### FIGURE No. 4

| REF NO. | PART NUMBER | TITLE | NO. REQ. |
|---|---|---|---|
| 1 | 97-61327-5 | Sleeve - Blast Tube R.H. | 1 |
|  | 97-61327-9 | Sleeve - Blast Tube L.H. | 1 |
|  | 97-61327-3 | Sleeve - Blast Tube R.H. | 1 |
|  | 97-61327-2 | Sleeve - Blast Tube L.H. | 1 |
| 2 | B1251-1032-2 | Screw - Recessed Button Head | 4 |
| 3 | 97-61308 | Collar - Gun Blast Tube | 4 |
| 4 | 97-61309 | Spring - Gun Blast Tube | 4 |
| 5 | 97-61306 | Retainer - Collar Spring | 4 |
| 6 | AN4-16A | Bolt | 4 |
| 7 | AC365-428 | Nut | 4 |
| 8 | 97-54229 | Cover - Disconnect Box L.H. | 1 |
|  | 97-54229-1 | Cover - Disconnect Box R.H. | 1 |
| 9 | 97-61009 | Gun Post - Fixed Gun Trunnion | 4 |
| 10 | 38B-1942 | Trunnion And Post (G.F.E.) | 4 |
| 11 | AC365-1032 | Nut | 2 |
| 12 | 97-63070 | Bracket - Sector Support | 2 |
| 13 | AC365-1032 | Nut | 2 |
| 14 | AN210-1A | Pulley | 2 |
| 15 | AN3-7A | Bolt | 2 |
| 16 | 97-63011 | Bracket - Front Support L.H. | 1 |
|  | 97-63011-1 | Bracket - Front Support R.H. | 1 |
| 17 | 97-63062 | Spring - Actuating Bracket | 2 |
| 18 | 97-63059-2 | Sector Assem. - Actuating L.H. | 1 |
|  | 97-63059-3 | Sector Assem. - Actuating R.H. | 1 |
| 19 | AN3-6A | Bolt | 1 |
| 20 | AN201K3A | Bearing | 2 |
| 21 | AN380-2-3 | Pin | 2 |
| 22 | 97-63066 | Cable - Bomb Release Control L.H. | 1 |
|  | 97-63067 | Cable - Bomb Release Control R.H. | 1 |
| 23 | 97-61348 | Plug - Tube Retaining | 1 |

## WING AMMUNITION BOXES AND CHUTES
### FIGURE No. 5

| REF NO. | PART NUMBER | TITLE | NO. REQ. |
|---|---|---|---|
| 1 | 97-61314 | Link Chute - Inboard Gun Link Ejection L.H. | 1 |
|  | 97-61113 | Link Chute - Outboard Gun Link Ejection L.H. | 1 |
|  | 97-61314-1 | Link Chute - Inboard Gun Link Ejection R.H. | 1 |
|  | 97-61113-1 | Link Chute - Outboard Gun Link Ejection R.H. | 1 |
| 2 | 39G5332 | Aircraft Machine Gun (G.F.E.) |  |
| 3 | 97-61104 | Chute - Outboard Feed L.H. | 1 |
|  | 97-61104-1 | Chute - Outboard Feed R.H. | 1 |
| 4 | 97-61105 | Chute - Inboard Feed L.H. | 1 |
|  | 97-61105-1 | Chute - Inboard Feed R.H. | 1 |
| 5 | F-409-2 | Bushings - Ammunition Box And Feed Chute Roller | 16 |
| 6 | B1385 | Roller - Ammunition Box And Feed Chute | 8 |
| 7 | B1286-10-8 | Screw | 16 |
| 8 | 4010-18 | Washer - Ammunition Box And Feed Chute Roller | 16 |
| 9 | B1070-10-3 | Spacer | 16 |
| 10 | AN960-10L | Washer | 16 |
| 11 | 97-61346 | Spacer - Ammunition Box And Feed Chute Roller | 8 |
| 12 | 97-61144 | Handle - Wing 50 Caliber Gun Ammunition Box Rear | 2 |
|  | 73-61144 | Handle - Wing 50 Caliber Gun Ammunition Box Front | 6 |
| 13 | 97-61141 | Ammunition Box - Wing 50 Caliber Fixed Gun Front L.H. | 1 |
|  | 97-61141-1 | Ammunition Box - Wing 50 Caliber Fixed Gun Front R.H. | 1 |
| 14 | 97-61142 | Ammunition Box - Wing 50 Caliber Fixed Gun Rear L.H. | 1 |
|  | 97-61142-1 | Ammunition Box - Wing 50 Caliber Fixed Gun Rear R.H. | 1 |

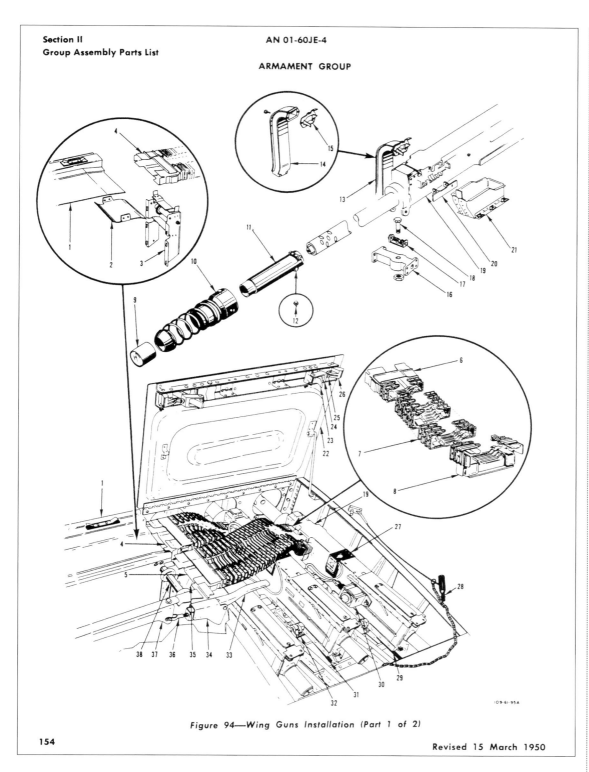

Diagram from an official P-51D Manual/Parts List showing the armament arrangement for the P-51D Mustang (left-hand wing shown). The guns were 0.5-in calibre M2 machine guns and the inner gun on each side was slightly staggered by being set back to allow the ammunition belts for the three guns to have an uninterrupted feed, thus avoiding the problems encountered on the P-51B and P-51C where the two guns in each wing were set at an angle and their awkward curved ammunition feed chutes often jammed particularly during combat manoeuvring *(Drawing: NAA)*

*Figure 94—Wing Guns Installation (Part 1 of 2)*

154

**Revised 15 March 1950**

each. A number of writers have noted that the outboard guns had 270 rounds each, making a total of 1,880 rounds. Certainly some armourers appear to have managed to load up to 270 rounds in the outer ammunition bays. The M2 Browning machine gun had a muzzle velocity of up to 800 rounds per minute, although this capability depended upon a number of factors, including the temperature and altitude at which the gun was fired, what type of rounds were fired (armour-piercing, tracer, etc), and the position of the gun in the wing. The effective range of the 0.5-in machine gun was some 2,400 ft (732 m), although many pilots had the guns on their Mustangs adjusted to converge at shorter distances for maximum effect in air combat. Interestingly, a number of writers have claimed that some of the later P-51B-series Mustangs had the six-gun wing of the P-51D-series installed. Despite extensive research this Author

has not been able to find any definite record of this being instituted on the NAA production lines, and it remains at best an unverified but possible if unlikely happening very late in the production of the P-51B. It is feasible that some P-51B-series Mustangs had the wings of P-51D-series Mustangs installed in the field, perhaps as the result of rebuilds or to repair major battle damage. There would have been possible interchangeability of the major airframe components such as this, but all the wiring and electrics relating to the guns would have needed to be changed in that case to make the wing compatible with the fuselage of a different mark.

All Merlin-Mustangs had attachments for underwing stores, eventually including underwing jettisonable fuel tanks, representing considerable foresight by NAA's designers. The largest load that was regularly carried by later marks of Mustang on the single underwing pylon beneath each wing was a bomb of 1,000 lb (454 kg). The P-51D-25 blocks and later were fitted and wired with attachment points for various types of unguided rockets and rocket launchers. These were most used during operations in the Korean War, although some specific employment was made of these hardpoints particularly in the Pacific and CBI late in World War Two for ground-attack sorties.

Gun aiming in the Mustang was by means of (for their time) advanced gunsights, with the excellent K-14 computing 'gyroscopic' gunsight becoming established during the P-51D production run. This was based on a British design, the Mk.IID, and was trialled in July and August 1944 for Mustang operations. It became standard on the production lines in the P-51D-series in its K-14A form from around October/November 1944 in the P-51D-20-NT/P-51D-25-NA and later blocks, although some were retrofitted, including the basic K-14, in earlier models that were still operational as well as in the P-51K. Modification was required to the cockpit

**Extract from an official P-51D Manual/Parts List** showing the 'zero-length' unguided rocket attachments that were introduced in late P-51D production, and were a great improvement on previous rocket attachments, including the unwieldy three-round bazooka-style rocket launchers used earlier in the war. Sometimes also called 'zero-zero' attachments, these little stub mountings allowed the rocket to become free almost at once it was fired, and usually carried a 5-inch unguided rocket. They were much used particularly in the Korean War. The full complement was five attachments and rockets beneath each wing of a Mustang, but if the normal Mustang pylon was fitted only three of the rocket attachments would be carried under each wing outboard of the pylon. On this drawing, the forward part of the mounting is numbered 11, and the rear mounting is numbered 26 (Drawing: NAA)

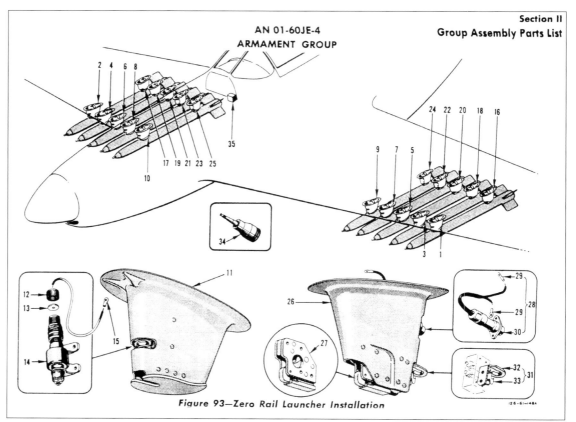

AN 01-60JE-4
ARMAMENT GROUP

Section II
Group Assembly Parts List

Figure 93—Zero Rail Launcher Installation

It is often forgotten that late in P-51D production, provision was made for the carriage of up to five unguided air-to-ground rockets beneath each wing. This involved the factory installation of 'zero-length' attachments, which were far better than the jury-rigged three-round long bazooka-type fittings which were carried by some early Mustangs in combat and which were mainly ineffective and caused problems to the type's aerodynamics. The 'zero-length' attachments worked very well and were used particularly in the Korean War to considerable effect. Illustrated here is the full quota of five sets of attachments and rockets beneath the right-hand wing of a Mustang. If the normal Mustang underwing pylon was fitted, however, only three of the rocket attachments would be carried under each wing outboard of the pylon, and if a bomb was carried on the normal pylon sometimes only two rockets would be fitted beneath each wing (Photo: NAA)

AN 01-60JE-4
ARMAMENT GROUP

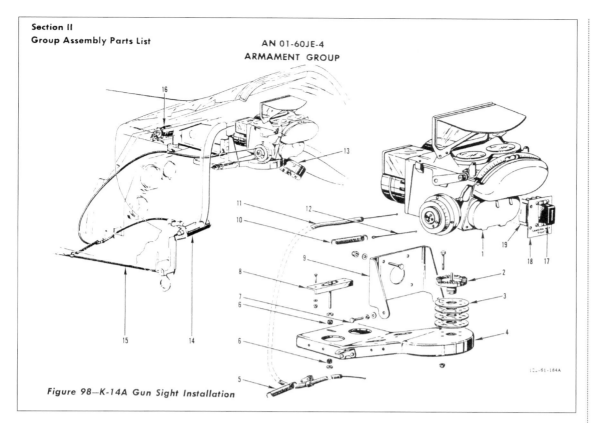

Figure 98—K-14A Gun Sight Installation

As far as gun sighting was concerned, the excellent K-14/K-14A computing 'gyroscopic' gunsight was installed in the later P-51D production, and was one of the most advanced gunsights to be fitted in any fighter during the Second World War. This extract from an official P-51D Manual/Parts List shows the comparatively bulky K-14A and its installation, including the heavy bracket (numbered 4 on the lower drawing) needed to hold it in place. The K-14A was introduced into P-51D manufacture at the factory during the D-25-NA and D-20-NT production blocks, although it is possible that some D-20-NA were factory-fitted with this type of gunsight as well *(Drawing: NAA)*

coaming to allow the bulky K-14 to fit. Prior to that time the N-9 had been used in earlier P-51D blocks, with the N-3B being standard for the P-51B and P-51C – although as with many aspects in operational conditions, there was some interchangeability between all the marks, and some pilots preferred the more 'hands on' approach to shooting needed with the earlier sights. The British Mk.VIII gunsight was also used in some Mustangs and in very early Mustangs a variety of gunsights could be found, including the ST1A – a ring-and-bead sight was also fitted on some initial production Mustangs. In contrast, by the time of the later versions of the P/F-82 Twin Mustang, an advanced K-18 gunsight was installed. Whichever sighting method was used, the Merlin-Mustang as a type ran up an impressive tally of air-to-air claims during the Second World War, making it one of the most successful fighters of all time.

Claimed by some historians to have been widely-used and highly-effective in combat, in fact the jury-rigged three-round long bazooka-type fittings which were carried by some early Mustangs in combat and shown in this NAA photograph were in reality anything but effective. Difficult to aim, unwieldy, drag-producing and definitely of no help at all if the Mustang got into a turning fight with an enemy fighter, they were in fact a poor addition to the Mustangs' arsenal of weapons. Later in the war, North American introduced 'zero-length' attachments on the production line beneath the wings for the carriage of up to five unguided rockets on each side, which did away with the need for the bazooka-type fittings. In this view a P-51B shows off the tube-like 'bazookas', three of which would normally be carried under each wing *(Photo: NAA)*

# Merlin and Twin Mustang Production

**M**ustangs, both Allison-engined and Merlin-powered, were built in large numbers. Nevertheless, surprisingly for such a well-known and well-documented aircraft, there has been a considerable amount of confusion in the past over the Mustang's production numbers and actual serial numbers. This appears to have been caused, in published sources at least, by typing errors and accidental duplication of batches. Some writers' arithmetic also appears to have gone astray, with batches of production aircraft being given an incorrect quantity without any attempt apparently being made to check how many serial numbers there are in a batch. The following is the most comprehensively-checked listing of Mustang serial numbers that has yet been published, although it is acknowledged that some of the serial number allocations within production batches remain contentious.

Fighter models of the Mustang in US service were designated P-51, with a prefix letter for the particular version (e.g. P-51D), the 'P' meaning 'Pursuit' – the original US Army name for a fighter. Following the creation of the independent US Air Force in 1947, out-dated designations such as this were eventually changed. The old Pursuit designation was altered in 1948 to 'F' for Fighter. Surviving Mustangs were thus redesignated, with the nomenclature F-51 being increasingly adopted – hence all Mustangs that served with the USAF in Korea were F-51 Mustangs.

A full listing of Allison-powered Mustangs was included in Part 1 of this two-part 'Modellers' Datafile' on the Mustang, which covered Allison-engined Mustangs. Merlin-Mustangs began, for the USAAF, with the P-51B, and for the RAF with the Mustang Mk III.

## Merlin-Mustang Production under US contracts, mainly for US use

| MODEL | NAA NO. | SERIAL NOS. | QUANTITY |
|---|---|---|---|
| XP-51B-NA | NA-101 | 41-37352, 41-37421 | 2 |
| P-51B-1-NA | NA-102 | 43-12093 to -12492 | 400 |
| P-51B-5-NA | NA-104 | 43-6313 to -7112 | 800 |
| P-51B-10-NA | NA-104 | 43-7113 to -7202 | |
| | | 42-106429 to -106538 | |
| | | 42-106541 to -106738 | 398 |
| P-51B-15-NA | NA-104 | 42-106739 to -106978 | |
| | | 43-24752 to -24901 | 390 |
| P-51C-1-NT | NA-103 | 42-102979 to -103328 | 350 |
| P-51C-5-NT | NA-103 | 42-103329 to -103778 | 450 |
| P-51C-10-NT | NA-103 | 42-103779 to -103978 | 200 |
| | | 43-24902 to -25251 | 350 |
| P-51C-10/11-NT | NA-111 | 44-10753 to -11152 | 400 |
| XP-51D-NA | NA-106 | 42-106539, 42-106540 | 2 |
| P-51D-5-NA | NA-109 | 44-13253 to -14052 | 800 |
| P-51D-10-NA | NA-109 | 44-14053 to -14852 | 800 |
| P-51D-15-NA | NA-109 | 44-14853 to -15752 | 900 |
| P-51D-20-NA | NA-122 | 44-63160 to -64159 | 1,000 |
| | | 44-72027 to -72626 | 600 |
| P-51D-25-NA | NA-122 | 44-72627 to -74226 | 1,600 |
| P-51D-30-NA | NA-122 | 44-74227 to -75026 | 800 |
| P-51D-5-NT | NA-111 | 44-11153 to -11352 | 200 |
| P-51D-20-NT | NA-111 | 44-12853 to -13252 | 400 |
| P-51D-25-NT | NA-124 | 44-84390 to -84989 | 600 |
| | | 45-11343 to -11542 | 200 |
| P-51D-30-NT | NA-124 | 45-11543 to -11742 | 200 |
| TP-51D-NT | | 45-11443 to -11450 | 8 |

**A USAAF North American F-6C Mustang from the 111th Tactical Reconnaissance Squadron.** *(Photo: USAF)*

CAC P51 Mustang A68-141, RAAF 24 'City of Adelaide Squadron', seen at RAAF Richmond in April 1958.
*(Photo: RAAF)*

| MODEL | NAA NO. | SERIAL NOS. | QUANTITY |
|---|---|---|---|
| | | 44-84610 to -84611 | 2 |
| P-51K-1-NT | NA-111 | 44-11353 to -11552 | 200 |
| P-51K-5-NT | NA-111 | 44-11553 to -11952 | 400 |
| P-51K-10-NT | NA-111 | 44-11953 to -12852 | 900 |
| XP-51F | NA-105 | 43-43332 to -43334 | 3 |
| XP-51G | NA-105 | 43-43335 to -43336 | 2 |
| P-51H-1-NA | NA-126 | 44-64160 to -64179 | 20 |
| P-51H-5-NA | NA-126 | 44-64180 to -64459 | 280 |
| P-51H-10-NA | NA-126 | 44-64460 to -64714 | 255 |
| XP-51J-NA | NA-105 | 44-76027 to -76028 | 2 |
| P-51M-1-NT | NA-124 | 45-11743 | 1 |

'NA' referred to NAA's Inglewood (Mines Field – Los Angeles Municipal Airport), California factory production, and 'NT' related to NAA's Dallas (Hensley Field), Texas, production facilities. Amongst these batches are deliveries to the RAF, therefore the totals referred to elsewhere in the text for deliveries to the USAAF do not necessarily tally with the overall total manufactured in specific batches as given here.

## Merlin-Mustang Production for Britain

| MODEL | NAA NO. | SERIAL NOS. | QUANTITY |
|---|---|---|---|
| Mustang Mk III | NA-104/111 | FB100 to FB399 | 300 |
| | | FX848 to FZ197 | 350 |
| | | HB821 to HB961 | 141 |
| | | KH421 to KH640 | 220 |
| Mustang Mk IV | | KH641 to KH670 | 30 |
| | | KM493 to KM743 | 251 |
| Mustang Mk IVA | | KH671 to KH870 | 200 |
| | | KM100 to KM492 | 393 |
| | | KM744 to KM799 | 56 |
| | | TK586, TK589 | 2 |

It is important to stress that not all the above aircraft were delivered to Britain – some were retained for trials in the US; some were taken for use by the USAAF; a small number crashed on acceptance or testing before delivery; similarly several were lost at sea in transit. In addition to these actual production aircraft for Britain, a number of other Mustangs found their way into British service or were allocated British serial numbers, sometimes for temporary service or test work. They include Mustang Mk IIIs FR411, and SR406 to SR440; a P-51H (KN987); the XP-51F (sometimes called a Mustang Mk V) FR409; and the XP-51G FR410. Five Mustangs were specifically employed by

Rolls-Royce as test aircraft for the installation of the Merlin engine - they were the former Allison-engined AL963, AL975, AM121, AM203, and AM208; they have often been called Mustang Mk X aircraft. A further Mustang, AG518, was evaluated for this programme but was not converted. AM121 was later passed to the Americans. It must also be remembered that Rolls-Royce also employed a number of other Mustangs at different times for various evaluation and test work.

## Merlin-Mustang Assembly/Production in Australia

| MODEL | NAA NO. | SERIAL NOS. | QUANTITY |
|---|---|---|---|
| CA-17 Mk 20 | (NA-110) | A68-1 to -80 | 80 |
| CA-18 Mk 21 | | A68-95 to -120 | 26 |
| CA-18 Mk 22 | | A68-81 to - 94 | 14 |
| | | A68-187 to -200 | 14 |
| CA-18 Mk 23 | | A68-121 to -186 | 66 |

The above were manufactured in Australia by the Commonwealth Aircraft Corporation. The first 80 (CA-17 Mk 20) were made up from 100 sets of components supplied from the US. Mustang assembly/production in Australia was definitely 200, and not 286 as claimed in some published sources.

However, in addition, Australia also received 299 Mustangs from US production, which wore the serial numbers A68-500 to -583, and A68-600 to -813. Most if not all the former were P-51K equivalents, the latter being P-51D equivalents. The '299th' was A68-1001, which was in effect a 'pattern aircraft' for the Australian production and is believed to have been a P-51D in origin.

### Reconnaissance Mustangs

Reconnaissance versions of the Mustang were designated F-6, where 'F' stood for 'Photographic' in the rather cumbersome designation allocations of the inter-war US Army Air Corps. All photo-reconnaissance Mustangs were originally serial numbered in the blocks of fighter P-51s, and therefore their production quantities should not be added to the total number of fighter Mustangs that were built for US forces. They included up to 55 F-6A converted from Allison-engined P-51 airframes, and 35 F-6B converted from Allison-engined P-51A examples. They were followed by 91 F-6C, this designation covering both P-51B or 'C' conversions - these and subsequent reconnaissance Mustangs were Merlin-powered, as described in this book; there were also some 146 F-6Ds that were former P-51D versions (44-13020 to -039; 44-13131 to -13140; 44-13181; 44-14547; 44-15453; 44-84509 to -84540; 44-84566; 44-84773 to -84778; 44-84835 to

-84855; and 45-11655 to -11689); and 163 F-6K that were originally P-51K models (including 44-11554; 44-11897 to -11952; 44-11993 to -12008; 44-12216 to -12237; 44-12459 to -12471; 44-12523 to -12534; and 44-12810 to -12852). It must be noted that these numbers are a guide only, the exact total of reconnaissance Mustangs is impossible to verify exactly, although these figures are a close approximation).

### Additional Mustang Serial Numbers

In addition to actual production, the USAF procured a number of Cavalier rebuilt Mustangs in the 1970s, chiefly for export. These received the following serial numbers – 67-14862 to -14865, and 67-22579 to -22582 for the single-seat Cavalier F-51D, and 67-14866 which was a two-seat TF-51D trainer. The US Army obtained two two-seat communications/chase F-51Ds, serial numbers 68-15795 to -15796. The prototype close-support Cavalier Mustang II received the civil registration N4222A, and the Cavalier Turbo Mustang III was N6167U. The original two-seat Cavalier Enforcer was N202PE, plus the single-seat Cavalier Enforcer N201PE. The two single-seat Piper PA-48 Enforcer aircraft were registered N481PE and N482PE. Some fifteen TF-51D conversions were made post-World War Two, including work carried out by Temco – known serial numbers being 44-84654 to -84658, 44-84660, 44-84662 to -84663, 44-84665 to -84670, and 44-84676 (it is quite possible that these were the only 15 so converted).

## P/F-82 Twin Mustang

| Model | NAA No. | Serial Nos. | Quantity |
|---|---|---|---|
| XP-82-NA | NA-120 | 44-83886 to -83887 | 2 |
| XP-82A-NA | NA-120 | 44-83888 | 1 |
| P-82B-1-NA | NA-123 | 44-65160 to -65168 | 9 |
| | | 44-65171 to -65179 | 9 |
| P-82C-NA | | 44-65169 | 1 |
| P-82D-NA | | 44-65170 | 1 |
| P-82E-NA | NA-144 | 46-255 to -354 | 100 |
| P-82F-NA | NA-149 | 46-405 to -495 | 91 |
| P-82G-NA | NA-150 | 46-355 to -383 | 29 |
| | | 46-389 to -404 | 16 |
| P-82H-NA | | 46-384 to -388 | 5 |
| | | 46-496 to -504 | 9 |

Note: the P-82H was a conversion from P-82F and P-82G production blocks, but is shown here separately for clarity. Most of the later versions of the Twin Mustang were actually known as F-82s virtually from the start, as the changeover from the old 'P' for 'Pursuit' designation to the new 'F' for 'Fighter' was starting to take place as they entered service or were taken on charge. Most historians now agree that a total of 273 Twin Mustangs of all types was built.

# RAF Merlin-Mustangs

**Appendix V**

I t is often forgotten that the RAF was the first air force to employ the Mustang of any type in combat, and successfully operated this iconic warplane from 1942 until the end of World War Two in Europe. Initially this involved Allison-engined Mustangs, latterly Merlin-Mustangs. As explained in Part 1 of this two-part 'Modellers' Datafile' on the Mustang, which covered Allison-engined Mustangs, some RAF squadrons flew Allison-engined Mustangs right up to the end of the war in Europe during May 1945. Indeed, RAF Mustangs went into action a year before the first USAAF Mustangs saw combat. Merlin-powered Mustangs started to reach the RAF in the latter part of 1943 and into 1944, and this type subsequently served with the RAF post-war until 1947, four squadrons actually continuing with their Merlin-Mustangs into that year. In addition, Mustangs also served with a variety of Commonwealth squadrons which operated under the umbrella of the RAF during World War Two, and several squadrons that were manned principally by personnel from occupied countries also used Mustangs and served under the auspices of the RAF. The following is a listing of these squadrons and their officially-assigned squadron code letters where applicable (although these were not always applied) with, where possible, details of their time on the Mustang – but it must as always be stressed that many units phased aircraft types in and out of service alongside their predecessors and successors, and sometimes spent time on working-up before becoming operational, and so exact dates in that context are only a guide.

A Royal Air Force North American Mustang Mark III (FX908) on the ground at Hucknall, Nottinghamshire following the installation of its 1,680-hp Packard Merlin engine by Rolls-Royce Ltd. This aircraft served with Nos.309 and 316 Polish Fighter Squadrons. *(Photo: RAF Archive)*

As far as the Merlin-Mustang service was concerned in the above units, some flew just the Mk.III while some operated only the Mk.IV/IVA, while some flew both Merlin-powered types. No.309 Squadron operated Allison-Mustangs before also serving on Merlin-powered Mustangs. An Australian-manned squadron within the RAF, No.450 based in Italy, received a small number of Merlin-Mustangs (possibly only one) but did not go operational on the type.

In addition to these squadrons, various other organisations flew Mustangs with or in conjunction with the British and Commonwealth forces, notably the test establishments at Boscombe Down and Farnborough. These latter formations did not usually carry their own distinguishing markings or codes on the aircraft that were (sometimes briefly) assigned to them. Additionally, a number of Mustangs served with training units; records of these are sketchy, but one of these organisations appears to have been No.61 OTU.

| SQUADRON/CODE | APPROXIMATE MUSTANG SERVICE DATES |
|---|---|
| 19 (QV) | 1/44 – 3/46 (Merlin only) |
| 64 (SH) | 8/44 – 5/46 (Merlin only) |
| 65 (YT) | 12/43 – early 1946 (Merlin only) |
| 93 (HN) | 1/46 – 12/46 (Merlin only) |
| 112 (GA) | 6/44 – 12/46 (Merlin only) |
| 118 (NK) | 1/45 – 3/46 (Merlin only) |
| 122 (MT) | 1/44 - 8/45 (Merlin only) |
| 126 (5J) | 12/44 – 4/46 (Merlin only) |
| 129 (DV) | 4/44 – 5/45 (Merlin only) |
| 154 (HG) | 2/45 - 3/45 (Merlin only) |
| 165 (SK) | 1/45 – 6/45 (Merlin only) |
| 213 (AK) | 5/44 – 2/47 (Merlin only) |
| 234 (AZ) | 9/44 – 7/45 (Merlin only) |
| 249 (GN) | 9/44 – 8/45 (Merlin only) |
| 250 (LD) | 8/45 – 1/47 (Merlin only) |
| 260 (HS) | 3/44 – 8/45 (Merlin only) |
| 303 (RF, later PD) Polish | 4/45 – 12/46 (Merlin only) |
| 306 (UZ) Polish | 3/44 - 1/47 (Merlin only) |
| 309 (WC) Polish | 10/44 - 1/47 |
| 315 (PK) Polish | 3/44 – 12/46 (Merlin only) |
| 316 (SZ) Polish | 4/44 – 12/46 (Merlin only) |
| 441 (9G) Canadian | 4/45 – 8/45 (Merlin only) |
| 442 (Y2) Canadian | 4/45 – 8/45 (Merlin only) |
| 541 (none) | 6/44 – 4/45 (Merlin only) |
| 611 (FY) | 1/45 – 8/45 (Merlin only) |

Warrant Officer C R Castleton of Bingley Yorkshire, bids farewell to his ground crew as he readies for take off in his North American Mustang Mark III of No. 122 Squadron RAF, armed with two 1000-lb bombs on wing racks, at B12/Ellon, Normandy. *(Photo: RAF Archive)*

# USAAF Merlin-Mustangs in Europe

**M**aking an outstanding contribution to Allied victory, the Merlin-engined P-51B/C and P-51D/K Mustang versions served with a number of significant USAAF fighter units in the ETO. All of these were a significant part of the overwhelming success of the Allied air forces against the Luftwaffe during the later stages of World War Two.

### Eighth Army Air Force

The best-known of the US Mustang operators in Europe were the 14 fighter groups that eventually operated the Merlin-Mustang within the Eighth Army Air Force from bases in England, as detailed here (assigned squadron code letters given in brackets) with their bases while flying the Mustang –

### 4th Fighter Group:

334th (XR, later QP), 335th (AV, later WD), 336th (MD, later VF) Fighter Squadrons; P-51 ops from 25/2/1944; based at Debden to end of war.

### 20th Fighter Group:

55th (KI), 77th (LC), 79th (MC) Fighter Squadrons; P-51 ops from 20/7/1944; based at King's Cliffe to end of war.

### 55th Fighter Group:

38th (CG), 338th (CL), 343rd (CY) Fighter Squadrons; P-51 ops from 19/7/1944; based at Wormingford to end of war.

### 78th Fighter Group:

82nd (MX), 83rd (HL), 84th (WZ) Fighter Squadrons; P-51 ops from 29/12/1944; based at Duxford to end of war.

### 339th Fighter Group:

503rd (D7), 504th (5Q), 505th (6N) Fighter Squadrons; P-51 ops from 30/4/1944; based at Fowlmere to end of war.

### 352nd Fighter Group:

328th (PE), 486th (PZ), 487th (HO) Fighter Squadrons; P-51 ops from 8/4/1944; based at Bodney to end of war, but also temporarily at Asch (Y-29), and Chièvres (A-84) in Belgium.

### 353rd Fighter Group:

350th (LH), 351st (YJ), 352nd (SX) Fighter Squadrons; P-51 ops from 2/10/1944; based at Raydon to end of war.

### 355th Fighter Group:

354th (WR), 357th (OS), 358th (YF) Fighter Squadrons; P-51 ops from 9/3/1944; based at Steeple Morden to end of war.

### 356th Fighter Group:

359th (OC), 360th (PI), 361st (QI) Fighter Squadrons; P-51 ops from 20/11/1944; based at Martlesham Heath to end of war.

**P-51 43-25050 of the 503rd FS, 339th FG, 8th AF and assigned to 1st Lt. Esteban A. Terrats and taken in the snow at RAF Fowlmere, England**
*(Photo: USAF)*

### 357th Fighter Group:

362nd (G4), 363rd (B6), 364th (C5) Fighter Squadrons; P-51 ops from 11/2/1944; based at Leiston to end of war.

### 359th Fighter Group:

368th (CV), 369th (IV), 370th (CS) Fighter Squadrons; P-51 ops from 5/5/1944; based at East Wretham to end of war.

### 361st Fighter Group:

374th (B7), 375th (E2), 376th (E9) Fighter Squadrons; P-51 ops from 12/5/1944; based at Bottisham until late September 1944, then Little Walden to end of war, but also temporarily at Saint-Dizier (A-64) in France, and Chièvres (A-84) in Belgium.

### 364th Fighter Group:

383rd (N2), 384th (5Y), 385th (5E) Fighter Squadrons; P-51 ops from 28/7/1944; based at Honington to end of war.

### 479th Fighter Group:

434th (L2), 435th (J2), 436th (9B) Fighter Squadrons; P-51 ops from 13/9/1944; based at Wattisham to end of war.

Note: Originally under the operational control of VIII Fighter Command, these fighter groups were divided on 15 September 1944 (effective 10 October 1944) under the auspices of fighter wings that were linked to the bombardment divisions that controlled the Eighth Air Force's heavy bombers. The assignments were as follows: the 4th, 355th, 361st, and 479th Fighter Groups came under the 65th Fighter Wing; the 55th, 78th, 339th, 353rd, and 357th Fighter Groups were assigned to the 66th Fighter Wing; and the 20th, 352nd, 356th, 359th, and 364th (and for a short time the 361st) Fighter Groups came under the 67th Fighter Wing.

### Ninth Army Air Force

In addition to the 14 Eighth Air Force fighter groups that flew the Mustang in north-west Europe, the following Ninth Army Air Force fighter groups also operated the Merlin-Mustang in that theatre –

| GROUP | SQUADRONS/CODE |
| --- | --- |
| 354th | 353rd (FT), 355th (GQ), 356th (AJ) |
| 363rd | 380th (D5), 381st (B3), 382nd (C3) |
| 370th | 401st (7F), 402nd (E6), 403rd (9D) |

### Fifteenth Army Air Force

In the Mediterranean/southern Europe, the following fighter groups operated the Merlin-Mustang as a part of the Fifteenth Army Air Force –

| GROUP | SQUADRON/CODE OR NUMBERS |
| --- | --- |
| 31st | 307th (MX), 308th (HL), 309th (WZ) |
| 52nd | 2nd (QP), 4th (WD), 5th (VF) |
| 325th | 317th (10-39), 318th (40-69), 319th (70-99) |
| 332nd | 99th, 100th, 301st, 302nd |

Note: the code letters carried by Mustangs of the Fifteenth Air Force's 31st and 52nd Fighter Groups were the same as those worn by the 78th and 4th Fighter Groups respectively of the Eighth Army Air Force. It is usually stated that this was carried out deliberately to confuse German intelligence.

**P-51D-20NA 'Glamorous Glen III', is the aircraft in which the future test pilot Chuck Yeager's achieved most of his 12.5 kills** (Photo: USAF)

# Air National Guard Merlin-Mustangs

**P**erhaps not surprisingly in view of its widespread regular air force service, the Merlin-Mustang actually holds the record of having been assigned to more National Guard/Air National Guard squadrons in the US than any other aircraft type. This service began in 1946, when the Guard was still called the National Guard, and continued into 1957 when the West Virginia ANG was the last state to operate the type. Mustangs of several versions served in the National Guard/Air National Guard, including the P-51D/F-51D, the F-51H, the RF-51D reconnaissance model and the TF-51D two-seat trainer. Remarkably, seventy-five of the active Guard squadrons during the post-World War Two period operated the Mustang in one mark or another. The following is a list of the National Guard/ANG squadrons that flew the single-seat Mustang in its F-51D and F-51H versions (some of these also operated examples of the rare two-seat TF-51D Mustang)

| SQUADRON | STATE | APPROX SERVICE |
|---|---|---|
| 101st | Massachusetts | 1951-54 |
| 103rd | Pennsylvania | 1953-54 |
| 104th | Maryland | 1951-55 |
| 107th | Michigan | 1952-54 |
| 108th | Illinois | 1952-55 |
| 109th | Minnesota | 1946-1956 |
| 110th | Missouri | 1946-52 |
| 111th | Texas | 1947-51, 1952-54 |
| 112th | Ohio | 1952-56 |
| 113th | Indiana | 1947-55 |
| 115th | California | 1953-54 |
| 116th | Washington | 1947-50, 1952-54 |
| 118th | Connecticut | 1952-53 |
| 119th | New Jersey | 1952-55 |
| 120th | Colorado | 1946-53 |
| 121st | Washington, D.C. | 1952-54 |
| 123rd | Oregon | 1946-51, 1952-53 |
| 124th | Iowa | 1946-53 |
| 125th | Oklahoma | 1947-50, 1952-54 |
| 126th | Wisconsin | 1947-49, 1952-53 |
| 127th | Kansas | 1946-50, 1952-54 |
| 128th | Georgia | 1952 |
| 131st | Massachusetts | 1951-54 |
| 132nd | Maine | 1950-54 |
| 133rd | New Hampshire | 1952-54 |
| 134th | Vermont | 1950-54 |
| 136th | New York | 1952-54 |
| 137th | New York | 1952-53 |
| 138th | New York | 1950-53 |
| 139th | New York | 1951-54 |
| 141st | New Jersey | 1952-55 |
| 142nd | Deleware | 1952-54 |
| 146th | Pennsylvania | 1951-54 |
| 147th | Pennsylvania | 1951-54 |
| 148th | Pennsylvania | 1950-51, 1952-55 |
| 152nd | Rhode Island | 1952-55 |
| 154th | Arkansas | 1946-50 |
| 155th | Tennessee | 1946-51 |
| 156th | North Carolina | 1949-51, 1952-53 |
| 157th | South Carolina | 1946-50, 1952-54 |
| 158th | Georgia | 1952-53 |
| 159th | Florida | 1947-48, 1952-55 |
| 160th | Alabama | 1947-50 |
| 162nd | Ohio | 1948-55 |
| 163rd | Indiana | 1947-54 |
| 164th | Ohio | 1948-53 |
| 165th | Kentucky | 1947-51, 1952-56 |
| 166th | Ohio | 1947-50, 1952-54 |
| 167th | West Virginia | 1952-1957 |
| 168th | Illinois | 1954-55 |
| 169th | Illinois | 1947-56 |
| 170th | Illinois | 1948-53 |
| 171st | Michigan | 1948-50, 1952-55 |
| 172nd | Michigan | 1947-54 |
| 173rd | Nebraska | 1946-48, 1950-53 |
| 174th | Iowa | 1947-50, 1951-53 |
| 175th | South Dakota | 1946-54 |
| 176th | Wisconsin | 1948-52, 1952-53 |
| 178th | North Dakota | 1947-54 |
| 179th | Minnesota | 1948-54 |
| 181st | Texas | 1946-50, 1951-54 |
| 182nd | Texas | 1947-50, 1952-55 |
| 185th | Oklahoma | 1947-51, 1953 |
| 186th | Montana | 1947-1953 |
| 187th | Wyoming | 1946-53 |
| 188th | New Mexico | 1947-53 |
| 190th | Idaho | 1946-53 |
| 191st | Utah | 1946-55 |
| 192nd | Nevada | 1948-55 |
| 194th | California | 1949-54 |
| 195th | California | 1946-54 |
| 196th | California | 1946-47, 1952-54 |
| 197th | Arizona | 1947-50, 1952-53 |

In addition to the above seventy-three squadrons, the following six ANG squadrons flew the reconnaissance-configured RF-51D (four of these are also in the list above, because they additionally flew other marks of Mustang, thus making a total of seventy-five ANG squadrons that flew the Mustang in one form or another)

| SQUADRON | STATE | APPROX SERVICE |
|---|---|---|
| 105th | Tennessee | 1952-54 |
| 153rd | Mississippi | 1952-55 |
| 154th | Arkansas | 1952-54 |
| 155th | Tennessee | 1951-52 |
| 160th | Alabama | 1952-55 |
| 185th | Oklahoma | 1951 |

Four North American F-51H Mustangs of the Maryland Air National Guard's aerobatic team 'Guardian Angels' in close formation. Maryland had an aerial demonstration team from 1952 to 1953. *(Photo: USAF)*

North American F-51H-5-NA 44-64255 of the California Air National Guard, photographed in 1952. *(Photo: USAF)*

F-51D-25-NT Mustang 44-84522 of the 160th Fighter Squadron, Alabama Air National Guard. *(Photo: USAF)*

Maryland Air National Guard mechanics work on a North American P-51H-10-NA 44-64505 assigned to the 104th Fighter-Bomber Squadron during their 1954 Summer Encampment at in Massachusetts. *(Photo: USAF)*

# Understanding the Subject

**North American P-51B Mustang (RAF Mk III)**

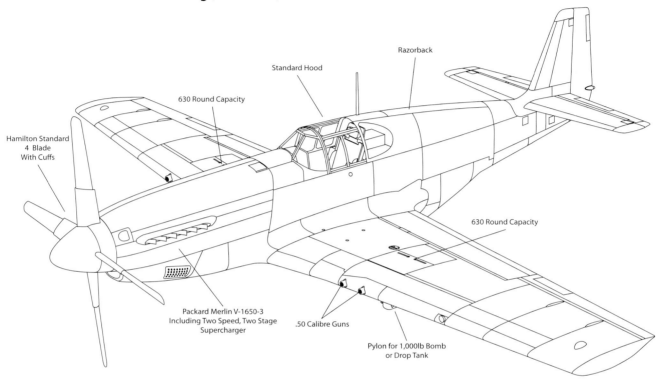

Razorback

Standard Hood

630 Round Capacity

Hamilton Standard
4 Blade
With Cuffs

630 Round Capacity

Packard Merlin V-1650-3
Including Two Speed, Two Stage
Supercharger

.50 Calibre Guns

Pylon for 1,000lb Bomb
or Drop Tank

**North American P-51B & C Mustang (Malcolm Hood)**

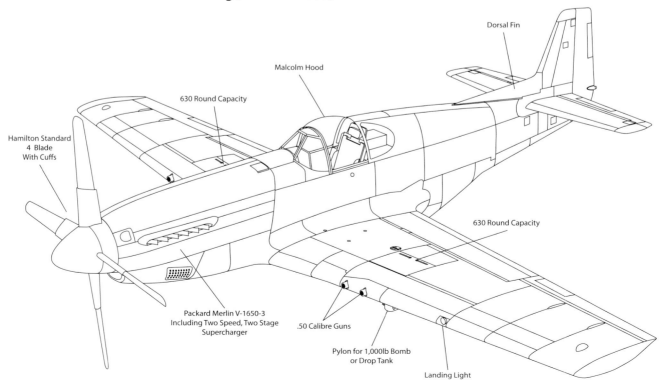

Dorsal Fin

Malcolm Hood

630 Round Capacity

Hamilton Standard
4 Blade
With Cuffs

630 Round Capacity

Packard Merlin V-1650-3
Including Two Speed, Two Stage
Supercharger

.50 Calibre Guns

Pylon for 1,000lb Bomb
or Drop Tank

Landing Light

## North American P-51D Mustang (RAF Mk IV)

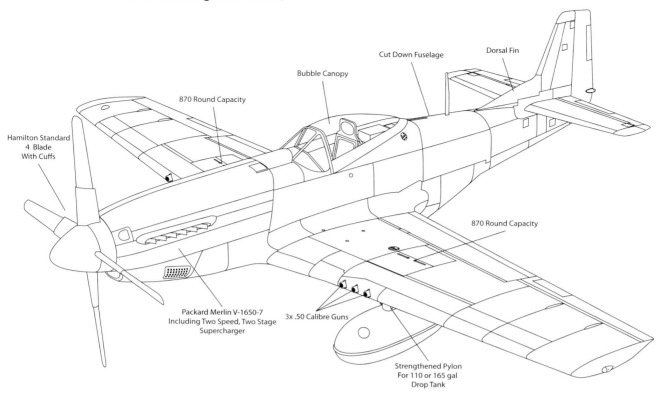

Cut Down Fuselage

Dorsal Fin

Bubble Canopy

870 Round Capacity

Hamilton Standard
4 Blade
With Cuffs

870 Round Capacity

Packard Merlin V-1650-7
Including Two Speed, Two Stage
Supercharger

3x .50 Calibre Guns

Strengthened Pylon
For 110 or 165 gal
Drop Tank

## North American P-51H Mustang

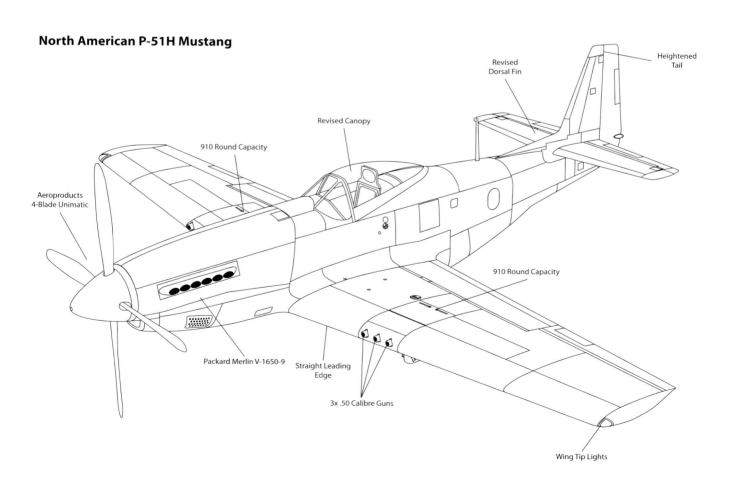

Heightened
Tail

Revised
Dorsal Fin

Revised Canopy

910 Round Capacity

Aeroproducts
4-Blade Unimatic

910 Round Capacity

Packard Merlin V-1650-9

Straight Leading
Edge

3x .50 Calibre Guns

Wing Tip Lights

## North American P-51K Mustang (RAF Mk IVA)

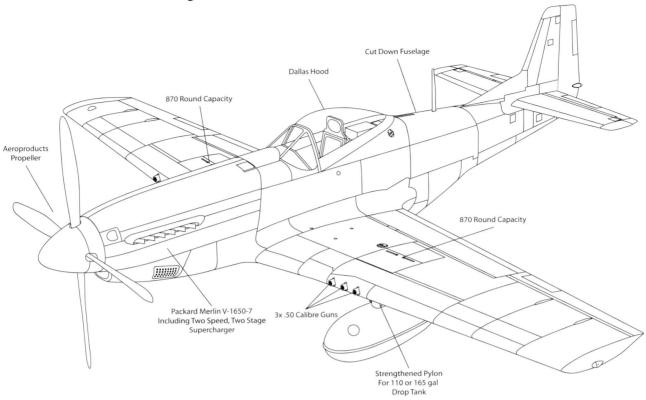

Cut Down Fuselage

Dallas Hood

870 Round Capacity

Aeroproducts Propeller

870 Round Capacity

Packard Merlin V-1650-7 Including Two Speed, Two Stage Supercharger

3x .50 Calibre Guns

Strengthened Pylon For 110 or 165 gal Drop Tank

## North American P/F-82B Mustang

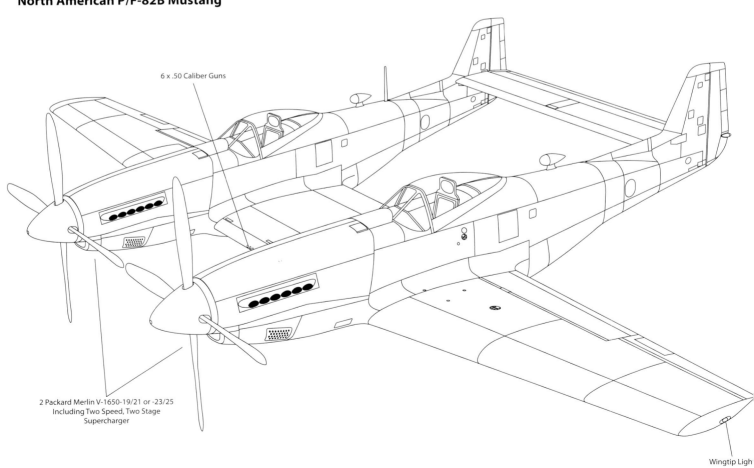

6 x .50 Caliber Guns

2 Packard Merlin V-1650-19/21 or -23/25 Including Two Speed, Two Stage Supercharger

Wingtip Ligh

# Kitography

## A Guide to Contemporary Mustang Kits Decals and Accessories*

## Kits

| | | |
|---|---|---|
| Academy AC12441 | 1:72 | North-American P-51C Mustang |
| Academy AC12464 | 1:72 | North-American P-51B Mustang 'Old Crow' |
| Academy AC12485 | 1:72 | North-American P-51B Mustang |
| Academy ACP51D | 1:72 | North-American P-51D Mustang |
| Accurate Miniatures ACM1020 | 1:72 | Air Legends North-American P-51B and Curtiss P-40 |
| Accurate Miniatures ACM0013 | 1:48 | North-American P-51C Bendix Transcontinental Racer |
| Airfix AX01004 | 1:72 | North-American P-51D Mustang |
| Airfix AX02047 | 1:72 | North-American P-51D Mustang |
| Airfix AX4001A | 1:24 | North-American P-51D Mustang |
| Airfix AX4003A | 1:24 | North-American P-51K Mustang |
| Dragon DN5407 | 1:72 | North-American P-51D Mustang |
| Dragon DN5530 | 1:48 | North-American P-51D Mustang |
| Hasegawa HAD25 | 1:72 | North-American P-51D Mustang |
| Hasegawa HAO1957 | 1:72 | North-American P-51B/P-51C Mustang Tuskegee Airmen |
| Hasegawa HAO1991 | 1:72 | North-American P-51D Tuskegee Airmen Combo |
| Hasegawa HAO2020 | 1:72 | North-American P-51D/P-51K Mustang ' Pacific Aces' Combo |
| Hasegawa HAO2054 | 1:72 | North American P-51B Mustang D-Day Marking Combo |
| Hasegawa HAJT030 | 1:48 | North-American P-51D Mustang |
| Hasegawa HAO9886 | 1:48 | North-American P-51D Mustang '4th Fighter Group' Debden Essex |
| Hasegawa HAO9903 | 1:48 | North-American P-51D Mustang 'Pacific Pin-up Girl' |
| Hasegawa HAO9947 | 1:48 | North-American P-51D Mustang 'Tuskegee Airmen' |
| HobbyBoss HB80230 | 1:72 | North-American P-51D Mustang IV 'Easy Build' |
| HobbyBoss HB80230 | 1:72 | North American P-51B Mustang |
| HobbyBoss HB80243 | 1:72 | North American P-51C Mustang |
| HobbyBoss HB85802 | 1:48 | North American P-51D Mustang IV |
| ICM 48121 | 1:48 | North-American P-51B Mustang USSAF with USAAF Pilots and Ground Personnel |

P-51D MUSTANG 'PACIFIC PINUP GIRL'

P-51B/C MUSTANG 'TUSKEGEE AIRMEN'

P-51D/K MUSTANG 'PACIFIC ACES COMBO'

| | | |
|---|---|---|
| ICM 48151 | 1:48 | North-American P-51D-5 Mustang |
| ICM 48153 | 1:48 | North-American P-51D Mustang with USAF Pilots and Ground Personnel |
| ICM 48154 | 1:48 | North-American P-51K Mustang |
| Italeri IT0086 | 1:72 | North-American P-51D Mustang |
| Pegasus Hobbies PH8404 | 1:48 | North-American P-51B Mustang Tuskegee Airmen |
| RS Models RSM192144 | 1:72 | North-American P-51H Mustang USAF |
| RS Models RSM192148 | 1:72 | North-American P-51H Mustang ANG |
| Revell RV4148 | 1:72 | North-American P-51D Mustang |
| Revell RV4142 | 1:72 | North-American P-51B Mustang |
| Revell RV4928 | 1:144 | North-American P-51B Mustang |
| Tamiya TA60749 | 1:72 | North-American P-51D Mustang Dallas canopy |
| Tamiya TA61040 | 1:48 | North-American P-51D Mustang 8th AF 'Lou IV' 'Nooky Booky IV', 'Petie 2nd' |
| Tamiya TA25151 | 1:32 | North-American P-51D Mustang Metal Plate Limited |
| Tamiya TA60322 | 1:32 | North-American P-51D Mustang |
| Tamiya TA60323 | 1:32 | North-American P-51D/K Mustang Pacific |
| Tamiya TA61042 | 1:48 | North-American P-51B Mustang |
| Tamiya TA61044 | 1:48 | North-American P-51D Mustang Korean War` |
| Tamiya TA92116 | 1:48 | North-American P-51B Mustang Blue Nose 352nd Fighter Group - standard and 'Malcolm Hood' canopies |
| Trumpeter TU02274 | 1:32 | North-American P-51B Mustang |
| Trumpeter TU02275 | 1:32 | North-American P-51B Mustang III RAF. |
| Trumpeter TU02401 | 1:24 | North-American P-51D Mustang IV |
| Trumpeter TU02402 | 1:24 | North-American P-51B/P-51C Mustang |

# Accessories and Conversions

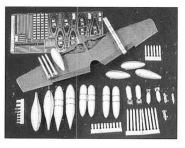

| | | |
|---|---|---|
| Aber ABR32018 | 1:32 | North-American P-51D Mustang Browning M2 Barrels (6) |
| Airwaves AEC72-47 | 1:72 | North-American P-51D/P-51K Mustang |
| Airwaves AEC7102 | 1:72 | North-American P-51B/P-51C Mustang |
| Aires AIRE2079 | 1:32 | North-American P-51B/P-51C Mustang Cockpit Set |
| Aires AIRE2091 | 1:32 | North-American P-51D Mustang Cockpit Set |
| Aires AIRE2082 | 1:32 | North-American P-51B Mustang Wheel Bay |
| Aires AIRE2092 | 1:32 | North-American P-51D Mustang Wheel Bay |
| Aires AIRE2097 | 1:32 | North-American P-51B/P-51C Mustang Gun Bay |
| Aires AIRE4072 | 1:48 | North-American P-51D Mustang Cockpit |
| Aires AIRE4082 | 1:48 | North-American P-51D Mustang Gun Bay |
| Aires AIRE4089 | 1:48 | North-American P-51D Mustang Detail Set |
| Aires AIRE4192 | 1:48 | North-American P-51B/P-51C Mustang Detail Set |
| Aires AIRE4219 | 1:48 | North-American P-51D Mustang Wheel Bay |
| Aires AIRE4233 | 1:48 | North-American P-51B/P-51C Mustang Cockpit Set |
| Aires AIRE4243 | 1:48 | North-American P-51B/P-51C Mustang Gun Gay |
| Aires AIRE4252 | 1:48 | North-American P-51D Mustang Engine Detail Set |
| Aires AIRE4257 | 1:48 | North-American P-51B/P-51C Mustang Engine Detail Set |
| Aires AIRE4557 | 1:48 | North-American P-51D Mustang Cockpit Set |
| Aires AIRE4613 | 1:48 | North-American P-51D Mustang Wheel Bay |
| Aires AIRE7074 | 1:72 | North-American P-51D Mustang Cockpit Set |
| Airscale AS24NAA | 1:24 | North-American P-51D Mustang Full Instrument Panel |
| Barracuda Studios BCR32012 | 1:32 | North-American P-51D Mustang Cockpit Sidewalls |
| Barracuda Studios BCR32013 | 1:32 | North-American P-51D Mustang Instrument Panel |
| Barracuda Studios BCR32015 | 1:32 | North-American P-51D Mustang Cockpit Upgrade Set |
| Barracuda Studios BCR32016 | 1:32 | North-American P-51D Mustang Paper Drop Tanks |
| Barracuda Studios BCR32029 | 1:32 | North-American P-51D Mustang Diamond Tread Pattern Tyres |
| Barracuda Studios BCR32030 | 1:32 | North-American P-51D Mustang Oval Tread Pattern Tyres |
| Barracuda Studios BCR32031 | 1:32 | North-American P-51D Mustang Octagonal Tread Pattern Tyres |
| Barracuda Studios BCR32032 | 1:32 | North-American P-51D Mustang Tyres |
| Barracuda Studios BCR32034 | 1:32 | North-American P-51D Mustang Main Wheel Hubs |
| Barracuda Studios BCR48051 | 1:48 | North-American P-51D Mustang Hexagonal Tread Wheels |
| Czech Master Kits CMK5051 | 1:32 | North-American P-51D Mustang Interior Set |
| Czech Master Kits CMK7063 | 1:72 | North-American P-51B Mustang Engine, Exhausts & Panels |
| Czech Master Kits CMK7064 | 1:72 | North-American P-51D Mustang Interior |
| Czech Master Kits CMK7065 | 1:72 | North-American P-51D Mustang Exterior |
| Czech Master Kits CMK7155 | 1:72 | North-American P-51D Mustang Detail Set |
| Czech Master Kits CMK7172 | 1:72 | North-American F-51D Mustang Korean War Interior Set |
| Czech Master Kits CMK7259 | 1:72 | North-American P-51D Mustang Interior Set |
| Czech Master Kits CMK7260 | 1:72 | North-American P-51D Mustang Armament Set |
| Czech Master Kits CMK7261 | 1:72 | North-American P-51D Mustang Engine set (Unshrouded) |
| Czech Master Kits CMK7267 | 1:72 | Packard V-1650-7 Engine |
| Czech Master Kits CMQ32125 | 1:32 | North-American P-51D Mustang Instrument Panel &  Gunsight |
| Czech Master Kits CMQ32126 | 1:32 | North-American P-51D Mustang Control Column |
| Czech Master Kits CMQ32127 | 1:32 | North-American P-51D/P-51K Mustang Rudder Pedals |
| Czech Master Kits CMQ32128 | 1:32 | North-American P-51D/P-51K Mustang Seat |
| Czech Master Kits CMQ32161 | 1:32 | North-American P-51D Mustang Wheels - Oval Tread Pattern |
| Czech Master Kits CMQ32161 | 1:32 | North-American P-51D Mustang Wheels Cross Tread Pattern |
| Czech Master Kits CMQ32183 | 1:32 | North-American P-51D Mustang Wheels Diamond Tread Pattern |
| Czech Master Kits CMQ32184 | 1:32 | North-American P-51D Mustang Wheels Diamond & Hole Tread Pattern |
| Czech Master Kits CMQ48039 | 1:48 | North-American P-51B/P-51D Mustang Wheels |
| Czech Master Kits CMQ48178 | 1:48 | North-American P-51D Mustang - Wheels Cross Tread Pattern |
| Czech Master Kits CMQ48179 | 1:48 | North-American P-51D Mustang - Wheels Diamond Tread Pattern |
| Czech Master Kits CMQ48180 | 1:48 | North-American P-51D Mustang Wheels Diamond & Hole Tread Pattern |
| Czech Master Kits CMQ48181 | 1:48 | North-American P-51D Mustang Wheels - Oval Tread Pattern |
| Czech Master Kits CMQ72032 | 1:72 | North-American P-51D Mustang Wheels |
| Czech Master Kits CMQ72033 | 1:72 | North-American P-51B/P-51C/P-51D Mustang Exhaust |
| Czech Master Kits CMQ72118 | 1:72 | North-American P-51D Mustang Tailplanes |
| Czech Master Kits CMQ72119 | 1:72 | North-American P-51 B/C Mustang Wheels |
| Czech Master Kits CMQ72120 | 1:72 | North-American P-51D Mustang Corrected Propeller |
| Czech Master Kits CMQ72169 | 1:72 | North-American P-51D Mustang Wheels - Oval Tread Pattern |
| Czech Master Kits CMQ72170 | 1:72 | North-American P-51D Mustang - Wheels Cross Tread Pattern |
| Czech Master Kits CMQ72171 | 1:72 | North-American P-51D Mustang Wheels Diamond & Hole Tread Pattern |
| Eduard EBIG3255 | 1:32 | North-American P-51D Mustang Detail Set (Dragon) |
| Eduard EBIG3274 | 1:32 | North-American P-51D Mustang Detail Set (Trumpeter) |
| Eduard EBIG3287 | 1:32 | North-American P-51D Mustang Detail Set (Trumpeter) |
| Eduard EBIG3310 | 1:32 | North-American P-51D Mustang Early Detail Set (Tamiya) |
| Eduard EBIG3312 | 1:32 | North-American P-51D Mustang Late Detail Set (Tamiya) |
| Eduard EBIG3329 | 1:32 | North-American P-51D/K Mustang Pacific Theatre (Tamiya) |
| Eduard ED23011 | 1:24 | North-American P-51D Mustang Placards |
| Eduard ED32010 | 1:32 | North-American P-51D Mustang (Hasegawa) |
| Eduard ED32013 | 1:32 | North-American P-51D Mustang (Revell) |
| Eduard ED32168 | 1:32 | North-American P-51D Mustang Exterior (Dragon) |
| Eduard ED32212 | 1:32 | North-American P-51B Mustang Wheel Wells |
| Eduard ED32213 | 1:32 | North-American P-51D Mustang Exterior (Trumpeter) |
| Eduard ED32214 | 1:32 | North-American P-51D Mustang Gun Bay |
| Eduard ED32226 | 1:32 | North-American P-51B Wheel Wells |
| Eduard ED32302 | 1:32 | North-American P-51D Mustang Exterior (Tamiya) |
| Eduard ED32307 | 1:32 | North-American P-51D Mustang Engine (Tamiya) |
| Eduard ED32515 | 1:32 | North-American P-51D Mustang Placards |
| Eduard ED32597 | 1:32 | North-American P-51D Interior Pre-Painted |
| Eduard ED32625 | 1:32 | North-American P-51B Mustang Placards |
| Eduard ED32626 | 1:32 | North-American P-51B Mustang Interior |
| Eduard ED32627 | 1:32 | North-American P-51D Mustang Interior |
| Eduard ED32712 | 1:32 | North-American P-51D Mustang Interior Early |
| Eduard ED32715 | 1:32 | North-American P-51D Mustang Interior Late |
| Eduard ED32721 | 1:32 | North-American P-51D Mustang Gun Bay Late |
| Eduard ED32715 | 1:32 | North-American P-51D Mustang Seat Belts |
| Eduard ED32721 | 1:32 | North-American P-51D Mustang Gun Bay Early |
| Eduard ED32731 | 1:32 | North-American P-51K Mustang Interior |
| Eduard ED32732 | 1:32 | North-American P-51D Mustang Gun Bay Early |
| Eduard ED32776 | 1:32 | North-American P-51K Interior |
| Eduard ED32778 | 1:32 | North-American P-51K Gun Bay |
| Eduard ED32793 | 1:32 | North-American P-51D Mustang Seatbelts |
| Eduard ED33007 | 1:32 | North-American P-51D Mustang Instrument Panel |
| Eduard ED33019 | 1:32 | North-American P-51B Mustang Interior |
| Eduard ED33021 | 1:32 | North-American P-51D Mustang Interior (Dragon) |
| Eduard ED33036 | 1:32 | North-American P-51D Mustang interior (Trumpeter) |
| Eduard ED33097 | 1:32 | North-American P-51D Mustang Interior Early #1 |
| Eduard ED33103 | 1:32 | North-American P-51D Mustang Interior Early #2 |
| Eduard ED33117 | 1:32 | North-American P-51K Mustang Interior |
| Eduard ED48199 | 1:48 | North-American P-51B Mustang Detailing Set |
| Eduard ED49216 | 1:48 | North-American P-51D Mustang Detailing Set |
| Eduard ED49219 | 1:48 | North-American P-51B Mustang Detailing Set |
| Eduard ED49268 | 1:48 | North-American P-51D Mustang Detailing Set |
| Eduard ED49603 | 1:48 | North-American P-51D Mustang |

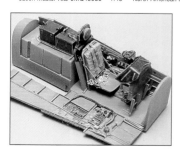

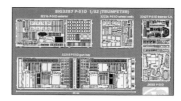

| | | | |
|---|---|---|---|
| Eduard ED632015 | 1:72 | North-American P-51D Mustang Wheels (Tamiya) | |
| Eduard ED648092 | 1:72 | North-American P-51D Mustang Wheels | |
| Eduard ED672016 | 1:72 | North-American P-51D Mustang Wheels (Tamiya) | |
| Eduard ED73206 | 1:72 | North-American P-51D Mustang Wheels | |
| Eduard ED73435 | 1:72 | North-American P-51D Mustang Detailing Set | |
| Eduard ED73451 | 1:72 | North-American P-51D/F-51 Mustang (Airfix) | |
| Eduard EDCX041 | 1:72 | North-American P-51D Mustang Mask | |
| Eduard EDCX052 | 1:72 | North-American P-51B/P-51C Mustang (Academy) | |
| Eduard EDCX056 | 1:72 | North-American P-51B Mustang Mask | |
| Eduard EDCX340 | 1:72 | North-American P-51D/F-51D Mustang (Airfix) | |
| Eduard EDEX034 | 1:48 | North-American P-51B Mustang (Tamiya) | |
| Eduard EDEX035 | 1:48 | North-American P-51D Mustang (Tamiya) | |
| Eduard EDEX102 | 1:48 | North-American P-51D Mustang (Hasegawa) | |
| Eduard EDEX171 | 1:48 | North-American P-51D Mustang Accurate Miniatures) | |
| Eduard EDEX359 | 1:48 | North-American P-51D Mustang (HobbyBoss) | |
| Eduard EDEFE216 | 1:48 | North-American P-51D Mustang Cockpit Set | |
| Eduard EDEFE219 | 1:48 | North-American P-51B Mustang | |
| Eduard EDEFE268 | 1:48 | North-American P-51D Mustang | |
| Eduard EDK1132 | 1:48 | North-American P-51D Mustang (Tamiya) | |
| Eduard EDJX047 | 1:32 | North-American P-51D Mustang (Hasegawa) Mask | |
| Eduard EDJX064 | 1:32 | North-American P-51D Mustang (Dragon) | |
| Eduard EDJX077 | 1:32 | North-American P-51B Mustang (Trumpeter) | |
| Eduard EDJX083 | 1:32 | North-American P-51D Mustang (Dragon) | |
| Eduard EDJX136 | 1:32 | North-American P-51D Mustang (Tamiya) | |
| Eduard EDJX156 | 1:32 | North-American P-51K Mustang (Tamiya) | |
| Eduard EDSS105 | 1:72 | North-American P-51B (Revell) Detailing set | |
| Eduard EDSS248 | 1:72 | North-American P-51D (Hasegawa) | |
| Eduard EDSS250 | 1:72 | North-American P-51B/C (Academy) | |
| Eduard EDSS250 | 1:72 | North-American P-51D Mustang (Italeri) | |
| Eduard EDSS451 | 1:72 | North-American P-51D/F-51 Mustang Interior (Airfix) | |
| Freightdog FDR72012 | 1:72 | North-American P-51D Mustang 108 gal Paper Tanks | |
| Freightdog FDR72013 | 1:72 | North-American Mustang Mk IV Conversion (Airfix) | |
| G-Factor GFAC3219 | 1:32 | North-American P-51D Mustang Landing Gear (Hasegawa) | |
| G-Factor GFAC3222 | 1:32 | North-American P-51D Mustang Landing Gear (Tamiya) | |
| G-Factor GFAC4804 | 1:48 | North-American P-51D Mustang Undercarriage Legs & Rear Wheel | |
| Isracast ISC32034 | 1:32 | North-American P-51D Mustang Rocket Rail Adaptors | |
| LF Models LF48012 | 1:48 | North-American TP-51B-1 Mustang Conversion | |
| LF Models LF72021 | 1:72 | North-American TP-51B-1 Mustang Conversion | |
| LF Models LF72022 | 1:72 | North-American TP-51B-1 Mustang Conversion | |
| Mastercasters MST32010 | 1:32 | North-American P-51D Mustang Weighted Resin Wheels | |
| Pavla Hobbies PAVC72035 | 1:72 | North-American P-51D/K Mustang Late Cockpit Details | |
| Pavla Hobbies PAVC72036 | 1:72 | North-American P-51D/K Mustang Early Cockpit Details | |
| Pavla Hobbies PAVS72034 | 1:72 | North-American P-51D Mustang Seat | |
| Pavla Hobbies PAVU72026 | 1:72 | North-American P-51D-10 Mustang Post 44-13902 | |
| Pavla Hobbies PAVU72027 | 1:72 | North-American P-51D-5 Mustang Tail Early | |
| Pavla Hobbies PAVU72028 | 1:72 | North-American P-51D/K Mustang Propellers | |
| Profimodeller PF32014P | 1:32 | North-American P-51D Mustang Gun Barrels | |
| Quickboost QB32057 | 1:32 | North-American P-51D Mustang Propeller | |
| Quickboost QB32061 | 1:32 | North-American P-51B Mustang Undercarriage Covers | |
| Quickboost QB32062 | 1:32 | North-American P-51B Mustang Pylons | |
| Quickboost QB32093 | 1:32 | North-American P-51B Mustang Exhaust | |
| Quickboost QB32144 | 1:32 | North-American P-51D/P-51K Mustang Propeller | |
| Quickboost QB32145 | 1:32 | North-American P-51D Mustang Propeller | |
| Quickboost QB48054 | 1:48 | North-American P-51D Mustang Exhausts | |

| | | |
|---|---|---|
| Quickboost QB48060 | 1:48 | North-American P-51D Mustang Exhaust Type B |
| Quickboost QB48097 | 1:48 | North-American P-51D Mustang Undercarriage Covers |
| Quickboost QB48113 | 1:48 | North-American P-51D Mustang Rear Wheel Well |
| Quickboost QB48198 | 1:48 | North-American P-51D Mustang Wing Flaps |
| Quickboost QB48225 | 1:48 | North-American P-51D Mustang Propeller |
| Quickboost QB48466 | 1:48 | North-American P-51D Mustang Propeller |
| Quickboost QB48551 | 1:48 | North-American P-51A Mustang/Mk IA Exhaust |
| Quickboost QB72274 | 1:72 | North-American P-51B/P-51C Mustang Exhaust Round |
| Quickboost QB72880 | 1:72 | North-American P-51B/P-51C Mustang Exhaust |
| Quickboost QB72292 | 1:72 | North-American P-51B/P-51C Mustang Propeller |
| Quickboost QB72299 | 1:72 | North-American P-51B/P-51C Mustang Propeller |
| Quickboost QB72369 | 1:72 | North-American P-51D/P-51K Mustang Propeller |
| Quickboost QB72391 | 1:72 | North-American P-51D Mustang Exhaust |
| Quickboost QB72397 | 1:72 | North-American P-51D Mustang Seat with Harness |
| Quickboost QB72432 | 1:72 | North-American P-51D/P-51K Mustang Propeller |
| RES-IM RESIM7211 | 1:72 | North-American P-51D Mustang - Control Surfaces (Airfix) |
| RES-IM RESIM7211 | 1:72 | North-American P-51D Mustang – Fuel Tanks (Airfix) |

*Scale Aircraft Conversions (SAC)*

| | | |
|---|---|---|
| SAC24006 | 1:24 | North-American P-51D Mustang Landing Gear |
| SAC 32054 | 1:32 | North-American P-51D Mustang Landing Gear (Tamiya) |
| SAC 32061 | 1:32 | North-American P-51D Mustang Landing Gear (Dragon) |
| SAC 32065 | 1:32 | North-American P-51D Mustang Landing Gear (Hasegawa) |
| SAC 48142 | 1:48 | North-American P-51D Mustang Landing Gear (Tamiya) |
| SAC 48177 | 1:48 | North-American P-51D Mustang Landing Gear (Tamiya) |
| SAC 72057 | 1:72 | North-American P-51D/F-51D Mustang IV Landing Gear |
| Squadron SQS9103 | 1:72 | North-American P-51D Canopy |
| Squadron SQS9114 | 1:72 | North-American P-51B Canopy |
| Squadron SQS9158 | 1:72 | North-American P-51D Canopy Dallas |
| Squadron SQS9181 | 1:72 | North-American P-51D/F-82 Twin Mustang Canopy |
| Squadron SQS9401 | 1:32 | North-American P-51D Canopy (Hasegawa) |
| Squadron SQS9402 | 1:32 | North-American P-51D Canopy Dallas |
| Squadron SQS9501 | 1:48 | North-American P-51D Canopy Dallas (Monogram) |
| Squadron SQS9519 | 1:72 | North-American P-51D Canopy |
| Squadron SQS9528 | 1:72 | North-American P-51B Canopy |
| Squadron SQS9529 | 1:72 | North-American P-51D Canopy Malcolm Hood |
| Squadron SQS9579 | 1:72 | North-American P-51D Canopy Dallas (Tamiya) |
| Squadron SQS9519 | 1:72 | North-American P-51D Canopy (Tamiya) |
| True Details TD32001 | 1:32 | North-American P-51D Mustang Wheels (Hasegawa) |
| True Details TD48008 | 1:48 | North-American P-51B/P-51D/Mk III Mustang Diamond Tread |
| True Details TD48025 | 1:48 | North-American P-51B/P-51D/Mk III Mustang Wheels |
| True Details TD48409 | 1:48 | North-American P-51D Seats |
| True Details TD48453 | 1:48 | North-American P-51D Cockpit Set (Tamiya) |
| True Details TD48486 | 1:48 | North-American P-51D Cockpit Set (Accurate Miniatures) |
| True Details TD72003 | 1:48 | North-American P-51D Wheels |
| True Details TD72412 | 1:48 | North-American P-51D Seats |
| True Details TD72460 | 1:48 | North-American P-51B/P-51C Mustang Cockpit Set |
| Verlinden VL0787 | 1:32 | North-American P-51D Mustang Cockpit Detail Set |
| Verlinden VL1164 | 1:72 | North-American P-51D Mustang Detail Set |
| Verlinden VL1170 | 1:48 | North-American P-51D Mustang Update Set |
| Verlinden VL1407 | 1:48 | North-American P-51D Mustang Underwing Stores |
| Verlinden VL1789 | 1:48 | North-American P-51D Cockpit/Moving Surfaces Set |

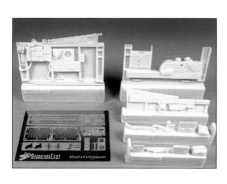

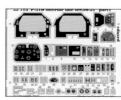

# Decals

| Aeromaster AMD32016 | 1:32 | P-51D Green Nose Mustangs of East Wretham #1 |
| Aeromaster AMD32017 | 1:32 | P-51D Green Nose Mustangs of East Wretham #2 |
| Aeromaster AMD48364 | 1:48 | P-51D Green Nose Mustangs of East Wretham #1 |
| Aeromaster AMD48365 | 1:48 | P-51D Green Nose Mustangs of East Wretham #2 |
| Aeromaster AMD48640 | 1:48 | P-51D Green Nose Mustangs of East Wretham #3 |
| Aeromaster AMD48646 | 1:48 | P-51B/P-51C Mustang D-Day Invasion Stripes |
| Aeromaster AMD48647 | 1:48 | P-51D Mustang D-Day Invasion Stripes |
| Aeromaster AMD48652 | 1:48 | Green Nose P-51D Mustangs 359FG #5 |
| Aeromaster AMD48653 | 1:48 | Green Nose P-51D Mustangs 359FG #6 |
| Aeromaster AMD48655 | 1:48 | Green Nose P-51D Yellow Nose Mustangs 361st FG #1 |
| Aeromaster AMD48656 | 1:48 | Green Nose P-51D Yellow Nose Mustangs 361st FG #2 |
| Aeromaster AMD48716 | 1:48 | Green Nose P-51D Southern European |
| Aeromaster AMD48772 | 1:48 | Green Nose P-51D Mustangs 356FG #2 |
| Aeromaster AMD48774 | 1:48 | Green Nose P-51D Mustangs 360FS/356FG #4 |
| Aeromaster AMD48775 | 1:48 | Green Nose P-51D Mustangs 360FS/356FG #5 |
| Aeromaster AMD72176 | 1:72 | P-51B SEA Mustangs #1 |
| Aeromaster AMD72177 | 1:72 | P-51B SEA Mustangs #2 |
| Aeromaster AMD72207 | 1:72 | P-51D Mustang Yellow Nose Mustangs 361st FG #1 |
| Aeromaster AMD72208 | 1:72 | P-51D Mustang Yellow Nose Mustangs 361st FG #2 |
| Aeromaster AMD72200 | 1:72 | P-51D Mustang Yellow Nose Mustangs 361st FG #3 |
| Aeromaster AMD72213 | 1:72 | P-51B Mustangs Southern Europe #1 |
| Aeromaster AMD72216 | 1:72 | P-51 Recce Mustangs Southern Europe #2 |
| Aztec AZD4814 | 1:48 | P-51D Latin Eagles #6 |
| Aztec AZD4830 | 1:48 | P-51D Latin Macho Mustangs #2 |
| Aztec AZD72030 | 1:76 | P-51D Latin Macho Mustangs |
| Barracuda BC3209 | 1:32 | P-51D Mustangs of the 8th AF |
| Barracuda BC3210 | 1:32 | P-51D Mustang Cockpit Stencils and Placards |
| Barracuda BC48011 | 1:48 | P-51D Mustangs of the 8th Air Force |
| Barracuda BC72009 | 1:72 | P-51D Mustangs of the 8th Air Force |
| Blue Rider BR309 | 1:72 | P-51D Mustang Costa Rica |
| Colorado CA48023 | 1:48 | P-51C/D Dijon/Italy |
| Colorado CA48024 | 1:48 | P-51B/D Colitishall |
| Colorado CA72048 | 1:72 | P-51B/D Colitishall/East Wretham/Somali/France |
| CAM CAM24004 | 1:24 | P-51D 4th FS/3rd ACG 'Bad Angel' |
| CAM CAM24005 | 1:24 | P-51D 357th FS/361st FG 'Detroit Miss' |
| CAM CAM24006 | 1:24 | P-51D 356th FS/354th FG 'Chicago's Own' |
| CAM CAM24007 | 1:24 | P-51D 356FS 'Ding Hao!' |
| CAM CAM24008 | 1:24 | P-51D 354FS 'Cherraine' |
| CAM CAM24009 | 1:24 | P-51D 385FS 'Look Homeward Angel' |
| CAM CAM24010 | 1:24 | P-51D 370FS 'Skeeter's Scooter' |
| CAM CAM24011 | 1:24 | P-51D 358FS 'Leaking Lizz' |
| CAM CAM24012 | 1:24 | P-51B 486FS |
| CAM CAM24013 | 1:24 | P-51B 38FS 'East Side Rat' |
| CAM CAM24014 | 1:24 | P-51B 38FS 362FS/357FG |
| CAM CAM24015 | 1:24 | P-51C VF-5 5FS/52FG |
| CAM CAM32153 | 1:32 | P-51D 'Bad Angel' & 'Chicago's Own' |
| CAM CAM32154 | 1:32 | P-51D 'Ding Hao!' |
| CAM CAM32155 | 1:32 | P-51D 'Cherraine' |
| CAM CAM32158 | 1:32 | P-51D 358FS/355FG D-Day Stripes |
| CAM CAM48115 | 1:48 | P-51D 'Bad Angel'/'Chicago's Own'/'Detroit Miss' |
| CAM CAM48116 | 1:48 | P-51D 'Ding Hao!' |
| CAM CAM48117 | 1:48 | P-51D 'Cherraine'/'Skeeter's Scooter'/'Look Homeward Angel' |
| Caracal 48020 | 1:48 | P-51D Air National Guard Units |
| Dutch Decal DD72070 | 1:72 | P-51s Indonesian Air Force |
| Eagle Cal EAG32103 | 1:32 | P-51D `Weaver's Nude'/`Passion Wagon'/`Hurry Home Honey' |
| Eagle Cal EAG32139 | 1:32 | P-51D 'Thunderbird'/'Duchess Arlene'/'Flying Dutchman' |
| Eagle Cal EAG32140 | 1:32 | P-51D 'Hun Hunter/Texas'/ 'Lou IV/Athelene' |
| Eagle Cal EAG32141 | 1:32 | P-51D 'Ridge Runner III'/'Ferocious Frankie' |
| Eagle Cal EAG32142 | 1:32 | P-51 Mustangs of Major George Preddy |
| Eagle Cal EAG48100 | 1:48 | P-51 Mustangs of Major George Preddy |
| Eagle Cal EAG48101 | 1:48 | P-51D 'Old Crow'/'Missouri Armada'/ 'Nooky Booky' |
| Eagle Cal EAG48102 | 1:48 | P-51D `Ol Flak Joe'/`Winged Ace of Clubs'/`Frenesi' |
| Eagle Cal EAG48103 | 1:48 | P-51D `Weaver's Nude'/`Passion Wagon'/`Hurry Home Honey' |
| Eagle Cal EAG48139 | 1:48 | P-51D 'Thunderbird'/'Duchess Arlene'/'Flying Dutchman' |
| Eagle Cal EAG48140 | 1:48 | P-51D 'Hun Hunter/Texas'/ 'Lou IV/Athelene' |

| Eagle Cal EAG48141 | 1:48 | P-51D 'Ridge Runner III'/'Ferocious Frankie' |
| Eagle Cal EAG48142 | 1:48 | P-51D 'Big Beautiful Doll'/'Da Quake' |
| Eagle Cal EAG72100 | 1:72 | P-51 Mustangs of Major George Preddy |
| Eagle Cal EAG72139 | 1:72 | P-51D 'Thunderbird'/'Duchess Arlene'/'Flying Dutchman' |
| Eagle Cal EAG72140 | 1:72 | P-51D 'Hun Hunter/Texas'/ 'Lou IV/Athelene' |
| Eagle Cal EAG72141 | 1:72 | P-51D 'Ridge Runner III'/'Ferocious Frankie' |
| Eagle Cal EAG72142 | 1:72 | P-51D 'Big Beautiful Doll'/'Da Quake' |
| Eagle Strike ESP48090 | 1:48 | P-51D Mustang 'Mary Mac'/'Stinker Pat'/'Shu Shu'/Chuck' |
| Eagle Strike ESP48103 | 1:48 | P-51D Mustang 'Double Trouble To'/'Betty-E' |
| Eagle Strike ESP48104 | 1:48 | P-51D Mustang 'Donna Mite'/'Dove of Peace' |
| Eagle Strike ESP48106 | 1:48 | P-51D Mustang 'Dallas Doll'/'Willit Run?' |
| Eagle Strike ESP48200 | 1:48 | P-51D Mustang 'Lady Eve'/ 'Big Dick' |
| Eagle Strike ESP48270 | 1:48 | P-51B/D Mustang 'Lady Beth III'/'Flying Dutchman'/ 'Miss Miami II' |
| Eagle Strike ESPI4810 | 1:48 | P-51BB Blue Nose Birds of Bodney, 'Lambie II'/The Flying Scot' |
| Eagle Strike ESPI7202 | 1:72 | P-51B Mustang 'Old Crow'/'Glamourous Glen'/'Nooky Booky' |
| Eagle Strike ESPI7203 | 1:72 | P-51D Mustang Yoxford Boys, 'Berlin Express'/'Pappy's Answer'/'Geronimo'/'Jersey Bounce' |
| Eagle Strike ESPI7204 | 1:72 | P-51D Mustang 'Ol Flak Joe'/'Hurry Home Honey'/'Arkansas Traveller'/'Nooky Booky III' |
| Eagle Strike ESPI7209 | 1:72 | P-51D Blue Nose Birds of Bodney, 'Petie 3rd'/'Moonbeam McSwine'/'Hell-er Bust' |
| Iliad Design ILD48024 | 1:48 | P-51D Air National Guard Mustangs |
| Iliad Design ILD72011 | 1:72 | P-51D Air ANG/Air National Guard Mustangs |
| Kits World KW144004 | 1:144 | P-51D Mustang Captain Charles Weaver's 'Passion Wagon' three aircraft, five versions |
| Kits World KW144004 | 1:144 | P-51D 'Sweet Arlene'/'Jan'/'Iron Ass'/'My Achin Back' |
| Kits World KW32001 | 1:32 | P-51D Mustang 'Passion Wagon' (2) |
| Kits World KW32002 | 1:32 | P-51D Mustang 'Daisy Mae'/'Temptation' |
| Kits World KW32003 | 1:32 | P-51D Mustang 'Passion Wagon' (3) |
| Kits World KW32005 | 1:32 | P-51B Mustang 'Ill Wind'/ 'Miss Dallas' |
| Kits World KW32006 | 1:32 | P-51D Mustang 'Sweet Arlene' (2) |
| Kits World KW32007 | 1:32 | P-51D Mustang 'Iron Ass'/ 'My Achin Back' |
| Kits World KW32008 | 1:32 | P-51B Mustang 'Shangri La'/'Salem Representative' |
| Kits World KW32009 | 1:32 | P-51B Mustang III |
| Kits World KW32026 | 1:32 | P-51D 'June Nite'/'Happy Jacks Go Buggy' |
| Kits World KW32027 | 1:32 | P-51D 'Panty Waste'/'Suzanne' |
| Kits World KW48008 | 1:48 | P-51B Mustang 4th FG Nose Art |
| Kits World KW48017 | 1:48 | P-51D Mustang 334th FS, 4th FG |
| Kits World KW48027 | 1:48 | P-51D Mustang General Markings |
| Kits World KW48028 | 1:48 | P-51B/D General Markings |
| Kits World KW48029 | 1:48 | P-51D Mustang - Nose Art Selection - Red Dog XII/Shillelagh/Happy Jacks Go Buggy/Heat Wave/Ridge Runner/Pin-up Girl/Missouri Mauler/Louisiana Heatwave |
| Kits World KW48054 | 1:48 | P-51D Mustang 357th FG |
| Kits World KW48055 | 1:48 | P-51D-20NA Mustang Captain Charles Weaver 'Passion Wagon' |
| Kits World KW48056 | 1:48 | P-51 Mustang Captain Charles Weaver 'Passion Wagon' |
| Kits World KW48060 | 1:48 | P-51D Mustang 20th FG 77th and 79th Fighter Squadrons |
| Kits World KW48061 | 1:48 | P-51D Mustang 20th FG 79th Fighter Squadron |
| Leading Edge LE3280 | 1:32 | P-51D Mustang RCAF Western Canada #1 |
| Leading Edge LE3281 | 1:32 | P-51D Mustang RCAF Eastern and MB Canada #2 |
| Leading Edge LE4880 | 1:48 | P-51D Mustang RCAF Western Canada #1 |
| Leading Edge LE4881 | 1:48 | P-51D Mustang RCAF Eastern and MB Canada #2 |
| Leading Edge LE7280 | 1:72 | P-51D Mustang RCAF Western Canada #1 |
| Leading Edge LE7281 | 1:72 | P-51D Mustang RCAF Eastern and MB Canada #2 |

| | | |
|---|---|---|
| LF Models LFMC4820 | 1:48 | P-51D Mustang in Swiss Service |
| LF Models LFMC4882 | 1:48 | P-51B Mustang in Swiss Service |
| LF Models LFMC4853 | 1:48 | P-51B Mustang Uruguay |
| LF Models LFMC4872 | 1:48 | P-51C Mustang Zirkus Rosarius #1 |
| LF Models LFMC4873 | 1:48 | P-51C Mustang Zirkus Rosarius #2 |
| LF Models LFMC72105 | 1:72 | F-51C Mustang Uruguay |
| LF Models LFMC72143 | 1:72 | P-51C Mustang Zirkus Rosarius #1 |
| LF Models LFMC72144 | 1:72 | P-51C Mustang Zirkus Rosarius #2 |
| Lifelike LL48015 | 1:48 | P-51B/P-51M #2 (4) 'Salem Representative'/ 'Big Mac'/ 'Skyczar'/ 'Nancy Lee' |
| LPS Hobby LPM7209 | 1:72 | P-51D British Silver Mustangs |
| LPS Hobby LPM7210 | 1:72 | P-51D British Camouflaged Mustangs |
| LPS Hobby LPM7211 | 1:72 | P-51D Tuskegee Mustangs |
| Matterhorn Circle MHN32011 | 1:32 | P-51D Swiss |
| Matterhorn Circle MHN48011 | 1:48 | P-51D Swiss |
| Matterhorn Circle MHN72011 | 1:72 | P-51D Swiss |
| Model Alliance ML48113 | 1:48 | P-51 Mustangs RAF, RAAF, RCAF & RNZAF |
| Model Alliance ML48195 | 1:48 | P-51 Mustang. WUB of 225 Squadron RAF, Algeria |
| Model Alliance ML72113 | 1:72 | P-51 Mustangs RAF, RAAF, RCAF & RNZAF |
| Model Alliance ML72195 | 1:72 | P-51 Mustang. WUB of 225 Squadron RAF, Algeria |
| MPD Mini Print MPD72550 | 1:72 | P-51B Mustang Black 63 |
| Microscale MS48002 | 1:48 | P-51B/P-51D Black & White European Theatre Stripes |
| Microscale MS48004 | 1:48 | P-51B/P-51C D-Day Invasion Stripes |
| Microscale MS48009 | 1:48 | P-51D D-Day Invasion Stripes |
| Microscale MS48009 | 1:48 | P-51D D-Day Invasion Stripes |
| Microscale MS48014 | 1:48 | P-51A/P-51B/P-51D National Insignia/Stencil Data |
| Microscale MS48017 | 1:48 | P-51 Lo-Vis Insignia |
| Microscale MS48017 | 1:48 | P-51 Lo-Vis Insignia |
| Microscale MS480914 | 1:48 | P-51D Mustang Aces 'Short Fuse' |
| Microscale MS480948 | 1:48 | P-51D-10-NA Mustang 'Tar Heel'/ 'Cookie' |
| Microscale MS32212 | 1:32 | P-51D Mustang PI-E 360 FS/356 The Virginia Squire' |
| Print Scale PSL48039 | 1:48 | P-51D Mustang 'Iron Ass'/ 'Big Dick' plus others |
| Print Scale PSL72039 | 1:72 | P-51D Mustang 'Iron Ass'/ 'Big Dick' plus others |
| Rafdec RAF7208 | 1:72 | P-51B Mustang AG367 63-X 400 (OTU) Sqn 1943 |
| Red Roo RRD4811 | 1:48 | P-51K Mustang A68-565 LB-V 84 Sqn |
| Red Roo RRD4812 | 1:48 | CAC Mk 20 Mustang A68-71 HU-A 78 Sqn 1946 |
| Red Roo RRD7205 | 1:72 | P-51D Mustang A68-766 FA-V 82 Sqn Japan 1948 |
| Sky Decals SD48021 | 1:48 | IDF P-51D Mustangs |
| Sky Decals SD72022 | 1:48 | IDF P-51D Mustangs |
| Superscale SS32257 | 1:32 | P-51D Mustang 'Sad Sack'/ 'Flying Girl' |
| Superscale SS32258 | 1:32 | P-51D Mustang 487 & 402 FS |
| Superscale SS480594 | 1:48 | P-51D Mustang 'Swede's Steed'/ 'Angels Playmate' |
| Superscale SS480615 | 1:48 | P-51D/P-51K Mustang 'Cheese Cake Chassis'/ 'Mrs Bonnie' |
| Superscale SS480732 | 1:48 | P-51D 'Grim Reaper' |
| Superscale SS480791 | 1:48 | P-51D 'The Prodigal Son' |
| Superscale SS480818 | 1:48 | P-51D/F-6K 'Palpitatin Pal'/ 'Jake the Snake' |
| Superscale SS480820 | 1:48 | P-51D Mustang 'June Nite' |
| Superscale SS480843 | 1:48 | P-51D Razorback 'Hun Hunter XIV' |
| Superscale SS480882 | 1:48 | P-51D 'Sad Sack' |
| Superscale SS480929 | 1:48 | P-51D Mustang 'Cheese Cake Chassis'/ 'Angel's Playmate' |
| Superscale SS480949 | 1:48 | P-51D Mustangs 'Chatanooga Choo Choo'/ 'Babe' |

| | | |
|---|---|---|
| Microscale MS480978 | 1:48 | P-51B Mustangs 'Shellelagh'/ 'Short Fuse Sallee' |
| Microscale MS481065 | 1:48 | P-51D Mustangs `Ol Flak Joe'/ `Cooler' |
| Superscale SS481081 | 1:48 | P-51D Mustang 'Gash Hound'/ 'Little Joe' |
| Microscale MS481097 | 1:48 | P-51D/K Mustangs 'Grim Reaper'/ 'Etta Jeanne II' |
| Superscale SS481098 | 1:48 | P-51D Mustangs 'Moose'/ 'Little Midget II'/ 'Missy' |
| Microscale MS481106 | 1:48 | P-51D Mustangs 'Buzzin Guzzin' |
| Superscale SS481107 | 1:48 | P-51D Mustangs Aces 8th Air Force 'The Shillelagh'/ `Dove of Peace' |
| Microscale MS481114 | 1:48 | P-51D Mustangs Aces 'Vivacious Virgin'/ 'Donald Duck' |
| Microscale MS481128 | 1:48 | P-51D Mustang 41FS/35 FG |
| Superscale SS481137 | 1:48 | P-51D Mustang `Little Joe'/ `Man O'War' 1945 |
| Superscale SS481144 | 1:48 | P-51D/P-51K Mustangs `Cheese Cake Chassis'/ 'Miss Bonnie' |
| Superscale SS481145 | 1:48 | P-51D Mustangs No 600 116TRS/23FG 14th AF |
| Superscale SS481152 | 1:48 | P-51D Mustang `Kwitcherbitchin'/ `Nip Nocker |
| Superscale SS481153 | 1:48 | P-51D Mustang `The Draggin' Lady'/ `Foxy' |
| Microscale MS481176 | 1:48 | P-51D Mustangs `Bad Angel' |
| Microscale MS481177 | 1:48 | P-51D Mustangs `Jumpin Jacques' |
| Microscale MS481178 | 1:48 | P-51C Mustangs (2) |
| Microscale MS481184 | 1:48 | P-51D Mustangs Iwo Jima `Hel-E-Ter'/ `Mary Alyce' |
| Microscale MS481186 | 1:48 | P-51C/1D Mustangs Tuskegee Airmen |
| Superscale SS481192 | 1:48 | P-51D Pacific Mustangs 'Blue Pickle'/ `Dirty Dick'/ `Dirty Old Man' |
| Microscale MS481194 | 1:48 | P-51B Mustang `Quick Check'/ `Geronimo'/ `Chicago Gun Moll' |
| Superscale SS481202 | 1:48 | P-51D Mustang `Tallahassee Lassie'/ `My Achin'! |
| Superscale SS481203 | 1:48 | P-51D/P-51K Mustangs Iwo Jima |
| Superscale SS481221 | 1:48 | P-51D Mustang Aces 334th and 335th FS |
| Superscale SS72774 | 1:72 | P-51D Mustang Aces 'Grumpy'/ 'Moonbeam McSwine'/ 'Butch Baby' |
| Microscale MS72806 | 1:72 | P-51D Mustang Aces 8th Air Force |
| Microscale MS72807 | 1:72 | P-51D Mustang Aces (3) |
| Microscale MS72851 | 1:72 | P-51D Mustang 354th FG Mustang Aces |
| Microscale MS72874 | 1:72 | P-51D Mustang 'Shellelagh'/ 'Short Fuse Salle' |
| Microscale MS72875 | 1:72 | P-51D Mustang Aces of the 352 FG |
| Microscale MS72906 | 1:72 | P-51B/P-51D Mustangs `Old Crow' (2) |
| Microscale MS72906 | 1:72 | P-51D Mustangs 357 FG 'Gash Hound'/ `Frenesi'/ `Little Joe' |
| Techmod TM32002 | 1:32 | P-51B Mustang III - Polish Pilots (8) |
| Techmod TM48002 | 1:48 | P-51B Mustang III - 315 Polish Sqn (4) |
| Techmod TM48028 | 1:48 | P-51B Mustang III - 351/306 Sqn (6) |
| Techmod TM48033 | 1:48 | P-51B Mustang III - 316/309 Sqn (4) |
| Techmod TM72009 | 1:72 | P-51B Mustang III - 316/309 Sqn (4) |
| Techmod TM72021 | 1:72 | P-51B Mustang III - 315 Polish Sqn (4) |
| Techmod TM72028 | 1:72 | P-51B Mustang III – 315/306 Polish Sqn (6) |
| Ventura VA3258 | 1:32 | P-51D Mustang New Mexico ANG |
| Ventura VA3268 | 1:32 | P-51D RNZAF No.1 Auckland Squadron |
| Ventura VA4855 | 1:48 | P-51B/K German Captured & RNZAF |
| Ventura VA4883 | 1:48 | P-51D RNZAF, Auckland & Wellington Sqns |
| Ventura VA4884 | 1:48 | P-51D RNZAF Canterbury and Otago Sqns |
| Ventura VA7276 | 1:72 | P-51D RNZAF Auckland, Wellington, Canterbury & Otago Sqns |
| Warbird WB14403 | 1:144 | P-51D Tuskegee Airmen |
| Warbird WB48001 | 1:48 | Tuskegee Red Tailed Mustangs #1 |
| Warbird WB48002 | 1:48 | Tuskegee Red Tailed Mustangs #2 |
| Warbird WB48003 | 1:48 | Tuskegee Red Tailed Mustangs #3 |
| Warbird WB48011 | 1:48 | P-51B/P-51C/P-51D Mustang Blue Nose Decals |
| Warbird WB48024 | 1:48 | P-51D Mustang 332nd FG |
| Warbird WB72001 | 1:72 | Tuskegee Red Tailed Mustangs (7) |
| Warbird WB72019 | 1:72 | P-51C/P-51D Mustang 332 FG |
| Monokio WD-48055 | 1:48 | P-51D Mustang 334th FS, 4th FG Early 1945 |
| Xtradecal X32043 | 1:32 | P-51D Mustang Mk IV RAF/RCAF/RAAF (6) |
| Xtradecal X48092 | 1:48 | P-51D Mustang in RAF service (6) |
| Xtradecal X72101 | 1:72 | P-51B Mustangs 4th Fighter Group RAF Debden (6) |
| Xtradecal X72124 | 1:72 | P-51B Mustang III - History of 19 Sqn RAF |
| Xtradecal X72131 | 1:72 | P-51D Mustang Mk IV in RAF service (6) |
| Zotz ZTZ32037 | 1:32 | P-51D Mustang 'American Beauty'/ 'Lovely Lila' (3) |
| Zotz ZTZ32038 | 1:32 | P-51D Mustang 'Jasper Joker II'/ 'Creaners Dream' (3) |
| Zotz ZTZ32042 | 1:32 | P-51D Mustang 'The Flying Undertaker'/ 'Snooks'/ 'Thunderbird'/ 'Straw Boss II/Little Sandra' |
| Zotz ZTZ32042 | 1:32 | P-51D Mustang Duxford Eagles 'Big Dick'/ 'Little Chick' |

*This listing features products that are at the time of printing readily available to the modeller, and does not show older or out of production items.*

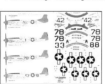

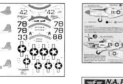

# Index

Please note: this index does not reference appendices

An interesting general view of the parking/maintenance area of No.112 Squadron, RAF, and its Mustang Mk.IIIs at an Italian airfield, showing the austere conditions in which many Mustangs were based – particularly those engaged in tactical operations where the aircraft had to follow the ground war very closely (Photo: R.L. Ward Collection)

A further view of the parking/maintenance area of No.112 Squadron, RAF, and its Mustang Mk.IIIs at an Italian airfield, with Mustang Mk.III GA-A in the foreground. Despite the austere conditions in which many Mustangs had to operate, the type was nevertheless generally able to stand up to these conditions well – although maintenance was very tough on the ground crews, who often had to look after the aircraft and even perform quite major maintenance, in the open air in less than perfect weather
(Photo: R.L. Ward Collection)

An NAA cutaway drawing of the Twin Mustang, specifically showing the P-82B layout. Envisaged as a long-range day fighter but with ground-attack capabilities, the P-82B was well-armed, and is shown in this drawing with one possible envisaged external armament layout, of clusters of air-to-ground unguided rockets. The P-82B was intended to be powered by Packard V-1650-23/25 engines - although interestingly 'handed' -19 or -9/-21 engines appear to have been specified, and it seems likely that some if not all the production P-82Bs used this combination *(Drawing: NAA)*

**A quartet of P-51D's from the 308th Fighter Squadron 31st Fighter Group**
*(Credit: USAF)*

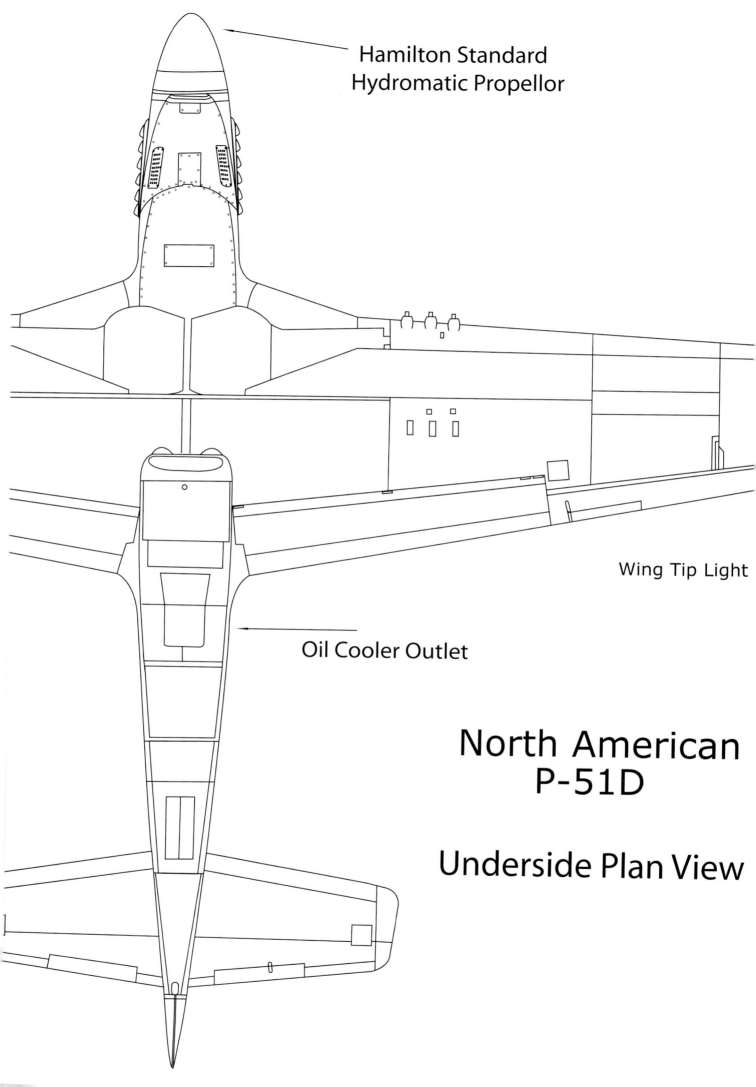

Hamilton Standard
Hydromatic Propellor

Wing Tip Light

Oil Cooler Outlet

# North American P-51D

## Underside Plan View

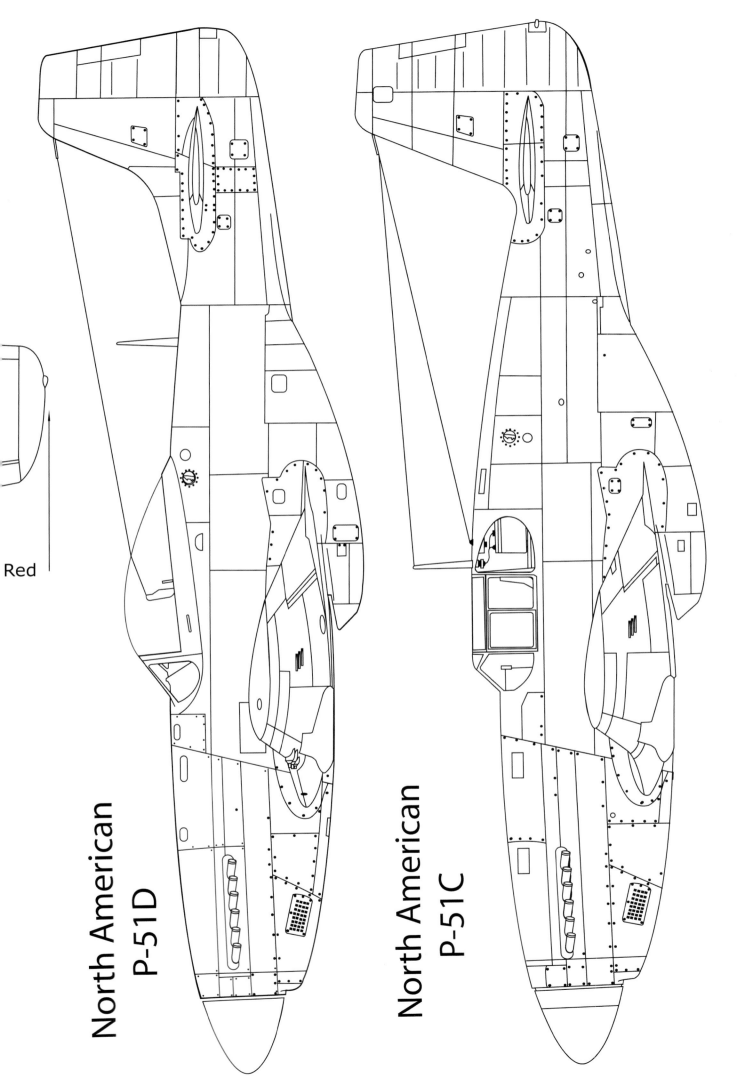

Red

North American
P-51D

North American
P-51C